REMEDIES FOR HUMAN RIGHTS VIOLATIONS

An innovative book that provides fresh insights into the neglected field of remedies in both international and domestic human rights law. Providing an overarching two-track theory, it combines remedies to compensate and prevent irreparable harm to litigants with a more dialogic approach to systemic remedies. It breaks new ground by demonstrating how proportionality principles can improve remedial decision-making and avoid reliance on either strong discretion or inflexible rules. It draws on the latest jurisprudence from the European and Inter-American Courts of Human Rights and domestic courts in Australia, Canada, India, Ireland, New Zealand, Hong Kong, South Africa, the United Kingdom and the United States. Separate chapters are devoted to interim remedies, remedies for laws that violate human rights, damages, remedies in the criminal process, declarations and injunctions in institutional cases, remedies for violations of social and economic rights and remedies for violations of Indigenous rights.

KENT ROACH holds the Prichard Wilson Chair in Law and Public Policy at the University of Toronto in Canada. He has written fifteen books including *Constitutional Remedies in Canada* (1994) and second edition (2013) and *The 9/11 Effect Comparative Counter-Terrorism* (2011). His work on remedies has been widely cited by courts. Acting pro-bono, he has been counsel in many of the Supreme Court of Canada's landmark decisions on remedies for rights violations.

CAMBRIDGE STUDIES IN CONSTITUTIONAL LAW

The aim of this series is to produce leading monographs in constitutional law. All areas of constitutional law and public law fall within the ambit of the series, including human rights and civil liberties law, administrative law, as well as constitutional theory and the history of constitutional law. A wide variety of scholarly approaches is encouraged, with the governing criterion being simply that the work is of interest to an international audience. Thus, works concerned with only one jurisdiction will be included in the series as appropriate, while, at the same time, the series will include works which are explicitly comparative or theoretical – or both. The series editor likewise welcomes proposals that work at the intersection of constitutional and international law, or that seek to bridge the gaps between civil law systems, the US, and the common law jurisdictions of the Commonwealth.

Books in the Series

Remedies for Human Rights Violations: A Two-Track Approach to Supra-national and National Law Kent Roach

Europe's Second Constitution: Crisis, Courts and Community Markus W. Gehring

A. V. Dicey and the Common Law Constitutional Tradition: A Legal Turn of Mind Mark D. Walters

Administrative Competence: Reimagining Administrative Law Elizabeth Fisher and Sidney A. Shapiro

Legal Sabotage: Ernst Fraenkel in Hitler's Germany Douglas Morris

Proportionality in Action: Comparative and Empirical Perspectives on the Judicial Practice Edited by Mordechai Kremnitzer, Tayla Steiner and Andrej Lang

Constitutional Dialogue: Democracy, Rights, Institutions Edited by Geoffrey Sigalet, Grégoire Webber and Rosalind Dixon

The Veiled Sceptre: Reserve Powers of Heads of State in Westminster Systems Anne Twomey

Vigilance and Restraint in the Common Law of Judicial Review Dean Knight

The Alchemists: Questioning Our Faith in Courts as Democracy-Builders Tom Gerald Daly

Australia's Constitution after Whitlam Brendan Lim

Building the Constitution: The Practice of Constitutional Interpretation in Post-Apartheid South Africa James Fowkes

Dimensions of Dignity: The Theory and Practice of Modern Constitutional Law Jacob Weinrib

Reason of State: Law, Prerogative, Empire Thomas Poole

Bills of Rights in the Common Law Robert Leckey

The Guardian of the Constitution: Hans Kelsen and Carl Schmitt on the Limits of Constitutional Law Translated by Lars Vinx, with an introduction, notes by Lars Vinx

Parliamentary Bills of Rights: The Experiences of New Zealand and the United Kingdom Janet L. Hiebert and James B. Kelly

Lawyering for the Rule of Law: Government Lawyers and the Rise of Judicial Power in Israel Yoav Dotan

Balancing Constitutional Rights: The Origins and Meanings of Postwar Legal Discourse Jacco Bomhoff

Judges on Trial: The Independence and Accountability of the English Judiciary Shimon Shetreet and Sophie Turenne

Proportionality and Constitutional Culture Moshe Cohen-Eliya and Iddo Porat

The Politics of Principle: The First South African Constitutional Court, 1995–2005 Theunis Roux

The New Commonwealth Model of Constitutionalism: Theory and Practice Stephen Gardbaum

Searching for the State in British Legal Thought: Competing Conceptions of the Public Sphere Janet McLean

Judging Social Rights Jeff King

Proportionality: Constitutional Rights and their Limitations Aharon Barak

Parliamentary Sovereignty: Contemporary Debates Jeffrey Goldsworthy

REMEDIES FOR HUMAN RIGHTS VIOLATIONS

A Two-Track Approach to Supra-national and National Law

KENT ROACH
University of Toronto

CAMBRIDGE
UNIVERSITY PRESS

CAMBRIDGE
UNIVERSITY PRESS

University Printing House, Cambridge CB2 8BS, United Kingdom

One Liberty Plaza, 20th Floor, New York, NY 10006, USA

477 Williamstown Road, Port Melbourne, VIC 3207, Australia

314–321, 3rd Floor, Plot 3, Splendor Forum, Jasola District Centre, New Delhi – 110025, India

79 Anson Road, #06–04/06, Singapore 079906

Cambridge University Press is part of the University of Cambridge.
It furthers the University's mission by disseminating knowledge in the pursuit of education, learning, and research at the highest international levels of excellence.

www.cambridge.org
Information on this title: www.cambridge.org/9781108417877
DOI: 10.1017/9781108283618

First published 2021

A catalogue record for this publication is available from the British Library.

ISBN 978-1-108-41787-7 Hardback
ISBN 978-1-108-40597-3 Paperback

BRIEF CONTENTS

CONTENTS

ACKNOWLEDGEMENTS

This book is in large part the product of my involvement with the Centre for Transnational Legal Studies in London, England. I first taught a seminar on remedies for violations of human rights in supra-national law and national law in the winter of 2016. I was able to return to teach the seminar in the winter of 2020. The centre has faculty and students from all the world. It encourages the type of blending of supra-national and comparative law that is found in this book. My students were eager to think about remedies, a subject that for most had been ignored in their legal education as I fear is typically the case. Classroom discussions about the differences between the European and Inter-American Court of Human Rights were particularly lively. In the winter of 2016, the seminar was also generously hosted by the European Court of Human Rights and its Committee of Ministers. We were scheduled to return in the winter of 2020 when COVID-19 disrupted our plans. I thank all my colleagues, staff and students at the Centre for their support.

I thank Robert J. Sharpe who commented on an earlier version of the manuscript and was the first to teach me about the importance of remedies. I also thank Ryan Beaton, John Borrows and Craig Forcese who made suggestions on earlier drafts of some of the chapters. Sooin Kim and Sufei Xu at the Bora Laskin Law Library were excellent in tracking down the wide-range of materials that were necessary to consult during the over six years it took to write this book. Maggie Morris, now a second year law student at the University of Toronto, provided excellent and cheerful editing and research assistance. I am also grateful to the Pierre Trudeau Foundation for providing funding during the early stages of this process. Thanks also to David Dyzenhaus editor of the *University of Toronto Law Journal* who provided funding for a symposium "Examining Remedies for Violations of Human Rights" published in (2019) 69 (Supplement 1) *University of Toronto Law Journal* 1–170. I am grateful to Brenda L. Gunn, David Landau, Robert Leckey, Robert J. Sharpe, Po Jen Yap and Katharine G. Young for their papers in the symposium and their engagement with my work. Both Geoff and Steven Budlender have assisted me in my understanding of the South African experience and the remaining errors are my own fault. The same applies to Jackie Hodgson who generously helped guide me through the complexities of European law when we wrote together on prisoners' voting rights. I thank the Victoria University of Wellington, which awarded me a Borrin Fellowship. They hosted a talk on damages, as did the University of Oxford's Faculty of Law.

I am also grateful to the David Asper Centre for Constitutional Rights and Cheryl Milne. They have allowed me to represent the Centre when it intervened in several of the Canadian remedies cases discussed in this book including *Ward* v. *Vancouver,* [2010] 2 SCR 28 and *Conseil scolaire francophone de la Colombie-Britannique* v. *British Columbia,* 2020 SCC 13 on damages; *G.* v. *Ontario*, 2020 SCC 38 on suspended declarations of invalidity and individual remedies and *Tanudjaja* v. *Attorney General (Canada)*, 2013 ONSC 5410 on complex remedies for socio-economic remedies. Hopefully, these "real life" experiences have sharpened some of my thinking about remedies. It also has convinced that all those involved in clinical legal education require and deserve the benefit of academic freedom even if the University of Toronto regrettably appears to have taken the opposite position.

Although re-written for the book, some of the material was first published as Kent Roach, "Polycentricity and Queue-Jumping in Public Law Remedies: A Two-Track Response" (2006) 66(1) *U.T.L.J.* 1; Kent Roach, "Remedies for Laws That Violate Human Rights" in John Bell et al. *Public Law Adjudication in Common Law Systems* (Oxford: Hart Publishing, 2016); Kent Roach, "Dialogic Remedies" (2019) 17 *I. Con.* 860; Kent Roach, "The Disappointing Remedy? Damages as a Remedy for Violations of Human Rights" (2019) 69 (1 supp) *U.T.L.J.* 33; and Kent Roach, "Reclaiming Prima Facie Exclusionary Rules in Canada, Ireland, New Zealand and the United States: The Importance of Compensation, Proportionality and Non-Repetition" (2020) 43(3)*Manitoba Law Journal* 1.

My most important debt is to my family who continue to offer me love, support and humour during these difficult times. I know this book was a burden for us all. Now, it is finally done.

TABLE OF CASES

African Court of Human and Peoples' Rights

Australia

Bahamas

Canada

Colombia

European Court of Human Rights

Hong Kong

India

Inter-American Court of Human Rights

Ireland

International Centre for the Settlement of Disputes

International Court of Justice

International Criminal Court

Jamaica

Kenya

Permanent Court of International Justice

New Zealand

South Africa

Janse van Rensburg NO and Another v. *Minister of Trade and Industry and Another NNO,* [2001] ZACC 18 220

Khosa v. *Minister of Social Development,* [2004] ZACC 11 414

Linkside v. *Minister for Basic Education,* [2014] ZAECGHC 111 420

Masiya v. *Director of Public Prosecutions Pretoria (The State) and Another,* [2007] ZACC 9 213

Mazibuko v. *City of Johannesburg and Others,* (2010) 3 BCLR 239 124, 415, 431

Minister of Health v. *Treatment Action Campaign (No. 2),* [2002] ZACC 16 57, 373–4, 385, 420, 422, 427, 527

Minister of Home Affairs v. *Fourie,* [2005] ZACC 19 178, 181, 208, 219–20, 227–8

Minister of Home Affairs v. *National Institute for Crime Prevention and the Re-integration of Offenders (NICRO) and Others,* [2004] ZACC 10 374

Minister of Justice v. *Ntuli,* [1997] ZACC 7 211

Minister of Justice and Constitutional Development and Others v. *Prince; National Director of Public Prosecutions and Others* v. *Rubin; National Director of Public Prosecutions and Others* v. *Acton and Others,* [2018] ZACC 30 210

Minister of Social Development and Others, Ex Parte, [2006] ZACC 3 211

Mlungwana and Others v. *S. and Another,* [2018] ZACC 45 209

Mistry v. *Interim Medical and Dental Council,* [1998] ZACC 10

Moise v. *Greater Germiston Transitional Council,* [2001] ZACC 21 203, 213

Mwelase and Others v. *Director-General for the Department of Rural Development and Land Reform and Another,* [2019] ZACC 30 57, 377, 420

N and Others v. *Government of Republic of South Africa and Others (No. 1),* 2006 (6) SA 543 (D) 375

National Coalition for Gay and Lesbian Equality v. *Minister of Home Affairs,* [1999] ZACC 17 199, 216, 414

National Treasury and Others v. *Opposition to Urban Tolling Alliance and Others (Road Freight Association Intervening),* [2012] ZACC 19 152–5, 162

Ngewu and Another v. *Post Office Ret. Fund and Others,* [2013] ZACC 4 197

Nthabiseng Pheko Occupiers of Bapsfontein Informal Settlement v. *Ekurhuleni Metropolitan Municipality,* [2011] ZACC 34 374, 425–6

Occupiers of 51 Olivia Road et al. v. *City of Johannesburg and Others,* [2008] ZACC 1 414, 447–8

Pheko and Others v. *Ekurhuleni Metropolitan Municipality,* [2011] ZACC 34 374, 426

Pheko and Others v. *Ekurhuleni Metropolitan Municipality and Others (No. 3),* [2016] ZACC 20 425

Port Elizabeth Municipality v. *Various Occupiers,* [2004] ZACC 7 21, 82–3, 100, 112, 410, 447, 450, 529

President of the Republic of South Africa and Another v. *Modderklip Boerdery (Pty) Ltd,* [2005] ZACC 5 267, 420, 437

Rail Commuters Action Group v. *Transnet Ltd t/a Metrorail,* (2005) (2) SA 359 (CC) 373, 385, 527

Saint Christopher (Kitts) & Nevis

Saint Lucia

Trinidad and Tobago

United Kingdom

United Nations Bodies

United States

1

The Importance and Complexity of Remedies

1.1 Introduction

We live in a world rich with rights. Alas, we live in a world poor in remedies.

Since World War II, the world has become much more concerned with human rights. Many new international and domestic laws have been enacted to "guarantee" rights. However, remedies have not been guaranteed. They are not always ordered. When ordered, they frequently fail to fully repair the harm of violations or prevent new ones.

Sometimes unarticulated concerns about whether remedies are manageable have deterred courts from finding that rights have been violated, especially with respect to socio-economic and Indigenous rights. Supranational courts have often assumed that their decisions that a right has been violated are a sufficient remedy.

Even when remedies are ordered, they have often been disappointing. Damages are frequently used, but their amount is often quite modest. They can fail to vindicate the many intangible and non-monetary values protected by various forms of human rights. Damages attempt to repair the past but may fail to prevent future and repetitive violations. They can also allow governments to buy their way out of supposedly mandatory human rights obligations. Nonetheless, both domestic and supra-national courts remain attracted to damages: they are an easy-to-manage remedy that ends judicial involvement in a case.

Another reason why we are poor with respect to remedies is that governments do not always fully comply with remedies. Lack of compliance with remedies ordered by international tribunals is well documented.[1] Less known is that governments, even in established democracies, have failed to comply with the spirit if not the letter of remedies ordered by domestic courts. Even when governments accept remedies, they often fail to take steps to prevent similar violations in the future.

Courts often rely on declarations about human rights obligations, but the parties do not always agree on how these general declarations should be implemented. At the same time, more prescriptive and mandatory remedies are not always the answer. Courts must be concerned about respecting limits on the judicial role in the separation of powers including limits on their own expertise and knowledge. The limits on the powers of supra-national courts are even greater.

Some domestic courts have powers to strike down laws that violate human rights, but such a remedy can be blunt. Alternative remedies such as suspending or delaying a declaration of invalidity or issuing a non-binding declaration of incompatibility, however, can leave litigants with no immediate remedy. Conversely, other remedies such as interpreting laws to comply with human rights may strain legislative intent and the separation of powers.

Systemic remedies designed to prevent similar violations in the future are important. Alas, they often depend on the ability of courts to persuade governments and society to respect human rights. As the ambitions of remedies increase, so too does the risk of failure. Human rights contemplate a perfect world. In contrast, remedies respond to our failures. They also create new failures. This book will attempt to confront the reality of remedial failure and the need for both domestic and supra-national courts to engage in iterative remedial processes.

Remedies are frequently a site for interest balancing but often in a manner that is less transparent and principled than occurs when determining whether limits on rights are justified and necessary to protect legitimate social interests. This book will argue that judges should apply proportionality principles to determine whether limits on remedies and

[1] The United States infamously executed Walter LaGrand in defiance of interim measures ordered by the International Court of Justice. *LaGrand (Germany* v. *United States)* [1999] ICJ Rep. 9; *LaGrand (Germany* v. *United States),* Judgment of 27 June 2001, [2001] ICJ Rep 466.

the use of less drastic alternative remedies are justified. This will make the exercise of remedial discretion more disciplined and transparent.

A final reason why we are poor with respect to remedies is that they have received much less attention than rights. Scholars, judges and litigators all devote less attention to remedies than the underlying human right. Many human rights instruments have remedial provisions, but they provide limited guidance in shaping remedies. Human rights law frequently seems to run out of steam when it comes to remedies.

1.1.1 Remedies as a Challenging and Neglected Subject

Why have remedies been neglected? Peter Schuck has suggested that "rights preoccupy a Don Quixote; remedies are the work of a Sancho Panza".[2] Canada's longest-serving chief justice, Beverley McLachlin, has observed that "'we are endowed with rights' slips off the legal tongue … 'we are endowed with remedies' has a more prosaic ring … Viewed as 'practical' but not necessarily 'exciting', remedies are relegated to the 'if I have room' or 'if I must' categories of most student and teaching timetables". Nevertheless, Chief Justice McLachlin eloquently defended remedies. They allow "us to mend our wounds and carry on – as individuals and as a society".[3]

Remedies are challenging to study because they cut across different fields of law even when, as in this book, they are limited to remedies for violations of human rights. Domestically, they involve criminal, civil, administrative and procedural law. Supra-nationally, they involve procedure and substance. They include the award of provisional measures and various follow-ups to remedial decisions. When remedies have received scholarly or judicial attention, there has been a tendency to focus on particular remedies while neglecting common issues throughout remedies. As Schuck has noted, "like many cross-speciality subjects" remedies languish "in a kind of academic no-man's land".[4]

This book will address a broad range of remedies including interim remedies, remedies for laws that violate human rights, damages,

[2] Peter Schuck, *Suing Government: Citizen Remedies for Official Wrongs* (New Haven: Yale University, 1983), p.27.

[3] Beverley McLachlin, "Rights and Remedies – Remarks" in Robert J. Sharpe and Kent Roach (eds.), *Taking Remedies Seriously* (Ottawa: Canadian Institute for the Administration of Justice, 2010), pp.22–23, 30.

[4] Schuck, *Suing Government*, p.xvi.

exclusion of improperly obtained evidence, stays of proceedings, sentence reductions, injunctions and declarations in order to highlight common issues and the possibility of a common approach to remedies. That said, remedies are inevitably contextual. Thus, separate chapters will be devoted to remedies used in the criminal process, in cases involving institutions such as the police and prisons and in the enforcement of socio-economic and Indigenous rights.

1.1.2 Supra-national Law and Remedies

Remedies engage both domestic and supra-national law. If domestic remedies have been exhausted and failed, recourse to supra-national law through the bodies associated with the United Nations or regional human rights courts is possible.

Some deride international law remedies because they only have persuasive force.[5] But this ignores the ingenuity of supra-national law. A central theme of this book is that domestic human rights lawyers can learn much about remedies from international law. Building on the work of the International Law Commission, the United Nations has developed *Basic Principles and Guidelines on the Right to a Remedy and Reparation for Victims of Gross Violations of International Human Rights Law and Serious Violations of International Humanitarian Law* (henceforth UN *Basic Principles*).[6] The UN *Basic Principles* recognize the importance of backward-looking forms of restitution, reparation and creative forms of satisfaction beyond damages but also forward-looking assurances of non-repetition. International criminal courts have broken new ground by using damages, sentence reductions and remedies for crime victims.

Domestic lawyers can learn much from international lawyers about the need for continuing and iterative attempts by all relevant public institutions and social actors to shape and revise remedies within a procedurally fair framework.[7] International law has grappled with the reality of

[5] Jack Goldsmith and Eric Posner, *The Limits of International Law* (Oxford: Oxford University Press, 2005).

[6] Adopted by the General Assembly 21 March 2006, A/Res/60/147 at para 18.

[7] For arguments that compliance or fidelity to international law depend on "interactive practices of legality" and "ongoing processes of interactional law-making" involving different institutions and social actors, see Jutta Brunée and Stephen Toope, *Legality and Legitimacy in International Law: An Interactional Account* (Cambridge: Cambridge University Press, 2010), pp.121–122. My colleagues' approach inspired by the work of Lon

remedial failure[8] and repetitive violations in a way that more established domestic courts have not.

As a newcomer to international law, I have been inspired by the international law distinction between specific measures to benefit litigants and general measures to prevent the reoccurrence of violations. From this practice emerges the major argument of this book: we should understand remedies as a two-track process. On the first track, courts should play the dominant role in providing meaningful remedies for the litigant. On the second systemic track, they should engage dialogically with the state to prevent similar rights violations in the future.

1.1.3 Outline of This Chapter

Section 1.2 of this chapter will outline a range of common issues that run throughout the individual remedies discussed in subsequent chapters. They include the multiple goals of remedies and the influence that the separation of powers, subsidiarity and competing social objectives play in constraining remedies.

Section 1.3 will discuss the legal process and interactionalist dialogic methodology used in the book and why it is suitable to the study of the complex subject of remedies.

Section 1.4 will examine the interactions between remedies in supranational and national law and the rationale for studying them together with examples taken from influential prior scholarship.

Section 1.5 will examine the relation between rights and remedies. A number of scholars have expressed concerns about "remedial deterrence".[9] This process operates when courts refuse to recognize rights because of concerns about the costs of remedies either for society at large or for the court itself. One source of remedial deterrence is the common idea that if courts recognize innovative and demanding rights, such as socio-economic rights and Indigenous rights, they must necessarily solve all of the remedial complexities of enforcing them. My interactionalist

Fuller also recognizes the importance of continual re-enforcement of norms including both softer attempts at persuasion and, when necessary, harder attempts at enforcement.

[8] Yuval Shany, *Assessing the Effectiveness of International Courts* (Oxford: Oxford University Press, 2014) pp.117–136; Dinah Shelton, *Remedies in International Human Rights Law*, 3rd ed. (New York: Oxford University Press, 2015), p.31.

[9] Daryl Levinson, "Rights Essentialism and Remedial Equilibration" (1999) 99 *Colum. L. Rev.* 4; Sonja B. Starr, "Rethinking 'Effective Remedies' and Remedial Deterrence in International Courts" (2008) 83 *N.Y.U. L. Rev.* 693.

and dialogic legal process methodology will suggest that when attempting to prevent future violations, courts generally do not and should not act alone. They should be assisted by other actors who can help them grapple with the complexities and challenges of remedies.

Section 1.6 will examine the main textual sources for remedies in domestic and supra-national law. These texts are most important when they specifically restrict remedies. For example, the UK's Human Rights Act 1998[10] denies courts the power to invalidate legislation and only allows non-binding declarations of invalidity. The 11th Amendment of the American Bill of Rights restricts the power of the Federal Courts over states. Remedial texts generally provide a broad and flexible framework for remedies by stressing vague admonitions to provide effective remedies. They have the virtue of allowing remedies to be shaped to the context, but they have the vice of not providing litigants or judges with principled criteria to apply to remedies.

Section 1.7 will draw on private law debates to outline different approaches to the exercise of remedial discretion.[11] Discretion plays a helpful and necessary role in remedial jurisprudence to the extent that it allows judges to adjust remedies to the context. At the same time, a strong discretion that simply allows judges to decline to grant a remedy without attempting to justify the remedial choice is a threat to rights and the rule of law. I will suggest that the answer to the dilemma of remedial discretion is not to try to reduce the necessary role of remedial discretion to rigid rules but rather to recognize broad principles that should guide rather than determine the exercise of remedial discretion.

What are the principles that should govern remedial decision-making? Section 1.8 will examine the need for courts at the domestic level to respect their appropriate role in the separation of powers and for adjudicators at the supra-national level to respect subsidiarity and the primacy of domestic legal systems. These concerns about the appropriate role of adjudicators should not, however, be rigid or static. Much will

[10] c. 42.

[11] Peter Birks, "Three Kinds of Objections to Discretionary Remedialism" (2000) 29 *W. Aust. L. Rev.* 1; private law scholars have since the legal realists devoted more time to understanding the importance of remedies as qualifying and often limiting rights. See Guido Calabresi and Douglas Melamed, "Property Rules and Liability Rules: One View of the Cathedral" (1972) 85 *Harv. L. Rev.* 1089; Stephen A. Smith, "Rights and Remedies: A Complex Relationship" in Robert Sharpe and Kent Roach (eds.), *Taking Remedies Seriously* (Ottawa: Canadian Institute for the Administration of Justice, 2010); Hanoch Dagan, "Remedies, Rights, and Properties" (2011) 4 *J. Tort L.* 1.

depend on the context and the respective performance of different institutions.

Section 1.9 will examine how principles of proportionality can help inform and discipline the way that competing social interests will constrain remedies, including questions of alternative remedies. Proportionality principles can assist courts in exercising remedial discretion in a more principled, transparent and disciplined manner. In particular, they can assist courts in determining whether governments can justify less drastic or even the award of no remedy because of competing social interests. Allowing competing social interests to compromise remedies is rightly controversial. It allows a second form of interest balancing after the state has failed to justify the human rights violation, sometimes on the basis of the same or similar social interests.[12] Nevertheless, ignoring compelling social interests will only increase the phenomena of remedial deterrence discussed in Section 1.5 of this chapter. In other words, it can lead to stunted interpretations of the underlying rights. Alternatively, ignoring competing interests can result in remedies that can cause serious and unanticipated social harms.

1.1.4 Outline of the Rest of the Book

I will argue in Chapter 2 that courts should take a two-track approach that distinguishes between remedies that compensate and protect litigants and more general and systemic measures to prevent or minimize similar violations in the future. Courts should recognize that they have a distinctive responsibility to provide individual remedies that is not shared by the executive or legislature. With respect to systemic remedies designed to prevent future violations, however, courts should play a more dialogic role that engages with the executive, the legislature, civil society and those who are supposed to benefit from the remedy. The judicial role should respect the separation of powers and subsidiarity. Nevertheless, courts should become interventionist if governments demonstrate that they are incapable or unwilling to take reasonable steps to prevent similar rights violations in the future.[13] Courts should also be responsive to requests for additional relief from those whose rights have or will be

[12] Paul Gewirtz, "Remedies and Resistance" (1983) 92 *Yale L. J.* 4; Robert Leckey, "The Harms of Remedial Discretion" (2016) 14 *I. Con.* 3, 584.

[13] Kent Roach and Geoff Budlender, "Mandatory Relief and Supervisory Jurisdiction: When Is It Appropriate, Just and Equitable" (2005) 122 *S.A. L. J.* 325.

violated again. International courts are much closer to the two-track approach than domestic courts. This chapter will also suggest that an exclusive focus on one of the individual or systemic tracks can produce remedial pathologies and that the two-track approach is attentive to remedial failure.

Chapter 3 will examine the important and often neglected role that interim remedies play in both domestic and increasingly in supranational law. Interim remedies can provide a first-track remedy that prevents irreparable harm to human rights. At the same time, they can be revisited by requests to amend the relief, by settlements or by a trial on the merits, all of which may be able to provide a more comprehensive approach to systemic relief. To be sure, interim remedies will not always be justified and should be tailored to reflect proportionality principles. A full application of these principles may require courts to take a closer look at the merits of the applicant's claim than has often been the case at the pre-trial stage. It may also require courts to assess the respective harms to applicants and respondents of not granting the interim relief. Without effective interim remedies, however, the promise of human rights will often ring hollow.

Chapter 4 will examine the range of remedies for laws that violate human rights. These include new remedies such as suspended declarations of invalidity and non-binding declarations of incompatibility. The two-track approach as applied to these new remedies will often require that successful litigants be given some tangible remedy even while courts provide legislatures an opportunity to craft the ultimate systemic remedies. A two-track approach can also, in some cases, justify the use of prospective rulings to accommodate competing social interests provided that litigants are given the benefit of the ruling. Interpretative remedies, including those that "read in" words to legislation, can be justified to the extent that they advance legislative objectives in so far as they are consistent with the court's interpretation of human rights. They can achieve both individual and systemic justice. Nevertheless, courts should generally allow legislatures to make choices if there are a variety of rights-compliant outcomes.

Chapters 5 and 6 will examine the traditional remedies of damages and remedies in the criminal process such as the exclusion of improperly obtained evidence. These remedies are best justified as individual remedies to compensate for past harms. At the same time, a failure by the state to take reasonable steps to prevent similar violations in the future should be relevant. Courts should encourage states to use the many remedies at their disposal to prevent similar violations in the future.[14] It will be suggested that supra-national courts, in part because of their more limited resources, have been more attentive to the dangers of repetitive violations than domestic courts.

The next three chapters will examine remedies in more innovative contexts. Chapter 7 will examine the range of remedies in cases where institutions such as prisons violate human rights. It will outline the implications of a two-track approach that compensates and prevents violations experienced by specific litigants while also supervising a more gradual systemic reform process designed to prevent future violations. Courts should often defer to the state that has the expertise, information and capacity to implement systemic remedies. At the same time, domestic courts should follow supra-national adjudicators by more frequently retaining jurisdiction to provide a transparent and fair process to entertain requests for additional relief. This chapter will advocate for a new intermediate remedy, the declaration plus, that combines the declaration's reliance on persuasion and deference to governments with the retention of jurisdiction that accompanies the use of injunctions. It will also be suggested that the two-track approach will be responsive to the reality of remedial failure in intractable institutional contexts. It can generate ongoing cycles of reform involving both individual remedies and enhanced systemic remedies.

Chapter 8 will examine remedies for violations of socio-economic rights such as housing and health rights. It will be argued that courts should be more willing to issue individual remedies. Individual remedies that prevent irreparable harm and compensate for harm, honour the integrity of adjudication as represented by traditional right to a remedy reasoning. They should not be disparaged as queue jumping, at least in cases where states have made unreasonable distributional or rationing choices. The South African and Colombian Constitutional Courts, like supra-national courts, have taken a two-track approach that combines individual remedies with more deferential systemic remedies.

Chapter 9 will examine remedies for violations of Indigenous rights. Interim remedies to prevent irreparable harm should play an important role. Courts have struggled with such remedies and have often failed to recognize or implement the priority of restitution of Indigenous land or even provide full compensation for pecuniary damages. Although they have been more generous with compensating for non-pecuniary harms, they

[14] Schuck, *Suing Government*.

need to guard against the dangers of, even with the best of intentions, imposing neo-colonial solutions on Indigenous communities. This chapter will examine the duty to consult that is playing an increasing role in domestic and supra-national law. It will suggest that the duty to consult is two-faced. It has often been used as a procedural checklist to justify resource extraction that limits Indigenous rights or claims. A better use of the duty to consult is as a source for creative remedies or modern Treaties based on the consent of the Indigenous community. The latter remedies, following the UN Declaration on the Rights of Indigenous Peoples, can be bi-jural in combining human rights and Indigenous law.

The final chapter will return to the common themes discussed in the first two chapters. It will revisit some methodological challenges in understanding remedies. It will suggest that proportionality reasoning can make the exercise of remedial discretion more disciplined and transparent. The two-track approach will be defended as a helpful way to think about the multiple goals and methodologies and the sad reality of remedial failure. It honours common expectations about adjudication and rights by providing individual remedies when possible to prevent and compensate for rights violations. It recognizes the need to prevent the reoccurrence of violations. Systemic remedies should not be crafted by the judiciary alone and should be done in a way that respects both separation of powers and subsidiarity. When systemic remedies fail, a new round of individual and systemic remedies will be necessary in a way that is more familiar to international than domestic human rights lawyers.

The topics of each of these chapters could, and in many cases have, commanded books in their own right. My hope, however, is to illuminate the common theoretical and institutional challenges faced throughout remedies for human rights violations.

1.2 Common Issues in Remedies

1.2.1 Remedies Defined

Following Professor Shelton, remedies will be defined in this book as "the range of measures that may be taken in response to an actual or threatened violation of human rights".[15] Remedies are what we use to

[15] Shelton, *Remedies in International Human Rights Law*, p.17. This is Professor Shelton's definition of remedies and, as she notes, remedies "thus embrace the substance of relief as well as the procedure through which relief is measured". Ibid.

prevent violations of human rights and, when prevention has failed, to make amends for their violation. In this sense, remedies have a dual function: responding to and sometimes preventing an unjust past and shaping a more just future.

The focus in this book will be on judicial remedies ordered by supranational adjudicators and domestic courts mostly from established democracies. It will be suggested that courts should often call on the executive and the legislature to play a role in devising systemic remedies to prevent the reoccurrence of human rights violations. It is in this sense that this book continues work that has already started on dialogic approaches to judicial review that recognizes that legislatures, the executive and the courts all play key roles in how rights are treated in democracies.[16]

1.2.2 The Goals of Remedies

Chapter 2 will examine the purposes or goals of remedies and the two-track approach that I propose. Nevertheless, a brief discussion of those issues is appropriate here because they are common issues that run throughout remedies.

As articulated in the *Chorzow Factory* case, a traditional goal of remedies is that they should, "as far as possible, wipe out all the consequences of the illegal act and re-establish the situation which would, in all probability have existed if the act had not been committed".[17] In *Marbury* v. *Madison*, Chief Justice Marshall appealed to a similar theory drawn from the common law as expounded by William Blackstone when he stated that "if the laws furnish no remedy for the violation of a vested legal right", the United States would no longer be subject to the rule of law.[18]

[16] The focus in this book will be on Western democracies, but dialogic approaches that are aware of the role of the executive and the legislature may play an even greater role with respect to authoritarian governments. See Po Jen Yap, *Constitutional Dialogue in Common Law Asia* (Oxford: Oxford University Press, 2015); Po Jen Yap (ed.), *Constitutional Remedies in Asia*, 1st ed. (London: Routledge, 2019).

[17] *Factory at Chorzow* (Judgment No. 13) [1928] PCIJ Series A No. 17, 22 at 47.

[18] In recognition that the petitioner in Marbury would not receive a remedy because of restrictions on the jurisdiction of the Federal Courts, Chief Justice Marshall stated that: "[i]f this obloquy is to be cast on the jurisprudence of our country, it must arise from the peculiar character of the case". *Marbury* v. *Madison*, 5 US 137 (1803) at 163. The theme of American exceptionalism in not granting judicial remedies runs throughout this book. For arguments that other countries should not look to the United States for guidance with respect to the damages for human rights violations because of residues of sovereign

A newer goal of remedies is to prevent violations of rights in the future. In 2005, the United Nations agreed on *Basic Principles*[19] that included not only the traditional remedial goals of restitution, compensation, rehabilitation and satisfaction but also "guarantees of non-repetition", including law reform. In the post-World War II era, domestic courts have been increasingly interested in preventing human rights violations in the future. Cases such as *Brown* v. *Board of Education II*[20] broke the close link between rights and personal remedies in an attempt to gradually desegregate public schools. This grew into public law litigation, now accepted in other parts of the world, where the courts are primarily concerned with attempting to end systemic rights violations in the future.

1.2.3 The Two-Track Approach to Individual and Systemic Relief

There is a tension between traditional approaches to remedies that focus on the litigant's right to receive a remedy designed to correct the past harms of the violation and more ambitious modern approaches that attempt to minimize future rights violations. As a means of recognizing and managing this tension, the two-track approach seeks, when possible, to combine these backward and forward-looking aspirations of remedies while recognizing that different approaches and remedies may be required on each track.

The two-track approach recognizes that an exclusive focus on either personal or systemic remedies is insufficient. It also seeks to respect the limits of judicial power with respect to devising effective and sustainable systemic remedies. Courts should assume primary responsibility for the traditional task of repairing and preventing the violation of a specific litigant's rights. At the same time, they should be more deferential

immunity and robust qualified immunity, see Gary Gilden, "Damages Caused by Violations of the Charter: The Relevance of American Constitutional Remedies Jurisprudence" (2009) 24 *Nat'l. J. Const. L.* 121; on the failure of American courts to provide effective remedies for human rights abuses in the war against terror, see James Pfander, *Constitutional Torts and the War on Terror* (New York: Oxford University Press, 2017); on how the United States Supreme Court has severely restricted the remedies of both exclusion of unconstitutionally obtained evidence and constitutional torts, see David Rudovsky, "Running in Place: The Paradox of Expanding Rights and Restricted Remedies" (2005) 2005 *U. Ill. L. Rev.* 5.

19 UN *Basic Principles* at paras 18, 23.

20 349 US 294 (1955) [henceforward *Brown II*].

towards the role and abilities of governments to select among various means to ensure future compliance with rights. Both in supra-national and national law, courts can attempt to engage legislatures and the executive to consult with those affected and take steps to prevent future violations. Such a deferential approach is supported by respect for subsidiarity in supra-national law and the separation of powers in domestic law. But neither of these concerns impose hard or immutable limits on judicial power. They are dependent on how governments respond. If governments prove to be incompetent or unwilling, stronger judicial remedies may be necessary.[21]

The two-track approach is an attempt to respond to the under-theorized nature of remedial discourse. Even if not possible in every case, it provides a guide for litigants and judges about remedial goals and means. However, the two-track approach also has a practical side. Concrete cases where domestic and especially supra-national courts have used the two-track approach will be discussed in each of the following chapters.

The two-track approach is an ambitious approach to remedies. It may not be possible and perhaps not advisable[22] in every case. In some cases, litigants may decide to only request individual or systemic remedies. These choices should generally be respected. Nevertheless, the dual ambitions of remedies should always be remembered. The repair of discrete violations suffered by individual litigants is an important component of the judicial role and judicial legitimacy. Judges also need to be attentive to the dangers of repetitive violations even while they recognize that they will need assistance from other parts of government and society to achieve these more ambitious remedial goals.

1.2.4 Remedial Failure

Remedies often fail. Systemic remedies are especially prone to remedial failure because they frequently fail to prevent similar rights violations in the future. Individual remedies, such as damages, may devalue the often-intangible harms that rights holders have suffered to their liberty, equality and dignity. This frequent failure of remedies may help to

[21] Roach and Budlender, "Mandatory Relief and Supervisory Jurisdiction".

[22] David Landau, "Choosing Between Simple and Complex Remedies in Socio-Economic Rights Cases" (2019) 69 (1 supp)*U.T.L.J.* 5, 105.

explain why they have not received the same attention as rights. Remedies are the rainy-day side of the sunny-day human rights story.

The two-track approach recognizes the tragic inevitability of remedial failure. Once systemic remedies have failed to prevent yet another individual violation, a new two-track cycle of remedies can start with new individual remedies that will focus attention on specific instances of rights violations. Courts may also begin devising less deferential systemic remedies to minimize future rights violations.

1.2.5 Choice of Remedies and Proportionality

Remedies are often subject to a balancing of competing interests and rights.[23] Courts ignore social interests that may be harmed by remedies at their peril. Nevertheless, they should resist the temptation to disguise the impact of these social interests on their remedial decisions by either refusing to recognize well-grounded rights claims or by relying on summary and inarticulate appeals to their remedial discretion.

Proportionality reasoning is increasingly used in other parts of human rights law. It can also assist in remedial decision-making in two main ways. First, it can structure and make transparent the balancing of interests. By requiring an explicit and legitimate objective to limit remedies, proportionality makes real the broken promise made by the United States Supreme Court in *Brown II*[24] that mere objections to rights should not be a legitimate factor in remedial decision-making. It can require courts to limit remedies as little as necessary to recognize competing interests and to compare the harms to society and rights-holders of limits to remedies.[25] Second, proportionality reasoning can play an important role in selecting the most appropriate of multiple remedies. The most drastic remedy such as a stay of proceedings that will stop prosecutions will not always be appropriate.[26] Less drastic remedies such as exclusion of evidence or sentence reductions may in some cases adequately address the damage caused by the violation and help prevent similar violations in the future. Damages may be adequate in some cases, but in other cases an interim or final injunction that prevents irreparable harm to rights may

[23] Gewirtz, "Remedies and Resistance".
[24] 349 US 294 (1955).
[25] Aharon Barak, *Proportionality* (Cambridge: Cambridge University Press, 2012).
[26] See *infra*, Chapter 6, Section 6.2.8.

be necessary. The role of proportionality in remedial decision-making will be discussed in greater detail in Section 1.9 of this chapter.

1.2.6 Separation of Powers and Subsidiarity

Another restraint on remedies is the appropriate role of courts. In domestic law, limits on judicial power are often based on concerns about the separation of powers. In supra-national law, these limits are also based on the principle of subsidiarity and concerns about the role of the nation state. These will be examined in greater detail in Section 1.8 of this chapter.

The limits on judicial power are often context-specific. Some countries accept that judges can strike down laws that violate human rights, but others do not. Some far-reaching judicial remedies that might ordinarily offend the separation of powers may be justified if the state is incapable or unwilling to take steps to prevent continuing or reoccurring violations. The role that courts play will often depend on how the executive and the legislature discharge their roles, especially with respect to the prevention of repetitive violations. It is in this sense that judicial remedies are "dialogic" because they respond to executive and legislative performance.

Judges should be candid about how concerns about institutional roles as well as competing social interests influence their remedial decisions. This is important if remedies are not to remain the under-examined underbelly of our modern commitment to human rights.

1.3 Methodology: Legal Process and Interactional/ Dialogical Approaches

My methodological approach is rooted in the legal process tradition of scholarship that examines the role of courts in light of the roles of other institutions and other processes of dispute resolution. Such an approach requires attention to interaction or dialogue between courts and the executive or legislature, often mediated by participation of civil society and the parties to a lawsuit who have an important role to play in proposing or objecting to particular remedies.

1.3.1 The Legal Process

The legal process approach has its origins in the course and teaching materials of Harvard law professors Henry Hart Jr. and Albert Sacks. It was based on the idea that courts, the legislature, the executive and more private processes based on negotiation and mediation all had essential roles in social ordering.[27] Hart and Sacks borrowed from law and society approaches in recognizing that most remedies were obtained not through court orders but through private settlements and other forms of non-adjudicatory ordering.[28] Their approach to public law remedies, however, ignored the work that was done even in their time to enforce *Brown*. Their understanding of the limits of judicial remedies reflected their heavy reliance on Lon Fuller's early work that suggested that courts were not well suited to making "managerial decisions" about "polycentric problems". Hart and Sacks argued that such problems "characteristically present so many variables as to require handling by the method of either *ad hoc* discretion or of negotiation or of legislation".[29]

1.3.2 Lon Fuller and the Challenges of Polycentric Problems

Hart and Sacks relied on an article that Lon Fuller finished in 1961, but that was not published until 1978, after his death. In it, Fuller argued that multi-faceted or polycentric problems were best suited to ordering through negotiation, the market or voting. In adjudication, they were simplified into "claims of right or accusations of fault".[30] Fuller's early work was influenced by Aristotle's dichotomy between matters of distributive and corrective justice. In 1954, Fuller wrote: that a "jury may be a useful device for determining how much *A* should pay for *B*'s broken leg, but it does not follow that it would be equally useful in allocating newsprint".[31]

At the same time, Fuller recognized that courts could grapple with multi-faceted or polycentric issues. The issue was not one of "distinguishing black from white. It is a question of knowing when the polycentric

[27] Henry Hart and Albert Sacks, *The Legal Process: Basic Problems in the Making and Application of the Law* (Westbury: The Foundation Press, 1994). They argued that regardless of the particular field of law, "problems arising in a court call for a perceptive awareness not only what courts are for but of what a legislature is for and sometimes also of what an administrative agency is for and of what matters can best be left to private decisions". Ibid., p.cxxxvii.

[28] Ibid., p.286.

[29] Ibid., p.647.

[30] Lon Fuller, "The Forms and Limits of Adjudication" (1978) 92 *Harv. L. Rev.* 353, 369.

[31] Lon Fuller, "Some Reflections on Legal and Economic Freedoms: A Review of Robert Hale's Freedom through Law" (1954) 54 *Colum. L. Rev.* 70, 81.

elements have become so significant and predominant that the proper limits of adjudication have been reached".[32] Remedies could accommodate polycentricity if the judge ordered a "tentative decree, with something like an order to show cause why it should not be made final".[33]

Remedial activism of judges is sometimes presented in popular critiques as a "one sided projection of authority"[34] that Fuller rightfully deplored. Nevertheless, Fuller's more nuanced notion of a "tentative decree" and "a difficult middle course" that uses "extra-curial processes of political adjustment and compromise" and avoids judicial decisions that were "too exacting and comprehensive" while still producing "a situation that was acceptable to the court"[35] describes much of the actual practice of complex relief. It also illustrates how the resulting decree gains legitimacy through the participation of the affected parties. It also gains legitimacy by judges being modest and fair in their dealings with all the parties. Fuller's warnings about the difficulties of courts dealing with polycentric problems still influences judges.[36] Nevertheless, it is noteworthy that he saw remedies as flexible enough to accommodate the complexity of polycentric issues. Part of the flexibility of remedies was that they could allow for participation by other institutions and could involve non-adjudicative processes.

At the same time, Fuller also stressed the importance of maintaining the integrity of adjudication by providing remedies for individuals that were responsive to their claim that their rights had been violated and that the defendant had committed a wrong.

One of Fuller's famous criteria of legality, the need for congruence between the law and official action, implicitly spoke to the need for remedies to both respond to past violations and prevent future rights violations. It also invoked a rule of law vision that suggested that officials were bound by law and should be liable for its violation.

Fuller lived in a more complex modern world than Blackstone did in the eighteenth century, one replete with multi-faceted and polycentric problems. This led him to recognize a second criteria of legality: that the law should not order the impossible. This second criteria could at times

32 Fuller, "Forms and Limits of Adjudication", 398.

33 Ibid., 389.

34 J. W. F. Allison, "Fuller's Analysis of Polycentric Disputes and the Limits of Adjudication" (1994) 53 *Cambridge L. J.* 367, 376.

35 Lon Fuller, *The Morality of Law* (New Haven: Yale University Press, 1969), p.178.

36 But for an important attempt to argue that much litigation is polycentric, see Jeff King, *Judging Social Rights* (Cambridge: Cambridge University Press, 2012), pp.190–210.

be at odds with his insistence on congruence between official conduct and the law.

The tension between congruence with law and not ordering the impossible captures many of the remedial dilemmas that judges and scholars continue to confront. My two-track approach to remedies is one attempt to ensure that congruence between law and official action is promoted, while also recognizing that judges should not order the impossible when it comes to preventing future rights violations through systemic reform.[37]

1.3.3 Alexander Bickel and the Recognition of Dialogic Remedies

Like Fuller, Alexander Bickel was a scholar influenced by the legal process. His approach to remedies was also nuanced. He recognized that effective remedies to desegregate schools could not be achieved by the courts alone. Desegregation would require both participation and buy in from other institutions such as school boards, states and, ultimately, American society. He recognized the novelty and the danger of the "all deliberate speed" remedial approach in *Brown II* that remanded cases throughout the US to local Federal Court trial judges. Bickel understood this remedy in dialogic terms: the trial courts would "engage in a continual colloquy with the political institutions, leaving it to them to tell the Court what expedients of accommodation and compromise they deemed necessary".[38]

At the same time, Bickel, like Fuller, recognized that courts were not a "collective poet laureate".[39] They must resolve cases on the basis of principles and reject proposals that "amounted to the abandonment of principle".[40] The US Supreme Court did this a few years after *Brown II* when it affirmed an order that nine Black students should be admitted to Central High in Little Rock.[41] In a decision signed by all nine Justices, it reversed lower court decisions that wanted to undo this individual remedy because of massive and racist state and social resistance.[42]

[37] For a more detailed discussion of polycentricity, see *infra* Chapter 8, Section 8.3.

[38] Alexander Bickel, *The Least Dangerous Branch* (New Haven: Yale University Press, 1986), p.254.

[39] Ibid.

[40] Ibid.

[41] *Cooper* v. *Aaron*, 358 US 1 (1958).

[42] Ibid. Alas the state responded by privatizing the high school and closing it to all students for the year.

Bickel rejected the idea that law was simply a matter of command. He understood Alexander Hamilton's admonition that courts were the least dangerous government branch that lacked the power of the sword or the purse. Despite the contempt powers of Federal Court judges, Bickel argued that "the problem was not simply one of enforcement. The task of the Court is to seek and foster assent, and compliance through assent . . . the task of judicial rather than legislative law was not to punish law breakers but to diminish their number".[43] He warned that:

> any rule of constitutional law not put into effect voluntarily by officials and other persons who acquiesce in it, or not taken up by legislation and made more effective by administrative or noncoercive means- any such rule is not in our system an effective rule of law . . . The Court thus interacts with other institutions, with whom it is engaged in an endlessly renewed education conversation . . . And it is a conversation, not a monologue.[44]

In other words, effective remedies require persuasion and voluntary compliance more than coercion. This understanding of law narrows the gap between domestic and supra-national law. Bickel laid the foundations for understanding remedies in both domestic and supra-national law in dialogic and interactionalist terms that includes not only courts but legislatures, the executive and society. He recognized that even remedies are not simply a matter of command. Like Fuller, Bickel knew that courts cannot order the impossible.[45] Bickel also knew that courts cannot save us from ourselves.

Bickel recognized the tragic side of remedies and their frequent failure. By 1970, he recognized how residential segregation and white flight to the suburbs and private schools placed real limits on the desegregation of public schools, even in the northern United States. Bickel warned that it was impossible for courts "to turn the clock back"[46] to eliminate racism in American society. He predicted that *Brown* might become irrelevant – an insight that Derrick Bell, a founder of critical race theory, would come

[43] Bickel, *The Least Dangerous Branch*, pp.250–251.

[44] Alexander Bickel, *The Morality of Consent* (New Haven: Yale University Press, 1975), p.111.

[45] He recognized that that "practical factors" could "make it impossible to achieve immediately a result called for by the Court's decision. Bickel, *The Least Dangerous Branch*, pp.246, 249.

[46] Alexander Bickel, *The Supreme Court and the Idea of Progress* (New Haven: Yale University Press, 1978 [first published 1970]), pp.150–151.

to share even though he had worked for many years as a lawyer trying to integrate schools.[47]

1.3.4 *Public Law Remedial Scholarship*

Other scholars have used legal process foundations to be even more imaginative and creative than Bickel in understanding remedies. Abram Chayes wrote seminal articles identifying a new style of public law litigation where courts tackled polycentric issues involved in, for example, desegregating schools, reforming prisons and dealing with relief for whole classes. He perceptively noted, however, that many complex remedies were a ratification of negotiation and mediation between the affected parties. He applied Fuller's insight that mixed forms of ordering that combined adjudication with negotiation, mediation and even voting could help tackle complex issues.[48] As will be discussed below, Chayes also applied some of this approach to supra-national law.

Another of Hart and Sacks' students, Owen Fiss, stressed the need for judges to ensure that the reasoned process of elaborating rights or constitutional values was not compromised by the demands and trade-offs of the new remedial environment.[49] He argued that remedial hierarchies that saw injunctions as extraordinary were broken down by the demands of school desegregation. Rather than using criminal or contempt sanctions to respond to lack of compliance, Fiss recognized that judges often responded to evolving polycentric problems by modifying existing orders or issuing supplemental ones.[50] As with Fuller and Bickel, remedies were a matter more of persuasion and adjustment than command. Again, this narrows the distances between domestic and supra-national human rights law.

Guido Calabresi also drew on legal process foundations to defend dialogical forms of judicial review that avoided the extremes of judicial and legislative supremacy. He stressed the remedial option of having

47 Derrick Bell, *Silent Covenants: Brown v. Board of Education and the Unfulfilled Hopes for Racial Reform* (Oxford: Oxford University Press, 2005).

48 Abram Chayes, "The Role of the Judge in Public Law Litigation" (1976) 89 *Harv. L. Rev.* 7; for a current recognition of the role that mediation can play in housing remedies, see *Port Elizabeth Municipality* v. *Various Occupiers*, [2004] ZACC 7, as discussed in Chapter 8, Section 8.6.

49 Owen Fiss, "Forward: The Forms of Justice" (1979) 93 *Harv. L. Rev.* 1.

50 Owen Fiss, *The Civil Rights Injunction* (Bloomington: Indiana University Press, 1979), p.36.

judges remand issues to legislatures and agencies. Calabresi and Melamed also contributed greatly to understanding remedial choice in private law through their famous distinctions between liability rules that only produce damages after the fact and property rules that are enforced by injunctions beforehand.[51] Finally, Calabresi, like Bickel, was a rarity among scholars who recognized the tragic nature of many of the choices[52] confronting judges, a view that can also be applied to the problem of remedial failure discussed throughout this book.

Fiss and Calabresi's sense of institutional role was more dynamic and contingent than previous legal process approaches. It has been characterized as the beginnings of a "new legal process" approach.[53] Courts for them should fill governance gaps created by legislative and administrative inertia or failure.[54] When necessary, courts could engage in activities that Hart and Sacks would have identified as exclusively reserved to the executive and the legislature.

A newer generation of scholars moved even farther away from original legal process understandings of essential institutional roles. These scholars had less faith in government than Hart and Sacks and confronted various pathologies in legislative, executive and judicial branches. Mark Tushnet defended weak and systemic remedies as the appropriate means to enforce socio-economic rights while recognizing that they could evolve into stronger remedies.[55] They defended various forms of remedial experimentation as a way of dealing with blockages in governance. They also observed a trend away from judge-dominated command and control strategies to ones that stressed monitoring and information gathering and focused more on outcomes.[56] This approach is more consistent with the lighter touch and realities of supra-national human rights law. Although the new experimentalists have influenced my approach to systemic relief, the two-track approach is built on

[51] Calabresi and Melamed, "Property Rules and Liability Rules".

[52] Guido Calabresi and Philip Bobbit, *Tragic Choices* (New York: W.W. Norton & Company, 1978). My approach to remedial failure, however, calls for more overt acknowledgment of failure and limits than contemplated by Calabresi and Bobbit.

[53] Kent Roach, "What is New and Old about the Legal Process" (1997) 47 *U.T.L.J.* 363.

[54] Guido Calabresi, *The Common Law in the Age of Statutes* (Cambridge: Harvard University Press, 1982).

[55] Mark Tushnet, *Weak Courts, Strong Rights: Judicial Review and Social Welfare Rights in Comparative Constitutional Law* (Princeton: University of Princeton Press, 2004), Chapter 8.

[56] Charles F. Sabel and William H. Simon, "Destabilization Rights: How Public Law Litigation Succeeds" (2004) 117 *Harv. L. Rev.* 1016.

the premise that experimentalists often discount the importance of individual remedies.

Finally, new remedial scholarship has reflected on comparative experiences, especially those in the global South. The Inter-American Court of Human Rights (IACtHR) has been the most creative of regional human rights courts. As will be discussed throughout the book, it has confronted challenges related to institutional atrocities, socio-economic rights and Indigenous rights. The Colombian Constitutional Court has supplemented its summary *tutela* jurisdiction, which has resulted in many individual remedies for socio-economic rights with a more systemic approach. As will be discussed in Chapter 8, Section 8.6, this has similarly occurred in recent housing rights cases in South African Courts.

1.3.5 Dialogic Judicial Review

Another variant of this new legal process approach is the still growing literature on judicial review as a form of dialogue with other institutions and society. Dialogic understandings of judicial review have been controversial. Some have argued that they disguise judicial power, independence and supremacy while others suggest that they threaten these qualities. While I will not re-engage in these broader debates in this work,[57] I will note that the two-track approach proposed in this book attempts to respond to some who have criticized dialogic remedies such as suspended declarations of invalidity in Canada and South Africa or declarations of incompatibility[58] in the UK, Australia and New Zealand on grounds that they sacrifice the traditional role of courts in providing immediate remedies for successful litigants.[59]

Courts should anchor their dialogic engagement with governments and society about systemic remedies to prevent future violations with individual remedies to prevent imminent violations or compensate for

57 See Kent Roach, "Dialogue in Canada and the Dangers of Simplified Comparative Law and Populism" in Geoffrey Sigalet, Gregoire Webber and Rosalind Dixon (eds.), *Constitutional Dialogue Rights and Institutions* (New York: Cambridge University Press, 2019); Kent Roach, *The Supreme Court on Trial: Judicial Activism or Democratic Dialogue*, rev'd ed. (Toronto: Irwin Law, 2016).

58 Leckey, "The Harms of Remedial Discretion".

59 Tom Hickman, "Bill of Rights Reform and the Case for Going beyond the Declaration of Incompatibility Model" (2015) *N.Z. L. Rev.* 35; Aileen Kavanagh, *Constitutional Review under the UK Human Rights Act* (Cambridge: Cambridge University Press, 2009).

past violations. Individual remedies are necessary to honour the integrity of adjudication. In doing so, these remedies make clear that courts contribute distinctive concerns about providing remedies for successful litigants to our ongoing and multi-faceted dialogues about the treatment of rights in our societies.

1.4 Methodology: Bridging the Gap between Supra-national and National Law

A potentially controversial feature of this book is its attempt to examine domestic and supra-national remedies for violations of human rights together. However, the availability of supra-national and domestic remedies is doctrinally intertwined because the availability of the former depends on the inadequacy of the latter.

Those who would stress that domestic remedies are different from international remedies often discount the degree to which many domestic remedies also rely on persuasion with only remote possibilities for coercive forms of enforcement that, in theory, are sometimes also available in the supra-national context.

Some of the scepticism about combining a study of supra-national and national remedies also reflects the increased specialization of the legal academy. Today, there is surprisingly little cross-over in the worlds of domestic and supra-national human rights law. This may limit the potential for creative cross-pollination. Fortunately, I can follow in the footsteps of two long-deceased scholars who profitably engaged with remedial questions both at the domestic and supra-national law levels.

1.4.1 Edwin Borchard and the Appeal of Persuasive Remedies Directed at the State

Edwin Borchard was an extremely prolific and creative Yale law professor who engaged with both international and comparative law. In 1916, he published an innovative treatise called *The Diplomatic Protection of Citizens Abroad.*[60] In this work, Borchard recognized the complex relationship between domestic and supra-national law. Aliens were only entitled to seek protection from their countries of citizenship when it was clear that local remedies were "insufficient, illusory or ineffective in

[60] Edwin Borchard, *The Diplomatic Protection of Citizens Abroad* (New York: Banks Law Publishing, 1916).

securing adequate redress".[61] This sets out principles of exhaustion of local remedies that still influence the work of supra-national adjudicators. Supra-national law of state responsibility is deeply interactional and dialogic: it responds to the performance of other bodies.

Borchard demonstrated an interest in both compensatory and preventive justice that is present in my two-track approach. For example, he contemplated that damages could be paid by states as a remedy for past abuses, but that countries might also request "the dismissal of delinquent police, the punishment of guilty offenders and the institution of measures considered adequate or likely to prevent the recurrence of the offence".[62]

Borchard's concern about preventive justice and his willingness to transfer ideas from international to domestic law was also seen in his extremely influential text advocating the use of declarations. He characterized the landmark *Chorzow Factory* supra-national case on remedies as "in the nature of a declaratory judgment".[63] He argued that declaratory judgements were the norm before international tribunals that have no coercive powers. As a consequence, their judgements "depend for their enforcement on the disposition of nations to carry them out".[64] In other words, "in our civilized communities it is the determination, and not the command, which evokes respect".[65] In short, Borchard's defence of declaratory judgements was related to his views that the essence of law, both domestic and international, was its persuasive force.

Borchard passionately urged domestic courts to use declarations to prevent future rights violations including in cases where litigants had not yet suffered an injury.[66] He recognized that courts often had "sound reasons" not to make mandatory orders against state officials as opposed to private defendants because officials have a "special position – a fact

[61] Ibid, p.33.

[62] Ibid, p.406. Unfortunately, Borchard maintained that such conditions would only be imposed on what he called a "backward country".

[63] Edwin Borchard, *Declaratory Judgments*, 2nd ed. (Cleveland: Banks: Baldwin, 1941), p.124.

[64] Edwin Borchard, "Declaratory Judgments in International Relations" (1935) 98 *World Affairs* 3, 161–162.

[65] Edwin Borchard, "Judicial Relief for Peril or Insecurity" (1931) 45 *Harv. L. Rev.* 791, 799.

[66] Borchard, *Declaratory Judgments*, pp.87–137. For a Canadian case demonstrating such a resistance to the award of declarations on the basis that "courts do not engage in legal consultations; they judge cases . . . The mere fear which a private individual may have that some day an action might possibly be brought against him does not *per se* entitle him to legal recourse", see *Saumur* v. *Quebec (Attorney General)* (1964), 45 DLR (2d) 627 (SCC) at 630.

which makes a declaration of their duty as effective as a command to perform it or an injunction not to transgress".[67]

Borchard's pioneering work on declarations reveals how attention to international law can expand the remedial imagination and enhance our understanding of a remedy that today is a staple of international and national rights litigation. Today, many laws allow declarations to be used against the state and state officials as a substitute for injunctions. To be sure, declarations, even when issued against the state, have disadvantages and injunctions may sometimes be necessary. In Chapter 7, Section 7.4, I will advocate for a new intermediate remedy – the declaration plus where courts issue declarations but retain jurisdiction. Following Borchard, the declaration plus seeks to bring the practice of supranational law into domestic law.

Borchard was also a comparatist and internationalist who recognized and criticized the American remedial exceptionalism that will also be criticized in this book. He argued that the absolute immunity of states from damages under the 11th Amendment was a "set back to democratic notions of responsible government".[68] He found support for theories of direct governmental liability in continental law. He argued that it was only in the United Kingdom and the United States that "we find the absolutist metaphysics of divine right and sovereign immunity arrayed in the full regalia of their theological vestments, reincarnating for a twentieth century society the ancient credo of Bodin and Hobbes".[69]

As will be seen in Chapter 5, Section 5.2, Borchard's vision of holding the state liable for rights violations is now the norm in Canada, India, New Zealand and the United Kingdom. Alas, the United States is still bound by the outdated idea of the absolute immunity of both the state and federal governments from damages and extremely robust qualified immunities that while ostensibly designed to protect individual officials from damage awards provide a huge obstacle to accountability for rights violations.

Whether with respect to diplomatic protection, damages or declarations, Borchard looked to the state as opposed to individual state officials as the proper defendant for rights violations. He was concerned that remedies both compensate for past violations and prevent future ones. Finally, he recognized that preventive remedies did not necessarily

[67] Borchard, *Declaratory Judgments*, p.876.
[68] Edwin Borchard, "Tort Liability of the State" (1930) 12 *J. Comparative Int'l. L.* 1, 1.
[69] Edwin Borchard, "Government Responsibility in Tort VI" (1926) 36 *Yale L. J.* 8, 3.

have to result in mandatory orders to be effective. Edwin Borchard's pioneering and still fresh work demonstrates the utility of using supra-national and comparative law to expand thinking about domestic remedies.

1.4.2 *Abram Chayes and Iterative and Persuasive Remedies*

Another scholar whose work spans domestic and supra-national law was Harvard law professor Abram Chayes. Chayes's work serves as a nice counter-point to Borchard's because it demonstrates how concepts first articulated in domestic law can migrate to international law.

In 1976, Chayes wrote the seminal article on the rise of complex public law litigation in American desegregation and prison cases. He depicted the traditional idea associated with Blackstone and Dicey that remedies could be deduced from the underlying right as part of a pre-realist vision where the powers of both judges and governments were "stringently limited".[70] In the new public law litigation, "right and remedy are pretty thoroughly disconnected"[71] so that judges could no longer look simply to the right to define the content of the remedy. Chayes challenged the retrospective focus of the traditional approach to remedies by arguing that judges in public law litigation were increasingly seeking "to adjust future behaviour" rather than attempting "to compensate for past wrong[s]".[72] The greater ambitions of public law decrees in governing the future also meant that judges would have to balance competing interests in the remedial process, including of those not represented in the lawsuit.[73]

Like Borchard, Chayes argued that new remedies were necessary in the age of the modern state. Whereas Borchard had championed the declaration and damage awards against governments, Chayes, writing almost forty years later, championed the injunction or the decree as a new

[70] Chayes, "The Role of the Judge in Public Law Litigation", 1288; see also Owen Fiss's similar argument that the idea that the relationship between right and remedy is "formal and deductive" is "impoverished" and not suitable for modern conditions: Fiss, "The Forms of Justice", 47.

[71] Chayes, "The Role of the Judge in Public Law Litigation", 1293.

[72] Ibid., 1298.

[73] Ibid., 1298, 1295; for a similar argument that victims of constitutional violations need not be the recipient of remedies because of the "instrumental nature of the remedy" and that injunctions are focused on the future and "does not require a judgement about wrong-doing, future or past", see Fiss, "The Forms of Justice", 22–23.

remedy fit for changing times. Borrowing from Lon Fuller's recognition of mixed form of ordering, Chayes was sensitive to the reality that the new public law injunction used to desegregate schools and reform custodial institutions was not simply a top-down formulation of a coercive court order. Rather, it was often the product of negotiation and mediation between the affected interests.[74]

Chayes's understanding of injunctions differed significantly from the traditional idea of the injunction as a precise judicial command. He noted that after finding violations, judges often relied upon the parties and others such as court appointed masters to submit plans to provide the content of the injunction. This meant that "the formulation of the decree in public law litigation introduces a good deal of party control over the practical outcome". The court's relief "tends to converge with relief through a consent decree or voluntary settlement".[75] He employed the legal process insight that private ordering such as negotiation and mediation was frequently used and had many advantages in dealing with complex and polycentric issues.[76]

The remedial process was not a top-down judicial driven process. He ended his seminal 1976 article by stating: "judicial participation is not by way of sweeping and immutable statements of *the* law, but in the form of a continuous and rather tentative *dialogue* with other political elements – Congress and the executive, administrative agencies, the profession and academics, the press and wider publics".[77] Like Borchard, Chayes understood remedies in persuasive terms even though he saw the injunction, rather than the declaration or damages, as the main remedy for violations of human rights

The legal process approach was also applied to Chayes's innovative teaching materials on the international legal process.[78] Writing with his wife, Antonia Handler Chayes, he argued for an approach to enforcing

[74] Chayes, "The Role of the Judge in Public Law Litigation", 1299 at fn 82 citing an unpublished version of Lon Fuller, "The Forms and Limits of Adjudication" and at 1304 citing Fuller's idea of "parasitic" or mixed form of ordering that combines legislative and executive function as well as negotiation and mediation.

[75] Ibid., 1299.

[76] In this his approach was distinct from that of Owen Fiss who viewed negotiation as a threat to rights and reason: Owen Fiss, "Against Settlement", (1984) 93 *Yale L. J.* 1073.

[77] "The Role of the Judge in Public Law Adjudication", 1316 (emphasis added).

[78] The book recognized the limits of adjudication and the role played by politics, economics and non-governmental organizations: Abram Chayes, Thomas Ehrlich and Andreas Lowenfeld, *International Legal Process* (Boston: Little Brown, 1968).

international law that depended on the "discursive process of explanation, justification and persuasion".[79] In supra-national law, "states are given ample opportunity to explain and justify their conduct. The reasons advanced to excuse noncompliant conduct point to avenues for improvement and correction".[80] Over time, the state's "promises of improvement contain increasingly concrete, detailed and measurable undertakings".[81] Similarly, public law decrees become more detailed over time. In both cases the process can become more prescriptive as the parties and the adjudicators become more knowledgeable and comfortable with complex contexts.

They stressed that "sanctioning authority is rarely granted by treaty, rarely used when granted, and likely to be ineffective when used".[82] As Harold Koh has noted, this approach has much in common with Chayes's approach to public law litigation in domestic law.[83] Koh points out that the threat of sanctions can play a role in both domestic and supra-national law even when not used. This insight, however, only bridges the gulf many see between supra-national and national law by illustrating that threat of sanction, if not actual use, can play a role in both.

As in domestic public law litigation, most international law disputes were resolved informally. This allowed supra-national decision-makers to reap the benefits of negotiation between the parties.[84] Like domestic public law litigation, supra-national processes frequently extended over time as an iterative process.[85] One of the most important contributions of dialogic accounts of legal interactions is that they expand the time frame beyond the moment of either judicial or legislative decision. The two-track dialogic approach contemplates remedies evolving over time as well as cycles of different reforms in response to remedial failures.

[79] Abram Chayes and Antonia Handler Chayes, *The New Sovereignty: Compliance with International Regulatory Agreements* (Cambridge: Harvard University Press, 1996), p.127.

[80] Ibid.

[81] Ibid., p.230.

[82] Ibid.

[83] Harold Hongju Koh, "Why Do Nations Obey International Law?" (1997) 106 *Yale L. J.* 2599, 2638–2641.

[84] Abram Chayes and Antonia Handler Chayes, *The New Sovereignty*, p.206.

[85] Koh, "Why Do Nations Obey International Law?", 2638; Alexandra Huneeus, "Reforming the State from Afar: Structural Reform Litigation at the Human Rights Courts" (2015) *40 Yale Int. L. J.* 1.

In both supra-national litigation and domestic public law litigation, third parties such as non-governmental civil society actors play a critical role in verifying and supplementing the information provided by the state.[86] Experts who can engage in on-site verification can also play a role. The work of the master in domestic public law litigation and special rapporteurs in the supra-national context have similarities.[87] As scholars versed in the legal process, the Chayes remained sensitive to the role of different institutions and actors each with their own strengths and weaknesses in supra-national remedial processes.

The "dynamics of dialogue" was central to achieving compliance. As in public law litigation, reporting by states on what they had or had not done in response to a ruling played a critical role and provided the state with powerful incentives to comply or face criticism.[88] Lack of compliance with international standards often reflected a lack of state understanding or capacity as opposed to outright defiance. The Chayes stressed the "interacting measures of assistance and persuasion" as opposed to "coercive sanctions".[89] Although they have been criticized for downplaying the need for enforcement to support the legitimacy of international law,[90] the Chayes also noted that "threats of exposure and shaming" played a role in achieving compliance: in many cases "there was considerable muscle behind the jawboning".[91] The Chayes's still relevant work provides a solid foundation for examining similarities between remedies for rights violations in international and national law that are too easily dismissed by those who stress the differences between international and national human rights law.

1.4.3 Interactionalist Accounts of International Law

My colleagues Jutta Brunée and Stephen Toope have articulated an interactional approach to international law that is consistent with dialogic approaches to domestic law because it recognizes that multiple institutions,

86 Abram Chayes and Antonia Handler Chayes, *The New Sovereignty*, pp.164, 249.

87 Ibid., p.171.

88 On the importance of reporting, see *infra* Chapter 7, Section 7.2.

89 Abram Chayes and Antonia Handler Chayes, "On Compliance" in Lisa L. Martin and Beth A. Simmons (eds.), *International Institutions: An International Organization Reader* (Cambridge and London: The MIT Press, 1993), p.205.

90 Koh, "Why Do Nations Obey International Law?"; Brunée and Toope, *Legality and Legitimacy*.

91 Abram Chayes and Antonia Handler Chayes, *The New Sovereignty*, p.230.

parties and civil society help to determine and re-enforce the degree to which there is congruence between state action and legal norms. They have criticized the Chayes for not exploring the ideas of legal obligation and the role of enforcement more deeply.[92] As with Koh's critique, Brunée and Toope's critique of the Chayes's iterative managerial approach can bring their approaches to international law even closer to domestic law.[93]

Brunée and Toope fundamentally agree with the Chayes that international law can work without reliance on "an explicit constraint matched by a sanction".[94] Similarly, they stress the important role of non-state actors in maintaining respect for the principles of international law,[95] and the fact that the meaning of law must be "reasserted again and again" so that "the hard work of international law is never done".[96]

Following Fuller, they recognize that the law cannot order the impossible but that over time there must be congruence between legal norms and the action of state officials. Interactionist and dialogic approaches apply throughout the law. Nevertheless, they are particularly relevant with respect to remedies that, by definition, reveal and then attempt to bridge a gap between legal norms and the reality of past and often future violations of these norms.[97]

The broad institutional and societal lens used by both legal process and interactionalist approaches to legal scholarship is necessary to understand the complexities of remedies and their failures. This helps recognize that courts, like other institutions, have both strengths and weaknesses. This opens space for understanding the important role that parties and other processes including negotiation and mediation can play in formulating remedies.

1.4.4 Summary

This book will examine remedies for violations of human rights in both domestic and international law for both intellectual and practical

92 Brunée and Toope, Legality and Legitimacy, pp.105–106, 109–114.

93 But note that the contempt power is rarely used in domestic law. See Nicholas Parrillo, "The Endgame of Administrative Law: Governmental Disobedience and the Judicial Contempt Power" (2018) 131 *Harv. L. Rev.* 685, 3.

94 Brunée and Toope, *Legality and Legitimacy*, p.2.

95 Ibid.

96 Ibid., p.102.

97 For my previous work on the dialogic aspect of remedies, see Kent Roach, "Remedial Consensus and Dialogue" (2002) 35 *U.B.C. L. Rev.* 202; Kent Roach, "Dialogic Remedies" (2019) 17 *I. Con.* 860.

reasons. Intellectually, the work of Borchard and Chayes has demonstrated how domestic and international law can cross-pollinate, enrich and deepen our thinking about remedies. Borchard made convincing and successful arguments that the use of declarations and direct government responsibility taken from supra-national law could improve domestic remedies. There are striking similarities between Abram Chayes's description of domestic public law litigation that relies on iterative attempts at persuasion, negotiation and monitoring to achieve compliance and his description of the operation of supra-national processes. In both cases, sanctions are something to be kept in reserve with an emphasis on obtaining voluntary compliance and building capacity and knowledge over time.

A practical reason for examining domestic and international remedies together is that petitioners have to exhaust domestic remedies before seeking supra-national ones. International remedies are a response to domestic remedial failure. In addition, supra-national processes rely on domestic processes to take steps to implement effective remedies. Remedial dialogue flows from the domestic to the international and then back to the domestic.

1.5 The Relation between Rights and Remedies and Remedial Deterrence

A book about remedies for violations of human rights should not ignore the question of rights. Although it is beyond the scope of this work to justify expansive understandings of rights, better appreciation of the remedial process can lay the basis to recognize rights, especially with respect to socio-economic rights and Indigenous rights.

Since the advent of legal realism, we know that courts do not decide questions of rights without worrying about remedies. Private law theory, however, has been more comfortable with this insight than public law.[98] As Daryl Levinson has argued, human rights law has been slow to recognize that remedies play an equilibrating role that qualifies rights.

[98] Levinson, "Rights Essentialism and Remedial Equilibration"; for one example, see L. L Fuller and William R. Purdue, "The Reliance Interest in Contracts" (1936) 46 *Yale L. J.* 1. For an assessment of a debate in private law between monist approaches that deduce remedies from an understanding of rights and dualist approaches that recognize a form of equilibration or interaction between rights and remedies, see Stephen Waddams, *Principle and Policy in Contract Law* (New York: Cambridge University Press, 2011), pp.209–231.

Instead, there has been what Levinson characterizes as "rights essentialism" where rights are considered as ideals divorced from the more messy, contingent, instrumental and pragmatic practice of remedies. Professor Levinson's cogent critique of rights essentialism helps explain why human rights scholars have traditionally neglected the field of remedies and why they have been wrong to do so. His analysis also explains why many discussions of remedial issues, including the gradual enforcement of rights in *Brown II* or the role of qualified immunities with respect to damages, have often been viewed as unwelcome threats to rights as opposed to qualifications of rights.[99]

Levinson has urged scholars to attend to how "rights and remedies operate as part of a single package"[100] and how "rights are almost inevitably impure, always already shaped by remedies".[101] I suspect that his insights were more readily accepted by litigators who instinctively understand how judicial fears of unmanageable remedies can easily sink a rights claim. Human rights scholars have been attracted to the ideal world of rights essentialism while human rights practitioners work in the practical world of rights equilibration.

Human rights scholars will expect "remedies 'to change' in response to rights and not the reverse".[102] The two-track approach outlined in the next chapter will recognize and provide one possible means to manage this tension. The first individual remedy track will attempt to preserve the ideal of rights by providing some recognition that a claimant's right has been violated. The second systemic track will be more flexible. It will evolve in response to the context and the behaviour of other actors. The court's initially deferential approach may assuage some concerns about

[99] Levinson suggests that the operation of remedial deterrence where rights shrink to avoid remedial consequences is often speculative because of the confidentiality of judicial deliberations. The historical record, however, is fairly clear that the US Supreme Court did not agree that desegregation was unconstitutional until it had decided to take a gradual remedial response. The Court rightly or wrongly was concerned that more immediate and drastic remedies would be too destabilizing. Richard Kluger, *Simple Justice: The History of Brown v. Board of Education and Black America's Struggle for Equality* (New York: Knopf, 1975); Michael Klarman, *Brown v. Board of Education and the Civil Rights Movement* (New York: Oxford University Press, 2007); Mark Tushnet, *Making Civil Rights Law: Thurgood Marshall and the Supreme Court 1936–1961* (New York: Oxford University Press, 1994), pp.217–234.

[100] Levinson, "Rights Essentialism and Remedial Equilibration", 914.

[101] Ibid., 924.

[102] Ibid., 935.

remedial deterrence. However, if the state fails to take reasonable steps to prevent future rights violations, courts may engage in remedial incorporation which go beyond rights and create prophylactic standards[103] in an attempt to prevent repetitive violations.

Sonja Starr has also applied the concept of remedial deterrence to the work of international criminal courts. She documents how international criminal courts have at times interpreted the rights of the accused narrowly, so as to avoid stays of proceedings that will prevent the accused from having a trial on the merits. Professor Starr urges courts to more directly confront the need to balance competing interests when devising remedies so as to avoid the distorting effect of not recognizing rights because of the fear of drastic, controversial or unmanageable remedies.[104]

Levinson and Starr are correct in identifying remedial deterrence as an important and frequent process where courts "shrink rights to avoid expansive remedies".[105] The approach taken in this book will attempt to bring such concerns into the open. It will confront remedial deterrence by incorporating proportionality analysis into remedial decision-making. In this way, courts can recognize competing interests to remedies in a transparent and familiar way that will be examined in Section 1.9 of this chapter. In Section 1.8, it will be suggested that when devising systemic remedies in particular, courts should defer to the limits on their role provided domestically by concerns about the separation of powers and supra-nationally by concerns about subsidiarity. At the same time, they should take a dialogic approach that recognizes that the judicial role may expand should states fail to prevent repetitive violations.

1.6 Textual Basis for Ordering Remedies

Although not all human rights instruments contain explicit provisions with respect to remedies, many do. Most of these provisions recognize the need for effective and appropriate remedies and the important role of remedial discretion. As such, they do not provide much guidance for remedial decision-making. The text of human rights laws are most relevant when they place restrictions on remedies.

103 Levinson calls this process "remedial incorporation" where courts define rights broadly in a manner designed to prevent future violations of the core right.

104 Starr, "Rethinking 'Effective Remedies'".

105 Levinson, "Rights Essentialism and Remedial Equilibration", 893.

1.6.1 Supra-national Laws

1.6.1.1 The Universal Declaration of Human Rights

Article 8 of the Universal Declaration of Human Rights adopted in 1948 by the General Assembly of the United Nations provides: "[e]-veryone has the right to an effective remedy by the competent national tribunals for acts violating the fundamental rights granted him by the constitution or by law".[106] The UK championed the right to a remedy, but it stopped short of advocating for a right that would allow individuals to petition for a remedy. This type of right was included in the 1948 American Declaration of the Rights and Duties of Man.[107] However, the UK delegation worried that "individual petitions might well pour in from Alabama, Nigeria, and even from Counties Fermanagh and Tyrone".[108] In other words, the lack of an individual right of petition reflected the realpolitik of remedies provisions drafted during the Cold War and the break-up of colonial empires. The fact that both the UK and the US were not enthusiastic about individual remedies can perhaps be seen as a testament to their importance.

1.6.1.2 The 1966 International Covenants

Although drafting was started at the time of the Universal Declaration, there was no agreement on separate International Covenants on Civil and Political Rights (ICCPR) and Economic, Social and Cultural Rights (ICESCR) until 1966.

Article 2(3) of the ICCPR[109] continued the Universal Declaration's focus on effective remedies. Article 2(3)(a) provided that the state party would ensure that any person whose rights or freedoms as recognized in the Covenant were violated "shall have an effective remedy notwithstanding that the violation has been committed by persons acting in an official capacity". This represented a rejection of the idea that the official capacity of those committing the violation should shield them from

[106] *Universal Declaration of Human Rights, 1948*, G.A. Res. 217(III)A, in force 10 December 1948, Art. 8.

[107] American Declaration of the Rights and Duties of Man, 2 May 1948 OAS. Res. XXX, Art. XXIV provided: "[e]very person has the right to submit respectful petitions to any competent authority, for reasons of either general or private interest, and the right to obtain a prompt decision thereon".

[108] A.W. Brian Simpson, *Human Rights and the End of Empire* (Oxford: Oxford University Press, 2001), pp.408, 524.

[109] International Covenant on Civil and Political Rights, 19 December 1966, in force 23 March 1976, 999 UNTS 171.

liability. Some domestic systems, especially the American, still retain remnants of such immunities. As discussed above, Edwin Borchard, informed by more state centred international law experience, was highly critical of the 11th Amendment of the American Bill of Rights that made individual American states immune from damage awards by American Federal Courts.

Article 2(3)(b) of the ICCPR refers to "competent judicial, administrative or legislative authorities" or "any other competent authority provided by the legal system of the State" providing remedies. This broad approach differs from many domestic constitutions that look to the courts as the exclusive source for remedies. Although there are dangers in relying on legislatures and the executive to provide remedies, the ICCPR contemplates that these institutions can be a source of effective remedies. In particular, executive and legislative participation in remedies is often necessary to prevent future violations of rights. This reflects a theme that will be seen throughout this book: that supra-national law and instruments often adopt a broader perspective on remedies than domestic law.

Article 2(3)(c) provides that "the competent authorities shall enforce such remedies when granted". This recognizes the importance of follow-up actions after the grant of the remedy. As such, the 1966 ICCPR foreshadowed Chayes's recognition of the limits of a one shot traditional remedial processes, often in the form of damages.[110] In some cases, effective remedies would require extended processes of enforcement.

In contrast to the ICCPR, the 1966 ICESCR[111] had no explicit remedial provision, reflecting concerns at the time about the justiciability of socio-economic rights. Article 2(1) stressed that each state was committed "to the maximum of its available resources . . . to achieving progressively the full realization of the rights . . . by all appropriate means, including particularly the adoption of legislature measures". This underlined a view prevalent in 1966 but increasingly challenged today that different methods of enforcement were required for economic, social and cultural rights because of their distributive implications than for political and civil rights.

In 1976, an optional protocol was created where countries could allow individuals to make complaints to the Human Rights Committee about

[110] Chayes, "The Role of the Judge in Public Law Litigation".

[111] International Covenant on Economic, Social and Cultural Rights, GA Res. 220A/XXI, 16 December 1966, in force 3 January 1976, 993 UNTS 3.

violation of their ICCPR rights. Some countries have not become party to this protocol, but the work of the Human Rights Committee will be examined in the next chapter. It will be seen that the Committee takes a two-track approach that includes individual or specific measures to benefit the petitioner and general or systemic measures to prevent the repetition of similar violations in the future.

A similar optional protocol for individual complaints was not added to the ICESCR until the end of 2008. Like the UN Human Rights Commission, the Committee on Economic, Social and Cultural Rights often recommends that individual complainants be provided with remedies such as compensation. It also makes recommendations about the state's "obligation to prevent similar violations in the future"[112] including the need to adopt legislative and administrative measures.

The degree of difference in the two International Covenants can be overstated, especially given the ICCPR's reference to the legislative and administrative authorities providing remedies. Indeed, the advent of individual complaints mechanisms under both Covenants has further narrowed the remedial differences between them and has helped cement the two-track approach to remedies in both systems. Both Covenants can now be used as standards for monitoring to achieve systemic justice and for individual complaints.

1.6.1.3 Other Global Instruments

There are a range of global human rights instruments and some have more developed remedial measures than others. Subject to some exceptions, there is a trend toward more specific remedial provisions that recognize the importance and complexity of the remedial process.

Article 6 of the International Convention on the Elimination of All Forms of Racial Discrimination[113] adopted in 1965 contemplates that states will ensure that their institutions and tribunals provide "effective protection and remedies". It also provides that petitioners can seek from tribunals "just and adequate reparation or satisfaction for any damage suffered" as a result of racial discrimination. The Convention on the

[112] *S.C. and G.P.* v. *Italy*, Views adopted by the Committee on Economic, Social and Cultural Rights Under the Optional Protocol to the International Covenant on Economic, Social and Cultural Rights No. 22/2017 E/C.12/65/D/22. 2017 adopted 28 March 2019, 14.

[113] GA Res. 2106/XX, 21 December 1965, in force 4 January 1969, 660 UNTS 195 Art. 6.

Elimination of All Forms of Discrimination Against Women[114] adopted in 1979 contains commitments for states to eliminate such discrimination by adopting "appropriate legislative and other measures", but otherwise does not specify specific remedial measures.

The Convention Against Torture[115] adopted in 1984 specifies a range of judicial remedies including compensation and the exclusion of improperly obtained evidence. Article 2 commits states to "take effective legislative, administrative, judicial or other measures to prevent acts of torture in any territory under its jurisdiction".[116] Article 14 provides for "fair and adequate compensation, including the means for as full rehabilitation as possible" for victims.[117]

The Convention on the Rights of the Child[118] adopted in 1989 provides that states "shall undertake all appropriate legislative, administrative, and other measures for the implementation of the rights recognized in the present Convention". Article 27(3) contemplates that states will "in accordance with national conditions and within their means" implement rights but "in case of need provide material assistance and support programmes, particularly with regard to nutrition, clothing and housing". This contemplates both immediate provision of basic sustenance rights for children and more gradual implementation of a fuller range of rights. This is consistent with a two-track approach to enforcing social and economic rights.

The International Convention for the Protection of All Persons from Enforced Disappearances[119] adopted in 2006 provides a particularly fulsome approach to remedies. It contemplates a variety of preventive mechanisms including: training; criminal offences and investigations; on-site visits by members of the Commission under Article 33; and interim measures to locate and protect those in danger of enforced disappearances under Article 31. Article 24 provides a broad remedial provision

[114] New York, GA Res. 341/180, 18 December 1979, in force 3 September 1981, 1249 UNTS 13 Art. 2(b).

[115] Convention against Torture and Other Cruel, Inhuman or Degrading Treatment or Punishment, New York, 10 December 1984, in force 26 June 1987, 1465 UNTS 85.

[116] Art. 2 of the Convention against Torture.

[117] Art. 14 of the Convention against Torture.

[118] New York, GA Res. 44/25, 20 November 1989, in force 2 September 1990, 1577 UNTS 3, Art. 4.

[119] New York, adopted by GA Res. 61/177, 20 December 2006, in force 23 December 2010, 2716 UNTS 3.

that provides generally for "fair and adequate compensation" for enforced disappearances including "restitution, rehabilitation, satisfaction, including restoration of dignity and reputation and guarantees of non-repetition".[120] In this way, this recent Convention incorporates *Basic Principles* enacted by the UN General Assembly in 2005.[121] These principles are not legally binding. They only apply to gross violations of human rights. Nevertheless, they are a persuasive source of remedial principles that elaborate on the bare bones of the remedial provisions in many international law texts.[122]

Article 3 of the UN *Basic Principles* requires both prevention of and reparation for rights violations. Article 18 provides "as appropriate and proportional to the gravity of the violation and the circumstances of each case" for "full and effective reparation". Reparation is defined broadly to include "restitution, compensation, rehabilitation, satisfaction and guarantees of non-repetition". Restitution is defined in Article 19 as restoration of the "original situation" before a violation occurred, including "restoration of liberty, enjoyment of human rights, identity, family life and citizenship, return to one's place of residence, restoration of employment and return of property". Compensation includes economically assessable material and moral damages "as appropriate and proportional to the gravity of the violation and the circumstances of each case".[123] Satisfaction is defined very broadly to include apologies, commemoration, investigation, "official declarations and judicial decisions restoring the dignity, the reputation and the rights of the victim and of persons closely connected with the victim" as well as "effective measures aimed at the cessation of continuing violation".[124] Guarantees of non-repetition are also defined broadly to include law reform, training and enforcement of "codes of conduct and ethical norms".[125] This recent remedial instrument recognizes the importance of full and effective reparation and prevention of rights violations. It also contemplates a broad range of mechanisms to achieve such ends.

[120] Art. 14(5) of the International Convention for Enforced Disappearances.
[121] UN *Basic Principles* at para 18.
[122] For a recent decision making reference to such principles and in particular the priority that should be given to restitution over-compensation, see *Mammadov* v. *Azerbaijan*, No. 15172/13, ECHR 29 May 2019.
[123] Art. 20 of UN *Basic Principles.*
[124] Art. 21 of UN *Basic Principles.*
[125] Art. 23 of UN *Basic Principles.*

1.6.1.4 Regional Instruments

1.6.1.4.1 The European Convention on Human Rights The 1950 European Convention on Human Rights stopped well short of giving the newly created European Court of Human Rights (ECtHR) full remedial powers to devise effective remedies. Despite the strong arguments of one renegade British official, Marguerite Bowie, that "[b]reaches of the Covenant will be wrongs done to individuals, and logically and morally the individual should have the right to complain",[126] the ECtHR would not have a right of individual petition until 1988.

The ECtHR does not have powers to annul domestic laws and administrative acts. Early proposals contemplated that it would, but the negotiation process leading to its adoption cut back remedial powers so that Article 50 (now Article 41) of the European Convention only makes reference to "just satisfaction" or damages to the injured party.[127] Pierre Henri Teitgen, a French resistance hero who had been instrumental in crafting the more ambitious remedial proposals, lamented the change. He argued that "if tomorrow, France were to sink into a dictatorship, and if her dictator were to suppress freedom of the press" all the new Court could do would be to award damages.[128]

As a supra-national instrument, the European Convention clearly looked to domestic systems to provide effective remedies. The main provision in this regard is Article 13. It provides that those whose rights were violated "shall have an effective remedy before a national authority notwithstanding that the violation had been committed by persons acting in their official capacity".[129] This followed the Universal Declaration in its reference to an effective remedy that, consistent with the rule of law, would apply even if state officials breached rights.

[126] Simpson, *Human Rights and the End of Empire*, p.524.

[127] Council of Europe, *Travaux Préparatoires on Article 50 of the European Convention on Human Rights*, Vol. 4 (Strasbourg: European Court of Human Rights, 30 April 1970) at 74; also the Committee of experts proposed that the court should not be able to examine the promulgation of legislative acts: Council of Europe, 1 January 2020, *Rules of Court: Registry of the Court,* online (pdf): www.echr.coe.int/Documents/Rules_Court_ENG .pdf; ibid. at 44; see also Ed Bates, *The Evolution of the European Convention on Human Rights* (Oxford: Oxford University Press, 2010), pp.86–87.

[128] *Travaux Preparatoire on Article 50* at 28.

[129] European Convention for the Protection of Human Rights and Fundamental Freedoms, Rome, 4 November 1950, in force 3 September 1953, 213 UNTS 221, Art. 13. Other provisions in the 1950 European Convention on Human Rights contemplated specific remedies with references to habeas corpus in Art. 5(4) and compensation for unlawful detention in Art. 5(5).

The UK appealed to the primacy of judicial remedies by arguing that remedies "should be provided by recourse to independent judicial authorities" (including administrative tribunals) because it was "particularly undesirable that a person whose freedom had been violated, in all probability, by the political authorities of the State, should have his right to a remedy determined by a political organ".[130] On the other hand, other states argued that "the omission of reference to political authorities would preclude the granting of remedies by the legislature or the executive, in cases where they might be the only, or most effective, agencies for that purpose".[131] This Cold War battle over whether remedies should come from the courts or the political branches of the government was eventually resolved in Article 13 of the European Convention by the use of the ambiguous phrase "national authority". Article 47 of the more recent EU Charter of Fundamental Rights reflects the current focus on remedies provided by tribunals and courts. However, the dialogic approach taken in this book suggests that there is much wisdom in a broader approach that includes a variety of national authorities, such as the executive and the legislature, while not excluding the judiciary in the remedial process.

The ECtHR's approach to remedies has evolved considerably. In early years, it relied on the declaratory effects of its rulings that states had violated rights. Over time, it has awarded damages as a form of just satisfaction but, as will be discussed in Chapter 5, Section 5.2.1.2, not in a particularly satisfactory or predictable manner. The most interesting remedial development, however, is that the Court and the Committee of Ministers, which is responsible for executing its judgements,[132] has become more concerned with general measures designed to prevent repetitive violations. Protocol 14 added in 2004 provides Articles 46(3)

[130] Council of Europe, 19 December 1962, *Annotations on the Draft International Covenants on Human Rights*, Doc A./2929, prepared by the UN Secretary General, at 18, online (pdf): www.echr.coe.int/LibraryDocs/Travaux/ECHRTravaux-ART13-DH(57)5-BIL1675402.pdf

[131] Ibid.

[132] The Committee of Ministers adds an interesting diplomatic aspect to the remedial process. During the time of the drafting, one UK official argued that "in our view, and taking the world as it is, political considerations may well justify restrictions on the enjoyment of these rights which are not strictly justifiable under the terms of the Convention. We have therefore desired that the mechanisms set up for enforcing the Covenant should not be purely judicial but should be competent to give due weight to political as well as legal considerations". Simpson, *Human Rights and the End of Empire*, p.719.

and (4). They allow the Committee of Ministers (by a two-thirds vote) to send a case back to the Court for further interpretation of a judgement or a finding of a lack of compliance. As will be discussed in the next chapter, the ECtHR has moved in the direction of a two-track remedial approach that at times separates out questions of specific and individual compensatory measures for successful litigants from general measures designed to reduce repetitive violations in the future.

1.6.1.4.2 The American Convention on Human Rights The 1969 American Convention on Human Rights[133] represented an advance from the limits placed on the ECtHR in only providing damages. Article 63(1) provides:

> If the Court finds that there has been a violation of a right or freedom protected by this Convention, the Court shall rule that the injured party be ensured the enjoyment of his right or freedom that was violated. It shall also rule, if appropriate, that the consequences of the measure or situation that constituted the breach of such right or freedom be remedied and that fair compensation be paid to the injured party.

As Professor Shelton has observed, "the plain language of Article 63 indicates the Court's power to order remedies other than compensation".[134] These include calls on states "to change impugned laws".[135] It also recognized a dual concern with compensating successful litigants for past violations and ensuring compliance in the future. The IACtHR takes responsibility for the execution of its own judgements whereas the Committee of Ministers performs this task for the ECtHR.

The American Convention's commitment to enforcement of rights was also underlined by the first recognition of the importance of pre-trial or interim remedies. Article 63(2) provides for "provisional measures" to be adopted "in cases of extreme gravity and urgency, and when necessary to avoid irreparable damage to persons". The concept of preventing irreparable damage is a fundamental one in both supra-national and domestic human rights jurisprudence.

Article 25 of the American Convention followed Article 13 of the European Convention in recognizing that individuals have a right to an effective remedy domestically. The American Convention made specific

[133] San Jose, Costa Rica, 22 November 1969, in force 18 July 1978, 1144 UNTS 123.
[134] Shelton, *Remedies in International Human Rights Law*, pp.228–229.
[135] Ibid.

reference to the need for "simple and prompt recourse" that is not present in the European Convention. This also reflects South American traditions of summary *amparo* or *tutela* relief. The American Convention also applies in North America, but unfortunately neither Canada nor the United States has accepted the jurisdiction of this important regional human rights court.[136]

1.6.1.4.3 Other Regional Rights Protection Instruments Article 5 of the 2012 ASEAN Human Rights Declaration[137] follows the ICCPR in providing that "every person has the right to an effective and enforceable remedy" determined by a court or other competent authority for violation of legal or constitutional rights. Unfortunately, there is no regional human rights court for Asia or Oceania.

Article 21 of the 1981 African Charter of Human and Peoples' Rights[138] provides for "the right to adequate compensation" for the "spoliation of resources of a dispossessed people". Article 27(1) of the Protocol establishing the African Court on Human and Peoples' Rights provides that "if the Court finds that there has been violation of a human or peoples' right, it shall make appropriate orders to remedy the violation, including the payment of fair compensation or reparation". Borrowing from the American Convention, Article 27(2) provides that "in cases of extreme gravity and urgency, and when necessary to avoid irreparable harm to persons, the Court shall adopt such provisional measures as it deems necessary".[139] Article 29 of the Protocol provides that the Executive Council of the African Union will monitor the execution of the Court's judgements. A proposal to establish a Committee of Ministers similar to that used in the Council of Europe system has not yet been implemented, but some support the Court itself being involved in implementation following IACtHR practice.[140]

136 Discussion of the remedial role of the Inter-American Human Rights Commission is beyond the scope of this work, which focuses on remedies available from supra-national and national courts.

137 Association of Southeast Asian Nations (ASEAN), ASEAN Human Rights Declaration, Phnom Penh, Cambodia, in force 18 November 2012.

138 Nairobi, 27 June 1981, in force 28 December 1988, 1520 UNTS 217 Art. 21.

139 Manisuli Ssenyonjo, "Responding to Human Rights Violations in Africa" (2018) 7 *Int'l. Hum. Rts. L. Rev.* 1.

140 Ben Kioko, "Perspective from the African Court on Human and Peoples' Rights" (2020) 12 *J. of H.R. Prac.* 163, 164.

1.6.2 National Laws

1.6.2.1 Early Silence on Remedies but the Legacy of Common Law Right to a Remedy Reasoning

Early constitutions were often silent about remedies. The 1788 American Constitution did not contain a specific remedies provision. It did, however, contemplate habeas corpus as a remedy that could be suspended in cases of war and rebellion as required by public safety.[141] This implicitly recognized an important remedy, but qualified it by setting out the circumstances in which it could be denied. The 5th Amendment, added in 1791, contemplated the payment of just compensation when private property was taken for public use.

Following common law traditions, the United States Supreme Court declared in *Marbury* v. *Madison* that it would provide remedies for violations of rights. Chief Justice Marshall cited William Blackstone for the proposition that "it is a settled and invariable principle in the laws of England that every right, when withheld, must have a remedy, and every injury its proper redress".[142] This case is rightly famous for establishing judicial review in which courts could invalidate laws that are inconsistent with the constitution. It was, however, bittersweet with regard to remedies. The Court interpreted the constitution as providing that the mandamus remedy requested by the petitioner was beyond its jurisdiction. The Court thus held it did not have the power to order the mandamus remedy to force the new Jefferson administration to hand over a commission as a justice of the peace even though the Court found that the petitioner had a "vested legal right" to such a commission.[143] As will be suggested throughout this book, the American experience with remedies has been influential in many parts of the world. Yet, it also reflects restraints on remedies that Federal Courts can order that have not been replicated in other countries.

It was not only the limits on the court's appellate jurisdiction in *Marbury* v. *Madison* that prevented American courts from ordering remedies. In 1795, the 11th amendment was added to limit the powers of the Federal Courts over the states. This amendment has been interpreted to prevent Federal Courts from awarding damages or injunctive

141 United States Constitution 1788, Art. 1, s. 9.
142 5 US 137 (1803) at 146.
143 Ibid.

relief against the states.[144] Similar restrictions have been imposed that limit the federal state from being directly liable for damages for violations of the Bill of Rights, at least in the absence of authorizing legislation. At the same time, following the rule of law right to a remedy reasoning that inspired *Marbury* v. *Madison*, American Federal Courts have held that individual state and federal officials can be subject to injunctions and damages in cases where they exceed their authority.[145] However, because of concerns about over-deterring individual officials, American courts have developed robust qualified and absolute immunities that make it difficult to obtain damages for violations of human rights. As discussed in Chapter 5, Section 5.2, however, many other countries with more modern constitutions recognize that the state can be held directly liable in damages.

The 1990 New Zealand Bill of Rights is a rare example of a modern bill of rights that makes no reference to remedies except to the extent that it denies the courts the right to invalidate legislation to the extent of its inconsistency with rights. Despite this, the New Zealand courts have held that they can exclude evidence obtained in violation of rights,[146] award damages for violations of rights[147] and issue declarations that legislation is inconsistent with rights.[148]

1.6.2.2 Remedies from Legislative and Administrative Bodies

As recognized in Article 2(3) of the ICCPR, the courts are not the only source of remedies. Federations including the United States and Canada were among the first to recognize that central legislatures could play a remedial role in enforcing rights that would not otherwise be respected at the local level.

The 13th Amendment of the American Bill of Rights was enacted after the Civil War. It bans slavery, but also provides that "Congress shall have power to enforce this article by appropriate legislation". Similar provisions are also attached to the 14th Amendment providing that states should not deny due process or equal protection of the law and the 15th Amendment providing that the right to vote shall not be denied on account of race, colour, or previous condition of servitude. The exercise

[144] *Hans* v. *Louisiana*, 134 US 1 (1890).
[145] *Ex Parte Young*, 209 US 123 (1908).
[146] *R.* v. *Butcher*, [1992] 2 NZLR 257.
[147] *Simpson* v. *Attorney General*, [1994] 3 NZLR 667.
[148] *Attorney General* v. *Taylor*, [2018] NZSC 104.

of Congressional jurisdiction under these provisions, especially in the 1960s, played a key role in enforcing voting and rights against racial discrimination with some commentators arguing that it was much more effective and important than the limited form of relief ordered by the courts.[149] The United States Supreme Court has, however, interpreted Congressional remedial jurisdiction more narrowly.[150]

One shortcoming of remedial legislation in enforcing human rights is that it requires the support of political majorities. The 1867 Canadian Constitution contained provisions to allow the federal Parliament to enact remedial legislation to protect the denominational school rights of religious minorities in the provinces. In 1890, the Manitoba Legislature enacted laws repealing public support for the schools of the Catholic minority. Remedial legislation restoring public funding was debated but not enacted.[151]

The Manitoba Act, 1870 provided for land to be granted to the Métis, an Indigenous people. The Canadian Supreme Court has recognized on two occasions that the Métis can seek declarations about failures to implement the requirements in order to assist in modern land claims negotiations.[152] In Chapter 9, Section 9.5, it will be suggested that remedies based on out of court agreements are a particularly important way to enforce Indigenous rights.

1.6.2.3 Modern Remedial Provisions and the Emphasis on Judicial Discretion

Farrell reports that 50 of 181 national constitutions have general provisions for judicial remedies and that another 62 have specific provisions for habeas corpus.[153] One pattern is to have a supremacy clause that indicates that laws are invalid to the extent of their inconsistency with the constitution and a separate clause providing for a broader range of

[149] Gerald N. Rosenberg, *The Hollow Hope* (Chicago: University of Chicago Press, 1991).

[150] *City of Boerne* v. *Flores*, 521 US 507 (1997).

[151] Judicial enforcement of the language rights of the francophone minority was no more effective until *Re Manitoba Language Rights,* [1985] 1 SCR 721 where the Supreme Court retained jurisdiction for seven years until unilingual laws were translated into French. See Kent Roach, "The Judicial, Legislative and Executive Role in Enforcing the Constitution: Three Manitoba Stories" in Richard Albert and David Cameron (eds.), *Canada in the World* (Cambridge: Cambridge University Press, 2018).

[152] *Dumont* v. *Canada*, [1990] 1 SCR 279; *Manitoba Métis Federation* v. *Canada*, 2013 SCC 14.

[153] Brian Farrell *Habeas Corpus in International Law*, pp.183, 205.

remedies. For example, Article 13 of the 1950 Constitution of the Republic of India[154] provides that inconsistent laws are "void" while Article 32 guarantees the right to petition the Supreme Court for a range of remedies. Similarly section 52(1) of Canada's Constitution Act, 1982 provides that laws are of no force and effect to the extent of their inconsistency with the Constitution while Section 24(1) of the Canadian Charter of Rights and Freedoms, 1982[155] provides that courts of competent jurisdiction can award remedies that are appropriate and just in the circumstances.

The Colombian Constitution, 1991[156] contemplates a particularly wide range of remedies. The Constitutional Court can issue remedies under Article 241 during and after the legislative process and can decide petitions by citizens claiming that bills, laws, international treaties, constitutional amendments or referenda are unconstitutional. The courts can also issue and review remedies provided by way of the summary tutela procedure, incorporated by Article 86. Article 90 provides that "the state will answer materially for any type of damages that can be attributed to an illegal action, or caused by deeds of commission or omission by the public authorities".

1.6.2.4 Socio-economic Rights

Some constitutions reflect the same reluctance to contemplate judicial enforcement of socio-economic rights as seen in the 1966 International Covenant of Economic, Social and Cultural Rights. For example, both Article 45 the 1937 Irish Constitution and Article 37 of the 1950 Indian Constitution preclude judicial enforcement of socio-economic rights.[157] As will be seen in Chapter 8, Section 8.2.6, however, the Indian courts have circumvented the above provision by interpreting the judicially enforced right to life to include some socio-economic rights. The trend seems to be towards enforcing socio-economic and cultural rights, but

[154] Art. 32(2) of the Constitution of India, 1950 provides: "The Supreme Court shall have power to issue directions or orders or writs, including writs in the nature of *habeas corpus, mandamus,* prohibition, *quo warranto* and *certiorari,* whichever may be appropriate, for the enforcement of any of the rights conferred by this Part".

[155] *Constitution Act, 1982,* s.52(1), being Schedule B to the *Canada Act 1982* (UK), 1982, c. 11; *Canadian Charter of Rights and Freedoms,* s. 24(1), Part I of the *Constitution Act, 1982,* being Schedule B to the *Canada Act 1982* (UK), 1982, c. 11.

[156] Political Constitution of Colombia, 1991.

[157] Constitution of Ireland, 1937, Art. 45; Constitution of India 1950, Art. 37.

such enforcement may require action by the executive and the legislature as well as by the courts.

1.6.2.5 Provisions Contemplating Delayed and Prospective Relief

The positive regulatory state means that fully retroactive relief that affects whole classes may be particularly disruptive to important competing social interests. Provisions for delayed and prospective relief also recognize the realist insight that courts may be deterred from recognizing some rights because of concerns about disruptive and drastic remedies.

The 1996 South African Constitution[158] broke new ground in many respects. It includes a variety of socio-economic rights. Section 38 contemplates that a competent court can grant "appropriate relief, including a declaration of rights". Section 26(3) provides that court orders are necessary for evictions or house demolitions and section 25(3) contemplates that compensation for expropriated property should reflect "an equitable balance between the public interest and the interests of those affected".

Section 172 of the South African Constitution contemplates delayed or prospective relief by providing:

> When deciding a constitutional matter within its power, a court
> a. must declare that any law or conduct that is inconsistent with the Constitution is invalid to the extent of its inconsistency; and
> b. may make any order that is just and equitable, including
>   i. an order limiting the retrospective effect of the declaration of invalidity; and
>   ii. an order suspending the declaration of invalidity for any period and on any conditions, to allow the competent authority to correct the defect.

Under this provision, the South African courts have limited the retrospective effect of a declaration of invalidity, often through the order of a suspended declaration of invalidity. The courts, under the broad reference to "just and equitable" relief, have also imposed conditions on how unconstitutional laws will be administered during the suspension. In Chapter 4, Section 4.4, it will be demonstrated that both suspended declarations of invalidity and prospective rulings can often be

[158] The Constitution of the Republic of South Africa, Act 108 of 1996.

administered in a two-track manner so as to give successful applicants some immediate and retroactive benefits of a ruling while imposing delays for systemic remedies that will recognize competing social interests.

1.6.2.6 Statutory Bills of Rights without Strike Down Powers

A different model has been used in some Commonwealth statutory Bills of Rights on the basis that courts should not be able to invalidate legislation. Section 4 of the UK's Human Rights Act, 1998[159] gives courts a discretion to make a declaration that legislation is incompatible with rights. The declaration does not affect the continuing operation of the law, but allows the responsible Minister to make fast-track remedial changes to the legislation with the approval of Parliament. These procedures are also available to respond to ECtHR decisions. Some state Bills of Rights in Australia also allow courts to make non-binding declarations of incompatibility with rights. The Australian High Court has pronounced declarations of incompatibility to be a non-judicial remedy because they provide no enforceable remedy for the successful litigant.[160] In contrast, the New Zealand Supreme Court has accepted a declaration of incompatibility as a judicial remedy.[161]

In a system without judicial power to strike down laws, an alternative to a declaration of incompatibility is to interpret laws so that they respect human rights. This gives both the successful litigant and all others the immediate benefit of the right.[162] Section 3 of the UK's Human Right Act, 1998, contemplates that courts can interpret laws to be compatible with the Convention rights contained in the document "so far as it is possible to do so".[163] This recognizes that it may not always be possible to interpret a law in a manner that complies with human rights, depending on the words and intent of the legislation.

Section 8 of the Human Rights Act, 1998, allows courts to grant appropriate and just relief with respect to any act or proposed act of a public authority. These remedies can include the award of damages by a

[159] c. 42.

[160] *Momcilovic* v. *The Queen*, [2011] HCA 34 at paras 89–90, 95 per French CJ.; at para 146 per Gummow J.; and at paras 533–534 per Crennan J. and Kiefel J.

[161] *Attorney General* v. *Taylor*, [2018] NZSC 104. See *infra* Chapter 4, Section 4.2.1.6.

[162] Another alternative contemplated in Ireland's European Convention on Human Rights Act 2003 s.5(4) is for an ex gratia payment of compensation to the litigant who has obtained the declaration of incompatibility.

[163] Human Rights Act 1998 s.3, c. 42.

competent court where damages are necessary to afford "just satisfaction". Section 8 instructs UK courts to consider the jurisprudence of the ECtHR when awarding damages. This reflects the intent of the Human Rights Act, 1998 to provide for domestic enforcement of rights in the European Convention. It has, however, been criticized for blurring the distinctive role of domestic courts in providing effective remedies with the residual role played by supra-national courts. It may also have a tendency to replicate the ECtHR's inconsistent and generally modest approach to the award of damages.[164] Although the UK remains subject to the ECtHR after Brexit, it will be interesting whether it develops a more nationally distinctive approach to remedies including damages in the years to come.

1.6.2.7 Summary

Some human rights laws are silent on remedies. Others simply make vague references to effective or just remedies. Although the text of human rights laws can limit remedies, they fail to provide a full theory or rationale for the grant of remedies. The study of remedies requires commentators to go beyond the text of human rights laws.[165] As Owen Fiss has stated, "the choice of remedy should not turn on generalized propositions" but rather upon "an appreciation of the technical advantages of each remedy and a judgment, made in light of the substantive claim".[166] Indeed, there is a danger that conclusions as to whether a certain remedy is or is not just or effective will simply be a disguise for the exercise of unreasoned and unjustified remedial discretion.

1.7 Conceptualizing Remedial Discretion

As discussed in the last section, many human rights laws implicitly or explicitly embrace discretion as a vital component of the remedial process. This recognizes that what makes a remedy "effective", "necessary" or "appropriate" will vary with the particular circumstances of the violation and other factors. In this sense, discretion is unavoidable in the remedial process. Yet, the idea that judges simply exercise discretion

164 Jason Varuhus, *Damages and Human Rights* (Oxford: Hart Publishing, 2006).

165 Robert Leckey, "Remedial Practice beyond Constitutional Text" (2016) 6 *Am. J. Comp. L.* 1.

166 Fiss, *The Civil Rights Injunction*, p.91.

when formulating remedies contributes to the overall neglect of remedies by judges, litigants and scholars that this book aims to redress.

Human rights lawyers can benefit from an extensive debate among private law lawyers about the role and dangers of remedial discretion. The late Peter Birks was an influential scholar of private law who strongly criticized the idea of discretionary remedialism. He raised concerns about a strong distinction between questions of right and remedy.[167] He warned that such strong remedial discretion would not allow the successful litigant "to have rights. To make room for the discretion, it has to reduce the plaintiff to a supplicant seeking the exercise of discretion in his favour".[168] Strong discretion depended on the "intuitive justice"[169] of the judge.

There is much to Professor Birks's criticism of strong discretion. A sharp distinction between rights and remedies can undermine both the value and the meaning of the right. That said, there is a danger of overreaction in rejecting strong discretion if the expectation is that remedial discretion can be reduced to rules that are "applicable in an all-or-nothing fashion"[170] or closely governed either by the text of the human rights law or precedent. A rule-based approach will inevitably be over- or under-inclusive of the range of circumstances and factors that judges must consider when devising remedies. A textual approach may result in conclusions that follow the text but avoid a reasoned justification about the result.[171]

Rather than relying on strong discretion, strong rules or assertions that follow remedial text, judges should be guided by general principles as they relate to both the goals of remedies and the constraints placed upon remedies. Judges can then decide how the principles apply to the particular circumstances and how much weight should be given to each remedial goal and constraint in each context. Principles are something

[167] Birks, "Three Kinds of Objections to Discretionary Remedialism".

[168] Ibid., 13.

[169] Ibid., 16.

[170] Ronald Dworkin, *Taking Rights Seriously* (Cambridge: Harvard University Press, 1977), p.24.

[171] In the early years of the Canadian Charter, judges often stressed the text of s.24(2), which mandates courts to exclude evidence if its admission would bring the administration of justice into disrepute. They followed a textual approach, but their conclusions depended on often implicit and varying ideas about what the reputation of the administration of justice depended upon. See Kent Roach, "Constitutionalizing Disrepute" (1986) 44 *U. Toronto Fac. L. Rev.* 209.

that always should be considered. They include the two-track goals of compensating and preventing violations and constraints such as the appropriate role of courts and the need to be fair to all parties.

Remedial decision-making is not amenable to hard and fast rules. An example of a rule-based approach can be seen in the categorical decision of American and Canadian courts that permanent dismissals of a criminal prosecution are the minimum remedy for violations of speedy trial rights.[172] Such an inflexible approach fails to recognize that pre-trial delay may harm one accused more than others and that the state's interests in a trial on the merits differ. A rule-based approach also does not address a central question in proportionality analysis – namely, whether a less drastic remedy will serve the relevant remedial purposes while better respecting competing interests. As will be discussed in Chapter 6, Section 6.2.2.2, this may also trigger a process of remedial deterrence where courts restrict rights to avoid what they fear are disproportionate remedies.

Another danger of a rule-based approach to remedial discretion is that the lack of fit between rules and complex remedial circumstances may persuade judges to abandon rules for the sort of strong and unreasoned discretion that Professor Birks rightly criticized. In Chapter 4, Section 4.2.5.2, we will see how, in Canada, an attempt to create rules that limited the use of suspended declarations of invalidity to only three factual situations (threats to the rule of law, public safety and the nullification of under-inclusive benefits)[173] had the opposite effect of forcing the Court to exercise a strong discretion with respect to the remedy. This created unpredictability in when courts will suspend the remedy. Some have argued that the result has undermined both rights and the rule of law.[174] Rules and strong discretion may be polar opposites.[175] Nevertheless, they are united by a crude legal positivism that demands that the law must be reduced to predictable rules or else simply be an exercise of unrestrained power and will.

Fortunately, there is viable middle ground between the extremes of rules and no rules. It is found in Ronald Dworkin's understanding of principled reasoning. Professor Dworkin's approach is best known both

[172] *Strunk* v. *United States*, 412 US 434 (1973) at 440; *R.* v. *Rahey*, [1987] 1 SCR 588.

[173] *Schachter* v. *Canada*, [1992] 2 SCR 679.

[174] Leckey, "The Harms of Remedial Discretion".

[175] Kent Roach, "Principled Remedial Discretion under the Charter" (2004) 25 *S.C.L.R.* (2d) 101.

for the distinction between principles as rights and policies as matters involving collective welfare and his sense that judges should aim to find right answers in difficult cases.[176] At the same time, however, Dworkin recognized that principles could play a somewhat more modest role. Principles could operate as factors that should be taken into account when making a decision. Dworkin recognized that such principles can be "competing and conflicting".[177]

In late 2020, the Supreme Court of Canada endorsed the need for a principled approach to the exercise of remedial discretion. Justice Karakatsansis stated: that the "categorical approach in *Schachter* has been overtaken by the underlying remedial principles that animated those categories". Under the principled approach, suspended declarations of invalidity are justified when the government discharges "the onus of demonstrating that a compelling public interest ... supports a suspension".[178] The Court added that the principled approach "would be more stringent than the categorical approach, because any suspension must be specifically justified".[179] The Court listed as the operative principles 1. the safeguard of rights through effective remedies, 2. the public's interest in legislation that complies with the constitution, 3. the public's interest to the benefit of legislation and 4. the different institutional roles of courts and legislatures.[180] These four principles can be simplified to provide that the court must ensure effective remedies while respecting the roles of the courts and legislatures including the public's interest in legislation that complies with human rights. This judgement is an important vindication of a principled approach to the exercise of remedial discretion that rejects either categorical or rule-based approaches and those based on the exercise of strong and unreasoned forms of discretion.

[176] Dworkin, *Taking Rights Seriously*, pp.26, 72.

[177] Ibid.

[178] *Ontario* (*Attorney General* v. *G.*) 2020 SCC 38 at para 126. For discussion and endorsement of a principled approach that avoids the extremes of hard and fast rules and strong discretion see ibid. at para 90–99. Three judges in dissent rejected the principled approach as too vague and indeterminate. One of the judges would have limited suspended declarations of invalidity to the three finite categories in Schachter. Ibid. at 190–199. Two other judges stressed the lack of a textual basis for a suspended declaration of invalidity in Canada's constitutional mandate to strike down laws to the extent of their inconsistency and the threat to the rule of law. They would only allow a suspension when an immediate declaration would threaten the rule of law or public safety. Ibid. at 244–246.

[179] Ibid. at 132.

[180] Ibid. at 158.

Remedies are complex and fascinating because the relevant principles rarely always point in the same direction. A remedy that provides compensation for a past violation may not address the risk of similar violations in the future and vice versa. Competing social interests and concerns about exceeding the legitimate role of courts may press against the need for remedies to compensate for past harms and to prevent new ones. Some of the multiple (and, at times, conflicting) principles relevant to decision-making include: 1. the need to consider what is necessary to recognize and compensate for a past violation; 2. what is necessary to reduce similar violations in the future; 3. restraints imposed by the appropriate role of the court; and 4. what is necessary to strike a proportionate balance between remedial principles and legitimate competing social interests and rights.

Principled remedial decision-making is amenable to structured debate that is not free from disagreement. Judges will not agree on the content of each principle or the weight it should be given in particular circumstances. Even if judges agree in a particular case, the parties certainly will not. Debates about the principled exercise of remedial discretion will be more sophisticated than debates about rules or appeals to strong discretion. For example, a rule that an unreasonably delayed trial always results in a stay of proceedings will simply transfer the remedial debate into whether the right has been violated. A party who seeks to persuade a judge to exercise a strong discretion will not know what factors may be relevant to the judge's decision.[181]

One final issue is the degree to which appellate or supra-national courts should defer to first level decisions about the exercise of remedial discretion. Appellate deference under strong or rule-based forms of remedial discretion exists, but primarily on the basis that the first level decider is closer to the facts and should be given a degree of deference on that basis. Under a model of principled remedial discretion, deference to the first level decider is only warranted if that judge considers all the relevant principles and applies them in a reasonable manner. A failure to consider one of the relevant principles would generally suggest that the first level decider has missed an important consideration. This may require a new and fully informed exercise of remedial discretion.

[181] Robert J. Sharpe, *Good Judgment: Making Judicial Decisions* (Toronto: University of Toronto Press, 2018), pp.217–218.

1.8 Constraints on Remedies: Separation of Powers and Subsidiarity

One of the principles that enters into all remedial decision-making is the need to consider the appropriate role of courts when devising remedies. In the domestic context, such concerns are generally expressed in terms of the separation of powers or the appropriate role of courts in relation to the executive and legislatures. In the supra-national context, such concerns are generally expressed in terms of subsidiarity or the primary role of nation states.

Both separation of powers and subsidiarity are excellent examples of the type of principles that should guide the exercise of remedial discretion. Both are matters that should always be considered, even though there may be legitimate disagreement about their exact content or weight that they should be given in a particular context.

1.8.1 Restrictions on the Jurisdiction to Award Remedies

The clear preclusion of certain remedies from a court's jurisdiction may place such remedies out of bounds. As examined in Section 1.6 of this chapter, some domestic and international human rights law prevent courts from awarding certain remedies. For example, neither the ECtHR or the UK courts can invalidate legislation that violates human rights. As will be examined in Chapter 4, Section 4.2.2.2, such restrictions on remedies may force courts to use other remedies in a way that may affect the separation of powers and subsidiarity. In Chapter 6, Section 6.2.1.4, we will see that the absence of jurisdiction for many common law domestic criminal courts to award damages limits a remedial choice that is available to the International Criminal Court.

As part of its remedial exceptionalism, the United States Supreme Court has increasingly taken a formal and rigid approach to the separation of powers. The United States Supreme Court has repeatedly decided that in the absence of specific Congressional authorization, Federal Courts should not even award damages against federal officials. For example, Justice Kennedy has stated that "[i]t is a significant step under separation-of-powers principles for a court to determine that it has the authority, under the judicial power, to create and enforce a cause of action for damages against federal officials in order to remedy a constitutional violation ... there are a number of economic and governmental concerns to consider".[182] In this case, damages were not available for mass immigration detentions after the 9/11 terrorist attacks. Other courts including the New Zealand courts have determined that they have inherent powers to award damages.[183]

1.8.2 A Flexible and Dialogic Approach to the Separation of Powers

Even when courts have a broad and unfettered discretion to award remedies, they should consider whether a particular remedy is appropriate for a court to order in a particular context. The Supreme Court of Canada has indicated that courts with full remedial discretion still "must employ means that are legitimate within the framework of our constitutional democracy".[184] They "must strive to respect the relationships with and separation of functions among the legislature, the executive and the judiciary. This is not to say that there is a bright line separating these functions in all cases. A remedy may be appropriate and just notwithstanding that it might touch on functions that are principally assigned to the executive".[185] Nevertheless, courts must not "depart unduly or unnecessarily from their role of adjudicating disputes and granting remedies that address the matter of those disputes".[186]

Consistent with a dialogic approach, the Canadian Court added a temporal dimension to its understanding of the separation of powers. It stressed that "[i]t will not be appropriate for a court to leap into the kinds of decisions and functions for which its design and expertise are manifestly unsuited"[187] while holding open the possibility that stronger remedies may be available over time. Courts that retain jurisdiction over a case frequently adjust their relief over time in response to changed circumstances.

The South African Constitutional Court has taken a similar approach to the Canadian Court. It has indicated that "although there are no bright lines that separate the roles of the legislature, the executive and the courts

[182] *Ziglar* v. *Abbasi*, 138 S.Ct. 1843 (2017) at C.
[183] *Simpson* v. *Attorney General (Baigent's Case)*, [1994] 2 NZLR 667.
[184] *Doucet-Boudreau* v. *Nova Scotia*, 2003 SCC 62 at para 56.
[185] Ibid.
[186] Ibid.
[187] *Doucet-Boudreau* v. *Nova Scotia*, 2003 SCC 62 at para 57.

from one another, there are certain matters that are pre-eminently within the domain of one or other of the arms of government and not the others". The Court added: "[w]here a breach of any right has taken place, including a socio-economic right, a court is under a duty to ensure that effective relief is granted . . . Where necessary this may include both the issuing of a mandamus and the exercise of supervisory jurisdiction".[188] The judgement made reference to the laws of other democracies and international law to find support for its flexible approach to the separation of powers. Courts in India and Colombia have been even bolder than South African courts in ordering remedies.[189]

The above Canadian and South African cases examined the separation of powers in the course of complex cases where courts were asked to order injunctions as a final remedy and to retain jurisdiction to enforce them. Such cases are important and one of the main arguments in this book is that domestic courts should be less reluctant to retain jurisdiction. At the same time, separation of powers concerns should be less pressing when courts are asked to provide more traditional remedies such as damages, exclusion of evidence or declarations. These remedies are traditional judicial remedies that are not typically provided by other branches of government. Those whose rights have been violated have a legitimate expectation that courts will award them. The weight that should be given to separation of powers concerns will vary with the type of remedies provided, as well as by the government's conduct.

1.8.3 A Flexible and Dialogic Approach to Subsidiarity

Subsidiarity involves an apparent paradox: supra-national institutions including courts must generally respect the autonomy of the nation states and its subgroups but may intervene in cases where it is clear that those states are not acting in a reasonable and justified manner.[190] The ECtHR

188 *Minister of Health* v. *Treatment Action Campaign (No. 2)*, 2002 SA 721 (CC) at paras 98, 106. See also *Mwelase and Others* v. *Director-General for the Department of Rural Development and Land Reform and Another*, [2019] ZACC 30 at para 48.

189 David Bilchitz and David Landau (eds.), *The Evolution of the Separation of Powers* (Northampton: Edward Elgar, 2018); Daniel Maladonado, *Constitutionalism of the Global South* (Cambridge: Cambridge University Press, 2013).

190 As Carozza suggests: "a subsidiarity-oriented understanding of human rights and international law does not care to ask whether 'state sovereignty' must either resist or give way to international harmonization and intervention but, instead, whether the good that

has used subsidiarity most explicitly in constructing a margin of appreciation in judging whether states have justified limits on rights. Even if one rejects subsidiarity at this level as a threat to human rights, it is more difficult to deny that it plays a role in remedies. As Paolo Carozza has suggested, subsidiarity is more flexible than more absolute concepts of sovereignty. It produces judgements that "will always be contextual and dynamic, containing the fluidity and flexibility of phronesis (practical judgment)".[191] These are precisely the type of judgements that adjudicators must make when devising remedies.

The ECtHR clearly recognizes "remedial subsidiarity".[192] Under Article 41 of the Convention, the Court will only award damages if the reparation provided at the domestic level is inadequate. Subsidiarity promotes a "sequencing of judicial monitoring" in which both domestic and supra-national courts have the ability to award remedies.[193]

The ECtHR also recognized subsidiarity when it stated in 1979 that its judgements are "essentially declaratory" and leave "to the State the choice of the means to be utilised in its domestic legal system for performance of its obligation".[194] In 1988, the Court again stressed that states "have a wide discretion in the choice of the means to be used".[195] At the same time, subsidiarity does not mean that in every context, the Court cannot order specific relief. For example, it has indicated that Georgia shall release a wrongly detained person[196] and that Ukraine shall reinstate a judge wrongly removed from office.[197] The ECtHR and especially the

human rights aim at realizing can be accomplished at the local level, and if not, what assistance is necessary from a more comprehensive association to enable the smaller unit to realize its role". Paolo G. Carozza, "Subsidiarity as a Structural Principle of International Human Rights Law" (2003) 97(1) *Am. J. of Int'l. L.* 38, 66.

191 Ibid., 79.

192 Samantha Besson "Subsidiarity in International Human Rights Law – What is Subsidiarity about Human Rights" (2016) 61 *Am. J. Jurisprudence* 69, 82–83.

193 Ibid., 92.

194 *Marckx* v. *Belgium*, No. 6833/74, [1979] ECHR 2 at para 58.

195 *Plattform "Ärzte für das Leben"* v. *Austria*, No. 10126/82, [1988] ECHR 15, para 31. See also *Öcalan* v. *Turkey*, No. 46221/99, [2005] ECHR 12 at para 210.

196 *Assanidze* v. *Georgia*, No. 71503/01, ECHR 2004-II, ECHR 8 April 2004 at para 203.

197 *Volkov.* v. *Ukraine*, No. 21722/11, [2013] I ECHR 73. For criticisms of the Court's inconsistency in this regard see Krzysztof Wojtyczek, "Judicial and Non-Judicial Elements in the Enforcement Mechanism of the European Convention on Human Rights" in Paulo Pinto de Albuquerque and Krzysztof Wojtyczek (eds.), *Judicial Power in a Globalized World* (Berlin: Springer, 2019).

Committee of Ministers has taken a greater interest in preventing repetitive violations. Nevertheless, the Council of Europe still stresses the primacy of each of its forty-seven member states developing their own mechanisms to respect rights and provide effective domestic remedies for their violation.

The IACtHR administers its own remedies whereas this task is done for the ECtHR by the Committee of Ministers. In both cases, however, domestic states are given time to implement systemic remedies that involve changes in legislation and executive practice. The Inter-American approach is more transparent with hearings with the parties represented. But in some cases, these hearings are closed to the general public. Even though principles of subsidiarity bind and limit the role of supra-national courts, those principles are responsive to how the various institutions of the nation state exercise their actual power.

1.8.4 *Summary*

Concerns about respecting the separation of powers and subsidiarity are important remedial principles that will be considered throughout this book. Consistent with the general nature of principles, these considerations will rarely provide definitive answers. Consistent with the expanded time horizon of dialogical theories, the history of a particular violation and the state's response to it will often be relevant in how much weight will be accorded to either principle. What might be judicial overreaching in one context and at one point in time may not be in another. This is engrained in the principle of subsidiarity. Supra-national courts are more attentive to the repetitive nature of rights violations than domestic courts. Nevertheless, even domestic courts should be prepared to retain jurisdiction in the face of a demonstrated inability of states to prevent human rights violations.[198]

The flexible and dynamic approach to the separation of powers and subsidiarity outlined above fits well with the use of proportionality-based reasoning. As will be seen in the next section, such reasoning carefully explores why a state has failed to either provide an effective remedy or take reasonable measures to prevent similar rights violations in the future.

[198] Both the United States and Australia have more rigid views about separation of powers that affect the remedial decisions of courts.

1.9 Constraints on Remedies: Competing Interests and the Role of Proportionality

The rise of proportionality reasoning as a central part of human rights law has been widely documented.[199] Objections to it have been raised[200] and a full defence of proportionality principles is beyond the scope of this book about remedies. Many of these objections to proportionality have less force when applied to remedies. For example, Alexy's famous characterizations of rights as nothing more than "optimization principles"[201] has drawn criticisms that it undermines the normative force of rights. This criticism, however, has less bite when applied to remedies. It is widely accepted that remedies involve practical considerations about what is possible and when.[202]

Remedial proportionality should not duplicate the analysis that is undertaken in many human rights laws about whether the state has justified general limits on rights. By the remedial stage, the court will already have rejected some requested limits. There is a violation and the question is now what remedy, if any, the court should order. The starting point in most cases will be the remedy requested by the applicant. The government might oppose that remedy on the basis that it will impose excessive costs on government or on social interests such a criminal trial on the merits or reliance interests in a law or on competing rights. As will be discussed below, proportionality principles provide criteria for determining the legitimacy of those competing interests, for assigning burdens on the government and for selecting among multiple remedies.

Proportionality reasoning can be used to discipline and guide the exercise of remedial discretion. It can help ensure a structured debate both by litigants and judges about remedial choice. As with other principles, judges will not agree on how proportionality should be applied in every case. Nevertheless, it has the potential to provide a framework for reasoning and debate which sadly is often lacking in judicial remedial decision-making.

199 David Beatty, *The Ultimate Rule of Law* (Oxford: Oxford University Press, 2004); Barak, *Proportionality*; Mark Tushnet and Vicki Jackson, *Proportionality: New Frontiers New Challenges* (Cambridge: Cambridge University Press, 2017).

200 Gregoire Webber, *The Negotiable Constitution* (Cambridge: Cambridge University Press, 2009); see generally Tushnet and Jackson, *Proportionality: New Frontiers.*

201 Robert Alexy, "Proportionality and Rationality" in Tushnet and Jackson, *Proportionality: New Frontiers.*

202 Fiss, "The Forms of Justice"; Gewirtz, "Remedies and Resistance".

1.9.1 *Proportionality as a Remedial Principle*

Relatively little has been written about how proportionality principles may inform the exercise of remedial discretion.[203] The Supreme Court of Canada has indicated that damages for violations of human rights should be determined on the basis of "rationality and proportionality".[204] Moreover, the Court has suggested that the government should have an opportunity to establish that open-ended countervailing factors, including the adequacy of alternative remedies, justify not awarding damages or reducing their quantum.[205] It has also paid attention to the overall balance between what the applicant and the government receives by way of remedy when deciding cases that depart from fully retroactive relief.[206] Similarly, the Constitutional Court of South Africa has applied proportionality style reasoning in deciding whether an immediate or suspended declaration of invalidity is required.[207] In an early and influential case, Justice Sachs stated that courts would have "to make an assessment on a case-by-case basis as to whether more injustice would flow from the legal vacuum created by rendering the statute invalid with immediate effect, than would be the case if the measure were kept functional pending rectification".[208]

Proportionality analysis is also consistent with the dynamic nature of remedial decision-making over time. Proportionality analysis does not reveal eternal truths. Rather, it responds to the arguments and evidence presented by the parties in a specific context. This is one reason why judges have been so attracted to proportionality analysis. It does not require them to be Hercules or even a philosopher.

203 Kent Roach, *Constitutional Remedies in Canada*, 2nd ed. (Toronto: Thomson Reuters, 2013), pp.3.970–3.1090; Kent Roach, "A Promising Late Spring for Charter Damages" (2010) 29 *N.J.C.L.* 135; Robert J. Sharpe and Kent Roach, *The Canadian Charter of Rights and Freedoms*, 6th ed. (Toronto: Irwin Law, 2017), pp.428–429; Grant Hoole, "Proportionality as a Remedial Principle: A Framework for Suspended Declarations of Invalidity in Canadian Constitutional Law" (2011) 49 *Alta. L. Rev.* 107; Tracy A. Thomas, "Proportionality and the Supreme Court's Jurisprudence of Remedies" (2007) 59(1) *Hastings L. J.* 73 (discussing but rejecting proportionality as a remedial principle).

204 *Ward* v. *Vancouver*, [2010] 2 SCR 28 at 51.

205 Ibid. In *Mazraani* v. *Industrial Alliance Insurance and Financial Services Inc.*, 2018 SCC 50 at para 52 the Court stated: "a remedy cannot be disproportionate in relation to the scale of the language rights violation, its recurrence and its impact on personal dignity".

206 *Hislop* v. *Canada*, 2007 SCC 10.

207 Hoole, "Proportionality as a Remedial Principle", 147.

208 *Coetzee* v. *Government of the Republic of South Africa*, 1995 (4) S.A. 631 at para 76.

In some cases, new information may justify new limits on remedies. Courts may decide that the retention of jurisdiction is no longer needed because the applicant no longer faces irreparable harm or the state has introduced reasonable preventive measures. In other cases, new evidence of repetitive violations or of government indifference to preventing violations may justify stronger and more drastic remedies. Proportionality analysis is a good fit for remedial decision-making because of its attentiveness to evidence and context.

1.9.2 Proportionality as Practical and Disciplined Reasoning

Proportionality is generally used to review whether a decision made by the legislature or the executive is reasonable and justified. Proportionality as a remedial principle will be somewhat different. The judge will be the primary decision-maker. As Owen Fiss has suggested, judicial decision-making should limit the danger "that the remedy may distort the right".[209] Proportionality may be particularly helpful with respect to systemic remedies because, as Vicki Jackson has argued, it allows courts to build "a better bridge"[210] with legislatures and executive branches to assist them in structuring their responses to court decisions. This captures the "inherently dialogic" aspect of proportionality.[211] The structuring effects of proportionality analysis is especially important in remedies because of the need for governments to respond to remedies, especially when devising systemic reforms that attempt to prevent similar violations in the future. As Professor Jackson suggests, proportionality may be "democracy enhancing" both by providing a "shared language of justification" and being attentive "to process deficiencies reflecting entrenched biases against particular groups".[212] My colleague David Beatty has similarly stressed that proportionality is a fact-intensive "neutral" theory that commands support over a broad range of constitutions and contexts.[213] He also argues that it can integrate the world of law and politics

[209] Fiss, "The Forms of Justice", 53.
[210] Vicki Jackson, "Constitutional Law in an Age of Proportionality" (2015) 124 *Yale L. J.* 3094, 3103.
[211] Kent Roach, *The Supreme Court on Trial*, p.392 in reference to the Canadian limitation clause, which has been interpreted with reference to proportionality principles.
[212] Jackson, "Constitutional Law in an Age of Proportionality", 3194.
[213] Beatty, *The Ultimate Rule of Law*, pp.183–184.

with ideals and practical realities.[214] Paul Gewirtz has made similar claims for an "interest balancing" approach to remedies in a 1983 article that was written before proportionality became the dominant legal construct that it is today.[215]

The disciplinary effects of proportionality apply not only to the executive and the legislature but also to judges. It forces judges to engage in what Justice Robert J. Sharpe has called "disciplined judicial making".[216] Judges should no longer be able to hide in the silence or perfunctory reasoning that too often has accompanied the exercise of remedial discretion, including the discretion not to order any remedy. Proportionality may help discipline judges who might otherwise resort to vaguer concepts such as the equities of the case, the balance of convenience or the public interest. Such vague concepts have, at times, been interpreted in majoritarian ways that do not give due consideration to the rights of unpopular minorities.

1.9.3 Proportionality and International Law

Sonja Starr has made a persuasive case that interest balancing should be recognized in international law remedies and is preferable to a lack of judicial candour or extreme shrinkage of rights in order to avoid drastic remedial consequences.[217] She also suggests that equity may be a ground for an interest balancing approach to remedies.[218] Equity can play a role in both supra-national and national law in justifying broad and practical remedies that may not easily be justified on corrective principles that require causal connections between remedies and proven violations.[219] Nevertheless, the vagueness of equitable standards and open-ended

214 Ibid, p.174. Beatty writes: "[p]roportionality provides a metric on which both rights and democracy, law and politics, can do better. The only politics that proportionality prohibits is the politics of extremism and hate".

215 Gewirtz, "Remedies and Resistance", 591–592. Indeed, proportionality analysis can be seen as a means of bridging the analytical dichotomy that Professor Gewirtz posed between "rights maximizing" and "interest balancing" approaches to remedies. As he notes, under both approaches a remedy may not fully undo or prevent the harms of a rights violation.

216 Sharpe, *Good Judgment*, pp.125–145.

217 Starr, "Rethinking Effective Remedies", 764–766.

218 Ibid.

219 Kent Roach, "The Limits of Corrective Justice and the Potential of Equity" (1991) 33 *Ariz. L. Rev.* 859; Starr, "Rethinking Effective Remedies", 766 (in reference to Inter-American Court's use of equity).

interest balancing have dangers. Proportionality analysis is a way of making the exercise of broad equitable remedial discretion more transparent.

International law has been more willing to incorporate proportionality principles into remedial decision-making than domestic law. Article 35 of the International Law Commission's *Principles of State Responsibility* illustrates how proportionality can be relevant to decision-making. It provides that states shall make full restitution for wrongful acts, unless re-establishing the situation before the wrong is impossible or "involves a burden out of all proportion to the benefit deriving from restitution instead of compensation".[220] Restitution is a preferred remedy, but courts should be concerned about disproportionate burdens imposed on the state. In addition, Article 35 is consistent with the "half a loaf is better than none" zeitgeist of proportionality analysis because it suggests that even when restitution is impossible or disproportionate, the victim should receive compensation. While proportionality reasoning can justify less drastic remedies, it will often require some remedy. The cases where governments can justify no remedy under a full proportionality test may be quite rare. Following proportionality analysis, such a result would have to be necessary to support a compelling social objective. Moreover, it would have to strike a reasonable and fair overall balance between the interests of those whose rights have been violated and competing social interests and rights. As will be discussed below, the final overall balance stage of proportionality analysis will often be critical in such analysis.

1.9.4 Proportionality and Competing Public Interests and Rights

In a leading damages case under the New Zealand Bill of Rights, Justice McGrath observed that "the remedy should be proportionate to the breach but also have regard to other aspects of the public interest".[221] When unpacked, this helpful statement suggests that proportionality can inform remedial decision-making in two ways: 1. disciplining state claims that damages or other remedies should not be awarded or reduced because of important competing public or social interests; and 2. with

[220] International Law Commission, *Principles of State Responsibility*, of the Commission's fifty-third and fifty-fifth sessions, 23 April–1 June and 2 July–10 August 2001, GA Supp. No. 10, A/56/10. See also James Crawford et al., *The Law of International State Responsibility* (Oxford: Oxford University Press, 2010), pp.537ff.

[221] *Tauna* v. *Attorney General*, 2007 NZSC 70 at para 369.

respect to comparing a particular remedy requested by the parties with alternative remedies.

Proportionality analysis can help judges determine whether the state's objective is important enough to limit a remedy. It will be suggested below that some objectives are not suitable for limiting a remedy. It can also help the parties and judges address whether the proposed limit on the remedy is truly necessary to advance the social objective. Finally, it can determine the overall balance between limiting the remedy that the applicant and others receive and the benefits that society or other rights holders will gain by either limiting a remedy or perhaps ordering no remedy at all.

1.9.5 *Proportionality, Remedial Choice and Less Drastic Remedies*

Proportionality analysis assists remedial decision-making in determining whether alternative remedies would be a more proportionate response to a violation. An important issue in remedial decision-making is selecting among different kinds of remedies. For example:

> Are damages a sufficient remedy or should an interim injunction be issued to prevent irreparable harm?
>
> Should the entire statute be declared invalid and inconsistent with rights or should part of the law that may be consistent with rights or justified limits on rights be saved?
>
> Should damages be awarded in addition to the judgement and should aggravated damages be awarded?
>
> Is a permanent stay or dismissal of criminal proceedings an appropriate response to a violation or will a less drastic remedy, such as a sentence reduction, be sufficient?
>
> Would a declaration or an injunction be more appropriate in a particular context?
>
> Is restitution and return of Indigenous land justified or should the less drastic alternative of compensation be justified?

These are some of the most central questions of remedial choice. They will be examined throughout this book. It will be suggested that proportionality analysis can help guide these critical remedial choices.

1.9.6 *Proportionality and the Onus of Proof*

The Supreme Court of Canada has held that once an applicant had established a rights violation and a functional need for damages, the burden shifts to the state to demonstrate that damages are not an appropriate and just remedy. The state may argue that any grant of damage will harm good governance or that a less drastic remedy such as a declaration will suffice.[222] The Canadian Court has also made clear that there is a presumption that remedies would be fully retroactive, but that the government can justify the use of less drastic prospective remedies through an open-ended list of good governance factors, including those related to the allocation of public resources.[223] To the extent that remedies for violations of human rights raise issues of public capacity and costs, placing an onus on governments to justify why less drastic or even no remedy is necessary makes eminent sense. This is especially so since the applicant has already established a rights violation.

Aharon Barak has argued that placing the burden of persuasion on the government in proportionality analysis is particularly justified when the relevant facts and evidence are primarily in the purview of the government.[224] Remedial decision-making is often fact specific. Many of the most relevant facts about the operation of state systems will only be available to the government, or at the least, easier for the government to establish than the applicant. Indeed, one of the values of dialogical systemic remedies is that courts can require governments to collect and make public information that will allow better monitoring of compliance with human rights.[225]

That said, the state's superior command of facts does not mean that courts should not pay attention to facts that parties and other non-governmental actors may be able to present. The parties should also be able to make adversarial challenges to the remedial facts and proposals that the government presents. Applicants may also be in the best position to demonstrate the harms that a less robust remedy proposed by the government or no remedy at all would cause. Applicants should be able to propose their own remedies and this may assist in identifying the alternatives that are central to proportionality reasoning and remedial choice.

1.9.7 The Objectives of Limits on Remedies

Paul Gewirtz argued for an "interest balancing" approach to remedies that would include social interests (like costs) apart from practical limits on maximizing the available remedy for the victim. Consistent with most

222 *Ward* v. *Vancouver (City)*, 2010 SCC 27.
223 *Hislop* v. *Canada*, 2007 SCC 10 at para 100.
224 Barak, *Proportionality*, pp.443–444.
225 Sabel and Simon, "Destabilization Rights".

forms of proportionality reasoning, Professor Gewirtz recognized that not all competing interests should qualify. For example, objections to the right in question, such as racist objections to school desegregation, would not qualify.[226] This rejection of interests that are antithetical to the right mirrors the rejection of some objectives for limiting rights.

Some supra-national instruments provide a limited list of objectives for limiting rights such as the need to protect order or the rights of others, while others are open-ended. Even when there is an open-ended list, however, courts will reject objectives for limiting rights that are antithetical to the underlying right. For example, the objective of preferring one religion over another or discriminating against a minority are not acceptable objectives in proportionality analysis.[227] As Chief Justice McLachlin has explained in striking down restrictions on prisoner voting, "a simple majoritarian political preference for abolishing a right altogether would not be a constitutionally valid objective"[228] for limiting a right, or in the remedial context, for limiting a remedy. On the other hand, other considerations such as the ability to conduct voting safely or in time for an upcoming election would be a valid objective for limiting or delaying a remedy. Proportionality-based reasoning can be seen as a commitment to evidence-based remedial decision-making. This commitment may be strained if governments fuelled by populism start to offer heckler's veto-type objections to rights and remedies.[229]

The social or state objective that could be harmed by a remedy should be defined as precisely as possible. This should avoid vague and symbolic objectives that may be used as another means to resist the underlying rights. Although concerns about respecting the separation of powers or subsidiarity are, as discussed above, a legitimate constraint on remedies, courts should address these concerns directly. They should not be vague, symbolic and all or nothing reasons for limiting remedies.

1.9.8 Rational Connection between Objectives and Limits

The next step in proportionality analyses is establishing that there is a rational connection between an important and legitimate governmental objective and

[226] Gewirtz, "Remedies and Resistance", 606–607.

[227] See for example *R.* v. *Big M Drug Mart*, [1985] 1 SCR 295; *Vriend* v. *Alberta*, [1998] 1 SCR 493.

[228] *Sauve* v. *Canada (Chief Electoral Officer)*, [2002] 3 SCR 519 at para 20.

[229] On these dangers, see Roach, "Dialogue in Canada" in Sigalet, Webber and Dixon (eds.), *Constitutional Dialogue Rights and Institutions.*

the delay or less drastic remedy that the government proposes. The rational connection requirement imposes a relatively deferential standard on the state because it simply has to demonstrate that a limit will at least partially advance the purpose and not whether "the means are proper and correct, or whether there are other, more proper and correct means".[230]

The rational connection test provides the court with a means to ensure that the state's purpose for the limitation is truly proper and not over-inflated. For example, it is possible to argue that an objective of preserving the state's financial resources is a proper basis for limiting remedies. Yet, it is not clear that the limits placed on the modest damages in the thousands of dollars are rationally connected to preserving state budgets measured, by contrast, in millions or billions of dollars. Similarly, governments may resist remedies in the criminal process such as the exclusion of evidence on the inflated basis that granting such remedies will harm its ability to combat crime. On closer examination, however, such extravagant claims may lack a rational connection to the limitation of the remedy.

Rational connection analysis could result in the state interest being reformulated into less grand objectives such as the government's interest in deciding the particular case on the merits. Consistent with the importance of facts to much proportionality reasoning and the government's general superior ability to discover such facts, it would be important for the government to demonstrate as precisely as possible the adverse effects that might follow from awarding the particular remedy. The focus should be on the damage caused by the remedy and not the damage found by the court's finding that a right has been violated.

Proportionality analysis may play out differently depending on the remedy requested. A convincing argument by the government that a floodgate of claims for a similar remedy will follow may convince the court to lower the amount of damages awarded to an individual. At the same time, evidence of repetitive violations might indicate that courts should pursue stronger systemic remedies to prevent such violations in the future.

1.9.9 *Least Restrictive Means to Limit the Remedy*

Even if the government has demonstrated that a limit on remedies would rationally advance an important and legitimate governmental objective, it should still demonstrate that its proposed remedy limits the applicant's

[230] Barak, *Proportionality*, p.305.

remedy as little as possible while advancing the important countervailing social interest or competing right. This least restrictive means test is widely seen as the most demanding part of proportionality analysis. This stage of remedial decision-making will present risks for both governments and applicants. If the government proposes no remedy or a nominal remedy, the court may well find that such a limit on the applicant's claim for a remedy has not been justified. Conversely, if the applicant proposes a demanding remedy, this may increase the chance that the court will find such a remedy to be excessive and disproportionate. Settlements may be encouraged if parties know that governments will apply proportionality reasoning to their remedial decision-making.

Courts should avoid a mechanical approach. A declaration will always be less drastic than an injunction, but the real question is whether it will serve the relevant remedial purposes as well as the more drastic remedy. Proportionality will be especially useful where there are more alternative remedies. Although remedial choice with respect to systemic remedies has traditionally been conceived as a choice between declarations and injunctions,[231] it will be argued in Chapter 7, Section 7.4, that there is a place for an intermediate remedy, the declaration plus, that combines elements of both declarations and injunctions. Similarly, in Chapter 6, Section 6.3.8, it will be suggested that the ability of the International Criminal Court to award damages, reduce sentences or order disciplinary actions against prosecutors provides them with more remedial tools than domestic criminal courts that only exclude evidence or stay proceedings.

An important component in determining the necessity or least restrictive means test will be what Aharon Barak suggests is "common sense". For example, "a limitation that applies only to some individuals is less limiting than a limitation that applies to all".[232] Following this common sense, the Supreme Court of Canada has recognized that interim remedies that exempt only a smaller number of people from a law limits the public interest in that law less than would a remedy that suspends the operation of the law for larger groups.[233] Similarly, the Court has recognized that it is less drastic to extend an under-inclusive statute to apply to a smaller group than to add a much larger group to the group that receives the benefit under the statute.[234]

[231] Fiss, *The Civil Rights Injunction*.
[232] Barak, *Proportionality*, p.328.
[233] *Manitoba (A.G.)* v. *Metropolitan Stores*, [1987] 1 SCR 110.
[234] *Schachter* v. *Canada* (1992), 1992 CanLII 74 (SCC).

The least restrictive means test also accords with a sense that remedies should be proportionate to a violation. There is much intuitive sense to the proposition that more harmful violations should receive more drastic remedies than less serious and harmful violations. In the next chapter, however, it will be suggested that it is important to consider the dual purposes of the remedy. Some violations require a greater remedy because of the harm that they cause to the litigant. Other violations may require a more drastic remedy because they indicate that the state has ignored the right and is likely to do so again in the future.

1.9.10 Overall Balance between the Limited Remedy and the Competing Objectives

Proportionality analysis as applied to remedial decision-making should be completed by the final overall balance stage. As Aharon Barak has argued, this overall balance stage plays a fundamental role in proportionality analysis.[235] This final stage of proportionality analysis raises the difficult issue of balancing the incommensurable values of rights against social benefits. As Barak notes, the overall balance stage is more driven by normative factors than the more evidence and fact-based analysis that plays a large part in both the rational connection and necessity stages of analysis.[236]

There are reasons to believe that the overall balance may be easier for judges to determine at the remedial stage. In part, this is simply because the finding of a violation of a human right remains intact and directs the court towards ensuring that litigants receive some tangible remedy. Litigants in turn can be expected to explain why some remedies will be ineffective given their circumstances. In addition, governments should be in a good position to demonstrate the social harms of requested and alternative remedies.

A two-track remedial strategy may also be better able to manage the problem of incommensurability between rights and competing social interests. This is because it allows the court to separate out the question of what remedy is required to compensate or protect a particular litigant's rights from the more contingent harms caused by broader systemic remedies. The ability of the state to justify proportional limits on remedies may be different when applied to the litigant and others similarly

235 Barak, *Proportionality*, pp.340–370.
236 Ibid., pp.350, 357, 366.

situated including potential future victims of similar rights violations. Specifically, it may be more difficult to justify limited remedies or no remedies for those who have gone to the time and expense of litigating and establishing a violation of human rights. Conversely, governments may more easily be able to justify limits including delays on systemic remedies. As suggested in the next chapter, courts will generally be more aggressive and less deferential towards governments in crafting remedies for individual litigants than when crafting systemic remedies to prevent future violations.

The Supreme Court of Canada has demonstrated how the overall balance stage of proportionality reasoning can be applied to remedies. The Court defended only applying pension benefits to same sex couples retroactive to 1999 (as opposed to 1985 when equality rights came into effect) as striking "an appropriate balance between fairness to individual litigants and respecting the legislative role of Parliament" with respect to policy making and the distribution of resources. The Court was clear that this result would not leave the applicants with "a hollow victory".[237] This decision demonstrated the importance of the final overall balance stage of proportionality reasoning as applied to remedies. It also confirms that proportionality reasoning may frequently result in remedial compromises that will leave neither those whose rights have been violated or the government fully satisfied with the remedy that the court orders.

In the final overall balance stage of proportionality reasoning, judges should articulate clearly why the full remedy requested in the case will harm social interests and the degree to which the limited remedy will satisfy these competing objectives. On the other hand, judges should pay attention to the effects of limited or even no remedies on both the litigants in the case and others who will be affected by the remedy (or lack thereof).

1.10 Conclusion

This chapter has sought to convince the reader that even though remedies for human rights violations have often been neglected by judges and scholars, they are important, challenging and worthy of more study. Most human rights law only provides vague admonitions about the need for appropriate or effective remedies. Some human rights laws restrict the

[237] *Hislop* v. *Canada*, 2007 SCC 10 at para 116.

type of remedies that courts can order. Some contemplate the need for courts to craft prospective or delayed remedies. Nevertheless, the answer to the many challenges of remedial decision-making will rarely be found in the text of human rights law.

This chapter has suggested that remedies have been under-theorized, but that recent work in the separation of powers and proportionality can provide some sound principles to guide and discipline remedial decision-making. To be sure, not all will agree with the exact content or weight that should be given to these principles. Nevertheless, discussion and debate about such general principles is better than relying on unfettered remedial discretion including the discretion not to award a remedy. Reliance on general principles is also better than making rules that will inevitably be under- and over-inclusive given the contextual and dynamic nature of remedial decision-making.

Following in the path of Edwin Borchard and Abram Chayes, it has been suggested that domestic law can be enriched by international legal practices such as the use of declarations and retention of jurisdiction. International human rights law reveals the importance of persuasion rather than command with respect to remedies. It also reveals the frequent reality of remedial failure and repetitive violations, something that domestic courts complacently ignore. The next chapter will also suggest that domestic courts can learn much from the supra-national practice of devising both individual remedies for litigants and systemic measures to prevent similar violations in the future.

2

A Two-Track Approach to Individual and Systemic Remedies

2.1 Introduction

Domestic and international human rights laws generally provide only vague admonitions about the need for effective remedies and the breadth of remedial discretion. Judges have placed too much reliance on the concept of remedial discretion. This chapter responds to the under-theorization of remedies by outlining a general conceptual approach to remedies that I call a two-track approach. The two-track approach is symbolized by the Monet painting on the cover of the book showing two different trains leaving Gare St Lazare in Paris at the same time. Even if the two-track approach cannot be implemented in every case, it remains a useful way to think about the dual goals of remedies and the different means that can be used in an attempt to achieve those goals.

The two-track approach combines attempts to repair past violations suffered by litigants with attempts to prevent future and repetitive violations. Its origins lie in the distinction that supra-national courts have drawn between individual measures (often compensation for the litigant) and general measures directed at states.[1] In addition, the two-track approach provides a mechanism for responding to remedial failure, particularly the frequent failure to prevent future violations.

On the first-track, courts should play a dominant and traditional role in providing restitution or compensation for litigants who have established that their rights have been or will be violated. This does not mean that litigants always get the remedy they want or that there are no remedial constraints that may justify proportionate limits on remedies or the selection of a less drastic remedy that better reconciles remedies with competing interests. Nevertheless, the separation of powers recognizes that courts play a special role in providing remedies to litigants.

Interim remedies pending a full trial, examined in the next chapter, can also be seen as a first-track remedy to prevent irreparable harm to rights that will make restitution impossible. Interim remedies are necessary to ensure that the court can adjudicate a dispute and, if rights are violated, provide a full and effective remedy.[2] Whether at the pre-trial interim remedy stage or post-trial stage, the two-track approach features a demanding approach to relief for litigants. It will be suggested that this lies at the core of widely held expectations about adjudication, courts and human rights.

Both supra-national and domestic human rights law has recognized a second important purpose for remedies: preventing similar human rights violations in the future. In the circumstances of the modern bureaucratic state, such an approach generally requires systemic remedies. The relevant bureaucracy should take reasonable steps to ensure that the

[1] The European Court of Human Rights has increasingly drawn distinctions between individual measures generally compensation and general measures designed to prevent future violations. Hellen Keller and Cedric Marti, "Reconceptualizing Implementing: The Judicialization of the Execution of European Court of Human Rights Judgements" (2016) 26(4) *E. J. L.* 829; Lize Glas, "The European Court of Human Rights Supervising the Execution of Its Judgments" (2019) 37(3) *Netherlands Q Hum. Rts.* 228.

[2] Keller and Marti, "Reconceptualizing Implementation", 833–834.

violation will not be repeated. Sometimes, the legislature will have to enact new laws or revise old laws that violate rights. This second systemic track also attempts to accommodate criticisms that it will result in judges "running prisons or police forces" and be "democracy by decree"[3] by respecting subsidiarity and the separation of powers as constraints on remedial decision-making discussed in Chapter 1, Section 1.8. It also attempts to make room for participation at various junctures including legislative debates in the wake of declarations of incompatibility and suspended declarations of invalidity, as well as participation through engagement and consultation in the formulation of complex relief.[4]

The two tracks of individual and systemic relief have been recognized in the literature since Abram Chayes's pioneering work contrasting a new public law form of litigation with a traditional common law model.[5] Much prior scholarship, including some of my own,[6] has emphasized tensions between the individual and systemic functions of remedies. The two-track approach recognizes these tensions but suggests that both individual and systemic remedies are necessary. It recognizes the legitimacy of both backward-looking concerns about correction and forward-looking concerns about prevention.[7] Moreover, it suggests that both forms of remedies can be complementary and mutually re-enforcing.

[3] David S. Schoenbrod and Ross Sandler, *Democracy by Decree* (New Haven: Yale University Press, 2003).

[4] For an account of how some supra-national adjudicators and South African courts have tried to make room for participation, including by those who are supposed to benefit from remedies, see Sandra Liebenberg, "Participatory Justice in Social Rights Adjudication" (2018) 18 *Hum. Rts. L. Rev.* 623.

[5] Abram Chayes, "The Role of the Judge in Public Law Litigation" (1976) 89 *Harv. L. Rev.* 7.

[6] Kent Roach, "The Limits of Corrective Justice and the Potential of Equity" (1991) 33 *Ariz. L. Rev.* 859; Aruna Sathanapally, *Beyond Disagreement* (Oxford: Oxford University Press, 2012), p.11 (recognizing corrective justice and systemic justice as the "two generally recognized functions" of remedies).

[7] The debate between Chayes's traditional and public law models reflects what my colleague Stephen Waddams has said about some elements of remedies in private law, namely: "there have been sharp differences of academic opinion on this point, both as among leading writers, and in the mind of individual writers over time. This strongly suggests that there is likely to be truth on both sides of this debate. Opinions in legal controversy that appear at first sight implacably opposed may often be reconciled by the consideration that each is describing a different dimension of a complex phenomenon, or by the consideration that each is addressing a slightly different question. Thus both, of seemingly opposite views, or several, of seemingly diverse views, may be correct. It is not possible to select one criterion exclusively as definitive: from a historical perspective the courts have been influenced by various factors". Stephen Waddams, *Principles and Policy in Contract Law* (Cambridge: Cambridge University Press, 2011), p.198.

Chayes's work is well known. What is new in my account of the two-track approach is an insistence that courts should travel both tracks at the same time and that exclusive focus on either track will be radically incomplete and produce remedial pathologies. If courts are only concerned with individual relief they will provide inadequate remedies, such as damages while ignoring larger questions about repetitive violations and compliance. If courts only pursue systemic remedies, they will strain their competence, stray away from the concerns of those the remedy is supposed to benefit and risk losing legitimacy as courts.

The emphasis that courts place on the individual or systemic track will depend on the context including the remedial demands of particular litigants and whether it is possible to provide effective relief for litigants without achieving systemic reform. Sometimes, both tracks may not be pursued at the same time.[8] Nevertheless, even if it cannot always be implemented, a two-track approach to individual and systemic remedies remains a useful way of thinking about remedies.

A final innovation of the two-track approach is that it is responsive to the reality of remedial failure. Consistent with dialogic forms of judicial review, it assumes a broader time perspective than most scholarship, which tends to focus on a single moment of decision.[9] It recognizes that few systemic reforms will be able to prevent all future violations. It thus contemplates subsequent cycles of reform when rights are violated again. Courts will generally provide remedies for these new harms, but also consider whether additional and perhaps more intrusive systemic reforms are also necessary. Courts should generally intensify systemic remedies if faced with evidence that the government is still not taking reasonable steps to stop repetitive violations. Relief in complex domestic cases is much closer to the focus on persuasion and iterative attempts used in supra-national law than most realize.

2.1.1 Outline of This Chapter

Section 2.2 will examine first-track remedies for successful litigants. The focus on providing successful litigants with remedies that provide

[8] David Landau, "Choosing between Simple and Complex Remedies in Socio-Economic Cases" (2019) 69 *Supp. 1 U.T.L.J.* 105.

[9] Kent Roach, "Dialogue in Canada and the Dangers of Simplified Comparative Law and Populism" in Geoffrey Sigalet, Gregoire Webber and Rosalind Dixon (eds.), *Constitutional Dialogue Rights and Institutions* (New York: Cambridge University Press, 2019).

restitution or compensation has roots in Aristotle's understanding of corrective justice. It is also reflected in the "right to a remedy" reasoning celebrated by Blackstone and Dicey. Despite its ancient roots, it is a mistake to dismiss this remedial purpose as an archaic artefact of history. It has recently been reaffirmed in the *Basic Principles and Guidelines on the Right to a Remedy and Reparation for Victims of Gross Violations of International Human Rights Law and Serious Violations of International Humanitarian Law* (henceforward *Basic Principles*).[10] To be sure, modern litigants often expect more than individual remedies when they engage in adjudication, but they still often and legitimately expect individual remedies.

Section 2.3 will examine how remedies in both domestic and supra-national human rights law have increasingly been concerned with preventing future violations. International law principles recognize the importance of providing guarantees of non-repetition of rights violations. Moreover, the practice of many supra-national rights adjudicators is to retain jurisdiction and to try, through follow up judgements and reports, to ensure better compliance by nation states with human rights in the future. Public law litigation where courts retain jurisdiction started in the United States, but has now spread to many other democracies.

Section 2.4 will outline my proposed two-track approach that combines the pursuit of both individual and systemic remedies. The two-track approach is more firmly established in supra-national law than domestic law. Supra-national adjudicators often make distinctions between specific measures that provide remedies for individual litigants and general measures designed to ensure greater governmental compliance with human rights in the future. Different types of remedies are often pursued in each track.

Section 2.5 will argue that an exclusive focus on either individual or systemic remedies will be incomplete and prone to produce remedial pathologies. This may occur if evidence is excluded as an individual remedy while the police continue routinely to violate the same right. In such cases, governments will simply be able to pay an occasional price for violating rights. Conversely, courts that only pursue systemic remedies will often produce remedies that lack legitimacy and may fail to respond

[10] *Basic Principles and Guidelines on the Right to a Remedy and Reparation for Victims of Gross Violations of International Human Rights Law and Serious Violations of International Humanitarian Law*, Adopted and Proclaimed by the CA Res 60/147 of 16 December 2005 UN Doc. A/Res/60/147.

to the most pressing needs of those whose rights have been violated.[11] A lack of individual remedies may also promote cynicism about both rights and remedies.

Section 2.6 will examine how the two-track approach recognizes and responds to the reality of remedial failure. It does so by outlining how cycles of individual and systemic remedies can occur. This allows both litigants and courts to adjust their approach in response to new evidence and new concerns. It allows courts, when warranted, to escalate their remedies for state failures to take reasonable steps to prevent future violations and to remind society of the human consequences and costs of continued violations by the award of individual remedies.

2.2 Individual Remedies to Compensate and Prevent Imminent Violations

2.2.1 Corrective Justice and Private Law

Aristotle described corrective justice as "that which plays a rectifying part in transactions between man and man" and contrasted it with "distributive justice which is manifested in distributions of honour or money or other things that fall to be divided among those who have a share in the constitution".[12] Leaving aside for now his hint that constitutional matters involved distributional issues, Aristotle's vision of corrective justice animates many deontological understandings of private law as well as Chayes's description of the traditional model of adjudication.

Justice in corrective justice "consists in having an equal amount before and after the transaction".[13] The law is only concerned with "the distinctive character of the injury".[14] Consistent with formal ideas of equality, corrective justice "treats the parties as equal, if one is in the wrong and the other being wronged, and if one inflicted injury and the

[11] Joshua Dunn, *Complex Justice: The Story of Missouri v. Jenkins* (Chapel Hill: University of North Carolina Press, 2008) (complex magnet school ordered to achieve desegregation fails to achieve that goal and not supported by African-American community); Anuj Bhuwania, *Courting the People Public Interest Litigation in Post-Emergency India* (Cambridge: Cambridge University Press, 2017) (public interest litigated dominated by judges and their appointed amicus and excluding litigants producing more homelessness).

[12] Aristotle, *The Nicomachean Ethics*, D. Ross (trans.), J. L Ackrill and J. O Urmson (rev. eds.), (Oxford: Oxford University Press, 1980), Book III.

[13] Ibid. at V.

[14] Ibid.

other has received it. Therefore, this kind of injustice being an inequality, the judge tries to equalize it" by "taking away the gain of the assailant".[15] Corrective justice demands remedies that do no more, but also no less, than repair the adverse consequences of the violation.

The causal connection between the wrong and harms caused is central in corrective justice. It is only just to require the defendant to compensate for harms that are the direct cause of the defendant's wrong and the plaintiff's suffering. If the harm would have inevitably occurred without the wrong, it should not be remedied. This vision of corrective justice fails, however, to capture all of private law.[16] For example, intentional torts such as assault and trespass that may be most similar to human rights violations impose damages without proof of harm in order to vindicate the importance of the underlying right or interest.[17] In either approach, however, right and remedy are closely matched: the remedy should be deduced from the nature of the right violated and the harms caused by the rights violation. The remedy was designed to make the individual litigant whole. In this tradition, it would be wrong for a judge to give the plaintiff an undeserved remedy in an attempt to prevent the defendant from violating rights in the future.

2.2.2 Corrective Justice and Constitutional Law

In the common law tradition, constitutional law was first seen as a form of private law. Not surprisingly, commentators such as William Blackstone implicitly appealed to corrective justice when he argued that "it is a settled and invariable principle in the laws of England, that every right when withheld must have a remedy, and every injury its proper redress".[18] This approach found favour in the rhetoric but not the actual result in *Marbury* v. *Madison*. Chief Justice Marshall claimed the United States would no longer be subject to the rule of law "if the laws furnish no remedy for a violation of a vested legal rights" before he refused to order a requested remedy on the basis of limits on the Supreme Court's jurisdiction.[19] A leading theorist of corrective justice, Ernest Weinrib,

[15] Ibid. at IV.
[16] L. L. Fuller and William R. Purdue, "The Reliance Interest in Contracts" (1936) 46 *Yale. L. J.* 1, 373; Waddams, *Principles and Policy in Contract Law*, pp.209–231.
[17] Jason Varuhas, *Damages and Human Rights* (Oxford: Hart Publishing, 2016).
[18] William Blackstone, *Commentaries on the Laws of England* (Oxford: Clarendon Press, 1765) at Book III, Chap. VII, pp.100–101.
[19] 5 US 137 (1803) at 163; see also *The Apollon*, 22 US 362 (1824) at 366–367.

has acknowledged that Blackstone's statement that remedies "redress the party injured, by either restoring to him his right, if possible, or by giving him an equivalent" is "a paradigmatic expression of corrective justice".[20]

Albert Venn Dicey argued that the principle that underlined the whole English Constitution is that "the courts give a remedy for the infringement of a right whether the injury be great or small".[21] Like Blackstone, he could celebrate the close connection between rights and remedies in large part because of their assumptions that violations of rights could be adequately redressed by simple remedies such as damages or the granting of writs that were "properly and singularly adapted" to a "particular grievance" so that "as little as possible is left to the breast of the judges whom the law appoints to administer and not prescribe the remedy".[22] Remedial discretion did not loom large. Dicey stressed that remedies were the result of applying private law principles to public law. He cheerfully acknowledged that "moral or political wrongs" would not result in a "legal remedy".[23] His approach assumed a minimal state and a minimal concept of rights.

The idea that remedies should compensate for the past harms of a violation and restore victims to the position they occupied before a violation is also found in international law. In 1928, the predecessor to the International Court of Justice stated in the *Chorzow Factory* case that remedies should, "as far as possible, wipe out all the consequences of the illegal act and re-establish the situation which would, in all probability have existed if the act had not been committed".[24] This make whole aspiration was also reflected in the drafting of the European Convention on Human Rights which emphasizes giving "just satisfaction to the injured party" if domestic laws of a member state provide only "partial

[20] Ernest Weinrib, *Corrective Justice* (Oxford: Oxford University Press, 2012), p.91 citing Blackstone, *Commentaries*, Book IV. Chap. IX. Even under Weinrib's approach, courts exercise some degree of remedial discretion and can award damages instead of specific performance or an injunction because of "the difficulty of constant curial supervision, the futility of the remedy, the absence of mutuality, the plaintiff's failure to do equity, and the reluctance to enforce a decree of personal service" so long as such factors relate to "the system of rights" even though these factors go beyond an examination of "a given right in isolation". Ibid., p.11.

[21] A. V. Dicey, *Introduction to the Study of the Law of the Constitution*, 10th ed. (London: MacMillan, 1959), pp.211–212.

[22] Blackstone, *Commentaries*, Book III, Chap. XVI, p.244.

[23] Dicey, *Introduction to the Study of the Law*, p.55.

[24] *Factory at Chorzow Case* (Jurisdiction), [1928] PCIJ Series A No.17, 22, 47.

reparation".[25] The focus was on repairing the past, not preventing future violations.

Following its common law origins, damages are often seen as a remedy for human rights violations that is driven by traditional corrective justice concerns about restoring the victim to the position that he or she occupied but for the violation. For example, the leading Canadian case on damages for violations of Charter rights quoted a leading European Court of Human Rights (ECtHR) case on just satisfaction that "the goal is to compensate the claimant for the loss caused by the *Charter* breach: 'the applicant should, in so far as is possible, be placed in the same position as if his Convention rights had not been infringed.'"[26] The South African Constitutional Court has similarly stated "it would be strange if damages could not be claimed for, at least, loss occasioned by the breach of a right vested in the claimant by the Supreme law".[27] Although sometimes accepted in constitutional law, punitive damages are deeply problematic within the corrective justice tradition. This is because they provide a windfall not tied to the harm suffered by the plaintiff and because they are designed to denounce and deter violations and not simply to compensate for the harms caused by violations.

As will be examined in Chapter 5, Section 5.2, damages have emerged as a disappointing remedy in large part because of the low amounts of damages awarded to repair the often intangible values such as dignity, liberty and equality protected by human rights. It may be that no award of damages will ever fully place some victims of human rights violations in the same position that they occupied before the violation. Nevertheless, the state should in theory be held responsible by the court for the pecuniary and non-pecuniary damages and losses that were caused by the human rights violation.

Jason Varuhas contends that public law and supra-national approaches have sapped damages of their private law vitality in dealing with rights violations. He appeals to Blackstone and Dicey in arguing that a person should receive robust damage awards for even the slightest unlawful infringement of liberty. Varuhas argues for a vindicatory tort approach taken from intentional common law torts, such as false

25 European Convention for the Protection of Human Rights and Fundamental Freedoms, Rome, 4 November 1950, in force 3 September 1953, 213 UNTS 221, Art. 41 and former Art. 50.

26 *Ward* v. *Vancouver (City)*, 2010 SCC 27 at para 27.

27 *Fose* v. *Minister of Safety and Security*, [1997] ZACC 6.

imprisonment and trespass.[28] In Chapter 5, Section 5.3, I will argue that his approach neglects many of the benefits of a public law approach, especially one inspired by recent work in international law. Nevertheless, I agree with Varuhas that a vindicatory approach should be taken to awarding damages for human rights in addition to a compensatory approach and that this should result in higher awards. In Chapters 5, Section 5.2.2.4, and Chapter 6, Section 6.2.2.1, I will also suggest that American courts have made a mistake in seeing damages and exclusion of evidence in purely instrumental terms and ignoring the corrective justifications of such remedies as deserved compensation for proven harms.

English commentators, as well as the Australian High Court, have expressed scepticism about declarations of incompatibility because they fail to provide litigants with tangible remedies.[29] Commentators have criticized suspended declarations of invalidity for not providing immediate remedies.[30] In Chapter 4, Section 4.4, I will suggest that these criticisms should be taken seriously and that, where possible, successful litigants should receive an individual remedy.

2.2.3 *Corrective Remedies and Queue Jumping*

Corrective justice is based in part on a dichotomy that distinguishes the transactional logic of corrective justice from larger concerns about distributive justice. In contexts involving human rights and especially socio-economic rights, it may be difficult to maintain such dichotomies. For example, the South African courts were initially hesitant to grant individual remedies for socio-economic rights because of concerns about queue jumping.[31] Justice Albie Sachs worried that individual remedies would allow those with "the sharpest elbows"[32] to go to the front of the line. His concern has, however, diminished over time. In *Port Elizabeth*,

[28] Varuhas, *Damages and Human Rights*, pp.60–61, 78.

[29] *Momcilovic* v. *The Queen*, [2011] HCA 34; Tom Hickman, "Bill of Rights Reform and the Case for Going Beyond the Declaration of Incompatibility Model" (2015) 2015 *N.Z. L. Rev.* 35, 46–47; Aileen Kavanagh, *Constitutional Review Under the UK Human Rights Act* (Cambridge: Cambridge University Press, 2009), pp.49–165.

[30] Bruce Ryder, "Suspending the Charter" (2003) 21 *S.C.L.R.* 2d 267; Robert Leckey, "Enforcing Laws That Infringe Rights" (2016) *Public Law* 206.

[31] *Soobramoney* v. *Minister of Health*, [1997] 12 BCLR 1696 at paras 28, 58–59.

[32] Albie Sachs, "The Judicial Enforcement of Socio-Economic Rights: The Grootboom Case" (2003) 56(1) *Current Legal Problems* 579, 598.

he more cheerfully recognized that while courts alone cannot solve "macro injustices", they can repair "micro injustices"[33] by granting successful litigants effective remedies. One way of seeing Justice Sachs's increased concern with "micro injustices" is that he has become inclined to see them as a form of corrective justice, or at least as something that litigants with a proven rights violation should be able to expect from the courts.

A common distributional concern with individual court-ordered remedies is that they constitute a form of queue jumping with respect to executive or legislative criteria for allocating scarce resources.[34] Queues are often venerated as a means of allocating scarce resources. As Calabresi and Bobbitt have demonstrated, however, they are only one of many methods.[35] Queue jumping may be part and parcel of right to a remedy reasoning that encourages judges to award successful litigants meaningful remedies. To be sure, individual queue-jumping remedies can have disruptive and regressive effects, especially in healthcare and housing contexts. That said, reply legislation could also address and minimize harms caused by individual remedies.[36] A challenge to reply legislation also provides the court with an opportunity to re-consider in light of new evidence whether the state has made reasonable and proportionate choices in allocating scarce resources.[37] Queue jumping is a concern, but it should not trump "right to a remedy" reasoning.

2.3 Systemic Remedies to Prevent Future Violations

The rise of the modern state combined with legal realist insights about the importance of remedial discretion make Blackstone and Dicey's attempts to deduce remedies automatically from the nature of rights and writs seem archaic. Declarations emerged as an important preventive

[33] *Port Elizabeth Municipality* v. *Various Occupiers*, [2004] ZACC 7 at para 38.

[34] Katharine G. Young, "Rights and Queues" (2016) 55 *Colum. J. Transn'l, L.* 65.

[35] Guido Calabresi and Philip Bobbit, *Tragic Choices* (New York: W. W. Norton & Company, 1978).

[36] Quebec legislation in response to *Chaoulli* v. *Quebec (Attorney General)*, [2005] 1 SCR 791 (Bill 33, *An Act to amend the Act respecting health services and social services and other legislative provisions*, 2nd sess., 37th Leg, Quebec, 2006, assented to 13 December 2006) that could have authorized queue jumping through the purchase of health insurance actually dampened such demands by improving the efficiency of the public system. See Kent Roach, "Polycentricity and Queue Jumping in Public Law Remedies" (2016) 66 *U.T.L.J.* 3, 38–40.

[37] Mark Tushnet, *Weak Courts, Strong Rights: Judicial Review and Social Welfare Rights in Comparative Constitutional Law* (Princeton: Princeton University Press, 2004), p.257.

remedy both in domestic and supra-national law[38] even though Blackstone and Dicey would have derided them as toothless.

Brown v. *Board of Education II*[39] demonstrated how remedies could be separated from rights and how delayed or weaker remedies were sometimes the price paid for more robust rights. The Court remanded the case for trial courts to proceed "with all deliberate speed"[40] in desegregating schools. The school boards would simply have to make "a prompt and reasonable start towards full compliance" and they would have "the primary responsibility" for solving practical problems. In a nod to the fact that all courts – domestic or supra-national – lack the power over the sword or the purse[41] and have to rely on the persuasive force of their judgements, the courts would simply judge whether governments had engaged in a "good faith implementation of the governing constitutional principles".[42] Remedies for Black children and parents who suffered discrimination and exclusion were effectively postponed indefinitely.

The Court's decision to take a gradual approach to desegregation remedies has been both controversial and influential. Its template for providing governments an opportunity to justify delay as "necessary in the public interest"[43] allowed governments to propose less drastic alternative remedies. It failed to produce prompt or effective remedies. Yet, its model of adjudication was celebrated by Chayes. Moreover, it migrated to prison cases in the United States and to many other jurisdictions. Echoes of the Court's incremental and iterative approach are also seen in supra-national processes, where the judicial retention of jurisdiction is even more commonplace than with respect to domestic courts.[44]

[38] Edwin Borchard, *Declaratory Judgments*, 2nd ed. (Cleveland: Banks Baldwin, 1941).

[39] 349 US 294 (1955) [henceforward *Brown II*].

[40] Ibid. at 301.

[41] As Alexander Hamilton said in *The Federalist No. 78*, 1788, the judiciary "has no influence over either the sword or the purse . . . It may truly be said to have neither FORCE nor WILL, but merely judgment; and must ultimately depend upon the aid of the executive arm even for the efficacy of its judgments". Hamilton's acceptance of the limits of judicial powers did not, however, devolve into an acceptance of co-ordinate construction that Jefferson and later Jackson embraced. For example, Hamilton wrote: "The interpretation of the laws is the proper and peculiar province of the courts. A constitution is, in fact, and must be regarded by the judges, as a fundamental law. It therefore belongs to them to ascertain its meaning, as well as the meaning of any particular act proceeding from the legislative body."

[42] *Brown II*, 349 US 294 (1955) at 299–300.

[43] Ibid. at 300.

[44] Alexandra Huneeus, "Reforming the State from Afar: Structural Reform Litigation at the Human Rights Courts" (2015) 40 *Yale L. J.* 1.

Chayes depicted the traditional idea that remedy could be deduced from the underlying right and would normally result in damages as part of a pre-realist vision where the powers of both judges and governments were "stringently limited".[45] He argued that the twentieth century had seen the rise of equitable relief where "right and remedy are pretty thoroughly disconnected"[46] and where judges must balance competing interests including those not represented in the lawsuit. Moreover the public law injunction was not "imposed but negotiated".[47] Like Alexander Bickel,[48] Chayes understood that the powers of courts ultimately depended on their ability to persuade. He contemplated justice as an ongoing process and "the subject of a colloquy in which legislators, officials and ordinary people – not just lawyers and judges – take part".[49] Perhaps because of his familiarity with international law, Chayes did not oppose public law litigation simply because it did not rely on coercive and immediate command and control remedies.

Chayes recognized that in many cases involving institutions and the environment, "it is hard to conceive individual relief apart from class relief".[50] This is an important factor that places limits on the two-track approach to remedies that will be discussed in greater depth later at Section 2.4.4 of this chapter. At this juncture, however, it should be noted that even in those contexts where Chayes is correct that only class-wide or institutional-wide relief is effective, he discounted the distinct ability of courts to focus on the effects of non-compliance with human rights on specific individuals. In his understandable eagerness to have the judiciary respond to the bureaucratic nature of modern government, Chayes discounted the need for a "warm body" and proof of some injury in fact[51] or "to compensate for past

[45] Chayes, "The Role of the Judge in Public Law Litigation", 1288; see also Owen Fiss's similar argument that the idea that the relationship between right and remedy is "formal and deductive" is "impoverished" and not suitable for modern conditions. Owen Fiss, "Forward: The Forms of Justice"(1979) 93 *Harv. L. Rev.* 1, 47.

[46] Chayes, "The Role of the Judge", 1293.

[47] Ibid., 1302.

[48] Alexander Bickel, *The Least Dangerous Branch,* rev'd. ed. (New Haven: Yale University Press, 1986).

[49] Abram Chayes, "How Does the Constitution Establish Justice?" (1988) 101 *Harv. L. Rev.* 1026, 1039.

[50] Ibid., 27.

[51] Abram Chayes, "Public Law Litigation and the Burger Court" (1982) 96 *Harv. L. Rev.* 4, 25–26. Chayes elaborated that "in much contemporary litigation, the named plaintiff has no role in the conduct of the litigation", ibid., 45.

wrong[s]".[52] He discounted the importance of this more individualistic approach to the legitimacy of the courts,[53] the effectiveness of their remedies[54] and in capturing public and political support for systemic reform.[55]

Owen Fiss stressed the role of the judge in giving meaning to constitutional values that could transform institutions and society going forward. The older idea of litigants being entitled to specific remedies was for him "rooted in a world that no longer exists".[56] At the same time, Fiss recognized that the structural injunction designed to reform schools and prisons to comply with future rights also had a reparative characteristic, if only because "at least as a practical manner, a past wrong is required . . . the mere threat of a wrong in the future is not likely to be deemed sufficient to trigger the reform enterprise".[57] He also questioned why victims and beneficiaries of the remedy had to be represented in the lawsuit[58] even though, as will be suggested in Chapters 7 and 8, they have their own form of expert knowledge about the harms that they suffered. Like Chayes, Fiss discounted the importance of past harms to judicial legitimacy, the effectiveness of the remedy and public and political support for a judicially led reform process.

There is much that is persuasive in Chayes and Fiss's sense that right to a remedy reasoning was not well suited to the modern age. However, their total rejection of the received tradition set public law litigation up for heavy criticism on the basis that it empowered judges beyond their roles and expertise. Judges as reformers at large is a difficult sell. As Fiss recognized, the forward-looking nature of public law litigation could threaten rights by making judges liable to conflate what was possible in a complex modern state with what rights required.[59] Fiss did not,

[52] Chayes, "The Role of the Judge in Public Law Litigation", 1298; for a similar argument that victims of constitutional violation need not be recipients of remedies because of the "instrumental nature of the remedy" and that injunctions are focused on the future and "even does not require a judgment about wrongdoing, future or past" see Fiss, "The Forms of Justice", 22–23.

[53] Lon Fuller, "The Forms and Limits of Adjudication" (1978) 92 *Harv. L. Rev.* 2.

[54] Dunn, *Complex Justice*; Bhuwania, *Courting the People*.

[55] Charles R. Epp, *Making Rights Real* (Chicago: University of Chicago Press, 1993).

[56] Fiss, "The Forms of Justice", 44.

[57] Fiss, *The Civil Rights Injunction*, p.11.

[58] Fiss, "The Forms of Justice", 18–22.

[59] Fiss was alive to this danger when he identified that a judge's need for success and clearing the docket was a threat to rights when it resulted in premature termination of structural reform efforts: ibid., 53.

however, anchor his concerns about rights in the need to provide some individual remedy for past harms to rights. Like Chayes, he saw that as anachronistic.

Chayes and Fiss's important arguments about the priority of preventing future rights violations rather than compensating for past harms fit well with the instrumental and forward-looking nature of much American remedial doctrine.[60] Since the 1960s, exclusion of unconstitutionally obtained evidence has been justified as a means to deter future police misconduct, not to repair specific rights violations suffered by the accused.[61] Similarly, damages are not awarded unless officials have clearly violated established law because of concerns about over-deterring state officials in the future exercise of their duties.[62] One searches modern American constitutional jurisprudence in vain for recognition of traditional right to a remedy reasoning.

The instrumental and preventive turn in remedies has been fiercely contested. Critics argue that future-directed remedies take courts well beyond their proper role and expertise.[63] The increased systemic and instrumental ambitions of remedies produce more frequent failures.[64] Even those who defend the remedial activism of American courts concede that the activism is a form of "experimentation"[65] that responds to governmental pathologies, as opposed to something that aggrieved litigants have a right to expect.

In supra-national law, there is recognition that remedies should in part be designed to prevent violations in the future. The work of the

[60] One of the challenges in remedial scholarship is that civil and even many constitutional lawyers like Chayes and Fiss tend to ignore the importance of remedies in the criminal process. I am grateful to the late Joe Arvay OC, QC who first made this point to me 30 years ago.

[61] *Elkins* v. *United States*, 364 US 206 (1960) at 217.

[62] *Ziglar* v. *Abbasi*, 137 S.Ct. 1843 (2017); *Ashcroft* v. *al Kidd*, 563 US 731 (2011) (Attorney General cannot be sued personally for use of material witness warrant as a form of preventive detention because of danger of deterring national security decision-making); see generally Stephen Vladek, "The New National Security Canon" (2012) 61 *Amer. Univ. L. Rev.* 1295; James Pfander, *Constitutional Torts and the War on Terror* (Oxford: Oxford University Press, 2017).

[63] Donald Horwitz, *The Courts and Social Policy* (Washington: Brookings Institute, 1977); John Yoo, "Who Measures the Chancellor's Foot: The Inherent Remedial Authority of the Federal Courts" (1996) 84 *Calif. L. Rev.* 1121.

[64] Fiss, "Forms of Justice", 50 ("failure is always possible with any instrumental activity"); Dunn, *Complex Justice* (failure of magnet school plan); Schoenbrod and Sandler, *Democracy by Decree*.

[65] Charles F. Sabel and William H. Simon, "Destabilization Rights: How Public Law Litigation Succeeds" (2004) 117 *Harv. L. Rev.* 1016.

International Law Commission on the principles of state responsibility recognized both cessation and assurances of non-repetition as core obligations of states involved in internationally wrongful acts.[66] The 2005 UN *Basic Principles*[67] included not only the traditional remedial goals of restitution, compensation, rehabilitation and satisfaction but also "guarantees of non-repetition" including law reform. Supra-national courts including the ECtHR have become increasingly concerned about preventing repetitive violations if only to ease their caseload, which has dramatically increased as Turkey and countries from the former Soviet Union have joined the Council of Europe. Under-resourced supra-national courts have a particular interest in preventing repetitive violations.[68] They are much more inclined than domestic courts to see systemic remedies to prevent future violations as a practical necessity for their own survival.

2.4 A Two-Track Approach to Individual and Systemic Remedies

The two-track approach encourages adjudicators to separate out the question of the appropriate remedy to protect and compensate specific litigants from the broader questions of appropriate measures to prevent the repetition of similar violations in the future. It combines the traditional "right to a remedy" task long articulated for courts in both domestic and supra-national law with the more modern task of promoting systemic reforms.

The two-track approach suggests that different remedies, different separation of powers considerations and different proportionality analysis of competing social interests will often be necessary in the different tracks. In particular, courts should assume primary responsibility for the traditional first-track task of repairing the violation of the rights of litigants. Courts should, at least initially, be more deferential towards the role and abilities of governments engaged with civil society to select

[66] International Law Commission, *Principles of State Responsibility*, of the Commission's fifty-third and fifty-fifth sessions, 23 April–1 June and 2 July–10 August 2001, GA Supplement No. 10, A/56/10. Art. 30.

[67] UN *Basic Principles* at paras 18, 23.

[68] Gerald L. Neuman, "Bi-Level Remedies for Human Rights Violations" (2014) 55 *Harv. J. Int'l. Law* 2. On the effects of lack of resources see Alice Donald, Debra Long and Anna-Katrin Speck "Identifying and Assessing the Implementation of Human Rights Decisions" (2020) 12 *Journal of Human Rights Practice* 125.

among various means to ensure future compliance with rights. The social interests that may be harmed and that compete with systemic remedies may also be greater than those which may be harmed and compete with individual remedies. Domestic courts should follow supra-national courts in devising both individual measures for litigants and more general measures to prevent future violations.

On the first track, courts should provide, wherever possible, some remedy for successful litigants who have suffered past violations. In the case of interim remedies, first-track remedies may be necessary to ensure that litigants do not suffer irreparable harm to their rights At the same time, such an individualistic approach to remedies may be too demanding in some institutional and distributive contexts. For example, the award of an entitlement to one litigant may have a precedential effect, implying that many others would also be entitled to receive the benefit. At this point, courts may have to choose whether to refuse the remedy because of concerns that it, writ large and applied to others, would be disproportionate or otherwise unworkable. Such a conclusion should not, however, detract from a finding that the successful litigant should have received a remedy. The violation should be noted and there may be a case for awarding some remedy, even a nominal one, to recognize this fact, even though others similarly situated may not be able to receive the remedy. Such a remedy can be criticized as irrational queue jumping in the larger distributional context. Nevertheless, it can also be justified on the basis that the particular litigant has already jumped the queue by establishing a rights violation and by the idea that courts should normally award successful litigants some remedy.

Even if the court orders the individual remedy, it should recognize that the remedy may be inadequate to ensure non-repetition of the violation in the future. On this second systemic track, courts should engage the legislature and the executive to devise broader remedies to ensure better compliance with human rights in the future. Courts would, at first, defer to the other institutions. They may, however, become more active in response to failures to make reasonable and effective efforts to prevent future violations. This second stage may also involve active encouragement of participation by the parties and other stakeholders. Both Fuller and Chayes recognized that broader participation was required when courts tackle complex polycentric problems.[69]

[69] See *infra* Chapter 1, Section 1.3, for discussion.

2.4.1 General Considerations

The two-track approach will vary with the context. Applicants may not ask for it in every case and, even if they do, it may not always be possible. It is presented as a way of thinking about and structuring the remedial process. Adjudicators should be open to a range of compensatory remedies that litigants propose, including not only damages but apologies and other informal acts of reparation. The two-track approach also contemplates a dynamic, iterative and interactive approach to systemic remedies that will often involve courts engaging with other institutions, the litigants and society. In this second systemic track, adjudicators may become less deferential over time if states are unwilling or unable to take steps to prevent future violations.

In some cases, litigants may also decide to only request individual or systemic remedies. Although these choices to prefer one track over the other should generally be respected, the dual ambitions of remedies should always be remembered. As will be more fully argued in the next section, obtaining individual remedies without systemic remedies will often ring hollow. Courts may be justified in pursuing two-track remedies even when applicants do not request them if there is evidence of repetitive violations.

Systemic remedies that are not supported and justified by the award of individual remedies will strain judicial competence and legitimacy. They may also drift away from those they are meant to benefit. An exclusively systemic approach may make adjudicators appear as reformers at large with little to support their remedial efforts and even less to distinguish their role from that of other parts of the state. It may also result in remedies that are not meaningful to those who had their rights violated.

2.4.2 Support for the Two-Track Approach in Existing Remedial Scholarship

Alexander Bickel, discussed in Chapter 1, Section 1.3, argued that *Brown II* used the flexible and broad equitable powers of trial courts "to engage in a continual colloquy with the political institutions, leaving it to them to tell the Court what expedients of accommodation and compromise they deemed necessary". He stressed, however, that courts would reject executive and legislative proposals "only when a suggested expedient amounted to the abandonment of principle".[70] This referred to the

[70] Bickel, *The Least Dangerous Branch*, p.254 referring to *Cooper* v. *Aaron*, 358 US 1 (1958) where the Court asserted its remedial authority.

Court's 1958 decision in the famous Little Rock High School segregation case. It reversed a trial judge's decision that would have allowed two and a half years delay in desegregating Central High because of fierce resistance to the admission of Black students by both the state and mobs. The Court quoted *Marbury* and Chief Justice Marshall that: "[i]f the legislatures of the several states may at will, annul the judgments of the courts of the United States, and destroy the rights acquired under those judgments, the constitution itself becomes a solemn mockery".[71] Bickel's nuanced understanding of remedies establishes much of the foundation for a two-track approach where courts recognize their obligations to give successful litigants meaningful remedies to protect principles while also engaging in a "colloquy" with political institutions and society about the ultimate systemic response.

Another constitutional theorist who has integrated remedies into his work and laid some of the foundations for a two-track approach is Mark Tushnet. Following the realist legacy, Tushnet is sensitive to how remedial consequences will affect the determination of rights. He has recognized links between *Brown II*'s incremental remedial strategy and the development of structural reform litigation that abandoned the Diceyean understanding of remedies as "personal and present" for successful litigants.[72] Tushnet has carried his influential work on strong and weak form judicial review into remedies. He has drawn distinctions between "strong remedies", such as mandatory injunctions that establish "specific deadlines" and "spell out in detail" what government officials must do, and "weak remedies" such as declarations or requirements that governments develop plans that encourage "negotiations among the parties over the contours of a more detailed plan".[73] Consistent with his recognition of the fine and dynamic line between weak and strong form judicial review, Tushnet observes that, over time, courts may "convert weak remedies into strong ones",[74] especially if they are frustrated with the

71 *Cooper* v. *Aaron*, 358 US 1 (1958) at para 18.

72 Mark Tushnet, "Public Law Litigation and the Ambiguities of Brown" (1992) 61 *Fordham L. Rev.* 23; desegregation remedies before *Brown II* were personal and present in ordering named African American plaintiffs to be admitted to segregated schools, see *Sweatt* v. *Painter*, 339 US 629 (1950); the Supreme Court may not have agreed to *Brown I* had they insisted on such an immediate right to a remedy approach.

73 Mark Tushnet, *Weak Courts, Strong Rights*, pp.248–251.

74 Ibid., p.256.

government's progress. This suggests that a systemic approach to remedies can evolve over time and become less deferential towards government.

Although at times he recognizes the ability of weak remedies to evolve into stronger remedies and back again, Tushnet also has a tendency to ignore individual remedies. For example, he has argued that weak remedies such as the general declarations in the South African housing rights case of *Grootboom* are best suited to the enforcement of socio-economic rights.[75] But, as will be suggested in Section 4.3.4 of this chapter, this discounts a more individual remedy that was provided in that case and more recent trends to combine anti-eviction remedies for litigants with engagement orders as a systemic remedy.[76]

The two-track approach combines remedies that provide immediate benefits to litigants with remedies designed to allow other institutions of government to achieve systemic reforms, ideally in consultation with civil society. Tushnet's dichotomy between declarations as a weak remedy and injunctions as a strong remedy is accepted in much of the common law world. Drawing in part on international law and Canadian practice, however, I will suggest in Chapter 7, Section 7.4, that a new remedy – the declaration plus – can allow governments flexibility to devise precise responses while allowing a judge to continue to monitor and respond to changing situations.[77] Under such an approach, Tushnet's dichotomy between strong and weak remedies is often a false choice.[78]

Richard Fallon and Daniel Meltzner have constructed a theory of constitutional remedies in the American federal system that is also relevant to a two-track approach to remedies. They recognize an idea rooted in corrective justice and articulated in *Marbury* that "for every violation of a right, there must be a remedy". At the same time, they argue that this demand for individual remedies confronts a second "more structural" idea that constitutional remedies should be "adequate to keep government generally within the bounds of the law".[79] They argue that both principles can justify withholding remedies in individual cases especially in cases where judges make new laws. Fallon has recently defended American qualified immunity doctrine in the face of cogent

75 Ibid.

76 See generally Brian Ray, *Engaging with Social Rights* (Cambridge: Cambridge University Press, 2016).

77 See *infra* Chapter 7, Section 7.4.

78 See generally Kent Roach, "Dialogic Remedies" (2019) 17 *I. Con.* 860, 874–875.

79 Richard H. Fallon and Daniel J. Meltzer, "New Law, Non-Retroactivity and Constitutional Remedies" (1991) 94 *Harv. L. Rev.* 8, 1778–1779, 1790–1791.

criticisms that it has become " Dicey's nightmare"[80] in the sense of denying damages to the vast majority of victims of executive wrong-doing.[81] Like Tushnet, these commentators identify elements of the two-track focus on individual and systemic remedies, but do not provide a basis for coherently combining both forms of remedies.

2.4.3 *Examples from Supra-national Law*

The two-track approach is an attempt to theorize remedies, but like any theory about remedies, it must also deal with practicalities. Here and in the chapters that follow, I will point to concrete examples where courts are applying the two-track approach. Consistent with the argument advanced throughout this book – that domestic law can learn much from supra-national law – the two-track approach is much more common in supra-national law than in domestic law.

2.4.3.1 United Nations Bodies

The 2005 UN *Basic Principles*[82] define the purposes of remedies for violations of human rights in terms of restitution including restoration of liberty, compensation for material and moral damages, rehabilitation, satisfaction including public apology and guarantees of non-repetition including training and law reform. In November 2016, the UN Human Rights Committee divided these remedial purposes in a manner consistent with the two-track approach. The Committee provided that in its decisions, it will set "out measures designed to make full reparation to the victims (restitution, compensation, rehabilitation and measures of satisfaction), as well as measures aimed at preventing the reoccurrence of similar violations in the future (guarantees of non-repetition)".[83] A similar two-track approach is contemplated in its General Comment 31.[84] The Committee has rightly, in my view, rejected calls that it

[80] James Pfander, "Dicey's Nightmare: An Essay on the Rule of Law" (2019) 107 *Calif. L. Rev.* 737. He also recognizes tensions between "wholesale" approaches and more limited "retail" approaches focused on the facts of specific cases: ibid., 781.

[81] Richard Fallon, "Bidding Farewell to Constitutional Torts" (2019) 107 *Calif. L. Rev.* 933.

[82] UN *Basic Principles* at paras 19–23.

[83] Guidelines on Measures of Reparation under the Optional Protocol to the International Covenant on Civil and Political Rights, November 2016 CCPR/C/158 at para 2.

[84] General Comment No. 31 of the Human Rights Committee also contemplates a two-track approach involving reparation and measures "beyond a victim-specific remedy ... to avoid recurrence of the type of violation in question. Such measures may require changes

abandon individual petitions and focus on General Comments and periodic country reports.[85] To be sure, the Committee could benefit from more court-like procedures, practices and resources, but the communication of its views demonstrates how individuals are affected by violations.

With respect to compensation, the Committee does not generally specify specific sums of money[86] though compensation can extend to non-pecuniary harms and be supplemented by the rehabilitation of victims and their families.[87] The Committee defines satisfaction broadly to include symbolic forms of satisfaction such as apologies and commemoration and other measures such as investigations that also seem related to non-repetition. The Committee also defended the sometimes controversial remedy of the reduction or commutation of sentence as a form of satisfaction.[88]

The Committee has accepted the legitimacy of the second systemic track. It has stressed that "[g]uarantees of non-repetition are general in scope and are essential in order to prevent subsequent human rights violations of the type that gave rise to the communication considered by the Committee".[89] Examples of general or systemic measures include recommended amendments or repeals of laws that violate rights or "[i]f the violation stems from the absence of certain legal provisions, the measures of reparation should include the adoption of the necessary laws

in the State Party's laws or practices". Human Rights Committee, General Comment No. 31 on the International Covenant on Civil and Political Rights, *The Nature of the General Legal Obligation Imposed on State Parties to the Covenant*, CCPR/C/21/Rev.1/ Add. 13, 29 March 2004 at para 16.

85 Henry Steiner, "Individual Claims in a World With Massive Rights Violations: What Role for the Human Rights Committee?" in Phillip Alston and James Crawford (eds.), *The Future of UN Human Rights Treaty Monitoring* (New York: Cambridge University Press, 2000). As Steiner has pointed out, the Committee risks being overwhelmed with petitions. Such a reality can, however, make the Committee more sensitive than domestic courts to repetitive violations. As Steiner points out, there is also a case for the Committee to focus more on interpreting the International Covenant on Civil and Political Rights and improving its "views" so that they more resemble judicial judgements. But on the utility of individual petitions, see also Kate Fox Principi "Implementation of UN Treaty Body Decisions: A Brief Insight for Practitioners" (2020) 12 *Journal of Human Rights Practice* 185.

86 Guidelines on Measures of Reparation under the Optional Protocol to the International Covenant on Civil and Political Rights, November 2016 CCPR/C/158 at para 9.

87 Ibid. at para 8.

88 Ibid. at para 11(c).

89 Ibid. at 12.

or regulations".[90] It also includes recommended "changes to procedures and practices" including training various government officials to respect human rights. In 2011, a special rapporteur position was created that is concerned with a mandate to monitor the promotion of truth, justice, reparation and non-reoccurrence.[91]

Noticeably absent from the UN Human Rights Committee's list of second-track systemic or general measures are requests that states and parties submit plans to prevent reoccurrence and subsequent reporting mechanisms. This omission is unfortunate because the parties, civil society groups and governmental defendants, may have information and expertise not available to the Committee.

The UN Human Rights Committee has conducted follow-up reports to ensure that both individual and systemic remedies are implemented. In one such case, it observed that the state paid compensation and apologized for police abuse. With respect to systemic remedies, it noted that the Victoria Police Act had been amended to ensure that in cases where individual officers were unable to pay damages because of bankruptcy,[92] the state would still be held liable for damages for rights violations. Consistent with adjudicative fairness, the Committee heard from both parties in the follow-up procedure. The complainant expressed dissatisfaction with aspects of the reply legislation, the lack of payment of legal fees and lack of police discipline of the officer who committed the assault. The Committee, nevertheless, gave the state an A rating for providing an effective remedy and ensuring non-repetition. Since 2012, the Committee has systemically reviewed state responses in a demonstration of the iterative process often used to enforce international norms.[93]

Other UN human rights adjudicators also follow a two-track approach. For example, the Committee on the Elimination of Racial

[90] Ibid. at para 13(a).

[91] UN Human Rights Council, *Special Rapporteur on the Promotion of Truth, Justice, Reparation and Guarantees of Non-Recurrence*, Res. 18/7, October 2011.

[92] Victoria Police Act, 2013 s.79; as the complainant noted, however, this amendment was enacted before the Committee released its views.

[93] *Horvath* v. *Australia*, CCPR/C/110/D/1885/2009, 27 March 2014 at paras 10–11 (giving state 180 days to review legislation to ensure that violations of the right to an effective remedy would not be repeated), Follow Up Information on *Horvath* v. *Australia*, 1885/2009, CCPR/C/113/3 at 2 (the follow-up grading system is also assisted and monitored by a civil society group), see Centre for Political and Civil Rights, Follow-Up Procedure of the Human Rights Committee (online) at http://ccprcentre.org/follow-up-and-assessment.

Discrimination ordered Denmark to pay adequate compensation for "material and moral injury caused" to the petitioners who were refugees who had a "no blacks allowed" sign posted near their house and had their house attacked by a mob of thirty-five people. At the same time, the Committee also asked Denmark to review its policies and procedures about prosecuting cases involving racial discrimination after only four people were prosecuted and received suspended sentences. Denmark was also asked to provide the Committee information in ninety days about the measures it had taken to give effect to the Committee's opinion.[94] In some ways, this resembles public law litigation where courts retain jurisdiction.

The Committee on the Elimination of Discrimination Against Women employed a two-track remedial approach in cases dealing with domestic violence. In one case, it ordered a range of individual remedies including compensation and re-opening custody proceedings against an abusive ex-partner. As a systemic measure, it also ordered an independent review of Finland's response to domestic violence and increased training about domestic violence for prosecutors and judges.[95] In another case, the Committee ordered Canada to provide compensation and housing for an Indigenous woman who was the victim of domestic violence. As a systemic measure, it indicated that a legal aid system in a northern territory be reviewed to ensure that Indigenous women who are victims of domestic violence receive appropriate access to justice.[96] Refinements of this second systemic remedial track would include asking all parties, and non-governmental organizations with expertise, to submit and comment on plans for reforms in order to increase information available to the Committee and more follow-up reporting.

The Committee on the Rights of the Disabled ordered an individual remedy of investigation and full compensation for a person whose arm was cut off because he had albinism. At the same time, the Committee suggested Tanzania implement a variety of systemic remedies including public education, training, prompt investigations and prosecutions in similar cases.[97] A feature of these cases is a clear distinction between

[94] *Dawas and Shava* v. *Denmark*, CERD C/80/D/46/2009, Comm. No. 43/2008, 16 June 2009 at paras 9–10.
[95] *J. I.* v. *Finland* (2018), UN Doc CEDAW C/69/D/103/2016, 25 April 2018 at para 10.
[96] *Kell* v. *Canada* (2012), UN Doc CEDAW C/51/D/19/2008, 27 April 2012 at para 11.
[97] *X* v. *Tanzania* (2017), UN Doc CRPD C/18/D/22/2014, 31 August 2017 at para 9.

individual compensatory measures and systemic measures to prevent similar violations in the future.

As will be discussed in more detail in Chapter 8, Section 8.6, the two-track approach can be applied to social and economic rights. In a 2019 case in Italy, the Committee on Economic, Social and Cultural Rights indicated that compensation and costs should be provided to specific complainants but also that Italy should, within six months, submit a written response about what legislative and administrative measures it had taken to prevent similar violations in the future.[98] As suggested above, plan submission is an important part of the second systemic track. It can, however, be made more consistent with norms of adjudicative fairness by providing all relevant parties with an opportunity to submit plans and to comment on those submitted by others.

2.4.3.2 The European Court of Human Rights

As discussed in Chapter 1, Section 1.6, the ECtHR was only given the power to order just satisfaction when not provided by domestic law. It still does not have power to invalidate laws or to order mandatory remedies. As Council of Europe membership has grown however, the remedial approach has evolved. The Court has moved away from its previous traditions of conceiving of its judgements itself as sufficient remedies or even of relying on awarding damages to individual applicants. A more sophisticated remedial approach involving the Committee of Minister's supervision of execution is now being used for more complex cases. This approach is driven by practical concerns about the Court's crushing caseload and the many repetitive violations it encounters.

In 2000, the Court explained that a state that had violated rights was responsible not only to pay sums awarded by way of just satisfaction, but "to choose, subject to supervision by the Committee of Ministers, the general and/or, if appropriate, individual measures to be adopted in their domestic legal order to put an end to the violation found".[99] In 2004, the Grand Chamber repeated this reminder in a case from Russia where it also awarded €150,000 and indicated that the applicant should be released.[100] The Court stressed the importance of preventing repetitive violations. At the same time, it noted that its "judgments are essentially

98 *S. C. and G. P.* v. *Italy*, E/C.12/65/D/22/2017, 7 March 2019 at paras 13–14.

99 *Scozzari and Giunta* v. *Italy*, Nos. 39221/98 and 41963/98, [2000] 249 ECHR 2000-VIII at para 249.

100 *Assanidze* v. *Georgia*, No. 71503/01, ECHR 2004-II at para 198.

declaratory in nature and that, in general, it is primarily for the State concerned to choose the means to be used in its domestic legal order in order to discharge its legal obligation under Article 46 of the Convention, provided that such means are compatible with the conclusions set out in the Court's judgment".[101] In this way, the Court respects subsidiarity perhaps even more with respect to general measures than individual measures.

Consistent with the two-track approach, the Committee of Ministers considers both individual and general measures when it executes judgements.[102] The former are defined as those "taken to ensure that the violation has ceased and that the injured party is put, as far as possible, in the same situation as that party enjoyed prior to the violation of the Convention".[103] Such individual remedies can include damage awards, striking out of an unjustified criminal conviction, and re-opening of proceedings when warranted. "General measures" are defined as those designed to prevent "new violations similar to that of those found or putting an end to continuing violations".[104] They typically include legislative or regulatory changes as monitored and recorded by the Committee of Ministers.[105] As Professor Antoine Buyse explains, this approach "is both looking forward and backward". He adds that the Strasbourg approach is consistent with "general public international law" because it recognizes that "there is not only a duty to repair, but also a duty of non-repetition".[106]

Some commentators have argued that guarantees of non-repetition are not explicitly included in the mandate of the ECtHR.[107] Judge Sicilianos has effectively rebutted this argument by arguing that Articles 46, 19 and 32 of the European Convention on Human Rights all provide ample

101 Ibid. at para 202.

102 Council of Europe, *Rules of the Committee of Ministers for the Supervision of the Execution of Judgments and of the Terms of Friendly Settlements*, adopted by the Committee of Ministers on 10 May 2006 (last amended 18 January 2017) online: https://rm.coe.int/16806eebf0

103 Ibid., Rule 6(2)(b)(ii).

104 Ibid.

105 For a helpful country-by-country review of complex cases subject to execution by the Committee of Ministers see Council of Europe, Department for the Execution of Judgments of the European Court of Human Rights, *Country Factsheets*, online: www.coe.int/en/web/execution/country-factsheets

106 Antoine Buyse, "The Pilot Judgment Procedure at the European Court of Human Rights: Possibilities and Challenges" (2009) Greek L. J. 1, 8–9.

107 Octavian Ichim, *Just Satisfaction under the European Convention on Human Rights* (Cambridge: Cambridge University Press, 2015), p.256.

support for the ECtHR's remedial powers.[108] Rule 61 of the ECtHR's rules of court contemplates that the Court itself shall identify "both the nature of the structural or systemic problem" and the general remedial measure that the state should take including imposing deadlines. The Court may reserve the question of just satisfaction and adjourn similar applications, but both of these issues can be revisited at the Court's discretion "where the interests of the proper administration of justice so require".[109]

Judge Helen Keller and Cedric Marti refer to the ECtHR's "dual judicial function".[110] On the one hand, the Court has traditionally been concerned with ensuring that applicants whose rights are violated receive satisfaction or compensation. On the other hand, the Court is increasingly concerned that the state, under supervision by the Committee of Ministers, take general measures to ensure future compliance with the right and prevent repetitive violations. The latter systemic measures are newer and more controversial. They can, however, be defended on the basis that subsidiarity is a flexible concept that depends on the performance of the member state.

2.4.3.3 Sacrificing Individual Remedies?

The ECtHR's newer approach has been criticized for sacrificing individual justice in an attempt to ensure systemic justice that prevents repetitive violations. This is most evident in pilot judgement procedures where the Court can suspend individual claims pending resolution of the systemic issue.[111] One famous example is its refusal to order damages for prisoners in the UK who continued to be denied the vote.[112] Such a denial of individual remedies is inconsistent with the two-track approach to the extent that it both denies litigants an individual compensatory

[108] Linos-Alexander Sicilianos, "The Involvement of the European Court of Human Rights in the Implementation of its Judgments" (2014) 32 *Netherlands Q. Hum. Rts.* 235, 253–257.

[109] Council of Europe, *Rules of Court*, European Court of Human Rights, in force 1 January 2020, Rule 61(6)(c).

[110] Keller and Marti, "Reconceptualizing Implementation", 838 fn 59.

[111] Dilek Kurban, "Forsaking Individual Justice: The Implications of the European Court of Human Rights Pilot Judgment Procedure for Victims of Gross and Systemic Violations" (2016) 16 *Hum. Rts. L. Rev.* 731, 768 ("a faulty assumption that contracting parties who were repeat violators in the past are no longer so, by virtue of a remedy they introduce to win a pilot judgment"); Tatiana Sainati, "Human Rights Class Actions: Rethinking the Pilot-Judgment Procedure at the European Court of Human Rights" (2015) 56(1) *Harv. Int'l. L. J.* 147.

[112] For criticism, see Jacqueline Hodgson and Kent Roach, "Disenfranchisement as Punishment: European Court of Human Rights, UK and Canadian Responses to Prisoner Voting" (2017) *Public Law* 450.

remedy and fails to place pressure on governments to respond to the systemic problems behind the repetitive violation.

An exclusive focus on systemic remedies can sacrifice individual justice. In a 2009 case, six applicants complained that Moldova had not honoured a judgement that they receive social housing. The ECtHR adjourned all similar cases, indicating that the Moldavian government had six months to enforce final domestic judgements for social housing and twelve months to provide redress for victims of non-enforcement.[113] The Court provided no interim remedy for the six applicants during the adjournment. This can be unfavourably contrasted with the approach taken in some second-generation South African housing cases where courts provided applicants with immediate remedies that prevented evictions or provided temporary housing, while also recognizing that governments should develop systemic remedies after consultation with those affected.[114]

A former president of the ECtHR has explained that a key feature of the pilot judgement procedure is that legislative and administrative measures to address the systemic problem should apply retroactively. This allows the ECtHR to defer any decision about just satisfaction until the state adopts a systemic solution.[115] This has the potential to ensure that the litigants receive some remedy. At the same time, the Court itself has an interest in accepting whatever systemic remedy the state provides, both to clear its backlog and to support the efficacy of the systemic process. Owen Fiss similarly worried that American courts involved in structural review would succumb to expediency and opt for a solution, or even a settlement, over justice.[116]

In the first pilot judgement case involving the property rights claims of over 80,000 people, the Committee of Ministers accepted Poland's legislative solution, which capped the compensation that the applicants could

[113] *Olaru and Others* v. *Republic of Moldova*, Nos. 476/07, 22539/05, 17911/08 and 13136/07, [2009] 21 ECHR IV; the ECtHR subsequently deferred and required other applicants to exhaust a new domestic remedy that Moldova introduced in 2011, *Balan* v. *Republic of Moldova*, No. 19247/03, ECHR 10 Feb 2012.

[114] *Port Elizabeth Municipality* v. *Various Occupiers*, [2004] ZACC 7.

[115] Luzius Wildhaber, "Pilot Judgments in Cases of Structural or Systemic Problems on the National Level" in Rudiger Wolfrum and Ulkrike Deutsch (eds.), *The European Court of Human Rights Overwhelmed by Applications: Problems and Possible Solutions* (Berlin: Springer, 2009), p.71.

[116] Fiss, "The Forms of Justice".

receive for land lost in World War II at 20 per cent of market value. The applicants subsequently challenged the Polish law, but the ECtHR upheld it.[117] This approach demonstrates the danger that courts that have prompted a systemic remedy may be inclined to defer to whatever systemic remedy the state provides. Ultimately, the remedy received by those who lost land was a legislative remedy and it factored in social interests by significantly limiting the amount of damages.

In a more recent case involving repetitive financial claims relating to savings held in Yugoslavian currency, the Court used the pilot judgement procedure and eventually held that legislation enacted by Serbia and Slovenia was adequate.[118] This demonstrates the same tendency to accept legislative replies as seen in the first pilot judgement procedure used against Poland. At the same time, however, the ECtHR helpfully held that it would continue to hear individual claims should the administration of the remedial legislation prove ineffective.[119] This demonstrates the ability of a two-track remedial approach to be attentive to remedial failure. It can, if necessary, generate remedial cycles where ineffective systemic remedies are revealed by the order of individual remedies and, potentially, more intrusive and prescriptive systemic remedies.

2.4.3.4 The ECtHR Wisely Rejects the Wise Persons Report That It Abandon Individual Remedies

During the height of the ECtHR's concern about its caseload, proposals were made by Lord Woolf and a Wise Persons group that the Court should delegate the task of ordering individual measures either to national courts or the Committee of Ministers.[120] On one level, these recommendations were understandable given that the Court's jurisprudence on awarding individual compensatory remedies is not consistent and in some contexts even influenced by guidelines that are not public.[121]

117 *Broniowski* v. *Poland Application* [GC], No. 31443/96, ECHR 22 June 2004.

118 *Ališić and Others* v. *Bosnia and Herzegovina, Croatia, Serbia, Slovenia and the Former Yugoslav Republic of Macedonia* [GC], No. 60642/08, 2014 ECHR-IV.

119 *Muratovic* v. *Slovenia* [GC], No. 6799/02, ECHR 13 April 2017; *Hodzic* v. *Slovenia*, No. 3461/08, ECHR 4 April 2017; for a similar approach, see also *Taron* v. *Germany*, No. 53126/07, ECHR 29 May 2012.

120 Lord Woolf et al., Review of the Working Methods of the European Court of Human Rights (2005), online: (pdf) www.echr.coe.int/Documents/2005_Lord_Woolf_working_methods_ENG.pdf at pp.6, 40–41; Report of the Group of Wise Persons to the Committee of Ministers, 46 ILM 77 (2007), 15 November 2006.

121 Ichim, *Just Satisfaction*; see also *infra*, Chapter 5 Section 5.2.4.

If the Court was not prepared to do a good job of ordering remedies, it is perhaps best to get out of the business altogether.

Professor Greer supported the move away from deciding individual remedies and argued that the Court should focus on "constitutional rather than individual justice".[122] He correctly pointed out that under the current approach to damages, "the justice delivered to the lucky few … tends to be more symbolic than instrumental".[123] Yet, Greer's own article implicitly illustrates some dangers of courts only engaging in systemic matters. He points out that for its first thirty years, the Court and the Convention were "largely ignored by just about everybody, including victims of human rights abuse, lawyers, jurists, politicians, and social scientists".[124] This was at a time where the Court did not entertain petitions from individuals.[125] While correlation is not causation, this does suggest that the ECtHR only became arguably one of the world's most important courts when it started to hear individual complaints and (however inadequately) provide individual remedies.

Following Fuller, Bickel and others in the legal process tradition examined in Chapter 1, Section 1.3, the two-track approach is based on the legal process insight that one of the primary functions of any court is to hear individual petitions and provide successful litigants with remedies. A court, perhaps especially a European court, that simply provides systemic remedies, risks becoming simply another policy interlocutor in a crowded governance space.[126] As will be suggested throughout the book, an exclusive focus on systemic concerns can produce a variety of pathologies. This includes remedies that are not effective or meaningful to the actual rights holders and threats to the court's legitimacy as a court.

122 Stephen Greer, "What's Wrong with the European Convention on Human Rights" (2008) 30 *Hum. Rts. Q.* 680.

123 Ibid., 686.

124 Ibid., 682; Greer also notes that France is a frequent violator of the Convention and "this is best explained by the lack of an individual right of constitutional complaint". Steven Greer, *The European Convention on Human Rights: Achievements, Problems and Prospects* (Cambridge: Cambridge University Press, 2006), p.91. For a defence of the right of individual petition and remedies, see J. Wadham and T. Said, "What Price the Right of Individual Petition: Report of the Evaluation Group to the Committee of Ministers on the European Court of Human Rights" (2002), 2 *Eur. Hum. Rts. L. Rev.* 169, 174. They also note that many NGOs opposed proposals that would restrict the right of petition.

125 Greer, *The European Convention of Human Rights*, p.33.

126 For somewhat similar criticisms of forms of dialogue that are not backed by rulings and remedies, see Tom Hickman, "Constitutional Dialogue, Constitutional Theories and the Human Rights Act, 1998" (2005) *Public Law* 306.

2.4.3.5 Supervision of Judgements by the Committee of Ministers

The ECtHR delegates the supervision of its judgement to the Committee of Ministers of the Council of Europe. Some critics who want the court to take a more robust remedial role might argue that such delegation offends the separation of powers by taking enforcement away from the courts. Others who want the court to take a less robust remedial role and only order just satisfaction might argue that the assignment of supervision to a political body demonstrates that the task is beyond the capacities of the courts. Consistent with the contextual and flexible approach to the separation of powers advocated in Chapter 1, Section 1.8, however, attention should be paid to the substance of the supervision rather than its form. When this is done, it suggests that the ECtHR is increasingly drawn to a two-track remedial approach that provides different remedies so as to compensate individual litigants and prevent similar violations in the future.

A recurring problem for the ECtHR has been excessive delay in the legal system. The Committee of Ministers' supervision of a German case dealing with such delay demonstrates the logic of the two-track approach. The case consolidated seventy-one different cases involving excessive delay. Damages were awarded according to the facts of the particular case, ranging from €500 to a high of €59,000.[127] Such individual remedies are important in meeting expectations and affirming the legitimacy of the Court.

With respect to general measures, there was a tailored approach that resulted in complementary judicial, administrative and legislative remedies. There was a joint federal-Lander conference to discuss the issue of delay. Germany enacted new legislation to provide for both acceleratory and compensatory remedies. Interestingly, the latter was set at €1,200 for each year of delay. This amount was both modest and more uniform than the just satisfaction awarded by the ECtHR. The ECtHR responded to the new legislation by declaring delay claims from Germany to be inadmissible while litigants exhausted their own domestic remedies. At the same time, it was careful to note that its views on inadmissibility could change

[127] European Council Committee of Ministers, *Execution of the Judgments of the European Court of Human Rights*, Res. CM/ResDH(2013)244 71 cases against Germany; adopted 5 December 2013, Appendix 1.

should domestic remedies not be effective in stopping excessive delay. The Committee of Ministers ended its implementation of the judgement only after examining the adequacy of domestic remedies in a number of contexts and courts.[128] As will be elaborated in Section 2.6 of this chapter, this demonstrates the ability of the two-track approach to measure and respond to remedial failure, as well as to start new cycles of reform where courts might award more generous remedies and begin to supervise systemic remedies more closely should rights continue to be violated in the future.

2.4.3.6 Inter-American Court of Human Rights

The Inter-American Court of Human Rights (IACtHR) awards individual and systemic remedies in a manner generally consistent with the two-track approach. Indeed, it is heavily invested in the systemic approach, with Alexandra Huneeus estimating that a quarter of the IACtHR's cases require states to undertake systemic reforms, in part because of South America's history of repressive and violent rule.[129] Some readers may question the emphasis in this book on the jurisprudence of the San Jose court which has often dealt with authoritarian atrocities.[130] Alas, it may become only more relevant as many democracies seem to be moving towards more repression of dissent and populist resistance to courts.[131]

The IACtHR is more aggressive than the ECtHR with respect to both remedial tracks. The IACtHR orders not only damages, but other forms of satisfaction relating to restitution of land, rehabilitation, acknowledgement of wrongs, memorials and apologies. This utilizes the full range of satisfaction-based remedies in the UN's *Basic Principles.* Some

[128] Ibid. A former deputy registrar of the ECtHR has defended the Committee of Ministers on the basis that the only way of persuading reluctant states to comply is through "the techniques of diplomacy, persuasion, or cajoling" as quoted in Clara Sandoval, Philip Leach and Rachel Murray "Monitoring, Cajoling and Promoting Dialogue: What Role for Supra-National Bodies in the Implementation of Individual Decisions?" (2020) 12 *Journal of Human Rights Practice* 71 at 79.

[129] Huneeus, "Reforming the State from Afar", 3.

[130] In their argument that independent international courts are not effective, Eric Posner and John Yoo single out the IACtHR as not effective: "Judicial Independence in International Tribunals" (2005) 93 *Calif. L. Rev.* 1, 44.

[131] On this danger, see Kent Roach, "Dialogue in Canada and the Dangers of Simplified Comparative Law and Populism" in Geoffrey Sigalet, Gregoire Webber and Rosalind Dixon (eds.), *Constitutional Dialogue Rights and Institutions* (New York: Cambridge University Press, 2019).

commentators have argued that in pursuing its remedies, the IACtHR has been influenced by restorative justice and is more victim centred than is the ECtHR.[132] The IACtHR tends to be more specific than other supranational bodies in its remedies. It also holds formal hearings to monitor implementation of remedies and has interpreted and expanded its own remedies in subsequent judgements.[133]

With respect to systemic remedies, the IACtHR (much more than the ECtHR) indicates that states should change their laws, enact training and undertake investigations and prosecutions. These remedies are related to the need to prevent future and often repetitive violations. Like the ECtHR, the Court stresses the state's commitments to abide by the Convention and the court's judgement. An important difference between the IACtHR and the ECtHR, however, is that the IACtHR does not delegate implementation issues to a separate body. In complex cases, the Court may also issue follow up judgements, sometimes three or more over a decade. In 2019, it was monitoring compliance with 223 cases that contained 11,153 measures of reparation.[134] This statistic is itself a measure of the Court's two-track approach because it reveals that the court ordered on average about five different remedies in each case.[135]

The IACtHR has encountered particular problems with remedial compliance where it orders state bodies – often independent prosecutors and judges – to investigate and prosecute. This problem will be discussed in greater depth in Chapter 6, Section 6.2.6. Another problem especially apparent in Indigenous rights cases (examined in Chapter 9, Section 9.2.3.1) is that states often comply with first-track compensatory

[132] Thomas M. Antkowiak, "An Emerging Mandate for International Courts: Victim-Centered Remedies and Restorative Justice" (2011) 47(2) *Stanford J. Int'l. L.* 279, 289. Antkowiak suggests in an extra-judicial killing the Strasbourg court would order €50,000 while the San Jose court would award greater non-pecuniary sums, and then order the state to: apologize, initiate a criminal investigation, locate the victim's remains, publish excerpts of the Court's judgement in national newspapers, and possibly grant psychological treatment to close family members of the deceased.

[133] Rachel Murray and Clara Sandoval, "Balancing Specificity of Reparation Measures and States' Discretion to Enhance Implementation" (2020) 12 *Journal of Human Rights Practice* 101, 112; Clara Sandoval, Philip Leach and Rachel Murray, "Monitoring, Cajoling, and Promoting Dialogue: What Role for Supra-National Bodies in the Implementation of Individual Decisions?" (2020) 12 *Journal of Human Rights Practice* 71, 81–83.

[134] Inter American Court of Human Rights, *Annual Report* (Organization of American States: Washington, 2019), p.61.

[135] Ibid., p.62.

remedies but not more ambitious systemic remedies.[136] This underlines the need for strong monitoring of state compliance with two-track remedies.[137] Professor Huneeus has stressed that international courts, unlike domestic courts, have no contempt powers, cannot appoint special masters to provide information[138] and cannot place institutions that continue to violate rights into receivership. This may discount the rarity of such coercive remedies even in American public law litigation.[139]

2.4.3.7 The African Court of Human and Peoples' Rights

The jurisprudence of the relatively new African Court of Human and Peoples' Rights is still developing. A new court trying to gain acceptance may be reluctant to follow the ambitious two- track approach to remedies in every case. Nevertheless, the Court followed the two-track approach by awarding both an individual remedy of USD$50,000 and indicating that Burkina Faso should amend its defamation laws to better accommodate freedom of expression and remove imprisonment as a remedy.[140] In its monitoring, the Court found that within a year of the judgement Burkina Faso had decriminalized defamation.

2.4.3.8 Summary

Supra-national courts could ignore the need for systemic remedies because of concerns about preserving comity with states who can renounce their jurisdiction. The same incentives may motivate them to rely upon low damage awards. Given these incentives, it is inspiring that supra-national adjudicators so often take the more demanding two-track

[136] Darrin Hawkins and Wade Jacoby, "Partial Compliance: A Comparison of the European and Inter-American American Courts for Human Rights" (2010) 6 *J. Int'l. L. & Int'l. Rltns.* 35, 55 Figure 2A (finding 40 per cent compliance with apology and material damage awards, 40 per cent with moral damage awards and 7 per cent compliance with more complex orders).

[137] My focus is on the work of the Court and not the Commission. But for arguments that the Commission should separate out individual and systemic matters in settlements with the latter involving more parties and institutions, see Jorge Contesse, "Settling Human Rights Violations" (2019) 60 *Harv. Int'l. L. J.* 317, 370.

[138] The Inter-American Commission on Human Rights may play a similar role in litigation before the IACtHR, and an execution department assists the Committee of Ministers in supervising ECtHR judgements.

[139] She recognizes, however, that non-American domestic courts including those in South America use "more dialogic soft power mechanisms". Huneeus, "Reforming the State from Afar", 23.

[140] *Lohe Issa Konate* v. *Burkina Faso* (2014), No. 004/2013, Merits, African Court on Human and Peoples" Rights, 1 AfCLR 314.

approach to remedies. In the many cases where adjudicators do take a two-track approach, they commonly monitor state compliance. Even well-resourced courts in established democracies are unfortunately more reluctant to retain jurisdiction for similar purposes and to take an interest in repetitive violations. This is another example where domestic courts could learn something about remedies from supra-national courts.

2.4.4 *Examples from National Law*

2.4.4.1 The United States

The Court's decision in *Brown II* to take a gradual approach to remedies has been both controversial and influential. Lawyers for the plaintiffs, including Thurgood Marshall and Roger Carter, argued for an immediate remedy on the basis of prior precedents where the Supreme Court had ordered individual applicants to be admitted into university programs in cases where there were no equivalent programs.[141] At the same time, many of the Justices were only prepared to sign the original opinion if there was a gradual remedial approach. Justice Hugo Black, who was from the south, also argued privately (and consistent with Fuller's approach to legality) that "nothing could injure the court more than to issue orders that cannot be enforced".[142]

Although it failed to intervene to stop much delay in implementing *Brown* and subsequently imposed limits on busing and other remedies, the Court insisted on a limited individual remedy in the form of its 1958 order signed by all nine Justices that nine brave Black students could continue to attend Central High in Little Rock, Arkansas, even in the face of violent and racist opposition from the government and the public.[143] This decision insisted that a limited individual remedy be maintained even in the face of massive resistance. It was an important affirmation of the rule of law and commitment to human rights. Alas, it failed in the short term because Central High School was closed for a year rather than re-admitting the African American students. Nevertheless, *Cooper* v. *Aaron* was a symbolic re-affirmation of the Court's commitment to both *Brown* and a successful litigant's individual right to a

141 *Sweatt* v. *Painter*, 339 US 629 (1950); Roger Carter, "The Warren Court and Desegregation" (1968) 67 *Mich. L. Rev.* 2.

142 Michael Klarman, *Brown* v. *Board of Education and the Civil Rights Movement* (New York: Oxford University, 2007), p.80.

143 *Cooper* v. *Aaron*, 358 US 1 (1958).

remedy. *Cooper* itself might have followed a two-track approach if an early draft of the opinion written by Justice Brennan had retained the requirement that school boards set deadlines for desegregation.[144]

Another example of a two-track approach by American courts is the tendency to exempt the successful applicants so that they receive the benefit of the ruling when making prospective rulings in constitutional cases.[145] This is responsive to systemic concerns about the disruptive effects of retroactive application of new rights, while the exemption of the applicant recognizes legitimate expectations that successful litigants should receive a remedy from the court.

2.4.4.2 Declarations of Incompatibility and a Two-Track Irish Twist

The two-track approach may be more difficult to implement in jurisdictions that deny courts powers to invalidate laws to the extent of their inconsistency with human rights. Commentators in the UK have favoured the use of robust interpretative remedies under section 3 of the Human Rights Act, 1998, on the basis that they, unlike non-binding declarations of incompatibility, provide effective remedies for individual litigants.[146] The declaration of incompatibility's lack of an individual remedy has led the Australian High Court to dismiss it as a non-judicial dialogic remedy.[147]

Section 5(4) of Ireland's European Convention of Human Rights Act, 2003,[148] has an interesting twist that moves in the direction of a two-track approach. It provides that litigants who have obtained a declaration of incompatibility can also obtain damages calculated on the basis of the principles of just satisfaction that would be applied by the ECtHR. The English courts in at least one case similarly combined a declaration of incompatibility with an interpretation that avoided applying a discriminatory buggery offence to the successful applicant.[149] The essence of the

[144] Klarman, *Brown* v. *Board of Education*, p.108.

[145] *Linkletter* v. *Walker*, 381 US 618 (1965); *Stovall* v. *Denno*, 388 US 293 (1967); M. L. Friedland, "Prospective and Retrospective Judicial Lawmaking" (1974) 24 *U.T.L.J.* 170.

[146] Kavanagh, *Constitutional Review*, 118–121.

[147] *Momcilovic* v. *The Queen*, [2011] HCA 34.

[148] No. 20. Alas and inconsistent with the two-track approach, the Irish courts cannot award damages along with the declaration of incompatibility and any award must be made ex gratia by the executive.

[149] *Re McR's Application for Judicial Review*, [2002] NIQB 58; for criticisms of this decision, see Fergal Davis and David Mead, "Declarations of Incompatibility, Dialogue and the

two-track approach is the use of one remedy to provide justice to the applicant before the court and a recognition that another remedy, often one that initially defers to governments for reasons related to subsidiarity or the separation of powers, is also required to prevent or minimize similar rights violations in the future.

2.4.4.3 Canada

As will be discussed in greater detail in Chapter 4, Section 4.2.5, the Canadian courts have relied heavily on suspended declarations of invalidity to enforce human rights under the 1982 Canadian Charter of Rights and Freedoms.[150] From the start, however, the Court held out the possibility that it might provide individual remedies during a suspension if necessary to prevent an injustice. Yet, Canadian courts have exercised this power infrequently.[151] This has led to criticisms that the Court is abdicating its traditional function of providing remedies for litigants.[152]

This issue came to a head in an assisted dying case. The Court ruled that an offence against assisted suicide violated the rights of adults who made a voluntary decision to end their life yet, because of a disability, required assistance in doing so.[153] The Court recognized the need for legislative regulation and suspended the declaration of invalidity for a year. Whether the litigants should be exempted from this suspension and receive an immediate remedy was not considered because the two individual plaintiffs had passed away by the time of the Court's decision. The government subsequently asked for an extension of the suspension. The Court divided 5–4, with a narrow majority holding that while it would extend the suspension for another four months, it would now allow qualified adults to obtain a court-ordered exemption during this

Criminal Law" (2014) 43 *Common L. World Rev.* 62; for praise, see Kent Roach, "Remedies for Laws That Violate Human Rights" in John Bell et al. (eds.), *Public Law Adjudication in Common Law Systems* (Oxford: Hart Publishing, 2016), pp.289–292.

150 Part I of the *Constitution Act, 1982*, being Schedule B to the *Canada Act 1982* (UK), 1982, c. 11.

151 In one case, *R.* v. *Demers*, 2004 SCC 46 the Court even seemed to suggest that courts were powerless to award individual remedies under s.24(1) of the Canadian Charter of Rights and Freedoms after having made systemic remedies related to unconstitutional laws under s.52(1) of the Constitution Act 1982.

152 Ryder, "Suspending the Charter" (2003) *S.C.L.R.* (2d); Robert Leckey, "The Harms of Remedial Discretion" (2016) 14 *I. Con.* 3.

153 *Carter* v. *Canada (Attorney General)*, 2015 SCC 5.

period.[154] Four judges in dissent would not have allowed any exemptions, on the basis that it would interfere with Parliamentary intent. However, the dissenters' approach was not balanced. It focused simply on the systemic problem that required legislation. It ignored the fact that the overbroad assisted suicide offence already violated rights and imposed suffering on adults who may make voluntary decisions to end their lives but were unable to do so. After this ruling, lower courts crafted exemptions in about thirty reported cases before new legislation was enacted to govern assisted dying. In a demonstration of the ability of the two-track approach to produce cycles of reform, the legislation itself was successfully challenged as too restrictive.[155] The judge in this case again suspended the declaration of invalidity but exempted the individual applicant from the exemption.[156]

In another recent case, Canadian courts have taken a two-track approach by suspending a declaration that a sex offender registry law was overbroad, while ordering that the applicant be immediately taken off the registry.[157] Doherty J. A. justified this approach, reasoning that "the courts have, in many cases, responded to this apparent injustice, by allowing the litigant who brought the claim the advantage of a finding of unconstitutionality, even though the declaration of invalidity is suspended for some period ... The court should be able to fashion a meaningful remedy for the rights-claimant".[158] This remedy was upheld by the Supreme Court on the basis that the government had justified the one-year suspension for reasons of public safety and the courts were capable of determining that the specific applicant should be exempted from the suspension because he was not dangerous. The Court noted that it was possible that the applicant would not be exempted from new legislation. It also accepted that litigants could be exempted from a suspension when "others similarly situated" would not because of the applicant's investment in a case and because "an individual remedy for the claimant will often be appropriate and just. The importance of safeguarding constitutional rights weighs heavily in favour of an individual remedy. The concern for vindicating individual rights with effective

[154] *Carter* v. *Canada (Attorney General)*, 2016 SCC 4.

[155] *Truchon c. Procureur général du Canada*, 2019 QCCS 3792 (CanLII).

[156] Ibid. at 746, 768. In a subsequent case the judge followed *Carter II* by extending the suspension but allowing any qualified person to seek a court-ordered exemption: *Truchon c. Procureur general du Canada*, 2020 QCCS 772 (CanLII) at para 22.

[157] *G* v. *Ontario (Attorney General)*, 2019 ONCA 264; aff'd 2020 SCC 38.

[158] Ibid. at 151, 153.

remedies reaches back to Blackstone and Dicey, and continues to have force in the present day".[159] This provides supports for a two-track approach that combines remedies for litigants with systemic remedies and that recognizes that different considerations may apply to the two different forms of remedies.

2.4.4.4 South Africa

Like the Supreme Court of Canada, the South African Constitutional Court has used the suspended declaration of invalidity to frequently remand the crafting of systemic remedies to the legislature. However, it has been more willing than the Canadian court to craft interim orders designed to minimize individual rights violations during the suspension. In some respects, these orders go beyond the two-track approach because they often do not simply allow the successful litigants to obtain a remedy. They also direct the government about how it should administer the unconstitutional legislation during the suspension. The South African courts seem committed to the idea that if they grant a litigant a remedy, all other similarly situated people should receive it too. Robert Leckey has defended this approach on the basis of "horizontal equity".[160] The strengths and weaknesses of the different Canadian and South African approaches will be examined in Chapter 4, Section 4.2.5. At this juncture, the important point is that the court provides immediate remedies even while it provides legislatures an opportunity to craft a systemic remedy.

The South African Court issued a declaration aimed at systemic relief in its first housing rights case.[161] Mark Tushnet defended this approach on the basis that "for practical reasons, the remedies for violations of social and economic rights cannot be 'personal and present'".[162] He compared it to the retreat from individual remedies in *Brown II* and other public law litigation cases. Even in *Grootboom*, however, the Court

[159] *Ontario (Attorney General)* v. *G.* 2020 SCC 38 at paras 152 and 147 citing Roach "Dialogic Remedies" (2019) 17 *I Con* 860 at 862–865. Three judges in dissent would have created a presumption against exemptions except in cases of irreparable harm to rights in large part because of concerns that they would create horizontal inequity with respect to others similarly situated. Ibid. at paras 215, 274 and 287. Even this more restrictive approach would allow for a two-track approach in cases where a suspension of a declaration of invalidity would irreparably harm a sucessful litigant.

[160] Robert Leckey, *Common Law Bills of Rights* (Cambridge University Press, 2015), pp.103–105.

[161] *Government of the Republic of South Africa and Others* v. *Grootboom and Others*, 2000 (11) BCLR 1169.

[162] Tushnet, *Weak Courts, Strong Rights*, p.247.

was concerned that the applicants receive some remedy that prevented their eviction.[163] Subsequent South African cases have more overtly used a two-track approach that combines immediate and personal relief through orders to stop evictions or provide temporary housing while also using more deferential remedies that allow the executive, after consultation, to devise systemic remedies for the future. In the *Port Elizabeth* case,[164] for example, the Constitutional Court stressed that a "relatively small group" of illegal occupiers of land should not be evicted unless some other (even temporary) housing solution was devised. Justice Sachs explained:

> [t]he inherited injustices at the macro level will inevitably make it difficult for the courts to ensure immediate present-day equity at the micro level. The judiciary cannot of itself correct all the systemic unfairness to be found in our society. Yet it can at least soften and minimise the degree of injustice and inequity which the eviction of the weaker parties in conditions of inequality of necessity entails.[165]

Such a two-track approach allows courts to transcend the difficult choice that Tushnet posed between weak remedies that may produce no effective remedy for successful litigants and strong remedies that may tax judicial competence. It does so by using stronger approaches for individual relief and weaker approaches for systemic relief.

The South African housing cases provide immediate protection from eviction while acknowledging the need for a more dialogic and incremental approach to systemic reform. The provision of individual remedies against eviction affirms common expectations that courts should provide remedies to successful litigants. It also helps counter inequality of bargaining in the systemic engagement process by ensuring that the conditions of those with inadequate housing do not become even more desperate. At the same time, the court's systemic approach is both dialogic and deferential. It allows the executive and those who are supposed to benefit from the remedy to lend their expertise to crafting a sustainable systemic remedy. These cases suggest that it is possible to combine strong but individualized and potentially temporary remedies with weaker and more dialogic remedies designed to produce systemic reform.

163 See *infra* Chapter 8, Section 8.6.2, for discussion.
164 [2004] ZACC 7 at paras 28, 59.
165 Ibid. at para 38.

The granting of individual remedies plays to judicial strengths by focusing on the specific facts of particular cases. The ability of the court to correct "micro injustices" may also increase its legitimacy and gain public attention and produce momentum for reform. Those who advocate that courts should take an "experimental",[166] "incremental",[167] "catalytic"[168] or "weak"[169] approach to systemic reform are not wrong to describe the systemic remedy side of the equation in these ways. Nevertheless, they may underestimate the potential costs to judicial legitimacy if courts act only in that manner. They may also underestimate how an individual remedy may help stimulate systemic reform.

2.4.4.5 New Zealand

The two-track approach can also be applied to less complex remedies, such as damages. In a leading damages case, the New Zealand Supreme Court indicated that the damages it awarded to prisoners that had been subject to a harmful solitary confinement regime might have been greater had the state not discontinued the program.[170] In another case, New Zealand courts indicated that damages might have been higher if the state had not disciplined officers who flagrantly violated rights by assaulting a prisoner.[171] This elegant approach places incentives on the state to use the great variety of instruments at their disposal to prevent future violations. It avoids the spectre of judges appearing to run prisons or police forces while also demonstrating an admirable judicial concern about preventing similar rights violations in the future.

2.4.4.6 Colombia

The Colombian Constitutional Court frequently engages in abstract review in the tradition of European constitutional courts as well as summary tutela jurisdiction in the South American tradition of amparo. The former can be seen as a form of systemic review that focuses on the constitutionality of legislation. The latter is an accessible form of individual remedies. The two-track approach, however, requires some combination of these.

166 Simon and Sabel, "Destabilization Rights".
167 Jeff King, *Judging Social Rights* (Cambridge: Cambridge University Press, 2012).
168 Katharine Young, *Constitutionalizing Economic and Social Rights* (Oxford: Oxford University Press, 2012).
169 Tushnet, Weak Courts, Strong Rights.
170 *Taunoa* v. *Attorney General*, [2007] NZSC 70 at paras 268, 371.
171 *Falwasser* v. *Attorney General*, [2010] NZAR 445 at paras 36–37, 124.

The Colombian Court moved towards a two-track approach when it aggregated a number of individual actions in 2004 in relation to the socio-economic rights of those displaced by internal conflict[172] and in 2008 in relation to healthcare rights.[173] In both cases, the Court declared that repetitive violations created an unconstitutional state of affairs. As in the ECtHR system, the Court's own interest in dealing with repetitive violations spurred a more systemic approach.[174] In both cases, the Court ordered tutela relief for the individual applicants. The Court also initiated systemic reform in the 2004 case by requiring greater co-ordination among the many government departments responsible for providing services to displaced persons and in the 2008 case, by requiring the government to update the services and drugs covered in the public healthcare system and to move towards universal healthcare.

Individual enforcement remains important in demonstrating to governments and society the real-life consequences of systemic and regulatory failures. They also demonstrate the institutional advantages that courts have in deciding cases on the basis of all the facts and ordering remedies to benefit successful litigants. With respect to systemic reform, the Court indicated that it "must make decisions that indicate that the bodies overcome failures of regulation that have led to the repeated violation of the right".[175] Nevertheless, because of the need to respect "the process of public debate, decision and policy implementation, characteristic of a democracy"[176] the Court was more modest and less prescriptive with respect to systemic as opposed to individual remedies.

One of the main features of the Court's systemic orders were orders calling for the collection of information.[177] The Court ordered that statistics about tutelas be kept, noting "[i]f the actions of regulatory bodies are ideal, people will not be forced to seek the actions of *tutela* and its proportion will be reduced".[178] In this respect the Colombian Court's approach to remedies was similar to that taken by supra-national regional human rights courts that devote much effort to collecting

[172] "Decision T-025 of 2004" in Manuel José Cepeda Espinosa and David Landau, *Colombian Constitutional Law* (New York: Oxford University Press 2017), pp.179–190.

[173] Ibid., "Decision T-760 of 2008", p.172.

[174] Neuman, "Bi-Level Remedies".

[175] "Decision T-760/08 of 2008", at 3.3.2, 6 online (pdf): www.escrnet.org/sites/default/files/English_summary_T-760.pdf

[176] Ibid. at 3.3.15.

[177] Ibid. at Resolves: nineteenth and twentieth orders.

[178] Ibid. at 9.

information from the state and making it public. What courts lack in terms of information in devising systemic remedies can be partially remedied by systemic orders that require its collection and publication. The adversarial features of courts also make them concerned with transparency and participation. In both the Colombian cases and the supra-national systems, systemic measures are directed at preventing and avoiding repetitive cases that could overwhelm the adjudicator.

As Professors Garavito and Rodriguez-Franco suggest, the Court's approach "promotes the reform process, but does not decide its contents, since most of its orders are means-oriented rather than outcome-oriented".[179] They also draw a useful distinction between monologic remedies where the court dominates and dialogic remedies where the court is responsive to input from the parties and civil society. In their terms, "monologic judgments involve detailed, outcome-oriented orders," while "dialogic judgments tend to outline goals and procedures and, in line with the principle of separation of powers, place the burden on government agencies to design and implement policies".[180] They praise the dialogic process used in systemic remedies and argue that it demonstrates a false dichotomy between judicial activism and democracy. However, they devote little attention to individual remedies. The terms "monologic" and "dialogic" are improvements on the terms of "weak" and "strong" because they are less court centric. They invite analysis of institutional and societal responses to court decisions.

In 1997, the Court took a systemic approach by legalizing doctor-assisted euthanasia while indicating that the legislature could regulate in the area. But in 2004, the Court took a more two-track and dialogic approach when it approved a tutela action to recover the costs of euthanasia for an individual's estate while also calling for new regulations to be formulated within thirty days for euthanasia.[181] Subsequent decisions in 2017 dealt with the case of children and also resulted in legislation.[182] In 2018, the Court took a two-track approach in two cases where it ordered both an individual remedy of re-admitting a student to school and allowing two prisoners to conduct religious ceremonies, while

[179] Cesar Rodriguez-Garavito and Diana Rodriguez-Franco, *Radical Deprivation on Trial: The Impact of Judicial Activism on Socio-Economic Rights* (Cambridge: Cambridge University Press, 2015), p.195.

[180] Ibid., p.172.

[181] "Decision T-970 of 2014"in Espinosa and Landau, *Colombian Constitutional Law*, p.64.

[182] Decision T-544 of 2017, Colombian Constitutional Court, online: www.corteconstitucional.gov.co/english/Decision.php?IdPublicacion=9298

indicating the need for new guidelines to prevent similar violations in the future.[183] The Colombian Court in these cases is pursuing a two-track remedial approach quite similar to that taken by the IACtHR. Comparative lawyers should be aware of the influence of regional human rights courts on domestic courts especially in monist jurisdictions.

One common objection to systemic reforms is that they exceed the institutional role and expertise of the judiciary. The Colombian cases, however, suggest that courts can be more modest when ordering systemic as opposed to individual orders. It also suggest that courts have some process-based expertise that can assist in achieving the policy reforms necessary for systemic reforms. The Court attempted to structure a process that was fair and transparent. It also ordered the collection of statistics that would allow it and society to understand better the relevant systemic problems.

2.4.5 The Problem of Relief for the Whole Class

Another possible objection to the two-track approach is that in some institutional contexts, it may be impossible to provide relief for individual litigants without providing systemic relief for the whole class.[184] For example, it may be impossible to provide a prisoner litigant with proper conditions of confinement without extending the relief to all inmates in the institution. At the same time, it is notable that both the ECtHR and the IACtHR tend to include some individual remedies in their orders even as they seek longer-term systemic reforms in prison and other institutional cases. Some American commentators have suggested that resources should not be diverted to individual remedies.[185] The Supreme Court of Canada has recognized that concerns for "judicial economy"[186] in cases affecting many people might justify not issuing immediate individual remedies in some cases where the courts suspend a declaration of invalidity for systemic reasons. Nevertheless, this discounts how

[183] Decision T-364 of 2018, Colombian Constitutional Court, online: www.corteconstitucional.gov.co/english/Decision.php?IdPublicacion=9300; Decision T-363 of 2018, Colombian Constitutional Court, online: www.corteconstitucional.gov.co/english/Decision.php?IdPublicacion=9299 (proportionate accommodation of religion).

[184] Fiss, "The Forms of Justice".

[185] Kathleen Noonan, Jonathan Lipson and William Simon, "Reforming Institutions: The Judicial Function in Bankruptcy and Public Law Litigation" (2019) 94 *Indiana L. J.* 491.

[186] *Ontario* v. *G.* 2020 SCC 38 at para 151.

individual remedies provide some limited remedial success and also help humanize and publicize the consequences of violations.

David Landau has argued that while my two-track approach captures much of the complex Colombian jurisprudence, it is best in some political and legal contexts to focus simply on one track.[187] The early jurisprudence of the African Court of Human and Peoples' Rights also suggests that even supra-national courts seeking to establish their mandate will not always pursue the ambitious and demanding two-track strategy. To some extent, it will be a matter of litigation strategy whether litigants seek individual remedies or systemic reform or both. Litigants may decide to abandon the quest for individual remedies, but they do so at some risk in terms of judicial legitimacy and publicizing the effects of policies on specific individuals. Conversely, they may abandon systemic remedies as too demanding, but at the risk of repetitive violations. As will be suggested in the next section, an exclusive focus on either individual or systemic remedies produces many risks.

2.5 The Inadequacy and Pathologies of Single-Track Approaches

In what follows, I will suggest that an exclusive reliance on either individual or systemic remedies can produce dysfunctions and even pathologies. Such a conclusion supports attempts to undertake a two-track approach whenever possible.

2.5.1 The Dangers of Relying Only on First-Track Remedies Addressing Past Violations

Courts that order only individual remedies without regard to future compliance run the risk of simply taxing the state for violations of human rights of those who are able to litigate their claims. This pathology is particularly evident in cases where litigants receive damages, a remedy that many consider an awkward fit for the intangible values protected by human rights. This is a particular concern for the overburdened ECtHR where damages are the main remedy awarded. Hillebrecht documents how Russia often pays the relatively modest damage awards awarded by

[187] David Landau, "Choosing between Simple and Complex Remedies in Socio-Economic Rights Cases" (2019) 69 *U.T.L.J.* 5.

the ECtHR as specific measures, while failing to implement general measures, especially investigations and prosecutions.[188] Similar patterns have been documented with respect to the IACtHR.[189]

Similar concerns are present even when courts order more drastic and socially costly individual remedies than damages. For example, the Supreme Court of Canada placed restrictions on the ability of police to conduct strip searches in 2001[190] but there were subsequent problems with compliance especially by the Toronto police. One study found eighty-nine subsequent reported cases where courts had found a violation of rights related to strip searches. In ten of these cases, the judges expressed concerns about the adequacy of police training but made no formal orders in that regard. The lack of reliable and uniform statistics made it difficult to make conclusions about overall compliance or the repetitive nature of the violation.[191] Even when courts are prepared to order drastic individual remedies such as stays of proceedings and exclusion of evidence in individual cases, this may simply place a heavier tax on continued violations of rights if the systemic basis for violations is not addressed.

Another Canadian case demonstrates the inadequacy of relying only on remedies that recognize past violations, but do not attempt to ensure future compliance. In 2000, the Canadian Supreme Court issued a declaration that customs officials had violated the rights of a small bookstore catering to sexual minorities by targeting its imports as obscene material. The Court rejected a request for mandatory orders and retention of jurisdiction. A strong and prophetic dissent warned that declarations might not be sufficient. It stressed that "systemic problems call for systemic solutions".[192] The bookstore continued to have problems with customs officials. It started a second round of litigation but had to abandon it after it was denied advance costs to finance the litigation.[193]

[188] As quoted in Courtney Hillebrecht, *Domestic Politics and International Tribunals: The Problem of Compliance* (New York: Cambridge University Press, 2014), p.120.

[189] Alexandra Huneeus, "Courts Resisting Courts: Lessons from the Inter-American Court's Struggle to Enforce Human Rights" (2011) 44 *Cornell Int'l. L. J.* 3.

[190] *R.* v. *Golden*, 2001 SCC 83.

[191] Office of the Independent Police Review Director, *Breaking the Golden Rule* (March, 2019).

[192] *Little Sisters Book and Art Emporium* v. *Canada (Minister of Justice)*, 2000 2 SCC 69.

[193] *Little Sisters Book and Art Emporium* v. *Canada (Commissioner of Customs and Revenue)*, 2007 1 SCR 38.

2.5.2 *The Dangers of Relying Only on Second-Track Remedies That Address Future Violations*

Courts that only order systemic remedies also risk losing their way. In 2011, a divided US Supreme Court upheld a controversial remedy to reduce overcrowded prisons in California as a means to improve horrible prison healthcare. It did so purely as a systemic remedy and without providing any remedies for the inmates who had established that they had suffered from inadequate healthcare.[194] The systemic remedy of reducing state prisons to 137.5 per cent of capacity ignored the individual violations suffered by many prisoners who had suffered and even died as a result of inadequate healthcare. A few individual remedies may have helped the court demonstrate the irreparable harms of inadequate healthcare. In an illustration of the complex polycentric nature of the problem, this decision led to a realignment of Californian criminal justice. California eventually complied with the order but more prisoners are now confined in county jails that are not covered by the Court's order.[195] Moreover, concerns about inadequate healthcare in the state prisons persist with courts so far refusing to intervene during the COVID-19 crisis.[196]

Scholars of the American remedial experience have observed how remedies can facilitate negotiations between the affected parties[197] and even engage in destabilizing experiments that respond to bureaucratic inertia and under-funding.[198] I am sympathetic to forward looking "public law" approaches to remedies and this book will draw on much of that learning. Nevertheless, there is a cost to abandoning traditional first-track "right to a remedy" reasoning. American law has thoroughly embraced the forward-looking and instrumental approach to remedies. But such systemic remedies have often failed to deter future rights violations by the police and in prisons. As the ambitions of remedies increase, so too does the likelihood of remedial failure.

194 *Brown* v. *Plata*, 563 US 493 (2011).

195 Margo Schlanger, "Plata v. Brown and Realignment" (2013) 48 *Harv. C.R. - C.L.L. Rev.* 145.

196 *Plata* v. *Newsom*, 2020 WL 1675775 (N.D. Cal.); *Plata* v. *Newsom*, 2020 WL 1908776 (N.D. Cal.).

197 Chayes, "The Role of the Judge in Public Law Litigation".

198 Simon and Sabel, "Destabilization Rights"; Margo Schlanger, "Civil Rights Injunctions over Time: A Case Study of Jail and Prison Court Orders" (2006) 81 *N.Y.U L. Rev.* 2.

Another consequence of the American abandonment of first-track right to a remedy reasoning are frequent refusals to award damages or exclude evidence because of speculative judgements that such remedies will over deter executive officials in the exercise of their duties. The fact that American courts have not provided even nominal damages to the many victims of post 9/11 human rights violations is an embarrassment that undermines the American commitment to human rights and the rule of law. Providing even an inadequate remedy for a discrete violation can serve important purposes.[199] To society, it illustrates that rights do not exist simply on paper and that real people are harmed, sometimes irreparably, when those rights are violated. It also demonstrates that the court is prepared to do something about the violation, even if the individual remedy cannot nullify the violation. Fortunately, other courts have picked up the rule of law slack. British and Canadian courts as well as the ECtHR have all ordered indirect remedies for post-9/11 abuses in what I have argued elsewhere is imperfect but important substitute justice litigation.[200]

Exclusively systemic approaches to remedies are not only a problem in the United States. In India, concerns have been raised that public law litigation has become a top-down affair that often ignores those that it is designed to protect. This is especially so when cases are effectively taken over by amicus curiae who have no particular duties to represent or even consult with those whose rights have been violated.[201] Justice Bhagwati, an early proponent of this form of litigation, argued that adherence to the rule of adversarial litigation would fail to protect the disadvantaged.[202] He accepted jurisdiction over cases on the basis of letters written to him. In one of these cases, Justice Pathak concurred but issued what has been called "a lone voice in the wilderness"[203] that later proved prophetic. He warned that "[t]he lives of large sections of people, some of whom have

[199] Pfander recommends nominal awards of US$1: Pfander, *Constitutional Torts in the War against Terror* (New York: Oxford University Press, 2017), p.148.

[200] Kent Roach, "'Substitute Justice?' Indirect Challenges to American Counter-Terrorism Activities in non-American Courts" (2012) 82 *Miss. L. J.* 4.

[201] Bhuwania, *Courting the People*; see also Chintan Chandrachud, "Structural Injunctions and Public Interest Litigation in India" in Po Jen Yap (ed.), *Constitutional Remedies in Asia*, 1st ed. (London: Routledge, 2019); see also Paul Craig and S. L. Deshpande, "Rights, Autonomy and Process: Public Interest Litigation in India" (1989) 9 *Oxford J. of Leg. Studies* 356.

[202] P. N. Bhagwati, "Judicial Activism and Public Interest Litigation" (1985) 23 *Colum. J. of Transn'l. L.* 561.

[203] Bhuwania, *Courting the People*, p.122.

had no voice in the decision, are shaped and ordered by mandatory Court action extending into the future".[204] My point is not that the systemic aspirations of public law litigation are illegitimate or should be abandoned. It is simply that they should be anchored in the reality of discrete violations and individual remedies.

2.5.3 The Need to Combine Backward and Forward-Looking Remedies

The extremes of the American and Indian approaches demonstrate that courts need to have regard for their primary duty to provide remedies for litigants who have established that their rights have been violated. Providing remedies to these litigants who have established that their rights have been violated is well within the zone of judicial competence. It responds to widely held expectations about courts. Judicial attention to the individual circumstances of litigants helps distinguish courts from the legislature and the executive. An exclusive judicial focus on systemic reform can downplay the reality that many individuals will have suffered rights violations before a court embarks on the difficult task of structural reform.

The two-track approach seeks to integrate traditional right to a remedy reasoning with its focus on compensatory individual remedies with the more ambitious modern approach that focuses on ensuring compliance with human rights in the future. It also attempts to do so in a manner that recognizes the need to respect domestic concerns about the separation of powers and supra-national concerns about subsidiarity. Multiple remedies, as frequently ordered by supra-national courts, should be used more frequently at the domestic level. A remedy that compensates a litigant will often be unable to prevent future violations and vice versa. The two-track approach should also be attentive to the possibility of remedial failure and should encourage domestic courts to follow supra-national courts by being more concerned about repetitive violations.

2.6 Remedial Failure and Cycles of Reform

One of the reasons why remedies attract less scholarship and excitement than rights is that they force us to confront gaps between what rights

[204] *Bandhua Mukti Morcha* v. *Union of India* (1984), 3 SCC 161 at para 163.

promise and what remedies deliver. If there is certain triumphalism in much discussion of human rights, there is a sense of pragmatism and even defeatism in the discussion of remedies. Remedies respond to proven violations, and they often fail to fully correct the harmful effects of past violations or prevent future ones. An awareness of remedial failure should produce a more honest and candid jurisprudence that places less reliance on simplistic slogans about a "right to a remedy" or an "effective remedy".

Domestic human rights lawyers can learn much from international lawyers about the reality of remedial failure. In his concurring judgement in the *Street Children* case, Judge Cançado Trindade, in justifying the award of over USD$500,000 to the families of deceased children, candidly admitted that the full reparation promised by remedial doctrine was impossible. He argued "[t]he evil committed does not disappear: it is only fought against, and mitigated ... In other words, the reparations granted mean that, in the concrete case, the human conscience has prevailed over the impulse of destruction". He added while the reparations were "not full" they are "endowed with an unquestionable importance" in safeguarding rights.[205] In the above case, the court ordered a range of systemic remedies in addition to damages. It determined years later that Guatemala had not been implemented the remedies.[206]

Courtney Hillebrecht has documented compliance with close to 600 judgements of the ECtHR and the IACtHR. She has found a 49 per cent compliance rate with judgements of the former and 34 per cent with judgements of the latter. She also notes that some countries, such as Russia and Italy, are chronic non-compliers. There is significantly greater compliance with reparation remedies for individuals as opposed to systemic non-repetition measures.[207] As the ambitions of remedies

[205] *Villagrán-Morales et al.* v. *Guatemala (Street Children case)* (2001), Inter-Am. Ct. H.R. (Ser. C.), (26 May 2001) at para 43, online (pdf): https://iachr.lls.edu/sites/default/files/iachr/Court_and_Commission_Documents/Villagr%2B%C3%ADn%20Morales%20et%20al.%20v.%20Guatemala.Reparations%26Costs.05.26.01.pdf

[206] *Street Children (Villagrán Morales et al.)* v. *Guatemala*, (2014) 36 *Loy. L.A. Int'l. & Comp. L. Rev.* 5, 1836.

[207] Hillebrecht, *Domestic Politics and International Tribunals*, p.13 finding 82 per cent compliance for reparations in ECtHR and 55 per cent in IACtHR but only 38 per cent and 23 per cent compliance with non-repetition remedies of those respective courts. She does find lower compliance rates for individual measures that do not involve monetary payments such as frequent orders by the IACtHR that bodies of the disappeared be provided to families for burials. On the benefits of aggregating similar cases of non-compliance to provide greater visibility and pressure on governments see Clara Sandoval, Philip Leach and Rachel Murray "Monitoring, Cajoling, and Promoting

increase, so too does the risk of non-compliance.[208] Both domestic and supra-national courts should monitor compliance with systemic remedies. This may often require that states collect and publicize relevant statistics to be examined by the parties and the public.

Professor Hillebrecht's findings are consistent with the idea that courts should not abandon individual remedies that will gain greater levels of compliance. This will create some remedial success even if restitution or full reparation of the many intangible values protected by human rights is impossible. The willingness of states to buy their way out of rights violations, however, underlines the need to pursue systemic remedies and to award individual remedies again if, as is likely, those remedies fail to prevent all future violations.

Although it is important to make remedies as effective and successful as possible, it is necessary to confront remedial failure. Remedial failure is better documented in international law than in domestic law. Domestic courts too often complacently assume that their remedies are effective. They do not have to prove this effectiveness or legitimacy in the way that supra-national courts do. As will be seen, international courts have struggled with violations of interim remedies. Because of their limited resources, they have been forced to try to reduce repetitive breaches. In domestic systems, each trial judge considers each remedy anew and without the burden of having to reduce repetitive violations that will more often than not end up in another colleague's courtroom.

Remedial failure should not be ignored or denied. A lack of compliance or even a failure of a particular remedy can serve to prompt new attempts at reform. It can also illustrate the need to adjust remedies. The success of remedies often depends on their persuasive force as well as the evidence that is available to formulate remedies. Again, this feature of remedies is better understood in international than domestic law. Understanding remedies as rights without pretensions means that we should acknowledge that multiple attempts will sometimes be necessary to produce truly effective remedies.

2.6.1 Remedial Cycles

As discussed in the examination of the legal process methodology in Chapter 1, Section 1.3, one of the defining features of dialogic

Dialogue: What Role for Supra-National Bodies in the Implementation of Individual Decisions?" (2020) 12 *Journal of Human Rights Practice* 71 at 82–83.

[208] Yuval Shany, *Assessing the Effectiveness of International Courts* (New York: Oxford University Press, 2014), pp.117–136.

understandings of judicial review is that they take a broader time frame than the moment of judicial or legislative decision. This broader time frame allows us to track cycles of remedies that respond to past remedial failure. Depending on the circumstances, second and third cycles may require courts to issue more robust remedies at both the individual and systemic level.

Requests for individual remedies provide a means to recognize remedial failures to prevent repetitive violations. The result can be to trigger a new cycle of individual and systemic remedies. The need for additional individual remedies will depend in part on how the legislature or the executive has responded to previous remedies. Legislatures will have incentives to enact new legislation quicker if the granting of individual remedies is fiscally or politically costly. In this regard, the UK government seemed more poised to enact new legislation on prisoner disenfranchisement when it believed that prisoners could obtain damage awards for each time they were denied the vote in an election.[209] The granting of individual remedies can also help mobilize civil society lobbying and media coverage, thus placing more pressure on the legislature to respond and shape its response.

Initially weak remedies such as declarations may, depending on the government's response, evolve into stronger ones that involve the retention of jurisdiction.[210] To the extent that dialogic systemic remedies invite legislative replies, however, courts may be inclined to accept the state's response as reasonable.[211] At the same time, however, the two-track approach will remain attentive to those who fall through the cracks of new programs and laws. This might include providing individual remedies and starting another cycle of both individual and systemic remedies and reform.

2.7 Conclusion

The two-track approach recognizes that the main purposes of remedies for violations of human rights can frequently be reduced to: (1) the need

[209] Hodgson and Roach, "Disenfranchisement as Punishment".

[210] Tushnet, *Weak Courts, Strong Rights*.

[211] Rosalind Dixon, "Creating Dialogue about Socio-Economic Rights" (2007) 5 *I. Con.* 391; see, for example, *Mazibuko* v. *City of Johannesburg*, 2010 3 BCLR 239 and *infra* discussion of reasonableness and proportionality in Chapter 8, Section 8.4. For a recognition that the more recent South African cases involve "a strong but temporary remedy that prevents eviction where the state is unable to provide alternative accommodation", see Ray, *Engaging with Social Rights*, p.210.

to respond through restitution or compensation to the violation and the harms it causes; and (2) the need to ensure ongoing compliance with human rights and the non-repetition of future violations. Both these backward- and forward-looking remedial purposes are important. They combine the traditional judicial concern of providing successful litigants with individual remedies as an incident of corrective justice with the broader ambitions of public law litigation and international law in reducing future rights violations.

The two-track approach urges courts to play a dominant role with respect to individual remedies. They include damages, exemptions for litigants from suspended declarations of invalidity and remedies in the criminal process but also interim remedies that prevent violations of human rights that cannot be adequately compensated by damages. At the same time, courts play a less dominant and more dialogic role with respect to systemic remedies. They include declarations of incompatibility, suspended declarations of invalidity and declarations that recognize that legislatures and the executive may be better positioned than courts to devise systemic remedies to govern the future.

A systemic approach where a court dialogically interacts with an expanded range of parties and institutions also has the potential to devise more creative, participatory and effective remedies than even the most determined judges could achieve on their own. For example, a lighter judicial touch when crafting systemic remedies makes room for Indigenous participation in determining the content of the remedy. At the same time, individual remedies restraining resource extraction that can cause irreparable harm can, in some cases, counteract imbalances of political and bargaining power. Consistent with the flexible approach taken to both the separation of powers and subsidiarity, systemic remedies ordered by courts may become stronger over time should governments not respond reasonably.

The fact that individual remedies such as orders for treatment or orders against evictions may result in queue jumping or treat litigants in a preferential manner should not be a decisive objection to such remedies. Queue jumping remedies respond to long standing expectations that courts should provide successful litigants with effective remedies. While there is some truth to the critique of queue jumping, such distributive critiques could be applied to all remedies that do not apply to everyone similarly situated. It denies the corrective logic of individual remedies and the nature of adjudication that provides privileged access to parties who chose to litigate.

A common objection to systemic remedies is that they require courts to go beyond their institutional capacities and engage in what Lon Fuller described as polycentric tasks. Again, there is some truth to this objection. But even Fuller, in his later work, recognized that courts could compensate for their institutional weakness by drawing on the expertise of the executive, the legislature and the parties. He also recognized that courts could provide fair processes and be willing to adjust their remedies in the face of new evidence. In addition, the parties could engage in negotiation and mediation as a way of dealing with the complexity of polycentric problems.

The two-track approach is ambitious. It may be displaced by a litigant's decision to pursue only individual or systemic remedies. It may not be possible in every case. But the two-track approach is rooted in the practice of many supra-national adjudicators. It is also found in the practice of fewer domestic courts, such as South African courts in their second-generation housing rights cases and the Canadian court in its assisted dying cases. Courts have also used the two-track approach when they exempt successful litigants from suspended declarations of invalidity that invite the legislature to formulate the systemic remedy.

An exclusive focus on either the individual or systemic track can produce remedial dysfunctions and even pathologies. Courts that exclusively order individual remedies may be overwhelmed with individual cases and ignore the larger institutional context of the violations. The experience of the ECtHR demonstrates how a court faced with an overwhelming case load and repetitive violations may be driven to devote more attention to systemic or general measures. At the same time, the ECtHR has wisely rejected calls for it to abandon its traditional functions in providing individual remedies. Even if the damages it awards to individual litigants are inadequate, they are important in distinguishing the ECtHR as a court and not simply as another advocate for better governance. Courts that focus only on systemic reforms risk undermining their core function. The California prison case has been widely praised in the United States in apparent ignorance that the ECtHR would, in a similar case, award both individual remedies including release for treatment and pursue systemic reforms with states that would go beyond the controversial and limited judicial remedy of reducing prison populations.

American courts have often concluded that evidence should be excluded or damages awarded only when necessary to deter future misconduct. But, this instrumental approach often leaves those whose rights have been violated without a remedy. Ignoring the right of individuals to remedies contributes to the cynicism about the rule of law and rights that flourishes in the United States. Courts that ignore individual remedies undercut their legitimacy and efficacy. But the answer cannot be to return to the simpler world contemplated by Blackstone and Dicey in the eighteenth and nineteenth century. Courts that ignore systemic remedies allow states to pay an occasional price for violations while condoning continuing and repetitive violations.

Courts must be concerned with both individual and systemic justice. A court that simply awards individual remedies will ignore issues of future compliance while a court that only awards systemic remedies will often be blind to the harms suffered by individuals. Courts need to recognize that different approaches and remedies are required to achieve compensatory and preventive remedial goals. Even if one does not accept this chapter's normative argument that courts should pursue a two-track approach to remedies, this chapter nonetheless makes the important descriptive point that some remedies focus on preventing or repairing harm to specific litigants while other remedies focus more on preventing future violations of rights. It also has indicated the frequency and importance of recognizing and responding to remedial failure.

3

Interim Remedies

3.1 Introduction

Interim relief refers to injunctions and stays of the operation of legislation awarded before a full trial on the merits. In order to obtain such interim or interlocutory relief, applicants must establish a risk of irreparable harm. In domestic human rights law, they must also establish that granting relief before trial is consistent with the balance of convenience or the public interest.

Even in the understudied field of remedies, interim remedies have been neglected.[1] This is most unfortunate. People look to courts to protect them from immediate and irreparable harms that cannot be fully repaired by damages or other remedies after trial. A court that tersely denies a request for interim relief as a mere matter of discretion and procedure can fail in its most basic function of protecting litigants from human rights violations. Interim remedies respond to widely held understandings of the nature of rights as something that places duties on the state to protect rights holders from suffering irreparable harm. No theory of remedies for human rights can be complete without reference to interim relief. It is not an exaggeration to say that interim remedies are critical to both the meaning of human rights and the judicial role in making rights meaningful.

The need to prevent irreparable harm is closely tied to both the obligation of states to respect human rights and the frequent inability of damages to fully repair all the harms and consequences of such violations. The common law tests for granting interim relief were developed in the private law. They use mechanisms, such as undertakings that applicants who obtain interim relief pay damages caused to defendants by such relief if they lose on the merits, that are not appropriate in the human rights context where the defendant is the government.

Interim remedies serve as a form of triage of rights. They illustrate where courts are prepared to enforce human rights through injunctions in a manner akin to property rules and when they determine that human rights are only a liability rule that, when violated, will result in the payment of damages.[2] In Chapter 5, Section 5.2, we will see that damages as a remedy for human rights violations are often nominal and

[1] For example, Dinah Shelton's leading text on remedies in international law does not have a chapter on interim remedies: *Remedies in International Human Rights Law*, 3rd ed. (New York: Oxford University Press, 2015).

[2] Guido Calabresi and Douglas Melamed, "Property Rules and Liability Rules: One View of the Cathedral" (1972) 85 *Harv. L. Rev.* 1089.

disappointing. This insight should inform how courts exercise their discretion to award interim remedies.

Both domestic and supra-national courts have been cautious, often too cautious, in granting interim relief. In 1994, Judge Bergenthal argued that interim relief should be "exceptional" and should have a "shock value". He warned that supra-national courts could undermine their status by granting such relief too frequently.[3] Since that time, however, international courts have become increasingly willing to grant interim relief to prevent irreparable harm to rights to life, liberty and security.[4] Judge Cançado Trindade has argued that interim remedies have emerged as an autonomous and obligatory legal regime that reveals that international law can respond to the desperate plight of real people.[5]

In early 2020, the International Court of Justice (ICJ) issued provisional measures that Myanmar take steps to prevent and "not commit any acts" of genocide against the Rohingya. Myanmar was also ordered to report back to the court in four months and subsequently every six months on the measures taken.[6] This demonstrates how interim remedies normalize the retention of jurisdiction that, as we will see in Chapters 7–9, can be controversial with respect to final judgements. A nimble and robust approach to interim remedies can also serve as a model for other forms of remedies, including remedies ordered during a

[3] Thomas Burgenthal, "Interim Measures in the Inter-American Court of Human Rights" in Rudolf Bernhardt (ed.), *Interim Measures Indicated by International* Courts (Berlin: Springer, 1994), p.93.

[4] Indeed, a leading international law treatise on interim remedies is simply called *Preventing Irreparable Harm*: Eva Rieter, *Preventing Irreparable Harm Provisional Measures in International Human Rights Adjudication* (Antwerp: Intersentia, 2010). See also Cameron Miles, *Provisional Measures before International Courts and Tribunals* (Cambridge University Press, 2017).

[5] He has argued: "[i]n sum, provisional measures of protection have enabled international tribunals to secure gradually, besides the protection of a preventive character, a continuous monitoring of the compliance, on the part of the States at issue, with the aforementioned measures ordered by them, thus fostering the strengthening of this procedural remedy of crucial importance to the protection of the fundamental rights of the human person". Cançado Trindade, *International Law for Humankind*, 2nd ed. (Leiden: Martinus Nijhoff Publishers, 2013), p.47. See also A. A. Cançado Trindade, "The Evolution of Provisional Measures of Protection under the Case-Law of the Inter-American Court of Human Rights (1987–2002)" (2003) 24 *Hum. Rts. J.* 162.

[6] *Application of the Convention on the Prevention and Punishment of the Crime of Genocide* (*The Gambia* v. *Myanmar*), Request for the Indication of Provisional Measures, Order of 23 January 2020 online (pdf): www.icj-cij.org/files/case-related/178/178-20200123-ORD-01-00-EN.pdf. Subsequent reporting has been delayed in part because of the COVID-19 pandemic.

period in which a declaration of invalidity is suspended to allow for a legislative response. This will be examined in Chapter 4, Section 4.2.5.

Domestic human rights law has focused less on irreparable harm to rights and people and more on whether interim relief is consistent with the public interest, the balance of convenience or the balance of equities. Some courts have failed to reconcile such potentially majoritarian and utilitarian concepts with the human rights that protect unpopular individuals and minorities. Vague concepts such as the "balance of convenience" and the "public interest" should be disciplined by application of proportionality principles. This will require precise articulation of the competing social objective, the degree of tailoring of relief to accommodate the competing objective and the overall balance between the harms inflicted by ordering or not ordering interim relief. Proportionality analysis should be sensitive to the comparative stakes of the rights claimant and the government, as well as the overall effects on them caused by granting or not granting interim relief.

A decision to deny interim relief may end the dispute, especially if those adversely affected truly suffer irreparable harm. In contrast, a decision to grant interim relief does not preclude a court from finding at trial that rights were not violated on the basis of full evidence and argument. It also does not stop the court from altering relief in response to changed circumstances including delay in litigation on the merits. The asymmetrical effect of decisions on interim relief is demonstrated by the United States Supreme Court's regrettable 5–4 decision to reverse interim relief against the so-called Muslim travel ban.[7] It has effectively ended the legal dispute. None of the judges doubted their ability to decide the case at the interim stage without a full trial.

Interim remedies should play a central role in the domestic and supranational enforcement of human rights. This does not, however, mean that they should be granted in every case. Interim remedies are generally reserved for the most urgent and grave situations.[8] They will be easier for

[7] *Trump* v. *Hawaii,* 138 S.Ct. 2392 (2018). For an earlier affirmation of tailored interim relief from a previous version of the travel ban to benefit those with existing connections to the United States see *Trump* v. *International Refugee Assistance Project* 137 S.Ct. 2080. 2087–2088 (2017). See also *Roman Catholic Diocese of Brooklyn* v. *Cuomo* 592 US (2020) reaching the opposite conclusion that a COVID restriction violated freedom of religion and also deciding to grant an interim injunction on the merits.

[8] Pamela McCormick, "Risk of Irreparable Damage: Interim Measures in Proceedings Before the European Court of Human Rights" (2010) 12 *Cambridge Y.B. Eur. Leg. Stud.* 313.

courts to justify when they are designed to protect discrete numbers of vulnerable individuals and groups. This chapter will encourage courts to apply the irreparable harm standard with a view to both the strength of the applicant's claim and the purpose of the human right in question. It will suggest that supra-national courts can learn from domestic courts in being prepared to order interim relief with respect to a wide range of rights and not only with respect to threats to life and health. International courts can also learn from those domestic courts that have recognized that in some contexts they can and must engage in merits-based review at the interim remedy stage. International courts, perhaps because they generally have no appeal structure with respect to interim remedies, are often too concerned that they will pre-judge a dispute when deciding an interim remedy. In a world beset with urgent situations where the most basic human rights are increasingly in peril, all courts must learn to accept that they will increasingly face "now or never" situations when deciding whether to grant interim relief.

Interim remedies will play an important role in the two-track approach to remedies advocated for in this book. In my view, they should be seen as a first-track individual remedy that is an inherent part of the judicial role in deciding disputes. In a world with massive access to justice problems and impending rights violations, judges must become more comfortable working in the "legal emergency room" as they face urgent motions for interim remedies. Something can be learned from South American traditions of the use of summary procedures to provide individual remedies and the willingness of American courts to take a merits-based approach to resolving questions of interim relief.[9] Judges should be more confident in applying their knowledge about rights and proportionality reasoning at the interim remedy stage. At the same time, they should also recognize that they may make mistakes. They should lean towards protecting rights from irreparable harm but also recognize that they may need to alter initial orders of interim relief in light of new evidence and changed circumstances.

3.1.1 Outline of This Chapter

Section 3.2 will examine leading interim relief cases in international and domestic human rights law. It will demonstrate how various

[9] During the COVID-19 crisis, the United States Supreme Court in a 5–4 decision on an application for interim relief held that California's restrictions did not violate freedom of religion. *South Bay United Pentecostal Church* v. *Newsome* 590 US (2020). This mirrored the same merits-based approach taken in the Muslim ban case.

international adjudicators have recognized the importance of interim relief in enforcing rights and protecting their ability to adjudicate. Domestic courts have applied a number of common law concepts that may not be appropriate to the human rights context.

Section 3.3 will examine the importance of the irreparable harm standard that is common in both international and domestic human rights law. It will also suggest that, in some contexts, courts should engage in a closer review of the merits of the applicant's case.[10] This may be especially important if courts consider a broad range of rights claims and do not focus, as supra-national courts have tended to, on threats to life.

Section 3.4 will examine how proportionality principles can guide and discipline decision-making about interim relief. Once the applicant establishes irreparable harm and the strength of its case, governments opposing interim relief should articulate a clear and legitimate social interest that will be harmed by the grant of interim relief. Courts should pay particular attention to whether interim relief can be tailored so as to accommodate competing social interests and competing rights. The overall balance between irreparable harm to the applicant and the harm to a clearly articulated and legitimate social interest, including harm to the rights of third parties, should also be a critical factor in deciding whether to grant interim relief.

Section 3.5 will outline the role that interim relief can play in the two-track remedial approach. It should be seen as an individual remedy that lies well within the domain of the judiciary in ensuring its ability to adjudicate and remedy a dispute. Interim relief is practically related to the adequacy of damages that, as examined in Chapter 5, Section 5.2, is also an individual remedy. It will also be suggested that courts should not be deterred by the prospect of remedial failure. Even when interim relief is not obeyed (as has sometimes been the case with supra-national courts) courts can respond by awarding increased damages and other remedies. The breach of interim remedies can itself also focus public attention on the irreparable harm caused by some rights violations.

3.2 Existing Practice

Interim remedies have long been seen as an adjunct to the idea that nation states accept the jurisdiction of a particular supra-national

[10] Robert J. Sharpe, "Interim Remedies and Constitutional Rights" (2019) 69 *Supp. 1 U.T.L.J.* 9.

tribunal and commit to not frustrating its ultimate judgement or aggravating the dispute. In recent years, many international courts have stressed the binding nature of interim remedies. They have maintained jurisdiction to assess penalties for violations.

At the same time, there are disadvantages in the way that supra-national courts approach interim measures. Many courts do not publish their decisions on interim remedies and do not hold full hearings. The European Court of Human Rights (ECtHR) and UN treaty bodies both tend to confine interim remedies to a small number of discrete factual situations, such as impending executions and deportations. They have not always been open to the possibility that applicants may be able to establish irreparable harm in other contexts. International courts are very concerned that their judgements on interim remedies may pre-judge the dispute. Finally, there have been flagrant and high-profile violations of interim remedies issued by supra-national courts.

3.2.1 *The International Court of Justice*

In a 1939 case, what is now the ICJ explained that a "principle universally accepted by international tribunals" was that "parties to a case must abstain from any measures" that would aggravate the dispute or "the performance of acts likely to prejudice, for either of the Parties to the case or for the interests concerned, the respective rights which may result from the impending judgment".[11]

As Chester Brown has argued, the power to grant interim relief can be seen as a general principle of international law that is justified even when enabling statutes are silent on their jurisdiction to do so.[12] The idea that courts have inherent powers to grant interim remedies can be deduced, on the one hand, from the authoritative nature of courts in dispute resolution and, on the other hand, by the nature of rights. The former

[11] *Electricity Company of Sofia and Bulgaria (Belgium* v. *Bulgaria)* (1939), PCIJ Ser A/B. No. 79 at para 199.

[12] Chester Brown, *A Common Law of International Adjudication* (New York City: Oxford University Press, 2007), pp.126–128 citing ibid. at paras 194, 199. To similar effect, see Sir Gerald Fitzmaurice, *The Law and Procedure of the International Court of Justice*, Vols. I–II (Cambridge: Grotius Publications Limited, 1986), p.542. See also *Aegean Sea Continental Shelf (Greece* v. *Turkey)*, [1978] ICJ Rep. 3 at paras 15–16; *LaGrand Case (Germany* v. *United States of America)*, Merits [2001] ICJ Rep. 466, (2001) 40 ILM 1069, 1093–1094; *Indonesia Amco Corporation and Others* v. *Republic of Indonesia*, ICSID Case No. ARB/81/1 at 412.

rationale is well summarized by Brown when he notes that "if international courts were unable to make orders preventing any prejudicial action and safeguarding their jurisdiction to render an effective decision, their function in settling the dispute would be undermined".[13] The latter rationale is recognized in Article 41 of the enabling statute of the ICJ, which provides that the court can order provisional measures to "preserve the respective rights of either party . . . if it considers that circumstances so require".[14]

Although it only considers interstate claims, the ICJ has increasingly ordered provisional measures in cases involving human rights. Many of these cases relate to the right to life in capital punishment cases, but some also relate to the protection of culture and the environment.[15] The ICJ has not hesitated to order interim remedies that require states to take a variety of positive measures, even though it has been hesitant to make similar mandatory orders as final remedies.[16]

In the *LaGrand* case, Germany obtained provisional measures to restrain the execution of a German national in the United States. The ICJ took a generous approach to the right to consular access by holding that "it is immaterial for the purposes of the present case whether the LaGrands would have sought consular assistance from Germany, whether Germany would have rendered such assistance, or whether a different verdict would have been rendered". It granted relief because "Germany and the LaGrands were in effect prevented by the breach of the United States from exercising" their rights "had they so chosen".[17] The Court then determined that its interim measures have binding effect because such measures are "based on the necessity, when the circumstances call for it, to safeguard, and to avoid prejudice to the rights of the parties as determined by the final judgment of the Court".[18] Although Germany in the *LaGrand* case sought to justify interim relief as necessary

[13] Brown, *A Common Law of International Adjudication*, p.128.

[14] United Nations, *Statute of the International Court of Justice*, in force 18 April 1946, 33 UNTS 993.

[15] Stegan Kdelbach, Thilo Rensmann and Eva Rieter (eds.), *Judging International Human Rights: Courts of General Jurisdiction as Human Rights Courts* (Cham: Springer International Publishing Company, 2019), pp.133–137.

[16] Christine Gray, *Judicial Remedies in International Law* (Oxford: Clarendon Press, 1990), p.70.

[17] *LaGrand Case (Germany* v. *United States of America)*, Merits [2001] ICJ Rep. 466, (2001) 40 ILM 1069, 1093–4 at para 74.

[18] *LaGrand Case (Germany* v. *United States of America) (Merits)*, Judgment of 27 June 2001 [2001] ICJ No. 2001/16, at para 102.

to preserve the status quo, the ICJ did not rely on this concept.[19] The preservation of the status quo is not helpful in the human rights context because the rights alleged to be violated and impugned state law or practice can all be characterized as part of the status quo.

The Court found that the United States had breached the interim measure. It accepted an apology, but indicated that this would not be sufficient reparation if there was a subsequent breach.[20] *LaGrand* has been an influential decision in a larger trend of supra-national courts and adjudicators asserting their powers to order binding interim measures. The Court has avoided narrow positivism that only views laws as enforceable commands by concluding that "the fact that the Court does not itself have the means to ensure the execution of orders is not an argument against the binding nature of such orders".[21] In general, the ICJ has not ordered damages or other remedies when states have breached provisional measures even though such breaches can be seen as an international wrong in its own right.[22] Breach of interim measures might also result in aggravated damages on the merits and the award of costs.

Since the 2001 *LaGrand* decision, the ICJ has restricted the availability of interim relief by requiring a tighter link between the relief claimed and the alleged legal violation.[23] In the subsequent case of *Avena and other Mexican Nationals,*[24] the Court only issued interim measures to prevent the execution of three of fifty-two people subject to the death penalty in the United States. This raises many concerns about the relation between rights and remedies and remedial deterrence discussed in Chapter 1, Section 1.5. As will also be discussed in Section 3.4, it may often be easier to justify interim relief when it is focused on preventing irreparable harm to strong rights claims by an individual or a smaller group of litigants.

[19] Brown, *A Common Law of International Adjudication*, p.121.

[20] *LaGrand Case (Germany* v. *United States of America) (Merits)*, Judgment of 27 June 2001 [2001] ICJ No. 2001/16.

[21] Ibid. at para 108.

[22] *Application of the Convention on the Prevention and Punishment of the Crime of Genocide (Bosnia and Herzegovina* v. *Serbia and Montenegro),* Judgment of 26 February 2007, ICJ. Rep. 2007 at para 469. For criticism, see Kdelbach, Rensmann and Rieter, *Judging International Human Rights,* p.166.

[23] Miles, *Provisional Measures*, p.295; Yoshiyuki Lee-Iwamoto, "The Repercussions of the *LaGrand* Judgment: Recent ICJ Jurisprudence on Provisional Measures" (2012) 55 *Japanese Y.B Int'l L.* 237.

[24] *Avena and Other Mexican Nationals (Mexico* v. *United States of America)*, Order of 31 March 2004, [2004] ICJ Rep. 12.

In 2020, the ICJ issued a range of interim measures to prevent genocide against the Rohingya, including requiring Myanmar to report in four months and every six months after on the measures taken.[25] Unlike in its previous decision restraining countries in the former Yugoslavia from committing genocide,[26] the ICJ effectively retained jurisdiction over the Myanmar case by requiring periodical reports back to the Court. Thought should be given, however, to allowing the parties (and perhaps others) to participate in the reporting process. In a nod to the role of the ICC, it also issues an obligation to retain evidence. The case demonstrated how interim measures can result in retention of jurisdiction and reporting requirements similar to the domestic public law model.

The majority of the ICJ in the Myanmar case required that the applicant establish a "plausible claim" that rights have been violated[27] and a "real and imminent risk of irreparable prejudice".[28] In a concurring judgement, Judge Cançado Trindade expressed his long-standing concerns that the plausible rights requirement undercut the fundamental nature of the right against genocide. Courts should take the irreparable harm approach seriously, but also allow applicants to strengthen their case for relief by demonstrating even at the interim stage that their claims are more than simply plausible or not frivolous. Alas, the ICJ and many supra-national adjudicators seem excessively concerned about appearing to pre-judge the merits in any way.

[25] *Application of the Convention on the Prevention and Punishment of the Crime of Genocide (The Gambia* v. *Myanmar)*, Request for the Indication of Provisional Measures, Order of 23 January 2020 online (pdf): www.icj-cij.org/files/case-related/178/178-20200123-ORD-01-00-EN.pdf

[26] *Application of the Convention on the Prevention and Punishment of the Crime of Genocide (Bosnia and Herzegovina* v. *Serbia and Montenegro)*, Order of the Court on Provisional Measures, Order of 8 April 1993, ICJ Rep. 1993.

[27] *Application of the Convention on the Prevention and Punishment of the Crime of Genocide (The Gambia* v. *Myanmar)*, Request for the Indication of Provisional Measures, Order of 23 January 2020 at para 43. The Court added: "[a]t this stage of the proceedings, however, the Court is not called upon to determine definitively whether the rights which The Gambia wishes to see protected exist; it need only decide whether the rights claimed by The Gambia on the merits, and for which it is seeking protection, are plausible. Moreover, a link must exist between the rights whose protection is sought and the provisional measures being requested". Ibid. at para 44. Ad hoc Judge Kress also stressed that the plausibility standard was not stringent especially with regards to genocidal intent and did not pre-judge the merits.

[28] Ibid. at paras 65, 75. For discussion of this difference and a defence of the plausibility requirement, see Cameron Miles, "Provisional Measures and the 'New' Plausibility in the Jurisprudence of the International Court of Justice" (2018) *Br. Y.B Int'l L.* bry011, online: https://doi.org/10.1093/bybil/bry011

3.2.2 *United Nations Human Rights Bodies*

The UN Human Rights Committee (UNHRC) has considered requests for interim measures even in cases where domestic remedies have not been exhausted and the admissibility of the complaint is not clear.[29] In a series of cases where the Committee has tried to stop executions, it has stressed that states that have committed themselves to the Optional Protocol should not frustrate the Committee's ability to hear the case by committing the irreversible act of an execution. It has used strong language when a number of states have gone on to execute people. In one case, it stated that Trinidad and Tobago's execution was "a shocking failure to demonstrate even the elementary good faith required of a State Party to the Covenant and the Optional Protocol".[30] The Human Rights Committee views its interim measures as binding.[31] As will be explored below, there is also a potential role for domestic courts to enjoin irreversible acts such as executions, extraditions and deportations pending decisions by UN and other supra-national bodies.

Interim remedies can matter a great deal. Trinidad and Tobago and Jamaica both denounced and opted out of the Optional Protocol as a result of death penalty cases.[32] The possible role of remedial deterrence in terms of courts not ordering remedies so as to avoid drastic consequences will be examined in Section 3.5.

The Committee has defined irreparable harm as harm that cannot be compensated for in damages. In the deportation/extradition context, it is harm caused when the individual is not able to return to the country that deported or extradited them.[33] The irreparable harm requirement is an important device for rationing interim relief. At the same time, the degree of likelihood of irreparable harm may not always be clear in often summary applications for relief. In one extradition case, the Committee

[29] Gino Naldi, "Interim Measures in the UN Human Rights Committee" (2004) 53 *Int'l. & Comp. L. Q.* 445, 447.

[30] *Ashby* v. *Trinidad and Tobago* (21 March 2002), Report of the UNHRC, UN GOAR, Comm. No. 580/1994, UN GAOR A/57/40, UN Doc CCPR/C/54/80/1994, at 10.9.

[31] UNHRC, "General Comment No. 33: The Obligations of States Parties under the Optional Protocol" International Covenant on Civil and Political Rights, in force 25 June 2009, CCPR/C/GC/33 at para 19.

[32] Sandy Ghandi, "The Human Rights Committee and Interim Measures of Relief" (2007) 12 *Canterbury L. Rev.* 203, 223.

[33] *Stewart* v. *Canada* (1993), Report of the UNHRC, UN GOAR, Comm. No. 538/1993, 58th Sess., Supp. No. 40, UN Doc A/52/40, Annex Vi, Vol. II.

asked for more information to establish irreparable harm, but unfortunately the state extradited the applicant in violation of the Optional Protocol before the Committee had made its decision.[34] Judges who make decisions in the legal emergency room of interim relief will often have to act without full information. They should adopt a precautionary principle with respect to rights but then be prepared to revise their orders in light of new evidence.

The Committee has been reluctant to order interim measures to benefit large groups or the population at large. For example, it refused to enjoin French nuclear testing in the South Pacific, holding that irreparable harm had not been established.[35] It will be suggested in Section 3.4 that proportionality principles favour the granting of relief to protect specific rights holders or smaller groups of rights holders.

The Committee Against Torture also orders interim measures. The Committee confirmed the mandatory nature of its interim measures in a case where Canada breached such measures by deporting a person to India. It emphasized that interim remedies are only ordered when it is "essential to protect the person in question from irreparable harm".[36] Even when interim measures are not obeyed by countries or enforced by domestic courts, they may still alert civil society and focus attention on the plight of the individual who has received the remedy.

3.2.3 *European Court of Human Rights*

Interim remedies have been granted by the ECtHR even though the European Convention on Human Rights does not specifically provide for them.[37] Alas, many provisional measure decisions are generally not

[34] *Weiss* v. *Austria* (2003), Report of the UNHRC, UN GOAR, Comm. No. 1086/2002, 77th Sess, Supp. No. 40, UN Doc CCPR/C/77/D/1086/2002, Annex V, Vol. VIII at para 1.2 (emphasis added).

[35] *Bordes* v. *France* (1996), Report of the UNHRC, UN GAOR, Comm. No. 645/1995, 51st Sess, Supp No. 40, UN Doc A/51/40, Annex IX, Vol. II at para 116.

[36] *T.P.S.* v. *Canada* (2000), Report of the UNCAT, UN GAOR, Comm. No. 99/1997, 55th Sess, Supp. No. 44, UN Doc A/55/44, Annex VIII, at 16.1 (16 May 2000); see also Joanna Harrington, "Punting Terrorists, Assassins and Other Undesirables: Canada, the Human Rights Committee and Requests for Interim Measures of Protection" (2003) 48 *McGill L. J.* 55, 55–88.

[37] Clara Burbano-Herrera and Yves Haeck, "Letting States off the Hook? The Paradox of the Legal Consequences Following State Non-Compliance with Provisional Measures in the Inter-American and European Human Rights Systems" (2017) 28(3) *Neth. Q. Hum. Rts.* 330, 336–340.

reasoned or published.[38] The Court generally limits interim relief to allegations of breaches of life and against torture and mistreatment.

Some cases from the ECtHR underline the temporary and dynamic nature of interim relief. In 2019, the Court granted interim measures in relation to medical and other assistance for forty cases. In *Yordanova and Others* v. *Bulgaria*,[39] the Court indicated that the applicants should not be evicted. It lifted the interim remedy when adequate alternative housing was made available even though the applicants would have preferred to stay in their original homes and in their Roma community. Judge Keller and Cedric Marti have suggested that this case represents a less generous approach taken to interim relief than that taken by the UN Human Rights Committee when it enjoined evictions of Roma persons in Bulgaria.[40]

In *Mamatkulov and Askarov* v. *Turkey*,[41] the Grand Chamber affirmed the mandatory nature of its orders of interim relief. It noted the general trend described above with respect to the ICJ and UN Human Rights Committee holding that states must follow interim measures. It reasoned that irreparable harm to the asserted Convention right would frustrate the effective exercise of the right of individual petition under Article 34 of the European Convention on Human Rights.[42] It also made reference to the right to an effective remedy in Article 13, concluding: "it is hard to see why this principle of the effectiveness of remedies for the protection of an individual's human rights should not be an inherent Convention requirement in international proceedings before the Court, whereas it applies to

[38] Yves Haeck, Clara Burbano-Herrera and Leo Zwaak, "Non-Compliance with a Provisional Measure Automatically Leads to a Violation of the Right of Individual Application … or Doesn't It: Strasbourg Court Takes Away Any Remaining Doubts and Broadens Its Pan-American Protection" (2008) 4 *Eur. Const. L. Rev.* 41, 57.

[39] No. 25446/06, ECHR 24 August 2012. The Court explained: "the general measures in execution of this judgement should include such amendments to the relevant domestic law and practice so as to ensure that orders to recover public land or buildings, where they may affect Convention-protected rights and freedoms, should, even in cases of unlawful occupation, identify clearly the aims pursued, the individuals affected and the measures to secure proportionality. In so far as individual measures are concerned, the Court is of the view that the execution of the present judgement requires either the repeal of the order of 17 September 2005 or its suspension pending measures to ensure that the authorities have complied with the Convention requirements, as clarified in the present judgment". Ibid. at paras 166–167.

[40] Keller and Marti, "Interim Relief Compared", 358, 371.

[41] [GC] Nos. 46827/99 and 46951/99, ECHR 4 February 2005.

[42] Ibid. at para 108.

proceedings in the domestic legal system".[43] Finally, it made reference to interim measures assisting the Committee of Ministers in the execution of final judgements under Article 46 of the Convention.[44] The Grand Chamber stressed the rights protecting nature of interim relief. It concluded that "the purpose of interim measures is to preserve the parties' rights, thus enabling the body hearing the dispute to give effect to the consequences which a finding of responsibility following the adversarial process will entail".[45] The Court also awarded each applicant €5,000 in damages for Turkey's breach of interim measures restraining their extradition to Uzbekistan and €15,000 in legal costs.

The ECtHR has taken an increasingly strict approach to enforcing its interim measures. For example, after the UK transferred detainees to Iraq, the Court found a breach of interim measures and the right to petition. It indicated that the UK should attempt to obtain assurances that the death penalty would not be applied in these cases.[46] In *Paladi* v. *Moldova*, the Court restrained the transfer of an ill applicant from a neurological centre to a correctional facility without adequate medical services. This measure was not observed for a number of days before the applicant was returned to the neurological centre where he was receiving adequate medical treatment. The Grand Chamber held that "the intentions or reasons" behind the lack of compliance or whether irreparable harm was in fact caused "are of little relevance".[47] The Grand Chamber ordered €15,000 in non-pecuniary damages, €2,080 in pecuniary damages and €7,000 in costs. A number of judges, however, dissented on the bases that the lack of compliance lasted only three days, caused no risk of irreparable harm and the government did not act in bad faith. In another case, the ECtHR rejected a waiting list for medical treatment as a legitimate reason not to comply with an interim measure.[48] Domestic courts would be less likely to conclude that states had violated interim remedies in similar circumstances, in part because of potentially punitive effects of holding the state or named state officials to be in contempt for violating an interim injunction.

[43] Ibid. at para 124.
[44] Ibid. at para 125.
[45] Ibid. at para 113.
[46] *Al-Saadoon and Mufdhi* v. *the United Kingdom*, No. 61498/08, [2010] II ECHR 61.
[47] *Paladi* v. *Moldava* [GC], No. 39806/05, ECHR 10 March 2009 at paras 87–88. The Court also indicated that Moldova was at least negligent in the breach: ibid. at para 104.
[48] *Makharadze and Sikharulidze* v. *Georgia*, No. 35254/07, § 35, 101, ECHR 22 February 2012.

3.2.4 *Inter-American Court of Human Rights*

Article 63(2) of the American Convention on Human Rights provides: "in cases of extreme gravity and urgency, and when necessary to avoid irreparable damage to persons, the Court shall adopt provisional measures as it deems pertinent in matters it has under consideration".[49] The Inter-American Court of Human Rights (IACtHR) publishes its reasons for all decisions on provisional measures, often holding public hearings and giving state respondents a chance to respond.[50] It considers its interim measures binding.[51] Unlike the ECtHR, however, it does not award damages for their breach.[52] In a 2006 case, Judge Trindade observed: "over 11,500 people (including members of entire communities), residing in countries of Latin America and the Caribbean, are under the protection of provisional measures ordered by this Court".[53] A leading commentator has concluded that the Court's interim remedies "save lives rather than merely provide reparations after a human rights violation".[54]

As in other supra-national courts, there has been evolution from a traditional international law focus on preserving the Court's ability to resolve the dispute on the merits towards a greater emphasis on protecting rights and rights bearers from irreparable harm.[55] In practice, the Court has ordered interim measures to protect a wider range of rights holders than the ICJ or the ECtHR. For example, the IACtHR has ordered provisional measures to protect "witnesses, human rights advocates, members of Indigenous communities, prisoners, journalists, [and]

[49] American Convention on Human Rights, San Jose, Costa Rica, 22 November 1969, in force 18 July 1978, 1144 UNTS 123.

[50] Clara Burbano-Herrera, "The Inter-American Court of Human Rights and Its Role in Preventing Violations of Human Rights through Provisional Measures" in Yves Haeck, Oswaldo Ruiz-Chiriboga and Clara Burbano-Herrera (eds), *The Inter-American Court of Human Rights: Theory and Practice, Present and Future* (Antwerp: Intersentia, 2015), pp.372–374.

[51] *Constitutional Court* v. *Peru* (2001), Provisional Measures, Order of the President of the Court, Inter-Am. Ct. H.R. (Ser C), (14 August 2000).

[52] For criticism, see Burbano-Herrera and Haeck, "Letting States off the Hook?", 332, 345.

[53] Concurring Opinion of Judge A. A. Cançado Trindade in the case of *Communities of Jiguamiandó and Curbaradó* v. *Colombia* (2006), Provisional Measures, Order of the President of the Court, Inter-Am. Ct. H.R. (Ser. C), (February 7, 2006) at para 1.

[54] Jo Pasqualucci, *The Practice and Procedure of the Inter-American Court of Human Rights*, 2nd ed. (Cambridge: Cambridge University Press, 2013), p.253.

[55] Ibid., p.252.

political candidates".[56] There are, however, concerns that expansion of interim remedies may strain the Court's limited resources and undermine state compliance with its judgements.[57]

The IACtHR has been willing to adjust its interim measures. It sometimes even sets a date within four to six months of its original decision to revisit the matter.[58] It has taken an active interest in compliance.[59] It has ordered provisional measures after the state has denounced the relevant human rights provisions on the basis that the Court had assumed jurisdiction over the case before the denunciation.[60] The Court has also ordered provisional measures as a means to ensure compliance with final judgements.[61] In subsequent chapters, it will be suggested that courts should consider applying the irreparable harm standard to other remedies, including suspended declarations of invalidity (Chapter 4, Section 4.4.7) and declarations (Chapter 7, Section 7.5.4) and that interim remedies can play a critical role in enforcing social, economic and cultural rights (Chapter 8, Section 8.2.1), and Indigenous rights (Chapter 9, Section 9.2.1).

The IACtHR tends to articulate provisional measures in general terms that allow the state, sometimes in consultation with the beneficiary,[62] to

[56] Thomas Antkowiak and Alejandra Gonza, *The American Convention on Human Rights* (Oxford: Oxford University Press, 2017), p.315.

[57] Pasqualucci, *The Practice and Procedure of the Inter-American Court of Human Rights*, p.263.

[58] Clara Burbano Herrera, *Provisional Measures in the Case Law of the Inter-American Court of Human Rights* (Antwerp: Intersentia, 2010), pp.169–170.

[59] Genevieve Sauberli, "Revision Procedures: Revisiting the Case of *Mapiripán Massacre* v. *Colombia*" in Yves Haeck, Oswaldo Ruiz-Chiriboga and Clara Burbano-Herrera (eds.), The Inter-American Court of Human Rights: Theory and Practice, Present and Future (Antwerp: Intersentia, 2015), p.51.

[60] *James et al.* v. *Trinidad and Tobago* (2000), Provisional Measures, Order of the Court, Inter-Am. Ct. H.R. (Ser. C), (16 August 2000) at *Considering* para 6.

[61] *La Rochela Massacre* v. *Colombia* (2009), Provisional Measures, Order, Inter-Am. Ct. H.R. (Ser. C), (19 November 2009), considering paras 6–10; *Mayagna (Sumo) Awas Tingni Community (Nicaragua)* (2002), Provisional Measures, Order, Inter-Am. Ct. H.R. (Ser. C), (6 September 2002), Res. 1; *Caballero Delgado and Santana* v. *Colombia* (1994), Provisional Measures, Order, Inter-Am. Ct. H.R. (Ser. C), (16 December 1994) at *Considering* paras 1–2, Res. 1; *Blake* v. *Guatemala* (2000), Provisional Measures, Order of the President, Inter-Am. Ct. H.R. (Ser. C), (18 August 2000); Herrera reports fifteen cases where provisional measures were maintained after a judgement on the merits and four cases where they were entered for the first time after a judgement on the merits. Herrera, *Provisional Measures in the Case Law of the Inter-American Court of Human Rights*, p.171.

[62] For example, it has also indicated that "provisional measures must be designed and implemented with the full participation of the beneficiaries and their representatives, taking into account their special protection needs in conformity with the specific

decide what precise steps must be taken to avoid irreparable harm.[63] It has avoided granting final relief in the form of freeing a prisoner or reinstating a worker, but rather focused on more limited measures to protect applicants from irreparable harm.[64] The Court will terminate provisional matters when there is no longer an urgent situation of grave harm that will cause irreparable harm. In one case, the Court terminated such measures after the parties agreed to a plan to reform Brazilian prisons.[65] It has also expanded interim measures to protect those related to the original applicant.[66]

Provisional measures will only be ordered where there is an urgent situation of extreme gravity and where there is a threat of harm that cannot be compensated for by damages. The Court has held that the damages caused by losing one's job through the closing of a radio station was not irreparable harm and neither was the diffuse harm that all listeners would suffer if the radio station closed.[67] In another case about the censorship of the movie *The Last Temptation of Christ*, the Court did not order interim measures despite eventually finding against Chile on the merits.[68]

Compliance with the Court's interim measures has been far from perfect. Non-compliance has resulted in loss of life.[69] Cases of non-compliance have been reported to the General Assembly of the Organization of American States but the General Assembly has not taken action.[70]

circumstances in the matter". *Gladys Lanza Ochoa* v. *Honduras* (2010), Provisional Measures, Order of the President, Inter-Am. Ct. H.R. (Ser. C), (2 September 2010) having seen para 2 decides para 1; see also *Juan Almonte Herrera* v. *Dominican Republic* (2010), Provisional Measures, Order of the President, Inter-Am. Ct. H.R. (Ser. C), (25 May 2010) at *Considering* para 16.

63 Pasqualucci, *The Practice and Procedure of the Inter-American Court of Human Rights*, pp.275–276.

64 Burbano-Herrera, *Provisional Measures in the Case Law of the Inter-American Court of Human Rights*, p.182.

65 *Urso Branco Prison* v. *Brazil*, Provisional Measures, Order of the President, Inter-Am. Ct. H.R. (Ser. C), (25 August 2011), Res. 1.

66 Rieter, *Preventing Irreparable Harm*, p.1095.

67 *Belfort Istúriz et al.* v. *Venezuela* (2010), Provisional Measures, Order of the President, Inter-Am. Ct. H.R. (Ser. C), (15 April 2010) at *Considering* paras 19–20.

68 *"The Last Temptation of Christ" (Olmedo Bustos et al.)* v. *Chile* (2002), Monitoring Compliance with Judgement, Order, Inter-Am. Ct. H.R. (Ser C), (28 November 2002).

69 Burbano-Herrera, Provisional Measures in the Case Law of the Inter-American Court of Human Rights, p.189.

70 Ibid., pp.209–211.

3.2.5 *African Court of Human and Peoples' Rights*

The new African Court of Human and Peoples' Rights has rendered many more decisions on provisional measures than on final remedies. This affirms the importance of interim remedies, especially to the supra-national enforcement of human rights. In one case, it held that ordering the release of a newspaper editor held on criminal libel charges would prejudge the case at an interim measure stage. At the same time, the Court ordered that the editor have access to health care and medication when in prison. Three judges made strong arguments in dissent that the editor should be released and could still be jailed should he fail on the merits after a full trial.[71] The editor succeeded on the merits and the court ordered material and moral damages and the expungement of his criminal record.[72] Many interim remedies directed at states such as Libya and Tanzania have resulted in non-compliance.[73] Courts could, however, use the naming and shaming effect of interim remedies to manage their dealings with recalcitrant states and to reward and praise states for complying with interim remedies. Its continuing nature allows courts to adjust interim relief in response to changed circumstances.

3.2.6 *Domestic Law in Aid of Supra-national Law*

In *Lewis* v. *Jamaica*,[74] the Privy Council enjoined the execution of six death row prisoners until an application for interim relief in the Inter-American system had been decided. The Court acknowledged the legitimacy of Jamaica's concerns about delays. Nevertheless, it stressed the importance of due process when the death penalty was in play. The Court indicated that the executive should be required to explain why it did not agree with conclusions reached by international human rights bodies.[75] Lord Hoffmann dissented. He characterized supra-national proceedings as simply those before a "non-governmental body"[76] that could not bind Jamaica.

[71] *Lohe Issa Konate* v. *Burkina Faso* (2014), No. 004/2013, Merits, African Court on Human and Peoples' Rights, 1 AfCLR 314.

[72] Ibid.

[73] *African Commission on Human and Peoples' Rights* v. *Libya* (2013), No. 002/2013, Order of Provisional Measures, African Court on Human and Peoples' Rights, 1 AfCLR 153.

[74] [2000] UKPC 35.

[75] Ibid. at 64. For praise of the majority's decision, see Lord Mance, "Justiciability" (2018) 67 *I.C.L.Q.* 739.

[76] *Lewis* v. *Jamaica* [2000] UKPC 35 at para 109.

A different approach has been taken by Canadian courts. After the Supreme Court of Canada held that a man would not face a significant risk of torture in Iran,[77] the man tried to have his deportation restrained pending a decision by the UNHRC, which had already issued a provisional measure that he not be deported to Iran. The majority of the Ontario Court of Appeal would not restrain the deportation because neither the UNHRC's interim remedies nor its final views were binding on Canada. Any remedy for Canada's actions would be a matter "for the court of international or public opinion but not for a court of law".[78] In a strong dissent, Rosenberg J.A. held that Ahani had already been detained by Canada as a security risk for almost nine years and it was appropriate to detain him pending the UNHRC judgement on the merits.

The UNHRC ultimately concluded that Ahani faced a real risk of torture in Iran and it rejected Canada's arguments that its interim remedies were not binding. It affirmed that its interim measures are "essential to this Committee's role under the protocol. Flouting of the Rule whether by irreversible measures such as the execution of the alleged victim or his/her deportation from a State party to face torture or death in another country, undermines the protection of Covenant rights under the Optional Protocol".[79]

The approach taken by the Privy Council in *Lewis* v. *Jamaica* is preferable to the approach taken in *Ahani* because it recognizes the irreversible and irreparable harm that can be caused by execution or deportation. The Privy Council's decision also demonstrates how domestic and supra-national remedies can interact and re-enforce each other, with the latter providing a safeguard when domestic remedies are exhausted. The approach taken by the majority in *Ahani* and Lord Hoffmann in *Lewis* is based on a stark sense of dualism between international and domestic law. It is also based on a sense of positivism that views law as matters of enforceable commands. The relevant question under this approach is simply whether Canada is bound by the supra-national decisions. In contrast, restraining domestic states until supra-national bodies have made their decisions allows for better

[77] *Ahani* v. *Canada*, [2002] 1 SCR 72.

[78] *Ahani* v. *Canada* (2002), 2002 CanLII 23589, 58 O.R.(3d) 107 (Ont. CA) at paras 121–122.

[79] *Ahani* v. *Canada* (2004), UNHRC, 80th Sess, UN Doc CCPR/C/80/D/1051/2002 at para 1.2.

informed and more rights conscious decisions even if the supra-national body does not ultimately have the ability to bind the domestic state.

3.2.7 *The Influence and Limits of the Common Law*

As Robert Sharpe has argued, there is a tendency in the common law to see interim remedies as extraordinary both because they depart from a traditional preference for damages over injunctions and because they are decided before a full trial on the merits. At the same time, Justice Sharpe also recognizes that interim remedies may be necessary to make real the common law's traditional promise of a right to a remedy.[80]

There is also a need to adapt common law tests that apply to disputes between private parties to the human rights context where the government will generally be the defendant. The private law focus on whether the plaintiff can pay damages caused by interim relief if not successful on the merits is not appropriate in a public law context in which individuals are claiming rights from the state. Similarly, the private law focus on whether the defendant – in most cases governments – will suffer irreparable harm is also not appropriate. The private law concept that injunctions should preserve the status quo is not helpful because both the challenged government action and the rights claimed are part of the status quo. Conversely, as the Supreme Court of Canada has recognized, the idea of preserving the status quo discounts that one of the very purposes of human rights "is to provide individuals with a tool to challenge the existing order of things or status quo".[81]

Another common law concept that is not appropriate is the idea that applicants need to establish a stronger case for an injunction that mandates positive action as opposed to one that prohibits action.[82] Placing a higher onus on applicants to establish the merits of their case when they invoke such rights creates different categories of rights.[83] To be sure, rights claims may be weak and the burdens of some interim remedies

[80] Sharpe, "Interim Remedies and Constitutional Rights".

[81] *R. J. R. Macdonald Inc.* v. *Canada (Attorney General)*, [1994] 1 SCR 311.

[82] This distinction has been imposed in the rights context in *R.* v. *Canadian Broadcasting Company*, 2018 SCC 5. In contrast, The Irish Supreme Court, however, applied the lenient *American Cyanamid* test to mandatory interim injunctions: *Campus Oil* v. *Ministry of Energy*, [1983] IR 88.

[83] For criticisms, see Roach, *Constitutional Remedies in Canada*, 2nd ed. (Toronto: Thomson Reuters, 2013), p.7.171; for criticism of the general distinction between positive and negative rights and remedies, see ibid., pp.3.260–3.310.

may be great. These factors, however, should be evaluated directly by considering the merits and the balance of convenience, not by relying on a distinction drawn from the private law that has the effect of making it more difficult to protect some rights from irreparable harm.

The traditional three-part common law test for interim relief involves consideration of: 1. the strength of the applicant's case; 2. whether the applicant will suffer irreparable harm in the absence of interim relief; and 3. whether the balance of convenience favours granting interim relief.

3.2.8 Canada

The Supreme Court of Canada has slightly modified the above three-part test in the public law context. The Court did so by providing that the public interest should always be considered in constitutional cases when applicants request an interlocutory injunction or an interim stay of the implementation of pending legislation. The Court also suggested that courts should presume harm to the public interest from interim relief and avoid judgements about the effectiveness of government action.[84] The public interest will be presumed to be represented by legislation.[85] However, the applicant may also be able to establish that their case for an interim remedy is in the public interest because "'[p]ublic interest' includes both the concerns of society generally and the particular interests of identifiable groups".[86] Alas, the idea that an applicant for interim relief may represent the public interest has not emerged as a powerful remedial tool, even in the context of Indigenous rights where courts sometimes recognize a public interest in honourable dealings with Indigenous peoples.[87]

84 *Manitoba (A.G)* v. *Metropolitan Stores,* [1987] 1 SCR 11; *R. J. R. Macdonald Inc.* v. *Canada (Attorney General),* [1994] 1 SCR 311; on the Canadian jurisprudence, see Kent Roach, *Constitutional Remedies in Canada*, Chapter 7.

85 *Harper* v. *Canada (Attorney General),* [2000] 2 SCR 764 at para 9. In this case, the Court reversed an interim stay of third party spending limits during the election largely on the basis of the public interest. As Robert Sharpe has argued, however, it would have been more persuasive for the Court to have assessed the case on the merits. When the case was decided after a full trial, the Court held that third party spending limits were a reasonable limit on freedom of expression designed to ensure equality in political participation. *Harper* v. *Canada*, [2004] 1 SCR 827. For cases where the Canadian court's decision on interim relief diverged from its ultimate decision on the merits see Roach *Constitutional Remedies in Canada* at 7.70.

86 *R. J. R. Macdonald Inc.* v. *Canada (Attorney General),* [1994] 1 SCR 311 at para 71.

87 See *infra* Chapter 9, Section 9.2.1.

The Canadian Court has also drawn a potentially useful distinction between interim remedies that are more intrusive to the public interest because they suspend a law, as opposed to those that are more narrowly focused and only result in exemptions from a law. The latter cases generally benefit "a relatively limited number of individuals and where no significant harm would be suffered by the public".[88] For example, interim injunctions preventing the mandatory retirement of fifteen doctors has been characterized as a less intrusive exemption case,[89] whereas a request for an interim stay of restrictions on tobacco advertising should be seen as a more intrusive suspension.[90] It will be suggested in Section 3.4 of this chapter that this Canadian distinction between interim remedies that are limited exemptions and more intrusive and difficult to justify suspensions can be integrated into proportionality reasoning. It will also be suggested that proportionality reasoning can bring discipline and transparency into determining where the vague and potentially majoritarian concepts of the balance of convenience and the public interest lie.

The Canadian jurisprudence has been influenced by the fact that the leading cases have involved requests for interim stays of legislation. The courts have been concerned about deferring to democratically enacted legislation. The case for deference may be less compelling when interim injunctions are sought against executive action. For example, a judge restrained Canadian officials from interrogating a Canadian detained at Guantanamo Bay in 2005.[91] In another case, the Supreme Court took a merits-based approach to overturning an injunction that restrained a woman in the twenty-first week of her pregnancy from obtaining an abortion. It concluded that neither the father nor the foetus had relevant human rights at stake.[92]

3.2.9 The United States

The United States Supreme Court has stated that a "plaintiff seeking a preliminary injunction must establish that he is likely to succeed on the merits, that he is likely to suffer irreparable harm in the absence of

88 *Manitoba (A.G)* v. *Metropolitan Stores*, [1987] 1 SCR 11.
89 Ibid. in relation to *Vancouver General Hospital* v. *Stoffman*, 1985 CanLII 778 (B.C. C.A.).
90 *R. J. R. Macdonald Inc.* v. *Canada (Attorney General)*, [1994] 1 SCR 311.
91 *Khadr* v. *Canada* (2005), 257 DLR (4th) 577 (F.C.T.D.).
92 *Tremblay* v. *Daigle*, [1989] 2 SCR 530.

interim relief, that the balance of equities tips in his favour, and that an injunction is likely in the public interest".[93] This is similar to the traditional common law three-part test, but it requires an applicant to demonstrate a stronger case on the merits than simply a serious and non-frivolous case. Like the Canadian courts, the American courts make reference to the public interest when deciding whether to grant relief.[94] In the context of a stay, however, the United States Supreme Court has stated that the merits and irreparable harm requirements are more important factors than the public interest.[95] This is an improvement over the Canadian approach given the vagueness of the public interest concept.

Some lower Federal Courts use a sliding scale that blurs the different factors.[96] Such a flexible approach has the advantage of allowing courts, where possible, to focus on the strength of the applicant's case. Indeed, John Leubsdorf has argued that interim injunctions should be decided on the basis that the goal of a preliminary injunction is "to prevent irreparable injury to legal rights in light of a prediction of the final outcome of the case".[97] At the same time, a sliding scale test can degenerate into the exercise of strong forms of remedial discretion that fails to make clear the judicial reasoning behind the remedial decision.

The American courts, more than many other courts, seem willing to assess and decide the strength of the applicant's rights claims before ordering interim relief. From early times, the United States Supreme Court has held that "if the legal right is doubtful . . . the court is always reluctant to take a course of action which may result in material injury to either party".[98] The results-based focus of the American jurisprudence is well demonstrated in the Court's controversial 5–4 decision to uphold President Trump's third travel ban directed against countries with majority Muslim populations.[99] The Court had previously stayed nation-wide

93 *Winter* v. *Natural Resources Defence Council*, 555 US 7 (2008) at 21–22.

94 *Inland Steel Co.* v. *United States*, 306 US 153 (1939) at 157: "duty of court of equity granting injunctive relief to do so upon conditions that will protect all – including the public – whose interests the injunction may affect"); *Winter* v. *Natural Resources Defence Council*, 555 US 7 (2008).

95 *Nken* v. *Holder*, 556 US 418 (2009), 434.

96 See Bethany M. Bates, "Reconciliation After *Winter*: The Standard for Preliminary Injunctions in Federal Courts" (2011) 111 *Colum L. Rev.* 1522, 1530.

97 John Leubsdorf, "The Standard for Preliminary Injunctions" (1978) 91 *Harv. L. Rev.* 525, 565.

98 *Russell* v. *Farley*, 105 US 433 (1881) at 438.

99 Before that decision, the Supreme Court overturned a preliminary injunction barring the transfer of an American citizen held in Iraq on the merits, including allegations that he

interim injunctions against the initial ban, but later allowed them to go into effect to provide relief for those who had a credible claim of a bona fide relationship with a person or entity in the US.[100] This decision demonstrates that narrower and more carefully tailored interlocutory relief will be easier to justify than broader relief.

The Court's opinion in *Trump* v. *Hawaii* was largely devoted to the merits of the claim that the travel ban violated the First Amendment. Chief Justice Roberts for the majority concluded that the applicants for interim relief had not demonstrated a likelihood of a violation of religious freedom.[101] Justice Thomas, in his concurrence, voiced concerns that courts did not have the constitutional power to issue universal or nation-wide preliminary injunctions. He reasoned that courts of equity did not generally provide relief beyond the parties to the case. Justice Gorsuch joined him in a subsequent decision overturning another nation-wide interim injunction. He stressed that broad interim remedies that applied to all increased the risk of error, but such risk was minimized when interim relief is framed more narrowly and especially when limited to the parties.[102]

Four judges in dissent concluded that the travel ban violated the First Amendment respecting the establishment of religion. They determined that the plaintiffs were also likely to suffer irreparable harm not compensable in damages and that the balance of equities and the public interest both favoured interim relief.[103] The dissent stressed that the plaintiffs had made "concrete allegations of serious harm" compared to the government's "nebulous national security concerns". They also cited various amici briefs to conclude that the injunction was in the public interest, given concerns raised about the harm the travel ban would cause to higher education, national security, health care, technology sectors and the economy.

would be tortured and that the government was entitled to have the litigation against it decided and ended on the merits. *Munaf* v. *Geren*, 553 US 674 (2008); but see *Jones El et al.* v. *Berge et al.*, 164 F.Supp.2d 1096 (W.D Wis., 2001) for an interim remedy prohibiting prisoners with mental illness from being placed in solitary confinement.

100 *Trump et al.* v. *International Refugee Assistance Project et al.*, 137 S.Ct. 2080 (2017). Justice Thomas with Justices Alito and Gorsuch dissented and would have stayed the injunction even as it applied to foreign nationals with connections to the United States.

101 *Trump* v. *Hawaii*, 138 S.Ct. 2392 (2018) (slip op. at 34).

102 *Department of Homeland Security et al.* v. *New York et al.*, 589 US, 140 S.Ct. 599 (2020).

103 *Trump* v. *Hawaii*, 138 S.Ct. 2392 (2018) per Justice Sotomayer in dissent, citing the test in *Winter* v. *Natural Resources Defence Council*, 555 US 7 (2008) at 23.

In a subsequent case, the US Supreme Court refused to review a preliminary injunction that required 800 older inmates to be released or transferred from a dormitory style prison where COVID-19 was rampant. The trial judge found that the inmates were exposed to irreparable harm and that the balance of convenience favoured relief. The judge retained jurisdiction to supervise the most vulnerable inmates who had to be transferred or released. The 6th Circuit upheld the order and the Supreme Court denied leave, with three judges dissenting.[104] In another COVID-19 related case, the Court decided that California's restrictions on public events did not violate freedom of religion under the First Amendment with Justices Thomas, Kavanagh and Gorsuch arguing in dissent that it did and that an interim injunction should be granted.[105] The Court changed track and affirmed interim relief for religious institutions from COVID restrictions. It held there was a strong case of a First Amendment violation and irreparable harm. Over four dissents, it concluded that the public interest and public health would not be harmed by the interim relief.[106] Evaluating the merits of these decisions is beyond the scope of this work on remedies. What is important, however, is that the Court was prepared to make rulings on the merits in these emergency situations.

3.2.10 South Africa

The South African Constitutional Court applies something close to the three-part common law test for interim injunctions. The Court has, however, added concerns about respecting the separation of powers. It did so when it reversed a lower court judgement restraining the implementation of tolls on new highways. Moseneke DCJ stressed that "separation of powers harms" should be considered in the balance of convenience. The judge concluded: "a temporary restraint against the exercise of statutory power well ahead of the final adjudication of a claimant's case may be granted only in the clearest of cases and after a careful consideration of separation of powers harm. It is neither prudent nor necessary to define "clearest of cases".[107] Adding "separation of powers

[104] *Williams* v. *Wilson*, 590 US (26 May 2020), Order in Pending Case.

[105] South Bay v. Newsome 590 US (2020).

[106] *Roman Catholic Dioscese* v. *Cuomo* 592 US (2020).

[107] Moseneke DCJ warned: "[a] court must be astute not to stop dead the exercise of executive or legislative power before the exercise has been successfully and finally impugned on review. This approach accords well with the comity the courts owed to other branches of Government, provided they act lawfully". *National Treasury and Others* v. *Opposition to*

harms" and the mantra of "clearest of cases" to already demanding tests with respect to the balance of convenience and the public interest creates a danger that courts may rarely grant interim relief. Although the separation of powers is a legitimate and helpful principle in remedial decision-making, it should be applied with caution at the interim remedy stage. Should the government succeed on the merits, it will be able escape the restraints of interim relief. There is also a danger that simply invoking the abstract category of the separation of powers will avoid the need to specify the precise harms that will be caused by the grant of interim relief.

The Court was, however, on firmer ground when it overturned the injunction in the above case on the basis that those who would have to pay tolls would not truly suffer irreparable harm given evidence that they would be among the most affluent people in the region. Moreover, they should be able to recover the money they paid in tolls if they were eventually successful after a full trial.[108] This approach correctly rejects that idea that every allegation of a violation of a human rights constitutes irreparable harm.

Irreparable harm may also be connected with the merits of the claim. The Court appropriately considered the merits of the applicant's claims that the road tolls would violate their rights. It concluded that "one important consideration" in determining the balance of convenience "would be whether the harm apprehended by the claimant amounts to a breach of one or more fundamental rights warranted by the Bill of Rights. This is not such a case".[109]

Urban Tolling Alliance and Others (Road Freight Association Intervening), [2012] ZACC 19 at para 26. See also *International Trade Administration Commission* v. *SCAW South Africa (Pty) Ltd*, [2010] ZACC 6; *Glenister* v. *President of the Republic of South Africa and Others*, [2008] (1) ZACC 19. For a defence of the court considering separation of powers concerns in these cases, see Chuks Okpaluba and Mtendeweka Mhango, "Between Separation of Powers and Justiciability: Rationalising the Constitutional Court's Judgement in the Gauteng E-Tolling Litigation in South Africa" (2017) 21 L. Democ. & Dvpm't. 1; for criticisms, see Mia Swart and Thomas Coggin, "The Road Not Taken: Separation of Powers: Interim Interdicts, Rationality Review and E-Tolling in *National Treasury* v. *Opposition to Urban Tolling*" (2014) 5 *Constitutional Ct. Rev.* 346.

108 *National Treasury and Others* v. *Opposition to Urban Tolling Alliance and Others (Road Freight Association Intervening)*, [2012] ZACC 19 at paras 54, 62. The Court also held that the balance of convenience favoured not granting the remedy given that the roads had been built and that without toll revenue the government might default on its payments to contractors and that the harm to the government in this case outweighed the harms that toll users would suffer: ibid. at paras 58–59.

109 Ibid. at para 47. In a concurring judgement, Froneman J took a more nuanced approach and stressed that the clearest of cases tests should only apply "where national legislative or executive power will be transgressed by a temporary interdict". Ibid. at para 90.

The Court has granted interim relief in some subsequent cases. In one case, it restrained the eviction of traders from their stalls, noting that such actions threatened their dignity, earnings and the socio-economic rights of their children.[110] The interim injunction in this case demonstrates that even under new restraints, interim injunctions are still available in South Africa.[111]

3.2.11 Summary

The caution that domestic courts have demonstrated in frequently concluding that the grant of interim relief was not in the public interest or consistent with the balance of convenience can be contrasted with bolder approaches taken by many supra-national courts that tend to focus on the need to prevent irreparable harm to rights. At the same time, supra-national courts generally limit their grant of interim remedies to a few most basic rights, often raised by impending executions or deportations. Supra-national courts also do not generally inquire into the merits of the case for fear of appearing to pre-judge the trial on the merits. Domestic courts, especially those in the United States, are more inclined to engage in merits-based review.

In the next section, it will be suggested that both domestic and supra-national courts should apply the common irreparable harm requirement with increased attention to the merits of the claim that human rights will be violated. This will broaden the claims that can be recognized for interim relief but also intensify the judicial scrutiny of them.

3.3 Irreparable Harm and Merits-Based Review

A critical and controversial element in granting interim relief is the degree to which an applicant has to establish that rights will be infringed. Too demanding a test will place an impossible burden on applicants. Too easy a test may force courts ultimately to deny relief not on the basis of judgements about the merits but on the basis that interim relief is not in the public interest.

110 *South African Informal Traders Forum and Others* v. *City of Johannesburg and Others; South African National Traders Retail Association* v. *City of Johannesburg and Others*, [2014] ZACC 8.

111 Ngwako Raboshakga, "The Separation of Powers in Interim Interdict Applications" (2014) 5 *Constitutional Ct. Rev.* 366.

3.3.1 *The Need for a Public Law Approach*

Writing in the common law context, Douglas Laycock has expressed scepticism about the idea that courts will order interim remedies to protect applicants from irreparable harm. He suggests that in most cases, courts balance the risk of irreparable harm to the applicant against the risk of irreparable harm to the defendant in granting the relief.[112] Leaving aside whether such an approach is desirable in private law, it should be avoided in human rights law. In private law, applicants and defendants are individuals who, as Laycock recognizes, can be said to suffer irreparable harm. Undertakings by plaintiffs to pay damages caused should the interim relief be overturned on the merits often play an important role. Many private law disputes boil down to money. Human rights cases do not.[113]

In public law, the defendant will generally be governments. As such, it will often be unfair to require applicants to pay the damages that interim relief may cause to governments should the applicant eventually lose on the merits. The harm to the government and the public interest will be difficult to calculate. If calculated, the large sums will deter most from seeking interim relief. To be sure, governments and those they represent can be harmed by the grant of interim relief, but they will rarely suffer irreparable harm from one judicial act. As suggested above, it is better to conceive of the harms suffered by governments as harms to the public interest.

3.3.2 *The Importance of Irreparable Harm*

Although irreparable harm is often the sole focus in supra-national courts,[114] it is only a preliminary factor in domestic law. Nevertheless, domestic courts should avoid any temptation to gloss over the irreparable

[112] Douglas Laycock, *The Death of the Irreparable Injury Rule* (Oxford: Oxford University Press, 1991), pp.121–123.

[113] Jamie Cassels, "An Inconvenient Balance: The Injunction as a Charter Remedy" in Jeffrey Berryman (ed.), *Remedies, Issues and Perspectives* (Thomas Professional Publishing, 1991), pp.299–300.

[114] It is regrettable that Rule 39 of the ECtHR Rules of Court that governs requests for interim relief does not mention irreparable harm but only refers "to the interests of the parties or of the proper conduct of the proceedings before it". As suggested above, the concept of irreparable harm – like the grant of interim remedies in the human rights context – is asymmetrical in the sense that it only benefits applicants who unlike states possess human rights.

harm requirement.[115] It plays a key role in rationing out the use of interim remedies. Irreparable harm has traditionally been associated with harm that cannot be adequately remedied by damages awarded after a full trial. The focus on damages probably reflects the fact that common law tests for interim or interlocutory relief were developed in the private law context. In the human rights context, however, there would be nothing to prohibit evaluating the adequacy of alternative remedies after trial such as declarations, injunctions or declarations of invalidity or incompatibility.

Arguments have been made that there should be a presumption of irreparable harm whenever an applicant for interim relief alleges a violation of a human right. This argument is largely based on the strength of the qualified and absolute immunity rules used in the United States with respect to damages.[116] In my view, a presumption that every alleged violation of human rights constitutes irreparable harm should be rejected. Some human rights, especially those relating to property rights and economic loss, may not result in irreparable harm. Even in other contexts, the risk or imminence of irreparable harm may be so remote or speculative that courts should conclude that the applicant has not established irreparable harm. Many procedural rights will not be amenable to irreparable harm because of the ability of the state to conduct new procedures in accordance with rights. The irreparable harm requirement should be considered in each case in light of the purposes of the particular human right.

Courts should only take the risk of ordering interim relief before a full trial on the merits when they are faced with a significant risk of irreparable harm. The Supreme Court of Canada has been generous, perhaps too generous, in concluding that there was a risk of irreparable harm in cases under the *Canadian Charter of Rights and Freedoms*. In the Court's three leading cases,[117] it concluded that corporate applicants had

[115] But see *PT* v. *Alberta*, 2019 ABCA 158 at paras 69, 98 where the Alberta Court of Appeal avoided deciding the question of irreparable harm because it was difficult and speculative, and moved on to decide that the balance of convenience did not favour the grant of relief.

[116] Beatrice Franklin, "Irreparability, I Presume? On Assuming Irreparable Harm for Constitutional Violations in Preliminary Injunctions" (2014) 45 *Colum. Hum. Rts. Rev.* 362.

[117] *R. J. R. Macdonald Inc.* v. *Canada (Attorney General)*, [1994] 1 SCR 311; *Manitoba (A.G)* v. *Metropolitan Stores*, [1987] 1 SCR 11; *143471 Quebec Inc.* v. *Quebec (Attorney General)*, [1994] 2 SCR 311.

established a risk of irreparable harm that was "not susceptible or difficult to be compensated in damages" even though in two cases, the harm was financial in nature and in the third it related to diminished expectations of privacy. Lower Canadian courts have taken a more demanding approach to the irreparable harm requirement. For example, they have found no irreparable harm when protesters could still protest,[118] where restrictions on postering were applied fairly[119] and where doctors who had their fees reduced should be able to obtain damages if successful on the merits.[120]

3.3.3 *Merits-Based Review and the Strength of the Applicant's Case*

If courts take the irreparable harm requirement seriously, they may also often find themselves taking a harder look at the merits of allegations that the applicant's rights will be violated.

Borrowing from the private law, courts have frequently followed the *American Cyanamid*[121] test of simply requiring the applicant to advance a claim that "is not frivolous or vexatious: in other words that there is a serious issue to be tried". This test is compatible with the open-ended nature of many human rights. Yet, it can result in implausible rights claims being entertained as a candidate for interim relief.

Despite this lenient test, domestic courts have not hesitated to engage in merit-based reviews of the strength of a case at the interim relief stage. This follows from the common sense observation that courts should be more willing to grant interim relief in a case where they believe that the applicant has a 75 per cent likelihood of succeeding on the merits compared to a 25 per cent likelihood.[122] For example, in the *Factortame* case, Lord Bridge of the House of Lords justified a decision to grant interim relief restraining a British fishing restriction as violating EU law on the basis that "the most logical course in seeking a decision least likely to occasion injustice is to make the best prediction we can of

[118] *Vancouver (City)* v. *Zhang*, 2009 BCCA 210 at para 9; *Canadian Civil Liberties Association* v. *Toronto Police Service*, 2010 ONSC 3525 additional reasons 2010 ONSC 3698 (no irreparable harm to freedom of expression because other ways to protest).

[119] *Vezina* v. *Scarborough (City)* (1990), 1 MPLR (2d) 22 (Ont. H.C.J.); but see *Morrison* v. *Winnipeg (City)* (1988), 55 Man.R. (2d) 288 (C.A.) for interim injunction when by-law against posters used to single out anti-free trade posters.

[120] *British Columbia Society of Eye Physicians* v. *British Columbia*, 2018 BCSC 1923.

[121] *American Cyanamid Co.* v. *Ethicon*, [1975] AC 396, 407–408.

[122] Sharpe, "Interim Remedies and Constitutional Rights", 14.

the final outcome and to give to that prediction decisive weight in resolving the interlocutory issue".[123] My only reservation about *Factortame* is that the plaintiffs who wished to register to fish might possibly have been able to obtain damages if they succeeded on the merits in establishing that UK law breached EU law. A more generous approach to granting damages should limit the need for interim relief. Many of the economic harms suffered, especially by corporations, can be compensated for by damages. As such, they should not routinely be characterized as irreparable.[124]

Similarly, many recent US Supreme Court decisions on interim relief have effectively decided the issue on the merits of rights claims.[125] The Canadian courts have also, on occasion, engaged in merits-based review but generally only in such urgent situations where "the result of the interlocutory motion will in effect amount to a final determination of the merits".[126] One example is a famous case where the Court overturned an injunction obtained by a man to prevent his former partner from obtaining an abortion.[127] In this case, the Court devoted its attention almost exclusively to the merits, concluding that human rights laws did not support either the rights of the man or the foetus in the abortion context.

Increased attention to the merits also means that courts should be less reluctant at the interim stage to grant relief that will effectively be final. In a decision two months before an election, the South African Constitutional Court retained jurisdiction and required the electoral commission to report back to it on steps it has taken to allow prisoners to vote in an election held two months after the decision.[128] This case can favourably be compared to a similar Canadian prisoner voting rights where appellate courts overturned an interlocutory injunction that would have allowed prisoners to vote in a general election.[129] As one judge

123 *R.* v. *Secretary of State for Transport, ex parte Factortame Ltd (No. 2),* [1991] 1 AC 603 at 859.

124 Leubsdorf, "The Standard for Preliminary Injunctions", 552.

125 *Trump* v. *Hawaii,* 138 S.Ct. 2392 (2018); *South Bay United Pentecostal Church* v. *Newsome,* 590 US (2020); *Roman Catholic Diocese of Brooklyn* v. *Cuomo* 592 U.S. (2020).

126 *R. J. R. Macdonald Inc.* v. *Canada (Attorney General),* [1994] 1 SCR 311 at 344.

127 *Tremblay* v. *Daigle,* [1989] 2 SCR 530.

128 *August and Another* v. *Electoral Commission and Others* (CCT8/99), [1999] ZACC 3.

129 *Canada (Attorney General)* v. *Gould,* [1984] 2 SCR 124. The Court eventually ruled that prisoners could vote: *Sauve* v. *Canada,* [2002] 3 SCR 519.

noted in dissent, "the effect of denying immediate enforcement of a probable but fleeting right is to decide irrevocably against the right".[130] As Jamie Cassels has observed: "[t]he fact that the relief claimed is in substance final certainly increases the risks upon judicial error. But it increases that risk for both parties equally. By itself it is neither a reason for nor against granting the relief claimed".[131]

Supra-national courts have been even more reluctant than national courts to engage in merits-based review. Both Eva Rieter[132] and Cameron Miles[133] have argued that international courts should move towards merit-based review at the interim stage. As Rieter notes, linking the interim relief claim to the relevant jurisprudence on the right can make the interim relief decision more persuasive.[134] The ICJ has moved slightly in this direction by requiring that the applicant demonstrate a plausible case.[135] Alas, there is uncertainty about whether this merits-based review is directed merely at the existence of the right or at the specific claim, including whether the right would be violated in the circumstances. The latter should be the focus of the inquiry, especially because it will be relevant to the determination of irreparable harm. As suggested above, the questions of irreparable harm and the merits are closely linked.

There is a danger in the human rights context that applicants will win under the first two parts of the common law test by establishing a non-frivolous claim of rights and a risk of irreparable harm only to lose when these claims are set off against the public interest and the balance of convenience.[136] Both in domestic and supra-national courts, applicants should be encouraged to put forward their strongest case on the merits. Courts should be less reluctant to consider those merits when deciding whether to grant interim relief. A strong case on the merits may be

[130] *Gould* v. *Canada*, [1984] 1 FC 1119 at 1139 (C.A.) rev'd [1984] 2 SCR 124.

[131] Cassels, "An Inconvenient Balance", p.308.

[132] Eva Rieter, "Provisional Measures: Binding and Persuasive?" (2012) *Netherlands Int'l. L. Rev.* 191–196.

[133] Miles, "Provisional Measures and the 'New' Plausibility".

[134] Rieter, *Preventing Irreparable Harm*, p.195.

[135] *Application of the Convention on the Prevention and Punishment of the Crime of Genocide* (*The Gambia* v. *Myanmar*), Request for the Indication of Provisional Measures, Order of 23 January 2020.

[136] Interim Remedies and Constitutional Rights, 22. Sharpe suggests that this often amounts to a de facto assumption that the challenged law or executive action is constitutional, something that the Canadian courts have suggested is not proper given its constitutional Bill of Rights. For an observation that interim relief for Indigenous rights is often difficult to obtain, see *Haida Nation* v. *British Columbia (Ministry of Forests)*, [2004] SCR 511 at para 17.

required to justify the court risking providing a remedy before a full trial is possible on the merits. It will be suggested in the next section that the government should have to establish that interim relief is not justified in the public interest or on the balance of convenience.

3.4 The Balance of Convenience and the Role of Proportionality

One of the contributions that proportionality analysis can make to the often quick and even summary decision-making made at the interim remedy stage is to provide structure for the parties' arguments and the judge's reasons. Writing in the South African context, Ngwako Raboshakga has commented that the "balance of convenience test is strikingly similar to the reasonableness test that applies in socio-economic rights cases". Raboshakga elaborates that both tests allow for the consideration of "all relevant factors (i.e. a proportionality exercise)" and "both tests allows courts to consider the constitutional rights at stake".[137] Cameron Miles has observed that proportionality is a matter of "common sense" because "a balanced order for interim relief that is not unduly burdensome enhances the institutional legitimacy of an international court or tribunal and increases the likelihood of compliance".[138] None of these commentators, however, systemically outlines how the various elements of proportionality analysis can be applied when determining balance of convenience or the public interest.

3.4.1 Onus of Proof and Justification

Once the applicant has established that human rights are at risk of irreparable harm, the state should bear the onus of proving that granting an interim remedy to prevent that harm will be contrary to the balance of convenience or the public interest. This would be a major change from the current law, but one this is consistent with general principles of proportionality. As Aharon Barak has argued, the state is in the best position to produce evidence about the harms to governance and to third parties.[139]

[137] Raboshakga, "The Separation of Powers in Interim Interdict Applications", 371.

[138] Cameron A. Miles, *Provisional Measures Before International Tribunals* (Cambridge: Cambridge University Press, 2017), p.305.

[139] Aharon Barak, *Proportionality: Constitutional Rights and Their Limitations* (Cambridge: Cambridge University Press. 2012), pp.340–370.

3.4.2 *The Need for a Legitimate Objective*

Although the public interest has frequently been considered as a legitimate factor by domestic courts in deciding whether to grant interim relief, the government's objectives in seeking to deny interim relief should be articulated with greater precision than by the evocation of the vague and grand phrase "public interest".

In one (in)famous Canadian case, a trial judge granted an injunction that would have stopped a massive hydroelectric development on James Bay. He reasoned that by flooding their traditional lands, the development would cause irreparable harm to the rights of Cree Indigenous people of the area. Similar to international law judges, the trial judge was reluctant to even consider the balance of convenience, given his findings of a prima facie rights violation and irreparable harm.[140] Alas, the Quebec Court of Appeal stayed and then overturned the injunction on the crudely majoritarian grounds that the development was in "the interests of Quebec ... The public and general interests of the people of Quebec are thus opposed to the interests of some thousand of its inhabitants. It is our view that at this stage of the proceedings, the two interests are beyond comparison".[141] Such reasoning can be criticized as vague, majoritarian, colonial and even racist. What was really at stake was the social interests in economic and energy development. Only when such objectives are clearly considered and not couched in the vague, inflated and emotive terms of the national or public interest can judges consider whether there are ways to reconcile particular social interests with rights.

As a first step in applying proportionality reasoning, the state interests that will be harmed by the granting of interim relief should be defined with as much precision as possible. Judges should insist that the state's interest be related to the granting of interim relief and not allow the state to re-argue that the right itself was justified for some general purposes. The focus should be on the specific harms that would be caused by granting interim relief.

To be considered in proportionality analysis, social interests should not simply be objections to the right or to granting remedies to protect such rights. Courts should be reluctant to accept the legitimacy of

[140] *Gros-Louis c. Société dé développment de la Baie James* (1973), 8 C.N.L.C 188 (Que. S.C.).

[141] *Gros-Louis c. Société dé développment de la Baie James* (1973), 8 C.N.L.C. 414 (Que. C.A.) at 415.

symbolic and inflated objectives offered by the government including the South African Constitutional Court's vague reference to "separation of powers harms".[142] Overly broad or symbolic objectives tend to be all-or-nothing matters that are not easily amenable to the subsequent steps and evidence based reasoning used in proportionality analysis.[143] Competing rights such as freedom of expression would, however, be a legitimate objective to consider in deciding whether to grant interim relief to protect the right to a fair trial or privacy.

3.4.3 The Need for a Rational Connection

The government should establish a rational connection between its legitimate objective and the harm that interim relief will cause. There will often be no rational connection between inflated and symbolic objectives such as "protecting the economy" and a denial of a particular interim remedy. The rational connection test serves as a check to ensure that there is a real connection between the government's professed objective and the harm that could be caused by the grant of interim relief. The extremes of simply deferring to the government's assertion of a rational connection or requiring a certain demonstration of harms to the government's interest should be rejected at this stage of proportionality analysis.[144]

3.4.4 The Need for Least Restrictive Means

The heart of proportionality reasoning is the need for a proper tailoring or fit between the ends and the means. With respect to remedies, courts should be concerned with the proper fit between the requested remedy and the right claimed to be violated (applicant orientated proportionality) and the proper fit between the government objective and the limit or denial that the government seeks on the interim remedy (defendant orientated proportionality).

[142] *National Treasury and Others* v. *Opposition to Urban Tolling Alliance and Others (Road Freight Association Intervening)*, [2012] ZACC 19 at para 26.

[143] Kent Roach, "Dialogue in Canada and the Dangers of Simplified Comparative Law and Populism" in Geoffrey Sigalet, Gregoire Webber and Rosalind Dixon (eds.), *Constitutional Dialogue* (Cambridge: Cambridge University Press, 2019), pp.290–292, 300–302.

[144] Barak, *Proportionality*, pp.309–310.

With respect to the applicant, the court should be concerned that the interim remedy goes no further than is necessary to protect the applicant's rights from irreparable harm. More tailored relief, including interim relief that only exempts the applicants or a smaller group from the law, may be more proportionate. The Canadian courts have sensibly recognized this when they concluded that it will be easier to justify interim relief that exempts small numbers from a law than interim relief that would suspend the law for all.[145] The Canadian distinction between less intrusive exemptions and more intrusive suspensions of the law should be administered in a purposive manner to maximize the protection of vulnerable minorities.

The majority of the Quebec Court of Appeal took a formalistic approach to this issue in a recent case where it denied an interlocutory stay of legislation that would prohibit teachers and other public servants from wearing religious symbols. The Court of Appeal accepted evidence that this would cause irreparable harm to women who because of their religious beliefs wear a hijab. The majority claimed that a stay would suspend the law while downplaying its effects on minorities. A dissenting judge would have granted interim relief stressing that it would protect only small numbers from irreparable harm pending a full trial.[146] In Chapter 4, Section 4.3.3, it will be seen that when determining remedies, courts do not allow the form of legislation to dictate their remedial choices. By similar reasoning, courts should not conclude that an interim stay of a law that targets minorities is a more intrusive suspension case. If the purpose or effect the law is to single out minorities than an interim remedy should be characterized as a less intrusive exemption.

In the United States, there is a debate about whether interim injunctions should be national in scope. Justices Gorsuch and Thomas have opposed nation-wide injunctions.[147] They rely on the work of Professor Bray, who has argued against national injunctions on the basis of the history of American courts in granting injunctions that only apply to the immediate parties.[148] Other American commentators propose a less

[145] *Manitoba (A.G)* v. *Metropolitan Stores*, [1987] 1 SCR 11.

[146] *Hak c. Procureure générale du Québec*, 2019 QCCA 2145 at paras 68, 86, 115 leave to appeal dismissed; *Ichrak Nourel Hak, et al.* v. *Attorney General of Québec*, 2020 CanLII 26448 (SCC).

[147] *Trump* v. *Hawaii*, 138 S.Ct. 2392 (2018) per Thomas J.; *Department of Homeland Security et al.* v. *New York et al.*, 589 US, 140 S.Ct. 599 (2020) per Gorsuch J.

[148] Samuel Bray, "Multiple Chancellors: Reforming the National Injunction" (2017) 131 *Harv. L. Rev.* 418.

absolutist and rule based approach that depends on the scope of the challenged policy or law.[149] Although a rule against national injunctions is too blunt, it will generally be true that the broader the injunction the more harmful its effects on competing social interests may be. At the same time, attention should be paid to all aspects of proportionality analysis, including the overall balance.

With respect to the defendant, the court should be concerned about the fit between the legitimate interests that the government claims will be harmed by the remedy and the precise limit or denial of a remedy that the government is attempting to justify. For example, if the government's concerns are its financial interests in terms of costs or revenue, much may depend on the estimated costs of the interim remedy. A narrow interim injunction that only exempts a small number of applicants from an impugned law or policy will harm social interests in the enforcement of that policy less than would an injunction that suspends the enforcement of the law or policy for a wide group of people. In American terms, nation-wide injunctions will generally be more disruptive to state interests than narrower injunctions. At the same time, courts should also recognize that some rights, such as fundamental freedoms and rights to privacy, are designed to protect larger groups of interests.

In some cases, interim relief brings competing rights into play. For example, an injunction to protect privacy or fair trial rights may compete with freedom of expression. Competing rights are obviously important and legitimate objectives that can limit remedies. At the same time, courts should not make judgements on the abstract basis that one right inevitably prevails over another. They should strive for practical ways to reconcile the competing rights.[150]

Proportionality analysis seeks to find compromises that accommodate rights and remedies with competing interests. For example in a labour picketing case, the Supreme Court of Canada upheld an injunction against picketing court houses on the basis that the result was "wholly proportional to the objective of the order".[151] The United States Supreme Court in 2017 similarly exempted foreign nationals with connections to the United States from an early version Trump's travel ban as part of an

[149] Michael T. Morley, "De-Facto Class Actions? Plaintiff- and Defendant-Oriented Injunctions in Voting Rights, Election Law and Other Constitutional Cases" (2016) 39 *Harv. J. L. & Pub. Pol'y.* 487.

[150] *Dagenais* v. *Canadian Broadcasting Corporation*, [1994] 3 SCR 835.

[151] *B.C.G.E.U.* v. *British Columbia (Attorney General)*, [1989] 2 SCR 214 at para 72.

"appropriate balance of the equities".[152] A broader injunction that applied to other places or other people would likely have been more difficult to justify.

3.4.5 *Overall Balance*

The overall balance stage allows the court's understanding of the irreparable harm faced by the applicant to be compared with the estimated harms that the remedy will cause to the state and third-party interests. The open-ended nature of the overall balance stage of proportionality reasoning fits well with the recognized discretionary nature of remedial decision making, especially with respect to the equitable award of injunctions.[153] It also recognizes that the various parts of the test for granting interim injunctions are not watertight compartments and that they interact.

Courts should place considerable emphasis on the irreparable harm that the applicant seeks to avoid. This can counter the argument of critics that "proportionality is a one way street: it is used to protect defendants against disproportionate remedies, but plaintiffs do not receive comparable protection".[154] The overall balance stage allows the court to take a second, more searching look at the degree to which the requested remedy will harm both parties.

At this stage, courts should no longer be satisfied with a rational connection or even a tight fit between the limit requested on the remedy and the objective or right. Instead, they should explore the impact of the interim remedy on the governmental objective. This should then be compared to the harmful effects of not granting interim relief on the applicant.

Reconceiving determinations of the balance of convenience as an exercise in proportionality analysis can assist in recognizing the special status of human rights, as well as the special demands placed on governments to justify irreparable harm to human rights. Proportionality principles can bring greater structure and transparency to the often quick and

[152] *Trump et al.* v. *International Refugee Assistance Project et al.*, 137 S.Ct. 2080, 2087–2088 (2017). Justice Thomas with Justices Alito and Gorsuch dissenting would have allowed the ban to apply to all foreign nationals.

[153] Laycock, *The Death of the Irreparable Injury Rule*, p.113.

[154] Tracy A. Thomas, "Proportionality and the Supreme Court's Jurisprudence of Remedies" (2007) 59(1) *Hastings L. J.* 73, 98.

abbreviated decision-making utilized when deciding whether to grant interim relief. It can also provide litigants with a better idea of the relevant issues in deciding whether to grant interim relief.

3.4.6 *The Provisional Nature of Judgements about Proportionality*

Some may suggest that proportionality is fact intensive and that courts at the interim stage do not have the full factual record. Proportionality would be impossible to apply in ex parte cases where the government is not represented and does not have an opportunity to articulate its concerns about the granting of the remedy. In such cases, courts should focus on irreparable harm, but subsequently allow the government to make the case that the interim relief ordered is disproportionate.

Fortunately, decisions about interim remedies can be changed when new evidence is presented or when conditions have changed. In some cases, the full costs to competing social interests of an interim remedy will only become apparent after it has been granted. Conversely, the inadequacy of an interim remedy in preventing irreparable harm may also become apparent. This may justify an expansion of the interim relief. In Section 3.5 of this chapter, it will be suggested that interim remedies play an important role in the two-track remedial process, in part because they normalize the court's continued retention of jurisdiction, which has often been seen as problematic at the stage of devising final remedies.

3.5 Towards a Two-Track Approach

3.5.1 *Interim Relief as First-Track Individual Relief*

Interim remedies to protect small numbers of applicants from irreparable harm to their rights should be characterized as a first-track individual remedy where courts should be prepared to play a dominant role. In this respect, it is significant that a number of international courts, including the ICJ and the ECtHR, have asserted their power to award interim remedies as an incident of their power to decide the case and of the right of an applicant to bring the case. International courts have frequently stressed that interim remedies are required for a court to properly decide a dispute. This suggests that interim remedies are an essential attribute of a court. Courts should thus play an active role at the interim remedy stage. They should be less concerned about the limits placed on them by the separation of powers than when devising final remedies especially systemic remedies. Courts should recognize that a refusal to grant interim remedies can undermine both the promise of human rights and their role as courts.

Interim remedies should be seen as a first-track court-dominated remedy in part because they are not meant to resolve the larger dispute. They leave open the issue of any systemic or permanent remedy, including the possibility that the parties may agree to resolve their dispute without going to trial. Both Lon Fuller and Abram Chayes recognized the value of negotiation between the parties in dealing with the complex problems presented by polycentric issues. Yet, neither theorist examined interim remedies – perhaps because of the tendency at the time to dismiss such remedies as a mere procedural device. But had they done so, they might have seen interim remedies as a way for the court to contribute to ongoing dialogues between the parties that include negotiation and mediation. The courts can attempt to even unequal bargaining power by ensuring that the impending exercise of state power does not effectively cause irreparable harm and frequently end the dispute.

As a first-track remedy, interim relief should not attempt to do too much. In one case, the IACtHR was likely too ambitious when dealing with the grave systemic problem of people displaced by internal conflict in Colombia when it ordered, as an interim remedy, that the state provide the necessary conditions for their return.[155] Such a goal is better suited to systemic relief ordered after a trial on the merits. The same may often be true of the San Jose court's tendency to frame interim relief in general terms. This leaves the state with a wide margin of appreciation. It allows the details of interim relief to be negotiated between the parties. While these are all good techniques to achieve sustainable systemic relief, the focus at the interim remedy stage should simply be the prevention and minimization of irreparable harm. Given the stakes, the court may need to be specific about what is prohibited or required.

3.5.2 Property Rules and Restitution

As Judge Keller and Cedric Marti have argued, granting interim relief in appropriate cases can ensure that the restitution of the rights is truly

[155] *Peace Community of San José de Apartadó* v. *Colombia* (2000), Order of Provisional Measures, Inter-Am. Ct. H.R (Ser. C), (24 November 2000) at *Considering* para 8.

possible.[156] The International Law Commission's principles on state responsibility contemplate monetary compensation as a second-best remedy when restitution is not possible or disproportionate.[157] To be sure, there may be cases where the order of interim relief may be disproportionate. As suggested above, this should be established by the state. It should not be masked in vague conclusions that the public interest or the balance of convenience does not support the grant of interim relief.

The grant of interim relief is supported by the idea that human rights are often more akin to what Calabresi and Melamed describe as property rules that demand injunctive protection than they are to liability rules that only require the assessment of damages after a breach.[158] Damages may be an adequate remedy for some violations of human rights especially when the harms are pecuniary.[159] There may also be less drastic but more effective remedies than interim relief for violations of procedural rights including new procedures. But often, there may be no alternative to interim relief.

3.5.3 Interim Relief Should Not Be Seen as Extraordinary

The important role contemplated for interim remedies in my two-track approach might be the most radical change suggested in this book, both with respect to international and domestic human rights law. Writing in 1994, Judge Bergenthal stressed the exceptional nature of interim relief. He warned that broader use of interim measures could imperil the authority of supra-national courts and compliance with their judgements. In his view, the effectiveness of interim remedies depended on "their shock value" and "effect on public opinion", which "will determine whether or not the State will comply with the decision".[160] Since that time, however, the use of interim remedies by international courts has increased. Indeed, Judge Cançado Trindade has written that in the last

156 Helen Keller and Cedric Marti, "Reconceptualizing Implementation: The Judicialization of the Execution of the European Court of Human Rights Judgments" (2015) 26 *Eur. J. Int'l. L.* 4.

157 James Crawford, *The International Law Commission's Principles on State Responsibility: Introduction, Text and Commentaries* (Cambridge: Cambridge University Press), p.509.

158 Calabresi and Melamed, "Property Rules and Liability Rules".

159 But see *infra* Chapter 9, Section 9.2.1, for a discussion of the importance of a distinct parcel of land to many Indigenous peoples.

160 Burgenthal, "Interim Measures in the Inter-American Court of Human Rights", p.93.

two decades, interim remedies have become an autonomous international legal regime to protect the vulnerable. Part of this important evolution has been an increase in hearings and judgements about interim remedies. As Judge Bergenthal noted, hearings and reasoned judgements are necessary to give provisional measures "a solemnity that enhance[s] the chances of compliance and enables the Court to better assess the need for such measures".[161]

Perhaps even more than supra-national courts, domestic courts see interim remedies as extraordinary. As human rights conditions deteriorate, however, interim relief will become more important. Many of the legal battles waged against the Trump administration have been fought through interim remedies. While Judge Bergenthal and many domestic judges seem to see interim remedies as a "wasting power",[162] as Owen Fiss has suggested, they should be seen as "muscle" that will gain strength with more use. Increased use of interim remedies could make rights and remedies more meaningful in the lives of those whose rights are threatened by impending censorship, torture, destruction of the environment, state violence and discrimination.

A more aggressive judicial approach to interim remedies carries risks. Judges worry that they will lose legitimacy when their decisions and especially their injunctions are not obeyed. But perhaps judges should be less concerned about reserving interim remedies for truly shocking situations. The occasional lack of compliance by governments with an interim injunction will have a shock value. It will also confirm that courts are trying their best to protect rights and ensure that those whose rights are violated have meaningful remedies.

The idea articulated by Judge Bergenthal that interim remedies must remain exceptional continues to influence both international and domestic courts. For international courts, the exceptional nature of interim relief is seen in the tendency only to order such remedies in the face of urgent threats to life and health. Although this preferred rights approach may be a defensible "emergency room triage" done by supra-national courts with inadequate resources,[163] it is not optimal. Domestic courts have been truer to the expansive nature of human rights. They have considered requests for interim remedies with respect to a broader range

161 Ibid. at 94.

162 Owen Fiss, *The Civil Rights Injunction* (Bloomington: Indiana University Press, 1979), p.82.

163 Rieter, "Provisional Measures", 165, 177.

of human rights. This may reflect that they are often better resourced than supra-national courts and that they only grant interim relief when it is consistent with the public interest. In any event, all courts should consider interim remedies to protect all human rights, not only the most basic human rights.

Many domestic courts continue to view interim remedies as exceptional in part because they continue to view mandatory orders or injunctions as exceptional. As Owen Fiss has argued, however, the preference against injunctions must be examined in light of the substance of the claim of particular human rights.[164] Professor Fiss argues that injunctions should be the preferred remedy for enforcing the equality rights of groups. Similar arguments could, however, be made about other rights that protect the intangible values of liberty and dignity. This substantive approach recognizes the asymmetry of rights in the public law context, something that is generally not the case in private law.

3.5.4 *The Importance of Irreparable Harm*

Domestic courts can learn from supra-national courts that allow the irreparable harm requirement to do the heavy lifting in decision-making about interim remedies. Irreparable harm should be defined by what is known about the circumstances faced by the applicant and by the purposes and interests that the human right in question is meant to protect. The court should also evaluate the adequacy of what remedies will be available after trial if an interim remedy is not granted. In Chapter 5, Section 5.2, we will see that damages awards can be precluded by qualified and absolute immunities. Even when ordered, they are often quite low. In some cases, they risk trivializing and monetizing the important non-pecuniary values protected by human rights. In deciding whether to order interim remedies, judges should take a more realistic and critical look at whether damages would truly be an adequate alternative remedy.

3.5.5 *The Possibility of Error*

Owen Fiss, who is otherwise a champion of injunctive relief, warned that judgements about the future are "treacherous [and] fraught with

[164] Owen Fiss, *The Civil Rights Injunction*, p.14.

error".[165] His warnings about lack of process are well taken with respect to interim injunctions that are decided without giving the state an opportunity to be heard. However, they discount the fact that judges who issue interim injunctions can always re-assess the case in light of new evidence and changed circumstances as presented by the parties.

The state should have the resources to establish harms that will be caused by an interim remedy. An interim remedy will also give the state an incentive to collect and publish information about the costs of granting interim relief. Although the possibility of error increases when remedies are issued at the interim stage, courts can respond to new evidence. When necessary, courts can re-shape or even terminate the interim remedy.

Although they are a first-track individual remedy designed to prevent irreparable harm to rights, interim remedies can have positive dialogic effects. For example, many interim remedies issued by supra-national courts relate to preventing execution or extraditions. These individual orders are often effective in securing assurances from states that these results will not occur, even though they involve complex matters of prosecutorial discretion, penal policies and foreign affairs. When courts do their job of protecting people from irreparable harm to their rights, they may often find that states do their job in making necessary and sometimes complex arrangements that allow the state to discharge various obligations while also respecting rights. In Chapter 9, Section 9.2.1, it will be suggested that interim remedies are one of the most important judicial remedies to enforce Indigenous rights. They can address power imbalances while creating incentives for agreements based on free and informed Indigenous consent.

3.5.6 Interim Remedies as a Model for Other Remedies

Many concepts and practices developed in the interim remedy context may prove invaluable in administering second-track systemic relief after a full trial on the merits. Interim relief can help legitimize and normalize judicial retention of jurisdiction over a case that domestic courts too often view as problematic. It can also serve as a template for when courts should intervene in the systemic remedial phrase so as to prevent irreparable harm to vulnerable individuals and groups. It will be suggested in

[165] Ibid., p.80.

Chapter 4, Section 4.2.5, that courts should borrow from interim remedies by paying particular attention to the risk of irreparable harm to discrete individuals and groups when suspending declarations of invalidity.

Although courts should often defer to the parties and other institutions to develop systemic remedies in the two-track approach, it will be suggested in Chapters 7–9 that courts should be prepared to intervene during these longer systemic processes to prevent irreparable harm. For example, courts may be able to justify ordering that a specific prisoner receive needed medical care even while they pursue longer term systemic reforms. Similarly, they may prevent the eviction of people even as they engage with the government about better housing in the future. Interim remedies are first-track remedies that allow courts to order remedies to prevent irreparable harm to rights. They focus on immediate dangers that the court can prevent and as such are distinct from more complex second track systemic relief.

3.5.7 Non-Compliance and Remedial Failure

Those who see law as a positivistic system of commands may be sceptical about the recent increase in the use of interim remedies in international law. They will accurately note that some interim remedies, such as the ICJ's famous decision ordering the United States not to execute a German national, are not obeyed.[166] Interim remedies from the ECtHR have also been breached and the Court has awarded damages for such breaches.[167] Critics of interim remedies might argue that courts have overstepped their authority in the absence of a full and final ruling of the merits. Orders that are not obeyed may harm the legitimacy and reputation of the courts.

[166] *LaGrand Case (Germany* v. *United States of America)*, Request for the Indication of Provisional Measures, Order of 3 March 1999 Provisional Measures, ICJ Reports 1999, at 9.

[167] *Paladi* v. *Moldava* [GC], No. 39806/05, ECHR 10 March 2009. In one case where an applicant who received interim measures could not be located, a majority of the Grand Chamber held that it did not have enough information to find Turkey in breach of Art. 3., *Mamatkulov and Askarov* v. *Turkey* [GC], Nos. 46827/99 and 46951/99, ECHR 15 December 2004 at para 77. Three judges in dissent would have found a violation and, as Eva Reiter has suggested, the state should at least have a burden to demonstrate that rights were not violated. Rieter, *Preventing Irreparable Harm*, p.1063.

The interactionalist[168] and dialogic[169] approach taken in this book, however, situates failure to comply with interim remedies in the larger context of frequent remedial failure and the inevitably iterative nature of the difficult process of ensuring compliance with human rights. Interim measures can be valuable even when breached. One researcher has documented 102 deaths that were violations of provisional measures ordered by the IACtHR between 1987 and 2009. At the same time, she also calculates that there were a total of 19,023 beneficiaries of the Court's interim measures during this time. Trinidad and Tobago executed a person in defiance of an interim measure and eventually withdrew from the Court's jurisdiction. At the same time, however, Mexico also released a long-time prisoner just before the Court held a public hearing on his request for interim measures.[170] Paraguay responded to one interim measure with Presidential and Ministerial visits to a psychiatric hospital, and addressed its inhumane conditions.[171]

Interim remedies are risky – both for the court and the applicant. But the promise of human rights is worth the risk of failure. Courts should not be deterred from issuing interim relief simply because their orders are not always obeyed. A breach of an interim order can crystallize and publicize a flagrant human rights violation. It sends warnings to us all when governments are prepared to violate rights and flout the rule of law. Interim remedies can result in spectacular remedial failure. But they can also result in spectacular remedial success that literally saves lives and makes rights meaningful.

What should a court do when a state breaches an interim measure? The optimal approach to breaches depends on the context. They can legitimately differ from court-to-court and case-to-case. Some commentators have been critical of the IACtHR for not holding that breach of interim measures is a separate violation.[172] The award of damages for

[168] Jutta Brunée and Stephen Toope, *Legality and Legitimacy in International Law: An Interactional Account* (Cambridge: Cambridge University Press, 2010).

[169] Abram Chayes and Antonia Handler Chayes, "On Compliance" in Lisa L. Martin and Beth A. Simmons (eds.), *International Institutions: An International Organization Reader* (Cambridge and London: The MIT Press, 1993).

[170] Pasqualucci, *The Practice and Procedure of the Inter-American Court of Human Rights*, p.295.

[171] Case 60, Inter-Am Ct. H.R. (2003) cited by Jo M. Pasqualucci, "Interim Measures in International Human Rights: Evolution and Harmonization" (2005) 38 *Vand. J. Transna' L.* 1, 45–46.

[172] Burbano-Herrera and Haeck, "Letting States off the Hook?".

breach of an interim remedy risks trivializing a breach when someone has been executed or deported in violation of the interim remedy. Payment of such damages may also suggest that the state has somehow redeemed itself. Interim injunctions enforce rights from irreparable harm. They should not be reduced to liability rules that when breached only require the payment of damages.

More important than court-ordered sanctions are the persuasive and public reasons where the court justifies its order for or against interim remedies.[173] As Eva Rieter has suggested, interim measures in international law only employ the court's "authority and persuasion" and this makes fully reasoned judgements in admittedly urgent situations very important.[174] As the Chayes' recognized, naming and shaming and reputational harms are often more critical than actual enforcement of international law.[175] There is also some evidence that naming and shaming are important in domestic law.[176]

Judge Lauterpacht of the ICJ has suggested that an early trial on the merits may be an appropriate response to a breach of provisional measures.[177] This can also bring more attention to any breach of interim measures. Interim remedies even when breached – perhaps especially when breached – can be part of a continual process of publicity and persuasion that will hopefully lead to greater awareness and compliance in the future. In a world with pervasive remedial failure, a publicized and criticized breach of an interim remedy is alas sometimes the best that can be done.

3.6 Conclusion

Interim remedies are perhaps the most important remedy studied in this book. They involve existential questions about the purposes of courts and the meaning of human rights. They should be seen as a first-track individual remedy designed to protect specific litigants from suffering

[173] Haeck, Burbano-Herrera and Zwaak, "Non-Compliance with a Provisional Measure", 57.

[174] Rieter, *Preventing Irreparable Harm*, pp.1106–1107.

[175] Abram Chayes and Antonia Handler Chayes, "Compliance without Enforcement: State Behaviour under Regulatory Treaties" (1991) *Negot. J.* 311, 323–324.

[176] Charles Epp, *Making Rights Real* (Chicago: University of Chicago Press, 1993).

[177] *Application of the Convention on the Prevention and Punishment of the Crime of Genocide (Bosnia and Herzegovina* v. *Serbia and Montenegro), Counter-Claims,* Order of December 1997, [1997] ICJ Rep 243, 284 at para 18 (Sep. Op. Lauterpacht J.).

irreparable harm to their rights. Interim remedies are an inherent part of a court's power to decide a dispute and of the ability of a person to petition the court for an effective remedy.

The irreparable harm requirement is critical. It is found in both domestic and supra-national law. Although there is a temptation to assume that any violation of a human right will cause irreparable harm, it should be resisted. Courts should realistically assess the adequacy of remedies that will be available after trial should an interim remedy not be ordered. Courts should pay attention to the underlying purpose of each human right as well as the adequacy of damages or other alternative remedies. They should take a principled approach that focuses on these matters, rather than asserting either a strong discretion to grant or refuse a remedy or a rule-based approach based on specific factual categories.

Supra-national courts should re-examine their tendency to only order interim remedies in extreme cases such as impending execution, torture or deportation. They can learn from domestic courts that are more willing to order interim remedies for a broader range of rights. Domestic courts should recognize that a private law approach to interim remedies will not effectively protect human rights. Private law concepts of preserving the status quo and higher standards for mandatory relief are not helpful. They fail to recognize that human rights are part of the status quo and sometimes require positive action.

All courts should pay increased attention to the merits of the applicant's case. A lenient approach to the merits often results in potentially weak claims of rights violations being weighed against social interests at the balance of convenience stage. The American courts seem more willing than Commonwealth courts to take a harder look at the merits at the interim stage. Some questions of rights involve matters of interpretation and even proportionality that can be resolved without a full trial. In all cases, applicants should put the best case forward. Courts should also recognize that they can revise decisions on interim relief if new evidence becomes available. Interim remedies can help normalize the retention of jurisdiction. Indeed, the ICJ's recent Myanmar decision demonstrates how courts might require parties to report back after issuing an interim remedy.

Courts should apply proportionality principles that require the state to justify denial or diminution of interim relief on the basis of important and legitimate social interests as opposed to crude majoritarian interests. The applicant's remedial request should not be taken as an all-or-nothing proposition. More tailored and less drastic interim relief should be considered. This should not result in categorical rules against national injunctions in the United States, suspensions of impugned laws or policies in Canada or granting relief that will give the applicant a victory in the final case. What is required is a more nuanced examination of how the scope of the relief will harm or accommodate competing interests and rights. Courts should be particularly attentive to the overall balance. This will require comparisons of the adverse effects of granting interim relief on governments and others as compared to the adverse effects on the applicant of not granting such relief. The determination of such an overall balance may lead courts back towards a more substantive approach that more deeply examines the merits of the right claims.

4

Remedies for Laws That Violate Human Rights

4.1 Introduction

There are a surprising variety of remedies for laws that violate human rights. They include newer remedies such as suspended declarations of invalidity and non-binding declarations of incompatibility. The latter demonstrate that remedies that are "purely exhortatory" and "non-coercive"[1] are no longer limited to supra-national law. The Australian High Court has dismissed the declaration of incompatibility as a non-judicial remedy.[2] The domestic and especially the international impact of such declarations should not, however, be so easily dismissed. The need for legislatures to change laws when necessary to respect and implement rights is recognized in most international human rights laws.

Courts have used strong interpretative remedies in recognition of the limits of either facial declarations of invalidity or declarations of incompatibility. The United States Supreme Court effectively did this to allow same-sex marriage.[3] In contrast, the South African Constitutional Court used a suspended declaration of invalidity to provide the legislature with an opportunity to select among different ways to comply with human rights while making clear that same-sex marriage would eventually be available.[4]

The range of remedies for laws that violate human rights means that remedial discretion is no less a reality than with respect to other remedies.[5] As suggested in Chapter 1, Section 1.7,[6] this discretion should be exercised in a principled and transparent manner. In other words, courts should not rely on strong discretion that threatens the meaning of rights or inflexible rules that will dictate remedies that may be inappropriate in particular contexts. An important principle that should inform the exercise of remedial discretion is respect for the roles of courts and legislatures. Courts should respect the role of the legislature in making a wide range of policy choices that are not dictated by the need to respect human

[1] Aruna Sathanapally, *Beyond Disagreement: Open Remedies in Human Rights Adjudication* (Oxford: Oxford University Press, 2012), pp.4, 23.

[2] *Momcilovic* v. *The Queen*, [2011] HCA 34. The Australian High Court has also rejected another remedial innovation that will be examined in this chapter: the use of prospective rulings that depart from the normally retroactive effect of rulings that laws are invalid. *Ha* v. *New South Wales* (1997), [1997] 146 ALR 355 at 371–372 (per Brennan CJ, McHugh, Gummow and Kirby JJ) and at 381 (per Dawson, Toohey and Gaudron JJ).

[3] *Obergefell* v. *Hodges*, 135 S.Ct. 2584 (2015) at 2605.

[4] *Minister of Home Affairs* v. *Fourie and Another*, [2005] ZACC 19.

[5] Eric S. Fish, "Choosing Constitutional Remedies" (2016) 63 *U.C.L.A L. Rev.* 2.

[6] See also Chapter One Section 1.8.

rights.[7] Courts should also respect the purposes of the underlying right and their obligation to provide effective remedies. In this respect, both suspended declarations of invalidity and declaration of incompatibility fail to provide immediate remedies.[8]

Examining the range of remedies that are available for laws that violate human rights can contribute to our understanding of comparative law.[9] In particular, it can break down theoretical dichotomies between what Mark Tushnet identifies as strong and weak forms of judicial review.[10] Although the United States is seen as the paradigm of strong judicial review, its Supreme Court often uses limited "as applied" rulings of invalidity, constitutional exemptions or interpretative remedies as less drastic alternatives to facial invalidation of laws. Strong form judicial review in Canada, Germany and South Africa is sometimes softened by the use of suspended declarations of invalidity. In turn, courts that lack the power to invalidate laws can be driven to strained interpretations of statutes in order to reconcile them with human rights and to provide litigants with effective remedies.[11] Remedies are an important window into the contextual world of judicial review and human rights as they are and not simply as they are understood as a matter of theory.

Consistent with a two-track approach that is attentive to both individual and systemic remedies, courts need to be aware that remedies for laws that violate rights will affect both the litigants before them and others. In some cases, courts can fashion remedies, such as interpretative remedies, that achieve both individual and systemic relief. In other cases, however, difficult choices and trade-offs may have to be made. It may not always be possible to give litigants effective remedies while respecting either the intent of the legislature and/or its ability to make policy decisions.

[7] Ruth Bader Ginsburg, "Some Thoughts on Judicial Authority to Repair Unconstitutional Legislation" (1979) 28 *Clev. St. L. Rev.* 301; *Schachter* v. *Canada* [1992], 2 SCR 679 (SCC).

[8] Bruce Ryder, "Suspending the Charter", 21 *S.C.L.R.* (2d); Tom Hickman, *Public Law After the Human Rights Act* (Oxford: Hart Publishing, 2010); Robert Leckey, "Remedial Practice Beyond Constitutional Text" (2016) 6 *Am. J. Comp. L.* 1.

[9] Leckey, "Remedial Practice Beyond Constitutional Text"; Kent Roach, "Dialogue in Canada and the Dangers of Simplified Comparative Law and Populism" in Geofferey Sigalet, Gregoire Webber and Rosalind Dixon (eds.), *Constitutional Dialogue Rights and Institutions* (New York: Cambridge University Press, 2019).

[10] Kent Roach, "Remedies for Laws That Violate Human Rights" in John Bell et al. (eds). *Public Law Adjudication in Common Law Systems* (Oxford: Hart Publishing, 2016).

[11] *R.* v. *A.*, [2001] UKHL 25.

Conversely, it may not always be possible to respect legislative choices while providing litigants with effective remedies.

The two-track approach helps manage the competing tensions and multiple goals of remedies for laws that violate human rights. Courts that use suspended declarations of invalidity or prospective rulings can respond to "right to a remedy" concerns by exempting the successful litigant so that they receive individual relief.[12] Courts that lack the power to invalidate laws that violate human rights can still attempt to provide litigants who establish that their rights have been violated with some remedy. Even in cases when the two-track structure is impossible to implement, it will still provide a useful guide for identifying either individual or systemic remedial deficits.

4.1.1 Outline of This Chapter

Section 4.2 will outline the practice of courts in dealing with laws that violate human rights. It will start with an examination of the declaration of incompatibility and related supra-national remedies provided by adjudicators that do not have the power to invalidate laws. It will examine a range of interpretative remedies and partial declarations of invalidity, facial declarations of invalidity, suspended declarations of invalidity and prospective rulings. Not all of these remedies will be available in every case, but they underline the range of remedies.

Section 4.3 will examine general principles that should inform remedial discretion. Adjudicators should try to respect the legitimate roles of courts and legislatures. In general, this means that courts should attempt to reconcile the objectives of legislation with human rights. This can justify reading in words that are not present in the statute so long as it advances the general purpose of the legislation and the relevant human rights. Courts should not, however, make policy choices not justified by the interaction between human rights and legislative purposes. There should also be a presumption of fully retroactive relief that will benefit both the litigant and others similarly situated. Governments may be able to justify departures from this principle but courts should still, whenever possible, provide remedies for successful litigants.

[12] *Linkletter* v. *Walker*, 381 US 618 (1965); *Reference Re Remuneration of Judges*, [1998] 2 SCR 443 at para 20; *Corbiere* v. *Canada (Minister of Indian and Northern Affairs)*, [1999] 2 SCR 203 at paras 122–123 (noting general case for exempting applicants from suspended declaration of invalidity to achieve corrective justice but refusing to do so in case involving voting rights that would apply to a larger group).

Section 4.4 will examine how Canadian courts have used the two-track approach in assisted dying cases where they combined a suspended declaration of invalidity that allow Parliament to enact a systemic remedy with court-ordered individual remedies.[13] This approach will be compared to the use of broader interim remedies used in South Africa to govern how the executive applies a law that violates human rights during a suspended declaration of invalidity. Another variation is when the courts establish precise default remedies should the legislature not enact a new law during the suspension.[14] Care should be taken not to trench on the legitimate role of the legislature to make policy choices that are not dictated by the court's interpretation of rights. Finally, this section will discuss the ability of the two-track approach to respond to remedial failure. It will be suggested that it was unfortunate that both UK and European courts failed to provide individual remedies when the UK legislature refused to respond to a ruling that a total ban on prisoner voting could not be justified.[15] Individual remedies play a critical role in recognizing that legislatures may fail to enact new laws that respect human rights.

4.2 Existing Practice: The Range of Remedies

The non-binding declaration of incompatibility is the least intrusive or disruptive remedy for laws that violate human rights, while the facial declaration of invalidity is the most intrusive. Courts can use interpretative remedies, including partial declarations of invalidity and reading in remedies, to make laws consistent with rights both for litigants and all others. "As applied" declarations of invalidity or exemptions only provide remedies for specific litigants. Suspended declarations of invalidity and prospective rulings limit disruption and provide forward-looking remedies but may fail to provide retroactive individual remedies.

[13] *Carter* v. *Canada (Attorney General)*, 2016 SCC 4; *Truchon c. Procureur général du Canada*, 2020 QCSC 772. Another more limited two-track approach would be to allow rights holders to obtain damages for any abuse of rights during a suspended declaration of invalidity as contemplated by the Hong Kong courts. *Koo Sze Yiu and Another* v. *Chief Executive of HKSAR*, [2006] HKCU 1152;

[14] *Minister of Home Affairs* v. *Fourie and Another*, [2005] ZACC 19; *W* v. *Registrar of Marriages*, [2010] HKCU 2118; see Po Jen Yap, "New Democracies and Novel Remedies" (2017) *Public Law* 30.

[15] Jacqueline Hodgson and Kent Roach, "Disenfranchisement as Punishment: European Court of Human Rights, UK and Canadian responses to prisoner voting" (2017) *Public Law* 450.

4.2.1 *The Declaration of Incompatibility*

Non-binding declarations of incompatibility used in the United Kingdom, New Zealand and some Australian states have some resemblance to the non-binding declarations that supra-national adjudicators can make about laws that violate human rights. The New Zealand Supreme Court has recognized that declarations of incompatibility fit into a system involving supra-national adjudication.[16]

4.2.1.1 Lauterpacht and the Declaration of Incompatibility

The declaration of incompatibility is similar to a remedy that the famed international lawyer Hersch Lauterpacht contemplated in 1945 to enforce his proposed International Bill of Rights. In an effort to get jurisdictions that accepted Parliamentary supremacy on board, he proposed that domestic courts would be empowered "to declare that a statute is not in conformity with the Bill of Rights" even though "no immediate *legal* result would attach to any such declaration".[17] He argued that such a remedy would be "by no means nominal. It is of significant political potency in the domestic sphere; it constitutes a starting point for the international procedure of protection and enforcement".[18]

Lauterpacht's support of a non-binding declaration of incompatibility was related to his non-positivist understanding of the rule of law that applied both domestically and internationally. He believed "[t]he fact that the rule of law may break down ... can hardly be regarded as throwing doubt on its effectiveness as an instrument of preserving peace ... Absolute certainty would transform it into a law of natural science". As an international lawyer, Lauterpacht recognized that "[i]n international society the compulsion [of the law] is less direct" than in domestic law and that "frequently the only guarantee of the effectiveness of the legal decision is the impersonal authority of the law".[19] Remedial

16 *Attorney-General* v. *Taylor*, [2018] NZSC 104.

17 Hersh Lauterpacht, *The International Bill of Rights* (Oxford: Oxford University Press, 2014), pp.192–193 (emphasis in original). On the historical roots of the declaration of incompatibility, see Neil Duxbury, "Judicial Disapproval as a Constitutional Technique" (2017) 15 *I Con.* 649.

18 Lauterpacht, *The International Bill of Rights*, p.193.

19 Hersh Lauterpacht, *The Function of Law in the International Community* (Oxford: Oxford University Press, 2011), pp.405–406.

failure was not a complete failure because the courts had at least declared that an injustice had occurred.

For some, including the Australian High Court,[20] non-binding declarations of incompatibility are not a welcome development because they undermine "right to a remedy" reasoning long celebrated in the common law. In the UK, commentators have argued that courts should employ interpretative remedies so that litigants receive real remedies and are not left with a toothless declaration of incompatibility.[21] Such criticisms reveal the weaknesses of declarations of incompatibility in providing first-track individual remedies. That said, they discount that the declaration of incompatibility can, as Lauterpacht contemplated, interact with domestic politics, civil society and supra-national rights adjudication. The fact that remedies are not binding or coercive does not mean that they do not matter.

4.2.1.2 European Court of Human Rights

Donald and Leach caution that the UK's defiance of the prisoner right to vote case should not obscure the UK's high rate of compliance with ECtHR decisions.[22] They conclude that "stridently negative voices should not be permitted to obscure the resilience and achievements of the Convention system in protecting fundamental rights and freedoms over the past half century, in the face of tumultuous political events leading to the dramatic eastwards expansion of the Council of Europe".[23] Another study found that compliance with ECtHR judgements is often delayed but eventually achieved when legislative change is required in member states.[24]

Consistent with respect for both subsidiarity and the separation of powers, the ECtHR is generally deferential when requesting legislative change. For example, in one case involving property rights of landlords

20 *Momcilovic* v. *The Queen*, [2011] HCA 34.

21 Aileen Kavanagh, *Constitutional Review under the UK Human Rights Act* (Cambridge University Press, 2009); Hickman, *Public Law*.

22 See also House of Lords, House of Commons, Joint Committee on Human Rights, "Seventh Report of Session 2014–15" in *Human Rights Judgments*, HL Paper 130, HC 1088 (2015), para 2.12; Courtney Hillebrecht, *Domestic Politics and International Human Rights Tribunals: The Problem of Compliance* (Cambridge: Cambridge University Press, 2014), p.48.

23 Alice Donald and Philip Leach, *Parliaments and the European Court of Human Rights* (Oxford: Oxford University Press, 2016), p.311.

24 Oyvind Stiansen, "Delayed but not Derailed: Legislative Compliance with European Court of Human Rights Judgments" (2019) 23 *Int'l. J. Hum. Rts.* 8, 1241.

that were violated by rent control legislation, the Court stressed that Croatia "should take appropriate legislative and/or other general measures to secure a rather delicate balance … It is not for the Court to specify how the rights of landlords and lessees should be balanced against each other".[25] When the Court sets deadlines, it has some of the same dilemmas as domestic courts that suspend declarations of invalidity. As Judge Sicilianos has commented: "[i]f the time limit is too long the applicants in those cases risk being negatively affected. If it is too short it may prove to be non-realistic and create practical difficulties for the State concerned and for the Committee of Ministers".[26]

4.2.1.3 Inter-American Court of Human Rights

The Inter-American Court of Human Rights (IACtHR) also generally does "not specify the exact means required of the State to meet its international obligations. The State, in its sovereignty, is allowed a margin of appreciation as to what measures it will take".[27] After some initial delay, Chile enacted access to information legislation in response to the Court's judgement calling for such reforms and awarded compensation to environmental activists wrongly denied access to information.[28] Ecuador broadened its habeas corpus remedy after a case in which the Court ordered damages to a wrongly detained person, but also called for legislative change to comply with the Convention.[29] However, there are other cases where states have refused to change their laws, such as Nicaragua's refusal to change its electoral law.[30] Peru also renounced the Court's jurisdiction after a decision calling on it to revise its anti-terrorism and treason laws, but it eventually implemented legislative changes and the Court ended its supervision of the case.[31] Compliance

[25] *Statileo* v. *Croatia*, No. 12027/10 ECHR 10 July 2014 at para 165.

[26] Linos-Alexander Sicilianos, "The Involvement of the European Court of Human Rights in the Implementation of Its Judgments" (2014) 32 *Net. Q. Hum. Rts.* 3, 261.

[27] Jo Pasqualucci, *The Practice and Procedure of the Inter-American Court of Human Rights*, 2nd ed. (Cambridge: Cambridge University Press, 2013), p.216.

[28] *Reyes et al.* v. *Chile*, (2016) 38 *Loy. L.A. Int'l & Comp. L. Rev.* 4, 1186.

[29] *Chaparro Álvarez and Lapo Íñiguez* v. *Ecuador*, (2017) 40 *Loy. L.A. Int'l & Comp L. Rev.* 3, 1451.

[30] *YATAMA* v. *Nicaragua* (2005), (2015) 37 Loy. *L.A. Int'l & Comp. L. Rev.* 4 at paras 258–259, 267. In six subsequent compliance hearings, the Court has found a lack of compliance.

[31] *Loayza Tamayo* v. *Peru* (1998, 1999), (2014) 36 *Loy. L.A. Int'l & Comp. L. Rev.* 6. Peru even for a time withdrew from the Court's jurisdiction to protest these decisions but did subsequently make some amendments to the terrorism law. The Court has ceased

is not perfect, but even supra-national courts are not "transformed from arbiters of rights ... to a form of privileged pressure group"[32] simply because their declarations are not binding.

4.2.1.4 Declarations of Incompatibility under Section 4 of the UK Human Rights Act, 1998

Declarations of incompatibility are often used domestically because of an unwillingness to give unelected courts the power to invalidate laws enacted by elected legislatures. The best-known example is section 4 of the Human Rights Act, 1998. It provides that when it is not possible to interpret legislation in compliance with rights, UK courts may make a declaration that the legislation is incompatible with a Convention right. Such a declaration does not affect the validity, operation or enforcement of the legislation. It is not binding on the parties and damages cannot be awarded if the rights violation is specifically authorized by the legislation.[33] There is a fast track for remedial orders including ones with retrospective effects. Legislation generally applies only prospectively while judicial decisions generally apply retroactively.

Like other remedies, the discretion to make a declaration of incompatibility can only be understood in the context of alternative remedies. The House of Lords opted for a strong interpretative remedy under section 3 of the Human Rights Act, 1998, to preserve the accused's fair trial rights. It stated that a "declaration of incompatibility is a measure of last resort. It must be avoided unless it is plainly impossible to do so. If a clear limitation of convention rights is stated in terms, such an impossibility will arise".[34] Commentators warned that that "the full weight of Parliamentary sovereignty" would fall on litigants who obtained a declaration of incompatibility.[35] There has been an understandable reluctance to use the declaration of incompatibility in criminal cases because it

supervising this part of the judgement: *Castillo Petruzzi et al.* v. *Peru* (1999), (2014) 36 *Loyola* 6, 2349–2350.

32 Hickman, *Public Law*, p.61. Costa Rica in contemplation of an implementation hearing by the IACtHR passed executive decrees but not yet legislation allowing some in viro fertilization. Montserrat Solano Carboni, "The Role of National Human Rights Institutions in Implementing Decisions of the Inter-American System: Three Recent Examples from Costa Rica" (2020) 12 *J. Hum. Rights Pract.* 217.

33 Human Rights Act, 1998 c.42, ss.4(6), 6(2)(a).

34 *R.* v. *A.*, [2001] UKHL 25 at para 55.

35 Ian Leigh and Laurence Lustgarten, "Making Rights Real: The Courts, Remedies, and the Human Rights Act" (1999) 58 *Cambridge L.J.* 3.

provides no immediate individual remedy. The UK courts have been more inclined to use non-binding declarations in public law cases where the litigant would normally be able to enjoy the benefits of any legislative change.[36]

One controversial case involved an attempt by a woman who previously had sex reassignment surgery to have her marriage legally recognized.[37] The House of Lords used a declaration of incompatibility because there was a need for Parliament to address many possible implications of the ruling.[38] Tom Hickman has argued that the Court engaged in what he disparages as "principle-proposing dialogue" in doing so.[39] He suggests that the Court could have made a narrow ruling that would have provided the litigant with a remedy.[40] Aileen Kavanagh has defended the decision as one in which the Court recognized the limits of its expertise and capacity.[41] In response to the declaration of incompatibility and earlier ECtHR decisions indicating the need for flegislative reform,[42] Parliament enacted legislation that created a panel to recognize cases of gender change and addressed other matters such as birth certificates and privacy. Unfortunately, the new law, despite warnings from the Joint Committee on Human Rights, did not have retrospective effect. This meant that Mrs. Bellinger was precluded from having her twenty-year marriage legally recognized.[43] The legislature crafted a systemic remedy, but no individual remedy.

Lord Mance has indicated that when courts make declarations of incompatibility, the court "will be of maximum assistance to Parliament" if it "articulates options" for compliance with human rights[44] There is a danger if courts are overly prescriptive in this regard

[36] Sathanapally, *Beyond Disagreement*, pp.101–102; Rosalind Dixon, "A Minimalist Charter of Rights for Australia?" (2009) 37 *Fed. L. Rev.* 335.

[37] *Bellinger* v. *Bellinger*, [2003] UKHL 21.

[38] Ibid. at para 37.

[39] Hickman, *Public Law*, pp.69–71.

[40] Ibid., pp.91–93; see also Gavin Philipson, "Deference, Discretion and Democracy in the Human Rights Era" (2007) 60 *Curr. Leg. Probl.* 40.

[41] Kavanagh, *Constitutional Review*, p.139.

[42] *Goodwin* v. *UK* (2002), No. 28957/95, 35 EHRR 18, 11 July 2002; *Sheffield and Horshman* v. *The United Kingdom* [GC] (1998), 27 EHRR 163, [1998] ECHR 69.

[43] Gender Recognition Act, 2004 c.7, s.9. On the legislative process, including examples of other laws enacted after declaration of incompatibility that have retroactive effect, see Sathanapally, *Beyond Disagreement*, pp.166–178.

[44] *R (on the application of Nicklinson and another)* v. *Ministry of Justice; R (on the application of AM)* v. *DPP*, [2014] UKSC 38 at paras 204, 314.

that they may short circuit legislative deliberation and creativity.[45] But Aruna Sathanapally and Jeff King have found no evidence in their examination of legislative debates that Parliament has been dominated by judicial reasoning. Sathanapally suggests that the Gender Recognition Act, 2004 was actually more protective of the rights of transsexual people than would have been a narrow decision in favour of Mrs. Bellinger on the facts of her particular case.[46] It will be suggested in Section 4.4 of this chapter that the *Bellinger* case raises tensions between the individual and systemic remedial tracks.

In almost every case, Parliament has responded to a declaration of incompatibility with amending legislation.[47] Jeff King has, however, documented significant delays. The quickest reply came after the *Belmarsh* case. The government rapidly enacted control orders as a counter-terrorism measure. He also finds that many of the legislative replies were made on behalf of marginalized groups such as prisoners, non-citizens, mental health patients and sexual minorities.[48] In many of these cases, there was ECtHR jurisprudence that also supported the case for legislative reform and perhaps the award of damages. The supra-national echoes of the UK declaration of incompatibility distinguish it from similar remedies in Australia and New Zealand. As Baroness Hale has noted, the purpose of the declaration of incompatibility is "to warn Government and Parliament that, in our view, the United Kingdom is in breach of its international obligations"[49] under the European Convention. The UK's possible withdrawal from the Council of Europe and with it, the ECtHR's jurisdiction, would make the declaration of incompatibility a less effective remedy.

[45] Similar concerns will be raised about the use of detailed interim remedies after the use of a suspended declaration of invalidity.

[46] Sathanapally, *Beyond Disagreement*, p.171.

[47] Chintan Chandrachud, *Balanced Constitutionalism Courts and Legislatures in India and the United Kingdom* (Oxford: Oxford University Press, 2017), pp.189–236; Sathanapally, *Beyond Disagreement*, pp.131–164; Christopher Crawford, "Dialogue and Declarations of Incompatibility under Section 4 of the Human Rights Act 1998" (2013) 25 *Denning L. J.* 43.

[48] Jeff King, "Parliament's Role Following Declarations of Incompatibility" in Murray Hunt, Hayley Hooper and Paul Yowell (eds.), *Parliament and Human Rights* (Oxford: Hart Publishing, 2015) pp.169, 179.

[49] *R. (Animal Defenders International)* v. *Secretary of State for Culture, Media and Sport*, [2008] UKHL 15 at para 53; see also Anthony Mason, "Human Rights: Interpretation, Declarations of Inconsistency and the Limits of Judicial Power" (2011) 9 *New Zeal. J. Public & Int'l L.* 1, 11 for similar observations.

The ability to issue a declaration of incompatibility is discretionary. The UK Supreme Court refused to order a second declaration of incompatibility in the prisoner voting rights saga.[50] It also refused to order damages under the EU Charter of Rights and Freedoms on the basis that the applicants, as life prisoners, could have been excluded from voting under more proportionate restrictions on prisoner voting.[51] The ECtHR also refused to award damages for prisoners that continued to be denied the vote[52] as the Committee of Ministers subjected the original 2005 *Hirst* decision[53] to supervision that only ended in 2018 with the unsatisfactory explanation that nothing would (nor ever had) stopped convicted prisoners on leave from custody from voting.[54] Parliament simply refused to respond in any way to the unpopular declaration of incompatibility. Jacqueline Hodgson and I have argued elsewhere that a continued award of damages to prisoners denied the vote may have produced a quicker and more satisfactory result to this case.[55] The award of damages can place pressure on governments and promote continued public debate about the rights of the unpopular.

The ECtHR itself has refused to see the declaration of incompatibility as an effective remedy under Article 13 of the European Convention. In *Burden*,[56] the Grand Chamber indicated that the declaration of incompatibility was not an effective remedy in cases where monetary damage has been caused. It decided that it was premature to conclude that the declaration of incompatibility was an effective remedy in other cases on the basis that it was not yet "so certain" that Parliament would respond to

[50] *R. (on application of Chester)* v. *Secretary of State for Justice*, [2013] UKSC 63.

[51] Ibid. at paras 72–83.

[52] *Greens* v. *United Kingdom* (2011), 53 EHHR 21; *Firth* v. *United Kingdom* (2016), 63 EHHR 25.

[53] *Hirst* v. *United Kingdom* (2005) [GC], No. 74025/01, ECHR 2005-IX.

[54] Execution of the Judgments of the European Court of Human Rights, Five Cases against the United Kingdom, Adopted by the Committee of Ministers on 6 December 2018, Res. CM/ResDH(2018) 467, online: https://hudoc.exec.coe.int/ENG#{"EXECIdentifier":["001-188692"]}

[55] Hodgson and Roach, "Disenfranchisement as Punishment'.

[56] *Burden and Burden* v. *United Kingdom* (2007) [GC], No. 13378/05, 44 EHRR 51, 29 April 2008 at para 40 where the Grand Chamber concluded that "a declaration of incompatibility has been held not to provide an effective remedy because it is not binding on the parties to the proceedings in which it is made and cannot form the basis of an award of monetary compensation". See also House of Lords, House of Commons Joint Committee on Human Rights, "Monitoring the Government's Response to Court Judgments Finding Breaches of Human Rights" (2006–2007) HL 128/HC 728.

every such declaration.[57] It is ironic that a supra-national court that itself lacks the power to invalidate laws would disparage the declaration of invalidity because it is non-binding. The UK practice of responding to declarations of incompatibility is not perfect, either in timing or ensuring that litigants receive the benefits provided by the new legislation retrospectively. But it is not nothing.

4.2.1.5 Judicial Indications of Inconsistency

The UK Supreme Court has used less formal dicta to indicate its concerns that laws against assisted suicide may violate human rights.[58] This was done despite Lady Hale's strong arguments that a declaration of incompatibility would still give Parliament complete freedom about whether or how to respond.[59] Informal indications are "disadvantageous to both litigants and the public" because they provide a "less clear pathway toward legislative change"[60] than the more formal declaration of incompatibility. Indications are susceptible to the criticism that Tom Hickman perhaps extravagantly levelled at formal declarations of incompatibility. That is, they reduce the court to one of many institutions that criticize laws and provide advice to the legislature.[61]

4.2.1.6 The Irish Debate about Declarations of Incompatibility

Section 5 of Ireland's European Convention on Human Rights Act, 2003[62] follows section 4 of the Human Rights Act, 1998, by providing that courts can make a non-binding declaration of incompatibility in cases where it is not possible to interpret legislation as consistent with Convention rights. In a timid recognition of the absence of an individual remedy, however, section 5(4) allows the government to make an ex gratia payment of damages to the successful applicant based on damages that might be awarded by the ECtHR. This allows an individual remedy to be combined with a systemic remedy. The fact that a declaration of incompatibility provides no remedy for the litigant who has established

57 *Burden and Burden* v. *United Kingdom* (2007) [GC], No. 13378/05, 44 EHRR 51, 29 April 2008 at para 43.

58 *R (on the application of Nicklinson and another)* v. *Ministry of Justice; R (on the application of AM)* v. *DPP*, [2014] UKSC 38.

59 Ibid. at para 300.

60 Nicholas Petrie, "Indications of Inconsistency" (2019) 78 *Cambridge L. J.* 3, 613.

61 Hickman, *Public Law*; Tom Hickman, "Bill of Rights Reform and the Case for going Beyond the Declaration of Incompatibility Model" (2015) 1 *N. Zeal. L. Rev.* 35.

62 No. 20.

that rights have been violated makes it important that the litigant receive some individual remedy such as damages.

Fiona de Londras has argued that the declaration of incompatibility does not fit the legal constitutionalism of the Irish constitution with its emphasis on judicial remedies. She points to an early case where a declaration of incompatibility with respect to the rights of transgender people was, unlike in the UK, not taken up by the legislature. She warns of the danger that a declaration of incompatibility will be a "non-remedy".[63] True to her predictions, the Irish courts have not embraced the declaration of incompatibility. Instead, they have used suspended declarations of invalidity which "leave in place the legislative provision, permitting prima facie the continued operation of a law considered to be inconsistent with the Constitution for the period between the delivery of the judgment and the making of any formal order".[64] Concerns have been raised that the applicant may not receive an effective remedy when such a deferral is used.[65] Others are more cautiously optimistic about this remedy.[66] I have argued elsewhere that a suspended declaration of invalidity is preferable to a declaration of incompatibility because it assigns the burden of legislative inertia in favour of rights.[67] At the same time, the suspended declaration of invalidity provides no immediate remedy for the litigant who has established the violation of human rights. It will be suggested in Section 4.3.4 of this chapter that litigants should generally be exempted from the suspension so that they receive an immediate individual remedy.

4.2.1.7 The Australian Debate about Declarations of Incompatibility

The Australian High Court has held that declarations of incompatibility available under some statutory bills of rights are not judicial remedies or functions because they do not bind the parties. Heydon J stressed that a

[63] Fiona De Londras, "Declarations of Incompatibility under the ECHR 2003 Act: A Workable Transplant?" (2014) 35 *Statute L. Rev.* 50, 64.

[64] C. v. *Minister for Social Protection and the Attorney General,* [2018] IESC 57 at para 2.

[65] David Kenny, "Remedial Innovation, Constitutional Culture, and the Supreme Court at a Crossroads" (2017) 40 *Dublin U. L.J.(N.S.)* 85, 90.

[66] Eoin Carolan, "A 'Dialogue-oriented Departure" in Constitutional Remedies? The Implications of *NHV* v. *Minister for Justice* for Inter-Branch Roles and Relationships" (2017) 40 *Dublin U. L.J.(N.S.)* 191, 204.

[67] Kent Roach, "Remedies for Laws That Violate Human Rights" in John Bell et al. (eds.) *Public Law Adjudication in Common Law Systems* (Oxford: Hart Publishing, 2016), pp.292–294.

declaration of incompatibility "is merely advisory in character. It does not declare any rights of the parties. It decides nothing . . . [It] does not involve the exercise of a judicial function and it is not an incident of the judicial process".[68] This follows formalistic understandings of the separation of powers and positivistic theories that stress that law is a form of enforceable command. It disregards the reality in Australia and many other democracies that those denied remedies domestically often seek them supra-nationally.[69]

French CJ distinguished a declaration of incompatibility from other declarations on the basis that the former did not determine the rights and obligations of the parties and was only directed to Parliament.[70] Even those judges most sympathetic to the declaration of incompatibility concluded that it was not similar to the traditional declarations issued by courts and was a novel power, at most ancillary to the judicial function.[71] The Australian High Court appealed to the common law tradition of rights requiring immediate and simple remedies. It also disparaged the idea that a declaration of incompatibility could promote a dialogue between courts and legislatures.[72] The High Court observed that the use of a declaration of incompatibility in a criminal case would require the court in one breath to declare that a conviction was obtained in violation of the accused's rights but in the next affirm that conviction.[73] This is indeed an awkward and troubling result. It will be suggested in Section 4.4 of this chapter that such a result might be avoided by the use of a two-track approach that would combine individual and systemic remedies.

4.2.1.8 The New Zealand Debate about Declarations of Incompatibility

Unlike the Australian High Court, the New Zealand Supreme Court has accepted non-binding declarations of incompatibility as a legitimate judicial remedy. Elias CJ warned that there might be a "rule of law

[68] *Momcilovic* v. *The Queen*, [2011] HCA 34 at para 457.

[69] For an examination of Canadian cases where applicants subject to domestic legislative derogation of rights brought successful complaints to the United Human Rights Committee, which then may have influenced subsequent decisions to withdraw the derogation, see Kent Roach, "Constitutional, Remedial and International Dialogues about Rights: The Canadian Experience" (2005) 40 *Texas J. Int'l Law* 537.

[70] *Momcilovic* v. *The Queen*, [2011] HCA 34 at para 88.

[71] Ibid. at para 535.

[72] Ibid. For a forceful endorsement of this approach by a leading English barrister, see Hickman, "Bills of Rights Reform".

[73] *Momcilovic* v. *The Queen*, [2011] HCA 34 at para 604, per Crennan and Kiefel JJ.

deficit"[74] if declarations that are available when the executive or the judiciary violates rights were not also available when the legislature did so. She cited the importance of remedies confirmed in *Baigent's* case,[75] where the New Zealand courts held that they could award damages in the absence of a remedies provision in the Bill of Rights. As Claudia Geiringer suggested in her review of the lower court decisions in this case, this placed a common law spin on the declaration of incompatibility, but one that is in tension with a right to an individual remedy.[76] In Section 4.4, I will suggest that these tensions can be usefully analysed in terms of dialogic systemic remedies and more judicially dominated individual remedies.

Like Lauterpacht, the New Zealand court reasoned that even though a declaration of incompatibility would not affect the validity of legislation, it could assist review and complaints at the international level.[77] In the end, the New Zealand Supreme Court declared restrictions on prisoner voting to be inconsistent with its Bill of Rights. This declaration was more effective than a similar British declaration. A law was enacted before the 2020 election to allow prisoners serving less than three years in jail to vote. This returned to a position that existed before penal populist legislation in 2010 took the vote away from all prisoners.[78] This experience suggests that declarations of incompatibility can result in effective systemic remedies in countries that are attentive to rights declarations. That said, declarations of incompatibility will not produce immediate remedies nor individual remedies.

4.2.1.9 Summary

Although disparaged as non-binding, declarations of incompatibility should not be dismissed, especially when they operate in concert with

[74] Ibid. at 105.

[75] Ibid. citing *Simpson* v. *Attorney General*, [1994] 3 NZLR 667 (C.A.).

[76] Claudia Geiringer, "The Constitutional Role of the Courts under the NZ Bill of Rights: Three Narratives from *Attorney-General* v. *Taylor*" (2017) 48 *V.U.W.L.R.* 4.

[77] *Taylor* v. *Attorney General* [2018] NZSC 104 at para 55 per Ellen France J, at para 101 per Elias CJ.

[78] NZ, "Electoral (Registration of Sentenced Prisoners) Amendment Bill" (2020) of the 52nd Parliament No. 223-1 (Hon. Andrew Little), Royal Assent 29 June 2020. A report by the Treaty of Waitangi Commission had recommended that all prisoners be able to vote because of Treaty provisions and Maori over-representation in prison: Treaty of Waitangi Commission, "*He Aha I Pērā Ai?* The Maori Prisoner Voting Report" (2019) WAI 2870, online (pdf): https://forms.justice.govt.nz/search/Documents/WT/wt_DOC_160697181/He%20Aha%20i%20Pera%20Ai%20W.pdf; the Green Party moved a motion in Parliament to implement this recommendation, but it was defeated.

supra-national systems of rights protection. To be sure, such declarations provide no individual remedy for the litigant who has established a rights violation. They do not even guarantee systemic reform that will prevent rights violations in the future. They do, however, signal a violation of rights and draw attention to remedial failure that allows rights to be violated without a remedy and will allow future rights violations.

4.2.2 Interpretative Remedies: Reading Down and Reading In

There are a variety of interpretative remedies available to the courts. It is not possible to evaluate such remedies in the abstract without looking at the available alternative remedies. In the United Kingdom, New Zealand and some Australian states, the only real alternative is a non-binding declaration of incompatibility. In contrast, in the United States, Canada and South Africa, there are a variety of alternative remedies including partial, full or suspended declarations of invalidity.

4.2.2.1 Interpretative Remedies and the Passive Virtues in the United States

Although the United States is often associated with strong form judicial review, American courts often use remedies short of a full declaration of invalidity, including interpretative remedies. In arguing that the court should avoid a full constitutional decision in the 1930s, Justice Brandeis stated that "even if a serious doubt about constitutionality is raised, it is a cardinal principle that this Court will first ascertain whether a construction of the statute is fairly possible by which the question can be avoided".[79] Interpretative remedies are frequently used as part of what Alexander Bickel defended as the passive virtues, precisely because they avoid a full constitutional ruling and allow the legislature to craft a dialogic response. In the American context, interpretative remedies are a "mediating way between the ultimates of legitimation and invalidation". They can result in a "colloquy" or dialogue between the court and the legislature that avoids the relative finality of a constitutional judgement.[80]

The United States Supreme Court used this method in dealing with detention at Guantanamo Bay in the wake of the 9/11 terrorist attacks. It

[79] *Ashwander* v. *Tennessee Valley Authority*, 297 US 288 (1936).

[80] Alexander Bickel, *The Least Dangerous Branch: The Supreme Court at the Bar of Politics* (New Haven: Yale University, 1985), pp.132, 156.

first relied upon presumptions of statutory interpretation in cases decided in 2004 and 2006, before eventually holding in 2008 that the detainees had a constitutional right to apply for habeas corpus.[81] It also used an interpretative remedy to uphold "Obama care" from judicial invalidation.[82] As will be seen below, the United States also softens its ability to invalidate democratically enacted legislation by using partial declarations of validity or limited "as applied" invalidity.[83]

4.2.2.2 Interpretative Remedies and the Remedial Virtues in the United Kingdom and New Zealand

The UK courts have made robust use of its interpretative mandate under section 3 of the Human Rights Act, 1998, to interpret statutes to make them consistent with human rights. It has read down reverse onuses that require the accused to establish a defence on the balance of probabilities to only require an evidential burden raising a reasonable doubt.[84] In *R.* v. *A.*,[85] the House of Lords read down a so-called rape shield law that restricts the admissibility of a sexual assault complainant's prior sexual conduct to not apply if its exclusion would violate the accused's right to a fair trial. It stressed "where the line is to be drawn must be left to the judgment of trial judges".[86] It distinguished the case from others involving "social and economic policy" where there may be a need to "defer, on democratic grounds, to the considered opinion of an elected body".[87] The Court relied on judicial expertise with respect to the admissibility of evidence, but its remedy created uncertainty about the extent of privacy protections that complainants would enjoy. Moreover as Aileen Kavanagh suggests, there are not always bright lines between contexts that involve social and economic policy and those involving judicial expertise. Indeed, *R.* v. *A.* seems to be a case where these categories overlap.[88]

Although started in criminal cases, the robust UK approach has been extended to other contexts. It has been used to authorize an

[81] *Rasul* v. *Bush*, 542 US 466 (2004); *Hamdan* v. *Rumsfeld*, 548 US 557 (2006).
[82] *National Federation of Independent Business* v. *Sebelius et al.*, 132 S.Ct. 2566 (2012) at 2600–2601.
[83] *United States* v. *Salerno*, 481 US 739 (1987); see generally Eric Fish, "Choosing Constitutional Remedies" (2016) 63 *U.C.L.A. L. Rev.* 322.
[84] *R.* v. *DPP ex parte Kebilene*, [2000] 2 AC 326; *R.* v. *Lambert*, [2002] AC 545.
[85] [2001] UKHL 25.
[86] Ibid. at para 45; see also ibid. at paras 45–46.
[87] *R.* v. *DPP ex parte Kebilene*, [2000] 2 AC 326 at para 86.
[88] Kavanagh, *Constitutional Review*, p.202.

interpretation of a statutory reference to opposite sex couples to include same-sex couples.[89] Lord Nichols concluded that "even if, construed according to the ordinary purpose of interpretation, the meaning of the legislation admits of no doubt, section 3 may none the less require the legislation to be given a different meaning".[90] At the same time, the Court recognized some limits to interpretative remedies. It has warned that "Parliament cannot have intended that section 3 should require courts to make decisions for which they are not equipped".[91]

Courts in Australia and New Zealand have been less aggressive than UK courts in using interpretative remedies. In *R.* v. *Hansen*,[92] the New Zealand Supreme Court refused to read down a reverse onus on a balance of probabilities to an evidential burden. Some judges explained that "the English courts, in their difficult and more complicated supra-national environment, seem to have felt it more appropriate to strike the balance between the judicial and legislative roles in a rather different way" and even as a "judicial override of Parliament".[93] The New Zealand courts concluded that their duty was to "construe not to reconstruct".[94] The New Zealand approach is more respectful of the role of the legislature, but can result in no individual remedy. It could potentially lead to more uses of declarations of incompatibility.

The Australian High Court avoided a result similar to *Hansen* in *R.* v. *Momcilovic*,[95] but only by holding that a reverse onus did not apply in the particular case. Four judges suggested that that the Victorian Charter of Rights affirms the robust UK approach to interpretative remedies.[96] Three others suggested that it simply affirms ordinary principles of statutory interpretation.[97] To complicate matters, one of the four judges indicated that the UK approach would give judges an impermissible license to exercise legislative powers.[98] The more conservative Antipodean approach may be related to the absence of a regional human rights court in the background. Interpretative remedies, no less than

[89] *Ghaidan* v. *Godin-Mendoza*, [2004] UKHL 30.
[90] Ibid. at para 29.
[91] Ibid. at para 33.
[92] [2007] NZSC 7.
[93] Ibid. at paras 156, 158 per Tipping J.
[94] Ibid. at paras 290 per Anderson J.
[95] [2011] HCA 34.
[96] Ibid. at para 170 per Gummow J (Hayne J concurring); ibid. at para 684 per Bell J.
[97] Ibid. at para 50 per French CJ; ibid. at paras 544–545 per Crennan and Kiefel JJ.
[98] Ibid. at para 454 per Heydon J.

declarations of incompatibility, are influenced by the presence or absence of supra-national recourse and remedies.

4.2.2.3 The Limits of Interpretative Remedies

In early cases involving new constitutional protections of rights, both the Supreme Court of Canada and the Constitutional Court of South Africa refused to save legislation through interpretative remedies. In 1996, the South African Constitutional Court stated that attempting to perform "textual surgery" would result in impermissible judicial re-drafting rather than review of legislation.[99] In 1984, the Canadian court opted for a declaration of invalidity on the basis that it "should not fall to the courts to fill in the details in the legislation that will render legislative lacunae unconstitutional".[100] The Court subsequently elaborated that interpretative remedies should not be used by courts if the result "would amount to making ad-hoc choices from a variety of options, none of which are pointed to with sufficient precision by the interaction between the statute in question and the requirements of the Constitution. This is the task of the legislature not the courts".[101] These cases illustrate that for reasons related to the separation of powers, courts may prefer a declaration of invalidity to an interpretative remedy.

4.2.2.4 Quasi-Legislative Interpretative Remedies

The Supreme Court of Canada has not always followed the above restriction on interpretative remedies. It has saved a Criminal Code provision enacted in 1892 that allowed parents and teachers to use "reasonable" force when correcting children by imposing categorical and quasi-legislative limits on the use of force.[102] The judicially reformed and trimmed defence would not apply to force against children under two years of age or teenagers and would not allow the use of objects.

[99] *Case* v. *Minister of Safety and Security*; *Curtis* v. *Minister of Safety and Security*, [1996] ZACC 7 at para 73.

[100] *Hunter* v. *Southam*, [1984] 2 SCR 145.

[101] *Schachter* v. *Canada*, [1992] 2 SCR 679 at para 57.

[102] *Canadian Foundation for Children, Youth and the Law* v. *Canada (Attorney General)*, [2004] 1 SCR 76. The Court used a quasi-legislative interpretative remedy in another politically sensitive case to save a recently enacted but overbroad child pornography offence: *R.* v. *Sharpe*, [2001] 1 SCR 45 at para 242; for criticism, see Kent Roach, "Constitutionalized Interpretation, Reading Down/In and the Wisdom of Schachter" (2016) 36 *N.J.C.L.* 2; for a defense of the Court's use of interpretative remedies, see Hamish Stewart, "A Defence of Constitutionalized Interpretation" (2016) 36 *N.J.C.L.* 2.

These are praiseworthy restrictions from a policy perspective. Nevertheless, they created a large discrepancy between the law as written by Parliament and the law as interpreted by the Supreme Court. In other cases, the Court has refused to use exemptions because they create a "divergence between the law on the books and the law as applied" that "impairs the right of citizens to know what the law is in advance and govern their conduct accordingly – a fundamental tenet of the rule of law".[103]

The South African Constitutional Court has similarly read in quasi-legislative restrictions on an overbroad provision prohibiting the broadcast of material that would prejudice relations between sections of the population. It did so through "notional severance" or reading in parts of legislation that more narrowly restricted freedom of expression.[104] Borrowing from other parts of the legislation may help ensure that the reformulated legislation is more consistent with legislative objectives. But when formulating remedies for laws that violate human rights, courts should be concerned about respecting human rights as well as legislative intent. American courts have rightly been more inclined to use facial declarations of invalidity because overbroad but judicially read down laws might still chill freedom of expression.[105]

The South African Constitutional Court has taken the idea of notional severance or "cutting and pasting" to make a law consistent with human rights quite far. They have read in paragraphs from proposed legislation to cure an equality rights violation caused by male primogeniture.[106] They have used similarly robust techniques to make child protection laws consistent with human rights[107] and to provide equal benefits for divorced and married couples.[108] Robert Leckey concludes that the

[103] *R.* v. *Ferguson*, [2008] 1 SCR 96 at para 72.

[104] *Islamic Unity Convention* v. *Independent Broadcasting Company Authority and Others*, [2002] ZACC 3 at paras 56–60.

[105] Carol Rogerson, "The Judicial Search for Appropriate Remedies under the Charter: The Examples of Overbreadth and Vagueness" in Robert J. Sharpe (ed.), *Charter Litigation* (Toronto: Butterworths, 1987); see also *R.* v. *Zundel*, [1992] 2 SCR 31 where the Supreme Court refused to save an overbroad and old false news offence by reading in restrictions that would limit it to hate speech.

[106] *Bhe and Others* v. *Khayelitsha Magistrate and Others*, [2004] ZACC 17 at para 106, per Langa DCJ.

[107] *C. and Others* v. *Department of Health and Social Development, Gauteng and Others*, [2012] ZACC 1 at paras 92–94, per Yacoob J.

[108] *Ngewu and Another* v. *Post Office Retirement Fund and Others*, [2013] ZACC 4 at paras 18, 21, per van der Westhuizen J.

South African court is more comfortable with interpretative remedies than the Canadian court.[109] Po Jen Yap argues that new democracies may be justified in using more robust "reading in" interpretive practices as a means of dealing with blocked or corrupt legislatures.[110]

But there are limits. The Indian Supreme Court upheld recently enacted legislation but read in requirements that judges sit with a new access to information commission.[111] The Court correctly resiled from such a quasi-legislative remedy when the government requested a re-hearing.[112] More robust interpretative remedies are more vulnerable to criticism in India and other countries where courts can strike down laws. This underlines the importance of always focusing on what alternative remedies are available to a court.

4.2.2.5 Reading in and Laws That Violate Human Rights Because They Are Under-Inclusive

There is an increasing recognition that the remedial options open to courts should not be dictated by the way legislation is drafted.[113] In particular, courts should be able to "read in" or add words to legislation to make it consistent with human rights, provided that such a result is driven by the court's interpretation of the underlying human right and is consistent with the overall objectives of the legislation. Simply nullifying statutes will not protect the full range of human rights in the age of the positive state.

In early gender equality cases, the United States Supreme Court read in females to underinclusive laws that only provided benefits to males.[114] The late Ruth Bader Ginsburg defended this reading in as a "moderate extension" compared to the alternative of invalidation that "would be far more destructive of the legislature's will".[115] The Supreme Court of Canada took a similar approach when it decided that reading in the term

[109] Robert Leckey, "Remedial Practice Beyond Constitutional Text" (2016) 64 *Am. J. Comp. Law.* 1, 13.

[110] Po Jen Yap, "New Democracies and Novel Remedies" (2017) *Public Law* 30; Po Jen Yap, *Constitutional Remedies in Asia* (London: Routledge, 2019).

[111] *Namit Sharma* v. *Union of India*, (2013) 1 SCC 745.

[112] *Union of India* v. *Namit Sharma*, (2013) 11 SCALE 85; see Chintan Chandrachud, *Balanced Constitutionalism* (Oxford: Oxford University Press, 2017), pp.138–144.

[113] Eric Fish, "Judicial Amendment of Statutes" (2016) 84 *Geo. Wash. L. Rev.* 3.

[114] *Califano* v. *Westcott*, 443 US 76 (1979) at paras 79–80; see also *Weinberg* v. *Wiesenfield*, 420 US 636 (1975); *Heckler* v. *Mathews*, 465 US 728 (1984).

[115] Ginsburg, "Some Thoughts on Judicial Authority", 314–318.

"sexual orientation" to laws protecting people against discrimination was justified both by equality rights and the overall objectives of the legislation.[116] The South African Court also read in "same-sex spouses" to some underinclusive statutes.[117] Both Canadian and South African courts have noted that legislatures retain the option to fine tune or even abolish benefits that the courts read in.[118] This is true, but legislation is not costless. Where the burden of legislative inertia is assigned by the court's remedy can be decisive. Legislatures may have less incentives to alter interpretative remedies that achieve compliance with rights than in responding to remedies that invalidate whole or parts of legislation.

Equality rights will often require judicial remedies that expand laws to include vulnerable minorities. But expansion of underinclusive statutes through reading in is not justified in every case. The reading in remedy needs to be both consistent with both human rights and the objective of the law. The Supreme Court of Canada refused to expand a statute providing leave for adoptive parents to the much larger group of biological parents. It was concerned that such a remedy would significantly change the legislative scheme and have significant budgetary implications.[119] The Court also refused to read the inclusion of same-sex couples into a reference to "spouse" in family law legislation because of repercussions on many other laws.[120] In both cases, the alternative to a reading in remedy was a suspended declaration of invalidity that temporarily preserved the underinclusive law and allowed the legislature an opportunity to engage in more comprehensive reform. One shortcoming, however, was that the successful litigants received no remedy and would not receive any remedy if new legislation were enacted prospectively.[121] There is a surprising amount of choice among different remedies for laws

[116] *Vriend* v. *Alberta*, [1997] 1 SCR 493.

[117] *National Coalition for Gay and Lesbian Equality* v. *Minister of Home Affairs*, [2000] ZACC 17.

[118] *Gory* v. *Kolver NO and Others*, [2006] ZACC 20 at para 30; ibid. at para 76; *C. and Others* v. *Department of Health and Social Development, Gauteng and Others*, [2012] ZACC 1 at para 57, per Skweyiya J, concurring; *Vriend* v. *Alberta*, [1997] 1 SCR 493 at para 167.

[119] *Schachter* v. *Canada*, [1992] 2 SCR 679.

[120] *M.* v. *H.*, [1999] 2 SCR 3; the Ontario legislature responded with legislation providing for a new category of "same-sex partners" that symbolically but not functionally denied same-sex partners spousal status: *Vincent* v. *Ontario (Attorney General)*, (1999) CanLII 14912 (ON SC).

[121] Sujit Choudhry and Kent Roach, "Putting the Past Behind Us? Prospective Judicial and Legislative Constitutional Remedies" (2003), 21 *S.C.L.R.*(2d) 205.

that violate human rights. Some remedies focus on systemic remedies while other focus on remedies for individuals while others provide both types of remedies.

4.2.3 Partial Declarations of Invalidity: Severance, as Applied and Exemptions

Depending on how legislation is drafted, severance of part of a statute can have the same effect as a reading in remedy in extending a law. A year before its landmark decision recognizing reading in as a remedy, the Supreme Court of Canada effectively extended benefits by severing and striking part of a statute that had excluded senior citizens.[122] The Court subsequently used this case as a justification for asserting the power to read words in to a law to ensure compliance with rights and respect the overall purpose of the law.[123] The South African Constitutional Court has used severance to invalidate an overbroad prohibition on protests while retaining a prohibition on members of the Defence Force engaging in strikes.[124] As with reading in, the judicially pruned statute should be consistent with rights (including justified limits on rights) and legislative objectives.

Consistent with other legislative attempts to control remedial discretion, American legislatures have frequently attempted to instruct courts whether or not to employ severance. Some have argued that such severability clauses are an improper direction to the judiciary.[125] The courts, however, tend to see such instructions as indicative of legislative intent and defer to them without always considering whether the end result is consistent with rights.[126]

The American severance jurisprudence is complex but inconsistent. In 2005, the Court preserved federal sentencing guidelines but made them

[122] *Canada (Employment and Immigration Commission)* v. *Tetreault Gadoury*, [1991] 2 SCR 22.

[123] *Schachter* v. *Canada*, [1992] 2 SCR 679.

[124] *South African Defence Union* v. *Minister of Defence*, [1999] ZACC 7.

[125] Fred Kameny, "Are Inseverability Clauses Constitutional?" (2005) 68 *Alb. L. Rev.* 997, 1001.

[126] *Alaska Airlines* v. *Brock*, 480 US 678 (1987) at 685; *Ayotte* v. *Planned Parenthood*, 546 US 320 (2006) at 329–330; *Gonzales* v. *Carhart*, 550 US 124 (2007), at 140–142; see Eric Fish, "Severability as Conditionality" (2015) 64 *Emory L. J.* 1293, 1335–1336 raising concerns that severance required American courts to act as legislatures.

non-mandatory,[127] whereas the year before it struck down similar state guidelines.[128] Four conservative judges would have struck down the entire "Obamacare" Affordable Care Act after finding only part of it unconstitutional with the issue returning to the Court in late 2020.[129]

There is a need for courts to justify their use of remedial discretion to escape claims that they are using remedies to impose their personal preferences. Severance is appropriate when it produces a result that is consistent with both overall legislative objectives and the rights in question. In reaching such results, judges should have regard to legislative instructions about the preferred remedy but not blindly defer to them. In the end, it is the court and not the legislature that determines the appropriate remedy. In a 2020 case, the Court held it could sever content-based speech regulation from other provisions prohibiting "robocalls". Justice Kavanagh stressed that courts should presume severability to salvage rather than destroy legislation. At the same time, he suggested that courts should generally follow legislative instructions with respect to severability.[130]

4.2.3.1 The Indian Doctrine of Eclipse and Basic Structure Doctrines

The Indian Supreme Court also uses severance but supplements it with a "doctrine of eclipse", that allows even part of legislation declared unconstitutional to be revived. This doctrine is not only complex but encourages constitutional amendments with retroactive effect.[131] This reflects the frequent enactment of constitutional amendments to reverse judicial rulings in India. This has in turn spawned the equally complex notion that Indian courts can annul constitutional amendments that offend the basic structure of the Constitution.[132] The choice of remedies for laws that violate human rights implicates in a dialogic manner a country's particular political structure.

[127] *United States* v. *Booker*, 543 US 220 (2005).

[128] *Blakely* v. *Washington*, 542 US 296 (2004).

[129] *National Federation of Independent Business* v. *Sebelius et al.*, 132 S.Ct. 2566 (2012) at 2668.

[130] *Barr* v. *American Association of Political Consultants* 591 US (2020).

[131] *State of Bihar* v. *Shailabala Devi*, [1952], Air 1952 SC 329; *Shankari Prasdad* v. *Union of India*, [1952] 1 SCR 89; see the excellent analysis in Chandrachud, *Balanced Constitutionalism*, pp.33–48.

[132] *Kesavananda Bharati* v. *State of Kerala*, 1973 SC 1461.

4.2.3.2 Exemptions and as Applied Invalidity

American courts frequently use exemptions or "as applied" declarations of invalidity as a way of minimizing the intrusion of judicial remedies on the legislative product. In *United States* v. *Salerno*,[133] the United States Supreme Court articulated a general preference for narrow "as applied" declarations of invalidity. The Court warned that broader facial declarations of invalidity are only valid if "no set of circumstances exist under which the Act may be valid". The Court has justified such a preference in terms of judicial restraint. It may also reflect the greater difficulty of crafting new legislation in a Congressional as opposed to a Parliamentary system of government. The result is a form of constitutional and judicial minimalism that can maximize legislative and executive discretion. At the same time, the American courts do grant broader facial declarations of invalidity, especially in the First Amendment context because of concerns that leaving overbroad laws on the books might chill fundamental freedoms.[134] In general, courts should be concerned that their remedies provide fair and certain notice both to the public and the executive.

The Supreme Court of Canada has resisted "as applied" challenges or what it describes as constitutional exemptions. In response to a finding that a "rape shield" law restricting the admissibility of a complainant's prior sexual conduct was overbroad, the Court rejected the use of constitutional exemptions as a remedy that was both uncertain and contrary to legislative intent.[135] Instead, the Court employed the more drastic remedy of a declaration of invalidity. It takes a similar approach to mandatory minimum sentences.[136] The result is greater judicial disruption of legislation, but also in the "rape shield" context, creative legislative replies enacted by Canada's Parliament.[137] By saving laws, "as applied" declarations may encourage legislative inertia.

133 481 US 739 (1987) at 745; see also *Regan* v. *Time, Inc.*, 468 US 641 (1984) at 652; *Sabri* v. *United States*, 541 US 600 (2004) at 608.

134 *Edwards* v. *Aguillard*, 482 US 578 (1987) (striking down statute requiring Creationalism to be taught as violating First Amendment); see Richard H. Fallon, Jr., "Fact and Fiction about Facial Challenges" (2011) 99 *Calif. L. Rev.* 915, 918 finding more frequent use of facial challenges than more limited "as applied" challenges. Professor Fallon also demonstrates that in some cases, the underlying attitudes of the different judges towards the law drives them to either strike it down in its entirety or to save it through a more limited partial declaration of invalidity: ibid., 951–952.

135 *R.* v. *Seaboyer*, [1991] 2 SCR 577.

136 *R.* v. *Ferguson*, [2008] 1 SCR 96.

137 See Kent Roach, The *Supreme Court on Trial: Judicial Activism or Democratic Dialogue*, 2nd ed. (Toronto: Irwin Law, 2016), pp.302–308. Hope has been expressed that invalidation of mandatory sentences might lead to creative legislative replies: Benjamin

An alternative to an exemption is an interpretative remedy that limits the application of an otherwise rights compliant law.[138] Such a remedy can provide clearer direction to the executive about how to enforce a law to comply with rights in the future than a one off exemption or "as applied" declaration of invalidity. Judicial remedies for laws that violate human right engage both the legislature that may have to enact new laws and the executive that may have to administer judicially re-formulated laws.

4.2.4 Declarations of Invalidity

Courts have generally found that a declaration of invalidity effectively nullifies that effect of a law and does so retroactively. The United States Supreme Court declared in 1886 that "an unconstitutional law is not a law; it confers no rights; it imposes no duties; it affords no protection . . . it is, in legal contemplation, as inoperative as though it had never passed".[139] In 2015, the South African Constitutional Court similarly stated that a declaration of invalidity will render a law invalid from the date of its promulgation.[140] The logic of such rule is based on the declaratory theory of law that suggests that judges simply declare the law as it always existed.[141]

A number of doctrines have emerged to limit the destabilizing effects of a fully retroactive declaration of invalidity. They include the doctrine of res judicata, which preserves convictions under unconstitutional laws once appeals have been exhausted[142] and various forms of qualified immunity with respect to damages that are caused by laws subsequently

Berger, "A More Lasting Comfort? The Politics of Minimum Sentences, the Rule of Law and *R.* v. *Ferguson*" (2009), 47 S.C.L.R. (2d) 101, but this has not yet materialized.

[138] *Victoria* v. *Adams*, 2009 BCCA 563 at paras 165–166; *Yahey* v. *British Columbia*, 2020 BCSC 278 at para 70. But for some resistance to such an approach, see *UFCW Local 401* v. *Alberta*, [2013] 3 SCR 735 at paras 40–41.

[139] *Norton* v. *Shelby County*, 118 US 425 (1886) at 442; see generally Peter Hogg, *Constitutional Law of Canada* 5th ed (Toronto: Carswell, 2007), Chapter 55.

[140] *Cross-Border Road Transport Agency* v. *Central African Road Services (Pty) Ltd and Another*, [2015] ZACC 12 at para 20; see also *Moise* v. *Greater Germiston Transitional Council*, [2001] ZACC 21 at para 13 holding that "the declaration was retrospective to the moment the [final] Constitution came into effect. That is when the inconsistency arose. As a matter of law, the provision has been a nullity since that date".

[141] *Hislop* v. *Canada*, [2007] 1 SCR 429 at paras 83–91.

[142] *R.* v. *Thomas*, [1990] 1 SCR 713; *S* v. *Bhulwana*; *S.* v. *Gwadiso*, [1995] ZACC 11 at para 32.

ruled unconstitutional.[143] Article 172 of the South African Constitution examined in Chapter 1, Section 1.6.2.5, recognizes that exceptions to fully retroactive declarations of invalidity may be necessary. The final two subsections, 4.2.5 and 4.2.6, of this chapter will examine the main departures from fully retroactive declarations of invalidity: the suspended declaration of invalidity and prospective rulings.

4.2.5 *Suspended Declarations of Invalidity*

Suspended declarations of invalidity are a controversial but quite common remedy. They were first used by the West German Constitutional Court "to prevent the greater hardship or inconvenience that would flow from the complete voidance of a statute. How long and under what conditions an unconstitutional law but still viable-law can remain in force is a matter the Court reserves to itself".[144] In 1986, they were defended by the President of the Court as allowing "the legislature to make the political decision which will determine the nature of a future regulation".[145] The Court has used a three year suspended declaration of invalidity to allow the legislature to remedy flaws in election laws.[146] Suspended declarations of invalidity are a good fit for a modern constitutional democracy that often requires legislation to implement the full range of human rights.

4.2.5.1 United States

Suspended declarations of invalidity have spread to other jurisdictions. The United States Supreme Court stayed for three months a judgement holding that a bankruptcy court was unconstitutional.[147] Two years after

[143] *Mackin* v. *New Brunswick (Minister of Finance)* 2002 SCC 13; *Rice* v. *New Brunswick,* [2002] 1 SCR 405.

[144] Donald Kommers and Russell Miller, *The Constitutional Jurisprudence of the Federal Republic of Germany* 3rd ed. (Durham: Duke University Press, 2012), pp.353–356.

[145] Wolfgang Zeidler, "Federal Constitutional Court of the Federal Republic of Germany: Decisions on the Constitutionality of Legal Norms" (1986) 62 *Notre Dame L. Rev* .4, 511. Zeidler discusses how it was used to allow the court to enact constitutional legislation on complex matters such as the rights of children, women and prisoners and unconstitutionally underinclusive benefits: ibid., 513–517. For an even earlier discussion of suspended declarations of invalidity by another former member of the court, see Wiltraut Rupp-von Brunneck, "Germany: The Federal Constitutional Court" (1972) 20 *Am. J. Comp. L.* 3, 390–395.

[146] Federal Constitutional Court, 03.07.2008 – 2 BvC 1, 7/07 – BVerfGE 121 at 266.

[147] *Northern Pipeline Construction Co.* v. *Marathon Pipeline Co.*, 458 US 50 (1982) at 87–89; see also *Northern Pipeline Construction Co.* v. *Marathon Pipeline Co.*, 459 US 813 (1982) (granting stay) and *Northern Pipeline Construction Co.* v. *Marathon Pipeline Co.*, 459 US 1094 (1982) (denying stay).

the original judgement, Congress enacted amendments to make the bankruptcy court constitutional, but only after the courts had to develop emergency rules.[148]

Suspended declarations of invalidity are linked with systems of governance and legislative inertia. The loose party discipline and checks and balances of the Congressional system of government may prevent quick legislative responses that are generally contemplated by suspended declarations of invalidity. Suspended declarations of invalidity may also be less necessary in the United States given the court's preference for relying on interpretative remedies and limited as applied declarations of invalidity. In Chapter 8, Section 8.2.2.2, however, it will be seen that state courts in the United States have used legislative remands with respect to public school financing. Nevertheless, the suspended declaration of invalidity may be less required in the US's more libertarian constitutional culture which tends to place less emphasis on legislative regulation of speech, election spending and social benefits compared to other constitutional democracies.

4.2.5.2 Canada

The suspended declaration of invalidity was first used by the Supreme Court of Canada in 1985 to avoid having all of Manitoba's unilingual statutes rendered of no force and effect. The Court gave the unconstitutional laws temporary effect for the minimum time necessary to translate them into French.[149] This case also established that a court that issues a suspended declaration of invalidity would retain jurisdiction over the case. The Supreme Court continued to issue rulings on the scope of Manitoba's obligations to translate old laws until 1992.

The Court subsequently used suspensions in cases where an immediate declaration of invalidity would present a threat to public safety or achieve equality with a vengeance by depriving people, such as single mothers, of benefits only because they were not extended to single fathers. In two early cases involving the criminal law, the Court took care to provide that interim remedies could be provided to limit the adverse effects that an accused would suffer from the unconstitutional law during the period of suspension.[150] This has not always been done in

[148] Fish, "Choosing Constitutional Remedies" 361–362.

[149] *Reference Re Manitoba Language Rights*, [1985] 1 SCR 721. See *infra* Chapter 7, Section 7.4.5, for more discussion of this case.

[150] *R.* v. *Swain*, [1991] 1 SCR 933 (limits on detentions for those found not guilty by reason of insanity that could be enforced by way of habeas corpus); note that in this case, the

subsequent cases. Suspended declarations have been used in criminal cases without exemptions[151] and people have been convicted under laws that were maintained by a suspended declaration of invalidity.[152] This highlights their failure to provide individual remedies.

The Court has articulated a presumption – one that it also recognizes in cases involving prospective ruling – that the successful applicant should generally receive the immediate benefit of the ruling and be exempted from the suspension.[153] In many cases, however, Canadian courts have not crafted an exemption from a suspended declaration of invalidity. For example, in one case involving voting rights where the Court first articulated its presumption, the successful litigant had to wait eighteen months before receiving the benefit of a legislative remedy. Recent trends are more favourable to the use of exemptions from suspensions.

In the 1992 *Schachter* case, the Court appeared to confine suspended declarations to three limited factual categories: 1. threats to the rule of law;[154] 2. threats to public safety;[155] and 3. cases involving benefits that violated rights only because they were underinclusive. As discussed in Chapter 1, Section 1.7, this attempted to impose rules on the exercise of remedial discretion. The rules soon were discovered to be underinclusive. Alas, the court then moved to exercising a strong and often unexplained discretion whether to suspend declarations of invalidity. This led to criticisms that the result was unpredictable and inconsistent with rights and

six-month period of suspension was extended at the government's request for an additional three months; *R.* v. *Bain,* [1992] 1 SCR 91 (indicating that courts could fashion remedies for abuses of the unconstitutional law giving the prosecutor forty-eight stand asides in jury selection).

151 *R.* v. *Demers,* [2004] 2 SCR 489 as criticized in Kent Roach, "New and Problematic Restrictions on Constitutional Remedies" (2004) 49 *C.L.Q.* 253; *Bedford* v. *Canada,* [2013] 3 SCR 1101 as criticized in Robert Leckey, "The Harms of Remedial Discretion" (2016) 14 *I Con.* 3, 592.

152 Convictions under sex work criminal offences that were subject to a suspended declaration of invalidity in *Bedford* v. *Canada,* [2013] 3 SCR 1101 were upheld in *R.* v. *Mohsenipour,* 2020 BCCA 160 at paras 84–88 and *R.* v. *Ackman,* 2017 MBCA 78 at para 75.

153 *Corbiere* v. *Canada (Minister of Indian and Northern Affairs),* [1999] 2 SCR 203 at para 122 (though interim relief not granted in this case due to "strong administrative reasons" where granting such relief would be inconsistent "with the principles underlying constitutional remedies"), ibid. at para 124. *Ontario (Attorney General)* v. *G.,* 2020 SCC 38 at 147, 152.

154 *Reference Re Manitoba Language Rights,* [1985] 1 SCR 721.

155 *R.* v. *Swain,* [1991] 1 SCR 933.

the rule of law.[156] One reason why the *Schachter* rules were unsuccessful was that the Court in that case rejected the principle that courts should employ the suspended declaration of invalidity for reasons related to the comparative institutional competence of legislatures over courts in selecting the precise means by which to comply with human rights.[157] Respect for the roles of the courts and legislatures, as well as a need for the remedy to be fair to all those affected and a presumption of immediate and retroactive relief, have all been recognized by the Canadian court as general principles that should inform the use of remedial discretion.[158] The Canadian court has subsequently rejected the categorical approach in *Schachter* in favour of a principled approach that will require the government to justify the use of a suspension and its length in each case. Three judges dissented and would have maintained more categorical approaches to the use of suspensions because they believed such an approach would be more restrictive and promote the rule of law.[159]

The Canadian Supreme Court has used suspended declarations of invalidity of six, twelve or eighteen months in order to give governments time to consult and develop policies that would comply with the *Charter* and they have extended suspensions for good reasons such as Parliamentary time lost for an election.[160] Robert Leckey has suggested that the timelines of Canadian suspensions may be too short to allow for full societal and legislative deliberation.[161] As will be seen, South African courts have used longer periods but with broader interim guidelines to govern how the law should be applied during the suspension. In the recent *Ontario* v. *G* case, the Court has stressed that the government

[156] Ryder, "Suspending the Charter"; Leckey, "The Harms of Remedial Discretion"; Arthur Peltomaa, *Understanding Unconstitutionality* (Toronto: Teja Press, 2018) raises these concerns but argues that suspended declarations are inherently illegitimate because they are contrary to constitutional text that requires invalidation of laws found to be inconsistent with the Charter.

[157] *Schachter* v. *Canada*, [1992] 2 SCR 679 at 715–717. For criticism of this "pigeon hole" approach as one that was based on inevitably over- or under-inclusive rules but that has subsequently degenerated into unpredictable strong discretion while ignoring principles related to comparative institutional role, see Kent Roach, "Principled Remedial Decision-Making under the Charter" (2004) 25 *S.C.L.R.* (2d), 101.

[158] *Doucet-Boudreau* v. *Nova Scotia*, 2003 SCC 62; *Hislop* v. *Canada*, 2007 SCC 10.

[159] *Ontario (AG)* v. *G.* 2020 SCC 38.

[160] *Carter* v. *Canada (Attorney General)*, 2016 SCC 4.

[161] Robert Leckey, "Assisted Dying, Suspended Declarations and Dialogue's Time" (2019) 69 supp. 1 *U.T.L.J.* 64.

must be prepared to justify not only the use of suspension for compelling public interests but also the length of the suspension. This is consistent with the idea that a suspended declaration of invalidity must be justified under proportionality analysis.

The entire Court now accepts that a two-track approach to suspended declarations of invalidity is in some cases warranted with the majority of the Court holding individuals should generally be exempted from suspensions within the limits of judicial economy when the justification for the suspension does not apply to them. Thus the litigant in the *Ontario v. G.* case who successfully challenged a sex offender registry law as overbroad was exempted because the Court was satisfied that the particular litigant did not constitute a public danger.[162] Dissenting judges would not have an exempted the applicant in part because they concluded courts lacked the ability to determine dangerousness. Nevertheless, they held open the possibility of an individual remedy and an exemption if the suspension would cause irreparable harm to the applicant.[163]

4.2.5.3 Hong Kong

The Hong Kong courts have preferred the use of temporary validity over suspended declarations of invalidity.[164] The former remedy opens up the possibility that the state could be held liable for abuse of laws that violate human rights during a period of a suspension. This relies on ex post remedies, whereas the South African approach to be examined in Section 2.5.4 has used interim remedies to provide ex ante guidance to the executive about how they should administer laws during the suspension.

The Hong Kong courts have followed South African jurisprudence in its same-sex marriage case by making it clear that if the legislature did not respond within a year's suspension that transsexuals would be effectively read into marriage legislation.[165] As Po Jen Yap has commented, this approach "provides a baseline of protection for successful

[162] *Ontario (Attorney General)* v. *G.* 2020 SCC 38 at 150–152, 181–183.

[163] Ibid. at 274. They provided examples such as releasing applicants from prison or ensuring that they receive urgent medical treatment.

[164] *Koo Sze Yiu* v. *Chief Executive,* [2006] HKFCA 75; Kent Roach, "Dialogic Remedies" (2019) 17 *Int'l. J. Con. Law* 860; Po Jen Yap, "Remedial Discretion and Dilemmas in Asia" (2019) 69 supp. 1 *U.T.L.J.* 84.

[165] *W.* v. *Register of Marriages* (2013), 16 HKCFAR 112 at 123, 148. Taiwan's Constitutional Court followed a similar practice in its 2017 same-sex marriage case: *Judicial Yuan Interpretation No. 748 and Reasons* (24 May 2017). Yap, "Remedial Discretion'; Compare to *Minister of Home Affairs* v. *Fourie,* [2005] ZACC 19.

litigants if the government falters".[166] Such remedies should be justified on the basis of the court's interpretation of the underlying right including, where relevant, justified limits on rights. Courts should leave policy decisions not dictated by rights to the legislature.

4.2.5.4 South Africa

The South African Constitutional Court uses its power under Article 172 of the Constitution to suspend declarations of invalidity in a wide range of cases. These include cases where a suspension is necessary to prevent "disruption and disorder"[167] or where an immediate invalidation would also violate rights by expanding a criminal offence without giving fair notice to the accused.[168]

Although the South African Constitutional Court frequently uses suspended declarations of invalidity and often tempers them with interim remedies, it seems reluctant to use them in criminal cases. For example, the Court struck down, with immediate effect, a law allowing for imprisonment for a failure to pay civil debt, because civil debts could still be collected by other ways.[169] The Court also allowed an overbroad authorization of police force to be immediately struck down on the basis that the police had adequate constitutional powers.[170] The Court similarly struck down an offence that applied to public protesters, on the basis of improper notice to the protesters.[171]

The South African court is much more willing than the Canadian or Hong Kong courts to impose interim guidelines about how the legislation should be administered during the suspension.[172] This may make the Court more willing to suspend declarations even in some criminal cases. For example, the Court issued detailed interim guidelines when it suspended a declaration that marijuana offences were invalid for twenty-four months. It reasoned that "if no interim relief is granted, there are

[166] Po Jen Yap, "Constitutional Remedies in Asia: An Overview" in Po Jen Yap (ed.) *Constitutional Remedies in Asia* (Milton Park: Routledge, 2019), p.5.

[167] *Mistry* v. *Interim Medical and Dental Council*, [1998] ZACC 10.

[168] *Ex Parte Ministry of Safety and Security and Others: In Re S* v. *Walters and Another*, [2002] ZACC 6.

[169] *Coetzee* v. *South Africa*, [1995] ZACC 7.

[170] *Ex Parte Ministry of Safety and Security and Others: In Re S* v. *Walters and Another*, [2002] ZACC 6.

[171] *Mlungwana and Others* v. *S and Another*, [2018] ZACC 45 at paras 109–110.

[172] Leckey, "The Harms of Remedial Discretion"; Robert Leckey, *Bills of Rights in the Common Law* (Cambridge: Cambridge University Press, 2015).

many adult people who will continue to be arrested by the police and who will face criminal charges and, if convicted, possible imprisonment for the use or possession or cultivation of cannabis in private for personal consumption in private – something that this judgment says nobody should be arrested for or charged with".[173] This interim remedy gives direction to the executive about how a law should be administered in a manner to minimize the impact of the rights deficiencies in a law. At the same time, other courts might conclude that such interim remedies provide too much direction to the executive and legislatures. In a similar Canadian marijuana case, the Court refused a one-year suspension.[174]

In another case, the South African Court declared that declarations of invalidity for under-age sex offences would be suspended for eighteen months. At the same time, it also issued a robust interim remedy during the suspension. This included a moratorium on investigations, arrests and application of the unconstitutional law as it affected those who are twelve to sixteen years of age, as well as expungement of convictions for close in age consensual sexual activity.[175] This provided guidance that was not present in a Canadian case where the Court struck down three offences against sex work, but suspended the declaration for a year without any guidance about how the offences should be applied during that year with convictions being upheld under the law during the period of the suspension.[176] The South African approach suggests less trust in the executive than the Canadian approach.

An open question with respect to the South African Court's robust use of guidelines is whether they will strain judicial competence and legitimacy through the creation of quasi-legislative codes and whether they will unduly influence legislative deliberation. The Court appeared to think this was not a danger and stated: "[i]n our participatory democracy Parliament is institutionally best-suited to ensure that the ultimate statutory regime is decided upon in an open, inclusive and transparent

[173] *Minister of Justice and Constitutional Development and Others* v. *Prince; National Director of Public Prosecutions and Others* v. *Rubin; National Director of Public Prosecutions and Others* v. *Acton and Others*, [2018] ZACC 30 at para 104.

[174] *R.* v. *Smith*, 2015 SCC 34, where the Supreme Court refused to suspend a declaration relating to medical use of marijuana.

[175] *Teddy Bear Clinic for Abused Children and Another* v. *Minister of Justice and Constitutional Development and Another*, [2013] ZACC 35 at paras 111–112.

[176] *Bedford* v. *Canada*, [2013] 3 SCR 1101. For criticism see Carolyn Mouland, "Remedying the Remedy: Bedford's Suspended Declaration of Invalidity" (2018) 41:3 *Man L.J.* 281.

manner, with all relevant parties who so desire being given the opportunity to shape the debate and the eventual outcome".[177]

The South African Court has used longer suspensions than the Canadian court. Interim guidelines can minimize the harm caused by the suspended law, presuming that the executive and especially the police are informed and follow these guidelines. This again suggests that any court's use of remedies should only be judged holistically with attention to both alternative and ancillary remedies and legislative and executive responses to their rulings.

Like the Canadian courts, the South African courts require justification for the government's request that a suspension be extended,[178] They will not extend a period of suspension after it has lapsed[179] but will extend it "when the facts have changed" or "where the full implications of the order were not previously apparent".[180] Requests to extend suspensions provide domestic courts with some supervisory powers. They also make it possible for courts to use periods that are designed to ensure that the legislative process is used promptly but not so quickly that its deliberative and investigatory capacities are strained.

4.2.6 *Prospective Rulings*

Prospective rulings have much in common with suspended declarations of invalidity because both involve departures from the general retroactive nature of judicial rulings that laws are invalid to the extent that they violate human rights.[181] They are opposed by those wedded to traditional understandings of adjudication that stress that courts simply declare the law as it always existed. For example, the Australian High Court has reasoned "[t]his Court has no power to overrule cases prospectively . . . it would be a perversion of judicial power to maintain in force that which is

[177] *Teddy Bear Clinic for Abused Children and Another* v. *Minister of Justice and Constitutional Development and Another*, [2013] ZACC 35 at para 109.

[178] *S.* v. *Steyn*, [2000] ZACC 24 at para 45.

[179] *Minister of Justice v. Ntuli*, [1997] ZACC 7; *Minister of Social Development and Others, Ex Parte*, [2006] ZACC 3.

[180] *Zondi* v. *MEC, Traditional and Local Government Affairs and Others*, [2005] ZACC 18 at para 39. This is a more helpful test than that used by the Supreme Court of Canada, which has simply stressed the "heavy" burden on the government to justify an extension: *Carter* v. *Canada*, 2016 SCC 4 at para 2.

[181] The South African Constitutional Court has recognized the similarity between suspended declarations of invalidity and rulings that are fully or partially prospective: *Ramuhovhi* v. *President of the Republic of South Africa*, [2017] ZACC 41 at para 44.

acknowledged not to be the law".[182]This traditional approach is also reflected in the Court's decision to hold that declarations of incompatibility are not a judicial remedy.

Consistent with its more instrumental approach to remedies, the US Supreme Court has used prospective rulings to limit the disruption caused by the Warren Court's new rules of constitutional criminal procedure designed to protect the rights of the accused. The Court generally gave the accused who litigated the case the benefit of the new rule even though others similarly situated who had not engaged in the litigation would not receive the benefit of the rule. This approach of "selective prospectivity" was justified on the basis that it satisfied American constitutional requirements that federal courts only hear real cases and controversies. Justice Brennan recognized that "[i]nequity arguably results from according the benefit of a new rule to the parties in the case in which it is announced, but not to other litigants similarly situated" but concluded that that this was required to ensure that the Court resolved concrete cases and controversies are required by Article III of the Constitution.[183]

The Supreme Court of Canada has also engaged in some prospective rulings but, like the American court, has generally given the litigant the benefit of the ruling. In one *Miranda* like case, the Court made a ruling that police had thirty days before being required to tell suspects about the right to legal aid. The Court, however, gave the accused in the case the immediate benefit of its ruling.[184] In a case dealing with essential medical services for those who are deaf, the Court gave a province six months to implement sign language interpretation in public hospitals but with no exemption for the applicant.[185] It will be suggested in Chapter 7, Section 7.5, and Chapter 8, Section 8.6, that the management of delay is a key issue in formulating remedies in institutional cases and in cases involving social and economic rights.

The leading Canadian case on prospective rulings is *Hislop* v. *Canada*,[186] where the Court only provided partially retroactive relief for same-sex couples that had been discriminated against in the provision

[182] *Ha* v. *New South Wales*, [1997], 189 CLR 465 at 503–504 per Brennan CJ, McHugh, Gummow and Kirby JJ. and at 515 per Dawson, Toohey and Gaudron JJ.

[183] *Stovall* v. *Denno*, 388 US 293 (1967) at 300.

[184] *R.* v. *Brydges*, [1990] 1 SCR 190.

[185] *Eldridge* v. *British Columbia*, [1997] 2 SCR 13.

[186] [2007] 1 SCR 429.

of pension benefits. The applicants claimed fully retroactive relief to 1985, when constitutional equality rights came into force in Canada. The Court, however, only granted relief retroactive to 1999. It recognized that the norm should be fully retroactive relief, but also held that "fully retroactive remedies might prove highly disruptive in respect of government action", including "framed budgets" or "attempts to design social programs".[187] It decided that the government had justified a departure from the retroactive norm because of reasonable and good faith reliance on the state of equality law until 1999.

The South African Constitutional Court similarly recognizes retroactive relief as the rule.[188] It has used prospective rulings when they are supported by other human rights, such as rights against retroactive expansion of criminal sanctions[189] or the taking away of defences.[190] It has also used prospective rulings to protect those who, in good faith, completed estate matters that discriminated against women.[191] As in the related suspended declaration of invalidity context, the South African courts are hostile to American and Canadian style exemptions that give litigants, but not others similarly situated, the retroactive benefit of a ruling.

4.2.6.1 Summary

There are a wide range of remedies for laws that violate human rights. The declaration of incompatibility provides no immediate individual or systemic remedy but has resulted in changes to laws and is an important signal to supra-national processes. Reading in and severance can protect the rights of the individual litigant before the court and ensure that these rights are respected in the future, provided that the executive and the public are fully informed about how the court has altered the statute. More limited remedies such as applied declarations of invalidity or exemptions can protect the rights of the litigants before the court. They have a more uncertain systemic effect going forward. Finally, unless accompanied with an exemption for the litigant or an interim remedy with a similar effect, suspended declarations of invalidity and prospective

[187] Ibid. at para 101.

[188] *Moise* v. *Greater Germiston Transitional Local Council*, [2001] ZACC 21 at para 13.

[189] *Masiya* v. *Director of Public Prosecutions Pretoria (The State) and Another*, [2007] ZACC 9.

[190] *Ex Parte Ministry of Safety and Security and Others: In Re S* v. *Walters and Another*, [2002] ZACC 6.

[191] *Bhe and Others* v. *Khayelitsha Magistrate and Others*, [2004] ZACC 17.

rulings will fail to produce a remedy for the individual litigant. Like the declaration of incompatibility, the suspended declaration of invalidity promotes dialogue with the legislature. An important difference, however, is that rights will eventually be respected under the suspended declaration of invalidity if the legislature fails to act.

4.3 The Relevant Principles

The variety of remedies available for laws that violate human rights means that courts exercise remedial discretion even in the face of commands in human rights laws that they must or must-not invalidate laws. As Leckey suggests, remedial texts "are not self-applying".[192] They do not dictate what particular remedies will be awarded.

As argued in Chapter 1, Section 1.7, judges should not exercise a strong remedial discretion that does not require them to justify their decisions, nor should they bind themselves by rigid rules that will not accommodate the wide range of contexts that they will confront over time. Rather, they should exercise remedial discretion with attention to relevant principles. What then, are the principles that should govern choice of remedy in the context of laws that violate human rights?

4.3.1 Reconcile Human Rights and Legislative Objectives Whenever Possible

The basic principle that should govern all remedies for laws that violate human rights is that courts should select the remedy that best reconciles its interpretation of the relevant human rights with the objectives of the legislation. A first step in this process is for the courts to make clear what human rights are at play and how they interpret such rights. Some argue that interpretative remedies are not really remedies, but ordinary constructions of the law that make resort to presumptions or canons of statutory interpretation that legislatures intend to respect rights. The Supreme Court of Canada has, however, indicated that it is a "fallacy" to think that "reading down does not involve a determination of invalidity"[193] because the Court must interpret the underlying right. Courts should be candid about when concerns about human rights are influencing their interpretation of the law. They should also generally

[192] Leckey, *Bills of Rights*, p.124.
[193] *Osborne* v. *Canada (Treasury Board)*, [1991] 2 SCR 69.

factor in whether the limits on rights that are contemplated in the statute are justified.[194] This is required to take into account the legitimate objectives of the legislation. In cases where there are competing rights at play, courts should also be clear about how they interpret those rights and the limits they place on each right in their remedial decision.

A second step is for the court to define the objectives of the legislation. When deciding whether an interpretative remedy or a partial declaration of invalidity such as severance is consistent with legislative objectives, courts often speak in terms of the intent of the legislature. Yet, what the legislature intended has, by this point, already been found to be inconsistent with human rights.[195] Rather, the true principle should be whether the court's exercise of remedial discretion is consistent with the larger objectives of the legislation. Courts can use "tailored remedies" such as severance or reading in if such a remedy "can be granted without the court intruding on the role of the legislature" and "such a remedy will preserve a law's constitutionally compliant effects along with the benefit that law provides to the public. The rule of law is thus served both by ensuring that legislation complies with the Constitution and by securing the public benefits of laws where possible".[196]

4.3.2 Respect the Separation of Powers by Leaving Policy Choices to the Legislature

The idea that the courts should select remedies that best reconcile human rights with legislative objectives is related to the separation of powers. Courts should interpret and be concerned with human rights (including justified limitations on those rights) while recognizing that legislatures define the policy objectives of legislation. They should avoid "making ad hoc choices from a variety of options, none of which are pointed to with sufficient precision by the interaction between the statute in question and the requirements of the Constitution. This is the task of the legislature not the courts".[197] If an interpretative remedy would significantly change

[194] *Slaight Communications Inc.* v. *Davidson*, [1989] 1 SCR 1038.

[195] Nitya Duclos and Kent Roach, "Constitutional Remedies as 'Constitutional Hints': A Comment on *R.* v. *Schachter*" (1991) 36 *McGill L. J.* 1; Fish, "Choosing Constitutional Remedies".

[196] *Ontario (Attorney General)* v. *G.* 2020 SCC 38 at para 116.

[197] *Schachter* v. *Canada*, [1992] 2 SCR 679 at 706. The South African Constitutional Court took an almost identical approach eight years later. It reasoned that "[w]here, as in the present case, a range of possibilities exists . . . it will ordinarily be appropriate to leave the

the legislation, the more appropriate remedy may be to issue a declaration of invalidity or incompatibility and give the legislature an opportunity to decide between the range of options. Reading in words can be justified when the court is convinced that this is the only way to make the law consistent with human rights.[198] It "will not be appropriate to read words in, unless in so doing a court can define with sufficient precision how the statute ought to be extended in order to comply with the Constitution".[199] The principled concern is whether, by using interpretative remedies, courts are making choices and changing legislative objectives in a manner that is best left to the legislature.

As discussed in Section 4.2.2.2, UK courts have used strong interpretative remedies that may alter the legislation so as to achieve respect for human rights. In principle, stronger interpretative remedies are more easily justified where the alternative of a declaration of incompatibility will provide litigants with no effective remedy and not prevent the repetition of the rights violation in the future. An interpretative remedy achieves both individual and systemic justice and Parliament can intervene if it is not satisfied with the systemic effects of the interpretation. The reluctance of New Zealand courts to engage in strong remedial interpretations is not justified and could lead to excessive use of declarations of incompatibility. The Australian approach is divided, but courts only exceed their role and usurp the legislative role if they make quasi-legislative choices.

Some courts have inappropriately made quasi-legislative choices under the guise of interpretative remedies. The Canadian Supreme Court did this when it read in age limitations and other categorical restrictions to make a criminal defence authorizing the use of reasonable force consistent with the rights of children.[200] The Indian Supreme Court similarly did this by re-designing access to information legislation.[201] The South

legislature to determine in the first instance how the unconstitutionality should be cured. This Court should be slow to make those choices which are primarily choices suitable for the legislature". *Dawood and Another; Shalabi and Another; Thomas and Another* v. *Minister of Home Affairs and Others*, [2000] ZACC 8 at para 64. For a defence of this approach, see Roach, "Constitutionalized Interpretation" 224–228.

198 *Jaftha* v. *Schoeman; Van Rooyen* v. *Stoltz*, [2004] ZACC 25 at paras 63–64.

199 *National Coalition National Coalition for Gay and Lesbian Equality* v. *Minister of Home Affairs*, [1999] ZACC 17 at para 75.

200 *Canadian Foundation for Children, Youth and the Law* v. *Canada (Attorney General)*, [2004] 1 SCR 76.

201 *Namit Sharma* v. *Union of India*, (2013) 1 SCC 745.

African Constitutional Court did this through using notional severance, a form of "cutting and pasting", from other parts of the legislation to save overbroad legislative provisions.[202] These intrusions on the legislative role are particularly unnecessary when the alternative of immediate or suspended declarations of invalidity are available as they are in all three countries. Part of a dialogic approach to remedies is respecting the ability of each institution to do its job.

4.3.3 *Remedial Choice Should Not Be Constrained by Legislative Drafting*

Many courts have recognized that distinctions between reading down or partial invalidity as a legitimate judicial remedy and reading in or extension as an illegitimate legislative remedy are no longer tenable and should be abandoned. This is because whether the court extends an underinclusive statute should not depend on the vagaries of how the statute was drafted.

In 1991, the Supreme Court of Canada extended an underinclusive statute so that it would apply to those over the age of sixty-five by using a partial declaration of invalidity or severance to invalidate part of a statute that explicitly excluded that group.[203] The Court did not appear to see this remedy as problematic. For example, it did not assess whether the extension would have significant budgetary effects or distort the objective of the legislation. This may have been because the addition of a small group vulnerable to discrimination (senior citizens) to an unemployment insurance benefit scheme was consistent with both human rights and the overall objectives of the law. In *Schachter*, decided a year later, the Court conducted a much more sustained analysis before concluding that it would be inappropriate to read in a larger group of biological parents to a scheme that was provided to allow adoptive parents to take time off work after the completion of their child's adoption.[204] In that case, the Court recognized that it would be "arbitrary" to allow the choice of remedies to be determined by how the impugned statute was worded.[205]

[202] *Islamic Unity Convention* v. *Independent Broadcasting Company Authority and Others*, [2002] ZACC 3 at paras 56–60.
[203] *Tetreault-Gadoury* v. *Canada*, [1991] 2 SCR 22.
[204] *Schachter* v. *Canada*, [1992] 2 SCR 679.
[205] Ibid. at 698.

In the 2004 UK case of *Ghaidan* v. *Godin-Mendoza*,[206] the House of Lords similarly recognized that a refusal to allow a reading in interpretative remedy would make the available remedies "something of a semantic lottery". The Court elaborated that the scope of available judicial remedies should not depend "upon the particular form of words adopted by the Parliamentary draftsman".[207]

In both *Schachter* and *Ghaidan*, however, the courts recognized that reading in would not be appropriate if it went against "the grain of the legislation".[208] In *Ghaidan*, reading in was found to be consistent with the broad objectives of the legislation, though obviously not its particular verbal formulation. It also had the effect of adding in a minority vulnerable to discrimination – same-sex couples – to a law that applied only to opposite sex couples. In contrast, the Supreme Court in *Schachter* refused to extend parental benefits made available to adoptive parents to the much larger group of biological parents. It instead struck down the provision of benefits to adoptive parents and employed a suspended declaration of invalidity. Parliament accepted an earlier extension of the law, but reduced the benefits provided to all parents from fifteen to ten weeks for all.[209] Although criticized by some as regressive, this was the type of decision that Parliament was entitled to make.

Schachter and *Ghaidan* highlight how it is much easier to justify reading in remedies to include smaller groups who are vulnerable to discrimination than larger groups who are not vulnerable to discrimination in the legislative process. The addition of the vulnerable minority in many cases will effectively respond to an intentional or unintentional legislative decision to exclude the group and will generally be consistent with the underlying purpose of the law. This helps explain the frequent willingness of courts to use strong interpretative remedies to include sexual minorities when they were excluded. This is not to say, however, that reading in and extension remedies should be automatic in such cases.[210]

[206] [2004] 2 AC 557 at para 31.

[207] Ibid.

[208] Ibid. at para 33 citing Lord Rodger at para 121.

[209] Duclos and Roach, "Constitutional Remedies as 'Constitutional Hints'".

[210] Courts have not read in same-sex or transsexual partners because of concerns about the need for the legislature to engage in more comprehensive reform: *M.* v. *H.*, [1999] 2 SCR 3; *Bellinger* v. *Bellinger*, 2003 UKHL 21.

4.3.4 A Presumption of Immediate and Fully Retroactive Relief

There should be a presumption in favour of fully retroactive relief that provides an immediate remedy for both the litigant and other rights holders as opposed to remedies that suspend a declaration of invalidity or engage in prospective rulings.[211] The Supreme Court of Canada has recognized that courts as adjudicative bodies "generally grant remedies that are retroactive to the extent necessary to ensure that successful litigants will have the benefit of the ruling".[212] Adjudicators have a unique role in resolving disputes on the basis of claims of legal rights.[213] The South African Constitutional Court has also recognized that "[o]rdinarily a successful litigant should receive at least some practical relief. This, however, is not an absolute rule".[214] The presumption of immediate and retroactive relief is rebuttable. The state should bear the onus of providing that departure from the retroactive principle is justified and proportionate.

4.3.5 Allow Only Proportional Limits on Fully Retroactive Relief

In *Schachter*, the Canadian Supreme Court looked to proportionality analysis as a guide to the exercise of remedial discretion. It indicated that a reading in remedy would not be appropriate if there was no rational connection between a requested extension of a law and the legislative objective. Such a remedy would, however, be more appropriate if the inconsistency of the law with human rights related only to minimal impairment concerns or the overall balance stage of proportionality analysis. In other words, it would be easier to justify reading in if it made only minor adjustments to legislation that had not been carefully tailored or had a "disproportionate effect"[215] on the excluded group than it would be to justify a reading in remedy that made fundamental changes to the legislation. This represented an early recognition of the utility of proportionality analysis in providing structure to the exercise of remedial discretion.

Proportionality should also be used as a principle in cases where the state argues for a less intrusive remedy, such as a suspended declaration of invalidity or prospective ruling. Alas, the proportionality analysis in

[211] Choudhry and Roach, "Putting the Past Behind Us?" 248–249.

[212] *Hislop* v. *Canada*, 2007 SCC 10 at para 89.

[213] Lon Fuller, "The Forms and Limits of Adjudication" (1978) 92 *Harv. L. Rev.* 353.

[214] *Minister of Home Affairs* v. *Fourie and Another*, [2005] ZACC 19 at para 133.

[215] *Schachter* v. *Canada*, [1992] 2 SCR 679 at 704.

Schachter[216] was not carried through to this part of the analysis. The state should advance some legitimate objective, such as a reliance interest, that would be harmed by an immediate declaration of invalidity or a fully retroactive remedy. A legitimate objective, as discussed in Chapter 1, Section 1.9.7, cannot be something that is simply an objection to the underlying right or remedy. Legitimate objectives could, however, include concerns about the financial or other costs of a remedy as well as the interests of third parties and disruption or dangers caused by an immediate remedy. A legitimate objective is not, however, enough to justify a departure from the basic principle of fully retroactive relief. The state should also demonstrate a rational connection between the objective and the requested limit on the remedy. In addition, the limit should be carefully tailored. This requirement may limit the length of a suspended declaration of invalidity or the degree to which the ruling is prospective.

Justice O'Regan appealed to proportionality when she stated that in those cases where a suspended declaration of invalidity is used, interim orders should be "made to ensure that constitutional rights are infringed as little as possible in the period of suspension".[217] In *Ontario* v. *G.*,[218] the Supreme Court updated the proportionality analysis in *Schachter* and applied it to the justification and duration of suspended declarations of invalidity. Consistent with general proportionality reasoning, the government must justify suspensions for compelling public reasons and also pay careful attention to the harm that a suspension might impose including on a litigant who was not exempted from the suspension.

Finally, the remedial result must strike an appropriate overall balance between securing the state's objective and its adverse effects on the rights holders. The Supreme Court of Canada assessed overall balance and concluded a partially prospective ruling struck "an appropriate balance between fairness to individual litigants" and the government's competing reliance interest on the view widely accepted before 1999 that it could exclude same

[216] Grant Hoole, "Proportionality as a Remedial Principle: A Framework for Suspended Declarations of Invalidity in Canadian Constitutional Law" (2011) 49 *Alta L. Rev.* 107.

[217] *Minister of Home Affairs* v. *Fourie and Another*, [2005] ZACC 19 at para 171 in partial dissent. O'Regan J. cited the following majority judgements in favour of this proposition: *Dawood and Another; Shalabi and Another; Thomas and Another* v. *Minister of Home Affairs and Others*, [2000] ZACC 8 at paras 66–67; *Janse van Rensburg NO and Another* v. *Minister of Trade and Industry and Another, NNO* [2001] ZACC 18 at paras 29–30, *Zondi* v. *MEC, Traditional and Local Government Affairs and Others*, [2005] ZACC 18 at paras 130–131. For additional discussion of the *Fourie* case see *infra* Section 4.4.4.

[218] 2020 SCC 38 at paras 132–135.

sex couples from pension benefits. The Court stressed making the remedy retroactive to 1999 meant that the successful applicants would not receive a "Pyrrhic victory".[219] Proportionality principles provided an appropriate and transparent vehicle to govern the exercise of remedial discretion. The applicants received a meaningful remedy but one that accommodated legitimate and opposing state interests in a proportionate manner.

4.4 Towards a Two-Track Approach

The tension between the role of courts in providing effective remedies for individuals and providing systemic remedies to prevent rights violations in the future was recognized by Abram Chayes in his path-breaking work. Chayes was a champion of systemic remedies domestically.[220] Given his understanding of international law as iterative and persuasive, he likely would have been comfortable with the declaration of compatibility as a warning that a country "is in breach of its international obligations".[221] At the same time, Chayes prematurely dismissed individual remedies as a relic of by-gone days.

Robert Leckey has aptly described a tension between constitutional enforcement that results in a complete judicial remedy and legislative engagement in which the legislature completes the remedy.[222] Unlike Chayes, he suggests that the posture of "constitutional enforcement" and "legislative engagement" need not be mutually exclusive. I agree. In my view, the tension identified by both can be resolved by a two-track approach that combines remedies for litigants with systemic remedies that leave room for legislative responses.

Leckey has warned that suspended declarations of invalidity have "diminished what constitutional supremacy means in rights cases".[223] At times, he has equated them with declarations of incompatibility,[224]

219 *Hislop* v. *Canada*, 2007 SCC 10 at paras 116–117.

220 Abram Chayes and Antonia Handler Chayes, *The New Sovereignty* (Cambridge: Harvard University Press, 1995); on the persuasive nature of international law, see Jutta Brunnée and Stephen Toope, *Legitimacy and Legality in International Law* (Cambridge: Cambridge University Press, 2010).

221 *R. (Animal Defenders International)* v. *Secretary of State for Culture, Media and Sport*, 2008 UKHL 15 at para 53.

222 Leckey, *Bills of Rights*, pp.151–169; for arguments that suspended declarations of invalidity harm litigants and the rule of law, see Robert Leckey, "Enforcing Laws That Infringe Rights" (2016) *Public Law* 206; Leckey "The Harms of Remedial Discretion".

223 Leckey, *Bills of Rights*, pp.172, 193.

224 Leckey, "Enforcing Laws That Infringe Rights".

even though as the UK prisoner voting rights saga demonstrates, suspended declarations only delay remedies while in some cases declarations of incompatibility result in their complete denial.[225] Leckey would also object to a two-track approach to the extent it privileges the actual litigant who receives a remedy while denying or postponing it to others similarly situated. Consistent with much South African jurisprudence,[226] Leckey has argued that "horizontal equity" that treats all rights holders the same at the same time is much more important in human rights law than in private law.[227]

An ideal two-track system would allow courts to do justice in individual cases while at the same time engaging the legislature when necessary for assistance in determining systemic remedies. A good example of where a two-track approach would have been helpful is in both the UK case of *Bellinger* and the Canadian case of *M.* v. *H.*

In *Bellinger*,[228] the House of Lords refused to provide the successful applicant with any individual remedy because of the complex knock-on effects of recognizing the rights of transsexual people to be legally married. In *M.* v. *H.*,[229] the Supreme Court of Canada also denied an individual remedy to the litigant, but allowed the legislature to enact a comprehensive law dealing with the rights of same-sex couples. Because the reply legislation was prospective, the individual litigants in both cases were denied any remedy. The two-track approach would allow the court to give the successful applicant a remedy. In the UK, this would have to involve the interpretative remedy that Hickman argued was possible in

225 Kent Roach, "Remedies for Laws That Violate Human Rights" in John Bell et al. (eds.), *Public Law Adjudication in Common Law Systems* (Portland: Hart Publishing, 2016), pp.287–299; but for a combination of some individual remedy with a declaration of incompatibility, see Ireland's European Convention on Human Rights Act, 2003 No. 20, s.5(4).

226 For example, in *Dawood and Another; Shalabi and Another; Thomas and Another* v. *Minister of Home Affairs and Others*, [2000] ZACC 8 at para 66, Justice O'Regan noted that while a suspension was justified to allow the legislature to select from a number of options, the court should "ensure that appropriate relief is provided to the successful litigants in this case, and to those who are situated similarly to those litigants in the meantime".

227 Leckey, *Bills of Rights*, p.32.

228 [2003] UKHL 21.

229 *M.* v. *H.*, [1999] 2 SCR 3. The Supreme Court of Canada may have subsequently disapproved of *M.* v. *H.* when it observed that in that case "However, an immediately effective declaration would not have prevented the legislature from addressing the issues more comprehensively in light of the Court's decision." *Ontario* v. *G.* 2020 SCC 38 at para 130.

the case.[230] In Canada, the remedy would have involved an exemption from the suspended declaration of invalidity. Even though exemptions are supposed to be the norm in Canada,[231] they are often not ordered including in *M.* v. *H.*. In the UK, the only way to have provided Bellinger with an individual remedy was for the courts to craft an interpretative remedy. It would them have been up to Parliament whether to revise it.[232]

The two-track approach is most relevant when courts face choices and trade-offs between providing effective remedies for the individual litigant and pursuing systemic remedies that respect the separation of powers and competing social interests. As Justice Goldstone recognized in an early suspended declaration of invalidity case under the South African Constitution, "on the one hand" there are "the interests of the successful litigant in obtaining immediate constitutional relief and, on the other, the potential disruption of the administration of justice"[233] that would be caused by an immediate declaration of invalidity.

4.4.1 *The Limits of Purely Individual Remedies*

One of the virtues of the two-track approach is its ability to demonstrate the inadequacy of remedial approaches that focus exclusively on either individual or systemic tracks. Remedies such as constitutional exemptions or as applied declarations of invalidity that are used in the United States can be effective in obtaining justice for individual litigants by ensuring that laws will not be applied to those litigants in a manner that will violate their rights. They provide limited guidance for the future either to the executive or to those who may be affected by the law. The executive may have an incentive to interpret the case-specific remedy in a limited manner that maximizes their discretion. They may assume that they can do whatever is not clearly prohibited. Qualified immunities

230 Hickman, Public Law, pp.92–93.

231 *Corbiere* v. *Canada (Minister of Indian and Northern Affairs),* [1999] 2 SCR 203 at para 122.

232 Legislative remedies in a democracy will not be without controversy. A Conservative government in Ontario responded to *M.* v. *H.* with a separate definition of "same-sex partner", which was subsequently challenged but upheld under the Charter. See *Vincent* v. *Ontario (Attorney General),* (1999) CanLII 14912 (ON SC). This provision was repealed in 2005, c. 5, s. 32(9).

233 *J. and Another* v. *Director General Department of Home Affairs,* [2003] ZACC 3 at para 21.

from damage awards discussed in Chapter 5, Section 5.2.10, may also encourage such assumptions. Such an individualized approach may fail to prevent future violations.

4.4.2 *The Limits of Purely Systemic Remedies in Assisted Dying Cases*

Remedies that are only directed at future systemic reform such as the declaration of incompatibility will not secure justice for those whose rights are denied. Both the Supreme Courts of the UK and Canada have recognized the injustice of absolute bans on medically assisted dying. The UK court made a judicial indication of disapproval with some judges using a non-binding declaration of incompatibility.[234] The Canadian court also headed down the dangerous road of exclusive reliance on systemic remedies. In 2015, it suspended a declaration of invalidity with no attention to individual remedies either for the applicants or those similarly situated.[235] In 2016, however, the Supreme Court allowed lower courts to give competent adults exemptions from the law when it extended the suspended declaration of invalidity.[236] Four judges, however, dissented on the basis that the Court's long standing concerns about constitutional exemptions or "as applied invalidity" still applied and that case-by-case exemptions would "create uncertainty, undermine the rule of law and usurp Parliament's role".[237] This position, however, disregards

[234] *R. (on the application of Nicklinson and another)* v. *Ministry of Justice; R. (on the application of AM)* v. *DPP*, [2014] UKSC 38 at para. 119 per Lord Neuberger (Lords Mance and Wilson concurring). Lady Hale at para 324 and Lord Kerr concurring at para 326 would have ordered the declaration of incompatibility.

[235] *Carter* v. *Canada (Attorney General)*, 2015 SCC 5. This may have been related to the fact that both lead applicants had passed away by the time the Supreme Court rendered its decision.

[236] *Carter* v. *Canada (Attorney General)*, 2016 SCC 4. The courts were able to grant a significant number of exemptions to competent adults during the remaining four months of the suspension. In this context at least, the judiciary could manage and administer case-by-case exemptions in a manner that provided successful litigants with remedies while allowing Parliament to create a new regulatory regime. For example, the Alberta Court of Appeal approved an exemption during the period of the suspension on the basis that the Supreme Court's decision in *Carter* did not require that a person be terminally ill: *Canada (Attorney General)* v. *F.(E.)*, 2016 ABCA 155 at paras 33–44. This flaw in the law eventually enacted by Parliament has led to successful Charter challenges of the new law. The courts followed the majority in *Carter II* and used both a suspended declaration of invalidity and exemptions for both the applicant and others from it: *Truchon c. Procureur général du Canada*, 2020 QCCS 772 at paras 27–28. A subsequent extension of the suspension was conditioned on the government's agreement to pay individual's costs for seeking exemptions. *Truchon c. Procureur général du Canada*, 2020 QCCS 4388 at para 101.

[237] *Carter* v. *Canada (Attorney General)*, 2016 SCC 4. at para 6.

the fact that court-crafted exemptions would only be made during the temporary suspended declaration of invalidity and ancillary to that remedy. The dissenters also ignored past cases where the Court has exempted successful litigants from both suspended declarations of invalidity and prospective rulings.[238]

The two-track approach taken by the majority in the Canadian assisted dying case does place the burden on dying adults to litigate to obtain individual exemptions from courts. It is possible that South African courts would have used more wholesale interim remedies. The choice between individual exemptions and broader interim remedies is a close call, especially in the assisted dying context where the consequences of error are so serious. Regardless, courts should be concerned about both individual and systemic remedies. It is undeniable that Parliament has a vital role to play in regulating medical assistance in dying. The Canadian laws in this regard are complex and subject to legislative revision. Yet, there is something profoundly wrong with a court recognizing that a person's rights would be violated by a categorical restriction on medical assistance in dying while doing absolutely nothing to remedy that person's unnecessary suffering. Litigants expect courts to craft effective remedies, even while making room for legislatures to craft a broader response to govern the future.

4.4.3 *The Limits of Purely Systemic Remedies in Supra-national Cases*

A similar danger of focusing exclusively on systemic justice is also present in supra-national human rights law. Dinah Shelton has recognized that declaratory judgements have "an important role in human rights litigation, in particular, in preventing a violation that is threatened but has not yet caused measurable harm".[239] She quickly adds, however, that "a declaratory judgment will not, in and of itself, be an adequate remedy" because "it will rarely serve to redress the consequences of the harm already suffered".[240] As suggested in Chapter 2, Section 2.4.3, the two-track approach is increasingly taken by supra-national adjudicators who order individual measures to compensate and general measures to

[238] Kent Roach, *Constitutional Remedies in Canada* 2nd edn (Toronto: Thomson Reuters, 2013), pp.14.1790–14.830.

[239] Dinah Shelton, *Remedies in International Human Rights Law*, 3rd ed. (New York: Oxford University Press, 2015), p.297.

[240] Ibid., p.286.

prevent future rights violations. Another supra-national example of the deficiencies of a purely systemic approach is the refusal of the ECtHR to award damages to prisoners who continued to be denied the vote after the *Hirst* case.[241] This meant that the UK was not reminded by the court of its repetitive rights violations. Moreover, prisoners who were supposed to have rights to vote were at the mercy of the government's determination not to change its legislation. Under the two-track approach, the courts would have continued to award damages even as they took an approach that was more deferential to the state in terms of systemic remedies. Such an approach recognizes the historical and essential role of courts providing successful litigants with remedies.

4.4.4 Same-Sex Marriage Cases

Cases recognizing the ability of same-sex couples to marry have been one of the few genuine achievements in justice so far in the twenty-first century. The century is still young, but these cases may compete for the claim of being this century's *Brown* v. *Board of Education*. Like *Brown*, though, the remedial dilemmas faced by courts were difficult and under-discussed.

The United States Supreme Court in *Obergefell* v. *Hodges*[242] held marriage laws "invalid to the extent they exclude same-sex couples from civil marriage on the same terms and conditions as opposite-sex couples". Although this remedy is often described as striking down, Eric Fish has demonstrated that it effectively read in same-sex couples to the remaining marriage statutes that had excluded them. The result ensured both an immediate individual remedy and a systemic remedy. It also reflected the limits of the strike down in a context where the state provides benefits.

Four judges dissented in *Obergefell*. They would have left the issue to be resolved by legislatures in each state. The majority's decision would have been stronger if it had justified its decision not to give states any leeway on the basis that domestic partnership alternatives would have been clearly unconstitutional by denying same-sex couples the intangible or symbolic benefits associated with marriage. Justice Kennedy for the

[241] *Hirst* v. *United Kingdom* (2005) [GC], No. 74025/01, ECHR 2005-IX; *Firth and Others* v. *United Kingdom* (2014), No. 47784/09 (12 August 2014) (denial of damages and legal costs).

[242] 135 S.Ct. 2584 (2017) at 2605. See Eric Fish "Judicial Amendment of Statutes" (2016) 85 Geo Wash L.Rev. 563.

Court did, however, provide some reasons for not following the *Brown II*[243] model of remanding the case back to the states. He adverted to the dangers of a state-by-state approach that created "distressing complications"[244] for married same-sex couples.

The Court's immediate remedy in *Obergefell* created a risk of backlash. Eminent scholars including Cass Sunstein[245] and William Eskridge[246] proposed more minimalist and dialogic strategies that would have given legislatures more room to manoeuvre. The decision has probably played a role in subsequent decisions to pack the Federal Courts with conservative appointees. At the same time, the attempt in *Brown II* to avoid a backlash by avoiding immediate remedies failed to stop a backlash to desegregation. *Obergefell*, like the Court's decision in *Loving* v. *Virginia*[247] striking down a ban on inter-racial marriage, had power in part because of its combination of individual remedies and systemic remedies.

The South African Constitutional Court took a different approach. The majority of the Court in *Minister of Home Affairs* v. *Fourie*[248] used a twelve month suspended declaration of invalidity to allow the legislature to recognize same-sex marriage and ensure stability and broader support.[249] The Court made clear that should the legislature fail to legislate a

[243] 349 U.S. 294 (1955). This case is discussed in Chapter 7, Section 7.2.1.

[244] *Obergefell* at 2606.

[245] Cass R. Sunstein, "If People Would Be Outraged by Their Rulings, Should Judges Care?" (2007) 60 *Stan. L. Rev.* 155.

[246] William N. Eskridge, Jr., "Pluralism and Distrust: How Courts Can Support Democracy by Lowering the Stakes of Politics" (2004) 114 *Yale L.J.* 6.

[247] 388 US 1 (1967) (reversing conviction of Richard and Mildred Loving but effectively declaring invalid 16 state laws at the time banning inter-racial marriage).

[248] *Minister of Home Affairs* v. *Fourie and Another*, [2005] ZACC 19.

[249] Justice Sachs explained: "what is in issue is a question of status. Interim arrangements that would be replaced by subsequent legislative determinations by Parliament would give to any union established in terms of such a provisional scheme a twilight and impermanent character out of keeping with the stability normally associated with marriage. The dignity of the applicants and others in like situation would not be enhanced by the furnishing of what would come to be regarded as a stop-gap mechanism". Ibid. at para 153. The Canadian cases raised another issue. It was whether Parliament should be given an opportunity to use a derogation provision to deny sex same marriage or shield a civil union scheme from invalidation as inconsistent with equality rights. Two Canadian Courts of Appeal used suspended declarations of invalidity that kept that option alive. *Hendricks* v. *Quebec* [2004], RJQ 851 (C.A.); *EGALE* v. *Canada* [2003], 2003 BCCA 406 (CanLII). A third Court of Appeal decided that a suspension was not justified *Halpern* v. *Toronto* [2003], 2003 CanLII 26403 (ON CA) at paras 156, 161 and used an immediate reading in remedy similar to *Obergefell*. I have argued elsewhere that the suspended declaration of invalidity was preferable in part

rights compliant definition of marriage within a year, a reading in remedy would ensure that same-sex couples could marry.[250] The Court recognized that: "[t]he effect of the suspension of the order of invalidity will be to postpone the day when they can go to a registry and publicly say 'I do.'"[251] In other words, it recognized that it was delaying both systemic and individual remedies. Justice O'Regan dissented. She would have ordered an immediate remedy that would have achieved individual and systemic justice at the same time. She accurately pointed out that the ambit for "legislative choice" that complied with rights was "narrow".[252]

South Africa responded with new legislation that allowed same-sex marriages, albeit by an amendment of the Civil Union Act, 2006[253] and not the Marriage Act 25, 1961.[254] Some gay rights advocates who were initially suspicious of the one year delay commented that "the one-year period definitely opened up a space for visibility and vocality of queer folk . . . I think there was a claiming of citizenship and public space in the one-year process that was very important".[255] Professor Jacoby has

because the immediate reading in created vested rights which prevented the legislature from making (the regrettable) decision of using derogation powers that cannot be applied retroactively: Kent Roach, "Dialogic Judicial Review and Its Critics" (2004) 23 *S.C.L.R.* (2d), 83–88; Roach, *Constitutional Remedies in Canada*, p.14.1450.

250 *Minister of Home Affairs* v. *Fourie and Another,* [2005] ZACC 19 at para 158. As suggested above, such a ruling would have strengthened the reading in remedy in *Obergefell.* Courts that ducked the civil union issues have eventually had to rule on it. For example, the Massachusetts courts used a six-month delay but subsequently ruled that a bill providing for separate civil unions for same-sex couples still was unconstitutional: *Goodridge* v. *Department of Public Health*, 798 N.E.2d 941, 970 (2003), see also the *Opinion of the Justices to the Senate*, 802 N.E.2d 565, 568 (2004). The Colombian Constitutional Court in Decision C-577/11 gave the legislature two years to provide for same-sex marriages, but the Court eventually ruled in Decision SU 214/ 2016 that a separate civil union provision still violated protections of equality. This latter decision took a two-track approach in that it was an aggregation of six individual tutelas. The Court granted these remedies but in order to address the inequities created by the previous decision, it also issued the systemic remedy of declaring "all civil marriages between same sex couples celebrated after June the 20th of 2013, have full validity as they are adjusted to the constitutional interpretation of the sentence C-577 of 2011". English summary online: www.corteconstitucional.gov.co/english/Decision.php?IdPublicacion=9244

251 *Minister of Home Affairs* v. *Fourie*, [2005] ZACC 19 at paras 154.

252 Ibid. at para 168, 171.

253 No. 17. For conclusions that this Act allows marriages, see Holning Lau "Comparative Perspectives on Strategic Remedial Delays" (2016) 91 *Tul. L. Rev.* 259, 281–282.

254 Act No. 25.

255 As quoted in Lau, "Comparative Perspectives", 297. The noted South African scholar David Bilchitz commented: "[a] lot of LGBT people were upset originally, but I think

concluded: "[r]emedial delay can be justified because it is temporary".[256] At the same time, the South African same-sex marriage case was a departure from the two-track approach because it did not provide any immediate or individual remedy. In contrast, *Obergefell* provided both individual and systemic relief. Indeed, this remedy could have been further strengthened had the United States Supreme Court been prepared to decide that any alternative short of gay marriage was unconstitutional.

4.4.5 The Two-Track Approach

When courts employ the new remedies of a declaration of incompatibility, suspended declaration of invalidity or prospective rulings, the two-track approach will provide a salutary reminder not to forget about the litigant who has won the case. The two-track approach should also remind judges to assess whether individualized rulings such as exemptions or as applied rulings provide sufficient systemic guidance to the executive to prevent similar violations in the future.

The two-track approach draws on the traditions of the common law in ensuring that where there is a right, there is a remedy. At the same time, it also recognizes the legitimate role of legislatures and society to be involved in the broader issues raised by a particular claim of right. The tension between dialogic remedies that provide legislatures with policy-making opportunities and the traditional judicial role of providing successful litigants with immediate remedies is real. But it is manageable.

4.4.5.1 The Two-Track Approach and Declarations of Incompatibility

The two-track approach is more difficult to achieve in systems where courts lack the power to invalidate laws to the extent that they violate human rights. The declaration of incompatibility recognizes that the legislature should be allowed to go back to the drawing board to craft a new law that complies with human rights should it so desire. At the same time, it is utterly inadequate with respect to individual remedies. Even if the legislature does respond to the declaration of incompatibility with

many of us in the campaign changed our minds. I initially thought Justice O'Regan was right. I was rather outraged that the court hadn't gone in her direction. Today, I think the majority was actually right". Ibid. at 302.

256 Tonja Jacobi, "Sharing the Love: The Political Power of Remedial Delay in Same-Sex Marriage" (2006) 15 *L. & Sexuality* 11.56.

new legislation that complies with human rights, the new legislation will often only have prospective effect. This may mean that the "successful" litigant is left without any tangible benefit. Sathanapally has observed that only in the first case of a declaration of incompatibility did the UK issue a remedial order that had retroactive effect. As she observes: "[t]he tension between providing a speedy remedy to victims and taking the time to introduce primary legislation ... was resolved, in practice, in favour of primary legislation".[257] When viewed through the lens of the two-track approach, this suggests that the UK government has favoured systemic responses developed by Parliament and downplayed individual remedies for violations. This cuts against the common law grain of the right to a remedy tradition.

Is it possible for a declaration of incompatibility to be made consistent with the two-track model? This was done in one Northern Irish case where a court declared a buggery offence to be incompatible with the Human Rights Act, 1998, but also quashed charges under the Act, thus providing an individual remedy.[258] This case has been criticized by defenders of Parliamentary supremacy who argue that judicial remedies in individual cases should not ignore validly enacted laws.[259] Another possibility is the approach provided by Irish legislation that suggests that damages should be awarded to litigants who obtain a declaration of incompatibility.[260] This would be better in public law than in criminal cases where an accused might still be convicted under an offence that violates rights. Another possibility recommended by Sujit Choudhry and myself in 2003 is to encourage legislatures to depart from their norm of prospective legislation when responding to either a declaration of incompatibility or a suspended declaration.[261] Again the legislative remedy would come too late in criminal cases.

4.4.5.2 The Two-Track Approach and Suspended Declarations of Invalidity: The Choice between Exemptions and Broader Interim Remedies

There are two main ways that courts can make a suspended declaration of invalidity consistent with the two-track approach. One is to exempt

257 Sathanapally, *Beyond Disagreement*, p.142.

258 *McR, Re an Application for Judicial Review,* [2002] NIQB 58.

259 Fergal Davis and David Mead, "Declarations of Incompatibility, Dialogue and the Criminal Law" (2014) 43 *Common Law World Rev.* 62; but for support, see Sathanpally, *Beyond Disagreement,* p.180.

260 Irish European Convention on Human Rights Act, 2003 No. 20, s.5(4).

261 Choudhry and Roach, "Putting the Past Behind Us?'.

successful litigants from the suspension so that they receive the immediate benefit of the remedy. This is the same approach that American and Canadian courts have used when they have employed prospective rulings. This approach is consistent with "right to a remedy" traditions long associated with the common law.

The second means is to follow the practice of the South African Constitutional Court and issue interim remedies that apply not only to the litigant but all rights holders. These interim remedies typically tell the executive how to apply the law that violates human rights during the period of the suspension. In theory, this should leave the legislature free to decide on the ultimate systemic response in the form of new legislation.

Robert Leckey has defended the South African approach on the basis of the importance of "horizontal equality". He has argued that "the idea of horizontal equality between the litigant and other members of her group differentiates constitutional law from private law".[262] His approach is supported by the South African Constitutional Court's strong aversion to providing remedies for litigants but not others similarly situated. There is, however, a danger that robust interim remedies may strain the separation of powers by having the court engage in quasi-legislative rulings that could pre-empt legislative deliberation and policy-making after the court has issued a suspended declaration of invalidity. It may also facilitate an approach where the legislature races to the bottom and only provides the minimum in rights protection that the court is prepared to enforce by way of an interim remedy. This would run afoul of Edmund Burke's warning to legislators that they should do "what humanity, reason and justice tells me I ought to do" as opposed to "what a lawyer tells me I may do".[263]

A more modest, and in my view better, model for interim remedies is that they should only aim to prevent irreparable harms to rights during a suspension. The court should clearly state that the ambition of its interim

[262] Leckey, *Bills of Rights*, p.99.

[263] Edmund Burke, *Burke's Speech on Conciliation with America* (London: MacMillan, 1961). On the tendency of Canadian legislature to opt for the minimum of rights protection, see Kent Roach, "The Dangers of a Charter-Proof and Crime-Based Response to Terrorism" in Ronald Daniels et al. (eds.) *The Freedom of Security: Essays on Canada's Anti-Terrorism Bill* (Toronto: University of Toronto Press, 2001). On similarities between Bickel's understanding of the limits of judicial restraint and Burke's stress on practical reasoning, see Anthony T. Kronman, "Alexander Bickel's Philosophy of Prudence" (1985) 94 *Yale L. J.* 7.

remedy is only to prevent irreparable harm. In other words, the interim remedy may not necessarily be an adequate response if adopted by the legislature. In both the interim remedies and suspended declarations of invalidity context, it is critical that courts retain jurisdiction so that they can respond to perhaps unanticipated issues that arise and, when necessary, re-shape their relief to prevent irreparable harm to rights.[264] The British Columbia Court of Appeal took this approach when it suspended a declaration of invalidity involving correctional legislation that authorized solitary confinement, but then placed a number of restrictions on how the legislation should be used during the suspension.[265] The suspended declaration of invalidity discussed in this chapter, like interim remedies discussed in Chapter 3, help normalize judicial retention of jurisdiction. This brings national practice closer to supra-national practice and helps set the institutional stage for other remedies based on retention of jurisdiction.

In addition to interim remedies that are designed to prevent irreparable harms to others, the successful applicant should be exempted from a declaration of invalidity or a prospective ruling.[266] This will create some "horizontal inequality" but recognizes that adjudication requires that successful litigants receive some remedy. The horizontal equity argument is related to the critique that individual remedies constitute unfair "queue

[264] Canadian courts have held that people can be convicted of offences during a suspended declaration of invalidity. *R.* v. *Ackman*, 2017 MBCA 78 and *R.* v. *Mohsenipour*, 2020 BCCA 160. This may be a correct result provided the courts ensure that the conviction does not involve the constitutional flaws identified when the suspended declaration of invalidity was used and in that way impose irreparable harm to rights.

[265] *British Columbia Civil Liberties* v. *Canada*, 2019 BCCA 5 at para 33; additional reasons: 2019 BCCA 177; 2019 BCCA 233. See Roach, *Constitutional Remedies in Canada*, pp.14.1831–14.1832. Note that new legislation was not unduly influenced by these interim remedies: see *Act to amended the Corrections and Conditional Release Act*, S.C. 2019 c.27, Bill C-83 (Assented to 21 June 2019).

[266] For arguments that this should be required but is far from uniform in the Canadian practice, see Roach, *Constitutional Remedies in Canada*, pp.14.1790–14.1870. Brown and Cote JJ in a partially dissenting judgement have stated "[a] helpful consideration in determining whether an individual exemption [from a suspended declaration of invalidity] is necessary to provide an "effective" remedy is to ask the question the interveners, the David Asper Centre for Constitutional Rights, and the Attorney General of Canada, posit: whether an exemption is necessary to prevent "irreparable harm" to the interests the Charter was designed to protect during the suspension (Asper Centre factum, at para. 2; A.G.C. factum, at para 55; Roach, *Constitutional Remedies*, at §§14.60, 14.910, 14.930 and 14.1790). The case for irreparable harm must be so significant that it overcomes the weighty need to leave the manner of addressing a constitutional infringement to the legislature." *Ontario* v. *G.* 2020 SCC 38 at para 274.

jumping". In Chapter 8, Section 8.3.2, it will be suggested that the queue-jumping critique undercuts the justiciability of social and economic rights. More fundamentally, it misunderstands the nature of adjudication as based on claims by litigants about their rights but also their remedies.

In summary, the two-track approach would have the benefit of ensuring that successful litigants before the court receive a meaningful remedy and that others, as best as possible, would be protected from irreparable harm. At the same time, it would allow the legislature a finite time to enact a new law that complied with human rights. The suspended declaration of invalidity is superior to the declaration of incompatibility because it casts the burden of legislative inertia in favour of rights. It only delays the remedy. It does not allow the legislature's refusal to enact legislation to allow rights violations to continue without even taking responsibility for derogating from human rights, thus often triggering supra-national review.

The provision of an individual remedy in the form of an exemption accords with public expectations about how courts work. The remand of controversial public policy issues to Parliament also accords with public expectations about how democracies work. The use of interim remedies to prevent irreparable harm draws on long standing practices of domestic and supra-national courts.

4.4.6 Remedial Failure and Remedial Cycles

The two-track approach can respond to remedial failure. Supra-national courts and courts that must use a declaration of incompatibility may not be able to provide either individual or systemic remedies. But, they should use their reasons for judgement to clearly indicate the harms caused to litigants by violations. They should also register continued violations of the rights and if possible provide new individual and systemic remedies. On this view, the UK courts were wrong to not award damages and not to issue another declaration of incompatibility when prisoners continued to be denied the vote.[267] The ECtHR was also wrong not to award damages and the Committee of Ministers was wrong to end supervision in the prisoner voting rights case. Both domestic and supra-national systems failed with respect to protecting prisoner voting rights. For UK prisoners, voting rights remain a hollow right without a remedy.

[267] Hodgson and Roach, "Disenfranchisement as Punishment".

The two-track approach contemplates cycles of reform where the failure of systemic remedies to prevent future violations generates new individual and systemic violations. Such cycles can occur after the use of suspended declarations of invalidity.[268] As discussed in Section 4.2.5.2, the Supreme Court of Canada used a suspended declaration of invalidity to allow Parliament to regulate medically assisted dying.[269] The new legislation was subsequently successfully challenged as violating the rights of competent adults suffering irremediable pain but who would not inevitably die from their condition. In 2019, the trial judge issued both a systemic remedy in the form of another suspended declaration of invalidity that applied to the new legislation and an individual remedy that exempted the successful litigant from the delay.[270] In 2020, the declaration of invalidity was extended three times, once because of an election and then because of COVID-19. Following the Supreme Court's 2016 decision, however, both the applicant and all qualified adults were allowed to obtain court ordered exemptions and the government agreed to pay the litigation costs of individuals who obtained exemptions after the third extension.[271]

The Canadian cases reflect remedial failure because Parliament's first attempt at regulation still violated rights. Arguably, the space for legislative deliberation the second time around was more limited. At the same time, the government still conducted public consultations in 2020 on new legislation. The bill that has been introduced would still preclude people whose sole condition was a mental illness from obtaining medical assistance in dying. It also attaches more stringent conditions on those whose death is not reasonably foreseeable. It is not a "cut and paste" from the court decision.[272] The Canadian approach has placed burdens of individual litigation on vulnerable people who wish to receive medical assistance to end their lives. At the same time, it is possible that

[268] For an examination of additional Canadian "second look" cases and for arguments that courts should not be more deferential in them, see Roach, *Supreme Court on Trial*, pp.356–358, 400–406.

[269] *Carter* v. *Canada (Attorney General)*, 2015 SCC 5; *Carter* v. *Canada (Attorney General)*, 2016 SCC 4.

[270] *Truchon c. Procureur général du Canada*, 2019 QCCS 3792.

[271] *Truchon c. Procureur général du Canada*, 2020 QCCS 772 at para 22; *Truchon c. Procureur général du Canada*, 2020 QCCS 2019 at paras 27–28; *Truchon c. Procureur général du Canada*, 2020 QCCS 4388 at para 101.

[272] Bill C-7 (43-2) passed by House of Commons 10 Dec 2020.

South African interim guidelines might have short-circuited legislative policy-making and had increased errors in its administration. Although the issue of assisted dying is a difficult one, the two-track approach facilitates an iterative and dynamic approach to rights compliance that is routine in supra-national law.

4.5 Conclusion

There is a need for a better sense of the respective strengths and weaknesses of the expanding range of remedies for laws that violate human rights. Litigants and courts should pay increased attention to general principles that govern choice of remedies. They should avoid the extremes of using strong and unreasoned forms of discretion or attempting to bind remedial discretion by rules that will inevitably be under- or over-inclusive in some contexts. The principles that should govern choice of remedy for laws that violate human rights include respect for the human rights in play, respect for the separation of powers and the legislature's ability to make policy, a presumption for immediate and fully retroactive relief and the need for the state to justify departures from this norm.

In the last few decades, the remedy of courts reading in words to a statute to ensure compliance with human rights has rightly become less controversial despite the appearance that it is a form of judicial legislation. There has been an increased recognition that the remedial powers of courts should not depend on the vagaries of legislative drafting. This has occurred because of frequent litigation of under-inclusive benefits that excluded disadvantaged groups such as women or sexual minorities. At the end of the day, a judicial reading in remedy, no less than the severance or a partial declaration of invalidity, can be justified if it is consistent with the objectives of the legislation and the relevant human right.

Following the two-track approach, courts should be concerned about protecting the rights of litigants and preventing similar rights violations in the future. Fortunately, many of the remedies for laws that violate human rights, including interpretative remedies and full and partial declarations of invalidity, can often achieve both individual and systemic remedies at the same time. More difficult cases involving declarations of incompatibility, suspended declarations of invalidity and prospective rulings may require more difficult trade-offs between individual and systemic remedies.

The declaration of incompatibility has emerged as a new remedy accepted in New Zealand, disparaged in Australia and perhaps subject to change in the UK. The idea that it is a useless and non-judicial "non-remedy" ignores the role of such declarations in broader domestic and supra-national dialogues. In relying on the adjudicator's ability to persuade the legislator, the declaration of incompatibility narrows the distance between supra-national and domestic human rights law. Domestic courts can also enhance the effectiveness of declarations of incompatibility and honour their obligations to provide individual remedies by continuing to grant damages or other remedies should a legislature continue to violate rights in the face of such a declaration. This would mirror supra-national practice where adjudicators are often concerned with repetitive violations and take an iterative approach.

Courts have understandably been reluctant to use declarations of incompatibility in cases where the stakes for litigants are high, most notably in criminal cases. The alternative of interpretative remedies may distort legislative objectives and create discrepancies between laws as written by the legislature and interpreted by the courts that may cause confusion for the public and the executive. The exercise of remedial discretion, as always, requires an informed choice between competing remedies. Robust interpretative remedies are easier to justify in systems that lack strike down powers. This can be done on the basis of the need for effective remedies that avoid continued rights violations. Interpretative remedies that distort legislative intent are less easily justified when the alternative is invalidation of legislation that will allow the legislature to exercise its full range of legislative options. The responsible exercise of remedial discretion requires courts to compare alternative remedies.

A number of domestic courts can strike down laws to the extent that they violate human rights. In some contexts, invalidation of laws can provide effective and immediate individual and systemic remedies. At the same time, an immediate declaration of invalidity can be a drastic remedy that deprives the state and society of important regulatory and reliance interests. Suspended declarations of invalidity can accommodate the modern regulatory state and the need for legislative action to implement socio-economic and many other rights that require positive state action. At the same time, suspended declarations can fail to provide successful litigants with immediate and effective remedies or provide guidance to the government about what should happen during the delay.

There should be a presumption of full and immediate retroactive relief that produces both effective individual and systemic relief. The state should have to justify the use of suspended declarations of invalidity or prospective rulings as a proportionate and necessary limit on remedies. There should be an even stronger presumption that litigants who have established that their rights have been violated should be exempted from the suspension or transition period and receive the benefit of the ruling. Courts should also craft interim remedies when necessary to prevent irreparable harm to rights while making clear that such relief is not meant to preclude legislative deliberation by providing a permanent systemic remedy.

Remedies provide an important window into comparative judicial review. This chapter has demonstrated that Mark Tushnet's highly influential dichotomy between strong and weak form judicial review breaks down in remedial practice. American courts use interpretative and narrow "as applied" declarations of invalidity to soften their "strong form" judicial review. The latter remedies may provide inadequate guidance to the executive about how they should administer the law and inadequate notice to the governed about what is and is not prohibited. Suspended declarations of invalidity also soften judicial review in Germany, Canada and South Africa. Conversely, the UK courts have been willing to use sweeping interpretative remedies to avoid imposing harms on people under a law subject to a declaration of incompatibility. The detailed analysis in this chapter suggests that the polarized and ideological contest between weak and strong form judicial review does not hold up to the actual practice of remedies. This should re-enforce the message that comparative lawyers and theorists of public law ignore remedies at their peril.

5

Damages

5.1 Introduction

Damages have the longest history of all the remedies for violations of human rights discussed in this book. Non-pecuniary damages of £5 were awarded in a 1703 case for the denial of the right to vote.[1] That case articulated the proposition, later echoed by both Blackstone and Dicey, that "it is a vain thing to imagine a right without a remedy; for want of right and want of remedy are reciprocal".[2] Despite their historical role in enforcing the rule of law and optimism in the wake of encouraging cases in the United States in the 1960s,[3] in India in the 1980s,[4] in New Zealand in the 1990s,[5] and in Canada in 2010[6], damages have becoming disappointing.

In the UK, there has never been much enthusiasm for damages as a remedy under the Human Rights Act, 1998.[7] Section 8 instructs courts to have regard to the jurisprudence of the European Court of Human Rights (ECtHR) in awarding damages. Alas, the consensus has been that the ECtHR and now the UK courts have both failed to develop defensible principles to determine the modest damages they award for serious rights violations.[8] The award of damages by other supra-national courts such as the Inter-American Court of Human Rights (IACtHR) has been no more

[1] *Ashby* v. *White*, (1703) 92 ER 126 at 124, 136; see also *Entick* v. *Carrington*, (1765) 95 ER 807 (K.B.).
[2] Ibid.
[3] *Monroe* v. *Pape*, 365 US 167, (1961); *Bivens* v. *Six Unnamed Agents of the FBI*, 403 US 388 (1971).
[4] *Rudul Sah* v. *State of Bihar*, (1983) 4 SCC 141.
[5] *Simpson* v. *Attorney General (Baigent's Case)*, [1994] 3 NZLR 667.
[6] *Ward* v. *Vancouver*, 2010 SCC 27. I acted as counsel for the British Columbia Civil Liberties Association and the Asper Centre for Constitutional Rights, which intervened in this case at the Court of Appeal and Supreme Court of Canada in support of the award of damages.
[7] c. 42.
[8] Jenny Steele, "Damages and Tort under the Human Rights Act" (2008) 67 *C. L. J.* 606, 634; Jason Varuhas, *Damages and Human Rights* (Oxford: Hart Publishing, 2016), pp.437–438).

inspiring. The Court has relied on vague notions of equity and fair balance even when awarding pecuniary damages sometimes well below the financial costs caused by some violations.[9] UN human rights bodies often make recommendations that states provide compensation without assessing the damages.

The poor performance of supra-national adjudicators is especially troubling because damages are often their prime remedy. Poorly explained damage awards fail to apply sophisticated public international law principles developed by the International Law Commission (ILC)[10] and largely adopted into the 2005 UN Principles on the Right to a Remedy.[11] These Principles are consistent with a two-track approach because they stress both the importance of backward-looking reparation and forward-looking non-repetition. They also recognize the limits of monetizing rights violations by providing for many forms of just satisfaction, including apologies, commemoration and acknowledgement of responsibility. The IACtHR employs these remedies, but the ECtHR simply awards monetary damages, often in amounts that seem both inadequate and inscrutable.

The UK courts have been criticized for following the practice of the ECtHR and awarding low damage awards under the Human Rights Act, 1998. The UK courts have rejected the idea that damages can be increased in order to vindicate rights, even though the Judicial Committee of the Privy Council has increased damage awards in order to vindicate rights under Caribbean constitutions.[12] Some argue that the UK should abandon the public law paradigm of damages for violations of human rights and rely on intentional torts such as assault, false

[9] Thomas Antkowiak and Alejandra Gonza, *The American Convention on Human Rights* (Oxford: Oxford University Press, 2017), pp.295–296 referring to *Case of the Saramaka People* v. *Suriname* (2007), Preliminary Objections, Merits, Reparations and Costs, Inter-Am Ct. H.R. (Ser. C), (28 November 2007) at paras 199–200 in which US$75,000 for taking timber and a US$600,000 community fund was awarded for violations of the rights of an Indigenous community when the timber's market value had been estimated to be US$10 million.

[10] James Crawford, *The International Law Commission's Articles on State Responsibility* (Cambridge: Cambridge University Press, 2002).

[11] United Nations General Assembly, *Basic Principles and Guidelines on the Right to a Remedy and Reparations for Victims of Gross Violations of International Human Rights Law and Serious Violations of Humanitarian Law*, Adopted by the General Assembly 21 March 2006, A/Res/60/147.

[12] *Walumba Lumba (Previously referred to as WL) (Congo) 1 and 2* v. *Secretary of State for the Home Department*, [2011] UKSC 12 at para 101, per Lord Dyson compared to *Merson* v. *Cartwright*, [2006] 3 LRC 264.

imprisonment and trespass.[13] This is not a hypothetical issue given the UK's apparent determination to replace the Human Rights Act, 1998.

Damages are even more disappointing in the US. Both federal and state governments are effectively immune from damage awards in Federal Courts.[14] Qualified immunities for individual officials require breach of the most clearly established rights. A bill passed by the House of Representatives in the wake of the police killing of George Floyd proposes to end such qualified immunities for state and local law enforcement officials, but it is unlikely to be enacted.[15] Even under it, broad immunities for federal officials would remain. The Court refuses to extend *Bivens*[16] actions on the basis of speculations that Congress would not support the award of damages in most areas including national security.[17] The inadequate response of American courts has forced victims of rendition and torture to seek damages in other domestic courts and in supra-national forums. These episodes of "substitute justice"[18] confirm the need to examine remedies in a manner attentive to comparative and supra-national law. It also reveals American remedial exceptionalism and deference to legislative restraints on remedies.

5.1.1 *Outline of This Chapter*

Section 5.2 will outline some current practices of awarding damages for breaches of human rights, with an emphasis on the modest nature of the damages that both supra-national and national courts award. It will also examine the frequent use of qualified immunities that require proof of fault in addition to a violation of a human right.

13 Varuhas, *Damages and Human Rights.*

14 As discussed in Chapter 1, Section 1.4, American law has resisted the calls made by Edwin Borchard almost one hundred years ago to follow Europe and international law examples and accept state liability for human rights violations.

15 George Floyd Justice in Policing Act of 2020, H.R. 712 s.102 proposing amendments to 42 U.S.C. 1983 (passed by House of Representatives 25 June 2020).

16 403 U.S. 388 (1971).

17 *Ziglar* v. *Abbasi,* 137 S.Ct. 1843 (2017) (no constitutional tort for pretextual mass detention after 9/11 under immigration law); *Ashcroft* v. *Al Kidd,* 563 US 731 (2011) (qualified immunity for post 9/11 abuse of material witness warrants). See generally James E. Pfander, *Constitutional Torts and the War on Terror* (Oxford: Oxford University Press, 2017).

18 Kent Roach, "'Substitute Justice?' Indirect Challenges to American Counter-Terrorism Activities in non-American Courts" (2012) 82 *Miss. L. J.* 4.

Section 5.3 will argue that it is not the answer to the generally disappointing nature of damages as a human rights remedy to abandon a public law understanding of such damages in favour of one based on the private law of tort or delict. An improved public law approach that draws on public international law has a number of advantages over private law approaches. They include a focus on state responsibility to cease and not repeat human rights violations.[19] A private law approach to damages focuses simply on damages and allows governments to merely pay an occasional price for rights violations. It also may not vindicate the equality of all rights holders.

Section 5.4 will suggest that the social interests that could be harmed by damages can be accommodated better by the use of proportionality reasoning than through the blunt instruments of qualified immunities that require the applicant to establish fault or absolute immunities. Immunities provide rules to govern the exercise of remedial discretion to award damages that are inevitably under- and over-inclusive. The Supreme Court of Canada has shown the way by preferring proportionality-based limits on damages to qualified immunities.[20] International law is also helpful by introducing alternative forms of satisfaction to damages, including apologies and public acknowledgment of responsibility.

Section 5.5 will outline a two-track approach to damages where damages are used primarily as a first-track compensatory remedy, but can also be used to help prevent future violations. Introducing a theme that will be carried over to the next chapter, the individual and systemic tracks are not watertight compartments. The seriousness of the violation or the state's failure to take steps to prevent similar violations in the future can help justify damages including aggravated damages. If similar violations reoccur, more damages and perhaps other remedies may be necessary.

5.2 Existing Practice

Damages are frequently awarded as a remedy for human rights violations both in international and domestic law. The theoretical goal of such damages is often pitched high: undoing all of the effects of the violation and placing victims in the position they would have occupied but for the

[19] Peter Schuck, *Suing Government: Citizen Remedies for Official Wrongs* (New Haven: Yale University Press, 1983).

[20] *Ward* v. *Vancouver (City)*, 2010 SCC 27.

violation. Alas, the practical reality is that most damage awards are modest and disappointing.

As Dinah Shelton has suggested, "the law on state responsibility for injury to aliens can be viewed as a precursor to international human rights law".[21] In the 1923 *Lusitania* Cases, arbiter Parker stressed that the "remedy must be commensurate with the injury received ... The compensation must be adequate and balance as near as may be the injury suffered".[22] In other words, there should be full compensation for pecuniary and non-pecuniary losses, including "mental suffering, injury to his feelings, humiliation, shame, degradation, loss of social position or injury to his credit or reputation".[23]

The award may reflect state conduct both before and after the act. This includes whether there have been apologies, measures to prevent future recurrence and whether the wrongdoers have been prosecuted and punished.[24] From the start, the diplomatic and dialogic nature of international law has employed a wider time frame than domestic law include tort. This has produced a broader and more realistic view of just satisfaction that is not limited to money and includes concerns about non-repetition. Apologies and efforts to prevent similar violations in the future can help reduce the amount awarded in damages. Domestic courts in human rights cases could learn much from this important practice of international courts.

5.2.1 The International Court of Justice

The International Court of Justice (ICJ) has committed itself to full compensation that will "as far as possible, wipe out all the consequences of the illegal act and re-establish the situation which would, in all probability have existed if that act had not been committed".[25] At the same time, the Court has expressed a preference for state parties to negotiate reparations. If required, it will calculate both pecuniary and non-pecuniary losses based on "equitable considerations".[26] Equity is a flexible tool that allows for a balancing of interests. It also allows for

21 Dinah Shelton, *Remedies in International Human Rights Law*, 3rd ed. (Oxford: Oxford University Press, 2015), p.142.

22 (1923) 7 RIAA at 35 at 36.

23 Ibid. at 40.

24 Shelton, *Remedies in International Human Rights Law*, pp.156–157.

25 *Factory at Chorzow Case* (Judgement No. 13), [1928] PCIJ Series A No. 17 at para 47.

26 *Case Concerning Ahmadou Sadio Diallo (Republic of Guinea* v. *Democratic Republic of the Congo)*, Reports of Judgments, Advisory Opinions and Orders of 19 June 2012, [2012] ICJ Rep. 324 at para 10.

awards that go beyond what is strictly required by principles that require the state to remedy no less and no more than the damages it has caused.[27] Alas, in supra-national law, equity is often used as a shorthand reference to strong remedial discretion that allows courts to award inadequate damages.

The range of discretion is well illustrated by one case where the Republic of Guinea claimed US$11.5 million for an almost seven-year wrongful detention by the Democratic Republic of the Congo (DRC) of a Guinean national living in the DRC.[28] The ICJ awarded US$85,000 in non-pecuniary damages and US$10,000 in pecuniary damages. The Court stressed that damage awards "necessarily rests on equitable considerations".[29] To illustrate the flexibility of the equitable process, some judges expressed concerns that the award was higher than that made by other international courts,[30] and even excessive and disproportionate.[31] Other judges would have ordered a higher award.[32] Judge Cançado-Trindade argued in a scholarly concurring judgement that the ICJ was re-claiming an earlier natural law tradition in international law that recognized that reparation for individuals was an "indispensable" result of a finding of a violation.[33]

In 2018, Costa Rica requested US$6.1 million in damages from Nicaragua for environmental harms. After the states could not agree on damages, the ICJ awarded US$378,000 in damages.[34] The Court noted that compensation was appropriate when restitution "is materially impossible or unduly burdensome ... but should not have a punitive or exemplary character".[35] The Court relied on a vague "overall

[27] Kent Roach, "The Limits of Corrective Justice and the Potential of Equity" (1991) 33 *Ariz. L. Rev.* 859.

[28] It is notable that, in this case, the petitioner state did not offer evidence about the loss of property underlining Professor Shelton's warnings that lawyers and judges in international tribunals must receive better evidence and argument at the remedial stage: Shelton, *Remedies in International Human Rights Law*, p.375.

[29] *Case Concerning Ahmadou Sadio Diallo (Republic of Guinea* v. *Democratic Republic of the Congo)*, Reports of Judgments, Advisory Opinions and Orders of 19 June 2012, [2012] ICJ Rep. 324 at para 13.

[30] Ibid. per Judge Greenwood at para 11 (Sep. Op.).

[31] Ibid. per Judge ad hoc Mampuya at para 13 (Sep. Op.).

[32] Ibid. per Judge ad hoc Mahiou at para 13 (Sep. Op.).

[33] Ibid per Judge Cançado-Trindade at paras 21, 40. (Sep. Op.)

[34] *Certain Activities Carried out by Nicaragua in the Border Area (Costa Rica* v. *Nicaragua)*, Compensation Owed by the Republic of Nicaragua to the Republic of Costa Rica of 2 February 2018, [2018] ICJ Gen. List No. 150, at para 42.

[35] Ibid. at para 31.

assessment" and did not decide between Nicaragua's preferred replacement value and Costa Rica's preferred ecosystem repair approach.[36] Unfortunately, this is typical of the summary reasoning that too often accompanies remedial decision-making.

5.2.2 *The European Court of Human Rights*

The ECtHR will only award damages under Article 41 of the European Convention if the reparation provided by national courts is inadequate.[37] Like the ICJ, the ECtHR awards damages on an equitable basis without extensive fact-finding and reliance on precedents. It does not explain its decisions to award or not to award damages, despite the fact that it awarded between €53 million and €2 billion in damages each year from 2011 to 2017.[38]

Both the UK Law Commission and the House of Lords have concluded that the ECtHR's award of damages have not produced legal principles.[39] The Strasbourg Court's awards continue to be inconsistent and difficult to rationalize.[40] The Court even uses confidential tables to calculate some forms of damages that have not been disclosed to the parties or the public and that apparently take into account the different economic conditions in the forty-seven member states.[41] The strong and unreasoned discretion that the Court exercises over damages is also reflected in its unpredictable decisions to hold that they are not necessary because the

[36] Ibid. at para 78.

[37] Lize Glas, "The European Court of Human Rights Supervising the Execution of Its Judgments" (2019) 37 *Net. Q. Hum. Rts.* 3.

[38] Department for the Execution of Judgments of the European Court of Human Rights, "Just Satisfaction: Global Amount Awarded by the European Court" online: https://rm.coe.int/1-just-satisfaction-global/16807b9250

[39] *Greenfield, R (on the application of)* v. *Secretary of State for the Home Department,* [2005] UKHL 14 at para 19; *R (on the application of Faulkner)* v. *Secretary of State for Justice*; *R. (on the application of Sturnham)* v. *Parole Board,* [2013] 2 WILR 1157 at para 34; Kenneth Cooper-Stephenson concludes the position is "unsettled": Kenneth Cooper-Stephenson, *Constitutional Damages Worldwide* (Toronto: The Carswell Company Ltd, 2013), p.234.

[40] Compare *Kablis* v. *Russia*, Nos. 48310/16, ECHR 9 September 2019 at 111, 121(a)(i)(ii) awarding €15,000 in damages and *Savva Terentyev* v. *Russia*, No. 10692/09, ECHR 28 August 2018 at para 98 concluding findings of violation was sufficient reparation in two recent cases involving freedom of expression violations by Russia.

[41] Octavian Ichim, *Just Satisfaction under the European Convention on Human Rights* (Cambridge: Cambridge University Press, 2015), p.2.

judgement alone is sufficient. In short, the ECtHR's damage jurisprudence confirms the dangers discussed in Chapter 1, Section 1.7, that strong forms of discretion to award or not award remedies present to both rights and the rule of law.[42]

The Grand Chamber has stated that "there must be a clear causal connection between the damage claimed by the applicant and the violation of the Convention and that this may, in the appropriate case, include compensation in respect of loss of earnings".[43] At the same time, the Court has qualified the above by indicating that damages can be awarded on an equitable basis even if a "precise calculation of the sums necessary to make complete reparation (*restitutio in integrum*) in respect of the pecuniary losses suffered by the applicants may be prevented by the inherently uncertain character of the damage flowing from the violation".[44] In Section 5.5, it will be suggested that causation requirements are justified for compensatory aspects of damage awards but not with respect to aggravated damages.

The ECtHR has not hesitated to award high levels of pecuniary damages when property rights have been violated. There are many examples of awards of millions of euros to companies who have suffered such violations.[45] Octavio Ichim rightly criticizes the result as a "perversion of human rights" compared to the Court's modest awards of non-pecuniary damages less than €10,000 in cases of inhumane conditions of confinement.[46]

[42] *R. (on the application of Faulkner)* v. *Secretary of State for Justice*; *R. (on the application of Sturnham)* v. *Parole Board*, [2013] UKSC 23.

[43] *Z. and others* v. *United Kingdom* [GC], No. 29392/95, [2001] V ECHR 1 at para 119; see also Cooper-Stephenson, Constitutional Damages Worldwide, pp.160–162.

[44] *Z and others* v. *United Kingdom* [GC], No. 29392/95, [2001] V ECHR 1 at para 120. In some cases, the Court has awarded pecuniary damages on the basis of a loss of chance or probability reasoning while in other cases requiring a stricter demonstration of "but for" causation requirements: Cooper-Stephenson, Constitutional Damages Worldwide, pp.174–176.

[45] For a survey of some of these cases, see Shelton, Remedies in International Human Rights Law, pp.337–345.

[46] Ichim, *Just Satisfaction*, p.157 comparing *Oferta Plus S.R.L.* v. *Moldova*, No. 14385/04, ECHR 12 February 2008 at para 76 (€2,500,000 in pecuniary damages and €25,000 in non-pecuniary damages awarded) and *Dacia S.R.L.* v. *Moldova*, No. 3052/04, ECHR 24 February 2009 at para 62 (€7,237,700 in pecuniary damages and €25,000 in non-pecuniary damages awarded) with *Ciorap* v. *Moldova (No. 2)*, No. 7481/06, ECHR 20 July 2010 at paras 31, 33 (€4,000 in non-pecuniary damages awarded) and *Parnov* v. *Moldova*, No. 35208/06, ECHR 13 July 2010 at paras 43, 45 (€87 in pecuniary damages and €9,000 in non-pecuniary damages awarded).

In 2014, the Grand Chamber held that its equitable approach would apply even to the calculation of pecuniary damages so long as there was some reasonable relation to market value. It approved of damages for the expropriated property that was 75 per cent lower than some quoted market values. It stated that: "the Court finds that the compensation to be determined in the present case will not have to reflect the idea of a total elimination of the consequences of the impugned interference, nor the full value of the property in issue".[47] It will be suggested in Section 5.4 of this chapter that it is legitimate for courts to consider competing social interests, especially when evaluating requests for large amounts of damages. Nevertheless, this should be done in a more transparent and disciplined fashion through the use of proportionality reasoning.

The Grand Chamber has appealed to the principle of subsidiarity to accept Slovenia's proposed blending of awards for pecuniary and non-pecuniary damages for people whose identities were erased from official citizenship registries.[48] The subsidiarity principle recognizes the need to defer to states that are closer to local conditions. It could justify the award of greater damages in cases of repetitive violations on the basis that the state has not prevented the violation. Unfortunately, there is some evidence that the Court awards less damages in cases of repetitive violations than single violations, providing states with perverse incentives.[49]

Flexible equitable principles can be a double-edged sword. It can be used to justify both inadequate and overly generous damages. In 2017, the Grand Chamber awarded €50,000 in damages to a mother whose son was killed by Russian authorities at a public protest.[50] The Court made this award even though the applicant had not submitted the normally required documents to substantiate the claim. It also observed that that the rule of exhausting domestic remedies may not apply to just

[47] *Case of Vistiņš and Perepjolkins* v. *Latvia* [GC], No. 71243/01, ECHR 25 March 2014 at para 36. The Court also awarded €3,000 in non-pecuniary damages.

[48] *Kurić and others* v. *Slovenia* [GC], No. 26828/06, Judgment (Just satisfaction), [2014] I ECHR 321; *Preda and Others* v. *Romania*, Nos. 9584/02 et al., CEDH 123, ECHR 29 April 2014.

[49] Veronika Fikfak, "Changing State Behaviour: Damages before the European Court of Human Rights" (2019) 29(4) *E.J.I.L.* 1091, 1111 noting reductions to awards from €5,000 to €1,000 in cases involving Ukraine's non execution of judgements and from €1,500 to 700 in cases dealing with trial delay in Italy. See also Judge Keller's dissent in *Navalnyy* v. *Russia* [GC], No. 29580/12, ECHR 2 February 2017 criticizing the majority for under-compensating rights violations from seven different arrests.

[50] *Case of Nagmetov* v. *Russia* [GC], No. 35589/08, ECHR 30 March 2017.

satisfaction claims.[51] In an interstate case, the Court awarded €10 million against Russia to emphasize the seriousness of the violation. In both cases, the Court stressed that its "guiding principle is equity".[52] This award was attentive to very serious violations and the difficulties of obtaining reparation and exhausting domestic remedies in Russia.

In a 2001 case, the Grand Chamber awarded £32,000 in non-pecuniary damages as a "a substantial award to reflect the pain and suffering" of four applicants who had suffered serious abuse while in child care apprehension.[53] In a more recent case, the Grand Chamber awarded, on an equitable basis, €5,000 in combined pecuniary and non-pecuniary damages to applicants in Azerbaijan who had been displaced from their homes for over a decade because of military conflict.[54] As Jason Varuhas has effectively shown, it is difficult to rationalize these awards.[55] Moreover, awards at the level of €5,000 or less can be criticized as trivializing rights and the suffering of the successful applicants. The Court has also occasionally reduced damage awards because of judgements about the applicants and their involvement in crime.[56] It will be suggested in Section 5.2.3 of this chapter that such an approach is contrary to the equality of all rights holders.

In some contexts, the Court has brought some order to its damage awards by creating guidelines. Ichim has pointed to guidelines between €1,000 and 1,500 per year for unreasonable delay of legal proceedings (and even up to €2,000 if "what was at stake for the victim was particularly important") and €450–500 per day for detention without judicial review. Ichim suggests that these are a satisfactory starting point with some basis in the caselaw.[57] As he suggests, however, such guidelines cannot be applied mechanically and should be subject to justified exceptions based on the gravity of the violation and its effects on the specific applicant.[58] Ichim also suggests standards of €50,000–100,000 for torture and €20,000–40,000 for mistreatment.[59] A recent study has found that over thirteen years, almost 95 per cent of victims of torture and

[51] Ibid. at paras 66–67.
[52] Ibid. at paras 73; *Georgia* v. *Russia* [GC], No. 13255/07, ECHR 2 July 2014 at para 46.
[53] *Z and others* v. *United Kingdom* [GC], No. 29392/95, [2001] V ECHR 1 at para 130.
[54] *Sargysan* v. *Azerbaijan* [GC], No. 40167/06 [2017], ECHR 14 December 2011.
[55] Varuhas, *Damages and Human Rights*, pp.271–272.
[56] *McCann and Others* v. *the United Kingdom* [GC] [1995], 21 ECHR 97 at para 219.
[57] Ichim, *Just Satisfaction*, p.261.
[58] Ibid., p.262.
[59] Ibid., p.267.

inhumane treatment were awarded less than €20,000, while 95 per cent of victims of fair trial violations were awarded less than €10,000.[60]

There is ambiguity with respect to whether damages can be aggravated by state misconduct. In one 2009 case, the Court stated that "there is little, if any, scope under the Convention for directing governments to pay penalties to applicants which are unconnected with damage shown to be actually incurred".[61] But in another 2009 case, it stated that damages can be used as "a serious and effective means of dissuasion with regard to the repetition of unlawful conduct of the same type, without however assuming a punitive function".[62] This latter statement seems to contemplate some role for aggravated damages to signal concerns about repetitive violations. It will be suggested below that this is appropriate in a two-track approach to damages.

Judge Pinto de Albuquerque has argued that punitive damages should be used with respect to gross, continuing or deliberate violations.[63] His judgement has been praised by commentators who urge the court explicitly to award punitive and denunciatory damages in response to serious and repeated violations.[64] Writing extra-judicially, the judge also has argued that the Court has increased damages in response to government fault.[65] Alas, the Court's lack of reasoning when making most damage awards fails to send clear signals about when and why it has increased damages.

It is particularly disappointing that the ECtHR seems to view damages as an afterthought and has such an inconsistent and unsatisfactory jurisprudence. This is especially so because damages remain its prime remedy and as suggested below it could draw on international law principles of state responsibility to take a sounder approach.

5.2.3 *European Court of Justice*

The European Court of Justice has held that member states may be liable in damages for breaches of European Union (EU) law, but only if "the

60 Fikfak, "Changing State Behaviour", 1108.
61 *Varnava and others* v. *Turkey* [GC], No. 16064/90, [2009] V ECHR 13 at paras 223–224.
62 *Guiso-Gallisay* v. *Italy* (Just satisfaction) [GC], No. 58858/00, ECHR 22 December 2009 at para 85.
63 *Cyprus* v. *Turkey* [GC], No. 25781/94, Judgement (Just satisfaction), [2014], II ECHR 245 at para 18 (Pinto de Albuquerque J., concurring).
64 Fikfak, "Changing State Behaviour", 1124.
65 Pinto de Albuquerque and Anne Van Aaken, "Punitive Damages in Strasbourg" in Anne van Aaken and Julia Motoc (eds.), *The European Convention on Human Rights and General International Law* (Oxford: Oxford University Press, 2017), p.230.

full effectiveness of Community rules would be weakened if individuals were unable to obtain compensation when their rights are infringed by a breach of Community law for which a Member State can be liable".[66] This formulation, as well as the requirement that violations must be serious, seems to take an instrumental approach so that damages are only awarded when they are advantageous or necessary to enforce EU laws.[67] That said, once damages are sought, EU law then somewhat incoherently requires that a direct causal connection be shown between a breach and the damage to be remedied as well as full reparation be made for the damage caused.[68] These individualistic causation and standing requirements would fit better with a compensatory rationale for damages.

5.2.4 *Inter-American Court of Human Rights*

The IACtHR will award damages if those ordered by the national authorities are not reasonable or effective in making full reparation.[69] The IACtHR has recognized that in "most cases involving human rights violations ... full restitution (*restitutio in integrum*), which implies restoring the previous situation ... is not feasible".[70] Nevertheless it has been more willing to order restitution than the ECtHR.[71] This can perhaps be explained by the specific reference in Article 63(1) of the American Convention that "the Court shall rule that the injured party be ensured the enjoyment of his right or freedom" with subsequent reference to "fair compensation be[ing] paid to the injured party".[72] The

66 *Francovich and Bonifaci* v. *Italy*, [1991] I ECHR 5357 at para 33.

67 Varahus, *Damages and Human Rights*, p.437 concluding that damages under EU law are "a damp squib, a remedy rarely sought and very rarely granted".

68 *R* v. *Secretary of State for Transport, ex parte Factortame Ltd (No. 2)*, [1991] 1 AC 603 at para 51 requiring "a direct causal link between the breach of the obligation resting on the state and the damage sustained by the injured parties".

69 *Rodriguez Vera et al. (The Disappeared from the Palace of Justice)* v. *Colombia* (2014), Preliminary Objections, Merits, Reparations, and Costs, Judgment, Inter-Am. Ct. H.R. (Ser. C), (14 November 2014) at para 593.

70 *Aloeboetoe et al.* v. *Suriname* (1993), Reparations and Costs, Inter-Am. Ct. H.R. (Ser. C), (10 September 1993) at para 49.

71 In 1997, the IACtHR first ordered a person freed: *Loayza Tamayo v. Peru* (1997), Merits, Inter-Am. Ct. H.R. (Ser. C), (17 September 1997) whereas this was only done by the ECtHR in 2004.

72 American Convention on Human Rights, San Jose, Costa Rica, 22 November 1969, in force 18 July 1978, 1144 UNTS 123, Art. 63(1).

IACtHR will sometimes hold that its judgement itself is sufficient reparation, but much less often than does the ECtHR.[73]

Like the Strasbourg court, the San Jose court stresses an equitable approach even with respect to the calculation of pecuniary damages. On the one hand, this has allowed the payment of damages when applicants could not submit full documentation. On the other hand, it has also allowed the Court to award US$75,000 in damages for loss of timber in the face of expert evidence submitted by an Indigenous applicant that the loss was US$10 million.[74] In the absence of other information, the Court may determine lost earnings on the basis of the minimum wage in the country in question.[75] It has also remanded the determination of pecuniary damages to national authorities. This may be a solution, but it places the burden of additional litigation on the victim.[76] Similar to the ECtHR, the IACtHR has in some cases awarded less than market value for violations of property rights. This reflects a felt need to strike "a fair balance"[77] between the interests of the prior owner and the social interest. Nevertheless, the US$18.7 million award in one property rights case affirms that, as with the ECtHR, some of the most generous damage awards are for violations of the property rights of advantaged persons.

The Court also takes an equitable approach to non-pecuniary damages, often awarding between US$50,000 and US$100,000 in the most serious cases involving torture or loss of life.[78] As Jo Pasqualucci has argued: "evidence is not necessary to prove non-pecuniary damages to a person who has been subject to cruel, inhuman, and degrading treatment, extrajudicial execution, forcible disappearance or arbitrary detention. Moral suffering in such cases is self-evident".[79] The IACtHR will award

[73] *"The Last Temptation of Christ" (Olmedo Bustos et al.)* v. *Chile* (2002), Inter-Am. Ct. H.R. (Ser. C), (5 February 2001) at para 99.

[74] *Case of the Saramaka People* v. *Suriname* (2007), Preliminary Objections, Merits, Reparations and Costs, Inter-Am Ct. H.R. (Ser. C), (28 November 2007) at para 153 as discussed in Thomas Antikowiak and Alejandra Gonza, *The American Convention on Human Rights: Essential Rights* (Oxford: Oxford University Press, 2017).

[75] *Villagrán-Morales et al.* v. *Guatemala (Street Children case)* (2001), Inter-Am Ct. H.R. (Ser. C), (26 May 2001) at para 79.

[76] Jo M. Pasqualucci, *The Practice and Procedure of the Inter-American Court of Human Rights*, 2nd ed. (New York: Cambridge University Press, 2013), p.236.

[77] *Salvador Chiriboga* v. *Ecuador* (2011), Reparations and Costs, Judgment, Inter-Am. Ct. H.R. (Ser. C), (3 March 2011) at para. 98.

[78] Antikowiak and Gonza, *The American Convention on Human Rights*, p.297.

[79] Pasqualucci, *The Practice and Procedure of the Inter-American Court of Human Rights*, p.236.

damages to next of kin depending on their closeness to the victim and how they were affected by the violation.[80] It has, however, abandoned its attempt to award damages for harm to a victim's life plans while noting that these harms can be covered by other forms of satisfaction and guarantees of non-repetition.[81] Like the ECtHR, the Court has at times refused to award damages because of the wrongdoing of the applicant.[82] It will be suggested below that this approach denies the equality of rights holders.

Like the ECtHR, the IACtHR has not accepted a role for punitive or aggravated damages while at the same time admitting that the seriousness of the violation may affect the quantum of damages, especially for non-pecuniary damages. It has reasoned that "reparations should not make the victims or their successors either richer or poorer and they should be proportionate to the violations declared in their judgment".[83] Pasqualucci has defended this approach on the basis that punitive damages would be paid by developing states and provoke public backlash against the Court.[84] Others support punitive damages as a means to ensure that non-compliant states do not simply pay small damage awards while otherwise not complying with rights.[85]

Judge Cançado Trindade has argued in a series of concurring judgements that the Court has "quite an amount of leeway regarding reparations. In my opinion ... some reparations with dissuasive or exemplary purposes (relating to aggravated liability) may contribute to the struggle against impunity and to guarantee non-repetition of harmful events".[86] Some commentators have concluded that the differences between his

[80] *Bámaca Velásquez* v. *Guatemala* (2000), Inter-Am. Ct. H.R. (Ser. C), (25 November 2000) at para 163 citing *Timurtas* v. *Turkey*, No. 23531/94, [2000] ECHR 221 at para 95 and *Çakici* v. *Turkey*, No. 23657/84, ECHR 8 July 1999 at para 98.

[81] *Ibsen Cardenas and Ibsen Peña* v. *Bolivia* (2010), Merits Reparations and Costs, Inter-Am. Ct. H.R. (Ser. C), (1 September 2010) at para 277.

[82] *Cruz Sánchez et al.* v. *Peru* (2005), Preliminary Objections, Merits, Reparations, Costs, Judgment, Inter-Am. Ct. H.R. (Ser. C), (17 April 2015) at paras 145, 483.

[83] *Goiburu et al.* v. *Paraguay* (2006), Judgement, Inter-Am. Ct. H.R. (Ser. C), (22 September 2006) at para 143.

[84] Pasqualucci, *The Practice and Procedure of the Inter-American Court of Human Rights*, p.193.

[85] Lisa Laplante, "Bringing Effective Remedies Home: The Inter-American Human Rights System, Reparations and the Duty of Prevention" (2004) 22 *Net. Q. Hum. Rts.* 347.

[86] *Gomez Plamoino* v. *Peru* (2005), Merits, Reparations and Costs, Judgment, Inter-Am. Ct. H.R. (Ser. C), (22 November 2005) concurring opinion of Judge Cançado Trindade at para 9.

view and the majority view that eschews punitive damage is semantic, given the flexibility of awards for non-pecuniary damages without actual evidence or proof[87] and the Court's recognition that damages can be used in part as "guarantees of non-repetition".[88] This view is supported by cases in which damages have been awarded as a means of "transmitting a message of official condemnation of the human rights violations in question and commitment to the efforts to ensure that they do not happen again".[89] At the same time, however, principles governing aggravated or punitive damages might allow the court to send clearer signals to litigants, the community and the state about its particular condemnation of serious violations.

Consistent with the 2005 UN Basic Principles, the IACtHR frequently includes elements of commemoration and public acknowledgment of responsibility along with damages. Judge Trindade has also praised state apologies and public acknowledgements of responsibility that have been ordered by the IACtHR and often obtained.[90] The IACtHR has been more creative in devising reparations than the ECtHR.[91] This suggests that comparative law insights could be applied to the work of the regional human rights courts.

5.2.5 *African Court of Human and Peoples' Rights*

The African Court of Human and Peoples' Rights, in its early jurisprudence, refused to order damages for violations of political rights in the absence of evidence of harm. However, it has ordered that judgements be

87 Agnostina Cichero and Sebastian Green-Martinez, "Punitive Damages and the Principle of Full Reparation in the Case Law of the Inter-American Court of Human Rights" in Yves Haeck et al. (eds.), *The Inter-American Court of Human Rights: Theory and Practice, Present and Future* (Cambridge: Intersentia, 2015), p.337.

88 *Supreme Court of Justice (Quintanan Coella et al.)* v. *Ecuador* (2013), Preliminary Objections, Merits, Reparations and Costs, Judgment, Inter-Am. Ct. H.R. (Ser. C) as cited with approval in Shelton, *Remedies in International Human Rights Law*, pp.228–229.

89 *Villagrán-Morales et al.* v. *Guatemala (Street Children case)* (2001), Inter-Am Ct. H.R. (Ser. C), (26 May 2001); see also Leiry Cornejo Chavez, "New Remedial Responses in the Practice of Regional Human Rights Courts: Purposes Beyond Compensation" (2017) 15 *I. Con.* 372.

90 Antonio Augusto Cançado Trindade, "The Human Person and International Justice" (2008) 47 *Colum. J. Transnt'l. L.* 16, 21–22.

91 Gabriella Citroni, "Measures of Reparation for Victims of Gross Human Rights Violations: Developments and Challenges in the Jurisprudence of Two Regional Human Rights Courts" (2012) 5 *Inter-Am. & Eur. Hum. Rts. J.* 49–71.

published and that the state report back to the Court to ensure non-repetition.[92] It has also, like the IACtHR, accepted a broad meaning of "victim", including family members.[93]

5.2.6 *Summary of Supra-national Jurisprudence*

The damage jurisprudence of supra-national courts remains disappointing. In many ways, it is not really a jurisprudence, but an inconsistent practice that is justified by vague appeals to equitable principles. This is especially regrettable given the existence of public international law principles of state responsibility developed by the International Law Commission and in the 2005 UN Basic Principles could provide a better basis for these courts to award and assess damages.

5.2.7 *The United Kingdom*

In the 1703 case of *Ashby* v. *Wright*, the House of Lords affirmed a £5 damage award by a jury against a constable who had denied an eligible voter the right to vote. Although some doubt has been cast on the case's reliance on the simple syllogism of where there is a right, there must be a remedy,[94] the House of Lords decision has generally been seen as a vindication of Chief Justice Holt's dissent in the Queen's Bench when he famously argued "it is a vain thing to imagine a right without a remedy; for want of a right and want of a remedy are reciprocal".[95] He elaborated: "a man shall have an action against another for riding over his ground, though it do him no damage, for it is an invasion of property, and the other has no right to come there". He stressed that damages were justified because the plaintiff was "obstructed of his right" even though the injury "does not cost the party one farthing".[96] He also hoped that damages for

[92] *Mtikila* v. *The United Republic of Tanzania* (2014), No. 011/2011, Ruling on Reparations, African Court on Human and Peoples' Rights, 1 AfCLR 72.

[93] *Zongo and Others* v. *Burkina Faso* (2015), No. 013/2011, Ruling on Reparations, African Court on Human and Peoples' Rights, 1 AfCLR 258.

[94] For arguments that the historical record suggests that damages were only awarded on the basis that the defendant had maliciously and with fault denied the plaintiff the right to vote, see Ted Sampson-Jones, "The Myth of Ashby v. Wright" (2010) 8 *St Thomas L. Rev.* 40. This more restrictive view of the precedent was followed in subsequent cases: *Harman* v. *Tappendan,* (1801) 102 ER 217; *Williams* v. *Lewis,* (1797) 170 ER 232.

[95] *Ashby* v. *White,* (1703) 92 ER 126; 2 Ld. Raymond 938 at 953.

[96] Ibid. at 955.

denial of the right to vote "will make public officers more careful to observe the *constitution* of cities and boroughs, and not to be so partial as they commonly are in all elections, which is indeed a great and growing mischief, and tends to the prejudice of the peace of the nation".[97] The jury's award of £5 may strike one as modest until it is considered that average yearly earnings at the time were only slightly over £100.[98] In the famous 1753 case of *Entick* v. *Carrington* that affirmed rights against illegal searches and seizures, a jury awarded £300.[99] This again was generous, given that the average yearly earnings had barely increased since 1703.[100]

This approach can be compared with *Faulkner* v. *Secretary of State for Justice*[101] where the UK Supreme Court indicated that damages awarded under section 8 of the Human Rights Act, 1998 should follow the practice of the ECtHR in awarding damages in countries with similar standards of living as the UK. The Supreme Court held that damages for "frustration and anxiety" caused by delay "should be on a modest scale" and cited with approval ECtHR judgements that awarded about £1,000 for such non-pecuniary damages before approving an award of £300 in the case.[102] In a companion case, where there was evidence that the delay had caused not only frustration and anxiety but also ten additional months in prison, the Court awarded £6,500 in damages.[103] The English courts are awarding significantly more modest awards for violations of human rights than under the traditional common law. To be sure, any award of damages will have aspects of the conventional and even symbolic. Extravagant awards are not justified. At the same time, courts should not trivialize the importance of the right and penalize the expensive process of litigation by ordering low amounts of damages.

97 Ibid. (emphasis added).

98 See Pierre Marteau, "The Marteau Early 18th Century Currency Converter: Great Britain 1600–2000" online: www.pierre-marteau.com/currency/indices/uk-02.html

99 (1765) 95 ER 896.

100 See Pierre Marteau, "The Marteau Early 18th Century Currency Converter: Great Britain 1600–2000" online: www.pierre-marteau.com/currency/indices/uk-02.html

101 [2013] UKSC 23.

102 Ibid. at 13, 67, 97. For similar subsequent modest damages for non-pecuniary harms caused by rights violations, see *R. (on application of Hainey)* v. *Secretary of State,* [2014] UKSC 66. In an earlier case, the House of Lords had followed the practice of the ECtHR in not awarding non-pecuniary damages for a violation of a right to counsel on the basis that a declaration of a violation was sufficient: *Greenfield, R (on the application of)* v. *Secretary of State for the Home Department,* [2005] UKHL 14 at paras 30–31.

103 Ibid. at para 87.

Jason Varuhas has also raised concerns that modest approaches to damages under public law may adversely affect more generous damages for intentional torts.[104] He notes how the UK Supreme Court has recently rejected vindicatory damages for the tort of false imprisonment because it was not prepared to let "such an unruly horse loose on our law".[105] Even dissenting judges who were prepared to "set the horse loose" stressed that the awards should be modest and in the range of £500 to £1,000.[106] In contrast, the Privy Council has awarded much higher vindicatory awards under Caribbean constitutions.[107]

It may be better to award no damages than trivial damages. In 2006, the House of Lords held that no damages should be awarded for a deliberate and bad faith opening of a prisoner's mail that did not cause financial loss. This reversed an appeal decision that had awarded the prisoner £5.[108] The ECtHR upheld the decision not to award damages in this case. It suggested that the acknowledgment of the violation coupled with the availability of damage awards in the future was sufficient.[109]

104 Varuhas, *Damages and Human Rights.* See also *Watkins* v. *SOSHD,* [2006] 2 AC 395 at para 64 noting that ECtHR's awards are "ungenerous" compared to tort awards.

105 *Walumba Lumba (previously referred to as WL) (Congo) 1 and 2* v. *Secretary of State for the Home Department,* [2011] UKSC 12 at para 101.

106 Lady Hale reasoned: "[b]ut no-one can deny that the right to be free from arbitrary imprisonment by the state is of fundamental constitutional importance in this country. It is not the less important because we do not have a written constitution. It is a right which the law should be able to vindicate in some way, irrespective of whether compensatable harm has been suffered or the conduct of the authorities has been so egregious as to merit exemplary damages. Left to myself, therefore, I would mark the false imprisonment in these cases with a modest conventional sum, perhaps £500 rather than the £1000 suggested by Lord Walker, designed to recognise that the claimant's fundamental constitutional rights have been breached by the state and to encourage all concerned to avoid anything like it happening again. In reality, this may well be what was happening in the older cases of false imprisonment, before the assessment of damages became such a refined science". Ibid. at para 217.

107 *Trinidad and Tobago (Attorney General)* v. *Ramanoop,* [2005] UKPC 15; *Merson* v. *Cartwright,* [2005] UKPC 38; *Takitota* v. *Bahamas, (Attorney General)* [2009] UKPC 11. The International Court of Justice has also been more generous awarding US$85,000 in damages for non-material loss to Guinea in relation to the wrongful expulsion of a national of the Democratic Republic of the Congo: *Case Concerning Ahmadou Sadio Diallo (Republic of Guinea* v. *Democratic Republic of the Congo),* Compensation Owed by the Democratic Republic of the Congo to the Republic of Guinea, Judgement of 19 June 2012 at para 25.

108 *Watkins* v. *Home Office,* [2006] UKHL 17 at para 26.

109 *Watkins* v. *United Kingdom,* No. 35757/06, [2009] ECHR 1730.

In the 2005 *Greenfield* case,[110] the House of Lords held that damages under the Human Rights Act, 1998 were not the appropriate remedy for a fair hearing violation that resulted in a conviction for a prison disciplinary offence and an extra twenty-one days' imprisonment for the plaintiff. The House of Lords stressed that the ECtHR, in most cases involving fair trial rights, only makes declaration of a violation. Lord Bingham concluded that following the reference in section 8 of the Human Rights Act, 1998, English courts should follow the ECtHR jurisprudence. In a recognition that damages can be responsive to the need to avoid repetitive violations, he did note that "it may be different if there is felt to be a need to encourage compliance by individual officials or classes of official".[111]

5.2.8 Canada

A similar story about the disappointing nature of damages can be told in Canada. Damages as a remedy for human rights violations in Canada largely begins with the landmark case *Roncarelli* v. *Duplessis*, where the Supreme Court of Canada awarded Can$33,000 in damages to a restauranteur who had his liquor licence unlawfully suspended by Quebec Premier Maurice Duplessis in retaliation for posting bail for Jehovah's Witnesses. The damage award was influenced by pecuniary losses suffered by the restaurant after its liquor license was suspended. This raises the troubling issue that pecuniary damages may more easily be measured and awarded than the many non-pecuniary interests protected by human rights.[112] Nevertheless, the damage award was a significant sum. It would have purchased a house at the time. In increasing the damages that Frank Roncarelli received from the Can$8,000 awarded at trial, the Supreme Court admitted it did so "in a somewhat arbitrary fashion" and on the basis of the equitable principles that would inform the jury.[113] The result was a generous, indeed some maintain too

[110] [2005] UKHL 14.

[111] Ibid. at para 19.

[112] [1959] SCR 121. The Supreme Court awarded Can$2,500 in damages to a Jehovah's Witness who was wrongfully arrested in Duplessis's Quebec and held over the weekend. The Court did not attempt to justify the quantum but referred to it as "substantial damages": *Lamb* v. *Benoit,* [1959] SCR 321 at 344. See also *Chaput* v. *Romain,* [1955] SCR 834 at 854–855 awarding Can$2,000 in damages for illegally breaking up a meeting of Jehovah's Witnesses and citing Dicey in support.

[113] *Roncarelli* v. *Duplessis,* [1959] SCR 121 at para 160 per Martland J.

generous,[114] award of damages that has stood as a civil rights landmark. In 1964, Douglas Schmeiser concluded that damage awards were "the main protection afforded in our law to a person whose religious freedom has been violated" and are "his right of civil action".[115] Few would make similar statements today.[116]

From 1982 to 2010, there was much confusion about whether damages under the Canadian *Charter* would be based on a tort model[117] or a public law model,[118] and whether it would include qualified immunities. In *Ward* v. *Vancouver*, the Supreme Court of Canada, in a unanimous judgement by Chief Justice McLachlin, opted for the public law model. She concluded that damages were a "unique public law remedy"[119] well within the traditional powers of courts. Damages could be justified to compensate the individual whose rights had been violated, vindicate the right violated or deter state agents from committing future breaches. This decision seemed to set Charter damages on a solid public law foundation.[120]

[114] David Mullan has warned that one reading of the multiple judgements in the case would impose damages whenever the government acts illegally and argues that such an approach would be inconsistent with the Court's subsequent approach to damages in administrative law: David Mullan, "*Roncarelli* v. *Duplessis* and Damages for Abuse of Power: For What Does it Stand in 1959 and for What Does It Stand in 2009?" (2010) 55 *McGill L. J.* 587, 605ff. For a conclusion that Australian courts today would not award damages in a similar case, see Mark Aronson, "Some Australian Reflections on *Roncarelli* v. *Duplessis*" (2010) 55 *McGill L. J.* 615. Fauteux J denied the damage remedy in *Roncarelli* on this basis even though he found that Premier Duplessis had acted illegally. For an argument that this approach can be justified as judges recognizing that they are themselves restrained by the rule of law, see Robert Leckey, "Complexifying Roncarelli's Rule of Law" (2010) 55 *McGill L. J.* 721.

[115] Douglas Schmeiser, *Civil Liberties in Canada* (Oxford: Oxford University Press, 1964), p.114.

[116] For a review of the higher damage claims awarded by Canadian human rights tribunals as opposed to courts, see Michele Flaherty, "Trends in Human Rights Damages" (2017) 20 *Can. Lab. & Emp. L. J.* 355.

[117] As advocated by Kenneth Cooper-Stephenson, *Charter Damage Claims* (Toronto: Carswell, 1990).

[118] As advocated by Kent Roach, *Constitutional Remedies in Canada* (Aurora: Canada Law Book, 1994).

[119] *Ward* v. *Vancouver (City)*, 2010 SCC 27 at para 31.

[120] Kent Roach, "A Promising Late Spring for Charter Damages: Ward v. British Columbia" (2011) 29 *N.J.C.L.* 135, but expressing some reservation about the modest amount of damages award. For an examination of the generally low quantum of Charter damage awards, see W. H. Charles, *Understanding Charter Damages* (Toronto: Irwin Law, 2016), pp.104, 157.

The one shortcoming in *Ward* was the modest award of Can$5,000 in damages for an unwarranted strip search. The quantum of the award was not appealed, but the Court defended it on the basis that the plaintiff was not touched, his genitals were not exposed, the officials were acting pursuant to a policy at the lock-up facility and were not acting in a "malicious, high-handed or oppressive" manner.[121] This award compares unfavourably against the landmark 1959 *Roncarelli* case. Indeed, no economically rational plaintiff would pursue a similar case unless it was aggregated by means of a class action.[122]

The Court in *Ward* did not apply a qualified immunity standard but indicated that they could serve as a form of "practical wisdom".[123] Instead, the Court allowed the state to establish a range of countervailing good governance factors to limit damage awards. This open-ended process followed the proportionality analysis that the Court had long used for imposing reasonable limits on rights. It included directions to consider the adequacy of less drastic alternative remedies, such as declarations, the seriousness of the particular violation, fairness to competing public interests and the need for "rationality and proportionality"[124] in any damage award. On this basis, the government established that a Can$100 damage award for the unreasonable seizure of Ward's car was not necessary because he suffered no damages as a result and a declaration of a violation was sufficient. Again, sometimes no damages are better than trivial amounts.

In subsequent cases, however, the Supreme Court was more attracted to qualified and even absolute immunities. In 2015, the majority of the Court required a wrongly convicted man to prove not only that prosecutors violated his rights but that they knew or ought reasonably to have known that non-disclosure would damage his right to full answer and defence and cause harm.[125] The Court reasoned that such a fault standard was necessary to protect the exercise of prosecutorial discretion and avoid a flood of lawsuits even though the defendant in the suit was the state and not the prosecutor. This standard placed a less onerous requirement on the applicant than proof of malice. It was also more generous than the American standard of absolute immunity for the

[121] *Ward* v. *Vancouver (City)*, 2010 SCC 27 at para 72.
[122] The use of class actions will be discussed in Section 5.5.2 of this chapter.
[123] Ibid. at para 43.
[124] Ibid. at para 51.
[125] *Henry* v. *British Columbia*, [2015] 2 SCR 214.

exercise of core prosecutorial functions. At the same time, Chief Justice McLachlin dissented and argued that prosecutorial obligations with respect to disclosure were a key part of good governance and supported by international law obligations to compensate the wrongfully convicted.[126]

Another case came very close to imposing absolute immunity for those who exercised judicial functions.[127] Four judges were prepared to rule that damages would never be an appropriate and just remedy for a violation of rights by adjudicators given the alternative remedy of judicial review. They stressed the need for absolute immunity to prevent the diversion of resources in defending damage claims even under a qualified immunity standard. A fifth judge in concurrence expressed general agreement with this proposition,[128] but held that it was not necessary to decide whether a statutory absolute immunity clause was constitutional. Four judges in dissent rejected absolute immunity. They suggested that damages against the state could play a role in vindicating rights and deterring rights violations even given the alternative remedy of judicial review.[129]

Canadian courts also apply qualified immunities when the state acts pursuant to legislation[130] subsequently found to be unconstitutional. The qualified immunity requires applicants to establish that the government not only violated rights but "acted negligently, in bad faith or abusing its powers".[131] In 2020, the Canadian Supreme Court refused to extend this fault requirement and qualified immunity to acts done pursuant to government "policies". The Court stressed the vagueness and lack of transparency of policies as well as the ability of the government to justify limits on damages under the standard analysis set out in *Ward*.[132]

It will be suggested in Section 5.4.1 of this chapter that absolute and qualified immunities are inevitably under- and over-inclusive. The *Ward*

126 Ibid. at paras 129–136.

127 *Ernst* v. *Alberta Energy Regulatory*, [2017] 1 SCR 3.

128 Ibid. at para 123 per Abella J.

129 Ibid. at para 173: "[c]onsiderations supporting private law immunity from liability for negligent conduct do not automatically support absolute immunity from *Charter* damages claims for more serious misconduct, including conduct amounting to bad faith or an abuse of power".

130 *Mackin* v. *New Brunswick (Minister of Justice)*, [2002] 1 SCR 405.

131 Ibid. at para 82.

132 *Conseil scolaire francophone de la Colombie-Britannique* v. *British Columbia*, 2020 SCC 13 at para 164ff. I acted as counsel for the Asper Centre that intervened in opposition to the use of qualified immunities.

approach of giving the government an opportunity to justify, on the facts of a particular case, why an award of damages would be disproportionate and harmful to competing social interests is a superior method of remedial decision-making.

5.2.9 New Zealand

In the landmark *Baigent's* case,[133] the New Zealand courts implied a cause of action for damages in the absence of a specific remedial clause in the New Zealand Bill of Rights.[134] The case involved an erroneous and defective warrant and an unreasonable search and seizure of a home in which no incriminating evidence was discovered. This was the type of low-visibility rights violation where it was "damages or nothing".[135] Hardie Boys J argued that the Court had already developed an exclusionary remedy to enforce the right against unreasonable searches but "in frank words, it only benefits the guilty . . . Obviously there must be a different, and equally effective, remedy where there has been an infringement of the rights of an innocent person". In such cases "monetary compensation is an appropriate and proper, indeed the only effective, remedy. In the assessment of the compensation, the emphasis must be on the compensatory and not the punitive element".[136]

Cooke P cited with approval a Privy Council decision interpreting a Caribbean constitution where Lord Diplock had stressed that the state should be subject to direct liability not dependent on tort or vicarious liability.[137] He indicated that an award of "somewhat less than [NZ]$ 70,000 would be sufficient vindication" for a "serious" search and seizure violation "where no physical harm or lasting consequences appear to have ensued".[138] As one judge has subsequently noted, this amount of

133 *Simpson* v. *Attorney General,* [1994] 3 NZLR 667.

134 As it did in implying a right to make declarations of incompatibility in *Attorney General* v. *Taylor,* [2018] NZSC 104, the Court adverted to international law with Casey J stating that even in the absence of a specific remedial provision the court could still "'develop the possibilities of judicial remedy' as envisaged in art 3(b) [of the International Covenant on Civil and Political Rights]. . . I do not accept that Parliament intended it to be what most would regard as no more than legislative window-dressing, of no practical consequence, in the absence of appropriate remedies for those whose rights and freedoms have been violated". Ibid. at 703.

135 *Bivens* v. *Six Unnamed Agents of the FBI*, 403 US 388 (1971) at 410 per Harlan J.

136 *Simpson* v. *Attorney General,* [1994] 3 NZLR 667 at 703.

137 *Maharaj* v. *Attorney-General of Trinidad and Tobago (No. 2),* [1979] AC 385 at 399 quoted in *Simpson* v. *Attorney General,* [1994] 3 NZLR 667 at 677.

138 *Simpson* v. *Attorney General,* [1994] 3 NZLR 667 at 678; at 703–704 per Gault J.

damages must have been geared to compensation because it was "fanciful" to think that the inadvertent search and seizure violation would be repeated in the particular case.[139]

Despite recognizing that the state can be required to pay damages to compensate, vindicate or deter violations[140] and rejecting the idea that either statutes of limitations or qualified immunities apply to Bill of Rights actions,[141] "the number of cases in which public law damages have been sought since 1994 is small".[142] This suggests "that early predictions of a flood of claims to vex the administration of justice are well astray".[143]

In *Taunoa*, the New Zealand Supreme Court reduced damages awarded to prisoners subject to prolonged solitary confinement.[144] The lead plaintiff had his award reduced from NZ$65,000 to NZ$35,000 for thirty-two months spent in solitary confinement. Others had their awards halved from NZ$40,000 to NZ$20,000 and from NZ$8,000 to NZ$4,000. The majority of the Court appealed to cases under the Human Rights Act, 1998, where courts awarded modest damages to mirror ECtHR jurisprudence and expressed disapproval of the more generous approach to constitutional damages taken by the Judicial Committee of the Privy Council in cases involving Caribbean constitutions.

Blanchard J, who would have reduced the award, concluded that damages should not be based on tort standards, but that they "should be enough to provide an incentive to the defendant and other State agencies not to repeat the infringing conduct and also to ensure that the plaintiff does not reasonably feel that the award is trivialising of the breach".[145] He aptly warned that "nominal damages benefits neither the victim nor society. It may appear to trivialise the breach".[146] In a strong

139 *Taunoa* v. *Attorney General*, 2007 NZSC 70 at para 232 per Blanchard J. At the same, however, he added that he regarded the quantum as "pitched far too high for the relatively transitory, though deliberate, breach of Mrs. Baigent's rights". Ibid. at 274, see also at para 301 per Tipping J.

140 Ibid. at paras 109–112, 250, 315.

141 *PF Sugue Ltd* v. *Attorney General*, [2004] 1 NZLR 206 at para 69. See also Lisa Tortell, *Monetary Remedies for Breach of Human Rights* (Oxford: Hart Publishing, 2006), pp.66–67.

142 *Attorney General* v. *Chapman*, 2011 NZSC 110 at 5.

143 Ibid. at para 5. The Court did hold that damage awards would not apply to judicial functions even though the Privy Council held that it was possible if the state and not the individual judge had to pay the damages.

144 *Taunoa* v. *Attorney General*, 2007 NZSC 70 at para 109.

145 Ibid. at para 258.

146 Ibid. at para 264.

dissent, Chief Justice Elias argued that the damages awarded at trial were justified by the need to compensate, vindicate and deter rights violations because the "conditions were" as the trial judge found "not fit for human beings, even those behaving badly in prison".[147] In response to her colleagues who argued that damages must be "moderate", she "did not think that the adjective assists".[148]

5.2.10 *The United States*

The use of damages as a human rights remedy stems from implied *Bivens* actions[149] against federal officials and a Reconstruction era statute[150] that authorizes suits against individual state and local officials for violations of constitutional rights. One of the most important features of the American approach is that individual officers are the only defendants for both kinds of damage claims. Unlike in most democracies, the federal and state government are generally immune from damage awards the latter by virtue of the 11th Amendment.[151] Municipalities[152] are the only level of government that can be sued for "constitutional torts" in the Federal Courts. At the same time, municipalities are not vicariously liable for all of the actions of their officials, but only for their policies.[153]

With respect to individual defendants, there are absolute immunities for the exercise of judicial,[154] prosecutorial[155] and Presidential[156] functions. There are also good faith immunities for most state officials,

147 Ibid. at para 113.

148 Ibid. at para 109.

149 *Bivens* v. *Six Unnamed Agents of the FBI*, 403 US 388 (1971). There is also limited direct governmental liability under the Federal Tort Claims Act of 1946. See Schuck, *Suing Government* at 41–43.

150 42 U.S.C §1983.

151 The 11th Amendment has been interpreted not to preclude injunctions aimed at states through a fiction that the injunction is aimed at officials acting unlawfully: *Ex Parte Young*, 209 US 123 (1908). The American concerns about damages is also exceptional. It likely reflects the litigious nature of the society as promoted by unique fee rules that combined with contingency fees makes it much easier to bring lawsuits in the United States than anywhere in the world.

152 *Monell* v. *Department of Social Services of the City of New York*, 436 US 658 (1978).

153 *Owen* v. *City of Independence*, 445 US 399 (1980) at 411 emphasizing differences when damages come "not from an official's pocket but the public treasury".

154 *Pierson* v. *Ray*, 386 US 547 (1967); *Stump* v. *Sparkman*, 435 US 349 (1978).

155 *Imbler* v. *Pachtman*, 424 US 409 (1976).

156 *Nixon* v. *Fitzgerald*, 457 US 731 (1985); *Harlow and Butterfield* v. *Fitzgerald*, 102 S.Ct. 2727 (1982).

including prison[157] and police[158] officers. These immunities have been interpreted broadly to require officials to violate clearly established rights that would be known to a reasonable person.[159] There will be no liability if the right in question was not "sufficiently clear that every reasonable person would have understood that what he is doing violated the right and that the issue was beyond debate".[160] As Professor Jeffries has noted, this means that human rights are "defined not by what judges, in their wisdom think it should mean, but by the most grudging conception that an executive officer could reasonably entertain".[161] Qualified immunities can also be asserted before discovery and appealed before a full trial. Justice Sotomayer has criticized qualified immunities for decreasing police accountability. Other Justices in dissent have raised questions about whether they are truly necessary if officials will, as empirical studies suggest,[162] be indemnified for damages awarded against them.[163]

Unless actual injury is proven, only nominal damages in the form of a US$1 verdict will be awarded.[164] This approach ignores that fact that human rights protect "dignitary interests" that are more akin to those protected by intentional torts than interests protected by negligence actions.[165] The Court also requires a strict causal connection between the violation and harm for which the plaintiff seeks compensation. For example, a teacher who was dismissed after exercising free speech rights

[157] *Procunier* v. *Navarette*, 434 US 555 (1978).

[158] *Pierson* v. *Ray*, 386 US 547 (1967).

[159] *Harlow* v. *Fitzgerald*, 457 US 800 (1982). For a rare case where the qualified immunity was held not to apply to a prison guard's actions in tying a prisoner in Alabama to a hitching post on a hot day for eight hours without water, see *Hope* v. *Pelzer*, 536 US 730 (2002).

[160] *Ashcroft* v. *Al-Kidd*, 131 S.Ct. 2074 (2011) at 2085 citing *Anderson* v. *Creighton*, 483 US 635 (1987) at 3037.

[161] John Jeffries Jr., "Reversing the Order of Battle in Constitutional Torts" (2009) *Sup. Ct. L. Rev.* 115, 120. For a summary of the complex law in these matters, see John Jeffries Jr., "The Liability Rule for Constitutional Torts" (2013) 99 *Virg. L. Rev.* 207.

[162] James Pfander, Alexander Reinert and Joanna Schwartz, "The Myth of Personal Liability" (2020) 72 *Stan. L. Rev.* 561.

[163] *Kisela* v. *Hughes*, 138 S.Ct. 1148 (2018) at 1162 (Sotomayor, J, dissenting) (qualified immunity "tells officers that they can shoot first and think later, and it tells the public that palpably unreasonable conduct will go unpunished"); *Richardson* v. *McKnight*, 521 US 399 (1997) at 411 (exempting private prison guards from qualified immunity because of availability of insurance).

[164] *Carey* v. *Piphus*, 435 US 247 (1978); *Memphis Community School District* v. *Stachura*, 477 US 299 (1986) at 305–309.

[165] J. C. Love, "Damages: A Remedy for the Violation of Constitutional Rights" (1979) 67 *Calif. L. Rev.* 1242, 1261; see also Varuhas, *Damages and Human Rights*.

was denied damages because there were other grounds to justify his dismissal.[166] In Chapter 6, Section 2.2.1, we will see that American courts also demand a similar causal requirement between a violation and the discovery of evidence sought to be excluded. Causation standards makes sense if the purpose of the remedy is limited to compensation. But they make much less sense if, as the American courts often purport, the common purpose of both constitutional torts and exclusion of evidence is to deter constitutional violations.[167]

Punitive damages awarded by juries are possible against individuals[168] but not against municipalities (being the one level of government that can be sued).[169] Much of the American experience, both with respect to damages and qualified immunity, can be explained as a form of jury control that is not applicable in jurisdictions where judges assess damages.[170]

Bivens damages actions against federal officials allegedly violating rights are not available if there is an alternative remedy or if there are special factors counselling hesitation in the absence of clear Congressional authorization. Qualified immunities are applied to these claims despite Justice Harlan's concurrence in *Bivens* that stressed that damages should compensate for harm even if they were not an effective deterrent.[171] In any event, Biven's damage claim for violation of his right against search and seizure was eventually settled for either $US 500 or $US 1000.[172]

In 2017, the United States Supreme Court refused to apply the *Bivens* cause of action to claims for damages brought by non-citizens who alleged that they were abused in immigration detention after the 9/11 attacks. Justice Kennedy for the Court stressed that Congress would not

166 *Mt. Healthy City School District Board of Education* v. *Doyle*, 429 US 274 (1977); see also *Carey* v. *Piphus*, 435 US 245 (1978).

167 On the instrumental nature of American remedial decision-making, see Kent Roach "Dialogic Remedies" (2019) 17 *I. Con.* 3. On connections between qualified immunities in constitutional torts and good faith exceptions to the American exclusionary rule, see Jennifer Laurin, "Trawling for Herring: Lessons in Doctrinal Borrowing" (2011) 111 *Colum. L. Rev.* 670.

168 *Smith* v. *Wade*, 461 US 30 (1983).

169 *Newport* v. *Facts Concert*, 453 US 247 (1981).

170 Lord Scott, Justice Randy Holland and Chilton Varner, "The Role of Extra-Compensatory Damages for Violations of Fundamental Human Rights in the United Kingdom and the United States" (2006) 46 *Va. J. Int'l. L.* 475.

171 *Bivens* v. *Six Unnamed Agents* per Harlan J.

172 Pfander, Reinert and Schwartz, "The Myth of Personal Liability", 570.

have authorized such damage claims. Justice Breyer, in a strong dissent, argued that damage claims should be allowed "after the emergency is over, after emotions have cooled and when more factual information is available. In such circumstances, courts have more time to exercise such judicial virtues as calm reflection and dispassionate application of the law to the facts".[173] He appealed to damages, even inadequate amounts, as a marker of an act of injustice.

In *Ashcroft* v. *Iqbal*,[174] the Court held that *Bivens* damage claims related to post 9/11 immigration detentions must demonstrate that the defendant officials "purposefully adopted a policy of classifying post-September-11 detainees as 'of high interest' because of their race, religion or national origin". In *Hernandez* v. *Mesa*,[175] the Court applied much the same reasoning to refuse to hold that a *Bivens* action would apply to a border agent's shooting and killing of a fifteen-year-old Mexican boy at the border. The Court stressed the dangers that the damages could disrupt border security and that they had not been authorized by Congress. Justice Thomas with Justice Gorsuch would have overruled *Bivens*, noting that for forty years the Court has refused to extend *Bivens* and that it was time to put the unfollowed precedent out of its misery. The failure to apply basic rule of law reasoning in these cases is a sad and telling testament to how American extra-legalism[176] has produced a state of affairs where government officials are not held accountable in damages for the most egregious violations of human rights.

5.2.11 South Africa

The Constitutional Court of South Africa in *Fose*[177] struck out a claim for constitutional damages, even in the face of allegations of a pattern of assault and torture by the police. The Court concluded that "for awards to have any conceivable deterrent effect against the government they will have to be very substantial and the more substantial they are the greater the anomaly that a single plaintiff receives a windfall of such

173 *Ziglar* v. *Abbasi*, 138 S.Ct. 1843 (2017).
174 556 US 662 (2009).
175 589 US (2020).
176 See Kent Roach, *The 9/11 Effect* (Cambridge: Cambridge University Press, 2011) at 163–169, 235–237, 436–438.
177 *Fose* v. *Minister of Safety and Security*, [1997] ZACC 6.

magnitude".[178] As suggested above, American courts are reluctant to award damages against individual officials because of fears about over-deterrence.[179] Conversely, South African courts seem reluctant to award damages against governments because of fears of under-deterrence.[180] This divergence reflects a lack of knowledge about the precise effects of damage awards on either officials or government. This confirms the wisdom of the Canadian approach in *Ward* in allowing governments to establish countervailing good governance factors that justify not awarding damages or reducing the damages awarded.

Subsequently, the South African Constitutional Court declared that property owners whose property had been irregularly occupied by people seeking a home could receive damages.[181] This provided an elegant solution between competing property and housing rights that will be discussed in Chapter 8, Section 8.2.3. In a subsequent case, however, the Constitutional Court indicated that damage awards in the administrative context should only be made in "exceptional cases" and not for "incorrect or negligent but honest decisions". The Court, nonetheless, reserved the possibility of awarding damages for decisions "made in bad faith or under corrupt circumstances or completely outside the scope of the empowering provision".[182] This represents a much broader form of qualified immunity than that found in Canada and New Zealand but perhaps not as demanding as American standards.

5.2.12 India

In 1993, the Indian Supreme Court recognized damages as "a remedy available in public law, based on strict liability for contravention of fundamental rights to which the principle of sovereign immunity does not apply, even though it may be available as a defence in private law in an action based on tort".[183] In the same case, however, another judge

[178] Ibid. at para 71.
[179] Schuck, *Suing Government*.
[180] Daryl J. Levinson, "Making Government Pay: Markets Politics and the Allocation of Constitutional Costs" (2000) 67 *U. Chi. L. Rev.* 2.
[181] *President of the Republic of South Africa and Another* v. *Modderklip Boerdery (Pty) Ltd*, [2005] ZACC 5 at para 5.
[182] *Steenkamp NO* v. *Provincial Tender Board of the Eastern Cape*, [2006] ZACC 16 at para 30.
[183] *Nilabati Behera* v. *State of Orissa*, [1993] 2 SCR 581.

characterized damages somewhat differently. Anand J stated: "[t]he compensation is in the nature of 'exemplary damages' awarded against the wrongdoer for the breach of its public law duty and is independent of the rights available to the aggrieved party to claim compensation under the private law in an action based on tort".[184] On the one hand, this suggests that damages are a form of "strict liability" designed to compensate, but on the other that they are a form of exemplary damages designed to vindicate and perhaps even deter rights violation. As in Canada and New Zealand, the Indian courts accept that damages serve multiple remedial purposes and that the state is liable for such a public law remedy.

5.2.13 *Caribbean Constitutions*

The Judicial Committee of the Privy Council has recognized the importance of vindicatory damages in a series of cases. In one case, it remitted a US$53,000 damage award for false arrest and physical violence given by a court in Trinidad and Tobago to consider whether higher damages were necessary to reflect a "sense of public outrage, emphasise the importance of the constitutional right and the gravity of the breach, and deter further breaches".[185] It has also upheld an award of US$100,000 as vindicatory damages in a case of police abuse from the Bahamas.[186] In another case that reveals a lack of clear principles, the Privy Council awarded an arguably excessive award of US$175,000 to a magistrate who had been improperly suspended for eight years with pay.[187] In any event, these awards are much more generous than those awarded in the richer democracies of Canada and New Zealand that also allow damages to

[184] Ibid. at para 2.08.

[185] *Attorney General of Trinidad and Tobago* v. *Ramanoop (Trinidad and Tobago)*, [2005] UKPC 15 at paras 19–20.

[186] *Merson* v. *Cartwright & Anor (Bahamas)*, [2005] UKPC 38. In another police abuse case, the Privy Council upheld a US$45,000 award in constitutional damages but noted that it may have been on the low side: *Subiah* v. *The Attorney General of Trinidad & Tobago (Trinidad & Tobago)*, [2008] UKPC 47.

[187] *Durity* v. *The Attorney General (Trinidad & Tobago)*, [2008] UKPC 59 at para 35. In early litigation in the same case, the Privy Council rejected the idea that constitutional damage claims could be precluded by statutes of limitations. More modest vindicatory damages of US$10,000 (*Fraser* v. *Judicial and Legal Services Commission & Anor (Saint Lucia)*, [2008] UKPC 25) and US$50,000 (*Inniss* v. *The Attorney General of Saint Christopher & Nevis (Saint Christopher & Nevis)*, [2008] UKPC 42) were awarded in other cases dealing with judicial independence.

vindicate the importance of the right.[188] Even when mediated through the Privy Council in London, these cases fit into a pattern of courts in the global South being more committed to achieving effective remedies than their more complacent northern counterparts.[189]

5.2.14 *Summary of National Jurisprudence*

Some commentators argue that courts should be modest in awarding damages for human rights in light of possible drains on limited state resources and the risk of promoting a "blame culture" that may encourage frivolous lawsuits.[190] However, such arguments discount the financial costs and risks of litigation. This is especially true outside the United States, where a person who unsuccessfully sues the government may have to pay the government's legal costs. With few exceptions, domestic courts, like supra-national courts, have valued human rights quite cheaply. This helps to explain why damages have emerged as a disappointing remedy for violations of human rights.

5.3 A Defence of Damages as a Public Law Remedy

The low damage awards for violations of human rights has caused Jason Varuhas to question whether common law countries would be better off relying on intentional torts.[191] Although Professor Varuhas has done an important service in critiquing the low quantum of awards and arguing that intentional torts are a better analogy to human rights than negligence,[192] there are still a number of compelling advantages to continuing to conceive of damages as a public law remedy.

[188] The UK Supreme Court has rejected vindicatory damages under the Human Rights Act, 1998: *Walumba Lumba (Previously referred to as WL) (Congo) 1 and 2* v. *Secretary of State for the Home Department*, [2011] UKSC 12 at para 101 per Lord Dyson.

[189] Daniel Bonilla Maldonado (ed.), *Constitutionalism of the Global South: The Activist Tribunals of India, South Africa and Colombia* (Cambridge: Cambridge University Press, 2013).

[190] Carol Harlow, "Damages and Human Rights" (2004) *N.Z. L. Rev.* 429, 447–448; Carol Harlow, *State Liability: Tort Liability and Beyond* (Oxford: Oxford University Press, 2004).

[191] Varuhas, *Damages and Human Rights*. The late Allen Linden also concluded that the Canadian Charter damages would have a largely symbolic and minimal effect: Allen Linden, "Charter Damage Claims: New Dawn or Mirage?" (2012) 39 *Adv. Q.* 426.

[192] For an earlier recognition, see Cooper-Stephenson, *Charter Damages*, p.240.

5.3.1 *Holding States and Not Individuals Accountable*

The tort approach to damages generally imposes liability on individuals, often on the basis that they have acted beyond their legal powers and/or with fault. As Peter Schuck has argued, the traditional tort focus on the conduct of individual officials is at odds with the bureaucratic nature of the modern state, where many rights violations are the result of systems failures. The concern that damage awards against individual officials may over-deter their performance of legitimate public functions has led Americans courts to only award damages for the most clear and flagrant violations of human rights. Schuck imagined an ideal system where damages would be assessed directly against all levels of government and would be seen as just one of a range of remedies that would include declarations and injunctions.[193] He imagined the public law system that now applies in New Zealand, Canada and many other countries.[194]

Schuck's ideal system has not taken root in the United States, where both state and federal governments enjoy immunity from constitutional damages. Nevertheless, his basic point remains valid: many human rights violations are caused by complex state systems. The imposition of liability for damages on the state avoids problems of over-deterrence of individual officials. It also allows the state to use its own expertise and knowledge to take a range of steps that can prevent future violations.[195]

5.3.2 *A Focus on Rights as Opposed to Absolute or Qualified Immunities*

The idea that damages are a public law remedy against the state has the potential to avoid absolute immunities that render the state immune from damages and qualified immunities that require plaintiffs to establish some form of fault by the state and its officials in addition to the violation of rights. For example, the Privy Council avoided holding that judicial functions were subject to an absolute immunity when it held that the state was directly liable for breaches of human rights under the

193 Peter Schuck, *Suing Government.*

194 See generally Cooper-Stephenson, *Constitutional Damages Worldwide.*

195 Daryl J. Levinson has criticized Schuck's assumptions that governments will respond rationally to damage awards: Levinson, "Making Governments Pay". Under my two-track approach, however, courts could escalate remedies beyond damages should the state not take reasonable measures to prevent repetitive violations.

Constitution of Trinidad and Tobago.[196] It will be suggested in the next section that qualified immunities are almost always over- and under-inclusive. As under the Canadian case of *Ward*[197] they can be replaced with a more tailored inquiry into whether the award of damages would harm good governance.

5.3.3 *Damages as One of Many Alternative Remedies*

As Calabresi and Melamed famously observed, damages enforce liability rules that can be violated for a price, as opposed to property-type rules that are enforceable through injunctions.[198] One of the disadvantages of taking a private law approach to damages as a remedy for violations of human rights is that it tends to conceive of damages as the prime, if not exclusive, remedy for a violation. Article 30 of the ILC's Principles of State Responsibility responds directly to concerns that damages can operate as a form of tax or price on human rights violations. It does so by providing that states are under a duty to cease any continuing wrongful act and "to offer appropriate assurances and guarantees of non-repetition, if circumstances so require".[199] James Crawford has explained that the primacy of restitution and cessation reflect a concern "that states otherwise be able to avoid their international obligations by offering payment in lieu".[200] Even when they order compensation, judges should not lose sight of the larger issue of compliance with human rights.

The alternative remedies to damages are not only more intrusive remedies such as injunctions, but also less drastic ones such as declarations. The United Nations Basic Principles on remedies contemplates both restitution and apologies as alternatives to damages. The IACtHR has ordered states to provide apologies or other acts of commemoration either as an alternative or adjunct to damage awards.[201] Although there

[196] *Maharaj* v. *Trinidad and Tobago*, [1978] 2 All ER 670.

[197] [2010] 2 SCR 28.

[198] Guido Calabresi and Douglas Melamed, "Property Rules, Liability Rules and Inalienability: One View of the Cathedral" (1972) 85 *Harv. L. Rev.* 1089.

[199] International Law Commission, *Principles of State Responsibility*, of the Commission's fifty-third and fifty-fifth sessions, 23 April–1 June and 2 July–10 August 2001, GA Supplement No. 10, A/56/10, Art. 30.

[200] James Crawford *The International Law Commission's Principles on State Responsibility: Introduction, Text and Commentaries* (Cambridge: Cambridge University Press), p.509.

[201] Antkowiak and Gonza, *The American Convention on Human Rights*, pp.285–314. Apologies can also be ordered under Australian anti-discrimination laws. In one case

are always dangers in forced apologies,[202] there are also many advantages. Johannes Chan has similarly recognized that alternative remedies "such as a declaration or an apology, may serve the purpose of vindication".[203] An apology or similar form of intangible recognition may be far preferable to the award of US$1 in nominal damages that Professor Pfander has proposed in the American constitutional tort context.[204] As a famous article on apology as a legal remedy has stated: "there are some injuries that cannot be repaired just by saying you are sorry, there are others that can only be repaired by an apology".[205] A private law approach would have the tendency to monetize all remedies for human rights and ignore other potentially more meaningful remedies.

5.3.4 Recognizing the Equality of All Rights Holders

The public law approach to damages not only ensures the proper defendant in the form of the state, but it also stresses that all plaintiffs are equal to the extent that they possess human rights. In a leading New Zealand Bill of Rights damage case brought by prisoners, Justice Blanchard has argued that the "character of the victim" should not influence the damage award "in view of the public law purposes of the

where an Indigenous man was subject to racial discrimination before he died in custody, police officers were ordered to make apologies to his family and publicly in the local newspaper: *Russell* v. *Commissioner of Police,* [2001] NSWADT 32. But for an order refusing to order a reluctant newspaper columnist to apologize, see *Eatock* v. *Bolt, (No. 2)* (2011), 284 ALR 114. See generally Robyn Carroll, "Apologies as a Legal Remedy" (2013) 35(2) *Sydney L. Rev.* 317 at 328ff; Robyn Carroll, "You Can't Order Sorriness, so Is There Any Value in an Ordered Apology – An Analysis of Ordered Apologies in Anti-Discrimination Cases" (2010) 33 *U.N.S.W. L. J.* 2.

202 The ECtHR has found that an ordered apology is a "doubtful form of redress": *Kazakov* v. *Russia* (2008), No. 1758/02, [2008] ECHR 1737 at para 30. It has, however, found apologies ordered by domestic courts to be a justified limit on freedom of expression: *Öztürk* v. *Turkey* (2009), No. 17095/03, ECHR 9 June 2009. The Hong Kong Court of Appeal has held that an ordered apology would often "be futile or disproportionate and contrary to the interests of the administration of justice": *Ma Bik Yung* v. *Ko Chuen* (2001), [2002] 2 HKLRD 1 at para 50.

203 Johannes Chan, "Vindicatory Damages for Violations of Constitutional Rights: A Comparative Approach" in Mark Elliott, Jason Varuhas and Shona Stark (eds.), *The Unity of Public Law?* (Oxford: Hart Publishing, 2018), pp.329, 348.

204 Pfander, *Constitutional Torts and the War on Terror*, p.151.

205 Hiroshi Wagatsuma and Arthur Rosett, "The Implications of Apology: Law and Culture in Japan and the United States" (1986) 20 *L. & Soc'y. Rev.* 461, 487.

award".[206] Similarly, the Supreme Court of India has stressed that prisoners "are not denuded of their fundamental rights under Article 21" of the Indian Constitution and that the "limited liberty" left to prisoners is "rather precious".[207] This public law focus on the equality of rights holders should preclude the government from arguing that damages for rights violations should be reduced because the person whose rights were violated had a so-called pre-existing "cracked skull" that makes the value of the right less valuable.[208]

One of Canada's largest ever award of Charter damages was Can$7.5 million. It was designed to vindicate Ivan Henry's Charter right as an accused to disclosure of state held evidence critical to his defence, the non-disclosure of which contributed to his wrongful conviction and imprisonment for twenty-seven years.[209] This figure was far larger than the Can$530,000 awarded for special and pecuniary damages. In assessing the latter damages, the trial judge employed causation and "cracked skull" analysis to conclude that Mr Henry's pecuniary damages should be reduced because he was likely to have been incarcerated for half of the twenty-seven years in any event and unemployed for half the time he was out of jail.[210] Such common law reasoning demonstrates how causation analysis can undermine the equality of all rights holders and fail to vindicate the importance of rights that have caused even serious violations.

[206] *Taunoa* v. *Attorney General*, 2007 NZSC 70 at para 266. The Law Commission of New Zealand similarly disapproved of a NZ$20 damage award to a gang member's whose freedom of movement had been violated on the basis that damages should vindicate rights and rights do "not depend upon the identity or the character of the plaintiff". Law Commission, Te-Aka-Matua-o-te-Ture, *Report 37: Crown Liability and Judicial Immunity* (Wellington: Law Commission, 1997) at para 70. For persuasive criticisms of the tendency of English courts to deny human rights damages to prisoners, see Varuhas, *Damages and Human Rights*, pp.375–381.

[207] *Nilabati Behera* v. *State of Orissa*, [1993] 2 SCR 581 at para 31.

[208] For criticism of the use of such defences in tort litigation arising from Indigenous children being sent to residential schools, see Kent Roach, "Blaming the Victim: Canadian Law, Causation and Residential Schools" (2014) 64 *U.T.L.J.* 566. But for findings that the ECtHR awards more damages for procedural violations to those of higher social status and those who are acquitted as opposed to convicted, see Shelton, *Remedies in International Human Rights Law*, pp.366–367. For a recent decision that suggests that only nominal damages of Can$500 for five illegal searches of a suspected gang member's home should be granted, see *Everett* v. *McCaskill*, 2015 MBCA 107 leave to appeal refused: 2016 CanLII 32306 1 (SCC).

[209] *Henry* v. *British Columbia*, [2015] 2 SCR 214.

[210] *Henry* v. *British Columbia*, 2016 BCSC 1038 at para 370.

The equality of all rights holders means that the causation analysis that is central to negligence-based torts should play less of a role under a public law approach. To be sure, causation analysis may still be relevant under a public law approach with respect to the determination of financial damages and even non-pecuniary harms caused by the violation, but it should not play a role with respect to the role of damages in vindicating and deterring human rights violations.[211] This also recognizes that many rights violations are multi-causal given the complexity of the modern bureaucratic state.[212]

5.3.5 *Damages as a Judicial Remedy Protected from Legislative Curtailment*

Damages are the quintessential judicial remedy. In principle, they should be based on the inherent powers of courts or authorized by general remedial provisions. This should prevent the use of ordinary legislation to place conditions on the manner that the independent courts employ this remedy.[213] Alas, legislatures have placed conditions on the ability of prisoners to receive damage remedies in both the United States[214] and New Zealand,[215] two jurisdictions that lack a general remedial clause in their Bills of Rights. Both laws require exhaustion of administrative remedies which will often deprive prisoners of a damage award that

[211] This was recognized by Chief Justice McLachlin in *Ward* v. *Vancouver (City)*, 2010 SCC 27 at para 30 when she concluded that "the fact that the claimant has not suffered personal loss does not preclude damages when the objectives of vindication or deterrence clearly call for an award".

[212] Schuck, *Suing Government.*

[213] Damages in Canada are awarded under s.24(1) of the Canadian Charter of Rights and Freedoms. The courts have recognized that they and not legislatures should determine whether damage awards or injunctions or other remedies are appropriate and just in the circumstances: *Ward* v. *Vancouver (City)*, [2010] 2 SCR 28 at para 17; *Doucet-Boudreau* v. *Nova Scotia*, [2003] 3 SCR 3 at paras 51, 95.

[214] Prison Litigation Reform Act of 1996, Pub. L. No. 104–134 110 Stat 1321 ss.802, 803, 804, 807 (required inmates to exhaust administrative forms of redress, limiting damages for pain and suffering, increasing filing fees and providing that an inmate who brought three unsuccessful lawsuits could be barred from subsequent litigation). On how this has reduced prisoner lawsuits, see Derek Borchardt, "The Iron Curtain Redrawn Between Prisoners and the Constitution" (2012) 43 *Colum. H.R. L. Rev.* 469, 480–482. For a Canadian case that rejects the need for prisoners to exhaust administrative remedies before seeking damages see *Canada (Attorney General)* v. *McArthur*, 2010 SCC 63.

[215] Prisoner and Victims' Claims Act 2005, No. 74 ss.3, 13, 14(2), (requiring exhaustion of administrative remedies; consideration of whether prisoner contributed to harm and providing that crime victims should have access to any damages prisoners may receive).

can mark and publicize an injustice.[216] Both laws have diminished prisoner litigation in the United States and New Zealand. If damages for violations of human rights are simply understood as a tort remedy, then there is nothing to preclude legislatures from restricting or replacing them.

In one 2012 case, a prisoner was awarded NZ$600 when he was subject to a second unjustified strip search on one day.[217] He would not receive the damages because the New Zealand legislation allows crime victims to collect the award. Moreover the low award trivialized the underlying right. It echoed the restrictive legislation in suggesting that the rights and dignity of prisoners do not matter as much as those of other human beings.

5.3.6 *Summary*

Despite the disappointing record of damages, there are still important advantages in a public law approach to this remedy. It can ensure that governments as opposed to individual officials are the proper defendant. It may also ensure that damage awards are not restricted by populist legislation. Public law principles also help situate damages within a range of alternative remedies including stronger remedies (such as injunctions and restitution) and weaker remedies (such as declarations) as well as alternative forms of satisfaction such as apologies. Public law principles drawn from international principles of state responsibility allow damages to be used as an important marker of both the equality and worth of all rights holders and the injustice of the violation of rights. In the next section, it will be suggested that public law principles also allow the exercise of remedial discretion to be disciplined and made more transparent through the use of well-established proportionality principles

5.4 Restraints on Damages and Proportionality

Courts have generally taken what Paul Gewirtz characterized as an interest balancing approach to ordering damages.[218] Supra-national

[216] The visibility of damage claims may be a key factor with respect to both civil society activism and bureaucratic reform: Charles Epp, *Making Rights Real: Activists, Bureaucrats and the Creation of the Legalistic State* (Chicago: University of Chicago Press, 2009).

[217] *Forrest* v. *Attorney-General*, [2012] NZCA 125 at para 42.

[218] Paul Gewirtz, "Remedies and Resistance" (1983) 92 *Yale L. J.* 4.

courts use an equitable approach in assessing both non-pecuniary and pecuniary damages that seeks a "fair balance between the general interest and the [applicant's] interest".[219] Domestic courts often balance interests by creating rules of qualified immunity that require plaintiffs to prove not only a violation of a right and harm that merits damages, but also that state officials have acted with some degree of fault. The American courts have defined qualified immunities to place almost impossible burdens on plaintiffs.[220] They have also defined absolute immunities more broadly than other courts, extending them to prosecutorial functions.[221]

Both the equitable and qualified immunity approaches are inferior methods of remedial decision-making to the direct application of proportionality reasoning. As demonstrated in Section 5.2, the frequent appeal to equity by supra-national courts often masks a strong remedial discretion that makes damage awards unpredictable. As discussed in Chapter 1, Section 1.7, a strong discretion allows a court to both withhold a remedy and to provide a remedy in a summary manner without adequate reasoning. On the other hand, absolute and qualified immunities are a rule-based approach and as such are inevitably over and under-inclusive as a means to ensure that damage awards do not harm important social interests.

5.4.1 *The Under- and Over-Inclusive Nature of Qualified Immunities*

Qualified immunities are inferior to proportionality rules because they serve as rigid on-and-off rules that detract attention away from both the rights violation and the particular governmental interest that may be harmed by the award of remedies. They protect governments prophylactically by requiring some set level of fault without regard to the consequences of awarding damages in the particular case. Rules are

[219] *Salvador-Chiriboga* v. *Ecuador* (2008), Preliminary Objections and Merits, Inter-Am. Ct. H.R. (Ser. C), (6 May 2008) at para 84.

[220] Qualified immunities in the US are often successfully asserted even before discovery and in the face of serious allegations. For a proposal in Congress to end qualified immunities for local and state law enforcement officials, see The George Floyd Justice in Policing Bill s.102.

[221] *Imbler* v. *Pachtman*, 424 US 409 (1976). Absolute immunities are generally recognized for judicial function. The notable exception is *Maharaj* v. *Trinidad and Tobago*, [1979] AC 385, which, as discussed in Section 5.3.2 of this chapter, focused on state liability for judicial acts.

inevitably under- or over-inclusive guides to the exercise of remedial discretion.[222] In some cases, damages should be awarded to compensate the harms suffered by applicants even though the state officials have not acted with the degree of fault required by the qualified immunities. In other cases, the consequences of awarding damages may be great and have a disproportionate effect on legitimate governmental interests even though the requisite degree of fault required to defeat the government's qualified immunity is present.

An inability to establish fault required by qualified immunities in the United States often defeats rights claims at a preliminary stage before discovery of material that the defendant holds that may reveal fault. Qualified immunities place severe burdens on plaintiffs. They generate much pre-trial litigation that does not address the merits. They are also unnecessary to prevent over-deterrence of officials if the official will, as is generally the case in the United States, be indemnified by the state[223] or if, as in New Zealand or Canada, the state is held directly liable for the damage award.

5.4.2 *The Value of Public Law Proportionality Principles to Remedial Decision-Making*

In *Taunoa*, Justice McGrath observed that "the remedy should be proportionate to the breach but also have regard to other aspects of the public interest".[224] When unpacked, this helpful statement suggests that proportionality can inform remedial decision-making in two ways: 1. with respect to understanding damages in light of alternative weaker or stronger remedies; and 2. disciplining state claims that damages or other remedies should not be awarded or reduced because of important competing social interests.

The Supreme Court of Canada in *Ward*[225] took an approach that required the state to establish that a less drastic remedy, such as a declaration, was sufficient to fulfil the relevant remedial purposes of compensation, vindication and deterrence.[226] It would also allow the

[222] See also Kent Roach, "Principled Remedial Decision-Making under the Charter" (2004) 25 *S.C.L.R.* (2d) 101.

[223] Joanna C Schwartz, "The Case against Qualified Immunity" (2018) 93 *Notre Dame L. Rev.* 5; Joanna C. Schwartz, "How Qualified Immunity Fails" (2017) 127 *Yale L. J.* 2.

[224] *Taunoa* v. *Attorney General*, 2007 NZSC 70 at para 369.

[225] 2010 SCC 27.

[226] The Court required the applicant to establish a rights violation but also that damages were prima facie required for compensation, vindication or deterrence.

state to establish that countervailing interests would justify either not awarding damages or reducing the amount. Consistent with proportionality principles examined in Chapter 1, Section 1.9, the Court left the category of countervailing interests open-ended. It appropriately insisted, however, that they must relate to legitimate good governance concerns. This should preclude objectives that are really objections to the right or the court's role in providing a remedy.

Supra-national courts balance interests before awarding damages and often justify the result through vague appeals to equity. A better approach is contemplated by the ILC's principles of state responsibility. Article 35 provides that states shall make full restitution for wrongful acts unless re-establishing the situation before the wrong is impossible or "involves a burden out of all proportion to the benefit deriving from restitution instead of compensation".[227] Article 37 provides that "satisfaction shall not be out of proportion to the injury".[228] Article 37 requires proportionality between the violation and damages awarded while Article 35 contemplates that the state can justify a lesser remedy of compensation if the burdens of restitution are disproportionate to its benefits. This mimics the overall balance stage of proportionality reasoning.

Following the proportionality principles, the state would have to establish that limiting or not awarding damages would rationally advance an important objective and that there is no other reasonable way to advance such important competing social interests. Proportionality analysis as applied to remedial decision-making should also be completed by the more controversial final overall balance stage. This compares the harms to the applicant of denying or reducing damages to the benefits to the state and other rights holders by limiting damages.

The Supreme Court of Canada has demonstrated how the overall balance stage of proportionality reasoning could be applied to remedies when it concluded that its controversial decision not to award fully retroactive payments of survivor benefits to same-sex couples would not leave the applicants with "a hollow victory".[229] The Court concluded that same-sex couples would be left with a meaningful remedy, while the state would not have to pay for benefits between 1985 and 1999: a time period during which it concluded that the government had reasonably

227 International Law Commission, *Principles of State Responsibility*.
228 Crawford, *The International Law Commission's Principles on State Responsibility*.
229 *Hislop* v. *Canada*, 2007 SCC 10 at para 116.

relied on the exclusion of same-sex couples from the definition of spouses.

The overall balance stage of proportionality analysis might also help the IACtHR and especially the ECtHR to justify reductions of multi-million dollar damage awards that they have awarded to corporations in some cases for violations of property rights. Such awards have been criticized as a "perversion of human rights"[230] when compared to the low value placed on the many important but non-pecuniary harms caused when the rights of individuals and groups are violated. High damage awards for violation of property rights may in some cases be disproportionate to the seriousness and consequences of the violation. Even if this is not the case, the state might still be able to justify reduced awards as necessary to advance important state objectives and as striking an appropriate overall balance between the state and the litigant's interests.

5.5 Towards a Two-Track Approach

Damages play an important role in the two-track approach. They compensate for past pecuniary and non-pecuniary harms caused by a rights violation. This primary role for damages builds on traditional "right to a remedy" thinking found in both the common law and international law. At the same time, the two-track approach recognizes that an approach that focuses exclusively on compensating for past harms will be inadequate. The tension between these older and newer approaches have been recognized at least since Abram Chayes's pioneering work contrasting a new public law form of litigation with a traditional common law model based on long celebrated right to a remedy reasoning.[231] What is new in my account, however, is an insistence that courts should travel down both tracks at the same time and my argument that an exclusive focus on either track will be radically incomplete and produce remedial pathologies.

The UN Basic Principles on the Right to a Remedy helpfully situate damages in a broader remedial landscape that includes restitution,

[230] Ichim, *Just Satisfaction*, p.3.

[231] Abram Chayes, "The Role of the Judge in Public Law Litigation" (1976) 89 *Harv. L. Rev.* 1289; but for assertions contrary to the two-track approach to damages suggested here that damages "are inevitably retrospective", see Shelton, *Remedies in International Human Rights Law*, p.315.

rehabilitation, satisfaction including apologies and sanctions and guarantees of non-repetition and cessation of the violation.[232] They respond to concerns that paying damages will allow states to buy their way out of having to respect human rights by insisting on cessation and non-repetition of human rights violations. This is consistent with the two-track approach. Domestic courts sometimes recognize deterrence of future violations as one of the purposes of damage awards, but rarely combines them with alternative remedies that may more effectively prevent future violations. It will also be suggested that only the New Zealand courts have employed a simple and elegant dialogic technique of asking states what steps they have taken to prevent a similar violation and allowing the state's answer to influence their assessment of damage awards.

5.5.1 Why Damages Remain Important

Given the low amounts of most damage awards for violations of human rights, one option would be simply to give up on damages as a remedy. Both Lord Woolf and the Wise Persons committee concluded that the overburdened ECtHR should allow domestic courts or the Committee of Ministers to calculate damage awards. As argued in Chapter 2, Section 2.4.3.4, however, that would have been a serious mistake.

The award of damages – even inadequate damages – has a cathartic effect that highlights the harms done to particular individuals. Charles Epp has illustrated how damage awards in police abuse cases allow "graphic complaints" to receive publicity and create "powerful incentives for reform".[233] Likewise, Veronika Fikfak notes behavioural studies that suggest that "there is novelty and immediacy with one single victim" but "psychological numbing" when victims become faceless statistics.[234] Damages are hard-wired into the judicial system because they demonstrate that individual litigants matter.

One of the judiciary's core and distinctive features is to provide remedies for particular litigants. This instinct is felt by both domestic

[232] United Nations General Assembly, *Basic Principles and Guidelines on the Right to a Remedy and Reparations for Victims of Gross Violations of International Human Rights Law and Serious Violations of Humanitarian Law*, Adopted by the General Assembly 21 March 2006, A/Res/60/147 at paras 19–23.
[233] Epp, *Making Rights Real*, pp.93–165, 228.
[234] Fikfak, "Changing State Behaviour" 1113.

and supra-national adjudicators, as evidenced by the ICJ's oft-quoted statement that remedies should "as far as possible, wipe out all the consequences of the illegal act and re-establish the situation which would, in all probability, have existed if the act had not been committed"[235] An interesting facet of the famous *Chorzow Factory* case, however, is that the Court seemed prepared to award damages that went beyond the value of the illegally seized factory if necessary to respond to the illegality committed by the Polish state in seizing the German factory.[236] In other words, there was flexibility in calculating damages. It could be used to go beyond purely compensatory damages if necessary to respond to illegal state conduct. This means that damages can also operate as a second systemic track remedy even though they will primarily be a first-track compensatory remedy.

A two-track approach does not necessarily mean that damages should be awarded for every human rights violation. Applicants need to establish that damages are an appropriate remedy to compensate for pecuniary or non-pecuniary harms caused by the rights violation,[237] vindicate the importance of the right for the litigant and society and, if necessary, to deter future violations or signal judicial concerns about the repetition of similar violations.[238] In making these determinations, courts will have to evaluate the adequacy of alternative remedies. For many violations of procedural rights, an order that the procedure be redone with proper respect for the applicant's rights may be sufficient. In some cases, the state may be able to justify not awarding damages either on the basis of the adequacy of an alternative remedy or because not awarding the remedy is a proportionate and necessary way to avoid harming important state interests. That said, not awarding damages should not be justified under the two-track approach simply because of concerns that

[235] *Factory at Chorzow Case (Jurisdiction)*, [1928] PCIJ Series A No. 17, 22, 47.

[236] Ibid. The Court also appointed two experts to calculate the appropriate damages, but the countries settled before any award: Timothy Nelson, "A Factory in Chorzow" (2014) *J. Damages Int'l. Arb.* 77.

[237] This is another context where domestic law could learn from international law, which since the *Lusitania* case has recognized that non-material damages "are very real, and the mere fact that they are difficult to measure or estimate by money standards makes them none the less real and affords no reason why the injured person should not be compensated:" *Lusitania Case* (*US* v. *Germany)* 1923, 7 RIAA 32 at 40.

[238] Geoff McLay has noted that damages can be a "signalling device" and related this to a public law understanding of damages: McLay, "Damages for Breach of the New Zealand Bill of Rights: Why Aren't They Sufficient Remedy" (2008) 2008 *N.Z. L. Rev.* 333, 374; similarly, see Varuhas, *Damages and Human Rights*, pp.351–352.

the plaintiff is a "queue jumper"[239] or because others not before the court have suffered similar violations. Nor should refusing damages be justified on the basis that an award will open the floodgates to other damage claims. The focus in the first track is on doing justice to the individual litigant, not on the broader distributive implications of the ruling. That is, unless the state can justify no remedy or a reduced remedy as a proportionate response to a compelling social interest.

5.5.2 Class Actions

One challenge to the two-track approach to remedies occurs when claims are sought on behalf of large groups. For example, in Canada, there is considerable interest in aggregating Charter damage claims into class actions because the low quantum of most awards makes litigation by individuals uneconomical. The state's ability to justify departures from full compensation as a proportionate restriction on remedies may, however, increase when remedial claims including damages are aggregated. Even in class actions, however, courts should take care to document individual rights violations. They should guard against what Fikfak has noted is the "psychological numbing"[240] that comes when a group such as "prisoners" do not have a human face. Part of the value of first-track remedies is that they respond to intuitive and deontological senses that remedies respond to the suffering of particular individuals.

The aggregation of damage claims in class actions has the potential to make damage claims a powerful second track instrument to induce governments to take steps to prevent similar violations in the future. But it risks placing less attention on the harms that individual members of a class suffer. Class actions often result in procedural battles and frequently result in settlements. When awarding damages or reviewing settlements, judges should be concerned with both compensation for past harms and prevention of new ones.

A Canadian trial judge took a creative approach in a class action brought by prisoners who had their rights violated in solitary confinement. He awarded Can$20 million in general damages in order to vindicate the rights of the prisoners and to deter and prevent similar

[239] Katharine Young, "Rights and Queues: On Distributive Contests in the Modern State" (2016) 55 *Colum. J. of Trans'l. L.* 64. See *infra* Chapter 8, Section 8.3, for more discussion of the limitation of the queue-jumping epithet.

[240] Fikfak, "Changing State Behaviour", 1113.

future violations. This was a systemic remedy because he ordered that the large award less lawyer's fees not be distributed to the class, but used to fund programs for all mentally ill prisoners, including non-parties to the class action.[241] Consistent with the two-track approach, he allowed litigants in the class to seek compensatory individual remedies for the harms caused to them, albeit in individualized proceedings to be held at a later stage of the proceedings.[242] At the same time, his judgement was decided by summary judgement. It was long on general legislative facts and a "battle of the experts" about the effects of solitary confinement but short on adjudicative facts about specific individuals who suffered harm. In addition, the award only amounted to about $10,000 per class member.[243] The judge later defended this global award stating that over and under-compensation was inherent in class actions.

The Ontario Court of Appeal overturned the innovative award on the basis that it was "not fair to either the class or Canada and it amounted to an unjustifiable assumption of judicial control over a complex public institution".[244] This decision discounts that the class could still seek compensatory awards under the trial judge's approach. At the same time, it is not clear whether individual assessment of compensatory damages would have been economical. The award may have been unfair to the class because the trial judge did not allow the parties to comment on the novel distribution[245] or make submissions about how the award would be spent. In Chapter 7, Section 7.5, it will be suggested that such participation may be valuable in ensuring that systemic remedies are effective.

[241] *Brazeau* v. *Canada (Attorney General)*, 2019 ONSC 1888 at paras 448, 459.

[242] Ibid. at paras 455, 466–468. In a companion case involving harms claimed by solitary confinement, he awarded Can$20 million but held that the award should be distributed to the class and indicated about Can$9 million of the award was for compensation including mental suffering. *Reddock* v. *Canada (Attorney General)*, 2019 ONSC 5053. In a subsequent case, he awarded Can$30 million against provincial authorities for harms associated with solitary confinement in combined damages for compensation, vindication and deterrence: *Francis* v. *Ontario*, 2020 ONSC 1644 at para 634–635. In another case involving police violation of rights of demonstrators at the 2010 G20 summit, a Can$16.5 million settlement was reached and approved as fair and reasonable. The settlement also included more creative forms of satisfaction including apologies and state attempts to help protesters expunge their criminal records. *Good* v. *Toronto Police Services Board*, 2020 ONSC 6332.

[243] Ibid. at 446.

[244] *Brazeau v. Canada (Attorney General)* 2020 ONCA 184 at para 112.

[245] Ibid. at 107.

The Court of Appeal's conclusion that the Can$20 million award would interfere with prison administration ignores that the award did not attempt to micro-manage how the state would spend the money beyond directing that it be used to assist inmates with mental health issues. The Court of Appeal also held that the Can$20 million violated restrictions in Ontario's Class Proceedings Act on cy-pres distribution of class awards because no attempt was made to distribute the award to the class. This ignores Canadian decisions that hold that creative exercises of remedial power under Canada's constitutional Charter of Rights should not be restricted by ordinary legislation.[246]

On remand and despite the Court of Appeal's order that the damage award should be considered anew on the basis of proper principles, the same trial judge awarded the Can$20 million to the class, but now held that it also fulfilled the need to compensate the prisoners who had been held in solitary confinement. This raised concerns that the class now might be under-compensated for the harms they suffered given that the judge had calculated the original award without compensation in mind. The judge seemed to indicate that over- and under-compensation are inevitable in class proceedings.[247] This may be true, but it remains troubling. Combined awards for both compensatory and non-repetition are permissible under the two-track approach, but the blurring of the rationales suggests that a strong discretion is being applied to the award of the quantum. A better approach would have more clearly articulated what part of the award was required for compensation of past harms and what part was required to prevent future violations. The latter amount could be influenced by the steps that the federal government was taking with respect to the rights violations caused by solitary confinement.

The Ontario Court of Appeal upheld a similar Can$20 million award to a class who had been held in solitary confinement in a companion

[246] *Doucet-Boudreau* v. *Nova Scotia*, [2003] 3 SCR 3 at para 51. In part because of the acceptance of the deterrent power of class actions, American and Canadian courts have generally accepted cy-pres distribution of class awards more than Australian courts that have been more sceptical of such approaches. See Jeff Berryman and Robyn Carroll, "Cy-Près as a Class Action Remedy" in Kit Barker and Darryn Jenson (eds.), *Private Law: Key Encounters with Public Law* (Cambridge: Cambridge University Press, 2013), pp.340ff. They also noted the cy-pres awards should for deterrence reasons not be returned to the defendant, but, in the trial judgment in *Brazeau*, they were allocated to address the mischief in the violation.

[247] *Brazeau* v. *Canada (Attorney General)*, 2020 ONSC 3272 at 33–34.

case. At the same time, it noted the awards "seems modest"[248] because it had been calculated on the basis of Can$500 for each placement in solitary confinement of more than fifteen days.[249] Such a base award continues the regrettable undervaluing of rights violation even while presenting governments with stronger incentives to change its behaviour because of the aggregation of the awards.

Class actions can play a role in the two-track approach, but courts should be attentive to the dual need to compensate those within the class for past harms and to prevent similar violations in the future. Damage awards made by way of class actions may lack legitimacy and lose public support if they are seen simply as a systemic remedy that is not responsive to past harms suffered by real people within the class.

5.5.3 *Avoiding Remedial Pathologies of Exclusively Individual or Instrumental Approaches*

The two-track approach is built on the premise that an exclusive focus on either track will be inadequate. American courts in particular have been attracted to an exclusively instrumental approach to a range of remedies including damages. In many cases, this has resulted in no remedy for those whose rights have been infringed on the basis of speculative concerns that awarding damages will over-deter officials and, as such, harm good governance.[250] Yet, a thoroughly instrumental approach fails to take seriously the equal rights of the plaintiff or to mark the injustice of the violation of their rights.

Conversely, however, focusing simply on remedying the past violation when awarding damages suggests that damages are simply a tax or price that governments must absorb and redistribute for rights violations. Although the Supreme Court of Canada recognized that damages could fulfil societal based vindicatory and deterrence purposes in *Ward*, it failed to situate its award of Can$5,000 in damages in the broader context of concerns that state officials had often failed to comply with restrictions

[248] *Brazeau* v. *Canada (Attorney General)*, 2020 ONCA 184 at para 103.

[249] Ibid. at para 104.

[250] *Ashcroft* v. *Iqbal*, 556 US 662 (2009); *Ashcroft* v. *Al-Kidd*, 563 US 731 (2011); *Arar* v. *Ashcroft*, 585 F.3d. 559 (2d Cir., 2009); *Rasul* v. *Myers*, 563 F.3d 527 (D.C. Cir., 2009); *Padilla* v. *Yoo*, 678 F.3d 748 (9th Cir. 2012). On the instrumental nature of other American constitutional remedies including exclusion of evidence, see Roach, "Dialogic Remedies".

that the Court had placed on strip searches nine years earlier.[251] To be sure, an award of extra damages would not necessarily have prevented similar violations in the future. But it would have signalled to society, police services and other courts the importance of compliance in the future. It also would have laid the basis for stronger remedies in the future, if necessary.

Damages have a dual function under the two-track approach. They have traditional compensatory and vindicatory functions long associated with the common law. But damages also have a modern systemic and regulatory function associated with non-repetition of violations and deterrence of future violations. This does not mean that deterrence should be the exclusive basis for damage awards or that other remedies other than damages should not be used when necessary to prevent future violations. Courts should defer to the state's ability to reform its own house, while also being able to justify higher damage awards or if necessary use other remedies such as declarations and injunctions. That said, damages that are aggravated because of concerns about repetitive violations should have a legitimate role in both domestic and international human rights law.

5.5.4 *Aggravated Damages as a Second-Track Systemic Remedy*

Courts should be willing to order aggravated damages as a second-track systemic remedy in cases where there is evidence of repetitive violations and where the state has not taken reasonable steps to respond to or prevent them. The approach to aggravated damages under the two-track approach would be quite different from that presently taken by American and English courts. American courts have left open the possibility of punitive damages against individual officials who have been "shown to be motivated by evil motive or intent" or "reckless or callous indifference" to rights.[252] However, courts have denied punitive damages when municipal governments have been held responsible for rights violations.[253] The American approach is exceptional and individualistic in its focus on the ability of juries to award punitive awards against individuals and its

[251] *R.* v. *Golden*, [2001] 3 SCR 679. See generally Michelle Psutska and Elizabeth Sheehy, "Strip Searching of Women in Canada: Wrongs and Rights" (2016) 94 *Can. Bar Rev.* 241.

[252] *Smith* v. *Wade*, 461 US 30 (1983).

[253] *City of Newport* v. *Fact Concerts Inc.*, 453 US 247 (1981).

reluctance to award punitive damages against municipalities as well as states and the federal government.

Although the award of aggravated and even punitive damages have long and honourable histories in English law as means to respond to the abuse of state power,[254] English courts have regrettably held that they are not available under the Human Rights Act, 1998 because they are not awarded by the ECtHR.[255] Supra-national courts have generally eschewed punitive damages.[256] Nevertheless, Professor Dinah Shelton has made a convincing case that "additional awards and non-monetary remedies may be needed to guarantee non-repetition of the act . . . It is important that governments not continue to violate human rights after being nominal or low compensatory damages to victims".[257] Although formally eschewing punitive damages, the ECtHR has recognized that damages can be used as "a serious and effective means of dissuasion with regard to the repetition of unlawful conduct of the same type, without however assuming a punitive function".[258] This is consistent with the two-track approach and arguably with the practice of the court. Nevertheless, the ECtHR jurisprudence could be improved by more consistency on this issue and clearer signalling of why it is increasing damages because of concerns about repetition of the violations. The

[254] In 1709, it was stated that "if public officers will infringe rights, they ought to pay greater damages than other men to deter and hinder others from the like offence". *Ashby* v. *White*, (1703) 92 ER 126; 2 Ld. Raymond 938, 953; see also *Rookes* v. *Bernard*, [1964] 1 All ER 367 at 410–411 in reference to arbitrary, oppressive and unconstitutional conduct.

[255] *Watkins* v. *Secretary of State for Home Department*, [2006] UKHL 17 at para 64; but see now *Cyprus* v. *Turkey* (Just Satisfaction) [GC], No. 25781/94, [2014] II ECHR 245 at para 18 per concurring judgement of Judge Pinto de Albuquerque suggesting that punitive or exemplary damages may be warranted in response to continuing and long standing violations of human rights and related restrictions of access to the courts.

[256] They have not been recognized in the work of the International Law Commission on State Responsibility with James Crawford concluding that "the idea of punitive damages under international law is currently unsustainable". Crawford, *State Responsibility*, p.526.

[257] Shelton, *Remedies in International Human Rights Law*, pp.407, 419–420. Ichim similarly observes of ECtHR practice that "[t]he judges have wisely transformed a punishment, which operates for a past activity, into incentives for future conduct, but the effect is still the same: the wrongdoing state should avoid repetition". Ichim, *Just Satisfaction*, p.167; see also Fikfak, "Changing State Behaviour" suggesting that a law and economics approach supports the award of punitive damage including with retributive condemnation of the state.

[258] *Guiso-Gallisay* v. *Italy* (Just satisfaction) [GC], No. 58858/00, ECHR 22 December 2009 at para 85.

increases in damages need not be extravagant. The Court's justification for modest increases would serve mainly as a form of naming and shaming. This would be more consistent with international law traditions than the exceptional American instrumental approach, which uses punitive damages to deter individuals and sometimes assumes (likely implausibly)[259] that damages will deter state behaviour.

Under the public law and two-track approach, exemplary damages would be assessed directly against the state. This responds to concerns that aggravated damages may over-deter official conduct. That said, individual fault in relation to rights violations should be noted by courts and may be a proper basis for the state to take disciplinary actions against officials including firing. It will be suggested below that the New Zealand courts have properly inquired in a damage action whether police officers who had beaten a suspect have been disciplined and have indicated that their damage award against the state would have been higher had the state not disciplined the officers.[260] The amount of aggravated damages need not be excessive: they would be designed to signal to both governments and civil society the need for reform to prevent the repetition of human rights violations.

Some may object that such aggravated damages represent an undeserved windfall for the plaintiff and punishment for the defendant (in this context, the state). This ignores the traditional role of aggravated damages in responding to abuses of state power. Moreover, compensatory damages in human rights cases have been modest and may well fall short of full compensation. In any event, declarations and retention of jurisdiction may be an alternative second-track systemic remedial approach should courts conclude that aggravated damages would be an unjustified windfall to the applicant.

5.5.5 *Examples in Supra-National Law*

More frequently than domestic courts, supra-national adjudicators take a two-track approach that combines individual and systemic remedies. The IACtHR typically awards damages in conjunction with other remedies. These remedies are concerned both with preventing future violations and including non-monetary forms of satisfaction. Alas, there is a pattern of states being more willing to pay the often-modest amounts of damages

[259] Levinson, "Making Governments Pay".

[260] *Falwasser* v. *Attorney General*, 2010 NZAR 445 at paras 36–37, 124.

that the Court awards than to implement more ambitious and often more expensive systemic remedies. The ECtHR generally awards only damages but in more complex and repetitive cases combines damages with general measures that are designed to prevent repetitive violations.

The International Court of Justice has considered the need for damages combined with measures to ensure that violations cease and are not repeated in a number of cases though it has not always combined these remedies.[261] Unfortunately, it did not address the relation between damages and the duty to assure non-repetition of violations in its award of damages in the *Diallo* case and focused simply on compensation and proof of pecuniary and non-pecuniary harms.[262] This avoids Professor Shelton's apt warnings that "an award of compensatory damages alone can amount to an inexpensive sale of the option to commit the same wrong or others like it. Disincentives such as additional awards and non-monetary remedies may be needed to guarantee non-repetition of the act".[263]

As will be discussed in Chapter 6, Section 6.2.1.3, the International Criminal Court has powers to order damages for victims and require offenders to pay damages in conjunction with prosecutions of the most serious crimes. The ICC uses damages but in conjunction with other mechanisms that are designed to prevent future violations of human rights.

Both the UN Human Rights Committee and the ECtHR took a two-track approach in cases concerning abortion rights in Ireland. The Committee indicated that Ireland should provide adequate compensation to women forced to leave the country to terminate their pregnancies[264]

[261] *Application of the Convention on the Prevention and Punishment of the Crime of Genocide (Bosnia and Herzegovina* v. *Serbia and Montenegro),* Judgment of 26 February 2007, ICJ. Rep. 2007 at 233–234. See Shelton, *Remedies in International Human Rights Law*, pp.162ff.

[262] *Case Concerning Ahmadou Sadio Diallo (Republic of Guinea* v. *Democratic Republic of the Congo)*, Reports of Judgments, Advisory Opinions and Orders of 19 June 2012, [2012] ICJ Rep. 324

[263] Shelton, *Remedies in International Human Rights Law*, p.407.

[264] UN Human Rights Committee, *Mellet* v. *Ireland*, Comm. No. 2324/2013, UN Doc CCPR/C/116/D/2324/2013, adopted 31 March 2016. In other cases arising from sexual harassment and assault, the UN Human Rights Committee has both ordered compensation for individual complainants for moral and material damages suffered as well as non-monetary compensation in the form of counselling while also proposing general measures including law reform to prevent similar violations in the future: Committee on the Elimination of Discrimination against Women, *Belousova* v. *Kazakhstan*, Comm. No. 45/2012, UN Doc CEDAW/C/61/D/45/2012, adopted 2015; Committee on the

and the ECtHR awarded €15,000 in damages.[265] Even if such damages are inadequate, they underlined the consequences of the Irish policy for individual women. At the same time, both adjudicators stressed the need for Ireland to take systemic measures to prevent similar violations of the rights of women in the future. Indeed, the Committee of Ministers stated that supervision would only be relinquished once Ireland had enacted some reform legislation to make abortions available at least when the life of the woman was at stake.[266]

5.5.6 *Examples in National Law*

A few damage cases under the New Zealand Bill of Rights are consistent with the two-track approach. The New Zealand Supreme Court reduced damages in a controversial prison case involving an abandoned solitary confinement regime. The Court stressed that "there can be little or no likelihood that the conduct will ever be repeated".[267] Blanchard J elaborated that "[t]he level of the monetary sum should also reflect the other ways in which the State has acknowledged the wrongdoing: whether, and with what speed, it has brought to an end the wrongful conduct and put in place measures to prevent reoccurrence; and whether it has publicly apologized to the victim in appropriate terms".[268]

Damages should not be reduced to levels that fail to compensate plaintiffs or vindicate the importance of respecting their rights. Nonetheless, the approach taken by the New Zealand Supreme Court pays attention to legitimate interests in ensuring future compliance with rights even while awarding damages for the past violation of the rights of prisoners. In this sense, this remedy demonstrates some of the virtues of both public law and two-track approaches to the awarding of damages.[269]

Elimination of Discrimination Against Women, *R.P.B.* v. *the Philippines*, Comm. No. 34/2011, UN Doc CEDAW/C/57/D/34/2011, adopted 21 February 2014.

265 *A, B, and C* v. *Ireland* [GC], No. 25579/05, [2010] ECHR 2032.

266 *A, B, and C* v. *Ireland* [GC], No. 25579/05, [2010] ECHR 2032, Final Resolution CM/ResDH (2014) 273.

267 *Taunoa* v. *Attorney General*, 2007 NZSC 70 at paras 268, 371.

268 Ibid. at para 262.

269 As Geoff McLay has concluded, "if the refusal to change a practice that is in breach of the New Zealand Bill of rights is a factor that may increase an award of damages, there might be sufficient incentive for government to take possible breaches seriously": McLay, "Damages for Breach of the New Zealand Bill of Rights", 371. Jason Varuhas recognizes that part of the Court's concern in *Taunoa* is on "compliance" but then criticizes it as an administrative law approach to damages or "an enhanced form of declaratory relief":

An earlier New Zealand decision elegantly demonstrated how courts can use damages to encourage the state to take systemic actions that could not otherwise be imposed by the Court. The Court awarded NZ$30,000 in damages to a prisoner who was assaulted in a cell with batons and pepper spray by the police. The Court stressed the seriousness of the breach and the need for compensation and vindication. What makes the award consistent with the two-track approach, however, was that the Court indicated that it would have increased the damage award to achieve deterrence had the state not already disciplined the police officers and apologized to the claimant.[270]

This decision provides the state with an incentive to apologize for rights violations and to take steps to prevent their reoccurrence. The state has a wide variety of means including not only discipline but adjustments to training, recruitment and organizational structure that can be used to minimize the risk of repetitive violations. Apologies are rarely used in domestic human rights despite significant evidence that it can, in some circumstances, be quite meaningful and effective.[271]

Both of these New Zealand cases show a judicial concern with the broader systemic dimensions of the violation while initially placing the onus on the state to take its own preventive measures. They do not necessarily contemplate the award of extravagant aggravated damages should the state not take reasonable steps to prevent a reoccurrence of the violation, but they do contemplate that courts could issue strong dicta as well as increased awards if the state had done nothing to prevent similar violations in the future. This relatively minor change in the structure of damage awards has the potential to make them an effective two-track remedy. In Chapter 6, Section 6.4.5, it will be suggested that a similar approach should be used to ensure that remedies awarded in the criminal process also are more attentive to the risk of repetition.

Consistent with a two-track approach, the Supreme Court of India has recognized that remedies should not only attempt to compensate for unlawful acts such as custodial deaths, but also "to civilize public power" and "to assure the citizens that they live in a legal system wherein their

Varuhas, "The Development of the Damages Remedy", 237–230. The enhancement is that plaintiffs who suffered harm can receive additional damages if the harm is continuing.

270 *Falwasser* v. *Attorney General*, 2010 NZAR 445 at paras 36–37, 124.

271 Brent T. White, "Say You're Sorry: Court-Ordered Apologies as a Civil Rights Remedy" (2006) 91 *Cornell L. Rev.* 6; Gijs van Dijk, "The Ordered Apology" (2017) 37 *Oxf. J. Leg. Stud.* 562.

rights and interests shall be protected and preserved".[272] In some cases, the Court has taken a two-track approach by ordering the government to take disciplinary actions against officers who violated rights while establishing presumptive damage awards for those who suffered damages from the illegal acts.[273] In one recent case, the Court both awarded damages to a victim of malicious prosecution and ordered that a three person commission investigate whether officials should be prosecuted.[274] Such a two-track approach allows the Court to provide some meaningful remedy to the plaintiffs. It avoids the pathologies of some Indian public interest litigation that will be discussed in Chapter 7, Section 7.2.4, where the injustice of past violations and the place of the plaintiff become forgotten. The more aggressive second-track systemic remedies taken by the Indian court in these cases compared to the New Zealand approach may reflect concerns that the state was unwilling or unable to take reasonable steps to prevent such violations in the future.[275]

5.5.7 Remedial Failure

The award of damages under the two-track approach will help generate some remedial success to balance off the perhaps inevitable failures of more systemic remedies. For example, in response to cases holding that solitary confinement violated rights, Canada enacted new procedures for structured intervention units that are designed to allow inmates four hours a day out of their cell and two hours of human contact.[276] There are concerns, however, that the new law can still result in rights violations. The continued award of damages and other remedies will alert governments and society to subsequent violations.

[272] *Basu* v. *State of West Bengal,* (1997) 1 SCC 416 at para 314.

[273] *In Re: Ramlila Maidan Incident Dt.4/5.06.2011* v. *Home Secretary, Union of India & Ors.*, (Suo Motu Writ Petition (Crl) No. 122 of 2011 at paras 227–236.

[274] *S. Nambi Narayanan* v. *Siby Mathews and Ors.*, (2018) 10 SCC 804. In other cases, the Court has awarded damages but has also given interim directions to the state, appointed investigators and ordered both the state and investigators to report back to the court about what steps had been taken to prevent similar violations in the future: *Delhi Jal Board* v. *National Campaign Etc.& Ors.*, [2011] INSC 611 at paras 31–32.

[275] For arguments that courts should be attentive to whether governments are either unwilling or unable to engage in systemic reforms to prevent future violations, see Kent Roach and Geoff Budlender, "Mandatory Relief and Supervisory Jurisdiction: When Is It Appropriate, Just and Equitable" (2005) 122 *South African L. J.* 325.

[276] An Act to Amend the Corrections and Conditional Release Act (Bill C-83), S.C. 2019, c. 27, assented to 21 June 2019.

Damages play a particularly important role in dealing with repetitive rights violations that are not authorized by laws that can be challenged. Damage awards can help focus public attention on rights violations caused by the way that the executive exercises its low visibility discretion. It can start another two-track cycle of recognizing that the rights of specific litigants have been violated while engaging in perhaps stronger remedies to ensure that governments take reasonable steps to prevent future violations. One of the challenges faced with damages is that diffuse domestic courts seem less concerned with repetitive violations than supra-national courts. This is a pressing concern because repetitive violations that only result in continuing modest damage awards will allow governments to pay a small price for continuing to violate rights.

5.6 Conclusion

If courts are only concerned with damages as an individual remedy, they may promote the idea that damages are a kind of tax that governments must pay when human rights violations are occasionally brought to their attention by courts. Such an approach will reveal damages as a disappointing remedy, one that often values rights quite cheaply. If, on the other hand, courts only order damages when they believe they are necessary to deter clear governmental misconduct, as in the United States, damages will also be disappointing because of the judicial reluctance to find governmental misconduct and perhaps exaggerated concerns about over-deterring governmental functions.

A two-track approach attempts to combine the need to award damages to respond to harm suffered by individuals, while also having courts be attentive to the risk of repetitive violations. Under the two-track approach, the core purpose of damages is to compensate for violations of human rights and to vindicate those interests for specific applicants. At the same time, courts can award increased damages if they conclude that the state has failed to take reasonable steps to prevent the repetition of similar violations. This allows the states to employ a wider variety of remedies than what is available to the court, including discipline and training. It also provides the state with an incentive to mitigate damages through apologies and other remedial measures. Concerns that aggravated damages will be an unjust windfall for the applicant seems far-fetched given the modest nature of damage awards.

The award of aggravated damages should be a signal of the court's concern about future compliance more than a means of actual deterrence or punishment. Indeed, in cases where there is clear evidence of repetitive violations that will cause irreparable harm, courts should consider using declarations, injunctions and the retention of jurisdiction, to be discussed in Chapter 7. Unlike in private law, damages are not an end in themselves in human rights law. They should be situated in the context of the state's primary obligation to respect human rights including cessation and non-repetition. Following the IACtHR and the UN Basic Principles, courts, especially domestic courts, should be open to the use of non-monetary forms of satisfaction such as apologies that may be more responsive to the intangible values protected by human rights.

The two-track approach could restore a sense of perspective to the use of damages. It affirms the importance of recognizing and attempting to remedy specific violations suffered by individuals in the past as a core judicial function that should not be subject to legislative curtailment. It also recognizes that damages may not ensure future compliance with human rights or provide satisfaction to those who have suffered serious rights violations. The two-track approach recognizes that additional remedies including aggravated damages may be necessary to ensure that similar rights violations are not repeated in the future.

6

Remedies in the Criminal Process

6.1 Introduction

This chapter will examine remedies for rights violations in the criminal process. They are likely the most litigated and awarded form of remedies. Despite this extensive experience, the remedial approaches taken by many domestic courts are quite some distance from the two-track approach advocated for in this book. Supra-national courts are, however, closer to taking a two-track approach that combines individual and systemic remedies and also includes remedies for crime victims.

Courts are increasingly resistant to using strong and drastic remedies such as exclusion of evidence as a first-track compensatory remedy. The American courts, for example, used to exclude improperly obtained evidence on compensatory grounds.[1] Now, they only exclude evidence as a second-track systemic remedy designed to deter future violations of rights.[2] The courts have frequently downplayed the accused's interest in receiving a remedy in the criminal process. Although instrumental concerns about the deterrence and non-repetition of rights violations are legitimate, they should supplement the accused's primary claim to receive a remedy that will compensate and vindicate a rights violation. The fact that courts require that an accused have individual standing as a person who has suffered a violation and often require a causal connection between a rights violation and evidence sought to be excluded or the accused's subsequent trial underlines the neglected compensatory origins of both exclusion and stays of proceedings.

Although courts should be concerned with non-repetition of human rights, they may over-estimate their ability to control state behaviour in the criminal process. Neither police or prosecutors have direct financial interests in successful prosecutions. Domestic courts have often not been

1 *Weeks* v. *United States*, 232 US 383 (1914) at 393.

2 *Elkins* v. *United States*, 364 US 206 (1960); *Mapp* v. *Ohio*, 367 US 643 (1961).

dialogic enough in criminal cases. They have often failed to engage with the executive and the legislature to achieve systemic reforms. Again supra-national courts have been better at combining individual remedies with systemic general measures that allow the executive and legislature to take steps to prevent the repetition of violations.

The individual and systemic tracks for criminal remedies are not watertight compartments. Just as damages can be increased for systemic reasons, courts should consider whether regulatory concerns relating to the seriousness of the violation and the state's response to it helps justify the use of a stay of proceedings or exclusion of evidence. Cycles of individual and systemic remedies can respond to the inevitable failure of systemic measures to prevent all future violations.

As discussed in Chapter 1, Section 1.9, there is nothing inherently objectionable to balancing the goals of providing individual and systemic remedies against compelling social interests. Courts have, however, been resistant to using structured proportionality analysis. A complicating factor is that domestic criminal courts, unlike the International Criminal Court (ICC), lack the ability to award compensation both to the accused[3] and to crime victims as a less drastic alternative to stays of proceedings or exclusion of evidence.[4]

Courts that fail to address the social costs of remedies will likely be influenced by remedial deterrence, a process that occurs when courts do not recognize or reduce the content of rights in order to avoid drastic remedial consequences.[5] For example, both the United States and Canadian Supreme Courts have held that the drastic remedy of a stay of proceedings is the minimum remedy required for a violation of the right to a trial in a reasonable time.[6] Not surprisingly, they have defined this right in a more minimal fashion so as to avoid wholesale use of stays that permanently end criminal prosecutions. In contrast, the European Court of Human Rights (ECtHR) has used a range of remedies including damages, sentence reductions and general or systemic measures to address similar problems of delay.

[3] UN General Assembly, Rome Statute of the International Criminal Court (last amended 2010), 17 July 1988, 2187 UNTS 2187, Art. 85.

[4] Ibid., Arts. 75, 79.

[5] Daryl J. Levinson, "Rights Essentialism and Remedial Equilibration" (1999) 99 *Colum. L. Rev.* 4; Sonja B. Starr, "Rethinking Effective Remedies: Remedial Deterrence in International Courts" (2008) 83 *N.Y.U. L. Rev.* 693.

[6] *Strunk* v. *United States*, 412 US 434 (1973) at 440; *R.* v. *Rahey*, [1987] 1 SCR 588.

6.1.1 Outline of This Chapter

Section 6.2 will outline existing practices of awarding remedies in the criminal process first in supra-national and then national courts. In order to highlight issues of remedial choice, it will examine the range of remedies used, including novel remedies such as sentence reductions as well as more traditional remedies such as stays, exclusion and sentence reductions. It will also examine the remedies that supra-national adjudicators have ordered to protect the rights of crime victims.

Section 6.3 will examine how courts have tempered remedies available in the criminal process to recognize competing social interests, such as the importance of a trial on the merits and state interests in detaining or punishing the accused. It will be suggested that instead of focusing on judicial integrity or relying on strong forms of discretion, courts should require the state to justify restrictions on remedies. This should be done through proportionality reasoning including whether less drastic remedies strike a better overall balance between remedial goals and social objectives.

Section 6.4 will outline a two-track approach to remedies. Courts should focus on compensation to make sense of individualistic standing and causation requirements. They should encourage second-track systemic remedies by using concerns about the seriousness of a violation and an inadequate response by the state to prevent future violations as a supplementary justification for stays and exclusion. Courts should respect the ability of states to implement a variety of measures including training, investigations, prosecutions and discipline, all of which seek to minimize the risk of similar violations in the future. They should also be attentive to the reality of remedial failure, especially because police and prosecutors may have incentives to violate human rights. Courts should be prepared to embark on another cycle of individual and systemic remedies when the rights of the accused or crime victims are violated in the future, but hopefully in a way that learns from past failures.

6.2 Existing Practice

6.2.1 International Criminal Courts

International criminal courts face severe remedial dilemmas because of the seriousness of the offences they try.[7] That said, however, there is a danger of taking such reasoning too far because it could justify the idea

[7] Starr, "Rethinking Effective Remedies".

that the important ends of countering impunity for the most serious crimes could justify all means that violate human rights. Fortunately, and unlike most domestic courts, international criminal courts have a range of less drastic remedies including damages and sentence reductions that can compensate the accused as well as powers to discipline prosecutors.

6.2.1.1 Stays of Proceedings and Less Drastic Alternatives

Stays of proceedings are always a controversial remedy because they have the drastic effect of ending proceedings and preventing an adjudication on the merits. They have been particularly controversial for international criminal courts.

The International Criminal Tribunal for Rwanda (ICTR) stayed proceedings in 1999 as a remedy for eleven months of illegal pre-trial detention.[8] This decision was reversed in less than a year.[9] The Court found new facts that indicated that the delay was limited to twenty days' detention. It ordered the less drastic remedy of a sentence reduction or the award of compensation in the event that the accused was acquitted. William Schabas has criticized the second decision as a results-oriented "distortion of the law" that bowed to pressure by Rwanda to withdraw support for the criminal court.[10] Sonja Starr, however, has been less critical. With reference to the literature on remedial deterrence, she argues that courts will always "'peek ahead' to the remedial stage"[11] and that "sometimes insisting on the most effective remedy means that victims get no remedy at all".[12]The second decision did not leave the accused with no remedy. After his conviction, his sentence was reduced from life imprisonment to thirty-five years as a remedy for the illegal detention.[13]

The ICC's Appeal Chamber has awarded conditional stays of proceedings in cases where information has not been disclosed to the accused and confirmed that a stay of proceeding could be used to prevent an unfair trial. It reasoned that where a fair trial is impossible, "it would be a contradiction

[8] *Barayagwiza* v. *The Prosecutor,* ICTR-97-19-AR72, Decision, (3 November 1999) (International Criminal Tribunal for Rwanda, Appeals Chamber).

[9] *The Prosecutor* v. *Barayagwiza*, ICTR-9 7-19-AR72, Decision on the Prosecutor's Request for Review or Reconsideration, (31 March 2000) (International Criminal Tribunal for Rwanda, Appeals Chamber).

[10] William A. Schabas, "International Decisions: *Barayagwiza* v. *Prosecutor* (Prosecutor's Request for Review or Reconsideration)" (2000) 94 *Am. J. Int'l. L.* 563, 567.

[11] Starr, "Rethinking Effective Remedies", 738.

[12] Ibid., 766.

[13] *The Prosecutor* v. *Nahimana, Barayagwiza and Ngeze*, ICTR-99-52-T, Judgement and Sentence, (3 December 2003) (International Criminal Tribunal for Rwanda) at paras 1106–1107.

in terms to put the person on trial ... A fair trial is the only means to do justice".[14] The stay was subsequently lifted by the Trial Chamber after disclosure arrangements were made with other states. A second stay in the case was overturned by the Appeal Chamber on the basis that Trial Chamber had erred by using the stay as the first resort remedy.[15] It stressed less drastic remedies such as sentence reductions, adverse inferences and compensation for the accused. With respect to prosecutorial misconduct, the ICC can reprimand, temporally bar prosecutors from the courtroom, fine them up to a half year's salary and can dismiss them. It can also ask for investigations by an independent oversight mechanism. Consistent with second track concerns, the ICC has called on the prosecutor to take measures to prevent future violations by prosecutors and the response was a code of conduct for prosecutors.[16] These are all a much broader range of systemic or deterrent-based remedies than employed by national courts with respect to either prosecutors or the police. Continued controversy about the ICC should not obscure its remedial range and creativity.

6.2.1.2 Exclusion of Improperly Obtained Evidence

Article 69(7) of the Rome Statute[17] provides:

> Evidence obtained by means of a violation of this Statute or internationally recognized human rights shall not be admissible if:
>
> a. The violation casts substantial doubt on the reliability of the evidence or
> b. The admission of the evidence would be antithetical to and would seriously damage the integrity of the proceedings.

[14] *The Prosecutor* v. *Thomas Lubanga Dyilo*, ICC-01/04-01/06, Judgment on the Appeal of the Prosecutor against the Decision of Trial Chamber, (21 October 2008), (International Criminal Court Appeals Chamber) at para 77.

[15] *Prosecutor* v. *Lubanga*, ICC-01/04-01/06 OA 18, Judgment on the Appeal of the Prosecutor against the Decision of Trial Chamber I, (8 July 2010) (International Criminal Tribunal for Rwanda, Appeals Chamber).

[16] *Prosecutor* v. *Kenyatta*, ICC-01/09-02/11, Decision on Defence Application Pursuant to Article 64(4) and Related Requests, (26 April 2013) (International Criminal Court Trial Chamber) at 89–90, 97. See generally Jenia Iontcheva Turner, "Policing International Prosecutors" (2012) 45 *N.Y.U. J. Int'l. L. & Pol'y.* 1; Jenia Iontcheva Turner, "The Accountability of International Prosecutors" in Carsten Stahn (ed.), *The Law and Practice of the International Criminal Court* (Oxford: Oxford University Press, 2015), Chapter 17.

[17] UN General Assembly, Rome Statute of the International Criminal Court (last amended 2010), 17 July 1988, 2187 UNTS 2187, Art. 69(7).

The Trial Chamber has indicated that evidence obtained through rights violations would be excluded if it was unreliable under Article 67(a), regardless of the seriousness of the violation.[18] Under article 67)(b), which directs the court to the "vague"[19]concept of judicial integrity, the court would generally balance the seriousness of the violation against other factors. The Trial Chamber has suggested that this should not include the seriousness of the offence[20] or the importance of the evidence sought to be excluded.[21] As will be seen both of these factors are considered by domestic courts that use balancing tests. It will be suggested in Section 6.3.3 that the seriousness of the offence should not be considered because to do so is at odds with the presumption of innocence but that the importance of the evidence can be a legitimate consideration. At the same time, the Trial Chamber will not exclude all evidence obtained in violation of rights. It admitted reliable documents seized by Congolese authorities (albeit in the presence of an ICC prosecutor) in this case. The violation was "not particularly grave" and its impact on the proceedings was lessened by the fact that the privacy rights of third parties (as opposed to the accused) were violated.[22] The ICC will not exclude evidence simply to deter future violations, but as suggested above can use other instruments to respond to prosecutorial misconduct.

The Trial Chamber rejected the personal standing requirements imposed by many domestic courts by holding that "evidence does not become admissible simply because the violation did not involve the human rights of the accused".[23] Some commentators have suggested that the reference in Article 69(7) to evidence being obtained "by means" of a rights violation demands a causal connection between the violation and the evidence sought to be excluded.[24] However, the broad integrity-based rationale for exclusion might justify excluding evidence where there is a only a temporal connection between a violation and the obtaining of the evidence. In other words, relaxed standing and causation requirements

[18] *The Prosecutor* v. *Thomas Lubanga Dyilo*, ICC-01/04-0l/06, Decision on Admission of Material from the Bar Table, (24 June 2009) (International Criminal Court Trial Chamber Decision) at para 35.

[19] Petra Viebig, *Illicitly Obtained Evidence in the International Criminal Court* (Berlin: Springer, 2016), p.3.

[20] *The Prosecutor* v. *Thomas Lubanga Dyilo*, ICC-01/04-0l/06, at para 44.

[21] Ibid. at para 43.

[22] Ibid. at para 47.

[23] Ibid. at para 37.

[24] Viebig, Illicitly Obtained Evidence, p.192.

seem particularly appropriate when the focus is on systemic concerns. That said, individual standing and causation requirements are essential to justify exclusion as an individual remedy designed to place the accused in the position they would have occupied had their rights not been violated.

In its second decision on the exclusion of evidence, the ICC excluded a self-incriminatory but reliable and non-coerced statement taken when an accused was first interviewed by prosecutors without a lawyer present.[25] The Court focused more on protecting the accused's rights than competing social interests. It even suggested that the value of the evidence to the prosecution was not an important factor to its decisions.

This decision is another indication of how the text of remedial provisions generally provide weak guidance to the exercise of remedial discretion. The court was free to define the reference to the integrity of its proceedings as depending on protecting the accused's rights. Simply asserting under the Rome Statute that exclusion was or was not required to protect the integrity of the proceedings does not justify the exercise of remedial discretion. As suggested in Chapter 1, Section 1.6, textual approaches to the exercise of remedial discretion are not particularly helpful. They can mask the real reason why judges exercise their discretion the way they do.

6.2.1.3 Sentence Reductions and Damages as Less Drastic Alternatives

Sentence reductions used by international criminal courts have generally ranged from six months to five years. This is quite short relative to the length of the overall sentence – often, life imprisonment. Some have argued that such reductions cannot be a meaningful remedy.[26] Others, however, argue that any sentence reduction could minimize the severity of international crimes.[27] The truth is likely somewhere between these two extremes. Even a short reduction may give the offender hope of

[25] *The Prosecutor* v. *Katanga and Ngudjolo*, ICC-01/04/01/07, Decision on the Prosecutor's Bar Table Motions, (17 December 2010) (International Criminal Court Trial Chamber II) at para 63 concluding that "there are serious concerns that those statements were obtained from him in violation of his right to remain silent and of the privilege against self-incrimination".

[26] Daniel Naymark, "Violations of Rights of the Accused at International Criminal Tribunals: The Problem of Remedy" (2008) 4 *J. Int'l. L. & Int'l. Rltns.* 2, 5.

[27] Yahli Shereshevsky, "Monetary Compensation as a Remedy for Fair Trial Violations under International Criminal Law" (2015) *18 New Crim. L. Rev.* 71.

release. The court, by articulating what the sentence would have been in the absence of rights violations, can still denounce and deter the crime committed.[28] It will be suggested in the second part of this chapter that prosecutors should be able to propose and justify sentence reductions as less drastic and more proportionate remedies.

Both Articles 71 and 75 of the Rome Statute empower the ICC to award compensation for some rights violations, such as unlawful detention or miscarriages of justice. The award of damages have, however, been quite modest ranging from US$2,000 to US$5,000.[29] As discussed in the last chapter, nominal remedies risk trivializing rights and courts seem to consistently under-value the non-pecuniary harms of violations of human rights. At the same time, even an inadequate remedy serves as a marker of the violation.

6.2.2 *The European Court of Human Rights*

The ECtHR defines most questions about the admissibility of evidence as matters for the domestic courts to determine. In one case, the majority stated: "[t]he Court therefore cannot exclude as a matter of principle ... It has only to ascertain whether the trial as a whole was fair".[30] Four judges, however, dissented on the basis that a trial cannot be fair if it uses evidence obtained by unlawful means. In 2008, the Court suggested that evidence taken in custodial interrogation without access to a lawyer should be excluded. It has, however, subsequently retreated from this automatic approach.[31] This retreat means, as Professor Hodgson has

[28] Sonja B. Starr, "Sentence Reduction as a Remedy for Prosecutorial Misconduct" (2009) 97 *Geo. L. J.* 6.

[29] *Rwamakuba* v. *The Prosecutor*, ICTR-98-44C-A, Decision on Appeal against Decision on Appropriate Remedy, (12 September 2007) (International Criminal Tribunal for Rwanda), online: www.unictr.org/Portals/0/Case/English/Rwamakuba/decisions/070913.pdf; see also the dissenting judgement of Judge Robison awarding $5,000 in damages for excessive delay and detention in another ICTR decision: *Mugenzi* v. *The Prosecutor*, ICTR-99-50-A, Appeals Judgment, (4 February 2013), (Appeals Chamber), online: www.unictr.org/Portals/0/Case/ English/Mugenzi/Judgment/130204-Appeal%20Judgment.pdf.

[30] *Schenck* v. *Switzerland* (1988), No. 10862/84, [1988] ECHR 17 at para 46. The EU still takes this approach even to enforcing the right to counsel. Art 3 Para 2 Directive 2013/48/EU.

[31] *Salduz* v. *Turkey* (2008) EHRR 421 at para 72; *Ibrahim and others* v. *the United Kingdom* nos 50541/08, 50571/08 and 40351/08 13 September 2016 at para 294. Both of these cases, however, focus on whether fair trials rights have been violated. They pay scant attention to whether exclusion of evidence is a necessary remedy and indeed award damages rather

argued, "there is the appearance of due process, but the substance is often lacking".[32]

Even with respect to evidence obtained by torture or mistreatment, the ECtHR has been reluctant to exclude evidence.[33] A majority of the Court allowed evidence of the discovery of the body to be admitted that was obtained in the infamous *Gäfgen* case as a result of police violence against the accused. The Court seemed to suggest that exclusion was not necessary to protect the fairness of the trial because the case against the accused was already strong and the accused made a second confession at the end of his trial. It also noted the availability of alternative remedies including investigations and prosecutions of state officials who engaged in misconduct.[34] There were strong dissents in the *Gäfgen* case emphasizing the absolute nature of the prohibition on the use of evidence obtained by torture. This case demonstrates the danger of ignoring the two-track distinction between what remedy is necessary to compensate the accused for a rights violation and what systemic remedy is necessary to prevent similar violations in the future. Evidence obtained by torture should always be excluded even if exclusion is not necessary to prevent a repetition of such an extreme violation of human rights.

6.2.2.1 Sentence Reductions and Damages as Less Drastic Alternatives

The ECtHR has used both sentence reductions and damages as a remedy for delayed trials.[35] It held that an eight-day sentence reduction for sixteen days of detention in an improper police facility was adequate and rejected the applicant's claim for damages.[36] As discussed in Chapter 5, Section 5.2.2, the ECtHR's calculation of damages is equitable

than exclusion of evidence. For critiques of the ECtHR retreat from an individual rights protection approach see Dimitrios Giannoulopoulos *Improperly Obtained Evidence in Anglo-American and Continental Law* (Oxford: Hart Publishing, 2019), Chapters 5 and 6.

[32] Jacqueline S. Hodgson *The Metamorphosis of Criminal Justice* (Oxford: Oxford University Press, 2020) at 244.

[33] John D. Jackson and Sarah Summers, *The Internationalisation of Criminal Evidence* (Cambridge: Cambridge University Press, 2012), pp.151–198.

[34] *Gäfgen* v. *Germany* [GC], No. 22978/05, ECHR 3 June 2010 Rectifying Judgement of 1 June 2010 at para 119.

[35] *Eckle* v. *Germany* (1982), No. 8130/78, [1982] ECHR 4, 15 July 1982; *Salah* v. *Netherlands*, No. 8196/02, 44 EHRR 55, ECHR 6 July 2006 at paras 30–40, 74; *Beck* v. *Norway*, No. 26390/95, ECHR 26 June 2001 at paras 1, 14; *Yetkinsekerci* v. *United Kingdom*, No. 71841/01, 43 EHRR 4, ECHR 20 October 2005 at para 8.

[36] *Porchet* v. *Switzerland*, No. 36391/16, ECHR 7 November 2019.

but often not transparent. To its credit, however, the Court has taken a more rigorous approach for sentence reductions. It has warned that they require "an individualised assessment of the impact of the violation on the Convention rights and of the specific redress that should be afforded to the aggrieved individual". It has suggested that an "automatic" or "standard reduction ... is unlikely to be compatible with individualised assessment" and could "adversely affect the public interest in criminal punishment".[37] In short, sentence reductions must be justified as an individual remedy that is not inconsistent with legitimate public interests in punishment.

The main remedy that the Court uses in criminal cases remains damages. A finding of a violation of torture or degrading treatment "creates a strong legal presumption that such conditions have occasioned non-pecuniary damage to the aggrieved individual".[38] Damages may be justified as the result of the cumulative effect of conditions and do not have to be related to the conduct of individual officials. The Court also precluded certain justifications for not providing an effective remedy by noting "that neither a high crime rate, nor a lack of resources, nor other structural problems may be regarded as circumstances excluding or attenuating the domestic authorities' liability for non-pecuniary damage incurred through inhuman or degrading conditions of detention".[39] As will be discussed in greater detail in Chapter 7, Section 7.2.2, the ECtHR has shown a commitment to individual measures including damages in prison cases.

The Court awards pecuniary and non-pecuniary damages for arrests in violation of Convention rights. However, damage must be shown and there is no entitlement to any specific amount of damages. The Court will also defer to damages awarded in domestic systems unless they are manifestly unfit. The Grand Chamber awarded €2,000 in non-pecuniary damages as well as a re-trial and costs in a landmark right to counsel case.[40] In a later case also involving denial of the right to counsel, the Grand Chamber found that the judgement itself constituted just satisfaction.[41] As discussed in Chapter 5, Section 5.2.2, the ECtHR's approach to damages remains inconsistent and unsatisfactory.

[37] *Ananyev and Others* v. *Russia*, Nos. 42525/07 and 60800/08, First Section Judgment, ECHR 10 January 2012 at paras 224–225.

[38] Ibid. at para 229.

[39] Ibid. at para 225.

[40] *Salduz* v. *Turkey* [GC], No. 36391/02, [2008] V ECHR 59.

[41] *Dvorski* v. *Croatia* [GC], No. 25703/11, [2015] VI ECHR 405.

6.2.3 *Complex Systemic Remedies for Delay*

The approach to systemic trial delays in the Council of Europe system is quite sophisticated. In many member states, issues of excessive delay in legal proceedings have been subject to continued supervision by the Committee of Ministers under Article 46 of the European Convention. The result has respected both subsidiarity towards the states and the separation of powers, with states enacting a wide range of reforms. Some have moved towards selective decriminalization and bail reform, some have changed the structure of courts and prosecutorial systems and some have introduced a variety of domestic remedies for excessive delay. Some have engaged in all of these types of reforms.

The German reforms for delays are instructive. The ECtHR found that delay violated the rights of the accused to a fair trial as well as to an effective remedy.[42] The Court awarded relatively small amounts of damages as individual measures for an accused who brought their case to court before eventually moving to a pilot judgement proceeding.[43] More prosecutors, judges and court staff were hired and domestic legislation was drafted providing for both acceleratory remedies to prevent future violations and compensatory remedies for past violations.[44] The operation of these remedies was subject to de facto supervision by the Court, which generally held that the accused must seek remedies under German law or they would not have exhausted their domestic remedies as required under the European Convention. As discussed in Chapter 1, Section 1.8, the concerns of supra-national courts in respecting their subsidiarity role to domestic states often go hand in hand with respect for the separation of powers. This allows both the executive and the legislature to use their powers and expertise. Supra-national courts also have special incentives to encourage states to prevent repetitive violations that are often absent in domestic systems. Supra-national courts are frequently under-resourced and have their own interests in curbing repetitive violations that can produce a flood of similar cases.

[42] *Ommer* v. *Germany* (Nos. 1 and 2), Nos. 10597/03 and 26073/03, [2008] ECHR 1439.

[43] *Rumpf* v. *Germany*, No. 46344/06, ECHR 2 September 2010.

[44] European Court of Human Rights, "Execution of the Judgments of the European Court of Human Rights", Res, CM/ResDH(2013) 244, 71 cases against Germany, adopted by the Committee of Ministers, 5 December 2013, online: https://hudoc.echr.coe.int/eng#{"itemid":["001-140656"]}

6.2.4 *Release and Habeas Corpus*

The right to habeas corpus is protected under Article 5(4) of the European Convention. The Grand Chamber has affirmed the importance of release as a form of restitution. For example, it stressed that Azerbaijan must release Ilgar Mammadov who had been improperly prosecuted for political reasons.[45] The state refused to comply and the decision remains under enhanced supervision by the Committee of Ministers. The Committee of Ministers has focused on individual measures in this case.

The IACtHR has also confirmed the importance of habeas corpus as a remedy requiring the state to produce a prisoner to a judge to review the legality of detention. The right to the remedy can be breached by informal constraints on it, such as intimidation of lawyers or judges,[46] or the likely refusal of the state to release the prisoner upon a court order.[47] As under the common law, third parties can also initiate habeas corpus proceedings. One leading text has observed that the Court "frequently hears cases involving due process violations. Procedural abuses have resulted in Court orders to reverse criminal convictions, grant retrials, cancel death sentences, expunge criminal records, and waive fines. On only rare occasions have due process violations led the Court to demand the release of detainees".[48]

In a series of cases, the African Court of Human and Peoples' Rights have stopped short of clearly indicating that the accused should be released. They have done this even in cases where the accused had served a substantial part of their sentence and there were strong dissents that release would be an appropriate remedy.[49] This may demonstrate the incentive that international courts, especially new ones, may have to pull their remedial punches in order not to antagonize states.

[45] *Mammadov* v. *Azerbaijan* [GC], No. 15172/13, Proceedings under Art.46§4, ECHR 29 May 2019.

[46] *Velásquez Rodríguez* v. *Honduras* (1988), Merits, Judgment, Inter-Am. Ct. H.R (Ser. C), (29 July 1988).

[47] *Fairén Garbi and Solís Corrales* v. *Honduras* (1989), Merits, Judgment, Inter-Am. Ct. H.R (Ser. C), (15 March 1989).

[48] Thomas M. Antkowiak and Alejandra Gonza, *The American Convention on Human Rights: Essential Rights* (Oxford: Oxford University Press, 2017), pp.302–303.

[49] *Abubakari* v. *United Republic of Tanzania* (2016), No. 007/2013, African Court on Human and Peoples' Rights, 1 AfCLR 599; *Thomas* v. *United Republic of Tanzania* (2015), No. 005/2013, African Court on Human and Peoples' Rights, 1 AfCLR 465; but see *Onyachi* v. *United Republic of Tanzania* (2017), No. 003/2015, African Court on Human and Peoples' Rights, 1 AfCLR 599 for an indication of release.

6.2.5 Remedies for Crime Victims

The willingness of supra-national courts to order remedies for crime victims is not without controversy. Michael Mandel was one of the first to question how international law had become enthusiastic about the use of the criminal sanction.[50] Given the focus of this work on remedies, I will not join this debate directly. Nevertheless, both the ICC and regional human rights courts have broken new ground not ploughed by domestic courts in providing remedies for victims.

6.2.5.1 International Criminal Court

Anne Dutton and Fionnuala Ni Aolain have suggested that the ICC is path breaking in recognizing that the long entrenched right to a remedy in international law should be extended to crime victims.[51] The Appeal Chamber of the ICC has held under Article 75(2) of the Rome Statute that there must be a link between the crime of which an accused has been convicted and the harm suffered by the victim.[52] This must be proved on a balance of probabilities. The Court has explained that "reparations fulfil two main purposes (. . .): they oblige those responsible for serious crimes to repair the harm they caused to the victims and they enable the Chamber to ensure that offenders account for their acts".[53] Although

[50] Michael Mandel, *How America Gets Away with Murder* (London: Pluto Press, 2004); see also Kathryn Sikkink, *The Justice Cascade: How Human Rights Prosecutions Are Changing World Politics* (New York: W.W. Norton and Company, 2011); Alexandra Huneeus, "International Criminal Law by Other Means" (2013) 107 *Am. J. Int'l. L.* 1; Frédéric Mégret and Jean-Paul Calderon, "The Move towards a Victim-Centred Concept of Criminal Law and the 'Criminalization' of Inter-American Human Rights Law: A Case of Human Rights Law Devouring Itself?" in Yves Haeck, Oswaldo Ruiz-Chiriboga, Clara Burbano-Herrera (eds.), *The Inter-American Court of Human Rights: Theory and Practice, Present and Future* (Cambridge: Intersentia, 2015), p.419; see also Karen Engle, "Anti-Impunity and the Turn to Criminal Law in Human Rights" (2015) 100 *Cornell L. Rev.* 1069.

[51] Anne Dutton and Fionnuala Ni Aolain, "Between Reparations and Repair: Assessing the Work of the ICC Trust Fund for Victims" (2019) 19 *Chi. J. Int'l. L.* 490; see also Frédéric Mégret, "Justifying Compensation by the International Criminal Court's Victims Trust Fund: Lessons from Domestic Compensation Schemes" (2010) 36 *Brook. J. Int'l. L.* 123.

[52] *The Prosecutor* v. *Thomas Lubanga Dyilo*, ICC-01/04-01/06, Judgment with Amended Order for Reparations, (3 March 2015) (International Criminal Court, Appeals Chamber) at para 32. The accused was ordered to pay $10 million for victims; for criticisms that the lack of prosecution of gender related violence excluded such victims of damages see Louise Chappell, "The Gender Injustice Cascade" (2017) 21(9) *Int'l. J. Hum. Rts.* 1223.

[53] Ibid. at para 99.

damages may be a serious punishment for an accused who has resources, they will remain quite modest when applied to each victim of a human rights violation.

The ICC's Trust Fund constituted under Article 79 takes a broader approach to damages than the Court. It places less emphasis on the need for a causal connection between an international crime and the damage to victims to be remedied. It has provided rehabilitation assistance to over 200,000 people in the Congo. Fredric Mégret has described this relief as "a veritable hodgepodge of activities: community support, micro-credit, vocational training, counseling, social events, workshops, medical and orthopedic support, reconstructive surgery, reintegration, peace and reconciliation, shelters," etc.[54]

6.2.5.2 Inter-American Court of Human Rights

The IACtHR also ordered damages for victims of massacres, but also a wide range of forms of rehabilitation, commemoration and acknowledgment of wrongdoing. As with damages, international courts are much more creative with their remedies than domestic courts. The IACtHR has also taken a lead with respect to gender violence.

In *Gonzalez et al.* v. *Mexico*,[55] also known as the Cotton Field case, the IACtHR ordered a large number of remedies relating to the state's responsibility with respect to investigations and reparations in relation to three women (including two minors) found dead in a Mexican cotton field in 2001. In addition to US$800,000 in pecuniary and non-pecuniary damages for the families of the three women killed,[56] the Court ordered various reforms to criminal investigations designed to combat violence against women. They included the provision of information on the internet about the missing, full disclosure of the investigation to the victims' families, training for criminal justice officials, a memorial for the victims and treatment for surviving victims. The IACtHR was also

[54] Mégret, "Justifying Compensation", 141. See also Luke Moffatt, "Reparative Complementarity" (2013) 17(3) *Int'l. J. Hum. Rts.* 368.

[55] (2009), Inter-Am. Ct. H.R. (Ser. C), (16 November 2009).

[56] For an account of how the IACtHR is more generous than the ECtHR in awarding damages to family members of victims but also the limits of court ordered remedies compared to reparation programs, see Ruth Rubio-Marin, Clara Sandoval and Catalina Diaz, "Repairing Family Members: Gross Human Rights Violations and Communities of Harm" in Ruth Rubio-Marin (ed.) *The Gender of Reparations* (Cambridge: Cambridge University Press, 2009).

influenced by ECtHR caselaw stressing the importance of preventing discrimination in the state's response to crime.[57] Ruth Rubio-Marin and Clara Sandoval have praised the "holistic gender approach to reparation"[58] taken by the Court.

The Court recognized the limits of the traditional goal of restoring the situation to that which would have existed without the violation. It explained that given "the context of structural discrimination . . . the reparations must be designed to change this situation . . . re-establishment of the same structural context of violence and discrimination is not acceptable".[59] At the same time, there have been issues in implementing these structural remedies. None of the families of the three women who were killed attended the 2011 commemoration of a memorial.[60] This itself can be seen as a form of remedial failure, which allowed many to protest the inadequacy of Mexico's response to violence against women.

In a detailed thirty-six-page report in 2013,[61] the IACtHR found compliance with much of the Cotton Field judgement, including updating investigative protocols, creation of a website of the disappeared and payment of damages. The Court continued supervising the execution of the decision including the ongoing investigations that had not yet resulted in any arrests.[62] Although some important reforms had been made, no judicial remedy can guarantee arrests let alone convictions.[63] Remedies to benefit crime victims can require an ambitious structural approach similar to the institutional reform cases that will be examined in Chapter 7, Section 7.2.

[57] Ibid. at para 298 citing *Angelova and Iliev* v. *Bulgaria*, No. 55523/00, ECHR 26 July 2007 at paras 293–294.

[58] "Engendering the Reparations Jurisprudence of the Inter-American Court of Human Rights: The Promise of the 'Cotton Field' Judgment" (2011) 33 *Hum. Rts. Q.* 1062, 1064. See also Rubio-Marin, *The Gender of Reparations*, recognizing how a feminist approach could expand understandings of reparations especially with respect to non-repetition.

[59] *Gonzalez et al.* v. *Mexico* (2009), Inter-Am. Ct. H.R. (Ser. C), (21 May 2013) at para 150, online: https://iachr.lls.edu/sites/default/files/iachr/Court_and_Commission_Documents/Gonz%2B%C3%ADlez%20et%20al.%20v.%20Mexico.MonitoringCompliance.05.21.13.pdf

[60] Caroline Bettinger-Lopez, "The Challenge of Domestic Implementation of International Human Rights Law in the Cotton Field Case" (2012) 15(2) *N.Y. City L. Rev.* 315, 329.

[61] *Gonzalez et al.* v. *Mexico* (2009), Inter-Am. Ct. H.R. (Ser. C), (21 May 2013).

[62] Monica Rodriguez, "Case Comment on *González et al. (Cotton Field)* v. *Mexico*" (2014) 36 *Loy. L.A. Int'l. & Comp. L. Rev.* 1971, 2007–2008.

[63] Mégret and Calderon, "The Move towards a Victim-Centred Concept of Criminal Law", p.439.

6.2.6 *Investigations and Prosecutions as Remedies*

The UN Human Rights Committee has called for investigations and prosecutions. In one case, it stated: "[t]he State party is under an obligation to take effective measures to ensure that . . . criminal proceedings are initiated seeking the prompt prosecution and conviction of the persons responsible for the author's arrest and ill-treatment" in part because the "the State party is under an obligation to ensure that similar violations do not occur in the future".[64] Such an approach ignores the presumption of innocence. The IACtHR has also ordered states to investigate, prosecute and punish those responsible for crimes.[65] This has also raised compliance issues given that prosecutors and courts are independent actors.[66]

A better approach is to focus on the need for impartial and effective investigations to guard against forms of impunity that can result in state responsibility for the violation of the human rights of crime victims. The ECtHR has articulated a variety of requirements that there be effective investigations and adequate criminal offences. The implementation powers of the Committee of Ministers as a political body could be an asset in securing remedies for crime victims. For example, it supervised a case involving human trafficking between Russia and Cyprus. It noted that €42,000 in just satisfaction had been paid to the applicant as specific measures. With respect to general measures to prevent re-occurrence, an adequate investigation had been conducted and new offences created.[67]

6.2.7 *The United States*

6.2.7.1 Exclusion of Evidence

The most famous remedy awarded in the criminal process is the exclusion of improperly obtained evidence. Although this remedy has long existed in the common law with respect to involuntary confessions,

[64] *Njaru* v. *Cameroon* (2007), Report of the UNHRC, UN GOAR, Comm. No. 1353/2005 UN Doc CCPR C/89/D/1353/2005 (2007).

[65] See for example *Vereda La Esperanza* v. *Colombia* (2013), Preliminary Objections, Merits, Reparations, and Costs, Inter-Am. Ct. H.R (Ser. C), 42 *Loy. L.A. Int'l. & Comp. L. Rev.* 1356 at para 42.

[66] Alexandra Huneeus, "Courts Resisting Courts: Lessons from the Inter-American Court's Struggle to Enforce Human Rights" (2011) 44 *Cornell Int'l. L. J.* 3.

[67] European Court of Human Rights, "Execution of the Judgment of the European Court of Human Rights Rantsev against Cyprus and Russian Federation", Final Res. CM/ResDH (2017)95, online: https://hudoc.echr.coe.int/eng#{"itemid":["001-172518"]}

the idea that "the criminal is to go free because the constable has blundered"[68] remains controversial. Unlike the international courts examined above, criminal courts in common law systems generally do not have jurisdiction to award damages or injunctions and they have at times been reluctant to use sentence reductions as a remedy.

The exclusionary remedy was first applied to violations of search and seizure rights by federal officials in the early twentieth century. Justice Day reasoned that the exclusion of incriminating letters obtained from a warrantless search of a person's home was required if the right against unreasonable search and seizure was to have any meaning.[69] This reasoning followed from the traditional emphasis placed on a right to a remedy celebrated by Blackstone and Dicey and recognized but not honoured in *Marbury* v. *Madison.*[70] The fact that the police could have obtained the incriminating letters with a warrant did not mitigate the fact that the letters were obtained as a direct result of a warrantless search. In the early twentieth century, the United States Supreme Court was prepared to exclude unconstitutionally obtained evidence regardless of the seriousness of the violation by federal officials.[71]

After experimenting with vague judicial integrity tests, the Court extended the Fourth Amendment exclusionary rule to the states. In part to limit the retroactivity of the new rule, the Court now stressed that exclusion's "prime purpose" was as "the only effective deterrent to lawless police action".[72] The deterrence rationale was used to justify many limits on the exclusionary rule. There are a range of good faith exceptions when the police rely on a warrant, statute, precedent or even internal police

[68] *People* v. *Defore*, 150 N.E. 585 (1926) at 587 per Cardozo J.

[69] *Weeks* v. *United States*, 232 US 383 (1914) at 393: "If letters and private documents can thus be seized and held and used in evidence against a citizen accused of an offense, the protection of the Fourth Amendment, declaring his right to be secure against such searches and seizures, is of no value, and, so far as those thus placed are concerned, might as well be stricken from the Constitution".

[70] The Court did subsequently extend the exclusionary rule to illegal drugs seized in violation of the right against unreasonable search and seizure: *Agnello* v. *U.S.*, 269 US 20 (1925).

[71] In *Gouled* v. *U.S.*, 255 US 298 (1921) at 304 the Court emphasized that rights were harmed was much by "stealthy encroachment or "gradual deprecation . . . by imperceptible practice of courts or by well-intentioned but mistakenly over-zealous executive officers".

[72] *Linkletter* v. *Walker*, 381 US 618 (1965) at 635; see also *United States* v. *Calandra*, 414 US 338 (1974) at 348.

information.[73] In *Herring* v. *United States*, the Court refused to apply the rule to what is characterized as an isolated act of police negligence. Chief Justice Roberts stressed that "the exclusionary rule is not an individual right". It only applies when "the benefits of deterrence . . . outweigh the costs . . . To trigger the exclusionary rule, police conduct must be sufficiently deliberate that exclusion can meaningfully deter it, and sufficiently culpable that such deterrence is worth the price paid by the justice system".[74] The *Herring* case came close to subjecting the 4th Amendment exclusionary rule to a cost-benefits analysis.

The *Miranda* exclusionary rule also evolved from a right connected to the 5th Amendment to a deterrent rule subject to public safety exceptions[75] and cost benefit calculations.[76] Justice Scalia argued with some justification that the deterrence provided by police discipline, training and complaints were "incomparably greater" than exclusion of evidence.[77]

Although the American exclusionary rule is not dead, there are increasing concerns that the court will not exclude evidence in the absence of some form of fault on the part of the police.[78] The fault requirements for the exclusionary rule are similar to those required by qualified immunities on damage awards as discussed in the last chapter.[79] Until the late 1980s, the rights protection rationale was defended by judges such as Justices Brennan and Marshall and academic commentators.[80] Today, the rights protection rationale seems lost and abandoned. This may be related to larger patterns of cynicism about rule of law expectations that those whose rights have been violated should receive a remedy from the courts.[81]

[73] *United States* v. *Leon*, 468 US 897 (1984); *Illinois Petitioner* v. *Albert Krull et. al*, 107 S.Ct. 1160 (1987); *Arizona* v. *Evans*, 514 US 1 (1995).

[74] *Herring* v. *United States*, 129 S.Ct. 695 (2009) at 141.

[75] *New York* v. *Quarles*, 467 US 649 (1984).

[76] *Dickerson* v. *United* States, 530 US 428 (2000).

[77] *Hudson* v. *Michigan*, 547 US 586 (2006) at 599.

[78] Craig M. Bradley, "Is the Exclusionary Remedy Dead?" (2012) 102 *J. Crim. L. & Criminology* 1.

[79] Jennifer Laurin, "Trawling for Herring: Lessons in Doctrinal Borrowing" (2011) 111 *Colum. L. Rev.* 670.

[80] *United States*. v. *Leon*, 468 US 897 (1984); Yale Kamisar, "Does (Did) (Should) the Exclusionary Rule Rest on a 'Principled Basis' Rather than an 'Empirical Proposition'" (1983) 16 *Creighton L. Rev.* 565.

[81] Influenced by legal realism, some American commentators dismiss as naïve the idea that all rights violations should receive a remedy suggesting that this would lead to a contraction of rights, see Daryl J. Levinson, "Rights Essentialism and Remedial

The American Court has also continued to limit the application of the exclusionary rule in ways that do not fit with the rule's new deterrence rationale. It will not apply the rule if evidence could have been obtained properly from an independent source,[82] would have been inevitably discovered[83] or if there was an attenuated causal connection between the violation and the obtaining of the evidence.[84] Causation analysis is used to limit the social costs of exclusion. The American courts fail to recognize that police misconduct in violating a suspect's rights may actually be worse if the police could have obtained the evidence without violating the accused's rights.[85] Similarly, the requirement of individual standing has been maintained,[86] even though it can require courts to ignore evidence obtained through serious violations.[87] Causation and standing requirements make sense if exclusion is used as first-track compensatory remedy. Today, they sit uneasily with the second-track systemic deterrence rationale that the Court now uses as the exclusive justification for the exclusionary remedy.

6.2.7.2 Stays of Proceedings or Dismissal with Prejudice

The United States Supreme Court has held that dismissal of a case is "the only possible remedy"[88] for the violation of a right to a speedy trial. This decision has long been criticized as ignoring the ability of the court to award more tailored and responsive remedies including release from pre-trial custody, dismissal without prejudice to a new prosecution and exclusion of evidence that the accused cannot fairly contest because of the delay.[89]

Equilibration" (1999) 99 *Colum. L. Rev.* 4; John C. Jeffries Jr., "*The Right-Remedy Gap in Constitutional Law*" (1999) 109 *Yale L. J.* 87.

82 *Murray* v. *United States*, 487 US 533 (1988).

83 *Nix* v. *Williams*, 467 US 431 (1984).

84 *Utah* v. *Strieff*, 136 S.Ct. 2056 (2016).

85 This is recognized by the Supreme Court in Canada in the course of determining the seriousness of the violation. For example, "where a police officer could have acted constitutionally but did not, this might indicate that the officer adopted a casual attitude toward or, still worse, deliberately flouted the accused's rights". *R.* v. *Cole*, 2012 SCC 53 at para 89.

86 *Rakas* v. *Illinois*, 439 US 128 (1978). On these exceptions to the various American exclusionary rules, see James J. Tomkovicz, *Constitutional Exclusion: The Rules, Rights, and Remedies That Strike the Balance between Freedom and Order* (New York: Oxford University Press, 2011).

87 Donald L. Doernberg, "'The Right of the People': Reconciling Collective and Individual Interests under the Fourth Amendment" (1983) 58 *N.Y.U. L. Rev.* 240.

88 *Strunk* v. *United States*, 412 US 434 (1973) at 440.

89 Anthony Amsterdam, "Speedy Criminal Trial: Rights and Remedies" (1975) 27 *Stan. L. Rev.* 3.

In *Alvarez-Machain*[90] the Court held that a stay of proceedings was not appropriate in a case where the accused had been kidnapped from Mexico to stand trial in the United States. The majority reasoned that such conduct was not specifically prohibited by the relevant extradition treaty. In similar situations, courts in most other common law countries[91] including the United Kingdom,[92] Canada[93] and New Zealand[94] have ordered a stay to condemn and dissociate themselves from such abusive conduct. In a subsequent lawsuit brought by the person who was kidnapped, the Supreme Court held that damages could not be granted because the kidnapping took place outside of the United States and did not fall within eighteenth-century exceptions for extra-territorial claims such as piracy.[95] Again, the unwillingness of American courts to use either stays or damages after the fact contributes to American remedial exceptionalism and extra-legalism noted at various junctures in this book.

6.2.7.3 Sentence Reductions

The use of sentence reductions as a remedy "are essentially unknown in U.S. courts".[96] They have, however, been defended as an intermediate remedy that can serve the purposes of both compensation and deterrence. For example, Judge Guido Calabresi argues the exclusionary rule leads to remedial deterrence and that the use of the less drastic remedy of sentence reductions could lead to judges recognizing and enforcing more rights.[97]

Sentence reductions have been rejected as a remedy for violation of the right to speedy trial,[98] even though they have emerged as an important

[90] *United States* v. *Alvarez-Machain*, 504 US 655 (1992).

[91] Paul Michell, "English-Speaking Justice: Evolving Responses to Transnational Forcible Abduction after Alvarez-Machain" (1996) 29 *Cornell Int'l. L. J.* 2; Patrick M. McFadden, "Provincialism in United States Courts" (1995–1996) 81 *Cornell L. Rev.* 4.

[92] *R.* v. *Horseferry Road Magistrates' Court, ex parte Bennett* [1994] 1 AC 42. For an earlier American decision more consistent with the common law view, see *United States* v. *Toscanino*, 500 F.2d 267 (2d Cir. 1974).

[93] *United States of America* v. *Khadr*, 2011 ONCA 358.

[94] *R.* v. *Hartley*, [1978] 2 NZLR 199.

[95] *Sosa* v. *Alvarez-Machain*, 542 US 692 (2004); see also Scott J. Borrowman, "Sosa v. Alvarez-Machain and Abu Ghraib – Civil Remedies for Victims of Extraterritorial Torts by U.S. Military Personnel and Civilian Contractors" (2005) 2 *B.Y.U. L. Rev.* 371.

[96] Starr, "Sentence Reduction as a Remedy".

[97] Guido Calabresi, "The Exclusionary Rule" (2003) 26 *Harv. J. L. and Pub. Pol.* 112; but see Yale Kamisar, "In Defence of the Exclusionary Rule" (2003) 26 *Harv. J. L. Pub. Pol.* 119 arguing that sentence reductions would not serve deterrent purposes.

[98] *Strunk* v. *United States*, 412 US 434 (1973).

remedy for that right in international courts. They have, however, been used as a remedy for some forms of prosecutorial misconduct,[99] which is generally immune from damage awards.[100] Sentence reductions are sometimes used in cases where the accused fails to establish an entrapment defence. Nevertheless, federal sentencing guidelines now govern this use of sentencing, again illustrating how the remedial discretion of American Federal Courts is often restrained by statutes.

6.2.7.4 Habeas Corpus

In *Boumediene* v. *Bush*,[101] the US Supreme Court affirmed that habeas corpus was protected under the American Constitution and applied to military detainees at Guantanamo Bay. It stressed that habeas corpus was even more important in cases where there was no criminal trial. Justice Kennedy for the majority held that "the privilege of habeas corpus entitles the prisoner to a meaningful opportunity to demonstrate that he is being held pursuant to 'the erroneous application or interpretation of relevant law'".[102] As Amanda Tyler has noted, this was a guarantee of due process as opposed to release.[103] The DC Circuit, which hears Guantanamo Bay habeas petitions, has indicated that something less than a preponderance of evidence may be sufficient to justify continued detention.[104] Habeas corpus has not been an effective remedy for the forty men still subject to indeterminate detention by the United States at Guantanamo Bay.

The Court has denied habeas corpus as a remedy to stop the transfer of those held in American military detention to Iraqi custody[105] and to non-citizens subjected to expedited immigration removal.[106] In both cases, the Court justified its restrictive approach on the basis that habeas was not used for such purposes when the constitutional guarantee of the remedy

99 *United States* v. *Dicus*, 579 F. Supp. 2d 1142 (N.D. Iowa, 2008) at 1159–1161; see Sonja B. Starr, "Using Sentencing to Clean Up Criminal Procedure: Incorporating Remedial Sentence Reduction Into Federal Sentencing Law" (2008) 21 *Fed. Sent'g. Rep.* 29, 29.

100 *Imbler* v. *Pachtman*, 424 US 409 (1976).

101 *Boumediene* v. *Bush*, 553 US 723 (2008).

102 Ibid. at 779.

103 Amanda Tyler, *Habeas Corpus in Wartime* (New York: Oxford University Press, 2017), pp.275–276.

104 *Al Bihani* v. *Obama*, 590 F.3d 866 (D.C. Cir., 2010) at 878; *Al Adahi* v. *Obama*, 613 F.3d 1102 (D.C. Cir., 2010) at 1103; *Kiyemba* v. *Obama*, 555 F.3d. 1022 (D.C. Cir., 2009); *Qassim* v. *Trump*, 927 F.3d 522 (D.C. Cir., 2019).

105 *Munaf* v. *Geren*, 553 US 674 (2008).

106 *Department of Homeland Security* v. *Thuraissigiam*, 591 US (2020).

was adopted in 1789. Justice Sotomayor dissented in the immigration case and argued that the Court's approach "handcuffs the Judiciary's ability to perform its constitutional duty to safeguard individual liberty".[107]

The courts now often require proof of factual innocence as a gateway or threshold to limit the use of habeas corpus to challenge criminal convictions even while not recognizing factual innocence as an independent basis for granting habeas relief.[108] They have also consistently deferred to state criminal law processes unless they violate clearly established rights.[109] Only three per cent of the first 250 DNA exonerations in the United States were obtained by way of federal habeas corpus.[110]

A concern that Federal Courts will overreach is also a factor in explaining American remedial exceptionalism. Leading scholars have concluded that habeas corpus "is viewed by many as a prime source of vexatious, time-consuming, often abusive, and ultimately meritless litigation" even though, for most who have been convicted, "the Great Writ is a pipe dream".[111] This result is consistent with American "extra-legalism"[112] that involves extensive and complex litigation that holds out a largely false promise of remedies.

6.2.8 *Canada*

6.2.8.1 Exclusion of Evidence

Although Canadian courts excluded involuntary confessions, they resisted excluding evidence as a remedy under the statutory Canadian

[107] Ibid. at 2 (Slip Op.).

[108] *Herrera* v. *Collins*, 506 US 390 (1993); *In re Troy Anthony Davis*, 130 S.Ct. 1 (2009). On remand, the District Court found that Troy Davis had not established actual innocence by clear and convincing evidence so that no reasonable juror could have convicted despite most of the state's witnesses recanting the testimony that convicted him. The judge concluded that "a federal court simply cannot interpose itself and set aside the jury verdict in this case absent a truly persuasive showing of innocence. To act contrarily would wreck [sic] complete havoc on the criminal justice system". *In re Troy Anthony Davis*, 2010 US Dist. Lexis 87340 (S.S. Ga., 2010) at 214. Troy Davis was executed on 21 September 2011.

[109] *Harrington* v. *Ritchter*, 562 US 86 (2011); *Cullen* v. *Pinholster*, 563 US 170 (2011); *Cavazos* v. *Smith*, 565 US 1 (2011).

[110] Brandon Garrett, *Convicting the Innocent* (Cambridge: Harvard University, 2011), p.230.

[111] Nancy King and Joseph Hoffman, *Habeas for the Twenty-First Century: Uses, Abuses, and the Future of the Great Writ* (Chicago: University of Chicago Press, 2011), p.17.

[112] Kent Roach, *The 9/11 Effect: Comparative Counter-Terrorism* (Cambridge: Cambridge University Press, 2011), pp.161–238.

Bill of Rights enacted in 1960.[113] Section 24(2) was added to the 1982 Canadian Charter of Rights and Freedoms as a compromise between no exclusion and automatic exclusion. It provides that evidence "obtained in a manner that infringed or denied any rights or freedoms guaranteed by the Charter ... shall be excluded if it is established that, having regard to all the circumstances, the admission of it in the proceedings would bring the administration of justice into disrepute".[114] There was an initial tendency by Canadian courts simply to conclude whether or not the admission of evidence would cause disrepute.[115]

Starting in 1987, the Supreme Court of Canada developed a more structured and predictable test. It held that evidence such as statements and breath samples that were unconstitutionally conscripted or obtained from the accused should generally be excluded in order to protect the fairness of the trial. Other unconstitutionally obtained evidence such as guns and drugs obtained without the accused's participation would only be excluded after balancing the seriousness of the particular violation against the adverse effects on the administration of justice of excluding the relevant evidence.[116]

The Canadian rights protection approach was supported by decisions that held that the accused did not have standing to request exclusion of evidence on the basis of violations of the rights of third parties.[117] The Canadian fair trial test, like American jurisprudence in general, required a causal connection between a violation that involved the accused's participation and the discovery of evidence sought to be excluded. This causation approach[118] made sense if the purpose of the exclusionary remedy was the first-track corrective goal of placing the accused in no worse, but also no better, of a position than if their rights had not been violated. As Chief Justice Lamer, the chief architect of the fair trial test, explained: "discoverability is premised on the notion of corrective justice.

[113] *R.* v. *Hogan*, [1975] 2 SCR 574.

[114] *Canadian Charter of Rights and Freedoms*, s 24(2), Part I of the *Constitution Act, 1982*, being Schedule B to the *Canada Act 1982* (UK), 1982, c 11.

[115] See *infra* Chapter 1, Section 1.6, for discussion.

[116] *R.* v. *Collins*, [1987] 1 SCR 265; *R.* v. *Stillman*, [1997] 1 SCR 607.

[117] *R.* v. *Edwards*, [1996] 1 SCR 128. This decision, however, resulted in a strong dissent by LaForest J. that correctly warned that the court's individualistic approach could result in the court ignoring serious violations.

[118] The Court rejected a causation requirement for a preliminary requirement that evidence be obtained in a manner that violates rights: *R.* v. *Strachan*, [1988] 2 SCR 980. This made sense because evidence would be excluded for regulatory or systemic reasons under the serious violation test which was distinct from the fair trial test.

The purpose is to ensure that the accused is placed in no worse, but also no better, position than if he or she had been forced to participate in the state's case".[119] The Court eventually recognized that pre-existing real evidence could be excluded under the fair trial test if the police could not have discovered such evidence without unconstitutionally conscripting the accused to assist in building the state's case.[120] This increased the social costs of the fair trial rule of prima facie exclusion and eventually led to its demise.

The fair trial test was overturned in 2009 on the basis that it was "an all-but-automatic exclusionary rule for non-discoverable conscriptive evidence".[121] The Court allowed more balancing of competing interests and refused to exclude unconstitutionally obtained drugs and guns. The Court made much of the text of section 24(2) and in particular the idea that it directs the court's attention to the future effects of admitting evidence. Prospective tests of disrepute, like a focus on judicial integrity, are somewhat artificial. They ignore that the court's traditional focus is on finding adjudicative facts about and providing remedies for past violations. The idea that exclusion is based on how a reasonable person or the judges would react to exclusion creates uncertainty and maximizes discretion.

Under the new test, courts will consider: 1. the seriousness of the violation; 2. the effects of the violation on rights; and 3. the adverse effects of excluding evidence in all cases.

The Court will still generally exclude statements obtained from the accused through a violation of the right to counsel.[122] The Court also affirmed the importance of causation analysis in revealing how much harm a particular violation did to Charter protected interests. It stated that "discoverability retains a useful role ... in assessing the actual impact of the breach on the protected interests of the accused. It allows the court to assess the strength of the causal connection between the Charter infringing self-incrimination and the resultant evidence".[123] At

[119] Rt. Hon Antonio Lamer, "Protecting the Administration of Justice from Disrepute" (1998) 42 *St Louis U. L. J.* 345, 358; see also Kent Roach, "The Evolving Fair Trial Test" (1996) 1 *Can. Crim. L. Rev.* 69 and Kent Roach, "Constitutionalizing Disrepute: Exclusion of Evidence after *Therens*" (1986) 44 *U. Toronto Fac. L. Rev.* 209 for similar views.

[120] *R.* v. *Burlingham*, [1995] 2 SCR 206.

[121] *R.* v. *Grant*, [2009] 2 SCR 353 at para 64.

[122] Ibid. at para 105.

[123] Ibid. at para 122.

the same time and contrary to American exclusionary jurisprudence, the Court recognized that a determination that the police could have obtained the evidence without violating rights tends to make violations more serious.[124] In this way, the Canadian court has correctly noted that causation reasoning can point in different directions depending on whether the purpose of the exclusionary remedy is to compensate for a violation or to regulate police conduct.

The final group of factors as before balances the seriousness of the offence and the importance of the evidence against the seriousness of the violation. The Court could have won public support for its ruling if it had stressed that it was reluctant to exclude guns. Nevertheless, it was extremely ambiguous on the issue. It recognized that while weapons offences "raise major public safety concerns and that the gun is the main evidence in this case", the seriousness of the offence charged also suggested that it is "all the more important" that the accused's rights be respected. In the end, the Court found the final balance part of the test not to be of "much assistance".[125] The Court has, in subsequent cases, indicated it should generally operate as a tie breaker in cases where a strong case for exclusion does not emerge after considering the seriousness of the violation and its effects on Charter protected interests.[126] It will be suggested in Section 6.3 of this chapter that courts may be more comfortable with a balancing test based on proportionality.

The seriousness of the violation has emerged as the most important factor, but it is "fact specific"[127] and hence difficult to predict. For example, in *Grant,* the Court determined that the violations of the rights against arbitrary detention and to counsel of a young Black man in Toronto were not serious enough to justify exclusion of drugs and a gun despite the fact that he was subject to a proactive and coercive stop by one uniformed and two undercover police officers. The Court stressed that there was no evidence of profiling or discriminatory practices. Moreover, the Court found that "the point at which an encounter becomes a detention is not always clear, and is something with which courts have struggled". Hence the error made by the police was "an understandable one"[128] and was committed in good faith.

[124] *R.* v. *Coté,* [2011] 3 SCR 215; *R.* v. *Cole,* 2012 SCC 53.
[125] *R.* v. *Grant,* [2009] 2 SCR 353 at para 139.
[126] *R.* v. *Le,* 2019 SCC 34 at paras 141–142.
[127] *R. v. Grant* at para 108.
[128] Ibid. at para 133.

Reasonable people may differ about the seriousness of the breaches in *Grant*. The same is true about the companion case of *R.* v. *Harrison*,[129] where a police hunch about a rental car that had travelled a great distance in a short time turned out to be correct. The police found thirty-five kilograms of cocaine in the truck. The Court excluded this important evidence in part because the officer involved gave misleading testimony. The Court has moved away from a first-track compensatory/corrective approach to exclusion of evidence. Its new test, however, is less predictable. The Court also fuels concerns similar to those seen in the United States that its exclusionary decisions are a vehicle for judges to express their respective support for either the state's interests in crime control or the accused's interests in due process.

6.2.8.2 Stays of Proceedings

The Canadian approach to stays of proceedings has been influenced by the British approach. In the 1964 case of *Connelly* v. *DPP*,[130] the House of Lords related its power to stay proceedings to the need to protect its own judicial process from abuse by the executive.[131] More than twenty years later, the Canadian Supreme Court recognized a "residual discretion" to stay proceedings in cases where compelling the accused to trial "would violate those fundamental principles of justice which underlie the community's sense of fair play and decency" and when necessary "to prevent the abuse of a court's process through oppressive or vexatious proceedings".[132] In subsequent years, however, both the British and Canadian courts have recognized that a stay of proceeding can also be justified when the accused could not receive a fair trial.[133] Thus, in both countries, stays can be justified either as an individual remedy to protect the accused's fair trial rights or as a systemic remedy to respond to abusive state conduct that should be condemned and not repeated.

In one early Charter case, the Supreme Court followed American jurisprudence and held that a stay of proceedings was the minimum remedy for a violation of a right to a trial in a reasonable time. The Court concluded that allowing a trial to proceed would compound the violation

[129] [2009] 2 SCR 494.

[130] [1964] AC 1254.

[131] See generally Andrew Choo, *Abuse of Process and Judicial Stays of Proceedings*, 2nd ed. (Oxford: Oxford University Press, 2008), pp.22–70 for an accounting of such cases.

[132] *R.* v. *Jewitt*, [1985] 2 SCR 128 at para 25.

[133] *Beckford* v. *Regina*, [1996] 1 Cr. App R 94 at 100–110.

of the right.[134] Justice LaForest warned in a strong and prophetic dissent, however, that based on the American experience, courts would adjust to the remedial straitjacket by refusing to interpret the underlying right in a generous manner. The next year, the Supreme Court held that a stay was the minimal remedy for entrapment.[135] In both contexts there is evidence of remedial deterrence in which the court is less generous with the right or the defence, presumably to avoid the drastic remedy.[136] In any event, while not reversing either case, the Supreme Court has in all subsequent jurisprudence stressed that courts should consider less drastic remedies before ordering stays of proceedings.

In both Canada and the UK, courts are now more willing to grant stays of proceedings when necessary to protect the accused's right to a fair trial than to respond to state misconduct or abuse of process. The original abuse of process rationale is now characterized by the Supreme Court of Canada as a "residual" and "small" category while "in the vast majority of cases, the concern will be about the fairness of the trial".[137] The Court has only stayed proceedings on such integrity grounds in a small number of cases involving violence or threatened violence.[138] The House of Lords have, in an extra-legal extradition case, affirmed that a stay of proceedings can be justified even if a fair trial was possible. Lord Griffiths explained: "the courts, of course, have no power to apply direct discipline to the police or the prosecuting authorities, but they can refuse to allow them to take advantage of abuse of power".[139] Lord Lowry stated that a stay "will discourage similar conduct in future and thus will tend to maintain the purity of the stream of justice. No 'floodgates' argument applies because the executive can stop the flood at source by refraining from impropriety".[140] This approach

[134] *R.* v. *Rahey*, [1987] 1 SCR 588.

[135] *R.* v. *Mack*, [1988] 2 SCR 903.

[136] After the Supreme Court set demanding and inflexible standards for speedy trials in *R.* v. *Askov*, [1990] 2 SCR 1199, over 50,000 stays of proceedings were entered. In 1992, the Court endorsed a more limited and fact-specific approach to whether the right was violated: *R.* v. *Morin*, [1992] 1 SCR 771. The Court has subsequently used guidelines but they are less demanding on the state than the *Askov* standards and allow for transition periods and exceptions: *R.* v. *Jordan*, 2016 SCC 27.

[137] *Canada (Minister of Citizenship and Immigration)* v. *Tobiass*, [1997] 3 SCR 391 at para 89.

[138] *United States of America* v. *Cobb*, [2001] 1 SCR 587; *R.* v. *Bellusci*, 2012 SCC 44. See generally, Kent Roach, *Constitutional Remedies in Canada*, 2nd ed. (Aurora: Thomson Reuters, 2013), pp.9.90ff.

[139] *R.* v. *Horseferry Road Magistrates' Court, ex parte Bennett*, [1994] 1 AC 42 at para 62.

[140] Ibid. at para 77.

recognizes that a stay of proceedings has a special role as the strongest judicial signal of disapproval of abusive state conduct and that the executive can engage in discipline and training to ensure the abuse is not repeated. Like punitive damages, however, use of such a remedy may produce a windfall for the applicant.

In *R.* v. *Maxwell*,[141] the UK Supreme Court affirmed that proceedings could be stayed when "it will be impossible to give the accused a fair trial". In such cases "no question of the balancing of interests arises"[142] even though balancing of interests should take place when stays are used to respond to state misconduct. The Supreme Court of Canada has similarly stressed in *R.* v. *Babos*[143] that the balancing of competing interests will be mandatory and have a greater role in cases where stays of proceedings are being used to respond to an abuse of process by the state as opposed to protecting the accused's right to a fair trial. In Section 6.4 of this chapter, It will be suggested that the dual focus on both protecting the accused's right and judicial integrity taken by British and Canadian courts is consistent with a two-track approach to remedies.

6.2.8.3 Sentence Reductions

Justice Louise Arbour in a Canadian commission of inquiry report recommended that the reduction of sentences be used as one remedy for violations of rights during imprisonment that made punishment more punitive than intended. She reasoned that such a remedy would produce no windfall for the accused and was akin to reducing punishment to reflect conditions in pre-trial detention.[144]

In *R.* v. *Nasogaluak*,[145] the Supreme Court of Canada concluded that sentence reductions could be used as a remedy so long as any abuse of state power related to the offender and the offence. In that case, the Court approved of the use of a mandatory minimum sentence as a remedy for police use of extreme and unnecessary violence in making an arrest. Sentence reductions can be used when a violation produces no incriminating evidence that can be excluded[146] and sometimes where

[141] 2010 UKSC 48.
[142] Ibid. at para 13.
[143] [2014] 1 SCR 309 at paras 40–41.
[144] Commission of Inquiry into Certain Events at the Prison for Women in Kingston, *The Arbour Report* (Ottawa: Supply and Services, 1996), pp.183–185.
[145] 2010 SCC 6.
[146] *R.* v. *Grencke*, 2004 ONCJ 121; *R.* v. *Oryia*, 2014 ONCJ 609; *R.* v. *T(J)*, 2017 ONCA 250; *R.* v. *Brown*, 2017 ABQB 191.

the courts have found exclusion is not warranted.[147] They are also used in some cases where the accused has suffered from delay but where the delay itself did not violate the Charter, triggering what in Canada is the mandatory use of stays of proceedings for unreasonable trial delay.[148]

Sentence reductions in Canada cannot result in sentences below mandatory minimum sentences provided by the legislature.[149] They also cannot be used to respond, as Justice Arbour suggested, to abuses of human rights in prison such as solitary confinement on the basis that this does not relate to the circumstances of the offence or the offender.[150] The restrictions are unfortunate as Justice Arbour's rationale for the use of sentence reductions as a remedy is sound. It will be suggested in Section 6.4 of this chapter that sentence reductions can in some cases provide a meaningful first track remedy for those who are convicted but that they are unlikely to be an effective second-track systemic remedy.

6.2.8.4 Habeas Corpus

The Supreme Court of Canada has taken a generous approach to habeas corpus, using it to grant release to a prisoner who had been subject to thirty-seven years of indeterminate detention even though it was possible for him to seek the alternative remedy of judicial review of a decision made by a parole board.[151] Habeas corpus was also applied to a transfer of several inmates to a higher security prison, even though judicial review of that decision was a possible alternative remedy.[152]

Canadian courts have been sensitive to the fact that habeas corpus has procedural advantages over judicial review, including placing the onus on the state to justify the legality of the impugned detention.[153] Habeas corpus has been used to challenge conditions of immigration detention in part because courts hear habeas corpus applications as a matter of priority and because habeas corpus is not "a discretionary remedy".[154] As

[147] *Kennett* v. *R.*, 2019 NBCA 52 at para 4.
[148] *R.* v. *Bosley*, 1992 CanLII 2838 (ON C.A.) at para 169.
[149] *Québec (Procureur général) c. Chabot*, (1992) 77 CCC(3d) 371 (Que. C.A.); *R.* v. *Gowdy*, 2016 ONCA 989 at para 128; *R.* v. *Ferguson*, 2008 SCC 6.
[150] *R.* v. *A.S.*, 2019 ONCA 900 at para 29. The Ontario Court of Appeal has also used the same rationale to preclude them as a remedy for late disclosure: *R.* v. *Claros*, 2019 ONCA 626 at paras 70–75.
[151] *Steele* v. *Mountain Institute*, [1996] 2 SCR 223.
[152] *May* v. *Ferndale Institute*, [2005] 3 SCR 809.
[153] *Khela* v. *Mission Institute*, [2014] 1 SCR 502; *R.* v. *Bird*, 2019 SCC 6 at para 62.
[154] *Canada (Public Safety and Emergency Preparedness)* v. *Chhina*, 2019 SCC 29 at para 59.

Farbey and Sharpe write in criticism to a British approach that is more willing to see judicial review as an adequate alternative remedy, habeas corpus "retains an important constitutional function above and beyond judicial review".[155]

There are some limits to habeas corpus. It cannot be used as a substitute for a criminal appeal. Courts hearing a habeas corpus application dealing with poor conditions of detention do not have jurisdiction either to retain jurisdiction or issue declarations.[156] It will be suggested in Section 6.4 of this chapter that this limits the ability of habeas corpus to serve second-track systemic purposes. Habeas corpus remains a traditional first-track remedy that courts have long used to protect individuals from illegal forms of detention. It affirms the importance of individual remedies and individual liberty.

6.2.9 *New Zealand*

6.2.9.1 Exclusion of Evidence

The trajectory of the use of exclusion of evidence in New Zealand has followed a path similar to that of the Canadian approach. In the early days of the 1990 statutory New Zealand Bill of Rights, the courts created a prima facie rule of exclusion that went beyond even the Canadian rule. It applied to all evidence obtained in violation of rights, including search and seizure breaches that were necessary to obtain real evidence such as drugs and guns. As in Canada, the new rule was announced in a case where the police had violated the right to counsel.[157] The Court held that both the accused's confession and hidden evidence that could only have been discovered with the confessions were inadmissible. Nevertheless, weapons that would have been discovered even without the violation were admissible.[158] This approach demonstrated how causation analysis

155 Judith Farbey, Robert J. Sharpe and Simon Atrill, *The Law of Habeas Corpus*, 3rd ed. (Oxford: Oxford University Press, 2011), p.63.

156 *Ogiamien* v. *Ontario*, 2017 ONCA 839; see also *Lord* v. *Couter*, 2007 BCSC 1758; *Egan* v. *Quinte Detention Centre*, [2008] 2008 CanLII 19224 (ON SC); *R.* v. *Green*, 2009 ABQB 233. They also do not have jurisdiction to award damages: *Brown* v. *Canada*, 2018 ONCA 14.

157 *R.* v. *Butcher*, [1992] 2 NZLR 257.

158 Ibid. Richard J. explained that "[t]he prosecution should not be put in a better position than it would have been if no illegality had happened or in a worst position simply because of some earlier police error or misconduct". *R.* v. *H.*, [1994] NZLR 143 at para 150.

could be central to a first-track individual remedial approach that stresses both compensation and vindication of rights. The Court also required a real and substantial connection between the violation and the evidence to be excluded. It rejected the broader Canadian test that would accept a temporal connection in order to assess the whole transaction from a more regulatory perspective concerned with protecting the administration of justice from disrepute.[159] Consistent with a rights focused approach, the Court was also reluctant to give standing to third parties whose rights were not violated to argue that evidence should be excluded.[160]

The early New Zealand jurisprudence placed the onus on the state to establish reasons why evidence should not be excluded. Such reasons were described by Cooke P. as "analogous" to situations where there would be reasonable limits on rights. They could include "trivial or inconsequential" violations of rights and situations of urgency.[161] He suggested that "the right is the starting point" and that generally the good faith of officers would not be sufficient to justify admission.[162] The New Zealand courts, both in their damages and exclusionary jurisprudence, have come the closest to recognizing the helpful role that proportionality reasoning can play in remedial decision-making. It will also be suggested in Section 6.3.1 that the original New Zealand (and Irish) approaches of placing burdens on the state to explain why the exclusionary remedy would be disproportionate in a particular case is an appropriate burden for the state to bear.

In *Shaheed*, the New Zealand Court of Appeal abandoned its prima facie rule of exclusion and embraced a balancing test.[163] The Court was concerned that the prima facie rule "does not give the appearance of adequately addressing the interest of the community that those who are guilty of serious crimes should not go unpunished".[164] It expressed special concerns about some Canadian developments that suggested that even real pre-existing evidence such as guns and drugs could be excluded under the Canadian fair trial test.[165] Justice Blanchard explained that judges must decide whether exclusion "is proportionate" to the breach.[166]

159 Compare *R.* v. *Whareumu*, [2001] 1 NZLR 655 with *R.* v. *Strachan*, [1988] 2 SCR 980.
160 *R.* v. *Bruhns*, [1994] 11 CRNZ 656.
161 *R.* v. *Butcher*, [1992] 2 NZLR 257 at 266.
162 *R.* v. *Goodwin*, [1993] 2 NZLR 153 at 172.
163 *R.* v. *Shaheed*, [2002] 2 NZLR 377.
164 Ibid. at para 137.
165 Ibid. at para 90 citing *R.* v. *Burlingham*, [1995] 2 SCR 206.
166 Ibid. at para 156.

He elaborated: "[e]xclusion will often be the only appropriate response where a serious breach has been committed deliberately or in reckless disregard of the accused's rights or where the police conduct in relation to that breach has been grossly careless".[167] The reliability of the evidence and its importance to the prosecution were also relevant.[168]

This test was subsequently codified in a "laundry list" of factors that maximizes judicial discretion in determining when evidence should be excluded.[169] Although *Shaheed* made some potentially helpful statements that proportionality was an important factor in administering the test, the New Zealand courts have not developed a jurisprudence that systemically employs proportionality reasoning. To be fair, the New Zealand courts had also failed under the previous prima facie rule to develop "a comprehensive, fully rationalized jurisprudence of exceptions to the prima facie rule".[170] Under *Shaheed*, there is a judicial desire to balance competing interests, but a failure to develop clear and predictable tests to do so.[171]

6.2.9.2 Stays of Proceedings

New Zealand courts will use stays either to protect the accused's right to a fair trial or to respond to abusive conduct.[172] The latter ground is about preserving judicial integrity and not about deterring or disciplining past misconduct. As in the UK and Canada, balancing is required in the second category of cases. It includes factors like alternative remedies and the gravity of the misconduct. The Court refused to stay proceedings in the leading case because exclusion was an alternative remedy and the misconduct would not be repeated.[173]

167 Ibid. at para 148.

168 Ibid. at para 152.

169 *New Zealand Evidence Act*, 2006, No. 69, s.30; Scott L. Optican and Peter J. Sankoff, "The New Exclusionary Rule: A Preliminary Assessment of R. v. Shaheed" (2003) 2003 *N.Z. L. Rev.* 1, 19.

170 Ibid., 3.

171 For arguments that there is a growing global consensus towards balancing interests and considering less drastic alternative remedies before excluding evidence obtained through violations of human rights, see Kay Levine, Jenia Turner and Ronald Wright, "Evidence Laundering in a Post-*Herring* World" (2016) 106 *J. Crim. L. & Criminology* 627, 665ff.

172 *Wilson* v. *R.*, [2016] 1 NZLR 705.

173 Ibid. at para 60.

6.2.9.3 Sentence Reductions

In New Zealand, sentence reductions have been used as a remedy for a violation of the right to a trial in a reasonable time.[174] A number of judges have rejected both sentence reductions[175] and damages[176] as alternative remedies to exclusion of evidence.[177] In Section 6.3.8 of this chapter, it will be suggested that sentence reductions and damages can in some cases be more proportionate alternatives to exclusion of evidence, but also that there should not be a mechanical preference for the use of less drastic remedies.

6.2.10 Ireland

6.2.10.1 Exclusion of Evidence

Until 2015, the Irish Supreme Court took a rights protection approach to the exclusion of evidence. Basing their decisions on a general remedial provision in the Irish Constitution,[178] the Court stressed it had "a positive duty ... to restore as far as possible the person so damaged to the position in which he would be if his rights had not been invaded".[179] For example, it excluded evidence obtained under an invalid warrant and pursuant to a long-standing Gardai policy, even though two judges dissented on the basis that the violation was not sufficiently serious to merit exclusion. The Court limited the compensatory remedy through a causation requirement.[180] Consistent with the rights protection approach, it would not exclude evidence that the police would inevitably have obtained without a constitutional violation[181] or where there was not a direct causal connection between a constitutional violation and the obtaining of evidence.[182] The Court would also not grant those whose rights were not violated standing to argue that evidence should be

[174] *R.* v. *Williams,* [2009] 2 NZLR 750.
[175] *R.* v. *Shaheed,* [2002] 2 NZLR 377 at para 154.
[176] *Hamed & Ors* v. *R,* [2011] NZSC 101 at para 247.
[177] Peter Marshall, "Sentence Reductions as a BORA Remedy" (2012) 2012 *N.Z. L. J.* 24.
[178] *People* v. *Kenny,* [1990] 2 IR 110.
[179] *The State* v. *Governor of Mountjoy Prison,* [1985] ILRM 465 at 484.
[180] Declan McGrath, "The Exclusionary Rule in respect of Unconstitutionally Obtained Evidence" (2004) 26 *Dublin Univ. L. J.* 108, 114.
[181] *People* v. *O'Donnell,* [1995] 3 IR 551.
[182] *Walsh* v. *O'Buachalla,* [1991] 1 IR 56.

excluded.[183] Individual standing and causation requirements are justified under a first-track compensatory approach to exclusion of evidence.

In its 2015 decision in *DPP* v. *JC*,[184] the Irish Supreme Court overruled its prima facie exclusionary rule in favour of a new approach based on balancing of competing interests. This followed public criticism of the prima facie rule, including proposals for legislative imposition of a balancing test or even a constitutional amendment to achieve such ends.[185]

Courts in the United States, Canada, New Zealand and now Ireland have moved towards balancing tests because of concerns about the crime control costs of previous exclusionary rules, but without citing specific evidence about these costs or even specific cases where new balancing tests would have clearly produced a different result. Even in *JC*, however, the Court retained its approach of prima facie rules mandating exclusion while providing the state an opportunity to establish that the evidence should be admitted because the state was not at fault for violating the rights. It will be suggested in the next section that this approach appropriately places a burden on the state to demonstrate good reasons for not excluding evidence that was obtained through rights violations.

6.2.11 Summary

Many courts accept that a stay of proceedings can be justified to protect the accused's right to a fair trial, but are much more reluctant to stay proceedings as a remedy for police misconduct. These two grounds correspond with individual and systemic remedies in a two-track approach. Many courts have stressed the need to balance conflicting interests and consider alternative remedies before staying proceedings.

Courts have moved towards balancing of interests test for exclusion but at the cost of "an undesirable lack of certainty in future cases".[186] Although he was the most influential critic of Canada's fair trial test, David Paciocco has criticized Canada's new balancing test as a "legal lottery".[187] The idea that judges have a strong discretion not to award a

183 *People* v. *Lawless*, (1985) 3 Frewen 30 at 34–35; Robert Bloom and Erin Delaney, "When Rights Become Empty Promises: Promoting an Exclusionary Rule That Vindicates Personal Rights" (2012) 46 *Irish Jurist (N.S.)* 38, 68.

184 2015 IESC 31.

185 Bloom and Delaney, "When Rights Become Empty Promises", 64–65.

186 Richard Mahoney, "Exclusion of Evidence", in Paul Rishworth et al. (eds.), *The New Zealand Bill of Rights* (Oxford: Oxford University Press, 2003), p.773.

187 David Paciocco, "Section 24(2): Lottery or Law – The Appreciable Limits of Purposive Reasoning" (2011) 58 *C.L.Q.* 15.

remedy tends to undermine the very idea of rights. Section 6.3 of this chapter argues that proportionality reasoning and prima facie rules would provide a more structured framework for remedial decision-making than reliance on discretion and the frequent judicial mantra that stays should only be available in the "clearest of cases" and that interests should be balanced. It will also suggest that alternative remedies such as sentence reductions and damages more frequently used by international courts can play an important role in proportionality analysis.

6.3 Restraints on Remedies and the Role of Proportionality

Both Sonja Starr and Jenia Iontcheva Turner have written about how international criminal courts may be particularly susceptible to the process of remedial deterrence where they reduce rights to avoid drastic remedies.[188] They have both argued that a balancing of interests is appropriate. Professor Turner notes that many domestic jurisdictions take a balancing approach to ordering remedies and that it finds support in the idea of proportionality.[189] She helpfully stresses the importance of less drastic alternative remedies including sentence reductions as well as judicial referrals of prosecutors for disciplinary action.[190]

At the same time, attempts by both international and domestic courts to balance competing interests have not been a success. Some have argued that international courts have made unprincipled decisions to abandon stays in order to maintain political support for the court.[191] Even in the domestic context, there are concerns that governments may be inclined to appoint judges who are more reluctant to exclude evidence. Splits in courts on criminal remedies cases are often thought to reflect ideological differences within the court. In any event, remedial decision-

[188] Starr, "Rethinking Effective Remedies"; Turner, "Policing International Prosecutors"; see also Calabresi, "The Exclusionary Rule".

[189] Professor Turner comments that "the court would be guided by the principle of proportionality and choose a remedy that advances legitimate goals of international criminal justice, while imposing the least burden on individual rights". Turner, "Policing International Prosecutors", 182.

[190] Consistent with proportionality reasoning she argues: "[t]he court should examine alternative remedies and sanctions and determine whether less restrictive measures" that are "less costly to individual rights and the integrity of the judicial process will be sufficient": ibid., 215.

[191] Schabas, "International Decisions".

making that stresses balancing, judicial integrity and the need for clear cases is unpredictable.

Judicial integrity is a widely cited rationale for remedies in the criminal process, but it is problematic.[192] It can be used as an excuse for protecting courts from public criticism about excessive remedies. Remedies in the criminal process are particularly vulnerable to the criticism that the court allows the "criminal to go free because the constable has blundered".[193] Andrew Choo has argued that judges should not give emphasis to adverse public reactions when deciding whether a stay of proceedings is warranted.[194] Petra Viebig has defended the ICC's use of judicial integrity as a rationale for exclusion. She argues that it allows the court to protect its reputation from both claims that it condones violations (thus undermining the rule of law) and the loss of public confidence if it excluded evidence of a serious crime.[195] The problem, however, is how judges should transparently and fairly balance such competing goals. Although conclusions that the admission or exclusion of evidence would harm judicial integrity follow Article 69(7)(b) of the Rome Statute, they beg more questions than they answer.

What is required is a more transparent and predictable means to balance competing interests. As suggested throughout this book, proportionality analysis can strengthen remedial decision-making. In particular, it can facilitate clear discussion of the purposes of remedies and how remedies may harm legitimate social interests. It can also inform whether less drastic alternative remedies will serve remedial purposes while better respecting competing social interests.

6.3.1 Proportionality, Burden of Proof and Prima Facie Rules

One of the key benefits of proportionality reasoning in human rights law is that it assigns responsibility to the state to justify limits on rights for

[192] It could be argued that some remedial texts such as s.24(2) of the Canadian Charter of Rights and Freedoms in its reference to only excluding evidence if its admission would bring the administration of justice into disrepute mandate concerns about public reactions to controversial remedies. To its credit, the Court has recognized that such an approach would be contrary to its anti-majoritarian role: *R.* v. *Collins*, [1987] 1 SCR 265 at paras 32–33. It has, however, replaced the idea of public views with the idea of the reasonable person, which is as vague and likely quite similar to the idea of judicial integrity.

[193] *People* v. *Defore*, 242 N.E. 13 (1926) at 588–589.

[194] Choo, *Abuse of Process*, p.113.

[195] Viebig, *Illicitly Obtained Evidence*, p.125.

social objectives. This recognizes the state's superior ability to introduce social and legislative facts that can educate the court about the consequences of its rulings. A similar pattern should be pursued as proportionality is applied to the remedial context. This would involve requiring the applicant to demonstrate that a remedy was required for a legitimate remedial purpose. If such prima facie entitlement to a remedy was established, the onus would then be on the state to demonstrate that the impact of the remedy on legitimate social interests was disproportionate and that a less drastic alternative remedy (or perhaps no remedy at all) would strike a better balance between the remedial purposes and the harms that the remedy would cause.

Such prima facie rules would have the advantage of indicating that courts will not routinely accept that the ends of crime control or prosecution justify the means of rights violations. They would demonstrate in concrete terms that the court takes rights violations and its remedial function seriously. They would provide the state with an opportunity to demonstrate that the violation was not serious and that it has responded appropriately to the violation and has taken steps to prevent similar violations in the future.

6.3.2 Legitimate Objectives

Proportionality both protects and allows reasonable limits on rights,[196] or in this case, remedies. This raises the threshold question of whether some of the state's objectives in limiting remedies are important enough to limit the remedy or whether they are inconsistent with the ideas of rights and remedies. The Supreme Court of Canada has suggested that objectives that are the antithesis or negation of the underlying right[197] or are simply a political or symbolic explanation of why the state wants to limit a right[198] are not important enough to justify reasonable limits on rights under section 1 of the Canadian Charter. It is striking that courts

[196] *R.* v. *Oakes,* [1986] 1 SCR 103.

[197] *Quebec* v. *Quebec Protestant Schools,* [1984] 2 SCR 66; *R.* v. *Zundel,* [1992] 2 SCR 731.

[198] *Sauvé* v. *Canada,* 2002 SCC 68. For arguments that courts should not accept rhetorical or symbolic objectives such as abstract notions about the rule of law or controlling crime as a legitimate objective in proportionality analysis, see Kent Roach, "Dialogue in Canada and the Dangers of Simplified Comparative Law and Populism" in Geoffrey Sigalet, Gregoire Webber and Rosalind Dixon (eds.), *Constitutional Dialogue: Rights, Democracy and Institutions* (Cambridge: Cambridge University Press, 2019), pp.267, 300–302.

that have stressed balancing tests for remedies in the criminal process are generally unable to cite concrete evidence that exclusion under previous compensatory rationales was harmful to social interests.

6.3.3 *Is the Seriousness of the Offence a Legitimate Objective?*

The seriousness of the offence charged should not be considered a legitimate objective to limit remedies in the criminal process. First, considering this factor assumes that the accused is guilty, contrary to the presumption of innocence.[199] Second, considering it supports the normatively dubious proposition that the ends of combatting serious crime justifies a lack of remedy for a rights violation. Finally, the seriousness of the offence cuts both ways. Although society has a greater interest in the prosecution of a serious offence, the accused also has a greater interest in receiving remedies for rights violations. Given this toss up, both the ICC[200] and the Supreme Court of Canada concluded that the seriousness of the offence is not of "much assistance"[201] with respect to exclusion. It is also not a feature in the American, New Zealand or Irish exclusionary jurisprudence.

The seriousness of the offence is, however, considered more often with respect to stays of proceedings and sometimes sentence reductions. It may be considered with respect to stays of proceedings but more on the basis that a stay prevents any adjudication of the merits of the allegation to be examined below. This is analogous to considering the importance of evidence where exclusion of one critical piece of evidence will make an adjudication on the merits impossible. With respect to sentence reductions, there is no longer the same presumption of innocence problem. Nevertheless, assigning categorical weight to offence seriousness may not be necessary should the state suggest a sentence reduction as a less drastic alternative remedy. Nor is it necessary if the court ensures that even with the reduction for a rights violation, the overall sentence remains proportionate to the crime and the offender's culpability.

[199] As such, it is similar to a "law whose only purpose is to discriminate". Aharon Barak, *Proportionality: Constitutional Rights and Their Limitations* (Cambridge: Cambridge University Press, 2012), p.251.

[200] *The Prosecutor* v. *Thomas Lubanga Dyilo*, ICC-01/04-0l/06, Decision on Admission of Material from the Bar Table, (24 June 2009) (International Criminal Court Trial Chamber Decision) at para 44 ("the seriousness of the alleged crimes committed by the accused is not a factor relevant to the admissibility of evidence").

[201] *R.* v. *Grant*, [2009] 2 SCR 353 at para 139.

6.3.4 *Is the Importance of the Evidence a Legitimate Objective?*

Courts are generally more reluctant to exclude guns, drugs or other illegal substances discovered through a rights violation than statements taken from the accused. Judges are concerned that the exclusion of tangible evidence will often cause a prosecution to collapse, thus turning exclusion into the functional equivalent of a stay.

There is less of a presumption of innocence problem in considering the importance of the evidence that was actually discovered in the accused's possession. If there are arguments that the accused did not actually possess the drugs or guns, they can still be resolved in the accused's favour on the appropriate reasonable doubt standard.

The public also has a legitimate (though not absolute) interest that criminal cases be decided on the merits. If the importance of the evidence is considered a valid objective to limit remedies, it will still be necessary for the court to apply the remaining elements of proportionality reasoning. In other words, the importance of guns or drugs should not be a trump card and lesser alternative remedies such as sentence reductions should be considered as should the overall balance of the competing state and remedial interests.

6.3.5 *Is Lack of Seriousness of the Violation a Legitimate Objective?*

Most courts accept that the seriousness of a violation is a relevant factor in remedial decision-making. The seriousness of the violation should be unpacked as it relates to different remedial purposes. A violation can be serious because of its impact on the accused. Here, there is a focus on what harms the violation caused to the accused. Alternatively, a violation can be serious because it demonstrates that police and prosecutors are indifferent or even hostile to rights. This involves the remedial purpose of responding to and preventing misconduct. As the Supreme Court of Canada has recognized, conclusions that the state could have obtained the evidence without violating rights may suggest that the violation is more serious,[202] even if that same conclusion minimizes the harm caused to the accused.

[202] *R.* v. *Cote*, [2011] 3 SCR 215; *R.* v. *Cole*, 2012 SCC 53; *R.* v. *Le*, 2019 SCC 34. McLachlin CJ has similarly recognized in the context of Charter damages in *Ward* v. *Vancouver (City)*, 2010 SCC 27 at para 30 that causation analysis, while related to compensation, plays less of a role with respect to the vindicatory and deterrent purposes of the remedy. See also Roach, *Constitutional Remedies*, pp.10.1390–10.1440.

Is deterrence of rights violations a legitimate concern? The United States is the only jurisdiction that since 1960 justifies exclusion of evidence exclusively in deterrence terms. The deterrence rationale fails to make sense of personal standing requirements that require the accused's own rights to be violated before the remedy is sought. If taken to its logical conclusion, it would abandon all standing and causation requirements and I am aware of no jurisdiction that has done so. Thus, deterrence is best seen as a supplementary second-track rationale.

Deterrence can work either as a form of specific deterrence of individual officers or as general deterrence of the state. As Peter Schuck has argued in the context of constitutional torts, specific deterrence of individual officials can be difficult to achieve and may result in over-deterrence. For these reasons, Schuck suggests that courts should focus on general deterrence that imposes direct remedies on the state as opposed to individual officers. Such state-focused general deterrence allows the state to select what, if any, steps it will take to respond to the remedies that the court imposes on the state.[203]

6.3.6 *Are Competing Rights a Legitimate Objective?*

Another legitimate objective is competing rights. The international criminal courts have considered the rights of victims of war crime and genocide in determining the appropriateness of a remedy for the violation of the rights of the accused. There is a danger that the competing rights of crime victims will become a rhetorical and symbolic objective for limiting remedies in the criminal process. Some of this danger can be addressed by applying the other steps in proportionality analysis. The ICC can award damages to crime victims and, in many cases, this may be more appropriate than limiting the rights of the accused in a manner that does not directly assist the crime victim.[204] Common law domestic courts might be more willing to order remedies for the accused if they could also order remedies for crime victims.

[203] Peter H Schuck, *Suing Government: Citizen Remedies for Official Wrongs* (New Haven: Yale University Press, 1983). On the role of insurance companies in encouraging training and oversight to lessen damage cost awards in the United States, see John Rappaport, "How Private Insurers Regulate Public Police" (2017) 130 *Harv. L. Rev.* 6.

[204] On the dangers that the rights of crime victims will be used as a justification for the crime control interests of the state, see Kent Roach, *Due Process and Victims' Rights: The New Law and Politics of Criminal Justice* (Toronto: University of Toronto Press, 1999).

There is also a danger that remedies ordered by supra-national courts for crime victims may ignore the rights of the accused, including the presumption of innocence. It will be suggested in Section 6.4.7 that the two-track approach that separates first-track compensatory remedies for crime victims from systemic remedies that should not trench on the separation of powers may be helpful in thinking through remedial strategies to benefit crime victims.

6.3.7 Rational Connection

The rational connection requirement can serve a useful purpose with regards to disciplining symbolic objectives such as the rights of crime victims or the battle against crime that the state may propose to limit remedies in the criminal process. For example, in cases where there is no specific crime victim, there would be no rational connection between the rights of victims and a state argument proposing that drugs and guns that were unreasonably seized should not be excluded. Even in cases with a concrete victim, the specific human right claimed on behalf of the victim would have to be specified and a rational connection between the limit on the remedy established. In most cases, equality rights of victims and potential victims would be the most likely candidate to survive the rational connection check on the state's objectives. Conversely, when a court orders reparations for crime victims, it might be argued that this infringes the accused's presumption of innocence. This claim might not survive the rational connection requirement if it was demonstrated that the accused's rights would be respected in any subsequent trial.

6.3.8 Least Restrictive Means and Alternative Remedies

The critical stage in proportionality reasoning is asking whether a legitimate state objective can still be achieved while violating the right less. Transferred to the remedial context, this question would ask whether a less drastic remedy would serve the purposes of compensating the accused and preventing future violations. It is important that this stage of proportionality not be reduced to a mechanical search for any less drastic remedy. A less drastic remedy should only be used if it fulfils its remedial purposes, both in terms of compensation and deterrence as well as a more drastic remedy.

The idea of preferring less drastic but equally effective alternative remedies is an entrenched staple of remedial jurisprudence. For example, stays of proceedings will only be ordered when there are concerns that the less drastic remedies, such as exclusion of evidence or a declaration, would not be effective. As suggested in Section 6.2.1.3, the ICC uses a broad range of alternatives to stays and exclusion including damages, sentence reductions and recommendations that officials be disciplined. The ECtHR has used both damage awards and sentence reductions as a remedy in criminal cases. As Professor Starr has argued, refusing to consider alternative remedies may result in the accused being denied any remedy at all.[205]

There was some interest in the United States in using damages as a less drastic alternative to exclusion.[206] Criminal courts in common law countries, however, do not have jurisdiction to award damages and access to justice issues often preclude separate civil litigation. In any event, robust qualified immunities would often make damages an illusory remedy in American courts.

In a leading New Zealand exclusion case, Blanchard J stated that an award of damages or a sentence reduction "might look strange" and even bring "the administration of justice into disrepute".[207] He also doubted whether a declaration or a police complaint proceeding "possibly leading to a disciplinary proceeding against the transgressing police officer, could provide a form of redress which truly vindicated the right".[208] Alternative remedies should be evaluated in relation to their remedial purpose. Disciplinary proceedings will not compensate an accused, but it might help to prevent future violations. A sentence reduction "might look strange" but it could be a meaningful form of compensation to the accused – especially if the alternative is no remedy at all. At the same time, a sentence reduction may not provide an effective incentive for the state to take steps to prevent similar violations in the future. One of the strengths of proportionality principles is that it provides questions to

[205] Starr, "Rethinking Effective Remedies", 766.

[206] Burger CJ defended damages as a more proportionate remedy to exclusion in *Bivens* v. *Six Unnamed Agents*, 403 US 383 (1971) but also conceded the need for legislative reform including the creation of a special tribunal to award damages. He also contemplated that: "[i]n addition to awarding damages, the record of the police conduct that is condemned would undoubtedly become a relevant part of an officer's personnel file so that the need for additional training or disciplinary action could be identified, or his future usefulness as a public official evaluated". Ibid. at 424.

[207] *R.* v. *Shaheed,* [2002] 2 NZLR 377 at paras 154–155. For approval of these comments and predictions that New Zealand courts will not examine alternative remedies, see Mahoney, "Exclusion of Evidence", p.787.

[208] *R.* v. *Shaheed,* [2002] 2 NZLR 377 at para 153.

guide analysis while allowing the parties and the context provide the answers in the particular context.

If sentence reductions are used as a remedy, courts should take care, as suggested by the ECtHR, to apply an individualized approach that justifies the sentence reduction in relation to the purposes of the remedy.[209] This is a more focused approach than the Canadian court's vaguer and more holistic approach to sentence reductions.[210] At the end of the day, the use of alternative remedies such as sentence reductions might be a way to reconcile the state's interests in an adjudication on the merits with the accused's interest in a meaningful remedy.

Costs or damages might also have to be used to provide an accused with a remedy if the accused is acquitted. This may require enlargement of the jurisdiction of some domestic criminal courts.[211]Courts should be sceptical of conceiving of a separate civil action as an alternative remedy given the costs of litigation and the low amount of most damage awards for rights violations. Again, the principled proportionality inquiry is not whether any less drastic remedy can be imagined. Rather, it is whether the less drastic remedy will strike a better balance between achieving the relevant remedial purpose and the competing social objective. Courts should not limit themselves to only one alternative remedy in the two-track approach. In some cases, damages or a sentence reduction can provide effective compensation for the accused, but additional training or discipline may also be necessary to ensure that the violation is not repeated.

6.3.9 *Overall Balance*

The final check provided by proportionality reasoning is that there should be an appropriate overall balance struck between the interests of those whose rights have been violated and the state's competing interests. The overall balance stage is valuable in providing judges with a final look at the adverse effects of granting a remedy as opposed to the effects on the accused of not granting a remedy. The absence of any remedy for the

[209] *Ananyev and Others* v. *Russia*, Nos. 42525/07 and 60800/08, First Section Judgment, ECHR 10 January 2012 at paras 224–225. The ECtHR, reflecting its jurisdiction and the ability of many European criminal courts to award damages, seems to prefer to award damages than to reduce sentences as a remedy.

[210] *R.* v. *Nasogaluak*, 2010 SCC 6 at paras 55–56.

[211] The Canadian courts have, however, used costs as a remedy in the criminal process especially in relation to late disclosure: *Ontario* v. *974649*, [2001] 3 SCR 575.

accused or the victim should bear considerable weight in the overall balance. It also allows the judge, with the state's assistance, to take a realistic look at the harm that the state may face. It may also give states incentives to propose alternative remedies, such as sentence reductions, to provide some individual remedy and to demonstrate that it has taken steps to prevent a similar violation in the future, thus making a systemic remedy unnecessary.

6.4 Towards a Two-Track Approach

Following from the discussion in Chapter 2, Section 2.4, a two-track approach to remedies separates out questions about what individual remedy is required to compensate the victim for the rights violation from what systemic remedies are required to prevent non-repetition of the violation. The two-track approach is a positive theory because it builds on remedial practice. It is also a normative theory about the dual purposes of remedies and the inadequacy of approaches that rely only on a single track.

6.4.1 The Problems with Exclusively Systemic and Deterrent-Based Remedies

Since the 1960s, the United States Supreme Court has justified the exclusion of evidence in terms of its value in deterring police misconduct. Yet there is little evidence that the remedy has actually curbed police misconduct in that country. In any event, the American exclusionary rule is now riddled with many complex exceptions, as are the underlying rights that restrict police behavior.[212] The American jurisprudence still has complex independent source and inevitable discovery exceptions, but these are unmoored from the logic of corrective justice that gives them purpose.[213] They seem to be used simply as an instrument to limit the crime control costs of exclusion. The loss of any sense that the accused has a right to a remedy helps explain why the very existence of the American exclusionary rule is in doubt.

The remedies typically ordered in criminal trials are blunt and uncertain in achieving systemic goals. Both American and Canadian courts

[212] Craig Bradley, *The Failure of the Criminal Procedure Revolution* (Pennsylvania: University of Pennsylvania Press, 1993).

[213] See generally Ernest Weinrib, *Corrective Justice* (Oxford: Oxford University Press, 2012); see also *infra* Chapter 2, Section 2.2, discussion.

rely on stays of proceedings to enforce speedy trial rights. But, this approach invites remedial deterrence. It can also result in wholesale use of stays that will require the state quickly to take steps such as appointing more judges and hiring more prosecutors.[214] It will be suggested below that the Council of Europe approach tends to produce broader and more sustainable reforms to combat delay. In any event, the award of individual remedies in both systems can detect if trial delay again becomes excessive.

6.4.2 Problems with Exclusively Corrective or Compensatory Remedies

Although the two-track approach favours individual remedies because of the legitimate expectations that people receive compensatory remedies, it recognizes that this will often be ineffective in obtaining systemic reforms to minimize similar violations in the future. Individual remedies may only impose infrequent costs on the state for rights violations. This is a particular danger in the criminal justice system because the police may have incentives to breach rights and many of the often disadvantaged accused may lack the incentive or means to obtain a remedy or to publicize that their rights were violated. Because of their centralized nature and limited resources, supra-national courts are more responsive to repetitive violations than domestic courts. At the same time, it is not impossible for domestic courts to concern themselves with repetitive violations. For example, the New Zealand Supreme Court refused to order a stay of proceedings in one case but justified its decision in part on the basis that "there is no evidence of a systemic problem ... there is no likelihood of a repetition of the conduct at issue".[215]

In 2001, the Supreme Court of Canada restricted police use of strip searches to cases where there were reasonable and probable grounds to believe that such a search would reveal evidence or a weapon.[216]

[214] Michael Code, *Trial within a Reasonable Time* (Toronto: Carswell, 1992) documenting the response to speedy trial standards set out in *R.* v. *Askov*, [1990] 2 SCR 1199. The Supreme Court retreated from these standards in *R.* v. *Morin* [1992] 1 SCR 771 only to impose new standards in *R.* v. *Jordan* [2016] 1 SCR 631 because of renewed concerns about trial delays.

[215] *R.* v. *Wilson*, [2015] NZSC 189 at para 93. The Court has demonstrated the same concern about the non-repetition of violations in its leading damage case of *Taunoa* v. *Attorney General*, [2007] NZSC 70 discussed *infra* Chapter 5, Section 2.2.3.

[216] *R.* v. *Golden*, [2001] 3 SCR 679. I acted as counsel for Aboriginal Legal Services in this case.

Unfortunately, there is evidence of chronic non-compliance by some police services. From 2001 to the end of 2018, there were eighty-nine reported judicial decisions finding unconstitutional strip searches in Ontario, forty of which involved the Toronto Police Service.[217] In ten of these cases, judges made adverse comments about the training that the police received.[218] This demonstrates that judges are capable of hearing evidence about some of the organizational determinants of rights violations. The judicial response to these violations in terms of individual remedies was quite robust though not uniform: thirty-five cases resulted in evidence being excluded and twenty-four cases resulted in the even more drastic remedy of a stay of proceedings. Nine cases resulted in a sentence reduction. In fourteen of the cases, the court ordered no remedy.[219] There were also some civil actions seeking damages for unnecessary strip searches. In 2010, the Supreme Court awarded Can$5,000 in damages for one such search conducted in 2002 and without adverting to the ongoing compliance issue.[220]

None of the individual remedies of stays, exclusion of evidence, sentence reductions and damages ensured that all police services respected rights restricting the use of strip searches. In only one of eighty-nine cases did the trial judge even take the step to ask that the decision be conveyed to the chief of police in order to ensure that proper training be implemented. None of the cases required particular police services to respond with plans about how to reduce strip search violations in the future with better training and supervision.[221] As discussed in Section 6.2 of this chapter, the ICC and regional human rights courts employ a much broader range of remedies to respond to official misconduct.

Habeas corpus is a particularly ancient and important individual remedy. Eve Brensike Primus has concluded that statutory and judicial restrictions placed on habeas corpus in the United States has made it

[217] Office of the Independent Police Review Director, *Breaking the Golden Rule* (March 2019), p.35.

[218] Ibid., p.36: ten of the cases involved lack of supervisor authorization, fourteen lack of privacy during the search, ten done in the field without exigent circumstances and six lack of notes: all matters that were referenced in the Supreme Court's original 2001 judgement (*R.* v. *Golden*, [2001] 3 SCR 679).

[219] Ibid., p.42.

[220] *Ward* v. *Vancouver (City)*, 2010 SCC 27. I acted as counsel for the Asper Centre for Constitutional Rights in this case.

[221] *R.* v. *Wilson*, 2006 ONCJ 434 at paras 59–62.

almost useless as an individual remedy. She argues that the time has come for a more structural or systemic approach to habeas corpus. Her approach would, however, limit habeas corpus to cases where there are systemic and repeated violations of rights, abandoning its original purpose as an individual remedy.[222]

Brandon Garrett has argued that aggregation of rights litigation in the criminal justice system could have many benefits.[223] Some of these benefits are seen in recent COVID-19 related litigation. In one case, a preliminary injunction for a class of 800 vulnerable prisoners was obtained. It required them to be transferred or released from a dormitory style prison that could not allow for social distancing.[224] Canadian courts have been more resistant to a two-track approach to habeas corpus. They have held that a judge erred when he retained jurisdiction on a habeas corpus application to determine whether further detention of the applicant was justified.[225] This ruling suggests that Canadian judges cannot retain jurisdiction in a habeas corpus application, even if it raises complex issues concerning prisons. To be sure, release remains an important individual remedy, but in some cases it may be too blunt. The Canadian courts have largely dealt with the COVID-19 crisis through individual decisions with respect to bail.[226] They have not used habeas corpus or injunctions.[227] This places burdens on the courts and denies the benefit of combining individual and systemic relief.

[222] Eve Brensike Primus, "A Structural Vision of Habeas Corpus" (2010) 98 *Cal. L. Rev.* 1. She contemplates relief in the form of giving states the choice of remedying structural violations in a reasonable time or releasing the applicants: ibid., 32. In the American context this would also result in a dialogue between the federal and state courts: Robert M. Cover and T. Alexander Aleinikoff, "Dialectical Federalism: Habeas Corpus and the Court" (1977) 86 *Yale L. J.* 1035.

[223] Brandon L. Garrett, "Aggregation in Criminal Law" (2007) 95 *Cal. L. Rev.* 383; Brandon L. Garrett, "Aggregation and Constitutional Rights" (2012) 88 *Notre Dame L. Rev.* 2.

[224] *Williams* v. *Wilson*, 590 US (2020).

[225] *Ogiamien* v. *Ontario (Community Safety and Correctional Services)*, 2017 ONCA 839.

[226] See for example *R.* v. *Shingoose*, 2020 SKCA 45 and *R.* v. *Kazman*, 2020 ONCA 251 granting release of individuals and *R.* v. *Ledesma*, 2020 ABCA 194 and *R.* v. *Mohsenipour*, 2020 BCCA 112 denying release of individuals. In one case, a Court of Appeal judge held that there was no power to consider COVID related prison conditions when deciding whether to grant bail pending an appeal: *R.* v. *Robinson*, 2020 ABCA 222.

[227] For a decision holding that habeas corpus does not apply to the deprivation of liberty in the COVID-19 situation, see *Racicot c. Procureure générale du Québec*, 2020 QCCA 656 at para 21. For a decision denying habeas corpus in part by deferring to correctional officials, see *Nagle-Cummings* v. *Nova Scotia (Attorney General)*, 2020 NSSC 188. See also *Latham* v. *Canada*, 2020 FC 670 at para 71; *Canada (Public Safety and Emergency*

Courts may be particularly averse to ordering aggregate remedies in the criminal process even while recognizing that aggregate remedies are often sought and ordered in the civil and administrative process.[228]

6.4.3 *The Different Role of Causation Analysis in the Individual and Systemic Tracks*

With respect to the first compensatory track, causation analysis is central. The elaborate American jurisprudence that requires individual standing and denies exclusion of evidence if the evidence would inevitably have been discovered or could have been discovered through an independent source only makes sense if the purpose of the remedy is to compensate the accused for proven harms.[229] Causation is also critical in determining whether an abuse will make a fair trial impossible, thus meriting a stay of proceedings.[230] There must also be a causal connection between a violation and the offending behaviour when using sentence reductions as an individual remedy.[231]

With respect to second-track systemic remedies, a causal connection between the violation and some harm to the accused is much less important. Abusive conduct is no less abusive because it does not harm the accused either at the time or at a subsequent trial. The Canadian courts, unlike the American courts, have consistently recognized that a conclusion that the state could have obtained impugned evidence without violating rights could indicate that the state engaged in a serious and unnecessary violation that ought not to be repeated in the future.[232]

Preparedness) v. *Taino*, 2020 FC 427 (authorizing continued detention despite COVID-19 concerns).

228 See, for example, *Vancouver Fraser Port Authority* v. *Brett*, 2020 BCSC 876 granting interlocutory injunction to dismantle encampment of the homeless because of COVID-19 concerns. The Canadian courts have aggregated damage claims by prisoners in class actions and have in some cases distinguished between amounts awarded to compensate for past harms and to deter future violations. See *Reddock* v. *Canada (Attorney General)*, 2019 ONSC 5053 and *Brazeau* v. *Canada (Attorney General)*, 2020 ONCA 184 discussed *infra* Chapter 5, Section 5.2.

Damages can sometimes deter, but they differ from injunctions which allow courts to retain jurisdiction to ensure that the state complies with human rights.

229 Doernberg, "The Right of the People".

230 *R.* v. *Regan*, [2002] 1 SCR 297 at para 107, 121; *R.* v. *Maxwell*, 2010 UKSC 48 at para 13; *R.* v. *Wilson*, [2015] NZSC 189 at para 40.

231 *Ananyev and Others* v. *Russia*, Nos. 42525/07 and 60800/08, First Section Judgment, ECHR 10 January 2012 at para 225; *R.* v. *Nasogaluak*, 2010 SCC 6 at para 48.

232 *R.* v. *Collins*, [1987] 1 SCR 265; *R.* v. *Stillman*, [1997] 1 SCR 607 at para 105; *R.* v. *Coté*, [2011] 3 SCR 215 at para 70; *R.* v. *Cole*, 2012 SCC 53 at para 89.

Similarly, Elias CJ has persuasively argued in dissent that causation analysis is a distraction when determining whether a stay of proceedings is necessary to respond to abusive conduct such as police violence.[233]

The lack of proven harms to the accused, however, may help explain why courts have frequently been reluctant to order stays of proceedings simply as a future-orientated remedy. This also holds true for the exclusion of evidence with the exception of the American courts that embrace deterrence as the exclusive remedial purpose. A two-track approach would be open to considering the combined compensatory and deterrent justifications for a stay or exclusion. It would also recognize that these two remedies are blunt and likely ineffective remedies to prevent additional violations in the criminal process and be willing to explore whether declarations or injunctions were necessary.[234]

6.4.4 *National Examples of the Two-Track Approach*

The survey of remedial practice in Section 6.2 of this chapter provides support for the idea that elements of the two-track approach already exist in the law. Many courts distinguish between when remedies are necessary to protect the accused's rights and when they are necessary to respond to abusive conduct from the state.[235] Stays of proceeding jurisprudence in the UK, Canada and New Zealand all make a similar distinction. Similarly, exclusion of evidence started on a compensatory basis, but

[233] *R.* v. *Wilson*, [2015] NZSC 189 at para 123.

[234] William Stuntz suggested that in the early 1960s the United States Supreme Court started using exclusion of evidence but it "might have done well to choose another remedy . . . institutional injunctions – orders compelling police departments whose officers frequently violate search and seizure law to adopt better procedures". William Stuntz, *The Collapse of American Criminal Justice* (Cambridge: Harvard University Press, 2011), p.220. In the wake of the Rodney King riots, Congress enacted what is now 34 U.S.C. 12601, which allows the federal Attorney General to obtain "appropriate equitable or declaratory relief". Such investigations generally result in consent decrees approved, monitored and enforced by the court. They can deal with a wide range of matters including discrimination, use of force and community engagement. This experience again accords with remedies in the United States often being dependent on statutes and the structure of American federalism. See generally Civil Rights Division, US Department of Justice, "Pattern and Practice Police Reform Work 1994–Present" (January 2017), online (pdf): www.justice.gov/crt/file/922421/download

[235] On this dual approach to the use of stays of proceedings, see *R.* v. *Maxwell*, 2010 UKSC 48; *R.* v. *Regan*, [2002] 1 SCR 297; *R.* v. *Wilson*, [2015] NZSC 189. On the dual approach to exclusion of evidence, see *R.* v. *Collins*, [1987] 1 SCR 265; *R.* v. *Stillman*, [1997] 1 SCR 607.

now is only ordered after a balancing of interests that focuses on the seriousness of the violation. These domestic cases recognize the two-track approach, but tend to maintain them as watertight compartments.

6.4.5 *Away from Watertight Compartments and towards a Two-Track Approach*

As suggested in Chapter 5, Section 5.5.6, with respect to damages, courts should focus on whether remedies are justified to compensate for the harms caused by the violation. In close cases, however, courts may award an individual remedy such as a stay or exclusion that may not be fully justified as necessary to compensate the accused on the ground that it also signals to the state the seriousness of the violation. The seriousness of the violation should be evaluated both on the basis of adjudicative facts about why the violation occurred and legislative facts about what remedial steps the state has taken to respond to the violation and prevent similar violations in the future. In such cases, courts could provide both backward-looking compensatory and forward-looking preventative justifications for its remedies. Such an approach would give the state an incentive to implement any of a wide range of remedies open to it, including training and discipline of state officials that as Justice Scalia pointed out may be more effective in controlling police behaviour than exclusion of evidence.[236] Domestic criminal courts can become more concerned with preventing future violations while applying a light touch.

6.4.6 *Supra-national Examples of the Two-Track System*

Various supra-national courts are much closer than domestic courts in taking a two-track approach.

6.4.6.1 The International Criminal Court

As discussed in Section 6.2.1.3, the ICC stresses less drastic alternatives to stays and exclusion, but also directly targets official misconduct. With respect to the latter, it can use reprimands, fines and dismissals of prosecutors who engage in misconduct and can also ask for investigation of their misconduct. As Jenia Iochevia Turner has argued, the ICC has also demonstrated an interest in preventing prosecutorial misconduct by

[236] *Hudson* v. *Michigan*, 547 US 586 (2006) at 599.

successfully calling on the office of the prosecutor to proclaim a code of conduct.[237] In contrast, national courts often take a more hands off approach to prosecutorial misconduct.

The ICC's more overtly disciplinary and regulatory approach could be applied by domestic courts to repetitive police misconduct. To be sure, these approaches may not always be effective, but they would signal misconduct and allow for cycles of individual and systemic remedies. One challenge, including for the ICC, is to ensure that effective remedies to compensate the accused are provided while at the same time taking steps to prevent future violations.

6.4.6.2 Regional Human Rights Courts

The ECtHR has been flooded with claims related to delayed court proceedings. Its remedial approach, however, has been more balanced and consistent with the two-track approach than the approach of American and Canadian courts in relying on individual remedies in the form of stays of proceedings.

Consistent with the two-track approach, the ECtHR has distinguished between remedies designed to compensate litigants for delay and systemic remedies designed to prevent delay in the future. In one case, the Grand Chamber suggested that a state can "choose between a remedy which can expedite pending proceedings or a remedy post factum in damages for delay that has already occurred. While the former is preferred as it is preventative of delay, a compensatory remedy may be regarded as effective when the proceedings have already been excessively long and a preventative remedy did not exist".[238] The problem with this approach is that it suggests that states can select one of the backward-looking compensatory tracks or forward-looking preventive tracks instead of travelling down both at once. Indeed, Italy for quite a time focused on compensation in responding to trial delay but this, of course, failed to prevent new cases of excessive delay. The low level of damage awards that can be awarded also creates a risk of governments simply paying a tax for violating rights in the criminal process.

Many states have taken a two-track approach to remedying trial delay. *In Scordino* v. *Italy (No. 1)*,[239] the ECtHR noted that a variety of states including Austria, Spain, Poland and Slovakia have "understood the

[237] Turner, "The Accountability of International Prosecutors".

[238] *Macfarlane* v. *Ireland* [GC], No. 31333/06, Merits, [2010] ECHR 1072 at para 108.

[239] *Scordino* v. *Italy (No. 1)* [GC], No. 36813/97, [2006] V ECHR 11 at paras 186–188.

situation perfectly by choosing to combine two types of remedies, one designed to expedite the proceedings and the other to provide compensation". The Court typically establishes compensatory remedies while the Committee of Ministers works with the states on a broad range of preventive remedies.[240] This recognizes that the state is in a much better position than the court to use a wide range of general measures including selective decriminalization, bail reform, statutory reforms and the re-organization of prosecutorial services and the judiciary to combat delay. The Court has also stressed the importance of domestic states in providing effective remedies for delay. Although the Committee of Ministers as an executive and diplomatic body may have some advantages in encouraging states to adopt general measures, it could also play its role in a more transparent manner. This might be done by ordering the state to submit remedial plans and allowing the applicants and interveners to challenge the plan and present their own competing plans.

6.4.7 *The Two-Track Approach and the Rights of Crime Victims*

Another area where international courts have been more creative than domestic courts is ordering remedies to benefit crime victims. At the same time, they have been criticized for making orders that are not enforceable and have violated the separation of powers.[241] Concerns have also been expressed that reparations are often not sufficiently transformative with respect to gender violence.[242] Fortunately, the two-track approach provides a framework for making remedies for crime victims more workable and for recognizing that transformative remedies will require a dialogic approach that will engage with governments and society.

The individual remedy will be directed to the past. The ICC can order damages for crime victims but this requires a causal connection with the crime.[243] The ECtHR has also ordered damages to benefit crime

[240] Martin Kuijer, "The Right to a Fair Trial and the Council of Europe's Efforts" (2013) 13 *Hum. Rts. L. Rev*. 4. He also concludes, consistent with the two-track approach, that compensatory remedies have been more successful and consistent than preventive remedies adopted by the states.

[241] Huneeus, "Courts Resisting Courts".

[242] Rubio-Marin (ed.), *The Gender of Reparations*.

[243] *The Prosecutor* v. *Thomas Lubanga Dyilo*, ICC-01/04-01/06, Judgment with Amended Order for Reparations, (3 March 2015) (International Criminal Court, Appeals Chamber) at para 32

victims.[244] The IACtHR has ordered damages but also more creative forms of remedies including various forms of commemoration and acknowledgment of responsibility.[245] As with other first-track remedies, these remedies are well within the limits of judicial competence.

Courts should proceed more cautiously with preventive remedies to ensure that such rights violations do not continue in the future. As Huneeus has documented, states have frequently not complied with IACtHR's orders with respect to investigation, prosecution and punishment.[246] Although not in itself decisive, this is a sign that the Court is approaching the limits of its powers. Courts should not abandon the need for more ambitious systemic, preventive and even transformative measures with respect to crime victims. Nevertheless, they should initially take a deferential approach that encourages the state to develop its own measures in consultation with civil society and those that are meant to benefit from systemic remedies. This was done with some success by the IACtHR in the Cotton Field case examined in Section 6.2.5.2.[247] In some cases, courts should encourage consultation with respect to systemic remedies that can draw on the experience and expertise of crime victims and civil society. If the state fails to make reasonable efforts to prevent future violations, courts should consider more specific systemic orders. Those orders should also be made with the input of the affected parties. They should also respect the separation of powers and competing rights.

All courts should recognize that it is both impossible and improper to order that punishment occur, even as a remedy for state complicity or involvement in violations of the victim's human rights. As Anja Siebert-Fohr argues, the ECtHR appropriately stresses the need for proper investigations and laws and not "an individual right of the *victim* to have perpetrators criminally punished as a form of redress".[248] She contrasts

[244] See, for example, *Talpis* v. *Italy*, No. 41237/14, ECHR 2 March 2017 awarding victim of domestic violence whose rights were denied by the state €30,000 in non-pecuniary damages and €10,000 in costs.

[245] See, for example, *Massacre of Plan de Sanchez* v. *Guatemala* (2004), Reparations Judgement, Inter-Am. Ct. H.R (Ser. C), (19 November 2004) at para 100.

[246] Huneeus, "Courts Resisting Courts".

[247] *Gonzalez et al. ("Cotton Field")* v. *Mexico* (2009), Preliminary Objections, Merits, Reparations and Costs, Judgment, Inter-Am. Ct. H.R. (Ser. C), (16 November 2009).

[248] Anja Seibert-Fohr, *Prosecuting Serious Human Rights Violations* (Oxford: Oxford University Press, 2009), p.118. As she elaborates, "criminalization and the establishment of a law-enforcement machinery are sought in order to prevent repetition. This is an obligation which serves to aid prevention and thus is in the interests of society as a

this with the IACtHR jurisprudence, which is much closer to articulating state duties to investigate, prosecute and punish as an individual right.[249]

The two-track approach can allow courts to order compensation and various forms of satisfaction for crime victims while respecting the separation of powers and competing rights with respect to remedies to prevent future violations. When such systemic remedies fail, there will be a need for a new cycle of remedies.

6.4.8 *The Two-Track Approach and Remedial Failure*

The two-track approach is responsive to remedial failure. It should use new violations as a prompt for courts to issue compensatory remedies and revised and hopefully improved systemic remedies. Courts need to be more sensitive to chronic violations of rights in the criminal process. Supra-national courts, perhaps because of their own interest in limiting caseload, are more attentive to repetitive violations than domestic courts.

Domestic courts in high volume criminal justice systems decide thousands of requests for remedies. Nevertheless, trial judges and even appellate courts are reluctant to make linkages between them. They rarely make the same observations that supra-national courts do about repetitive violations. Decentralized domestic courts may lack the capacity to make linkages. They may also fear that making such linkages would be unfair to the government. This concern about pre-judgement should not, however, be a pressing concern at the remedial stage where a violation in the individual case has already been established.

As discussed above, the ECtHR has been quite effective in dealing with trial delay. There is, however, a danger that the low damages it awards could become a tax imposed on states for excessive delay. The Committee of Ministers may also have incentives to prematurely end supervision. An important safeguard against both these eventualities, however, is the

whole. . . . When the Court requests an investigation capable of leading to the punishment of those responsible it has been cautious not to proclaim an individual right of the victim for criminal punishment of the perpetrator. In those cases in which an inadequacy or lack of prosecution was criticized as contrary to the victim's rights it was not because of the lack of punishment". Ibid., p.148.

[249] *Öneryildiz* v. *Turkey* [GC], No. 48939/99, [2004] XII ECHR 79 at para 96 ("the national courts should not under any circumstances be prepared to allow life-endangering offences to go unpunished. This is essential for maintaining public confidence and ensuring adherence to the rule of law and for preventing any appearance of tolerance of or collusion in unlawful acts").

ability of litigants to go to the Court and ask for specific measures or individual remedies and better systemic remedies. This can result in cycles of reforms. In a delay case from Poland, the ECtHR recognized that "unreasonable length of proceedings in the respondent States is a multifaceted problem which may be caused by a range of factors of a legal, administrative or logistical nature".[250] It welcomed the general measures previously taken by Poland, but concluded it would not suspend pending cases under the pilot judgement procedure. This meant that Poland would have to pay damages in these cases even as it was given a two-year deadline to take new general measures to prevent similar violation in the future. Cycles of individual and systemic remedies can respond to remedial failure and the constant danger of backsliding on human rights and remedies.

6.5 Conclusion

Courts should first focus on whether a remedy is required to compensate and nullify the harms of a human rights violation. Competing social interests loom large with respect to remedies in the criminal process. The way courts balance interests, however, could be improved by using proportionality analysis used in other parts of human rights law. Vague social objectives and the seriousness of the offence charged should be rejected in this proportionality analysis. Domestic courts should follow the ICC in paying more attention to alternative remedies such as damages, referrals of state officials for discipline and sentence reductions. They should, however, avoid a mechanical search for the least drastic remedy. The overall balance stage provides a final safeguard against under-compensating the accused.

Courts should more deferentially consider second track systemic remedies. It is far from clear that the use of blunt and individual remedies such as exclusion of evidence or stays of proceedings will effectively achieve the systemic reform necessary to prevent violations in the future. Sometimes concerns about the repetition of violations will justify such remedies, but courts should consider alternative remedies including declarations and injunctions that are better suited to preventing future violations. Such a two-track approach employs the court's strength in responding to harms that the state has caused while recognizing that the

[250] *Rutkowski and Others* v. *Poland*, Nos. 72287/10, 13927/11 and 46187/11, ECHR 7 July 2015 at para 209.

executive and the legislature in consultation with society have better and more comprehensive tools to engage in reform measures to prevent repetitive violations.

The above two-track structure is already reflected in much remedial doctrine. Most courts recognize that stays are easier to justify when used to protect the accused's right to a fair trial and are more reluctant to use them to discipline or deter future violations. Courts in the United States, Canada, Ireland and New Zealand were all initially attracted to justifying exclusion of evidence on the grounds that it nullified the effects of the rights violation on the accused. They have now, however, moved towards tests that allow a more open-ended balancing of interests that should be sharpened by the use of proportionality analysis.

As suggested in Chapter 5 with respect to damages, two-track concerns about compensation and prevention should not be watertight compartments. In other words, a remedy that may not be quite justified solely on compensatory grounds could be warranted if the violation is serious or the state has failed to respond to it reasonably. Courts can give states incentives to take reasonable measures to prevent similar violations in the future without micro-managing those responses.

Domestic courts could learn from supra-national courts about the need to recognize and respond to repetitive violations, providing remedies for crime victims and using the fullest range of remedies in criminal cases. First-track remedies should compensate those individuals whose rights were violated. Systemic remedies need not be imposed in a heavy-handed manner. They should encourage the state to use a broad range of instruments to prevent similar violations in the future. They should draw on the expertise of the state in training and disciplining state officials. In the context of crime victims, systemic responses should draw on the experience and expertise of those victims and their supporters in civil society.

7

Declarations, Injunctions and the Declaration Plus

7.1 Introduction

Writing in 1976, Abram Chayes outlined a new form of public law litigation. It had started in the United States in school desegregation cases and had spread to cases dealing with conditions of confinement in custodial institutions.

The focus was on the future as opposed to the past. Specifically, the remedy was not dictated by past violations of rights. Rather it was a decree or injunction that had been "fashioned ad hoc". Such forward-looking decrees resembled legislation and administration more than traditional backward-looking adjudication.[1]

Chayes acknowledged that some questioned the legitimacy of the new form of public law litigation. Nevertheless, he suggested that the new approach might be justified because the judges were engaging in "a continuous and rather tentative dialogue"[2] with governments as well as an expanding range of participants in the lawsuit. The trial judge did not impose the details of the decrees from on high. Rather, the details were often negotiated between the parties. Procedural and remedial innovation was ultimately justified by the substantive justice of the claims made by minorities and prisoners and by the bureaucratic nature of modern government. American public law litigation – controversial from the start – has survived more than four decades of assault by legislatures[3] and by those who argue that it has allowed judges to exceed their legitimate role under the separation of powers.[4] It survives, however, by the thinnest of margins.

In 2011, the United States Supreme Court upheld in a 5–4 decision an order that California reduce prison overcrowding as a response to documented incidents of cruel and unusual punishment caused by deficient medical care for its inmates.[5] Today, academic defenders of public law litigation in the United States concede that it is best seen as "experimental" litigation that may only be justified given pervasive dysfunction in governance.[6] Some have predicted, however, that it may return given attempts by the Trump administration to dismantle the administrative state.[7]

[1] Abram Chayes, "The Role of the Judge in Public Law Litigation" (1976) 89 *Harv. L. Rev.* 7, 1294, 1297.

[2] Ibid., 1316.

[3] Prison Litigation Reform Act, 1996, Pub. L. No. 104–134, 110 Stat. 1321, 1367–68 (1996) (codified at 18 U.S.C. § 3626 (a) and (b) (2012)).

[4] Ross Sandler and David Schoenbrod, *Democracy by Decree: What Happens When Courts Run Government* (New Haven: Yale University Press, 2004); Donald Horowitz, *The Courts and Social Policy* (Washington: Brookings, 1977); John Yoo, "Who Measures the Chancellor's Foot: The Inherent Remedial Authority of the Federal Courts" (1996) 84 *Calif. L. Rev.* 1121.

[5] *Brown* v. *Plata*, 131 S.Ct. 1910 (2011).

[6] Charles Sabel and William Simon, "Destabilization Rights: How Public Law Litigation Succeeds" (2004) 117 *Harv. L. Rev.* 1016.

[7] Kathleen Noonan, Jonathan Lipson and William Simon, "Reforming Institutions: The Judicial Function in Bankruptcy and Public Law Litigation" (2019) 94 *Indiana L. J.* 491.

But public law litigation has done better as an American export. It was first embraced in India.[8] Public law litigation in India, as in the United States, has until recently focused almost exclusively on systemic remedies. At times, it has had unintended and even counter-productive effects such as authorizing evictions in the hope of better housing.[9] As in the California prison case, individual litigants who have been mistreated have not received individual remedies as courts focus on systemic reform such as reducing prison overcrowding. Public law litigation has also come to Canada, but often with judges deferring more to the state by using declarations than by retaining jurisdiction and issuing injunctions.[10]

Some other jurisdictions have engaged in public law litigation that follows a two-track approach in combining individual and systemic relief. The South African and Colombian Constitutional Courts have both combined individual and systemic relief. Litigants have been protected from eviction while governments were given time to engage with those who would benefit from systemic housing reforms. Individuals have received court ordered medical treatment while the court has engaged in a more deferential and inclusive process to achieve universal healthcare.

The two-track approach has also been used by supra-national courts. Both the Inter-American Court of Human Rights (IACtHR) and the European Court of Human Rights (ECtHR) have ordered individual remedies, such as compensation and necessary medical treatment, while also engaging with states around broader systemic reforms in an attempt to prevent similar rights violations in the future.[11] The IACtHR monitors compliance, whereas a Committee of Ministers administers complex relief under Article 46 of the European Convention on Human Rights. Although it remains dominant in the literature, there are many alternatives to the American model of public law litigation.

[8] P. N. Bhagwati, "Judicial Activism and Public Interest Litigation" (1985) 23 *Colum. J. Transnational L.* 561.

[9] Anuj Bhuwania, *Courting the People: Public Interest Litigation in Post-Emergency India* (Cambridge: Cambridge University Press, 2017).

[10] Kent Roach, "Charter Remedies" in Peter Oliver, Patrick Macklem and Nathalie Des Rosiers (eds.), *The Oxford Handbook of the Canadian Constitution* (New York: Oxford University Press, 2017), pp.689–692; Kent Roach, *Constitutional Remedies in Canada*, 2nd ed. (Toronto: Thomson Reuters, 2013), Chapters 12–13.

[11] Alexandra Huneeus, "Reforming the State from Afar: Structural Reform Litigation at the Human Rights Courts" (2015) 40 *Yale Int'l. L. J.* 1.

Public law litigation, however, remains a hard sell especially for domestic judges who are often reluctant to retain jurisdiction over a case.[12] Trial judges often face a stark choice between using declarations that will end their involvement in the case but may be the subject of continued dispute and ordering clear and precise injunctions which can be coercively enforced through the contempt power.

In this chapter, I will advocate for the use of a new intermediate remedy: the declaration plus.[13] This remedy combines the flexibility and deference to governments implicit in the declaration with the retention of jurisdiction that accompanies interim and final injunctions. It fills a gap when declarations alone would be ineffective in preventing rights violations but where a detailed injunction might demand too much of a court in confronting difficult polycentric problems. Retention of jurisdiction allows domestic courts, like supra-national adjudicators, to engage in naming and shaming should governments act unreasonably. It also allows courts, if necessary, to elaborate on what is required to comply with rights and to make their relief more specific and precise.

7.1.1 Outline of This Chapter

Section 7.2 of this chapter will discuss the practice of public law litigation starting in the United States but migrating to supra-national and other national courts. Contrary to popular caricatures of judges running schools and prisons, the reality is more nuanced. There are striking similarities between this practice of public law litigation and the understanding of international law as an iterative process than relies more on dialogue and persuasion than command. This part will also examine cases where public law litigation has gone off the rails because of an exclusive focus on systemic remedies that ignores individual litigants and the violations they have suffered. It will also be seen that the ECtHR and IACtHR, when they have confronted complex institutional cases, have used both individual and systemic remedies and appropriately recognized that the latter will be less dominated by the courts. This affirms how common concerns for the separation of powers and subsidiarity influence systemic remedies.

[12] See, for example, Beverley McLachlin, "The Charter: A New Role for the Judiciary" (1991) 29 *Atla. L. Rev.* 540, 552–553.

[13] See also Roach, *Constitutional Remedies in Canada*, p.12.700ff.

Section 7.3 will suggest that while courts should be cautious when dealing with polycentric or multi-faceted problems, they should not abstain from engaging with them. I will suggest that both domestic and supra-national courts should respect the important roles of legislatures and the executive in systemic reform. They should also recognize that negotiation, mediation and broad public participation can help resolve some of the complexities of polycentric issues.

Section 7.4 will present a new remedy: the declaration plus. It allows courts to articulate in a general sense what compliance with human rights requires while retaining jurisdiction to resolve disputes that may arise from the meaning of a declaration and from new evidence and changed circumstances. It avoids the need for courts to make very specific orders that give fair notice to defendants about what they must and must not do to avoid punishment for contempt. It will be suggested that the declaration plus is consistent with both the practice of supra-national courts and a few Canadian cases.

Section 7.5 will examine how complex institutional relief can be fitted into the two-track model advocated throughout the book. Public law litigation and structural injunctions are generally built on the back of multiple and repetitive human rights violations.[14] In the two-track approach, judges would be more willing to order individual relief while at the same time trying to fashion systemic relief to prevent future violations. Individual relief should redress past and continuing violations suffered by litigants and also include specific orders to prevent irreparable harm. Courts that order individual remedies can achieve some remedial success. They can also demonstrate the harms that dysfunctional state institutions cause to real people. At the same time, courts should engage with governments and the affected public in the development of longer-term systemic remedies. Judges who undertake the difficult task of systemic institutional reform should beware of the likelihood of remedial failure and when necessary take different approaches to prevent repetitive violations.

7.2 Practice

The traditional view of adjudication conceives of the court issuing one shot and simple remedies such as damages designed to restore identified

[14] Owen Fiss acknowledges that while the structural injunction is future orientated that there are reparative aspects to it: Owen Fiss, *The Civil Rights Injunction* (Bloomington: Indiana University Press, 1979).

plaintiffs to the position that they would have occupied but for the legal wrong done to them. Courts of equity, however, have always dealt with more complex issues that require them to retain jurisdiction. One example is bankruptcy proceedings where courts often put failing corporations into receivership, deal with multiple parties and manage complex polycentric issues.[15] The novelty of complex and systemic relief in public law litigation can easily be overstated. In the human rights context, there is a tendency to forget that courts only attempt structural reform of institutions in the context of repetitive and continued violations.

7.2.1 *American Public Law Litigation*

7.2.1.1 *Brown* v. *Board of Education II* and the Start of Public Law Litigation

The United States Supreme Court could not see itself to the conclusion that segregated schools were unconstitutional until it had decided to take a gradualist remedial approach.[16] This is an important reminder that those asking a court to recognize new and controversial rights ignore remedies at their peril. Ask for too much, and the court may simply reject the right. Ask for too little, and the remedy may be ineffective.

In *Brown* v. *Board of Education II*,[17] the plaintiffs, led by Thurgood Marshall, argued that the large numbers affected by *Brown* should not take away from the "personal and present rights" of the plaintiffs. Marshall stressed that "behind every numeral is a Negro child, suffering the effects" of segregation.[18] His argument appealed to a widely held

[15] Theodore Eisenberg and Stephen Yeazell, "The Ordinary and Extraordinary in Institutional Litigation" (1980) 93 *Harv. L. Rev.* 465; William Conklin and Jodi Morrison, "Public Law Issues in a Private Law World: The Appointment of a Receiver as a Case Study" (1986) 26 *Osgoode Hall L. J.* 45; Noonan, Lipson and Simon, "Reforming Institutions".

[16] Michael Klarman has concluded that "an informal deal had enabled the Court to be unanimous in *Brown I*. The more ambivalent judges supported the result in exchange for a gradualist remedy". Chief Justice Warren indicated that "the time element is important in the deep South". Justice Jackson stressed the limits of judicial remedies as did Justice Frankfurter, who observed that "a declaration of unconstitutionality is not a wand by which these transformations can be accomplished". Michael Klarman, *From Jim Crow to Civil Rights* (New York: Oxford University Press, 2004), pp.313, 302, 307, 311, 316.

[17] 349 US 294 (1955) [henceforward *Brown II*].

[18] Richard Kluger, *Simple Justice: The History of Brown* v. *Board of Education and Black America's Struggle for Equality* (New York: Vintage Books, 1975), p.728; Klarman, *From Jim Crow to Civil Rights*, p.316.

sense that courts are uniquely equipped to provide individual remedies. Nevertheless, the United States Supreme Court in *Brown II* rejected the individual remedy of ordering that the named litigants in the case be admitted into all-white schools, as it had done in prior cases ordering that African American litigants be admitted to universities.[19] Instead, the message that *Brown II* sent to governments and society was the ambiguous one of "all deliberate speed"[20] to achieve desegregation.

The Court stressed that local school boards had to make a prompt, reasonable and good faith start to full compliance with school desegregation. In response to the defiance it heard from lawyers representing the Southern states, the Court reminded them that disagreement with the constitutional principles in *Brown* was not a legitimate reason for delay. At the same time, the Court contemplated that the executive would "have the primary responsibility" for responding to local problems and proposing desegregation plans. The "courts will have to consider whether the action of school authorities constitutes good faith implementation of the governing constitutional principles".[21] The school boards would have to justify delay to trial judges. These judges would use their equitable powers to retain jurisdiction over the cases and to determine the adequacy of compliance plans.

Brown II failed. It was perceived at the time as backtracking from *Brown I*. Roger Carter, one of the plaintiff's lawyers, concluded that the Court's gradualist remedy in *Brown II* was "a grave mistake".[22] In the 1963–1964 school year, only 1.2 per cent of Black children in the South attended public schools with whites. The percentages were to increase with federal legislative action to 16.9 per cent in 1966–1967 and to 91.3 per cent in 1972–1973.[23]

[19] *Missouri ex rel. Gaines* v. *Canada et al.*, 305 US 337 (1938); *Sipuel* v. *Oklahoma*, 332 US 631 (1948); *Sweatt* v. *Painter*, 339 US 629 (1950); *McLaurin* v. *Oklahoma State Regents*, 339 US 637 (1950). Only Justices Black and Douglas showed support for a limited immediate remedy that would only apply to the named plaintiffs and not the entire class they represented: Klarman, *From Jim Crow to Civil Rights*, p.316.

[20] *Brown II* at 301.

[21] *Brown II* at 294.

[22] Robert L. Carter, "The Warren Court and Desegregation" (1968) 67(2) *Mich. L. Rev.* 236, 243.

[23] Gerald Rosenberg, *The Hollow Hope: Can Courts Bring about Social Change?*, 2nd ed. (Chicago: University of Chicago Press, 2008), p.50.

Although *Brown II* is derided today as "infamous",[24] it still establishes the basic procedural stance for public law litigation where courts retain jurisdiction and look primarily to the government to comply in good faith and to develop specific remedial plans.[25] As Wendy Parker has suggested, this asks those responsible for the violation to develop plans to remedy it.[26] The plan proposals are, however, subject to adversarial challenge.

Brown II appealed to the "practical flexibility" of equitable powers to adjust and reconcile the competing "public and private needs".[27] This contemplates a balancing of interests. However, the notion of "private needs" was not transparent. It was in tension with the Court's warning that objections to the underlying right was not a legitimate factor. As suggested in Chapter 1, Section 1.9, a more transparent approach to balancing would today employ proportionality reasoning.

The remedy contemplated in *Brown II* was systemic. In part, this reflected that the case involved combined litigation from different states, but it also reflected the Court's desire to take an incremental approach. In 1958, however, the Court insisted on an individual remedy in the famous *Cooper* v. *Aaron* case involving Central High School in Little Rock, Arkansas. All of the Justices signed an opinion that required the immediate desegregation of Central High by admitting nine Black students.[28] The high school was eventually desegregated, but by 1963 only 69 of its 7,700 students were Black.[29]

The Court's approach to the power of courts to order desegregation remedies waxed and waned in subsequent years. The breadth of equitable remedial powers allowed the courts subsequently to order remedies that went beyond the right to desegregated schools and included other remedial measures such as more funds for education.[30] These remedies were, however, not used until white flight to the suburbs made public school integration in the North often impossible. At the same time,

[24] Jim Chen, "With All Deliberate Speed: *Brown II* and Desegregation's Children" (2006) 24 *Law & Ineq.* 1, 3.

[25] Mark Tushnet, *Weak Courts, Strong Rights* (Princeton: Princeton University Press, 2004), pp.247–250.

[26] Wendy Parker, "The Supreme Court and Public Law Remedies: A Tale of Two Kansas Cities" (1999) 50 *Hastings L. J.* 475, 554–555.

[27] *Brown II* at 300.

[28] *Cooper* v. *Aaron*, 358 US 1 (1958) [henceforward *Cooper*].

[29] Rosenberg, *The Hollow Hope*, p.84.

[30] *Milliken* v. *Bradley II*, 433 US 267 (1977); *Missouri* v. *Jenkins*, 110 S.Ct. 1651 (1990).

equity was a double-edged sword. In the 1990s, the Court would appeal to equity to restrain remedial powers by stressing that courts should do no more than was necessary[31] and could relinquish jurisdiction because they had done all that was possible even if integration was not achieved.[32] Today, the Court seems to oppose the very idea of remedies designed to achieve racial balance.[33]

When the Court wanted to restrict remedies, especially metropolitan busing plans, it appealed to the traditional corrective ideal that the remedy could only respond to the proven effects of the violation.[34] Busing was a controversial systemic remedy. Judge Garrity in the Boston busing case acknowledged that "the plaintiffs in this case do not seek a remedy that would compensate them, as a class, for the injury already wrought by the defendants' long-practised racial discrimination. That injury, of course is immense ... The desegregation plan that the court orders cannot make the plaintiffs whole".[35]

Busing not only failed to make Black school children "whole". In some cases, it harmed them. Derrick Bell who acted for the plaintiffs in some of these cases increasingly became worried that the institutional litigator behind the case had placed its organizational interests in achieving integration over the educational and other needs of Black children.[36] Professor Bell would later imagine that the courts should have focused on improving educational quality for students left in predominately Black schools, such as improving teacher–pupil ratios and increasing the

[31] *Spallone* v. *United States*, 493 US 265 (1990).

[32] *Board of Education* v. *Dowell*, 498 US 237 (1991) at 248; *Freeman* v. *Pitts*, 503 US 467 (1992) at 492; *Missouri* v. *Jenkins*, 515 US 70 (1995) at 91.

[33] *Parents Involved in Community Schools* v. *Seattle School District*, 127 S.Ct. 2738 (2007) at 2769 where Chief Justice Roberts simplistically declared that "the way to stop discrimination on the basis of race is to stop discriminating on the basis of race" through race conscious remedies. This conclusory reasoning has rightly been criticized as "an Orwellian absurdity": Charles J. Jr. Ogletree and Susan Eaton, "From Little Rock to Seattle and Louisville: Is All Deliberate Speed Stuck in Reverse" (2008) 30(2) *U. Ark. Little Rock L. Rev.* 279, 287.

[34] *Milliken* v. *Bradley*, 418 US 717 (1974); *Missouri* v. *Jenkins*, 110 S.Ct. 1651 (1990); see generally Kent Roach, "The Limits of Corrective Justice and the Potential of Equity in Constitutional Remedies" (1991) 33 *Ariz. L. Rev.* 859.

[35] *Morgan* v. *Kerrigan*, 401 F. Supp. 216 (D. Mass., 1975) at 231. He placed the public-school system into receivership only returning it to local control in 1985; Peter Hoffer, *The Law's Conscience Equitable Constitutionalism in America* (Chapel Hill: University of North Carolina Press, 1999), p.193.

[36] Derick A. Bell Jr., "Serving Two Masters: Integration Ideals and Client Interests in School Desegregation Litigation" (1976) 85 *Yale L. J.* 470.

number of Black educators and paying them better while pursuing the longer systemic remedy of integration.[37] In other words, Bell's approach would have combined remedies that attempted to compensate for the harms of segregation while at the same time not abandoning the systemic remedy of an integrated non-discriminatory public-school system.

The desegregation cases have many remedial lessons. They laid the pattern for many subsequent cases involving complex institutional remedies. Courts could appeal to their equitable powers and discretion to justify a wide range of remedies. At the same time, they could also not escape the corrective ideal that remedies should be restricted to responding to harms caused by the specific violation. *Brown II* demonstrates the need for more transparency about approaches that balance interests. It must be clear that objections to rights are not a legitimate reason to limit remedies. The balancing of interests at the remedial stage should not allow a re-litigation of the original rights violation.

The desegregation cases also revealed the difficulty and perhaps even the impossibility of achieving systemic success in the face of executive, legislative and public opposition.[38] These cases also confirm the wisdom of Thurgood Marshall's warning to the Court in *Brown II* that it should not forget that they were dealing with real children who only had one chance for an education.[39] In other words, it affirms the importance of not forgetting about those individual litigants – such as the nine applicants in *Cooper* – who had established a rights violation and should receive some remedy.

7.2.1.2 Police Cases American courts dealt with police misconduct in the 1960s by extending the exclusionary remedy to the states. As discussed in Chapter 6, Section 6.4, the exclusionary remedy is a blunt and limited remedy in dealing with police misconduct. In a case in the 1970s, a trial judge found the Philadelphia police liable for a pattern of misconduct. The judge gave the city thirty days to submit a plan for revised complaints procedures. The Supreme Court reversed this attempt to reform policing. It held that the plaintiffs lacked standing and that

[37] Derrick Bell, *Silent Covenants: Brown* v. *Board of Education and the Unfulfilled Hopes for Racial Reform* (New York: Oxford University Press, 2005), pp.38–50.

[38] The courts were more effective when their decisions on segregation were linked with increased funding that the federal government made available for integrated schools: Rosenberg, *The Hollow Hope*, pp.97–99. Rosenberg also suggests that the courts provide "cover" for the executive to make reforms: ibid., p.102.

[39] Kluger, *Simple Justice*, p.728; Klarman, *From Jim Crow to Civil Rights*, p.316.

federalism prevented the Federal Court from using the extraordinary remedy of an injunction to prevent future violations.[40] In 1984, the Court held that a Black man who has been choked unconscious by the Los Angeles police after a traffic stop for a broken tail light did not have standing to seek injunctive relief.[41] This was because he had not established the likelihood that he would be subject to a similar choke hold in the future. This decision was made despite evidence of at least fifteen deaths caused by police chokeholds in Los Angeles.[42] In his dissent, Justice Marshall accurately noted that "the city is free to continue the policy indefinitely as long as it is willing to pay damages for the injuries and deaths that result".[43]

After the acquittal of four Los Angeles police officers in the beating of Rodney King, Congress enacted legislation allowing the United States Attorney General to seek declaratory and equitable relief if it established a pattern and practice of rights violations by local law enforcement.[44] After investigations, the federal Justice Department would often obtain consent decrees dealing with matters such as discrimination and the use of force. These decrees are approved and enforced by the court. Independent monitors are often appointed to measure compliance, sometimes for many years. Private individuals, however, cannot seek such remedies. This and related consent decrees that are available in cases involving the disabled fit into the American pattern of legislation as opposed to the courts playing a key role in either encouraging or discouraging judicial remedies. This illustrates that the strength of judicial review in the United States at least with respect to remedies often depends on legislative action.

7.2.1.3 Prison Cases The Court's gradualist approach in *Brown II* laid the foundation for litigation designed to bring American prisons into compliance with human rights.[45] Critics argued that these cases were

[40] *Rizzo* v.*Goode*, 423 US 362 (1976).

[41] *Los Angeles* v. *Lyons*, 461 US 95 (1983).

[42] Ibid.

[43] Ibid. at 113.

[44] See now 34 U.S.C. § 12601; see generally Civil Rights Division, US Department of Justice, "Pattern and Practice Police Reform Work: 1994 to Present" (2017), online (pdf): www.justice.gov/crt/file/922421/download; Myriam Gilles, "Reinventing Structural Reform: Deputizing Private Citizens in the Enforcement of Civil Rights" (2000) 100 *Colum. L. Rev.* 1384; Stephen Rushin, "Structural Reform Litigation in American Police Departments" (2015) 99 *Minn. L. Rev.* 1343.

[45] Mark Tushnet, "Public Law Litigation and the Ambiguities of *Brown*" (1992) 61 *Fordham L. Rev.* 23.

examples of judges becoming prison administrators, but the judicial role was much more nuanced. As contemplated in *Brown II*, courts would often ask the executive to devise remedial plans. When judges did not have the necessary information, they appointed expert administrators to act as masters or receivers to collect and analyse the needed information.[46] Following equitable traditions, courts were also prepared to modify their remedies if they had unanticipated consequences or if conditions changed. The Court allowed remedies that were designed to prevent violations, such as a thirty-day limit on solitary confinement,[47] rather than respond to the harms caused by the past violations. There was also an increasing trend toward consent decrees where courts approved and enforced remedial plans agreed to by the parties. The incremental reform achieved in these cases was done on the back of established rights violations that caused many prisoners to suffer and die in appalling prison conditions.

The opposition to complex prison litigation resulted in legislative backlash. Congress, with bi-partisan approval in 1996, enacted legislation that limited damage and injunctive remedies in cases brought by prisoners.[48] It limited one particularly unpopular remedy – the release of prisoners from overcrowded prisons. Under the legislation, only a special three-judge panel could order such a remedy and only if other remedies had been tried and failed. Judges were instructed to give substantial weight to public safety when making release decisions.[49] This continues the exceptional American practice of ordinary legislation restricting the remedies available for constitutional violations.[50] These legislative restrictions on judicial remedies were upheld from constitutional challenge.[51] They were successful in reducing prison litigation. In the early 1980s, 51 per cent and 43 per cent of prisoners in local and state prisons respectively were in institutions subject to judicial decree. By the mid-

[46] For an overview of these cases, see Malcolm Feeley and Edward Rubin, *Judicial Policy-Making and the Modern State* (Cambridge: Cambridge University Press, 1998).

[47] *Hutto* v. *Finney*, 437 US 678 (1978) (approving thirty-day limit on solitary confinement).

[48] Prison Litigation Reform Act of 1996, Pub. L. No. 104–134, 110 Stat. 1321, 1367–1368 (18 U.S.C. § 3626 (a) and (b) (2012)).

[49] 18 U.S.C. § 3626.

[50] It is also true that legislation sometimes encourages injunctions and other remedies, often by litigation by the Department of Justice. See Civil Rights Act of 1964, Pub. L. 88–352 Title IV; Violent Crime Control and Law Enforcement Act of 1994, H.R. 3355, Pub. L. 103–322 Title XXI.

[51] *Miller* v. *French*, 530 US 327 (2000).

2000s, only 20 per cent and 22 per cent of those in local and state prisons were subject to judicial supervision.[52]

7.2.1.4 Diminishing Enthusiasm for Public Law Litigation The American courts have demonstrated diminishing enthusiasm for public law litigation. The Court has warned trial judges not to become "enmeshed in the minutiae of prison operations".[53] It disapproved of the use of special masters and instead indicated that the executive itself should propose plans to respond to deficiencies in prisons.[54] In 1992, the Court categorically ruled out preventive or prophylactic remedies that went beyond constitutional entitlements by declaring: "[f]ederal courts may not order state or local governments, over their objection, to undertake a course of conduct not tailored to curing a constitutional violation that has been adjudicated".[55] This fit into the pattern also seen in school desegregation cases of courts using the corrective requirement of remedies being defined by the scope of the violation to limit injunctions.

The Court has stressed that "federal supervision of local school systems was intended as a temporary measure".[56] This drew a dissent from Justice Marshall, who argued that "the continued need for a decree" should "turn on whether the underlying purpose of the decree has been achieved".[57] Finally, the US Supreme Court has suggested that because of their effects on the separation of powers and federalism, structural injunctions aimed at institutions should be terminated earlier than injunctions addressing less complex issues.[58] This wrongly assumes that the more difficult task of systemic reform could be achieved more quickly than the simpler task of preventing or repairing more limited rights violations.

7.2.1.5 The California Prison Case In 2011, the US Supreme Court in a bitterly divided 5–4 decision upheld a decision of a special three-

52 Margo Schlanger, "Trends in Prison Litigation, as the PLRA Enters Adulthood" (2015) 5 *U.C. Irvine L. Rev.* 153, 169.

53 *Bell* v. *Wolfish*, 441 US 520 (1979) at 526.

54 *Lewis* v. *Casey*, 516 US 804 (1996).

55 *Ruffo* v. *Inmates of Sufolk County Jail*, 502 US 367 (1992) at 389. In 1978, the Court had earlier held that courts did not err in imposing a thirty-day limit on solitary confinement as a means to prevent cruel and unusual punishment: *Hutto* v. *Finney*, 437 US 678 (1978).

56 *Board of Education* v. *Dowell*, 498 US 237 (1991) at 248.

57 Ibid. at 267.

58 *Horne* v. *Flores*, 557 US 433 (2009); see generally Jason Parkin, "Aging Injunctions and the Legacy of Institutional Reform Litigation" (2017) 70 *Vanderbilt L. Rev.* 167.

judge panel that California be required to reduce in two years its prisons to 137.5 per cent capacity. The plaintiffs and some of the state's own experts supported a reduction to 130 per cent capacity, while a state panel recommended a less drastic reduction to 145 per cent capacity. The three judge panel split the difference. The Supreme Court upheld this exercise of remedial discretion, noting that there are "no scientific tools available to determine the precise population reduction necessary to remedy a constitutional violation of this sort".[59] In his dissent, Justice Scalia denounced the prisoner reduction order as "the most radical injunction issued by a Court in our nation's history" that would release "46,000 convicted criminals".[60]

The above description of the case might suggest that the California case was, like many other prison cases, about prison overcrowding. It was not. The California case merged two earlier lawsuits that alleged a failure of adequate healthcare in prisons leading to many documented premature and avoidable deaths of prisoners. The population reduction order expanded what was already a complex and polycentric problem involving struggles to hire more doctors and nurses and provide better facilities and funding for prison healthcare. The prison reduction remedy implicated virtually all of California's criminal justice system including its use of mandatory sentences and the interplay of state and local prisons. For example, California's criminal justice realignment has seen increased crowding in jails run by fifty-eight counties that were not included in the decree.[61] Nevertheless, the majority of the Supreme Court accepted the polycentric nature of the issue and held that it justified expanding the lawsuit into overcrowding issues. Justice Kennedy concluded: "[o]nly a multi-faceted approach aimed at many causes, including overcrowding, will yield a solution".[62] It will be suggested in Section 7.3 of this chapter, however, that the Court bit too deeply into the polycentric pie in this case and lost sight of the prisoners and their claims that they suffered inadequate healthcare.

As of November 2020, the case is still subject to judicial supervision. The 137.5 per cent population cap was achieved in 2015. Nevertheless, concerns about the adequacy of healthcare facilities and inadequate

[59] *Brown* v. *Plata*, 131 S.Ct. 1910 (2010) at 541.

[60] Ibid. at 550.

[61] Margo Schlanger, "Plata v. Brown and Realignment: Jails, Prisons, Courts and Politics" (2013) 48 *Harv. C.R.-C.L. L. Rev.* 145.

[62] Ibid. at 526.

suicide prevention remain.[63] An application for emergency relief related to COVID-19 has been denied.[64] Some scholars, such as Jonathan Simon, have praised *Brown* v. *Plata* as a remedy that addresses mass incarceration.[65] Others, however, point out that one possible response to caps on overcrowding has simply been to build new prisons.[66] What gets lost in this debate is the original complaint of the prisoners in the California case: inadequate physical and mental healthcare. It will be suggested below that Indian public law cases also demonstrate some of this same sense of drift in the search for systemic remedies that do not focus on the plight of individuals. Fortunately, there are other prison cases, including from supra-national courts, that combine individual and systemic remedies.

7.2.2 *The European Court of Human Rights*

The ECtHR takes a more deferential approach to prison reform than the American courts. It does not have the power to threaten contempt or even impose fines as a form of punitive damages if states do not comply with its judgements.[67] In a 2012 pilot judgement case (designed to respond to repetitive cases), the Court acknowledged, as in the California case, that overcrowding was at the root of the problem of poor prison conditions in Russia. Nevertheless, it stressed that the Court "does not have the capacity, nor is it appropriate to its function as an international court, to involve itself in detailed reforms".[68]

These issues would be resolved by negotiations conducted by the Committee of Ministers. The Court imposed deadlines of six and twelve months for Russia to submit reform plans including effective domestic remedies. Consistent with the two-track approach, these domestic laws would include both compensatory and preventive remedies. The Court awarded individual measures of €2,000 and €13,000 to the applicants

[63] *Coleman* v. *Brown*, 922 F. Supp. 2d 1004, 1008 (E.D. Cal./N.D. Cal., 2013).

[64] *Plata* v. *Newsom*, 2020 WL 1675775 (N.D. Cal., 2020); *Plata* v. *Newsom*, 2020 WL 1908776 (N.D. Cal., 2020).

[65] Jonathan Simon, *Mass Incarceration on Trial: A Remarkable Court Decision and the Future of American Prisons* (New York: New Press, 2014).

[66] Joshua Guetzkow and Eric Schoon, "If You Build It, They Will Fill It: The Consequences of Prison Overcrowding Litigation" (2015) 49(2) *L. & Soc. Rev.* 401.

[67] *Varnava and Others* v. *Turkey* [GC], No. 16064/90, [2009] V ECHR 13 at para 223.

[68] *Ananyev and Others* v. *Russia* [GC], Nos. 42525/07 and 60800/08, ECHR First Section Judgment, 10 January 2012 at paras 194, 214–231.

who were vulnerable because of health conditions.[69] The Court also refused to suspend similar cases under the pilot judgement procedure because of the seriousness of the violations and the need to "remind the respondent state on a regular basis of its obligations under the Convention".[70] The Committee of Ministers closed its examination of the case in December 2018. It noted that €763 million would be spent on prison upgrades. Moreover, steps had been taken to reduce pre-trial detention and implement domestic provisions providing for both compensatory and preventive remedies.[71] Some of the systemic remedies adopted by Russia were similar to those implemented by California in the wake of the prison reduction order. An important difference, however, is the use of individual remedies both in the ECtHR's judgement and in the reform legislation that Russia introduced. These individual remedies mean that should the Committee of Ministers have prematurely terminated its supervision that both Russian courts and eventually the ECtHR could award individual and systemic remedies for prison conditions, thus triggering another two-track cycle of reform.

In a case involving solitary confinement, the ECtHR ordered €10,000 in damages to a prisoner who had been held in solitary confinement from 1994 to 2006. Such an award is in itself inadequate given the profound damage caused by solitary confinement. The petitioner was also released after the judgement. The systemic response by France as supervised by the Committee of Ministers involved a combination of judicial, legislative and administrative measures limiting and regulating solitary confinement. The French courts expanded appeal rights and directed judges to inquire about the effects of solitary confinement on prisoners. Three legislative amendments were introduced limiting solitary confinement. Both lawyers and prison administrators were provided with copies of judgements and training on the new legal regime. The Committee of Ministers closed supervision on the basis that France's domestic remedies were now adequate.[72] As discussed in Chapter 1, Section 1.8, this case

[69] Ibid.

[70] Ibid. at para 236.

[71] *Ananyev and Others* v. *Russia* [GC], Nos. 42525/07 and 60800/08, ECHR Enhanced Procedure, online: https://hudoc.exec.coe.int/eng#{"EXECIdentifier":["004-14142"]}

[72] *Ramirez-Sanchez* v. *France*, No. 59450/00, Execution of the Judgment of the European Court of Human Rights, Ramirez Sanchez against France Judgment of 4 July 2006, Resolution CM/ResDH (2010)162, Adopted by the Committee of Ministers on 2 December 2010.

shows how supra-national concerns about respecting subsidiarity can dovetail with respect for the separation of powers.

The end of supervision by the Committee of Ministers in this and other prison cases is no guarantee of effectiveness going forward. A difference from the California case is that the willingness of courts to order individual remedies provides some safeguard should prison conditions not improve or worsen over time. The European cases allow the state to propose and implement a broad range of legislative and administrative remedies, albeit subject to supervision and publicity by the Committee of Ministers. They are also more concerned than the American case that individual applicants receive remedies including appropriate medical treatment when necessary.[73] Some of these orders have been by way of interim remedies.[74] The Committee of Ministers has visited prisons in some cases to verify that individual prisoners receive required medical treatment.[75] The European experience suggests that it is possible to combine individual and systemic remedies in combatting poor prison conditions.

7.2.3 The Inter-American Court of Human Rights

The IACtHR combines both individual and systemic remedies in its institutional cases. Unlike the ECtHR, the IACtHR monitors compliance with its own rulings, often issuing lengthy judgements years after the initial ruling,[76] as well as playing a mediating role in some closed

[73] *Tekin Yildiz* v. *Turkey* (1998), 52/1997/836/1042, ECHR 9 June 1998 at paras 62–66; *Dybeku* v. *Albania*, No. 41153/06, ECHR 18 December 2007 at paras 63–64, 41; *Kotsaftis* v. *Greece*, No. 39780/06, ECHR 12 June 2008 at para 50; *Slawomir Musial* v. *Poland*, No. 28300/06, ECHR 20 January 2009 at *Holds* para 4; *Gülay Çetin* v. *Turkey*, No. 44084/10, ECHR 5 March 2013 at paras 102–103; *Contrada* v. *Italy (No. 2)*, No. 7509/08, [2014] ECHR 142 at paras 97–103; *Mozer* v. *Moldova and Russia* [GC], No. 11138/10, ECHR 23 February 2016 at paras 225–235, 178.

[74] *Kondrulin* v. *Russia*, No. 12987/15, ECHR 20 September 2016 (finding that Russia breached interim measure under Rule 39 and subsequently Article 3 of the European Convention); *Aleksanyan* v. *Russia*, No. 46468/06, ECHR 22 December 2008; *Salakhov and Islyamova* v. *Ukraine*, No. 28005/08, ECHR 14 March 2013 at paras 216–224.

[75] Resolution CM/ResDH(2019)327, Six Cases against Italy, Adopted by the Committee of Ministers on 5 December 2019.

[76] *Baena-Ricardo et al.* v. *Panama* (2003), Judgment (Competence), Inter-Am. H.R (Ser. C), (28 November 2003) at paras 72–73, online (pdf): https://iachr.lls.edu/sites/default/files/iachr/Court_and_Commission_Documents/Baena-Ricardo%20et%20al.%20v.%20Panama.Competence.11.28.03.pdf Compliance hearings “can assist the Court in understanding the problems and challenges arising for the state in attempting to comply with

implementation sessions.[77] Also unlike the ECtHR, the IACtHR orders symbolic forms of reparation such as commemoration and public acknowledgements of responsibility.

Only five of eighty complex cases classified by Alexandra Huneeus to be the equivalent of structural injunctions have resulted in full compliance. Many of these problems relate to orders that require domestic prosecutors and courts to conduct investigations.[78] Professor Huneeus also notes that complex cases make up about a quarter of the IACtHR's contentious cases,[79] whereas estimates of complex cases under Article 46 of the European Convention range from 2 to 6 per cent of the ECtHR's much larger case load.[80] Professor Huneeus notes that the IACtHR involves the victims much more than does the European court. As she concludes, "the victim's participation could be viewed as a type of remedy in itself, and as a form of procedural justice".[81] Involving the victims of rights violations is good practice in all institutional cases. It can help counter the possibility that systemic remedies will not be responsive to the concerns of those who are meant to benefit from the remedy. Those who have had their rights violated have their own expertise that can supplement that of lawyers, judges, masters and bureaucrats.

One troubling pattern for the two-track approach is that governments are often more willing to pay damages to victims than to undertake more ambitious systemic reforms.[82] For example, Honduras paid US$123,000

its orders, as well as giving the opportunity to state authorities to put human faces to cases and better understand victims' views and situations." Clara Sandoval, Philip Leach and Rachel Murphy "Monitoring, Cajoling and Promoting Dialogue: What Role for Supranational Institutions in the Implementation of Individual Decisions?" (2020) 12 *J. of H.R. Prac.* 71 at 83.

[77] Huneeus, "Reforming the State from Afar", 31.

[78] Ibid., 36.

[79] Ibid., 15.

[80] Alice Donald and Anne-Katrin Speck, "The European Court of Human Rights' Remedial Practice and its Impact on the Execution of Judgments" (2019) 19(1) *Hum. Rts. L. Rev.* 83, 88.

[81] Huneeus, "Reforming the State from Afar", 37. See also Antkowiak and Gonza, *The American Convention on Human Rights* (New York: Oxford University Press, 2017), p.313; see also Jo Pasqualucci, *The Practice and Procedure of the Inter-American Court of Human Rights*, 2nd ed. (Cambridge: Cambridge University Press, 2013), pp.305–306 also noting low compliance with court orders for investigations.

[82] *Ximenes Lopes* v. *Brazil* (2006), (2017) 40(3) *Loy. L.A. Int'l & Comp. L. Rev.* 1371 (damages paid but not training or investigation after a death in a mental hospital); *Velez Loor* v. *Panama* (2010), (2014) 36 *Loy. L.A. Int'l & Comp. L. Rev.* 1143 (US$50,000 in damages paid but no compliance with general measures to separate immigration detainees from criminal detainees or improve conditions of detention); *Pacheco Teruel et al.* v. *Honduras*

in damages, but almost thirteen years after the original 2006 judgement had not complied with other remedial orders to investigate and improve prison conditions.[83] Sometimes, the state does not even pay damages. In a case involving fires and shootings that killed ten detainees and injured others in Paraguay, the Court awarded US$3.5 million in damages. It also ordered Paraguay to provide treatment and formulate a new policy with respect to youth in trouble with the law. Four years after the judgement, the Court found that only 18 per cent of the damages were paid and an overall lack of compliance with the systemic orders. The Court continues to supervise the case but young prisoners continue to die in the juvenile facility because of fires and use of force.[84] The Court has at least owned up to this remedial failure in its three follow-up judgements on compliance.

At the same time, it would be wrong to conclude that the IACtHR's general measures are never effective. Sometimes, even partial compliance can serve a valuable purpose. For example, Guatemala enacted new prison legislation paying more attention to rehabilitation after the Court had found a lack of compliance in two follow-up judgements.[85] In one case, the Court found compliance with general measures directed towards improving conditions of confinement in a specific prison and enactment of new prison legislation that complied with human rights standards. The Court also found compliance with respect to individual remedies for an American citizen wrongly convicted of terrorism.[86] In a Colombian case dealing with torture of prisoners, the state paid almost US$500,000 in damages, started criminal proceedings against one official, strengthened oversight and trained prison doctors.[87] Like the ECtHR, the IACtHR seems committed to both individual and systemic remedies in individual cases.

7.2.4 India

India was the first country to embrace public law litigation on the American model. Despite the Indian Supreme Court's embrace of

(2012), (2014) 36 *Loy. L.A. Int'l & Comp. L. Rev.* 1771 (referring to friendly monetary settlement but not reporting compliance on various general measures designed to improve prison conditions).

83 *López Álvarez* v. *Honduras* (2006), (2014) 36 *Loy. L.A. Int'l & Comp. L. Rev.* 2053.

84 *Juvenile Re-education Institute* v. *Paraguay* (2004), (2016) 38 *Loy. L.A. Int'l. and Comp. L. Rev.* 1446.

85 *Fermín Ramírez* v. *Guatemala* (2005), (2014) 36 *Loy. L.A. Int'l & Comp. L. Rev.* 2143.

86 *Lori Berensen Mejia* v. *Peru* (2004), (2014) 36 *Loy. L.A. Int'l & Comp. L. Rev.* 2609.

87 *Gutiérrez Soler* v. *Colombia* (2005), (2014) 36 *Loy. L.A. Int'l & Comp. L. Rev.* 1325.

public interest litigation, its ability to achieve meaningful remedies has been challenged. Upendra Baxi has noted that a 1986 case famous for recognizing housing rights nevertheless authorized evictions.[88] Anuj Bhuwania has criticized public interest litigation as a "slum demolition machine"[89] with those being evicted sometimes not even being made parties to the case and without provision of alternative accommodations. The editors of the 2016 *Oxford Handbook of the Indian Constitution* concluded that "the grandiosity of constitutional doctrine is not matched by the strength of remedies".[90]

The Supreme Court of India has recognized public interest litigation as "essentially a cooperative or collaborative effort on the part of the petitioner, the State or public authority and the court to secure observance of the constitutional or legal rights, benefits and privileges conferred upon the vulnerable sections of the community and to reach social justice to them".[91] The reference to cooperation and collaboration is consistent with what Abram Chayes identified in 1976 as one of the defining features of public law litigation in the United States: namely, that the remedy was often negotiated as opposed to being deduced from the rights violation or imposed by the judge.

In a 1988 case involving conditions of juvenile detention, the Supreme Court stated that it would proceed cautiously in recognition that "unduly harsh and coercive measures against the States and the authorities might themselves become counter-productive. In the matter of affirmative action, the willing co-operation must, as far as possible, be explored ... The coercive action would, of course, have to be initiated if persuasion fails".[92] In a 1996 prison case, the Court only provided vague directions to the government to consider a variety of reform proposals prepared by the Law Commission and other bodies.[93] This approach to remedies can, however, reduce the status and legitimacy of the court to one of an advisory body.

[88] Upendra Baxi, "Law, Politics and Constitutional Hegemony" in Sujit Choudhry, Madhav Khosla and Pratap Bhanu Mehta, *The Oxford Handbook of the Indian Constitution* (Oxford: Oxford University Press, 2016) in reference to *Olga Tellis* v. *Bombay*, (1986) 3 SCC 545.

[89] Bhuwania, *Courting the People*, pp.80, 85–87.

[90] Sujit Choudhry, Madhav Khosla and Pratap Bhanu Mehta, "Locating Indian Constitutionalism" in Choudhry, Khosla and Bhanu Mehta, *The Oxford Handbook*, p.9.

[91] *People's Union for Democratic Rights* v. *Union of India*, (1982) 3 SCC 235 at para 2.

[92] *Sheela Barse* v. *Union of India*, (1988) AIR 2211 at 2219.

[93] *Shri Rama Murthy* v. *State of Karnataka*, [1996] INSC 1660.

Another concern is the lack of participation by those whose rights have been violated and whom are supposed to benefit from the remedy. A 2018 case dealing with allegations of inhumane conditions in 1,382 different prisons was initiated by a letter from a former Supreme Court Justice. The Supreme Court directed the creation of an investigative commission headed by a retired Supreme Court Justice. Although much of the judgement dealt with the conditions for paying the judges who would conduct the investigation, the Court defended public interest litigation as giving "a voice to millions of marginalized Sections of society, women and children. Public interest litigation is one of the more important contributions of India to jurisprudence".[94] Although the procedural flexibility of Indian public law litigation has been defended as necessary to allow the poor to initiate cases, it can also be used in a way to maximize the interests of judges and amicus curia who belong to a very different class than those the remedy is supposed to benefit.[95]

In the 2018 prison case, the Indian Court focused on reducing overcrowding in prisons to 150 per cent capacity. It also ordered the creation of committees to limit the number of pre-trial detainees and recognized the need to fill over 27,000 vacant prison guard positions and improve access to medical facilities in prison. This followed the exclusively systemic approach taken in the California prison case. As will be discussed in Section 7.5.2, however, this case did move towards an individual first-track remedial approach when it ordered that courts investigate and, when appropriate, award damages for wrongful deaths in prisons.

In a 2015 case finding police torture, the Supreme Court issued quasi-legislative remedies,[96] such as ordering seven states to create human rights commissions. It also ordered the state to conduct investigations in cases involving death in custody.[97] Other orders made in the case, such

[94] *In Re: Inhuman Conditions in 1382 Prisons* v. *State of Assam* (2018), 18545/2013, (10) SCJ 35 at para 3.

[95] Jamie Cassels "Judicial Activism and Public Interest Litigation in India: Attempting the Impossible?" (1989) 37(3) *Amer. J. of Comp. Law* 495. On the use of the Supreme Court's power to initiate public law litigation on its own motion see Marc Galanter and Vasujith Ram "Suo Moto Intervention and the Indian Judiciary" in Gerald Rosenberg, Shishar Bail and Sudhir Krishnasawmy (eds.), *A Qualified Hope: The Indian Supreme Court and Progressive Social Change* (Cambridge: University of Cambridge Press, 2019) at 117.

[96] Surya Deva, "Public Interest Litigation in India" in Po Jen Yap and Holning Lau (eds.), *Public Interest Litigation in Asia* (London: Routledge, 2011), p.67.

[97] *Shri Dilip K. Basu* v. *State of West Bengal & Ors.*, [2015] INSC 508.

as requiring police to wear identifying badges and to install video cameras, seem more workable. The Court focused exclusively on guidelines to regulate the police without attention to the need for compensatory remedies for victims of police abuse.[98] To be sure, even partial compliance with some of the many systemic remedies ordered by the Indian Supreme Court could have considerable benefits.[99] Nevertheless, much Indian public law litigation focuses on systemic reforms without providing immediate or individual remedies. Nor do the cases always appear to be responsive to the concerns of those who are meant to benefit from the remedies.

7.2.5 South Africa

Like the Supreme Court of Canada,[100] the Constitutional Court of South Africa originally expressed a preference for declaratory relief. It overturned supervisory injunctions in two early cases dealing with housing and access to life-saving medicine.[101] In a case dealing with violence on commuter trains, the Court rejected a request to retain jurisdiction. It explained that "declaratory relief is of particular value in a constitutional democracy which enables courts to declare the law, on the one hand, but leave to the other arms of government, the executive and the legislature, the decision as to how best the law, once stated, should be observed".[102] The Court's decision not to retain jurisdiction in these early cases did not seem sensitive to the gravity of the harms of remedial failure.

The Court in the *Treatment Action* case upheld the ability of courts to retain supervisory jurisdiction if necessary to ensure an effective remedy. The Court suggested that retention of jurisdiction was not necessary in the particular case involving the supply of drugs to stop mother to child

[98] *People's Union for Civil Liberties* v. *State of Maharashtra* 2014, MANU/SC/0882/2014.

[99] Gerald Rosenberg, Shishar Bail and Sudhir Krishnasawmy, "Neither a Silver Bullet Nor a Hollow Hope" in Gerald Rosenberg, Shishar Bail and Sudhir Krishnasawmy (eds.), *A Qualified Hope: The Indian Supreme Court and Progressive Social Change* (Cambridge: University of Cambridge Press, 2019), pp.350–351.

[100] *Eldridge* v. *British Columbia*, [1997] 2 SCR 13; Kent Roach, "Remedial Consensus and Challenge: General Declarations and Delayed Declarations of Invalidity" (2002) 35 *U.B.C. Law Rev.* 211.

[101] *Government of the Republic of South Africa and Others* v. *Grootboom and Others*, 2000 (11) BCLR 1169 (CC); *Minister of Health* v. *Treatment Action Campaign (No. 2)*, [2002] ZACC 16.

[102] *Rail Commuters Action Group* v. *Transnet Ltd t/a Metrorail*, (2005) (2) SA 359 (CC) at para 108.

HIV transmission because governments had always followed declarations. As Geoff Budlender and I have argued elsewhere, this ignored that governments may fail to comply with rights because of incompetence and not simply defiance.[103] Incompetence is not, as some have suggested, a psychological state.[104] Rather, it is the frequent failure of large bureaucracies to comply with human rights because of a lack of resources and training. Governments may also fail to comply if the scope of the declaratory relief is too limited or too vague.

The Constitutional Court's failure to retain jurisdiction in *Treatment Action* (as the trial judge had) was a mistake. Commentators have observed that the implementation was "patchy at best". In some provinces, compliance did not start until there was litigation threatening contempt of court. Problems remain with the lack of programs to encourage mothers to get tested for HIV. Over 64,000 babies had HIV four years after the decision.[105] The costs of remedial failures in this case were especially grave.

In some subsequent cases, South African courts have retained jurisdiction. Following the original model in *Brown II*, they have required responsible officials to report back to the Court about their plans to facilitate prisoner voting[106] or the commutation of death sentences.[107] In a 2011 housing right case, the Court similarly required the municipality to file a report with the court by a specific date about the provision of alternative housing. Consistent with the adversarial process, it allowed the applicant to file a competing report.[108] In other housing rights cases that will be examined in Chapter 8, Section 8.2.6, the Court retained jurisdiction to provide the parties an opportunity to negotiate a systemic

103 Kent Roach and Geoff Budlender "Mandatory Relief and Supervisory Jurisdiction: When Is It Appropriate, Just and Equitable" (2005) 122 *S.A. L. J.* 325.

104 Helen Taylor, "Forcing the Court's Remedial Hand: Non-Compliance as a Catalyst for Remedial Innovation" (2019) 9 *Constitutional Ct. Rev.* 247, 252.

105 Amy Kapczynski and Jonathan M. Berger, "Story of the TAC Case: The Potential and Limits of Socio-Economic Rights Litigation in South Africa" in Deena Hurwitz and Margaret Slaitterwaite, *Human Rights Advocacy Stories* (New York: Foundation Press, 2009), p.70.

106 *August and Another* v. *Electoral Commission and Others*, [1999] ZACC 3 at para 39; *Minister of Home Affairs* v. *National Institute for Crime Prevention and the Reintegration of Offenders (NICRO) & Others*, [2004] ZACC 10 at *Order* para 5.

107 *Sibyia and Others* v. *Director Public Prosecutions: Johannesburg High Court and Others*, [2005] ZACC 6 at *Order* paras 2–6; *Sibiya and Others* v. *Director Public Prosecutions* [2006] ZACC 22 at paras 1–3.

108 *Nthabiseng Pheko Occupiers of Bapsfontein Informal Settlement* v. *Ekurhuleni Metropolitan Municipality*, [2011] ZACC 34.

remedy. This is consistent with Chayes' understanding of public law litigation as well as a new emphasis on participation by those who are supposed to benefit from the remedy.

In one case, a trial judge ordered the government to provide drugs to HIV-positive prisoners.[109] The judge ordered that the government submit a plan to the court that could be commented upon by the applicants. The judge also subsequently made an interim order requiring the drugs to be supplied. On appeal, the Court noted that the government's appeal was unlikely to succeed given that the plaintiffs had established a risk of irreparable harm. The Court also noted an affidavit filed on behalf of the prisoners detailing unnecessary deaths in prison from HIV-related causes. Justice Nicholson threatened contempt against some of the respondents that had not complied with the trial judge's orders and indicated that judges might have to resign if the central government was responsible for non-compliance.[110] A settlement between the parties occurred after the judgement.[111] The threat of contempt and even resignation seemed to have worked.

In recent years, South African courts have had to deliver on threats of punishment. In multiple cases involving contracting out social security payments, the Court issued a series of structural interdicts. A 2014 case would have supervised a new tendering process and placed various conditions on the government, such as no disruption of existing grants and respect for the privacy of personal data.[112] This case also recognized the reality of remedial delay. Justice Froneman observed: "a just and equitable remedy will not always lie in a simple choice between ordering correction and maintaining the existing position. It may lie somewhere in between".[113]

[109] On poor prison conditions in South Africa but the general lack of public interest litigation, see Rudolph Jansen and Emily Tendayi Achiume, "Prison Conditions in South Africa and the Role of Public Interest Litigation since 1994" (2011) 27(1) *S.A J. Hum. Rts.* 183.

[110] *N and others* v. *Government of Republic of South Africa and Others (No. 1)*, 2006 (6) SA 543 (D) at para 33.

[111] Sandra Liebenberg, *Socio-economic Rights: Adjudication under a Transformative Constitution* (Claremont, South Africa: Juta, 2010), pp.431–432.

[112] *AllPay Consolidated Investment Holdings (Pty) Ltd and Others* v. *Chief Executive Officer of the South African Social Security Agency and Others (No. 2)*, [2014] ZACC 12.

[113] Ibid. at para 39. The Court also stressed the importance of giving the parties continued access to the court in *AllPay Consolidated Investment Holdings (Pty) Ltd and Others* v. *Chief Executive Officer of the South African Social Security Agency and Others* (CCT 48/13) [2015] ZACC 7.

Rather than hold a new tendering process for private service providers, the government took over the distribution of payments and the Court ended its supervision. The government struggled to administer social security. The Court found another constitutional violation, but suspended the declaration of invalidity for a twelve-month period. During that time, social benefits had to be paid and the government was required to report to the Court every three months on its progress.[114] This approach, like that taken in Canada's *Reference re Manitoba Language Rights*,[115] demonstrates how a suspended declaration of invalidity requires a court to retain jurisdiction and to monitor and assist in the compliance process.

The South African court had continuing concerns about the government's performance. It hence appointed an auditor to monitor the payments of the grants.[116] The Court was candid that its new activism was "extraordinary" and only justified by "the very real threatened breach of the right of millions of people to social assistance . . . It is necessary to be frank about this exercise of our just and equitable remedial power. That power is not limitless and the order we make today pushes at its limits".[117] In this case, the Court was faced with a recalcitrant government as demonstrated by its requirement that the responsible Minister personally pay 20 per cent of the costs to the successful applicants and be considered for possible perjury prosecutions.[118]

In a 2019 case, the Constitutional Court upheld a lower court's order that granted a special master extensive powers to develop a plan and its budget for court approval with respect to land reform. The Court recognized that such a remedy was novel. Justice Cameron appealed to a

[114] See also *South African Social Security Agency and Another* v. *Minister of Social Development and Others*, [2018] ZACC 26 for an extension of an additional six months subject to exacting conditions.

[115] [1985] 1 SCR 721; supplemental reasons [1985] 2 SCR 347; [1990] 3 SCR 1417; [1992] 1 SCR 212. After declaring that most of Manitoba's laws were unconstitutional because they were only enacted in English, the Court retained jurisdiction for seven years and issued several supplementary decisions elaborating on the extent of Manitoba's obligations to translate laws into French. See generally Roach, Constitutional Remedies, paras 13.460–13.570.

[116] *Black Sash Trust* v. *Minister of Social Development and Others (Freedom under Law NPC Intervening)*, [2017] ZACC 8.

[117] Ibid. at paras 43, 51.

[118] *Black Sash Trust* v. *Minister of Social Development and Others (Freedom under Law NPC Intervening)*, [2018] ZACC 36 at paras 17–18. The Court held that such an order did not violate the separation of powers and would be governed by tests of bad faith and gross negligence.

flexible understanding of the separation of powers: "[i]n cases that cry out for effective relief, tagging a function as administrative or executive, in contradistinction to judicial, though always important, need not always be decisive". The judge elaborated that "when egregious infringements have occurred, the courts have had little choice in their duty to provide effective relief". In other words, the judicial role expands in response to "crises in governmental delivery, and not any judicial wish to exercise power".[119] The Court noted that American courts had frequently used special masters in public law litigation. Such experts may assist with either devising a remedial plan or implementing it. In implementing a remedy, the main task of a special master was to monitor rather than replace the executive.[120] Two judges of the Court, while also approving the use of special masters, concluded that determining the required budget was an executive function that should not be exercised by the court or its special master.[121]

There are signs that the South African courts are becoming more prescriptive and punitive in their approach to public law litigation. This may be warranted in the face of bureaucratic dysfunction, political neglect and intransigence.[122] At the same time, more prescriptive approaches that involve special masters may leave less room for the parties and others to shape the remedy.

7.2.6 Australia

In a case under the Victorian Charter of Rights and Freedoms, a judge not only issued declarations that the detention of juvenile offenders at an adult facility was unlawful but also issued prohibitive and mandatory injunctions prohibiting such detention and requiring transfer to a juvenile detention facility.[123] The judge was aware that the youth system

[119] *Mwelase and Others* v. *Director-General for the Department of Rural Development and Land Reform and Another*, [2019] ZACC 30 at para 48. See also Chapter 1, Section 1.8, for a similar discussion of the need for a flexible approach to the separation of powers.

[120] Ibid. at para 58.

[121] Ibid. at paras 104–108; see also Taylor, "Forcing the Court's Remedial Hand".

[122] One commentator has suggested that these recent cases "are best understood as remedial mechanisms aimed at addressing institutional dysfunction and political blockages that threaten rights at a systemic level, rather than punitive measures targeting the recalcitrance of individual public officials". Taylor, "Forcing the Court's Remedial Hand", 252.

[123] *Certain Children* v. *Minister for Families and Children & Ors (No. 2)*, [2017] VSC 251 at para 585.

was at capacity. The judge nevertheless questioned why the government had not devoted more resources to avoid what happened. The judge also restrained the prison authorities from using pepper spray on inmates until they had developed policies and guidelines on its use. The latter moves in the direction of a structural injunction but in ways that rely on the expertise of the executive and does not provide for any comment or participation by others. It also suggests that public interest litigation may emerge even in jurisdictions not known for judicial activism.

7.2.7 Summary

Public law litigation started in the United States with *Brown II* but has spread to many other democracies and even to supra-national courts. It does not involve judges running schools and prisons but rather fashioning remedies based on recommendations by the parties and sometimes by experts appointed as special masters. One danger of this approach, however, is that attempts at systemic reform may not always be responsive to the concerns and priorities of those the remedy is meant to benefit. Both the ECtHR and the IACtHR engage in public law litigation, but take a two-track approach that combines individual and systemic remedies.

7.3 Polycentric Problems and the Separation of Powers

In Chapter 1, Section 1.3.2, Lon Fuller's evolving approach to the ability of courts to deal with polycentric problems was discussed. To summarize, Fuller was originally attracted to an idea that courts, because of their focus on rights and wrongs, were ill equipped to deal with problems that had unanticipated effects. Such distributive issues were best left to private ordering or legislative and administrative decisions. At the same time, Fuller recognized that courts (especially at the remedial stage) could facilitate "extracurial processes of political adjustment and compromise" by avoiding judicial rulings that were "too exacting and comprehensive". At the same time, the end result should be "acceptable to the court".[124]

Fuller's approach anticipated the work of Abram Chayes[125] who concluded that judges in complex cases often mediated the competing

[124] Lon Fuller, *The Morality of Law* (New Haven: Yale University Press, 1969), p.178.
[125] Chayes, "The Role of the Judge".

claims of plaintiffs and governmental defendants. At the same time, Fuller, like Owen Fiss,[126] worried that judges who engaged in such mediation might lose sight of their obligations to adjudicate. Fuller warned that "courts have been instituted, not to mediate disputes, but to decide them . . . whereas mediation is directed toward *persons,* judgements of law are directed toward *acts*; it is acts, not people, that are declared proper or improper under the relevant provisions of law".[127]

Charles Sabel and William Simon recognize the polycentric nature of much litigation. They defend the ability of courts to address multiple issues "in a sequence determined in the course of problem-solving itself" so that over time judges address "reforms too complex to be addressed whole".[128] Their candid defence of public law litigation as destabilizing and experimental ignores Fuller's insight that much judicial legitimacy comes from focusing on remedying specific acts and wrongs – something that is the object of first-track remedies in my proposed two-track model.

Sabel and Simon are on firmer ground when they argue that the separation of powers critique of public law litigation is overly simplistic. In more recent work, Simon with colleagues has pointed out that courts face similar challenges in bankruptcy cases. In both cases, judges use their expertise in ensuring a fair process of dispute resolution between the stakeholders.[129] If such efforts to tackle polycentric problems are justified in bankruptcy, they should also be justified with respect to institutions that repetitively violate human rights.

The executive and the legislature are also involved in public law litigation. As Margo Schlanger has noted, officials in the executive are often happy to be the subject of public law litigation if it means they will receive adequate funds and training to do their jobs properly.[130] The American legislature has encouraged public law litigation in some contexts including with respect to the rights of the disabled and patterns and practices of police misconduct.[131] In other contexts, legislative and executive neglect and default may also help justify the court taking a more active role in managing an institution. Public law litigation is

[126] Owen Fiss, "The Forms of Justice" (1979) 93 *Harv. L. Rev.* 1.
[127] Lon Fuller, "Mediation – Its Forms and Functions" (1971) 44 *S. Cal. L. Rev.* 305, 328.
[128] Sabel and Simon, "Destabilization Rights", 1080.
[129] Noonan, Lipson and Simon, "Reforming Institutions".
[130] Margo Schlanger, "Beyond the Hero Judge: Institutional Reform Litigation as Litigation" (1999) 97 *Mich. L. Rev.* 6.
[131] Sandler and Schoenbrod, *Democracy by Decree.*

dialogic. It involves not only the judge but also the parties, including the executive.

Another objection to courts ordering remedies in institutional cases is that they will impact the polycentric budgeting processes of government. As the South African Constitutional Court has stated in the context of orders for temporary housing, the court's approach "cannot be restricted by budgetary and other decisions that may well have resulted from a mistaken understanding of constitutional or statutory obligations. In other words, it is not good enough for the City to state that it has not budgeted for something, if it should indeed have planned and budgeted for it in the fulfilment of its obligations".[132] There cannot be meaningful remedies in the institutional context without courts confronting some polycentric issues that require resources.

Nevertheless, Fuller's criticisms of the ability of courts to grapple with polycentric issues still holds weight with many judges. It makes them reluctant to retain supervisory jurisdiction. For example, former Canadian Supreme Court Chief Justice Beverley McLachlin has stated that "the image of a judge making day to day operational decisions in the running of a school – down to what kind of tennis balls to order in one case – is hardly one most Canadian judges would embrace".[133] It is perhaps not surprising that Canadian judges have avoided retaining jurisdiction and issuing injunctions in prison cases. Instead, they have employed individual remedies, such as damages and habeas corpus, and more recently suspended declarations of invalidity and large class action awards with respect to solitary confinement eventually leading to the enactment of reform legislation.[134]

Retention of jurisdiction and asking for information and assistance from states and parties is much less a problem with international judges. This is perhaps because they recognize that the law they administer is not a matter of enforceable command. In addition, regional human rights

[132] *City of Johannesburg Metropolitan Municipality* v. *Blue Moonlight Properties 39 (Pty) Ltd & Another*, [2011] ZACC 33 at para 74.

[133] McLachlin, "The Charter: A New Role for the Judiciary", 552–553.

[134] *British Columbia Civil Liberties Association* v. *Canada (Attorney General)*, 2019 BCCA 228 (declarations and suspended declarations of invalidity); *Canadian Civil Liberties Association* v. *Canada*, 2019 ONCA 243 (declaration of a fifteen-day limit on solitary confinement); *Pratt* v. *Nova Scotia (Attorney General)*, 2020 NSCA 39 (habeas corpus relief from solitary confinement); *Brazeau* v. *Canada* 2020 ONCA 184 (Can $ 20 million class action award in relation to harms caused by solitary confinement). The new reform legislation amends the corrections legislation. SC 2019 c. 27.

courts have a special interest in encouraging states to take actions to end repetitive violations that may swamp their limited resources in a way that domestic courts do not. In some ways, it is the comparative humility and dependence of international law judges that may make them more amenable to public law litigation. This is a paradox only to those who misconceive public law litigation as a simple act of judicial will and command.

7.3.1 The California Prison Case Re-visited

Although it is wrong to read Fuller as prohibiting all judicial encounters with polycentric problems, his cautions cannot be ignored. This allows us to revisit the California prison case discussed in Section 7.2.1.1.4. The lower court judgements provide much evidence about how courts could not avoid side issues such as the problems of attracting and retaining healthcare professionals in prisons. The mental healthcare case documented high numbers of prisoners with mental health issues and above average suicide rates. As late as 2018, the government was unsuccessfully appealing an order that it should transfer inmates to a mental health crisis bed within twenty-four hours of referral.[135] One judge justified putting the California prison system into receivership on the basis that it was "a textbook example of how majoritarian institutions sometimes fail to muster the will to protect a disenfranchised, stigmatized and unpopular subgroup of the population".[136] Three years later, however, 80 per cent of healthcare positions remained vacant.[137] It is clear that judges cannot turn away from such failing institutions that produce chronic rights violations.

My reservation about the California prison case is not that judges should not have retained jurisdiction or grappled with the polycentric issues involved in providing healthcare. It is that the three judge panel took on too much of the polycentric pie when they moved from the difficult task of improving prison healthcare to reducing prison capacity. This also subsequently applies to the majority of the United States Supreme Court. The move by both Courts introduced unnecessary side issues, such as whether prison release would threaten public safety. More fundamentally, however, it meant that California could eventually

[135] *Coleman* v. *Brown*, 756 Fed. Appx. 677 (9th Cir., 2018).
[136] As quoted in Simon, *Mass Incarceration on Trial*, p.107.
[137] Ibid., p.96.

comply with the Court's order that it reduce prison population to 137.5 per cent of capacity and still have prisons that provided inadequate healthcare that violated basic human rights.

The Court was not candid that it shifted to the prison reduction remedy because of failures to improve healthcare. This demonstrates a judicial reluctance to discuss or even admit remedial failure. The result was that prison reduction remedy was not responsive to the prisoners' original complaint. Courts that focus on ever widening circles of systemic reform may unintentionally lose sight of the underlying violations. They may also lose the legitimacy that comes from right to a remedy reasoning based in documented cases of horrific rights violations and the harm that they cause to specific litigants. The California prison case should have been about the unnecessary deaths of prisoners because of poor healthcare and not about the public safety effects of reducing the prison population.

The three-judge panel's 182-page judgement ordering the reduction to 137.5 per cent capacity focused on the question of whether the remedy was consistent with public safety.[138] Even the Supreme Court majority admitted that the public safety question, mandated by the terms of the Prisoner Litigation Reform Act, was speculative. A striking feature in reading the many judgements is how the aggrieved individuals – prisoners who needlessly died, suffered or committed self-harm because of inadequate mental healthcare – slid off the judicial and public radars. The voices of the prisoners and their needs and priorities were absent. My point is not that the courts cannot make rulings that affect polycentric policy issues, but only that they should be responsive to the rights violations that individuals have suffered.

Although overcrowding aggravates healthcare problems, the prison reduction remedy has distracted from the original focus on unnecessary deaths and suicides. Consistent with Fuller's claim that courts are at their best when dealing with allegations of rights and wrongs, the Court's judgement is most powerful when it occasionally goes beyond a sociological focus on public safety and a bureaucratic focus on healthcare metrics and examines the effects of cruel and unusual treatment on specific individuals. For example, Justice Kennedy notes that: a prisoner with severe abdominal pain died after a 5-week delay in referral to a specialist; a prisoner with "constant and extreme" chest pain died after an

[138] Ibid., p.112.

8-hour delay in evaluation by a doctor; and a prisoner died of testicular cancer after a "failure of MDs to work up for cancer in a young man with 17 months of testicular pain."[139]

Justice Alito in his dissent acknowledges these examples of "shockingly deficient medical care". He then attempts to dismiss them as mere "anecdotal evidence".[140] His approach ignores the task of the court in providing remedies for clear wrongs and rights violations. Justice Scalia in his dissent at least contemplated the possibility of individual remedies. He suggested that a judge could order the release of an individual prisoner if that was the only way the prisoner could obtain constitutionally required medical treatment.[141] As seen above, supra-national courts have employed such individual remedies alongside systemic remedies.

It remains an open and controversial question whether the courts were correct in concluding that the prison reduction remedy could be achieved without harming public safety. Even if the majority's predictions turn out to be correct, the case has expended both judicial resources and political capital on achieving a remedy that has not provided better healthcare for prisoners. There are also concerns that reducing the population of state prisoners has transferred some healthcare (and overcrowding) problems to local jails in fifty-eight different counties. It will be more difficult to achieve remedies for these problems on a county-by-county basis.

Courts can and must confront the polycentric issues raised by public law institutions that chronically violate rights. They should, however, be cautious and involve the parties in formulating workable and manageable remedies. They should be wary of taking on additional laudable systemic goals that are not responsive to the underlying rights violations and the priorities of those who are supposed to benefit from the remedy.

139 *Brown* v. *Plata*, 131 S.Ct. 1910 (2010) at 1925. He also poignantly observed: "[t]wo prisoners committed suicide by hanging after being placed in cells that had been identified as requiring a simple fix to remove attachment points that could support a noose. The repair was not made because doing so would involve removing prisoners from the cells, and there was no place to put them". Ibid. at 1934. The majority opinion also includes three pictures, one showing a telephone-like cage that prisoners awaiting a mental health bed were locked into.

140 Ibid. at 1962.

141 He explained that: "if the court determines that a particular prisoner is being denied constitutionally required medical treatment, and the release of that prisoner (and no other remedy) would enable him to obtain medical treatment, then the court can order his release; but a court may not order the release of prisoners who have suffered no violations of their constitutional rights, merely to make it less likely that that will happen to them in the future". Ibid. at 1958.

Public law litigation that results in evictions (as in India) or that promotes prisons operating significantly over capacity without adequate healthcare (as in the United States) is evidence of public law litigation that has lost its way. It will be suggested in Section 7.5 that a two-track approach that combines individual and systemic remedies can help public law litigation stay on track.

7.4 The Declaration Plus

7.4.1 The Advantages of Declaratory Relief

As discussed in Chapter 1, Section 1.4.1, Edwin Borchard was a prime advocate for the declaratory remedy. The eventual acceptance of this remedy can be seen as another instance of domestic courts learning from the practice of supra-national courts. The declaration has emerged as a widely used remedy in both supra-national and national human rights law. Emily Chiang has argued that American litigators should make greater use of declaratory relief. She points to the increasing restrictions on injunctive relief and the ability of broad declaratory relief to establish more wide-ranging precedents than fact specific injunctions.[142] These are valid points, but they discount that declaratory relief has not involved the retention of jurisdiction and with that the capacity for the court to manage compliance.[143]

The declaration has become a preferred remedy in those cases where governments have a variety of options in terms of complying with human rights in the future. The Supreme Court of Canada has explained that "a declaration will ensure that the appellants' rights are realized while, at the same time, leaving the government with the flexibility necessary to fashion a response which is suited to the circumstances".[144] In a case involving healthcare, the Supreme Court elaborated that "a declaration, as opposed to some kind of injunctive relief is the appropriate remedy in this case because there are a myriad of options available to the government that may rectify the unconstitutionality of the current system".[145]

[142] Emily Chiang, "Reviving the Declaratory Judgment: A New Path to Structural Reform" (2015) 63(3) *Buff. L. Rev.* 549.

[143] As recognized in Samuel L. Bray "The Myth of the Mild Declaratory Judgment" (2014) 63 *Duke L. J.* 1091 who, nevertheless, argues that declarations can be an important and meaningful remedy.

[144] *Mahe* v. *Alberta*, [1990] 1 SCR 342 at para 114.

[145] *Eldridge* v. *British Columbia*, [1997] 2 SCR 13 at para 96.

The South African Constitutional Court has made similar statements.[146] The United States Supreme Court has noted that declarations provide "a milder alternative to the injunction remedy".[147]

Declarations are often used as a dialogic device that allows the executive to decide what specific means to use to achieve the outcomes that courts have declared are required in order to comply with human rights. They assume that governments are both willing and competent to implement the declaration and that the declaration provides sufficient guidance about what should be done to comply with rights.

7.4.2 *The Disadvantages of Declaratory Relief*

The preference for declarations has not always worked despite somewhat complacent claims or assumptions by judges that Canadian and South African governments always comply with declarations.[148] For example, a judge in an early case declared solitary confinement to be cruel and unusual but provided no guidance about appropriate remedies.[149] Some of the corrective steps taken were perceived by prisoners as worsening their conditions.[150] After the Canadian government's delayed and lacklustre response to a declaration that it had violated the rights of Omar Khadr, a Canadian detained at Guantanamo Bay,[151] a trial judge held in follow-on litigation that the applicant had still not been given an effective remedy. The trial judge attempted to encourage consultation in the wake of general declarations by holding that the intended beneficiaries of the declaration have a legitimate expectation that the government will consult them. He then structured a plan submission process that allowed the

146 *Rail Commuters Action Group* v. *Transnet Ltd t/a Metrorail,* (2005) (2) SA 359 (CC) at para 108.

147 *Steffel* v. *Thompson*, 415 US 452, 467 (1974).

148 *Minister of Health* v. *Treatment Action Campaign (No. 2)*, [2002] ZACC 16; *Khadr* v. *Canada (Prime Minister)*, [2010] 1 SCR 44.

149 *McCann* v. *The Queen*, 1975 CanLII 1104 (FC).

150 Michael Jackson, *Prisoners of Isolation* (Toronto: University of Toronto Press, 1980), pp.141–142.

151 The Court reversed an injunction that Canada make a diplomatic request to the United States for Khadr's return. In reasoned that the injunction "gives too little weight" to the executives responsibility for "Canada's broader national interests" and that a declaration gives the government "a measure of discretion in deciding how to respond". *Khadr* v. *Canada (Prime Minister),* [2010] 1 SCR 44 at para 2. After a delay the government, which was opposed to Khadr's return to Canada, asked that the results of Khadr's interrogation by Canadian officials not be used in American military commission proceedings.

applicant to comment on the government's proposed course of action before the judge issued his final order, which could have included an injunction that the government ask the United States to return Khadr to Canada. The judge never issued that order because his judgement was stayed pending appeal and the appeal was declared moot after Omar Khadr pled guilty to an offence at Guantanamo in a successful attempt to be returned to Canada.[152] Declarations do not always get the job done and Khadr's self-help remedy by pleading guilty was a far more effective remedy than the Supreme Court's declaration. In its next case, the Canadian Supreme Court issued a mandatory order against a Minister to allow the operation of a safer injection site, but on the basis that this was the only result on the facts of the case that was consistent with human rights.[153]

A majority of the Supreme Court of Canada relied on declarations of past equality rights and freedom of expression violations in a case where customs officials had targeted and profiled imports to a small bookstore catering to sexual minorities. The majority denied the request that the Court retain jurisdiction concluding, "with some hesitation, that it is not practicable" to order "a more structured . . . remedy".[154] The Court noted that much time had elapsed since the trial judge's findings of fact and that a declaration about past violations would provide "a firm basis" should additional litigation be necessary. The declaration attempted to identify some of the causes of the past violations by singling out inadequate training of customs officials on the legal definition of obscenity as well as the failure to provide the bookstore with sufficient reasons and a speedy administrative appeal process.[155]

[152] *Khadr* v. *Canada (Prime Minister)*, [2010] 4 FCR 36 decision stayed pending appeal [2012] FCR 396 and appeal declared moot; see generally Roach, Constitutional Remedies in Canada, p.12.810ff; Kent Roach, "The Supreme Court at the Bar of Politics: The Afghan Detainee and Omar Khadr Cases" (2010) 28 *N.J.C.L.* 115; Amir Attaran and Jon Khan, "Solving the 'Khadr' Problem: Retention of Jurisdiction- A Comparative Analysis" (2015) 34 *N.J.C.L.* 145.

[153] *Canada* v. *PHS Community Services* [2011] 3 SCR 134 at para 152.

[154] *Little Sisters Book and Art Emporium* v. *Canada (Minister of Justice)*, 2000 2 SCC 69 at para 157.

[155] Ibid. at para 156. One factor here may be that the bookstore originally only sought declaratory relief. They requested retention of jurisdiction after the trial judgement but this request was denied by the trial judge on the basis that customs was implementing a process toward the necessary reforms. The trial judge did, however, order that customs no longer impose a look-out on the store's imports: *Little Sisters Book and Art Emporium* v. *Canada*, (1996) 134 DLR (4th) 293 (BCSC).

Justice Iacobucci issued a strong dissent in the above case. He noted that while declarations were flexible and deferential to governments, they also suffer "from vagueness, insufficient remedial specificity, an inability to monitor compliance and an ensuing need for subsequent litigation to ensure compliance".[156] He warned that declarations that ended the court's jurisdiction over the case would be inadequate in cases where administrators "have proven themselves unworthy of trust".[157] His warnings proved prophetic. The customs bureaucracy continued to prohibit books ordered by the small bookstore. The bookstore was required to start new litigation. Unfortunately, the subsequent litigation was never decided on the merits because the bookstore was forced to abandon it after the Supreme Court ruled that it was not entitled to advanced costs to finance the costly litigation.[158] Again, the Supreme Court's use of a declaration seems not to have produced an effective remedy. At the very least, it did not resolve the dispute between the rights-holder and the government.

7.4.3 *The Often Impossible Choice between General Declarations and Specific Injunctions*

Owen Fiss has recognized that "in many situations, injunctions and declaratory judgments are functionally equivalent".[159] The difference is that injunctions can be enforced through punitive powers of civil or criminal contempt. This "gives the defendant, one more chance" while the declaration that has generally ended the court's involvement in the case "gives the defendant two more chances".[160]

Although Fiss downplays this because of his focus on structural injunctions,[161] injunctions may often not be appropriate because they require specificity to provide fair notice to the defendants. Although the

156 *Little Sisters Book and Art Emporium* v. *Canada (Minister of Justice)*, 2000 2 SCC 69 at para 248.

157 Ibid. at para 257.

158 *Little Sisters Book and Art Emporium* v. *Canada (Commissioner of Customs and Revenue)*, [2007] 1 SCR 38.

159 Owen Fiss, "Dombrowski" (1977) 86 *Yale L. J.* 1103, 1122.

160 Ibid., 1124.

161 He wrote that "[t]he issuance of the injunction is not so much a coercive act, such as issuing a command, as it is a declaration that henceforth the court will *direct* or *manage* the reconstruction of the social institution, in order to bring it into conformity with the Constitution. The first ploy of any manager is to induce collaboration; authoritative directives are reserved as a last resort". Fiss, *The Civil Rights Injunction*, p.37.

detailed command and controls of American structural injunctions have often been interpreted as imposing the will of the "heroic judge"[162] or the results of negotiation,[163] they are also a requirement of due process in relation to possible contempt sanctions. The result is that courts are often faced with a stark choice between a general declaration and a specific injunction.

In their influential 2004 article, Sabel and Simon have suggested that contemporary public law litigation has moved away from "command and control" to focus more on "flexible and provisional norms with procedures for ongoing stakeholder participation and measured accountability".[164] Despite some disputes about the accuracy of their account,[165] it is clear that specific orders, including the one in the California prison case, place considerable demands on the limited information and expertise of judges. They may also require the judge to delegate the details of the remedy either to the parties or a special master, thus making the process technocratic and perhaps divorced from the priorities of those the remedy is intended to benefit. Finally, they may also encourage the executive to observe only the letter of the injunction and not its broader spirit.[166] The attractive vision of a dynamic, transparent and dialogic approach to public law relief[167] can be advanced by a remedy that combines the generality and flexibility of declarations with the retention of jurisdiction that in most domestic systems only occurs when the court is prepared to order specific injunctions. I have called such a new remedy "the declaration plus".[168]

7.4.4 The Declaration Plus: A New Remedy between the Declaration and the Injunction

What is the declaration plus? It is a declaration that provides in general terms what is required to ensure compliance with rights while the court

[162] Schlanger, "Beyond the Hero Judge".
[163] Chayes, "The Role of the Judge".
[164] Sabel and Simon, "Destabilization Rights", 1019.
[165] Margo Schlanger, "Civil Rights Injunctions over Time: A Case Study of Jail and Prison Court Orders" (2006) 81 *N.Y.U. L. Rev.* 550, 623–626.
[166] Sabel and Simon, "Destabilization Rights", 1053.
[167] Public reporting and monitoring responds to concerns that a "controlling group" within the litigation will capture the litigation: Sandler and Schoenbrod, *Democracy by Decree*, pp.113–161.
[168] Roach, Constitutional Remedies in Canada, at 12.700ff.

retains jurisdiction and the ability to alter relief and resolve disputes arising from the declaration in a procedurally fair manner. The declaration plus may already be available under American federal law because of a provision that allows a plaintiff who obtains a declaration to return to court and have the court grant "further necessary or proper relief based on a declaratory judgment".[169]

A declaration plus would focus on broad outcomes and goals while leaving the means to achieve them subject to the state's decision. It would also allow for stakeholder participation in the form of comments and challenges to reports by the state to the court about its plans and progress. The declaration plus recognizes that judges will not generally have sufficient information or expertise to impose detailed relief. It also recognizes that judges rarely use their contempt powers.[170]

The declaration plus is motivated by the legal process aspiration to allow courts to do what they do best: elaborate the meaning of rights and respond to dynamic contexts in a procedurally fair and evidence-based manner. It also allows governments to do what they do best: use their expertise and resources to select the means to implement the general goals of rights compliance articulated by the courts. It also allows rights seekers to do what they do best: monitor compliance, negotiate with governments and when necessary to bring disputes to the judge's attention.

Consistent with a theme in this book, the declaration plus would be a domestic version of a remedial process that is routine in international law. Supra-national adjudicators do not attempt specific command and control strategies. They know that they lack the information necessary to formulate them and the contempt powers necessary to enforce them. They also routinely retain jurisdiction and ask states and parties to report back to them about their response to proven rights violations.

[169] 28 U.S.C. s.2202 (2012). For an examination of relatively rare use of this power see Bray, "The Myth of the Mild Declaratory Judgment" at 1111–1113.

[170] On the reluctance of judges to use contempt in part because of its counterproductive effects, see James M. Hirschhorn, "Where the Money Is: Remedies to Finance Compliance with Strict Structural Injunctions" (1984) 82(8) *Mich. L. Rev.* 1815, 1841; Larry Yackle, *Reform and Regret: The Story of Federal Involvement in the Alabama Prison System* (New York: Oxford University Press, 1989), p.219ff (noting no evidence of any official going to jail for contempt for defying a structural injunction issued by a Federal Court); see also Nicholas Parrillo, "The Endgame of Administrative Law: Governmental Disobedience and the Judicial Contempt Power" (2018) 131 *Harv. L. Rev.* 685.

Those who embrace a stark dualist approach that separates international and domestic law may argue that the declaration plus will reduce domestic courts to a pleader without even the threat of enforcement powers. Such criticisms, however, ignore that domestic courts already use declarations and in many cases governments try to comply with their requirements. They also discount the ability of judges who retain jurisdiction if necessary to place contempt powers back on the table if and when they are prepared to make specific orders that can fairly be enforced through contempt powers. By that time in the dispute, the judge likely will have become familiar enough with the context to make specific orders that provide fair notice. For example, judges who issue declarations plus and retain jurisdiction could, if necessary, order injunctions to prevent irreparable harm to rights during a longer-term process of systemic reform.

7.4.5 The Canadian Experience with the Declaration Plus

The Canadian courts have been struggling to recognize an intermediate remedy between a general declaration that ends the court's involvement and injunctions that must be specific enough to give fair notice for contempt.

From 1985 to 1992, the Supreme Court of Canada retained jurisdiction to ensure that Manitoba's laws were translated into French in compliance with constitutional obligations.[171] The Court encouraged the parties to establish a schedule for translation by consent. In several hearings, the Court elaborated on the extent of translation requirements in response to

[171] The Court rejected a more experimental approach urged by some of the applicants and supporting intervenors that would have declared all of Manitoba's unilingual laws to be of no force and effect. The Court reasoned that this approach was inconsistent with the judicial role because it would rely "on a future and uncertain event", namely a constitutional amendment and use of executive power to enforce the Constitution: *Reference re Manitoba Language Rights,* [1985] 1 SCR 721 at 753. This approach was experimental in that it would have likely removed political blockages caused by the Conservative opposition who had thwarted a vote on a constitutional amendment by refusing to answer the division bells. The amendment would essentially have replaced any obligation to translate old laws for contemporary guarantees of French language services from the Manitoba government. See Gordon Mackintosh, "Heading Off Bilodeau: Attempting Constitutional Amendment" (1986) 15 *Man. L. J.* 271; Kent Roach, "The Judicial, Legislative and Executive Roles in Enforcing the Constitution: Three Manitoba Stories" in Richard Albert and David Cameron (eds.) *Canada in the World* (Cambridge: Cambridge University Press, 2018), pp.280–294.

what it characterized as genuine disputes about its original 1985 ruling. In 1990, the Court extended the time necessary to translate non-statutory legal instruments.[172] There was never any threat of the Manitoba government being held in contempt, though the Court did rule in 1992 that any future unilingual instrument would immediately be held of no force and effect. This focused on preventing new harms to language rights while recognizing the need for delay to achieve the massive translation process.[173] It is possible to see this case as a declaration plus because the Court declared the required outcome and retained jurisdiction without making specific orders that could be enforced by contempt. It resolved several subsequent disputes about what the rights in question required in a transparent and fair manner that resulted in subsequent judgements. The Court in 1992 made clear that it would not tolerate new violations of minority language rights.

Although it was defended as a structural injunction, the leading Canadian case of *Doucet-Boudreau* v. *Nova Scotia*[174] also combined the generality of a declaration with the trial judge's retention of jurisdiction. The case involved a long-standing failure in Nova Scotia to provide minority language public education. The Nova Scotia case involved five different locations, multiple parties including a province-wide francophone school board and a variety of means of achieving homogenous French language education, including the construction of new schools. The trial judge made an order that, while defended as an injunction, simply required the governmental defendants to make "best efforts" to comply with rights. Such a vague and aspirational order would have been difficult to enforce by contempt. At the same time, the trial judge required the government to submit progress reports in affidavit form that would be subject to adversarial challenge by the parties. The trial judge's "best efforts" order avoided what Fuller recognized as the evil of laws that ordered the impossible. It was based more on what he defended as a morality "of aspiration".[175] It was also consistent with Bickel's defence of judicial supervision of gradual desegregation where the judicial task "was not to punish law breakers but to diminish their number".[176]

[172] *Reference re Manitoba Language Reference*, [1990] 3 SCR 1417.
[173] *Reference re Manitoba Language Reference*, [1992] 1 SCR 212 at 233.
[174] [2003] 3 SCR 3.
[175] Fuller, *The Morality of Law*, p.170.
[176] Alexander Bickel, *The Least Dangerous Branch* (New Haven: Yale University Press, 1986), p.251.

Nova Scotia objected to the increased accountability that came with the retention of jurisdiction. It appealed the trial judge's retention of jurisdiction on the basis that the trial judge was functus. A majority of the Court of Appeal allowed the appeal. It displayed a long-standing antipathy among some Canadian judges towards American-style public law litigation. One dissenting judge defended the trial judge's approach as a "creative blending of declaratory and injunctive relief"[177].

The Supreme Court of Canada restored the trial judge's approach in a bitterly divided 5–4 decision. Justices Iacobucci and Arbour stressed the need to respect general principles about the need for effective and responsive remedies, adherence to a flexible understanding of the separation of power and fairness towards the defendant.[178] They stressed that the trial judge's best efforts order had left "detailed choices of means largely to the executive".[179] They concluded that while the reporting order could have been more precisely worded, it was not unfair to the government. As Justice Rouleau and Linsey Sherman have commented: "retaining jurisdiction allows the court to refrain from making decisions on the basis of incomplete information and on matters in which it has little expertise".[180] It also creates space for creative solutions such as using existing English language schools for French language instruction.

The four dissenting judges argued that the trial judge had exceeded his legitimate judicial role. They disparaged the progress report hearings as "a cross between a mini-trial, an informal meeting with the judge and some kind of mediation session".[181] In some ways, this echoed Fuller's observation that a mixed form of ordering could deal with the

[177] *Nova Scotia* v. *Doucet-Boudreau,* (2001) 203 DLR (4th) 128 at para 70.

[178] The majority elaborated that an appropriate and just remedy under s.24(1) would 1. vindicate the rights of the applicant given the violation and the applicant's circumstances; 2. must not "unduly or unnecessarily" depart from the judicial role in "resolving disputes"; 3. "vindicates the right while invoking the function and powers of a court"; and 4. would be "fair to the party against whom the order is made. The remedy should not impose substantial hardships that are unrelated to securing the right" and can include "novel and creative features" when necessary to respond to the "challenges" and "needs" of the particular case: ibid. at paras 56–59.

[179] *Doucet-Boudreau* v. *Nova Scotia,* 2003 SCC 62 at para 69.

[180] Paul Rouleau and Linsey Sherman, "Doucet-Boudreau, Dialogue and Judicial Activism" (2010) 41(2) *Ottawa L. Rev.* 171, 194.

[181] *Doucet-Boudreau* v. *Nova Scotia* at para 100. The dissenters also echoed Fuller when they stated: "[t]he judiciary is ill equipped to make polycentric choices or to evaluate the wide-ranging consequences that flow from policy implementation. This Court has recognized that courts possess neither the expertise nor the resources to undertake public administration". Ibid. at para 120.

complexities of polycentric issues. The trial judge, by holding the progress hearings, had crossed "the boundary between judicial acts and administrative oversight" and in doing so had acted "illegitimately and without jurisdiction".[182] If the judge was prepared to make more orders after an unsatisfactory progress report, he was treating the government unfairly. On the other hand, if he was only attempting to induce compliance by persuasion and transparency, he was acting like a leader of the opposition by placing the government's "feet to the fire" and placing "pressure on the government to act".[183]

The minority discounted that the trial judge had, as emphasized by the majority, treated all parties fairly. The trial judge rightly resisted the temptation to resort to what Fuller rightly denounced as informal "lunch time" methods of enforcement.[184] The progress reports simply collected information that would otherwise only be known to the government. Moreover, the trial judge's fidelity to adjudication facilitated adversarial and public debate about the significance of that information. If the judge had made any additional order, that order could be appealed, as indeed the government appealed his retention of jurisdiction. The government's appeal is ironic given that Canada's experience with retention of jurisdiction suggests that the government is most often its beneficiary. For example, the government could have asked for more time or elaboration of any lack of clarity in the original declarations, just as had occurred in the *Manitoba Language Reference* and when courts extend suspended declarations of invalidity.

The dissenters in *Doucet-Boudreau* distorted what the trial judge did as a heavy-handed and politicized assumption of the executive role. This echoes much critical commentary on complex remedies but like that commentary it ignores the complexities of what was actually done. For example, the minority focused only on part of the remedy, namely retention of jurisdiction. The majority recognized that the retention of jurisdiction balanced the best efforts order that appropriately deferred to the government's expertise in organizing education and building schools. The majority concluded that the overall result was rooted in "balance and moderation",[185] not judicial usurpation.

[182] Ibid. at para 117; see also ibid. at para 112.

[183] Ibid. at paras 127–128.

[184] Lon Fuller, "The Forms and Limits of Adjudication" (1978) 92 *Harv. L. Rev.* 353, 389.

[185] *Doucet-Boudreau* v. *Nova Scotia*, 2003 SCC 62 at para 13.

The minority's preferred remedy, a "construction deadline with the possibility of a contempt order",[186] was in many ways more extreme than what the trial judge did. It invoked what Fuller saw as a positivistic morality of duty that assumed that legal commands had to be precisely set out to be enforceable. The minority's focus on precision and enforceability assumed that the government was a "bad man" who must be given the clearest of orders that if breached could result in a stern sanction. It would also force the trial judge to make specific orders and set deadlines in a manner that would require detailed information about educational facilities and school construction in five different parts of the province. It would have taken away flexibility that both the government and the minority needed with the school year approaching.

Although the minority accepted that courts could use coercive injunctions, it is difficult to think that many judges would be prepared to issue such precise orders at least in the first instance. Indeed, the minority's insistence on clear rules that could be enforced by contempt has acted as a type of "poison pill" that has scared Canadian judges off from retaining jurisdiction. Unfortunately, the dissenters' position has become more widely accepted in the years since.[187] The threat of contempt continues to influence the form of injunctions by generally requiring that the injunction be clear and precise.[188] This is unfortunate because judges may often not have enough information to order a detailed injunction. Even if they could obtain such information, such command and control standards may be counter-productive by encouraging the government to abide by the letter but not necessarily the spirit of the order.[189]

Both the *Manitoba Language Reference* and *Doucet-Boudreau* are best conceived of as declaration plus cases in which the court retained jurisdiction because of the complexity of complying with minority language rights and the province's delay in complying. Neither the "best efforts" order in *Doucet-Boudreau* nor the flexible translation schedules in the *Manitoba Language Reference* could fairly be enforced by contempt. They

[186] Ibid. at para 143.

[187] The Kenyan Court of Appeal has also rejected retention of jurisdiction as contrary to the idea that judges should be functus after rendering their judgements: *Kenya Airports Authority* v. *Mitu Bell Welfare Society*, [2016] eKLR, Civil Appeal No. 218 of 2014.

[188] *Thibodeau* v. *Air Canada*, 2014 SCC 67 at paras 125–127 relying on a private law precedent stressing the importance of clarity in the injunction because a contempt holding could result in a fine or incarceration.

[189] See Sabel and Simon, "Destabilization Rights", on the move away from command and control.

were essentially declarations. In subsequent decisions in the *Manitoba Language Reference*, the Court expanded on the requirements of its original declarations and resolved legitimate and genuine disputes about them. The progress reports in *Doucet-Boudreau* seemed to have worked because the case was moot by the time it reached the Supreme Court.

A declaration plus is an intermediate remedy between general and unenforceable declarations and detailed and specific injunctions enforceable by contempt. It fills an important gap in the remedial arsenal. It allows courts to focus on interpreting the general requirements of rights while allowing the state to select the means of compliance, subject to adversarial challenge by the parties.

7.5 Towards a Two-Track Approach

Since Abram Chayes' identification of the public law model of adjudication, it has been widely accepted that the aim of institutional reform litigation is to achieve reforms so as to prevent future violations. Chayes recognized the traditional nature of compensatory remedies but dismissed them as anachronistic.[190] But in doing so, he under-estimated the importance of right to a remedy reasoning for judicial legitimacy and success. He may also have under-estimated the challenges and frequent failures of systemic reforms.

Systemic reform is necessary to prevent repetitive violations caused by institutions. Nevertheless it should be joined with individual relief that addresses the wrongs done to individuals caught in the grip of institutions that consistently violate rights. In a recurring theme in this book, supranational courts point towards a different and more balanced approach to remedies than that used by most domestic courts. Both the ECtHR and the IACtHR have taken a two-track approach to institutional reform: one that provides individual remedies for past violations while engaging with states to take actions to prevent future violations. The remedial record of these supra-national courts is not perfect. They do, however, recognize the inadequacy of approaches that focus only on individual or systemic remedies.

7.5.1 *The Pathologies of Exclusively Individual Remedies*

A range of individual remedies including damages and the exclusion of evidence have been examined in the last two chapters. Many of these

[190] Abram Chayes, "Foreword: Public Law Litigation and the Burger Court" (1982) 96(1) *Harv. L. Rev.* 4, 47ff; see also Fiss, "The Forms of Justice".

remedies have been directed at the police. These individual remedies have imposed considerable costs on society. Alas, they have left in place many police services that continue to violate rights.

At the starkest level, damages allow states to pay a fine (and raise taxes) for violating human rights. It is not a coincidence that states are often more willing to pay damages awarded by regional human rights courts than take measures to prevent future violations. Exclusion of evidence, stays of proceedings and release of individuals by way of habeas corpus are necessary to provide effective remedies for those whose rights are violated in the criminal process. Nevertheless, they leave in place institutions that continue to violate rights, including the rights of the disadvantaged and the unpopular. They provide little incentive for states to engage in systemic reform. Individual remedies can play a helpful role in reform, especially when they are well publicized and provide a human face to rights violations.[191] Nevertheless, a reliance on individual remedies will not bring complex bureaucratic institutions into compliance with minimal rights standards.

7.5.2 The Pathologies of Exclusively Systemic Remedies

Systemic remedies are necessary, but they need to be grounded by individual remedies and with that the lived experience of those whose rights have and will be violated. The California prison case, by spinning out into reducing overcrowding, lost its focus on the harms that inadequate healthcare causes to prisoners. Eventual compliance with the order that California prisons "only" be 137.5 per cent over capacity allowed California to operate a prison system well above capacity and with inadequate healthcare.

Another example of a purely systemic approach that seems to have spun out of control is *Missouri* v. *Jenkins*.[192] In that case, the United States Supreme Court authorized the creation of a magnet school and taxation scheme to fund city schools after the trial judge found that busing involving the suburbs was not permissible because the suburbs had not engaged in intentional segregation. The state complied and built a school with excellent facilities. It was known colloquially in Kansas City as the "Taj Mahal". Alas, the school was not supported by the Black

[191] Charles Epp, *Making Rights Real* (Chicago: University of Chicago Press, 1993).

[192] 495 US 33 (1990). The Court did indicate that the trial judge erred by raising taxes but rather should have required the elected authorities to do so.

community. It largely failed to achieve either integration or improved academic performance.[193] In 1995, the case returned to the Supreme Court, which tried to encourage an end to the failed US$500 million experiment. It ruled that the Court could not increase teacher salaries in pursuit of the desegregation plan.[194] The failure of this well-intentioned remedy combined with reservations that Derrick Bell and others have expressed about busing remedies reveals that purely systemic approaches are likely to fail and can have counter-productive effects. This is particularly so if the intended beneficiaries of the remedy do not participate in helping to formulate the remedy.[195]

William Simon and his colleagues have recently argued in favour of a purely systemic approach to both bankruptcy and public law litigation on the basis that individual claims may divert limited resources.[196] This ignores, however, that public funds in the human rights context are not as limited as the funds of a bankrupt corporation. It also ignores that damage awards for human rights violations are often modest. There is also a role for non-monetary alternative individual remedies, such as apologies and court orders that relate to specific litigants. More fundamentally, it ignores how individual remedies can enhance the legitimacy of the court and provide some success and marker of past injustices as the court continues to struggle to achieve reforms that will minimize future violations.

Courts faced with dire systemic problems may be tempted to focus on them exclusively. The Indian courts have frequently taken a purely systemic approach. In the next chapter, it will be acknowledged that the Indian courts have had some success with this approach in the right to food litigation. Nevertheless, in many other cases they have imposed harms on litigants by, for example, authorizing evictions and slum demolitions.[197]

As discussed in Section 7.2.4, an ongoing Indian prison case initiated by a complaint from a former Chief Justice has generally focused on

[193] Joshua Dunn, *Complex Justice: The Case of Missouri* v. *Jenkins* (Chapel Hill: University of North Carolina Press, 2008), p.1.

[194] *Missouri* v. *Jenkins II*, 515 US 70 (1995).

[195] Dunn details how the Black community was ambivalent or even hostile to the remedy: Dunn, *Complex Justice.* For other findings that the interests of institutions and lawyers have often been advanced in public interest litigation over those of intended beneficiaries, see Sandler and Schoenbrod, *Democracy by Decree.*

[196] Noonan, Lipson and Simon, "Reforming Institutions", 503–506.

[197] Bhuwania, *Courting the People*, p.86.

systemic remedies. More recently, however, it has started to address the distinctive needs of sub-groups of prisoners such as women and youth. The Court has also mandated local courts to investigate and, if appropriate, award damages with respect to over 500 "unnatural" deaths that occurred in India's prisons between 2012 and 2015.[198] This move demonstrates more concern for unnecessary deaths in prison than is seen in the California prison case. It also follows a pattern in the right to food litigation where the Court focused on the needs of sub-groups and also used documented starvation deaths as evidence of non-compliance.[199] By focusing on specific vulnerable groups and specific violations of rights such as prison and starvation deaths, the Indian Supreme Court has started to move towards a two-track approach that combines individual and systemic remedies.

In an attempt to manage its crushing caseload, the ECtHR has adopted a pilot judgement procedure that allows the Court to suspend pending claims while a systemic remedy is developed by the state in consultation with the Committee of Ministers. In its focus on systemic justice, this approach departs from the two-track approach and has been criticized for sacrificing individual justice.[200] The Court has recently expanded this approach by delegating over 12,000 individual claims against the Ukraine to the Committee of Ministers. Seven judges in the Grand Chamber issued a strong dissent. They argued that individual claims and access to the Court was being sacrificed for the sake of efficiency.[201] At the same time, even this approach is not as unbalanced as the California prison case. In order to comply with the right to an effective remedy, European states will often have to provide both individual and preventive remedies, including in the cases that were suspended pending a pilot judgement.

198 Supreme Court of India, Writ Petition (Civil) No. 406 of 2013, *In Re Inhuman Prison – 1382 Prisons* (15 September 2017), online (pdf): www.slsagoa.nic.in/Report%20WP%20No.406%20of%202013.pdf

199 *People's Union for Civil Liberties* v. *Union of India & Ors*, Writ Petition (Civil) No. 196 of 2001, Court Order of 3 May 2003, online: www.escr-net.org/caselaw/2006/peoples-union-civil-liberties-v-union-india-ors-supreme-court-india-civil-original See *infra* Chapter 8, Section 8.6.3, for discussion.

200 Antoine Buyse, "The Pilot Judgment Procedure at the European Court of Human Rights: Possibilities and Challenges" (2009) 57 *Nomiko Vima* 1890, 1902; Janneke H. Gerards and Lize R. Glas, "Access to Justice in the European Convention on Human Rights System" (2017) 35 *Netherlands Q. Hum. Rts.* 11, 27; Eline Kindt, "Giving up on Individual Justice?" (2018) 36 *Netherlands Q. Hum. Rts.* 173.

201 *Burmych and Others* v. *Ukraine* [GC], No. 46852/13 et al., ECHR 12 October 2017.

Systemic cases are ultimately about respect for the rights of individuals and groups. Harms to individuals both before and during the court's retention of jurisdiction should be taken seriously. Practically, attention to distinct harms and the award of individual remedies in a large systemic case may also produce some remedial success for the Court and also focus public attention on the consequences to individuals of systemic injustices.

7.5.3 *Examples of the Two-Track Approach*

As outlined in Chapter 2, Section 2.4, the two-track approach is both a descriptive account of what courts at their best can do and a normative account of what they should do.

7.5.3.1 Supra-national Adjudication

The Council of Europe system increasingly takes a two-track approach to complex cases under Article 46 of the European Convention. At times, the ECtHR has made some indications of the general or systemic measures that it concludes are necessary to prevent future violations. Professor Mowbry's thorough review of these indications, however, reveal them as quite general and declaratory in nature.[202] They are a far cry from the detailed orders associated with injunctions issued by domestic courts. They are better seen as a declaration plus remedy.

The Committee of Ministers has attempted to be more transparent about its interactions with states during the execution of judgements. In many, but not all cases, it issues public reports. It has an institutional incentive to end supervision, even in cases where there is less than full compliance. For example, it has ended its supervision of the UK's refusal to allow voting in prisons and of prison condition cases in Russia and Italy. The two-track approach should be attentive to the risk of remedial failure and backsliding if prisoners bring new cases where they can establish that their rights have been violated.

The IACtHR also follows a two-track approach. Unfortunately states have a tendency to comply with individual remedies such as damages more than with systemic remedies. Fortunately the IACtHR undertakes

[202] For a detailed discussion of the ECtHR practice in this regard and examples of what the Court says about general measures, see Alistair Mowbry, "An Examination of the European Court of Human Rights Indication of General Measures" (2017) 17 *Hum. Rts. L. Rev.* 451.

its own monitoring of its judgements, often for years after the original decision. Aided by the assistance of the Inter-American Human Rights Commission, the applicants and other interested parties, the IACtHR should be more specific in the face of non-implementation of systemic orders.[203] Such an escalation of response should not violate either the separation of powers or subsidiarity because it would be based on the state's failure to comply with the Court's remedy and to take reasonable steps to prevent violations.

7.5.3.2 Domestic Courts

As Derrick Bell's work suggests, a two-track approach to school desegregation might have involved remedies designed to improve educational equity while more gradual systemic remedies achieved greater integration.[204] In some cases, it may have followed the *Cooper*[205] approach of combining immediate remedies to allow named plaintiffs to attend previously segregated schools with broader systemic remedies such as a schedules for desegregation. This was an approach taken by Justice Brennan in an original draft of the *Cooper* v. *Aaron* decision, but the more ambitious two-track approach was dropped in order to maintain the unanimity of the Court.[206]

A two-track approach in prison cases would order immediate remedies in relation to healthcare and harmful practices while more gradually pursuing long-term systemic goals including better healthcare facilities in prison, more healthcare staff and the reduction of overcrowding. Longer-term systemic remedies also can create space and time for meaningful participation by a range of actors, including those who are supposed to benefit from the remedy. Systemic remedies should include participatory rights for those that the remedy is supposed to benefit, through allowing submissions and adversarial challenge to the government's remedial plans or requiring the government to consult with those affected before implementing a declaration. These participatory

[203] This is not to say that general orders in the first instance may not be of value in part because they create space for the state and the parties to focus on evolving priorities. On specificity see Rachel Murray and Clara Sandoval "Balancing Specificity of Reparation Measures and State's Discretion to Enhance Implementation" (2020) 12 *J of HR Prac.* 101.

[204] Bell, *Silent Covenants*, pp.20–29.

[205] 358 US 1 (1958).

[206] Michael Klarman, *Brown* v. *Board of Education and the Civil Rights Movement* (New York: Oxford University, 2007) at p.108.

mechanisms can respond to the danger that institutional litigants, amicus curiae and masters may not always represent the priorities and immediate interests of those who have suffered a rights violation.[207]

7.5.3.2.1 South Africa As will be discussed in Chapter 8, Section 8.6.10, the South African courts are increasingly taking a two-track approach that provides individual remedies against eviction (or temporary accommodation) with longer term systemic remedies to construct public housing. The declaration plus approach described in Section 7.4 of this chapter might strengthen the South African approach by requiring courts in general terms to provide a sense of what housing rights require rather than relying on open ended engagement orders as systemic remedies.[208]

One South African case focused on seven mud schools in some of the poorest areas of the country. Mobile classrooms with water supply, desks and chairs were provided pending the construction of permanent schools. By 2013, the construction of new schools for the original seven schools was almost complete. More systemically, 200 temporary classrooms were provided to mud schools and construction was started on ninety schools.[209] The success of this case is consistent with the two-track approach because it focused first on achieving remedies for the seven schools before expanding to other schools. Other litigation started with the appointment and payment of 140 teachers to unfulfilled vacancies. It has subsequently expanded to include teachers from ninety more schools.[210] Gilbert Marcus and Steven Budlender, in their important reports on South African public law litigation, have stressed the

[207] Bell, "Serving Two Masters".

[208] Sue-Mari Viljoen and Saul Porsche Makama, "Structural relief – A Context-Sensitive Approach" (2018) 34 *S.A J. Hum. Rts.* 209, 210, 229. For an argument that the relief ordered by the trial judge in the famous Grootboom housing rights was essentially a declaration plus, see Roach and Budlender, "Mandatory Relief and Supervisory Jurisdiction", 329.

[209] The applicant Legal Resource Action Centre did start new litigation in 2014 but aimed at requiring the school authorities to disclose plans and progress. The follow-on litigation may have been unnecessary had the court retained jurisdiction: Steven Budlender, Gilbert Marcus SC and Nick Ferreira, *Public Interest Litigation and Social Change in South Africa: Strategies, Tactics and Lessons* (The Atlantic Philanthropies, 2014), p.81 online (pdf): www.atlanticphilanthropies.org/wp-content/uploads/2015/12/Public-interest-litigation-and-social-change-in-South-Africa.pdf

[210] Ibid., pp.88–99.

importance of starting with narrowly framed cases and then building on their success.[211]

7.5.3.2.2 Colombia The Colombian Constitutional Court has also combined individual and systemic relief. In a 2004 case, it aggregated 108 individual tutela applications that requested a range of remedies relating to the health, housing and education rights of over 1,000 persons displaced by internal conflict. The Court recognized that the individual violations had "structural" causes. They involved "a social problem whose solution requires the intervention of various entities", additional budget and a "coordinated set of actions".[212] As with supra-national courts,[213] concerns about courts being overwhelmed with individual actions was one of the repeated factors that the Court cited in declaring an unconstitutional state of affairs and taking a more systemic or structural approach.

The Court ordered a wide variety of individual remedies and imposed deadlines on the state of eight to fifteen days for those relating to health and housing and thirty days for those related to education.[214] Some may criticize such individual remedies as "queue jumping".[215] Nevertheless, they honoured the purposes of tutelas or amaparos in providing individual remedies akin to habeas corpus in common law countries. These individual remedies were dominated by the court.

The Court's systemic remedies were more tentative and dialogic. The Court struck a modest tone noting that "[t]he *tutela* judge cannot solve each one of these problems, which corresponds to both the National Government and territorial entities, and to Congress, within their respective margins of jurisdiction".[216] These systemic remedies should be designed "to protect, based on the principle of equality, the rights of those found in a similar situation to the petitioner, but who have not filed tutelas".[217]The Court made clear that systemic remedies would require

[211] Ibid.

[212] Decision T-025 of 2004, translated in Manuel José Cepeda Espinosa and David Landau, *Colombian Constitutional Law* (New York: Oxford University Press 2017), p.182.

[213] Gerald L. Neuman, "Bi-Level Remedies for Human Rights Violations" (2014) 55 *Harv. J. Int'l. L.* 2.

[214] Decision T-025 of 2004 at paras 11–14 in Espinosa and Landau, *Colombian Constitutional Law*.

[215] This critique will be discussed in Chapter 8, Section 8.6.8.

[216] Ibid. at para 6.3.1.4.

[217] Ibid., p.182.

budgetary increases, but did not order them but rather called on the government to propose a budget. This has been identified as a factor in getting the government's attention and substantially increasing dedicated budgets.[218]

Like supra-national courts, the Colombian Court took a whole of government approach that required various ministries to respond to its judgement.[219] The systemic orders were designed both to minimize future violations and to reduce the caseload of the courts. The Court specifically ordered that the authorities should not make the filing of a tutela a precondition for recognizing the rights of displaced persons. This builds on an alignment between the institutional interests of the courts and the more principled interest in preventing future and repeated violations. Relative ease of action in filing tutelas meant that the Colombian courts were, like supra-national courts, moved to seek systemic remedies in part because of concerns about conserving scarce judicial resources.

The Colombian Court tried to empower internally displaced person in a way that could allow them to obtain benefits from the state without judicial enforcement. To this end, it ordered that displaced persons should be informed "in an immediate, clear, and precise manner about the rights that purport to secure them dignified treatment by the authorities, and to verify that this actually happens".[220] Such a clear articulation of rights, even as a matter of aspiration, has the potential to inspire a democratic process in which citizens are mobilized to demand that they be treated in a humane and dignified manner by their government. It also fits with a declaration plus model where courts focus

[218] Cesar Rodriguez-Garavito and Diana Rodriguez-Franco, *Radical Deprivation on Trial: The Impact of Judicial Activism on Socio-economic Rights* (Cambridge: Cambridge University Press, 2015), p.74: "T25's immediate effect was to shake up state bureaucracies responsible for attending to the IDP population. The Constitutional Court used socioeconomic rights as "destabilization rights", which were designed to provide the pressure needed for breaking the deadlock surrounding assistance to the displaced population. Such deadlock resulted from dispersion of responsibilities, poor coordination between the agencies in charge assisting IDPs, deficient budget, and sluggishness on the part of state entities".

[219] Huneeus identifies the whole of government approach taken by international court as a disadvantage, but it may be an advantage in some contexts: "Reforming the State from Afar".

[220] Decision T-025 of 2004 at para 10.1.4 in Espinosa and Landau, *Colombian Constitutional Law*.

on interpreting rights while leaving the implementation of rights to others.

As Cesar Rodriguez-Garavito and Diana Rodriguez-Franco argue, the systemic orders were not prescriptive. They involved an extensive articulation of the rights at stake and a strong commitment to monitoring. The Court should promote reform without deciding the precise means to achieve reform or the precise content of reform.[221] Nevertheless, the systemic remedies ordered did become more specific and prescriptive over time. A 2008 decision focused on the rights of women. It "ordered the creation of 13 programs to meet specific gaps in public policy toward displaced women and girls of all ages".[222] A 2009 decision focused on the rights of Indigenous peoples. It required "the adoption of thirty-four ethnic safeguarding plans, one for each of the indigenous peoples at risk of disappearing". It was "supplemented by three follow-up decisions, ordering urgent measures to protect specific groups within the indigenous population that are under greater risk".[223]Another 2009 order requiring five pilot projects for displaced persons with disabilities.[224]

7.5.3.2.3 India Indian courts have followed a similar pattern in both their right to food and prison cases in focusing on distinct needs of subgroups of those who are supposed to benefit from the systemic remedies. The Indian Supreme Court has also taken a two-track approach in a case where it ordered damages, the construction of housing and police patrols for an individual victim of sexual violence. At the same time, the Court implored "the State machinery to work in harmony" to prevent sexual violence and also indicated that public and private hospitals should provide free treatment and rehabilitation for all victims of sexual violence.[225] Courts in the west have much to learn from the remedial practices of these courts in the global South, which combine generous and creative individual remedies with a variety of systemic remedies.

[221] Rodriguez-Garavito and Rodriguez-Franco, *Radical Deprivation on Trial*, p.19 discussing Colombia Constitutional Court, ch.4.

[222] Constitutional Court, Decision 92 of 2008.

[223] Rodriguez-Garavito and Rodriguez-Franco, *Radical Deprivation on Trial*, p.47; Colombia Constitutional Court, Decision 6 of 2009 at para 47; Colombia Constitutional Court, Decision 382 of 2010; Colombia Constitutional Court, Decision 174 of 2011; Colombia Constitutional Court, Decision 173 of 2012.

[224] Rodriguez-Garavito and Rodriguez-Franco, *Radical Deprivation on Trial*, p.90.

[225] Re Woman gang-raped, (2014) 4 SCC 786 at paras 23–26.

7.5.4 Stopping Irreparable Harm during Systemic Reform

The order of urgent measures during the systemic phase of public law litigation also demonstrates the mutually re-enforcing nature of the two-track approach. Such orders should be patterned on interim remedies designed to prevent irreparable harm. Like interim remedies, they should be changed if the evidence warrants it. The IACtHR has even ordered such provisional measures after the final judgement on the merits.[226]

Individual remedies to stop irreparable harm could have ensured that prisoners in the California prison case received required medical treatment. It could have reminded the court of both continued right violations but also the priorities of the rights holders. Individual remedies can inject concerns about substantive rights into a remedial process that over time may have become technocratic and focused on procedure and the interests of small "working groups" of experts and lawyers[227] or the judge's own interests.

7.5.5 Remedial Failure and Remedial Cycles

Systemic reform is difficult to achieve. For this reason, it is important that courts retain jurisdiction. The two-track approach is responsive to the reality of remedial failure by providing that judges should be open to ordering new individual remedies and to re-considering their systemic remedies in light of new evidence. A continued willingness to order individual remedies respects the integrity of adjudication as related to claims of wrongs and entitlement to remedies by specific individuals.[228] It integrates traditional right to a remedy reasoning that was unwisely abandoned in early articulations of public law litigation.

Early defenders of public law litigation such as Chayes and Fiss disparaged individual remedies as archaic to the modern age. They were correct that we needed systemic remedies and that courts could use some assistance from others. They were wrong, however, that individual remedies should be abandoned. Individuals caught in institutions that continually violate their rights need remedies. Courts also need to issue such

226 Clara Burbano Herrera, *Provisional Measures in the Case Law of the Inter-American Court of Human Rights* (Antwerp: Intersentia, 2010) p.171 documenting fifteen such cases.

227 Sandler and Schoenbrod, *Democracy by Decree*.

228 Fuller, "The Forms and Limits of Adjudication".

remedies to confirm their legitimacy as courts and to achieve some remedial success.

Continued requests for individual and interim remedies should alert judges to problem areas. It may continue their education about the particular institution. It may also persuade them in cases where the state is unwilling or unable to prevent continued violations to take a more prescriptive approach. The declaration plus provides the procedural vehicle that allows the court to start with general declarations but if necessary move towards injunctive relief.

7.6 Conclusion

Domestic judges are often reluctant to retain jurisdiction as a means to reform complex public institutions that chronically violate rights. Judges remain much more comfortable with "one shot" individual remedies, such as damages and the exclusion of evidence discussed in the last two chapters. This is so even when the human rights violations in those cases are a product of the failure of public institutions.

Judges are haunted by doubts that they are ill-equipped to deal with polycentric or multi-faceted problems because they only hear one case at a time. To be sure, they should be cautious when confronting polycentric problems, but the idea that they should not or cannot consider such problems should be rejected. It would suggest that courts should rarely pursue systemic remedies designed to prevent future violations. It would also suggest that judges are not suited to enforce social and economic rights and Indigenous rights, to be examined in the next two chapters.

One way to deal with polycentric complexities is for courts to retain jurisdiction and to be open to hearing new evidence about problems that both governments and plaintiffs are encountering during complex processes of systemic reform. Domestic courts should be more willing to retain jurisdiction and adjust their approach when warranted by the production of new evidence. If under-resourced supra-national courts like the IACtHR can monitor compliance, better resourced domestic courts in democracies should be able to do so too.

Domestic courts may need a new remedy to encourage them to retain jurisdiction. They associate retention of jurisdiction with the need to put the government on notice that the court is prepared to use punitive contempt powers. This requires domestic courts to use specific command and control orders. Judges usually do not have the necessary information to formulate such standards at an early point in the remedial process.

Even if they do, such specificity could be counter-productive by insisting on rules that will often be over or under inclusive.

Judicial acceptance of the declaration plus would allow judges to issue declarations that define and declare the scope of rights and the general obligations that they place on governments. It will relieve them of the burden of having to specify in detail, at the early stage of a complex remedial process, the means and deadlines for compliance. Supranational courts do not live with the due process burdens of contempt powers. The processes that they follow essentially involve the declaration plus advocated for in Section 7.4. In other words, they cannot coerce, but they can and often do retain jurisdiction.

Both the ECtHR and IACtHR have recognized the importance of providing both individual and systemic remedies even in complex institutional cases. Some domestic courts in Colombia, South Africa and more recently India have on occasion followed this path, but all domestic courts need to do so more routinely and self-consciously. Individual remedies provide some remedial success and bolster judicial legitimacy. They counter the tendency seen in American public law litigation to ignore the need to repair or prevent discrete harms caused to individuals. They may also help counter the drift in such cases to systemic remedies that do not always seem to serve the interests of those they are intended to benefit.

A two-track remedial strategy accepts the traditional role of courts in providing individual remedies while recognizing that individual remedies in the modern state are often not sufficient to ensure compliance with human rights. The two-track approach allows courts to respond to the harms that non-compliance imposes on real people. Individual remedies can also make it easier to take the time that is necessary to allow participation in the formulation of systemic remedies and hopefully to get it right. They may also allow courts to avoid the "reformer at large" tendency seen in some American and Indian public law cases. In short, a two-track remedial approach can preserve the integrity of adjudication while recognizing the challenges that courts will confront in dealing with polycentric problems.

8

Remedies for Social, Economic and Cultural Rights

8.1 Introduction

Remedies are a problem for those who wish to have social, economic or cultural (SEC) rights recognized by the courts. Making clear that recognition of SEC rights will require costly and systemic remedies increases the chances that courts will simply not recognize the right. In turn, minimizing remedial demands by presenting the case as only an individual one-off remedy may mean that the right will not be effectively or equitably remedied.

Justice Albie Sachs has expressed concerns that "people with the sharpest elbows, with the best lawyers" will "get the water ... get the houses".[1] In other words, individual remedies may disturb queues for limited resources and even reward more advantaged people. The reluctance to recognize SEC rights or remedies is also related to the polycentric nature of such rights. Remedies that contemplate or require increased funding for housing may have unanticipated consequences on other budgets including health and education. As suggested in Chapter 7, Section 7.3, the answer to these difficulties is for courts to avoid judgements that are "too exacting and comprehensive" and that leave space for legislatures, the executive and processes of negotiation and mediation to allow for "adjustment and compromise"[2] in light of new information. The disruptive effects of individual queue-jumping remedies can also be mitigated by new legislation if it can be successfully defended by the government as a reasonable and proportionate allocation of scarce resources. Both proportionality principles and a two-track approach to individual and systemic remedies make room for the recognition and enforcement of SEC rights.

Considerable scholarly work over the last decade has provided detailed case studies of remedial strategies in SEC cases.[3] This work has also provided new taxonomies of different remedial strategies. Commentators have proposed the use of "weak",[4] "experimental",[5] "dialogic",[6] "incremental"[7] or "catalytic"[8] remedies as ways for courts to enforce SEC rights. As seen in Chapter 7, Section 7.5, a similar consensus has emerged that complex institutional cases should move away from detailed command and control. In this chapter, I will suggest that these

1 Albie Sachs, "Enforcement of Social and Economic Rights" (2006) 22 *Am. U. Int'l. L. Rev.* 673, 688.

2 Lon Fuller, *The Morality of Law* (New Haven: Yale University Press, 1969), p.178.

3 See, for example, Mal Langford, Cesar Rodriguez-Garavito and Julieta Rossi, *Social Rights Judgments and the Politics of Compliance: Making It Stick* (Cambridge: Cambridge University Press, 2017).

4 Mark Tushnet, *Weak Courts , Strong Rights* (Princeton: Princeton University Press, 2008); David Landau, "The Reality of Social Rights Litigation" (2012) 53 *Harv. J. Int'l. L.* 189.

5 Charles Sabel and William Simon, "Destablization Rights: How Public Law Litigation Succeeds" (2004) 117 *Harv. L. Rev.* 1016.

6 Kent Roach, "Constitutional, Remedial and International Dialogues about Rights: The Canadian Experience" (2005) 40 *Texas Int'l. L. J.* 537; Rosalind Dixon, "Creating Dialogue about Socio-Economic Rights" (2007) 5 *I. Con.* 391.

7 Jeff King, *Judging Social Rights* (Cambridge: Cambridge University Press, 2012).

8 Katharine G. Young, *Constituting Economic and Social Rights* (Oxford: Oxford University Press, 2012), pp.167–191.

developments can help guide courts as they pursue systemic remedies. Suspended declarations of invalidity examined in Chapter 4, Section 8.2.4, and the declaration plus examined in Chapter 7, Section 7.4, will allow the legislature and the executive to formulate housing, health and cultural policies in consultation with the intended beneficiaries of rights and remedies.

A refusal to ask for or provide individual remedies may be a mistake. If SEC rights are to be justiciable and treated like real rights, there should be individual remedies in deserving cases. The two-track approach of combining individual and general measures is taken by a number of supra-national adjudicators. The South African courts are combining individual remedies against evictions with longer-term systemic housing remedies. The Colombian Constitutional Court has ordered many individual remedies with respect to healthcare. It now also engages the executive, legislative and civil society in systemic healthcare reform. Again borrowing the words of Justice Sachs, these courts have found a way to prevent "micro injustices" while recognizing that more work needs to be done in collaboration with other institutions and society to remedy more systemic "macro injustices".[9] This two-track approach of combining individual measures for petitioners with more general and systemic measures is also used by supra-national adjudicators that address SEC rights.

With respect to systemic remedies, the South African courts have stressed that the state should engage with SEC rights holders. Participation by those who are supposed to benefit from remedies can result in creative remedies that reflect the priorities and consent of the rights holders. Alas, there is also a danger that engagement will become a procedural checklist that governments can use to limit SEC rights. It will be suggested both in this chapter and in the next (with respect to a similar duty to consult Indigenous people) that the engagement/consultation works best when it results in consensual remedies but that it can also be used to justify limits on rights.

Finally, the two-track approach is attentive to the reality of remedial failure. Individual remedies can play a role in triggering iterative processes of systemic reforms. At the same time, requests for new individual and systemic remedies may be rightly rejected should the state be able to

[9] *Port Elizabeth Municipality* v. *Various Occupiers*, [2004] ZACC 7 at para 38.

justify proportionate restrictions on SEC rights or limits and delays on providing remedies.

8.1.1 *Outline of This Chapter*

Section 8.2 will examine the range of remedies available for SEC rights in supra-national and domestic courts. It will also examine how American courts have interacted with legislatures over school finance cases. It suggests that interim remedies, suspended declarations of invalidity and the declaration plus may all play useful roles in enforcing SEC rights.

Section 8.3 will examine criticisms that individual remedies for SEC rights will produce inequitable queue jumping. Although individual remedies may jump the successful litigant to the front of the queue for limited resources, this is part and parcel of adjudication. This also suggests that an exclusive reliance on systemic, weak or dialogic remedies may undercut the judicial role in enforcing SEC rights.

Section 8.4 will examine the role of proportionality principles and reasonableness review with respect to limits on SEC remedies. My examination of proportionality principles in this chapter is expanded to include limits on rights. This is because the ability of states to justify limits on SEC rights is an important component of my response to critiques that individual remedies for SEC rights will constitute a regressive form of queue jumping. I will also examine how remedies may be limited in emergency situations, such as those created by the global COVID-19 pandemic.

Section 8.5 will examine engagement remedies ordered by the South African courts. It will suggest that individual remedies that prevent evictions or provide alternative accommodation can help address inequality of bargaining power in engagement. It will also outline an analytical distinction between engagement as a means to limit rights and authorize evictions and as a source for consensual and perhaps creative remedies. This distinction will also be carried over to the next chapter in my analysis of the analogous duty to consult Indigenous peoples.

Section 8.6 will outline a two-track approach to remedies. It will again stress the dangers of an exclusively systemic response while discussing some successes such as the Indian right to food litigation. It will also suggest that individual remedies can establish judicial success in enforcing SEC rights and help publicize the real-life consequences of their violations. The relation between individual remedies and the minimum core of SEC rights[10] will also be explored. Finally, it will be suggested that individual remedies play an important role in responding to remedial failures and can trigger cycles of remedies and reform.

8.2 Practice

8.2.1 Interim Remedies

Article 5 of the Optional Protocol to the International Covenant on Economic, Social and Cultural Rights (ICESCR) contemplates the use of interim remedies so as to avoid "possible irreparable damage". At the same time, it also states that such remedies will only "be necessary in exceptional circumstances".[11] The Committee on Economic, Social and Cultural Rights indicated that to prevent irreparable harm, the petitioner should have her eviction order suspended as an interim remedy or be provided with alternative housing after genuine consultation with her. The petitioner was, however, evicted. In its final views, the Committee failed to provide damages on the basis that the judgement finding a violation to both the petitioner's right to adequate housing and Article 5 of the Optional Protocol was itself adequate reparation.[12] As a general measure to ensure non-repetition, the Committee also indicated that the state should develop protocols for complying with interim remedies.[13]

The ECtHR issued a provisional measure against evictions of a Roma community. It lifted the measure when alternative accommodation was made available to them, even though the applicants were not willing to use it because it would affect their ability to earn a living.[14] Such a conclusion is potentially problematic and demonstrates the need for full reasoning at the interim remedy stage. The UN Human Rights Committee has granted provisional measures against evictions in a similar case. In a display of the value of retained jurisdiction, it expanded the measure to prevent the state from cutting off the water supply to the

10 Office of the High Commissioner for Human Rights, *General Comment No. 3: The Nature of States Parties' Obligations (Art.2, Para. 1 of the Covenant)*, CESCR, 5th Sess., UN Doc E/1991/23 (1991) at para 10.

11 Optional Protocol to the International Covenant on Economic, Social and Cultural Rights, GA Res. 832, UNGAOR, 63rd Sess., UN Doc A/RES/63/117 (2008), Art. 5.

12 *Rosario Gómez-Limón Pardo* v. *Spain*, Comm. No. 52/2018 Report of the Committee on Economic, Social and Cultural Rights, Adoption of Views, UN Doc E/C.12/67/D/52/2018 (14 April 2020) at paras 11–13.

13 Ibid. at para 14.

14 *Yordanova and Others* v. *Bulgaria*, No. 25446/06, ECHR 24 August 2012 at para 51.

Roma community.[15] The ECtHR has also ordered, as interim remedies, that prisoners be transferred to hospitals to receive necessary treatment. Even short delays by states in complying with such interim measures has been ruled an independent violation and resulted in the award of €15,000 in damages.[16] The IACtHR has ordered similar interim remedies that prisoners receive essential medical treatment.[17]

Domestically, courts often consider the balance of convenience before granting interim relief. As discussed in Chapter 3, Section 3.4.4, it may be easier to obtain interim relief that can be characterized as a less intrusive exemption for a finite group of individuals than for a larger group. This is also consistent with conclusions drawn by Steven Budlender and Gilbert Marcus that SEC litigation is more likely to succeed if it is narrow and focused. They suggest that applicants in several cases may have been in a better position had they obtained interim relief as a defensive remedy against evictions and cuts to essential services.[18]

The South African Constitutional Court granted interim relief to prevent the eviction of informal traders who did not have proper licences.[19] The Court found that the harm to those evicted was irreparable. It would deprive them of their livelihood and their ability to provide for their children. It criticized the government's promise to the destitute traders of damages after a full trial as bordering "on the cynical".[20] Conversely, the harm that the city would suffer from granting interim relief was much less.

Canadian courts have granted detailed interim relief in a number of cases to ensure the provision of minority language educational facilities for the start of the school year, sometimes revising their orders in

[15] *Naidenova et al.* v. *Bulgaria*, Comm. No. 2073/2911, Report of the Human Rights Committee, UNGAOR, 106th Sess., UN Doc CCPR/C/106/D/2/2073/2011 (2012) at paras 9–10.

[16] *Paladi* v. *Moldava* [GC], No. 39806/05, ECHR 10 March 2009 at para 108.

[17] *Cesti Hurtado* v. *Peru* (1998), Order of the Court, Inter-Am. Ct. H.R. (Ser. E), (21 January 1998), online (pdf): https://iachr.lls.edu/sites/default/files/iachr/Court_and_Commission_Documents/20142015/cesti_hurtado_v._peru.provisionalmeasures.1.21.1998.pdf

[18] Steven Budlender, Gilbert Marcus and Nick Ferreira, *Public Interest Litigation and Social Change in South Africa: Strategies, Tactics and Lessons* (The Atlantic Philanthropies, 2014), pp.69–70 online (pdf): www.atlanticphilanthropies.org/wp-content/uploads/2015/12/Public-interest-litigation-and-social-change-in-South-Africa.pdf

[19] *South African Informal Traders Forum & Others* v. *City of Johannesburg & Others*, [2014] ZACC 8 at para 24.

[20] Ibid. at para 34.

response to new evidence and new solutions.[21] Interim remedies remain an important and under-studied and under-used means to provide some protection for SEC rights.

8.2.2 *Remedies Involving Legislation*

Much SEC litigation will target legislation but will rarely ask for the immediate invalidation of such legislation. This recognizes the importance of legislative measures recognized in Article 2(1) of the ICESCR. In some cases, courts will lack the power to invalidate legislation and may issue only a declaration of incompatibility. Jeff King has defended this as a flexible remedial approach.[22] Mark Tushnet has observed that the impact of such declarations will depend on particular political cultures.[23]

In countries where courts can invalidate laws, partial invalidation or a reading in remedy that cures under-inclusion can provide both an immediate victory for the applicants and a systemic remedy that benefits others similarly situated as the applicants. At the same time, such "peremptory remedies"[24] may trigger remedial deterrence that could lead to rights being denied by the court because of fears about the costs of remedies.

As examined in Chapter 4, Section 4.2.2, the Canadian and South African courts have both indicated that while courts can extend benefits, they should only do so where it is clear that judicial extension of benefits is consistent with the main objectives of the statute as well as with the relevant right. The courts will be concerned about the budgetary impacts of an interpretative remedy.[25] If Canadian or South African courts conclude that interpretative remedies would result in too drastic a change to the law, they will often use a suspended declaration of invalidity as a less intrusive remedy.

[21] *Commission Scolaire Francophone* v. *North West Territories*, 2008 NWTSC 53 and revised order 2009 NWTSC 43; *Conseil Scolaire Fransaskois de Zenon Park* v. *Saskatchewan*, [1999] 3 WWR 743 var'd [1999] 12 WWR 742 (Sask. C.A.).

[22] King, *Judging Social Rights*, pp.284–285.

[23] Tushnet, *Weak Courts, Strong Rights*, pp.240–241.

[24] Young, *Constituting Economic and Social Rights*, p.162.

[25] *Schachter* v. *Canada*, [1992] 2 SCR 679; *Vriend* v. *Alberta*, [1998] 1 SCR 493; *National Coalition for Gay and Lesbian Equality* v. *Minister of Home Affairs*, [1999] ZACC 17 at para 75; *Khosa* v. *Minister of Social Development*, [2004] ZACC 11; *Occupiers of 51 Olivia Road et al.* v. *City of Johannesburg and Others*, [2008] ZACC 1 at para 49.

8.2.2.1 Suspended Declarations of Invalidity

A suspended declaration of invalidity provides the legislature with an opportunity to enact new legislation generally within a set period of time. The use of such a remedy can respond to some problems of remedial deterrence. Dissenting judges who were prepared to recognize SEC rights in a leading Canadian case tempered the recognition of rights with an eighteen-month suspended declaration of invalidity.[26] Similarly, the South African Supreme Court of Appeal that recognized water rights would have declared the use of pay-as-you-go water meters to be unconstitutional but only subject to a two-year suspension.[27] The Constitutional Court in a controversial decision overturned the decision on the merits.

As discussed in Chapter 4, Section 4.2.5, the suspended declaration of invalidity may leave applicants and others similarly situated without an immediate remedy. Courts can, however, order a variety of remedies during the suspension. They range from simply exempting the successful applicant to devising more systemic interim remedies. The German Constitutional Court created an interim or transitional remedy of enhanced payments when it ruled in 2012 that benefits paid to refugees that had not been revised since 1993 were unconstitutional. At the same time, the Court stressed that the legislature could displace its interim remedy with new legislation.[28]

Those concerned with the possible regressive effects of judicial remedies with respect to healthcare often point to the Supreme Court of Canada's controversial 2005 *Chaoulli* decision as an example of the dangers of such litigation.[29] In that case, a majority of the Court struck down Quebec's restrictions on private health insurance because of long wait times for hip surgery.

Consistent with an overall theme in this book, the remedy in *Chaoulli* was absolutely critical to the case but largely neglected. The *Chaoulli*

[26] *Gosselin* v. *Quebec (Attorney General)*, [2002] 4 SCR 429 at paras 291–293 per Bastarache J. in dissent; See also *Eldridge* v. *British Columbia*, [1997] 3 SCR 624 at paras 95–96 for a six-month delay in providing translation services.

[27] *Mazibuko and Others* v. *City of Johannesburg and Others*, [2008] ZAGPHC 128 rev'd [2009] ZACC 28 (CC).

[28] Federal Constitutional Court, Judgment of the First Senate, 1 BvL 10/10 (18 July 2012) online: www.bundesverfassungsgericht.de/SharedDocs/Entscheidungen/EN/2012/07/ls20120718_1bvl001010en.html

[29] See generally Colleen M. Flood, Kent Roach and Lorne Sossin (eds.), *Access to Care, Access to Justice: The Legal Debate Over Private Health Insurance in Canada* (Toronto: University of Toronto Press, 2005).

applicants made a shrewd tactical decision to ask for a deceptively simple and negative remedy: an immediate declaration that Quebec's prohibition on the purchase of private insurance was unconstitutional. The success of the *Chaoulli* case was closely related to this limited and negative remedy that the litigants requested. Chief Justice McLachlin and Justice Major observed with apparent approval at the start of the judgement that the litigants "do not seek an order that the government spend more money on healthcare nor do they seek an order that waiting times for treatment under the public healthcare scheme be reduced".[30] Justice Deschamps conceded that the declaration of invalidity would not "provide a complete response to the complex problem of waiting lists" and that "the solution must come from the state itself".[31] She then granted the declaration of invalidity on the basis that it was not up to the applicants "to find a way to remedy a problem that had persisted for a number of years ... Their only burden was to prove that" their rights have been infringed.[32]

Ironically, it was only the dissenters in *Chaoulli* who appeared open to the possibility that in a truly compelling case, courts could fashion an individual remedy that would require the government to spend money by, for example, paying for treatments outside of Quebec.[33] To be sure, such an individual remedy could have allowed queue jumping, but it would have responded to the proven suffering of a specific individual. As I have argued elsewhere, there may be a need for "increased judicial activism to protect those who suffer in the public system and the majority in *Chaoulli* should accept the minority's willingness to consider the case for individual remedies".[34]

The Supreme Court originally issued an immediate declaration of invalidity in *Chaoulli*. This could have resulted in an unregulated insurance market and given insurance companies rights under free trade agreements that would have allowed them to resist subsequent regulation. On a request by Quebec for a re-hearing, the Court suspended the declaration of invalidity for twelve months. The suspension gave Quebec

[30] *Chaoulli* v. *Quebec*, [2005] 1 SCR 791 at para 103.

[31] Ibid. at para 100.

[32] Ibid.

[33] They reasoned that their rejection "of the appellants' global challenge to Quebec's health plan would not foreclose individual patients from seeking individual relief tailored to their individual circumstances". Ibid. at para 264.

[34] Kent Roach, "The Courts and Medicare: Too Much or Too Little Judicial Activism?" In Flood, Roach and Sossin (eds.), *Access to Care, Access to Justice*, p.200.

an opportunity to reform its own health system. By the next year, Quebec enacted twenty-two pages of legislation that complied with the Court's ruling by allowing private insurance for knee, hip and cataract surgeries. At the same time, it expanded the policy debate in a way that the court could not by introducing centralized management of waitlists and a regulated system of out of hospital treatment.[35] This legislation can be seen as a dialogue between courts and legislatures. The Court played a role by listening to the claims of otherwise invisible people stuck on waiting lists. In turn, the legislature respected the Court's decision by allowing people to buy some private insurance while taking steps to quell the demand for such insurance by reducing wait times.

A suspended declaration of invalidity provides a vehicle for legislation to address polycentric issues implicated in SEC rights. Non-binding declarations of incompatibility would also give the legislature an opportunity to formulate remedial legislation in light of its other commitments. As discussed in Chapter 4, Section 4.2.1, however, it would also allow the legislature simply to do nothing in the face of the declaration. This is a danger where the beneficiaries of a declaration of incompatibility are unpopular or lack political power.

8.2.2.2 American School Finance Litigation

The United States is generally seen as an inhospitable environment for both SEC rights and suspended declarations of invalidity. Yet, school finance litigation under state constitutions demonstrates that both are possible. American courts have taken a dialogic rather than a managerial approach to school finance litigation. They frequently use remands to the legislature.[36]

In 1973, the United States Supreme Court effectively ended litigation in the federal courts over school funding by classifying education as not a

[35] Bill 33, *An Act to Amend the Act Respecting Health Services and Social Services and Other Legislative Provisions*, c. 43, 2nd Sess., 37th Leg., Quebec, 2006, assented to 13 December 2006. Colleen Flood described these proposals as a "sophisticated" and "measured" response to the decision that included "a variety of disincentives for a two tier system to flourish". Colleen Flood, "Chaoulli's Legacy for the Future of Canadian Health Care Policy" (2006) 44 *Osgoode Hall L. J.* 273, 305.

[36] George D. Brown, "Binding Advisory Opinions: A Federal Court's Perspective on State Court School Finance Decisions" (1994) 35(3) *B.C. L. Rev.* 543, 566–586. See also Peter H. Schuck, "Public Law Litigation and Social Reform" (1993) 102 *Yale L. J.* 1763, 1771–1772 (discussing "dialogic" nature of "interactions between courts, legislatures, agencies and other social processes").

fundamental interest protected under the US Constitution.[37] This shifted the battle to litigation under the state constitutions. In 1989, the Texas Supreme Court found that unequal funding of school districts violated the state constitution. It concluded: "[w]e do not now instruct the Legislature as to the specifics of the legislation it should enact; nor do we order it to raise taxes. The Legislature has the primary responsibility to decide how best to achieve an efficient system". However, the court warned: "[a] band-aid will not suffice; the system itself must be changed".[38] The Court stayed its response, effectively giving the state seven months to respond. The state responded, but its response was found to be inadequate in a second round of litigation. The Court again responded in a deferential and dialogic manner, noting that there were a wide variety of ways for the government to cure the underfunding problem.[39] It was only when the Court heard the case a fourth time that it decided that the school funding system – which now transferred tax revenues from wealthier school districts to poorer ones – was constitutionally sufficient.[40] Over the course of this litigation in Texas, school funding increased over US$1.9 billion, mainly for the benefit of children in poorer school districts.[41]

In an influential 1989 case, the Kentucky Supreme Court found funding of public schools to be unconstitutional under the state constitution. It enumerated seven specific learning goals that have subsequently been adopted by five other state Supreme Courts.[42] The next year, the Kentucky legislature responded with comprehensive school reform. This reform included broad public participation including by civil society groups who had participated in the litigation.[43]

Michael Rebell has argued that "[c]ourts have a unique capacity for ensuring that effective accountability measures are put into effect, not by micromanaging the day-to-day operations of a school system, but by making sure that legislatures, state education departments, and school districts do their jobs well". He notes that the availability of both

[37] *Rodriguez* v. *San Antonio School Board*, 411 US 1 (1973).

[38] *Edgewood Independent School District* v. *Kirby*, 777 S.W.2d 391 (Tex. 1989).

[39] *Edgewood II*, 804 S.W.2d 491 (Tex. 1991); *Edgewood III*, 826 S.W.2d 489 (Tex. 1992).

[40] *Edgewood IV*, 893 S.W.2d 450 (Tex. 1995).

[41] Michael Rebell, *Courts and Kids: Pursuing Educational Equity through the State Courts* (Chicago: University of Chicago Press, 2009), p.32.

[42] *Rose* v. *Council for Better Education*, 790 S.W.2d 186 (Ky. 1989).

[43] Molly Hunter, "All Eyes Forward: Public Engagement and Educational Reform in Kentucky" (1999) 28 *J. L. Edu.* 485.

standards and performance-based statistics "provide judges readily available tools for undertaking these responsibilities".[44] He used the language of democratic engagement[45] and advocated the use of representative committees that include parents, educators and experts to help inform the content of the remedy.[46] He also warned that "[r]emedial decrees drafted by a judge, even with input from the parties or a group of experts, often lack a clear understanding of the context of needed education reform or an understanding of how the remedy to a particular problem will affect other aspects of school district functioning".[47] As in Chapter 7, Section 7.3, this suggests that judicial use of command and control strategies are unlikely to be effective in complex polycentric contexts. It also highlights the importance of allowing broad participation when formulating systemic remedies.

8.2.3 Damages

The role of damages as a remedy to enforce SEC rights is controversial. The prospect of large damage awards can serve as a form of remedial deterrence and as a diversion of limited governmental resources. Canada's leading failed socio-economic rights case involved a class action seeking Can$389 million in damages. Even dissenters who would have found a rights violation rejected the requested damage award which they classified as "close to half a billion dollars".[48] They concluded that the damages would divert limited financial resources and could not be justified by the degree of governmental fault. Instead, they would have applied an eighteen-month suspended declaration of invalidity to a law limiting social assistance payments for younger recipients. In another Canadian case, Parliament reduced the amount of workplace parental leave benefits when lower courts extended such benefits originally available only to adoptive parents to biological parents as well. The Supreme

44 Rebell, *Courts and Kids*, p.76.

45 Michael A. Rebell and Robert L. Hughes, "Schools, Communities and the Courts: A Dialogic Approach to Education Reform" (1996) 14 *Yale L. Pol'y. Rev.* 99. See also Susan Sturm, "A Normative Theory of Public Law Remedies" (1991) 79 *Geo. L. J.* 1355.

46 Michael A. Rebell and Robert Hughes, "Efficacy and Engagement: The Remedies Problem Posed by Sheff v. O'Neill and a Proposed Solution" (1997) 29 *Conn. L. Rev.* 1115, 1147. In some desegregation cases, judges created and were advised by committees of parents and staff. See, for example, *Keyes* v. *School District* I 380 F. Supp 673 at 704 (1974).

47 Rebell and Hughes, "Schools, Communities and Courts", 129.

48 *Gosselin* v. *Quebec (Attorney General),* [2002] 4 SCR 429 at para 297.

Court eventually held that such an extension would constitute too drastic an expansion of the benefit scheme and used a suspended declaration of invalidity.[49] However, the Supreme Court recently upheld the award of over Can$7 million in damages caused by violations of minority school rights.[50]

Damages have played a useful role in some South African cases. They were made to a property owner to prevent the eviction of those who had established informal housing on the property.[51] This allowed the occupiers to remain on the land, did not require the state to provide alternate land and compensated the property owner for the land.[52] This damage award responded to the harms caused to the property rights of the land owner and prevented a violation of the housing rights of the irregular settlers or the need for complex remedies to ensure that they received adequate alternative accommodation. The South African courts have also used class actions to ensure that teachers in under-funded schools are paid.[53] This effectively used private law to circumvent the need for public law remedies to appoint and pay for more teachers in under-funded schools.[54]

One concern with damages is that they may constitute a windfall for the plaintiffs when others have also suffered similar harms. In Canada, a trial judge awarded Can$20 million in order to deter rights violations, but then ordered these damages be paid not to the class of prisoners who brought the action but to benefit all prisoners with mental health issues. Unfortunately, the judgement did not provide any opportunity for participation or engagement that involved the prisoners. In any event, the innovative remedy was overturned on appeal on the basis that it was not authorized by class action legislation, even though the judge was exercising remedial discretion under section 24(1) of the Canadian Charter of

[49] *Schachter* v. *Canada*, [1992] 2 SCR 679.

[50] *Conseil Scolaire Francophone de la Colombie Britannique* v. *British Columbia*, 2020 SCC 13. I acted as counsel for an intervenor who supported the award of the damage remedy.

[51] *President of the Republic of South Africa and Another* v. *Modderklip Boerdery (Pty) Ltd*, [2005] ZACC 5.

[52] Ibid. at para 20 in reference to *Fose* v. *Minister of Safety and Security*, [1997] ZACC 6 and *Minister of Health* v. *Treatment Action Campaign (No. 2)*, [2002] ZACC 16.

[53] *Mwelase and Others* v. *Director General for the Department of Rural Development and Land Reform and Another*, [2019] ZACC 10; *Linkside* v. *Minister for Basic Education*, [2014] ZAECGHC 111; *Centre for Child Law* v. *Minister of Basic Education*, [2012] ZAECGHC 60.

[54] James Rooney, "Class Actions and Public Interest Standing in South Africa: Practical and Participatory Perspectives" (2017) 33(3) *S.A. J. Hum. Rts.* 406.

Rights and Freedoms. The Court of Appeal also expressed concerns that even though the remedy was the traditional one of damages, it exceeded the legitimate role of the courts and that it was not fair to the class who brought the action.[55] On remand, the trial judge ordered that the damages be distributed to the class of prisoners that had been held in solitary confinement. Although the total award was considerable, it amounted to only Can$500 for each placement in solitary confinement.[56] This is consistent with the pattern of low damage awards for human rights violations seen in Chapter 5, Section 5.2.

Damages alone may fail to achieve systemic reform given that governments may not be responsive to the typically modest awards. The European Court of Human Rights (ECtHR) has awarded €14,000 in non-pecuniary damages in one forced eviction case.[57] Unfortunately, it did not address the risk of the repetition of the violation. The UN Human Rights Committee has urged that state parties pay compensation to prisoners who were denied food for a number of days, but also urged states to take measures to ensure non-repetition of the violation.[58]

Damages can still serve some purpose in calling attention to the existence and harms of a violation. Damages may also help publicize violations in a way that inspires political and civil society engagement and helps convince courts that they can play an effective but manageable role in enforcing SEC rights. It would be wrong to dismiss damages as a remedy for SEC violations, especially under a two-track approach.

8.2.4 *Declarations*

In two early SEC cases, the South African Constitutional Court overturned injunctions with retention of jurisdiction and relied on declaratory relief. In *Grootboom*, the Court declared that the city had an obligation to provide housing for those most in need in emergency situations.[59] It was not, however, until August 2003 that national and

55 *Brazeau* v. *Canada (Attorney General)*, 2020 ONCA 184.

56 *Brazeau* v. *Canada (Attorney General)*, 2020 ONSC 3272; ibid. at para 103.

57 *Connors* v. *United Kingdom*, No. 66746/01, ECHR 27 May 2014 at paras 114–115.

58 *Mukong* v. *Cameroon*, Comm. No. 458/1991, Report of the United Nations Human Rights Committee, 51st Sess., UN Doc CCPR/C/51/D/458/1991 (1994); *Lantsova* v. *The Russian Federation*, Comm. No. 763/1997, Report of the United Nations Human Rights Committee, 74th Sess., UN Doc CCPR/C/D/63/763/1997 (2002).

59 *Government of the Republic of South Africa and Others* v. *Grootboom and Others*, 2000 (11) BCLR 1169 at paras 36, 44, 68.

provincial governments adopted emergency housing plans.[60] In the interim, the applicants had settled with the government and subsequently obtained an order from the Constitutional Court requiring that their temporary shelters be waterproofed and that water and toilets be provided.[61]

In the *Treatment Action* case[62] the Court required national and provincial governments to provide a drug that would prevent transmission of HIV from mothers to newborns but refused to retain supervisory jurisdiction. It viewed retention of jurisdiction as an unwarranted penalty for a recalcitrant government by stressing the "government has always respected and executed orders of this Court. There is no reason to believe it will not do so in the present case".[63]

The Supreme Court of Canada has also relied on a declaration in *Eldridge v. British Columbia*[64] and even suspended the declaration for six months to allow the province to select among a range of options in providing sign language interpretation in the provision of medical care. Declarations can be effective if competent governments have simply been unaware of rights and if the court defines the relevant rights with sufficient clarity.[65]

In both *Eldridge*[66] and the *Treatment Action* case,[67] there is evidence that some provinces did not respond promptly to the court's declaration. David Bilchitz has concluded that in *Treatment Action* "[t]wo provinces in particular, Mpumalanga and Limpopo, had failed to make any progress in making nevirapine more widely available, despite reports by doctors and nurses that there was the capacity to do so. This situation is tragic and could have been avoided had the Court adopted a more

60 See David Bilchitz, *Poverty and Fundamental Rights* (Oxford: Oxford University Press, 2008), pp.151ff on the response to the declaration.

61 Sandra Liebenberg, *Socio-economic Rights: Adjudication under a Transformative Constitution* (Claremont: Juta, 2010), pp.400–401. As Liebenberg notes "the delays in implementing the program specified in the Grootboom orders undoubtedly has serious repercussions for those in urgent housing need. This has been mitigated to some extent by the reluctance of the courts to grant eviction orders without being satisfied that the authorities have made provision for some form of alternative accommodation". Ibid., p.408.

62 *Minister of Health* v. *Treatment Action Campaign (No. 2)*, [2002] ZACC 16 at para 129.

63 Ibid.

64 [1997] 2 SCR 13.

65 Kent Roach and Geoff Budlender, "Mandatory Relief and Supervisory Jurisdiction: When Is It Appropriate, Just and Equitable?" (2005) 122 *S.A. L.J.* 325.

66 See Kent Roach, "Remedial Consensus and Dialogue" (2002) 35 *U.B.C. L. Rev.* 225.

67 Roach and Budlender, "Mandatory Relief and Supervisory Jurisdiction", 333–334.

robust approach and sought to supervise the implementation of its order".[68] Similarly, not all provinces in Canada promptly responded to the *Eldridge* decision in part because the declaration was only directed at one province.

Retention of jurisdiction should not be seen as a form of punishment or probation for recalcitrant governments. It may simply respond to a dynamic situation where delays and unanticipated problems in responding to declarations can cause serious harms to rights. At the same time, courts may be reluctant to use detailed injunctions to enforce SEC rights. In the context of educational rights, the Irish Supreme Court has more categorically ruled that injunctions would violate the separation of powers.[69] As discussed in Chapter 7, Section 7.4, the choice between a general declaration and a detailed injunction often places courts in a difficult position. In such circumstances, a declaration plus where the court retains jurisdiction without making specific orders that could be enforced through contempt sanctions may be a valuable intermediate remedy.

8.2.5 *The Declaration Plus*

An example of a remedy that could be characterized as a declaration plus is the trial judgement in the famous *Grootboom* housing rights case. Justice Dennis Davis maintained in force an interim injunction against the eviction of the plaintiffs who had occupied higher land to avoid the rains. He then ordered each party, within three months, to submit remedial plans that could be commented upon by the other parties. He explained: "[i]t seems to me that the relief which can properly be granted at this stage on the available evidence is at best declaratory. The next step, is to endeavour to give some practical content to the declaration". As for the governmental defendants, he noted that "now that they know where their duty lies, they should be given an opportunity of proposing a practical solution. In fairness to the applicants, now that they know where their rights lie . . . [they] should furthermore have the opportunity of commenting on the proposals, and the respondents should be allowed to respond to such comment".[70] Taken on its own, such an order simply set out a procedure to gather information and allowed the Court to retain

[68] Bilchitz, *Poverty and Fundamental Rights*, p.163. See also ibid. for a similar conclusion.
[69] See, for example, *T.D.* v. *Minister of Education*, [2001] IESC 101 (Ir.).
[70] *Grootboom* v. *Oostenberg Municipality and Others*, 2000 (3) BCLR 277 (C) at 294–295.

jurisdiction. Justice Davis, however, provided some content to the declaration by indicating that while he did not:

> wish to be prescriptive about the solutions which the respondents are called upon to suggest to discharge their constitutional obligation. But in order to contain any future debate, I would say provisionally that tents, portable latrines and a regular supply of water (albeit transported) would constitute the bare minimum. Perhaps something better can be offered. The choice of an appropriate site presents another difficulty. The convenience of the applicants, and proximity to existing jobs, is but one factor to be taken into account. The applicants' immediate interests regarding location may have to yield to other constraints.[71]

This sort of a declaration provides some content to the relevant rights. As such, it responds to the concerns raised by David Bilchitz that supervisory jurisdiction with only vague direction for governments to be reasonable and consult will not be adequate and that the courts need to define the minimum core of the right.[72]

A number of Canadian courts have followed a similar remedial template in retaining jurisdiction while essentially making declarations about the content of the right. The leading case of *Doucet-Boudreau v. Nova Scotia*[73] was examined in Chapter 7, Section 7.4.5, as an example of what effectively was a declaration plus. This combined general declarations about what minority language schools were required in certain areas while leaving it up to the state to select the means to implement them while the judge retained jurisdiction. Variations on the declaration plus have been used in other cases. In a case involving claims for autism therapy, the British Columbia Court of Appeal employed "directions". The Court characterized this as a remedy that was stronger than a mere declaration but short of a mandamus or an injunction.[74] In another case, a trial judge specified that the parties must devise a dispute resolution process to address specified matters. The judge added: "ultimately, the court will always retain its power to review the issue of whether the decisions made meets the constitutional duty ... Hopefully, a well-considered dispute resolution process will avoid any further referrals to the Court".[75]

71 Ibid.
72 Bilchitz, *Poverty and Fundamental Rights*, pp.16ff.
73 [2003] 3 SCR 3.
74 *Auton (Guardian ad litem of)* v. *British Columbia (Attorney General)*, 2002 BCCA 538 at paras 92, 128 rev'd on merits [2004] 3 SCR 657.
75 *Assn. des parents francophones (Colombie-Britannique)* v. *British Columbia*, (1998) 61 BCLR (3d) 165 (S.C.) at para 58.

In another minority language school case, the Supreme Court of Canada upheld a trial judge's decision to bifurcate remedial proceedings while retaining jurisdiction. The Court stressed Canada's "tradition of state actors taking declarations seriously". It expressed hopes that the parties could resolve issues concerning "competing resource demands and the imperfect realities of day-to-day management of an education system".[76] The declaration plus allows the court to retain the benefits of making general declarations about SEC rights and retaining jurisdiction if necessary to resolve disputes. This space also provides the parties an opportunity to agree on the details of the remedy but in a way that is conscious and guided by the rights that the court has declared to exist.

8.2.6 Injunctions

As discussed in Chapter 7, Section 7.2.5, the South African Constitutional Court has moved towards more aggressive structural injunctions in recent years in response to chronic governmental failures. Like the Supreme Court of Canada,[77] it has stressed the need for injunctions to be clear and precise in order to be enforceable. Justice Nkabinde affirmed for a unanimous Court that:

> Supervisory orders arising from structural interdicts ensure that courts play an active monitoring role in the enforcement of orders. In an appropriate case, this guarantees commitment to the constitutional values of accountability, responsiveness and openness by all concerned, in a system of democratic governance. By granting the structural interdict a court secures a response in the form of reports and thereby prevents a failure to comply with the positive obligations imposed by its order. Generally, the court's role continues until the remedy it has ordered in a matter has been fulfilled.[78]

The Court noted that its original orders combined declaratory relief about a past violation with a "structural interdict". It noted that the latter remedy "is, by its nature, a much more interventionist remedy than declaratory relief". The Court ordered that the Municipality "identify land . . . for the relocation of the applicants and engage meaningfully with

[76] *Assoc. des parents de l'ecole Rose-des-vents* v. *British Columbia*, 2015 SCC 21 at paras 61, 65.

[77] *Thibodeau* v. *Air Canada*, [2014] 3 SCR 340.

[78] *Pheko and Others* v. *Ekurhuleni Metropolitan Municipality and Others (No. 3)*, [2016] ZACC 20 at para 1.

them on the identification of land" and "file a report . . . regarding steps taken . . . to provide access to adequate housing for the applicants".[79] Injunctions, including the ability to hold responsible officials in contempt, may be warranted in some circumstances. Nevertheless, they come with the price of the court having to be specific about what is required of governments. A somewhat more deferential approach based on the declaration plus may be a better starting point with respect to the enforcement of SEC rights.[80]

8.3 Weak Remedies and Queue Jumping

An impediment to the justiciability of SEC rights is the idea that judges should not order individual remedies because they constitute "queue jumping". As will be seen, such an approach does not appropriately recognize that courts acting within the separation of powers should provide litigants who have established rights violations with effective remedies wherever possible.

8.3.1 Weak Remedies?

Drawing on his distinction between strong and weak form judicial review previously discussed and criticized in Chapter 4, Section 4.4, Mark Tushnet defended the South African Constitutional Court's use of declaratory relief in *Grootboom*, including that "under the Court's order the individual plaintiffs need not receive any relief at all. The government's program would have been acceptable had it promised to provide some housing for people in desperate need 'within a reasonably short time'".[81] He elaborated that "for practical reasons, the remedies for violations of social and economic rights cannot be 'personal and present'".[82] This invoked the *Brown v. Board of Education II* formula discussed in Chapter 7, Section 7.2.1, where courts focus on systemic relief and not on providing immediate and individual remedies.[83]

[79] Ibid. at para 27. In reference to the Constitutional Court's original order in *Pheko and Others* v. *Ekurhuleni Metropolitan Municipality*, [2011] ZACC 34 at para 53.
[80] Robert J. Sharpe, "Injunctions and the Charter" (1984) 22(3) *Osgoode Hall L.J.* 474.
[81] Tushnet, *Weak Courts, Strong Rights*.
[82] Ibid., pp.247–248.
[83] At the same time, Professor Tushnet was well aware of the dynamic swings between strong and weak forms of both judicial review and remedies. Drawing on Simon's and Sabel's work on experimental remedies, he contemplated a process where weak remedies

In the wake of *Grootboom*, an academic consensus started developing that weak remedies were the preferable way to enforce SEC rights. Jeff King argues that polycentric issues can be accommodated by remedies that "leave latitude to the primary decision-maker to adjust to the ruling in a flexible way in future circumstances".[84] King points to declarations and suspended declarations of invalidity as two such remedies. I agree that these remedies can play a valuable role in enforcing socio-economic rights.[85] At the same time, I do not share King's considerable reservations about having judges retain jurisdiction and requiring governments to report back to the court.[86]

Katharine Young, like King, opposed strong forms of managerial or peremptory judicial review because they involve "a striking arrogation of power to the courts".[87] Her defence of a "catalytic court"[88] that interacts with the executive, the legislature and political and social movements has many dialogic features and much in common with King's defence of "non-intrusive remedies".[89] Generally, I share some of Young's optimism about courts acting dialogically as catalysts of reforms. Nevertheless, I doubt that courts will be legitimate or effective if they are solely concerned with systemic reform. There is a need for courts to recognize and enforce rights if they are to have legitimacy.[90] This is especially the case if SEC rights are to be recognized as justiciable. Neither Tushnet nor King address the lack of individual remedies in *Grootboom* or the lack of retained jurisdiction in *Treatment Action* as a problem.[91]

Some scholars disagree with the academic consensus in favour of weak and systemic remedies (such as declarations) as the sole means to enforce SEC rights. Both David Landau and Cesar Rodriguez-Garavito argue in

would be found to be ineffective, replaced by a strong remedy also found to be ineffective and finally replaced "by a different form of weak remedy, which promises to be effective". Ibid., pp.249, 255.

84 King, *Judging Social Rights*, p.203.

85 See Roach, "Remedial Consensus and Dialogue".

86 King, *Judging Social Rights*, pp.274–275.

87 Young, *Constituting Economic and Social Rights*, p.165.

88 Ibid., pp.133–191.

89 King, *Judging Social Rights*, pp.300–301.

90 For my arguments about the need for normative justifications of dialogical judicial review, see Kent Roach, *The Supreme Court on Trial: Judicial Activism or Democratic Dialogue*, 2nd ed. (Toronto: Irwin Law, 2016), pp.175- 207.

91 Young noted that "the apparent inattention of the Constitutional Court to the direct plight of the claimants registered dramatically when eight years after the judgement, Irene Grootboom passed away, still without a home". Young, *Constituting Economic and Social Rights*, p.147.

favour of respectively "strong structural reform"[92] and "dialogical activism".[93] They both cite the Colombian Constitutional Court's combination of large numbers of individual actions with respect to healthcare with judicial supervision but not dictation of the state's response. Brian Ray has also defended a recent trend in South African jurisprudence to combine individual anti-eviction remedies with structural remedies based on engagement.[94] In Section 8.6, I will build on this work in outlining a two-track approach to enforcing SEC rights that combines strong individual and systemic remedies and that accepts the need, even in the systemic track, for courts to use peremptory and managerial remedies when appropriate.[95]

8.3.2 Queue Jumping?

One of the justifications for weak systemic remedies to enforce SEC rights is the idea that individual remedies will allow successful litigants to jump queues for allocating scare resources. Writing in 2003, Justice Albie Sachs warned about courts giving "individuals with the sharpest elbows (and the best lawyers)" access to limited resources.[96] This idea is related to Aristotle's dichotomy between distributive justice and corrective justice in the sense that individual corrective remedies for individual litigants may disturb the distribution of scarce resources in a society.

Guido Calabresi and Philip Bobbitt have recognized that there are a variety of methods for allocating scarce resources. They include not only queues, but markets, lotteries, custom and politics. They argue that no one method is perfect. Societies will use different methods at different times as the shortcomings of each method become clearer.[97] Katharine Young has observed that the epithet of queue jumping has been deployed

92 David Landau, "The Reality of Social Rights Enforcement" (2012) 53 *Harv. J. Int'l. L.* 189.

93 Cesar Rodriguez-Garavito, "Beyond Enforcement: Assessing and Enhancing Judicial Impact" in Langford, Rodriguez-Garavito and Rossi, *Social Rights Judgments*, p.82.

94 Brian Ray, *Engaging with Social Rights: Procedure, Participation and Democracy in South Africa's Second Wave* (Cambridge: Cambridge University Press, 2016).

95 Young, *Constituting Economic and Social Rights*, p.161.

96 Albie Sachs, "The Judicial Enforcement of Socio-Economic Rights: The Grootboom Case" (2003) 56 *Current Leg. Prob.* 579, 598.

97 *Tragic Choices: The Conflicts Society Confronts in the Allocation of Tragically Scarce Resources* (New York: W.W. Norton & Company, 1978).

in South Africa "by officials and politicians in relation to housing policy",[98] in part because there are 1.8 million people on a waitlist for public housing. As she concludes, the shorthand of queue jumping is in some tension with the idea of rights. It also assumes that the government's allocation of scarce resources is sufficient and reasonable.[99]

The queue jumping effects of individual remedies can be justified on the basis of legitimate expectations that successful litigants should receive effective remedies from courts. Objections to SEC litigation on the basis of queue jumping smack of double standards and second thoughts about the justiciability of SEC rights. The queue-jumping epithet is rarely raised in the context of other rights even though it should be clear that not all who have suffered rights violations will seek and receive remedies. Judges simply cannot know how many similarly situated individuals have suffered similar injustices to the litigant before them. Nevertheless, their job is to do justice to the litigant before them. The South African Constitutional Court has recognized, alas not in the context of SEC rights, that it "cannot deny strong actual claims timeously asserted by determinate people, because of the possible existence of hypothetical claims that might conceivably have been brought by indeterminate groups".[100]

Rosalind Dixon and David Landau have examined the tendency of the middle class to benefit from socio-economic rights litigation. They concede that this can have regressive effects, but also argue that such litigation may assist the most marginalized by placing more attention on SEC rights and broadening support for reforms.[101] When joined with the importance of right to a remedy reasoning in courts, this also provides another rejoinder to those who would criticize the award of individual remedies in SEC litigation as regressive queue jumping.

8.4 Constraints on Remedies: Proportionality and Reasonableness Review

There is a large debate in both the SEC and administrative law literature about the role of reasonableness review. Some argue that reasonableness

[98] Katharine G. Young, "Rights and Queues: On Distributive Contests in the Modern State" (2016) 55 *Colum. J. Transnt'l. L.* 65, 94.

[99] Ibid., pp.126ff.

[100] *August and Another* v. *Electoral Commission and Others*, [1999] ZACC 3 at para 30.

[101] David Landau and Rosalind Dixon, "Constitutional Non-Transformation?" in Katharine Young (ed.), *The Future of Economic and Social Rights* (Cambridge: Cambridge University Press, 2019).

review is preferable to proportionality-based review because it makes more room for the positive state.[102] Others suggest that SEC jurisprudence lacks the rigour of proportionality review.[103] This debate is largely beyond the scope of this book on remedies. Nevertheless, it is relevant to the degree to which courts should scrutinize legislation that allocates scarce resources in the context of SEC rights and what limits should be placed on SEC remedies, especially individual remedies.

In *Grootboom*, the South African Constitutional Court employed a test that required more justification from the state depending on the impact of denying a right. The Court explained: "[t]o be reasonable, measures cannot leave out of account, the degree and extent of the denial of the right they endeavour to realise. Those whose needs are most urgent and whose ability to enjoy all rights is therefore most in peril, must not be ignored . . .".[104] This statement echoes the final overall balance element of proportionality analysis. As discussed in Chapter 1, Section 1.9, this is a critical yet sometimes controversial step in proportionality review. The overall balance stage is particularly helpful in many remedial contexts as it measures the effects of denying or limiting a remedy on the applicant against the benefits received by the state in remedial delay or other limits placed on remedies. This form of proportionality analysis can be very helpful in remedial analysis. If it had been applied to remedies (as opposed to rights) in *Grootboom*, it may have justified individual and immediate remedies for the applicants who were in quite desperate situations as part of the main judgement.[105]

[102] Cass Sunstein, "Social and Economic Rights? Lessons from South Africa" (2001) 11(4) *Constitutional Forum* 123.

[103] Katharine Young, "Proportionality, Reasonableness and Economic and Social Rights" in Vicki C. Jackson and Mark Tushnet (eds.), *Proportionality: New Frontiers, New Challenges* (Cambridge: Cambridge University Press, 2019).

[104] *Government of the Republic of South Africa and Others* v. *Grootboom and Others*, 2000 (11) BCLR 1169 at para 44.

[105] As Liebenberg noted, the Court did provide individual remedies before rendering judgement in the case by ordering that the municipality "provide basic sanitation services, water and R200,000 for the purposes of waterproofing the applicants' existing accommodation . . . Given the negotiated settlement which was made an order of court, the Constitutional Court was relieved of the burden of having to decide on direct relief for the Grootboom community in its judgment". Liebenberg, *Socio-Economic Rights*, pp.400–401. See also Albie Sachs noting that an individual remedy had been given which "left us free to deal with the level of unreasonableness". Sachs, "The Judicial Enforcement of Socio-Economic Rights: The Grootboom Case", 595. Alas, many commentators have ignored this individual remedy in their discussion of *Grootboom*.

Reasonableness review with respect to limits on rights may provide legislatures and the executive with a greater margin of appreciation to determine limits on or the exact content of SEC rights. For example, reasonableness review was used in *Mazibuko*[106] to overturn a trial judgement that urban residents were entitled to fifty litres of water a day. The Court of Appeal had altered the remedy to forty-two litres of water. This is the sort of line drawing that should be done by the legislature or the executive, at least in the absence of an unwillingness or inability of those institutions or some particularly adverse impact on the population. As Steven Budlender and Gilbert Marcus have argued, a better case would have sought a structural interdict aimed at providing water to the 750,000 residents of Johannesburg who do not have any access to residential water.[107]

As the Court recognized in *Mazibuko*, both reasonableness and proportionality standards, while not holding governments "to an impossible standard of perfection", still demand a "a detailed accounting"[108] from them. The ability of governments to justify reasonable limits on rights is a key aspect of a dialogic approach.[109] It means that even if courts order remedies for SEC rights violations that may be determined to be excessive (perhaps in response to other emergency demands on governments) or regressive, it is likely that the government will be able to respond and justify its distributive choices in allocating scarce resources.

The most worrying concern in *Mazibuko* is not the fine distinction between reasonableness and proportionality, but the Court's use of absolutist separation of powers rhetoric. For example, it stated that the Constitution does not "require courts to take over the tasks that in a democracy should properly be reserved for the democratic arms of government".[110] As argued in Chapter 1, Section 1.8, the best approach to the separation of powers is one that makes comparative assessments of the actual and not the imagined capacity of each institution in light of the actual harms that human rights violations have caused to individuals. One danger of overreaching on either rights or remedies is that it may

[106] *Mazibuko and Others* v. *City of Johannesburg and Others*, [2009] ZACC 28.

[107] Budlender, Marcus and Ferreira, *Public Interest Litigation and Social Change in South Africa*, p.64.

[108] *Mazibuko and Others* v. *City of Johannesburg and Others*, [2009] ZACC 28 at paras 161, 163.

[109] Dixon, "Creating Dialogue about Socio-Economic Rights"; Kent Roach *The Supreme Court on Trial* rev'd ed. (Toronto: Irwin Law, 2016) chs 9 and 17.

[110] *Mazibuko and Others* v. *City of Johannesburg and Others*, [2009] ZACC 28 at para 161.

cause the courts to retreat into restrictive and rigid conceptions of the separation of powers.

8.4.1 *Remedies in Emergencies*

The COVID-19 crisis makes particularly relevant what happens to remedies in an emergency where the state faces overwhelming demands with less financial resources. The two-track approach can accommodate the emergency most easily with respect to systemic remedies by allowing more time to implement systemic remedies. Even with respect to systemic remedies, however, courts should not simply accept governmental cries of emergency and lack of resources at face value. In a judgement delivered during the COVID-19 crisis, the Supreme Court of Canada appropriately held that a vague reference to the need "for a fair and rational allocation of limited public funds" was not a legitimate objective for limiting minority school rights.[111] Even in emergencies, governments need to justify why they cannot provide remedies.

The more difficult question is what effect emergencies should have on individual remedies. The idea of a minimum core of non-derogable rights is well accepted with respect to some rights such as rights against torture.[112] The minimum core concept has also been defended in SEC rights by David Bilchitz and others.[113] Using the 2008 financial crisis as an example, Jernej Černič has argued that courts should embrace the minimum core as part of their commitment to the rule of law with respect to SEC rights.[114]

A request for individual remedies may be warranted by the dire circumstances that individuals face in emergencies. It is a high-risk but sometimes necessary strategy for litigants to take. An individual remedy based on the minimum core concept can make clear to governments and the more advantaged the consequences of an emergency. Even if a state cannot provide the minimum core to everyone in an emergency, individual remedies can help ensure that the courts play a role in the emergency and that the public and history are reminded of the importance of rights and remedies.

[111] *Conseil scolaire francophone de la Colombie Britannique* v. *British Columbia*, 2020 SCC 13 at para 153.

[112] The Court noted in *Khocklich* v. *Moldova*, No. 41707/98, ECHR 29 April 2003 at para 181 that "lack of resources cannot in principle justify prison conditions which are so poor as to reach the threshold of treatment contrary to Article 3 of the Convention".

[113] Bilchitz, *Poverty and Fundamental Rights.*

[114] Jernej Letnar Černič, "The European Court of Human Rights, Rule of Law and Socio-Economic Rights in Times of Crises" (2016) 8 *Hague J. Rule Law* 227.

Remedial decision-making should be attentive to the reality of remedial failure and true tragedy. One of the strengths of remedies is that they force litigators and judges to depart from the heady perfectionism that permeates rights language. In times of crisis, there also may be a role for courts to say that while rights have been violated and while applicants would normally be entitled to a remedy to stop the violation and compensate for its effects, in present circumstances it is not possible for the court to award a remedy.

8.5 The Two Faces of Engagement: Consensual Remedies or Authorized Evictions?

The South African courts have increasingly ordered that governmental defendants engage with rights holders in SEC rights cases. Such engagement orders reflect the polycentric nature of SEC rights. They also have the potential to draw on the practical wisdom and resilience of the intended beneficiaries of the remedy. In one of the first engagement cases, Justice Sachs urged the government to respect and listen to occupiers facing eviction who had demonstrated "tenacity and ingenuity . . . in making homes out of discarded material, in finding work and sending their children to school . . . Justice and equity oblige them to rely on this same resourcefulness in seeking a solution to their plight and to explore all reasonable possibilities of securing suitable alternative accommodation or land".[115] As Sandra Liebenberg has argued: "participatory enforcement mechanisms can mitigate polycentricity and judicial competence concerns ... Novel solutions to seemingly intractable problems may be generated as parties analyse the root causes of rights violations, share local knowledge, deliberate and test policies through processes of trial and error".[116] In short, engagement can result in creative and consensual remedies.

In 1976, Abram Chayes identified participation and negotiation as a fundamental feature of public law litigation.[117] Susan Sturm subsequently formulated remedial theories designed to encourage consensual but

[115] Ibid. at para 41. See Liebenberg, *Socio-Economic Rights*, pp.278–279; Geoff Budlender, "The Right to Alternative Accommodations in Forced Evictions" in John Squires et al. (eds.), *The Road to a Remedy: Current Issues in the Litigation of Economic, Social and Cultural Rights* (Sydney: University of New South Wales Press, 2005).

[116] Sandra Liebenberg, "Participatory Approaches to Socio-Economic Rights: Tentative Lessons from South Africa's Evictions Law" (2014) 32(4) *Nordic J. Hum. Rts.* 312, 319.

[117] Abram Chayes, "Public Law Litigation and the Burger Court" (1982) 96 *Harv. L. Rev.* 4.

deliberative resolution of the remedy.[118] The South African courts were likely attracted to engagement in part because a number of housing rights were the subject of successful settlements. Engagement remedies can be seen as both dialogic and experimental. They recognize that there are a variety of legitimate ways to implement SEC rights. Rather than dictating a solution, the court gives the state and the rights holders an opportunity to shape the content of the remedy. At the same time, there is a danger that inequality of bargaining power will distort the engagement process. This is especially so if the courts do not protect the rights-holders from suffering irreparable harm and if they do not articulate in general terms what the right requires.

The South African emphasis on engagement has two faces. Engagement can produce consensual agreements that draw on the expertise of both governments and rights holder. The less happy face of engagement is when it is used as a means to limit SEC rights and authorize evictions.

In the *Joe Slovo Community* case,[119] the Court ordered the parties to engage with each other about the community's evictions, including with respect to the timing, the quality of any temporary accommodation[120] and the allocation of spaces in the new developments that were to be built fifteen kilometres from where the applicants lived.[121] The Court warned that the requirement to engage did not mean that those who would be evicted have a veto.[122] As will be seen in Chapter 9, Section 9.3.1, this is also a common refrain in the Canadian jurisprudence on the duty to consult Indigenous people. The "no veto" edict, however, can undermine the consultation process. As Kirsty McLean noted: "[o]ne would imagine

118 Sturm, "A Normative Theory of Public Law Remedies", 1391 noting that both Fuller and Fiss stress that participation is important to the legitimacy of adjudication but then do not apply this insight to remedial decision-making.

119 *Residents of Joe Slovo Community, Western Cape* v. *Thubelisha Homes and Others*, [2009] ZACC 16 at para 244.

120 The court was specific about the quality of the alternative accommodation, something that Young criticizes as a managerial approach that "despite its ability to address the immediate plight of litigants . . . may ultimately compromise judicial power by exacerbating concerns about competence and legitimacy". Young, *Constituting Economic and Social Rights*, p.161. Although some individual remedies may have managerial aspects they remain individual remedies and something that courts are expected to provide.

121 *Residents of Joe Slovo Community, Western Cape* v. *Thubelisha Homes and Others*, [2009] ZACC 16 at para 5.

122 Ibid. at paras 243–244 ("the goal of meaningful engagement is to find a mutually acceptable solution to the difficult issues confronting the government and the residents in the quest to provide adequate housing".).

that such limited engagement, with so little bargaining power and an eviction a *fait accomplii*, would be cold comfort for those facing eviction".[123]

Perhaps not surprisingly, the engagement was something of a top-down affair. The Court acknowledged these problems but held that the engagement was reasonable. Hence the community could be evicted from their homes and given temporary accommodation. O'Regan J. appealed to the queue jumping concept in concluding that while "[r]efusing an order of eviction in this case might give some temporary relief to the applicants" , it would harm the interests of others on waiting lists for housing. She also held open the possibility of some accommodation by stating that "the order of eviction that is made can seek to remedy, at least to some extent, the failure of government to engage meaningfully in consultation with the applicants up to this stage".[124]

Liebenberg has aptly characterized the *Joe Slovo Community* approach to engagement as a narrow "dispute resolution"[125] approach. Anashri Pillay has similarly criticized the engagement process as focusing on "rapid delivery" of re-development "at the expense of real engagement".[126] As she notes, the idea of meaningful engagement was watered down by the Court to reasonable engagement[127] with some judges refusing to really consider the applicant's concerns about re-location on separation of powers grounds. For example, Ngcobo J. stated that "it is not for the courts to tell the government how to upgrade the area".[128]

123 "Meaningful Engagement: One Step Forward or Two Back: Some Thoughts on Joe Slovo" (2010) 3 *Con. Ct. Rev.* 223, 240.

124 *Residents of Joe Slovo Community, Western Cape* v. *Thubelisha Homes and Others*, [2009] ZACC 16 at para 303.

125 Liebenberg, "Participatory Approaches".

126 Anashri Pillay, "Towards Effective Social Economic Rights Adjudication: The Role of Meaningful Engagement" (2012) 10(3) *I. Con.* 732, 744. Professor Pillay elaborates: "[g]ranting the evictions in the first place removed much of the 'sting' from the Constitutional Court's orders that further engagement take place and that the state take steps to improve the transport situation for people in Delft, for example. It is difficult to see how the Joe Slovo residents could be equal partners in a future engagement process under these circumstances". Ibid., 751.

127 *Residents of Joe Slovo Community, Western Cape* v. *Thubelisha Homes and Others*, [2009] ZACC 16 at para 117 per Yacoob J.; ibid. at paras 301–302 per O'Regan J.

128 Ibid. at para 253. At the same time, the Court engaged in what Young criticizes as "managerialism" by providing for minimum specifications for the temporary housing and minimum allocations in the new development: ibid. at para 10; Young, *Constituting Economic and Social Rights*, p.161. Such entitlements may have given the applicant some more power after their evictions, but did not address their resistance from being displaced from their existing homes.

Inequality of bargaining power between governments and those claiming housing rights will be especially acute in cases where the engagement is narrowly focused on evictions and alternative accommodations.[129] Respectful engagement may require a more flexible agenda that has not been set by the government.

But there appears to be happy ending to the *Joe Slovo Community* case. The government started the case with the goal of evicting and re-locating the residents fifteen kilometres away from their homes. In the end, the residents eventually convinced a new government that improvements to their existing housing was a better remedy, even after the Constitutional Court had approved of eviction after twenty-one months of engagement.[130] The case ended with a creative and consensual remedy, but it could also have ended with a forced eviction after a top-down engagement. Those are the two faces of engagement. As will be seen in Chapter 9, Section 9.3, similar patterns can be seen in the duty to consult Indigenous people.

8.6 Towards a Two-Track Approach

The two-track approach is based in part on the practice of supra-national courts that distinguish between individual remedies for applicants and general measures to prevent or reduce future rights violations. Different remedies are often necessary and desirable to achieve these different remedial goals. Individual remedies can include interim remedies to prevent irreparable harm, damages and exemptions from suspended declarations of invalidity. The systemic remedies include retention of jurisdiction, engagement orders, plan submissions and the use of declarations, the declaration plus, injunctions and legislative reform.

The two-track approach recognizes that SEC rights, like more complex forms of civil and political rights, raise complex polycentric problems. Even with the best of intentions, some judicial remedies may produce unanticipated and negative consequences. The two-track approach allows courts to pursue systemic remedies in an initially deferential and dialogic manner while also ordering individual remedies that affirm the justiciability of SEC rights and provide some measure of remedial success.

[129] In Chapter 9, Section 9.3, it will be suggested that a similar narrow focus on development allows an analogous duty to consult to limit Indigenous rights.

[130] Factors included a change of government and concerns about the costs of the new development. Liebenberg, "Participatory Approaches", 325.

8.6.1 *The Dangers of Exclusively Focusing on Individual Remedies*

It is widely accepted that individual remedies themselves will not be adequate to enforce SEC rights. In India, much school litigation has focused on admission to neighbourhood and private schools. It has been criticized for neglecting systemic educational reform.[131] Although damages as an individual remedy to compensate the property owner in *Modderklipp* had the effect of preventing evictions,[132] the need for broader systemic remedies with respect to public housing remains.

In South America, there has been considerable focus on the individual enforcement of SEC rights through summary procedures such as amparo. In the context of healthcare litigation in Brazil, Octavio Ferraz has argued that individual remedies had a greater impact than systemic remedies.[133] David Landau has also examined extensive tutela healthcare litigation in Colombia that has produced thousands of individual remedies. Both Professors Ferraz and Landau concede that such robust individual enforcement had regressive effects with better off litigants benefiting more than the poor. Landau has argued that "the judicious use of structural injunctions can more effectively target social rights interventions towards the poor".[134] In reply, however, Ferraz has argued that courts have encouraged regressive outcomes not so much by choice of remedy but by interpretation of rights.[135] In truth, both have a point. Courts in Brazil and Colombia have been too generous in ordering expensive treatments for individuals. This may be related to the summary nature of the individual action that has not always allowed governments to justify the reasonableness of their allocation of scarce resources.[136]

[131] Arghya Sengupta et al., "Legislating Human Rights" in Young, *The Future of Economic and Social Rights*, p.180.

[132] *President of the Republic of South Africa and Another* v. *Modderklip Boerdery (Pty) Ltd*, [2005] ZACC 5.

[133] Octavio Ferraz, "Brazil: Are Collective Suits Harder to Enforce?" in Langford, Rodriguez-Garavito and Rossi, *Social Rights Judgments*; Landau, "The Reality of Social Rights Enforcement", 218.

[134] Landau, "The Reality of Social Rights Enforcement", 191, 202.

[135] Octavio Luiz Motta Ferraz, "Social Rights, Judicial Remedies and the Poor" (2019) 18(3) *Wash. U. Global Studies L. Rev.* 569.

[136] A study of 1000 tutela actions found that the petitioner succeeded in 95.9 per cent of cases and generally received relief: Diego Gomez-Ceballos and Isabel Craverier, "Judicialization of the Right to Health" (2019) 34 *Int. J. Health Plan. Mgmt.* 1277. Insurance companies sometimes had incentives to support tutelas that would save them from paying for procedures.

Individual remedies on their own will not achieve justice for those most in need of remedies for violations of SEC rights.

8.6.2 *The Dangers of Exclusively Focusing on Systemic Remedies*

The South African Constitutional Court's general declaration in *Grootboom* that the state must devise a program for those without homes has been read by Tushnet as providing for no individual remedy.[137] This reading is re-enforced by the tragic fact that Irene Grootboom, the lead plaintiff, died without a permanent home. As discussed above, however, the case is more complex and more consistent with the two-track approach. This is because the Court had issued orders that provided sanitation, water and water-proofing to the Grootboom plaintiffs in their informal settlement.[138] As will be seen below, subsequent South African cases have more formally combined individual and systemic remedies.

A Canadian housing rights case that sought only systemic relief in the form of effective policies to reduce and eventually eliminate homelessness, plan submission and retention of jurisdiction failed. Asking only for a systemic remedy allowed the Ontario Court of Appeal to conclude that the application was not justiciable because it was based on the idea that the government has given inadequate priority to housing. With respect to remedies, it concluded that a mere declaration "would be so devoid of content as to be essentially meaningless" while judicial supervision of the government's response would take the court "well beyond the limits of its institutional capacity".[139] A search for purely systemic remedies will

[137] He argues "under the Court's order the individual plaintiffs need not receive any relief at all ... As the South African cases indicate, for practical reasons, the remedies for violations of social and economic rights cannot be 'personal and present'": Tushnet, Weak Courts, *Strong Rights*, pp.244, 247.

[138] Sachs, "The Judicial Enforcement of Socio-Economic Rights: The Grootboom Case", 595; Christopher Mbazira, "Non-implementation of Court Orders in Socio-economic Rights Litigation in South Africa: Is the Cancer Here to Stay?" (2008) 9(4) *ESR Rev.: Econ. Soc. Rts. S.A.* 2, 2–3; Marius Pieterse, "Coming to Terms with Judicial Enforcement of Socio-economic Rights" (2004) 20 *S.A. J. Hum. Rts.* 383, 407; Liebenberg, *Socio-economic Rights*, pp.400–401. See *infra* n.105 for discussion of the oft-neglected shadow or informal remedy for the successful litigants in the case.

[139] *Tanudjaja* v. *Canada (Attorney General)*, 2014 ONCA 852 at para 34. Even the one dissenting judge who would not have struck the claim out as disclosing no cause of action signalled concerns about remedial deterrence by stating that while the applicant "seeks, as one remedy, an order requiring the governments to implement strategies to reduce homelessness and inadequate housing and to consult with affected groups, under

often raise judicial alarm bells about their capacity to handle complex polycentric issues. Judges remain more comfortable with dealing with concrete adjudicative facts.

A purely systemic approach could make courts dependent on the willingness and ability of the government to devise and implement effective systemic remedies. Even governments in established democracies struggle to deliver public goods likes housing, health and education. The only option within the purely systemic approach that Tushnet contemplates is for courts to move from "weak" remedies such as declarations to stronger remedies such as injunctions. But this may demand too much of the courts. A two-track approach opens up a simpler judicial enforcement strategy: award new individual remedies while indicating that if necessary, stronger forms of systemic remedies may be forthcoming.

8.6.2.1 The Exception That Proves the Rule? Indian Right to Food Litigation

In Chapter 7, Section 7.2.4, some Indian public law cases that focused exclusively on systemic remedies were critically examined. At the same time, it must be acknowledged that some Indian SEC litigation with an exclusively systemic focus has been successful. The Indian right to food litigation is arguably the most successful SEC litigation in the world. It relied exclusively on systemic relief often tied to monitoring and existing statutes and programs.

The Indian Supreme Court retained jurisdiction for seventeen years until it ruled that subsequent issues of food insecurity could be litigated under new national legislation. Its first of over sixty interim orders dealt with eight different programs. Many of these orders were directions to the central and state governments to comply with existing legislation or support existing programs. Like supra-national courts, the Court frequently appeared reliant on governments to provide them with information. It also encountered much resistance and non-compliance. Nevertheless, the Court persisted. Poorvi Chitalkar and Varun Gauri have suggested that the success of this litigation is related to the

court supervision, the court need not make such a wide-ranging order if it finds a breach of the Charter. It may limit itself to granting declaratory relief only": ibid. at para 85 per Feldman JA in dissent. I acted as counsel at trial for an intervenor in this case, which supported the purely systemic remedy, and subsequently came to view this as a strategic mistake.

Court's early articulation of a clear constitutional right to food, surpluses that the court could order be released to the public and the Court's appointment of two experts as food commissioners to investigate violations of its interim orders. They also suggest that such success is related to political and media engagement with the issue in response to starvation deaths despite increases in India's wealth.[140]

There are some echoes of a two-track strategy in the right to food litigation. The Court declared that all households belonging to six "priority groups" should receive cards entitling them to free food. The priority groups included those over sixty years old, single women with no means of support, households with a disabled person, pregnant women and Indigenous people. The Court also ruled that starvation deaths would be taken as evidence that its orders had not been implemented and that the executive could be held responsible.[141] These decisions used individual instances of starvation deaths as evidence and focused on vulnerable groups.

The right to food litigation was a success, but there are other examples of purely systemic SEC litigation in India failing. For example, much housing litigation has failed to provide individual remedies against evictions.[142] Indian courts have grandly stated that "every Government, which has its priorities right, should give foremost importance to providing safe drinking water even at the cost of other development programs. Nothing shall stand in its way whether it is lack of funds or other infrastructure".[143] Nevertheless, the courts have failed to enforce the right to water.[144] There are many examples of purely systemic approaches that have failed in India and even had counter-productive

[140] "India: Compliance with Orders on the Right to Food" in Langford, Rodriguez-Garavito and Rossi, *Social Rights Judgments*.

[141] *People's Union for Civil Liberties* v. *Union of India & Ors*, Writ Petition (Civil) No. 196 of 2001, Court Order of 3 May 2003, online: www.escr-net.org/caselaw/2006/peoples-union-civil-liberties-v-union-india-ors-supreme-court-india-civil-original

[142] Anashri Pillay, "Revisiting the Indian Experience of Economic and Social Rights Adjudication: The Need for a Principled Approach to Judicial Activism and Restraint" (2014) *I.C.L.Q.* 385. Similar concerns have been raised by Atia Naznin and Shawkat Alam in "Judicial Remedies for Forced Slum Evictions in Bangladesh" (2019) 6(1) *Asian J. L. Soc.* 99.

[143] *Vishala Kochi Kudivella Samarkshana Samithi* v. *State of Kerala* [2006], 2006 (1) KLT 919 (High Court of Kerala) at para 3.

[144] Philippe Cullet, "The Right to Water in Rural India" in Malcom Langford (ed.), *The Human Right to Water: Theory, Practice and Prospects* (Cambridge: Cambridge University Press, 2017).

effects, such as authorizing evictions without providing alternative accommodation.[145]

Purely systemic approaches may simply result in the judiciary bouncing the complexities of polycentric problems back at the government. It may provide no real entry into or concrete illustration of the deficiencies being identified. The right to food litigation may well be the exception that proves the rule about the inadequacy of exclusively systemic approaches and even it had echoes of a two-track approach by using individual starvation deaths as evidence and assigning priorities to specific groups.

8.6.3 *Examples of a Two-Track Approach*

The two-track approach is rooted both in actual practice and theory. In her defence of the justiciability of SEC rights at the supra-national level, Tara Melish has suggested that it is a mistake to conclude that such rights can never result in individual and immediate remedies for individuals. At the same time, she also recognizes the need for "broader more structural relief". She suggests that the "precise details" of systemic remedies should be "deferred in the first instance to the "representative branches", in consultation with the victims and subject to both reasonable time-frames and the organ's continuing supervisory jurisdiction".[146] Fortunately, there are some concrete examples of such a two-track approach.

8.6.3.1 European Court of Human Rights

In *Yordanova and Others v. Bulgaria*,[147] the Court took a two-track approach to remedies when it stated that the applicants who were Roma about to be evicted were entitled "so far as individual measures are concerned" to the repeal or suspension of the eviction order. It then

[145] Upendra Baxi, "Law, Politics and Constitutional Hegemony" in Sujit Choudhry, Madhav Khosla and Pratap Bhanu Mehta, *The Oxford Handbook of the Indian Constitution* (Oxford: Oxford University Press, 2016) in reference to *Olga Tellis* v. *Bombay*, (1986) 3 SCC 545; Anuj Bhuwania, *Courting the People: Public Interest Litigation in Post-Emergency India* (Cambridge: Cambridge University Press, 2017) pp.80–111.

[146] Tara Melish, "Rethinking the 'Less as More' Thesis: Supranational Litigation of Economic, Social and Cultural Rights in the Americas" (2006) 39 *N.Y.U. J. Int'l. L. Pol'y.* 171, 339–340, 248. She also draws analogies to school litigation that focuses on the concrete situations of individual applicants and not simply aggregate disparities. Also consistent with the two-track approach, she recognizes that to obtain individual remedies, there must be a causal connection between what the state did or did not do and the specific harm to the individual to be remedied: ibid., 293–303.

[147] No. 25446/06, ECHR 5 June 2012.

expressed "the view that the general measures in execution of this judgment should include such amendments to the relevant domestic law and practice" to ensure that the state "even in cases of unlawful occupation" respected rights when recovering public lands or buildings.[148] The Committee of Ministers subsequently accepted that the eviction order, though not formally repealed or even suspended, would not be enforced. It noted with respect to general measures that a draft bill featuring proportionality principles had been prepared and that the relevant administrative court was now applying such principles.[149] As in institutional cases, this approach demonstrated a two-track concern with both individual and general measures.

8.6.3.2 Inter-American Court of Human Rights

In a case involving a prohibition on in vitro fertilization, the IACtHR provided individual remedies of counselling, US$5,000 in pecuniary damages and US$20,000 in non-pecuniary damages. The systemic remedies included changing the law and providing training to prevent similar rights violations in the future. All of these remedies were implemented except the change of law.[150] Systemic remedies may often be more difficult to implement than individual remedies.

In a case involving reduced pensions, the Court ordered Peru to compensate the five applicants but also to investigate and punish those responsible so as to prevent similar violations in the future. After six different compliance hearings between 2004 and 2011, the Court found that while the state had paid the non-pecuniary damages, it had not undertaken an investigation.[151] As discussed in Chapter 6, Section 6.2.1, the IACtHR's frequent orders that states conduct investigations are often the subject of non-compliance and may discount prosecutorial independence.

The two-track approach should allow courts to use a broad range of systemic remedies including declarations about what should be done to prevent the repetition of similar violations in the future. Systemic

[148] Ibid. at paras 166–167. Unfortunately these statements were not translated into the Court's actual order which simply stated that "that the finding of a violation of Article 8 of the Convention constitutes in itself sufficient just satisfaction for any non-pecuniary damage sustained by the applicants": ibid. at Order para 5.

[149] *Yordanova and Others* v. *Bulgaria*, No. 25446/06, Enhanced Procedure, Status of Execution, ECHR 29 September 2012, online: http://hudoc.exec.coe.int/eng?i=004-1924

[150] *Artavia Murillo et al. ("In Vitro Fertilization")* v. *Costa Rica*, (2016) 38 *Loy. L.A. Int'l. & Comp. L. Rev.* 1345.

[151] *Five Pensioners* v. *Peru*, (2014) 36 *Loy. L.A. Int'l. & Comp. L. Rev.* 2353.

measures will often be more challenging and subject to failure and a lack of full compliance than individual measures.

8.6.3.3 United Nations Bodies

The UN Committee on Economic, Social and Cultural Rights has taken a two-track approach to remedies. In one case, it provided an individual remedy by stating that Spain had an obligation to provide the successful applicant with an effective remedy "in particular to ensure that the auction of the author's property does not occur".[152] It then stated "that, in principle, the remedies recommended in the context of individual communications may include guarantees of non-repetition and recalls that the State party has an obligation to prevent similar violations in the future". It noted that such general measures would include appropriate legislative or administrative measures to ensure notice and challenge in cases of mortgage foreclosures. It then ordered Spain to report back to the Committee within six months. In another case, the Committee indicated that the applicants should receive adequate accommodation, financial compensation and costs. It did not stop at these individual remedies but suggested a range of systemic remedies including legislative and administrative measures to ensure genuine consultation before evictions and a comprehensive plan for adequate housing for low income persons.[153] Concerns about respecting the state's role will be greater with respect to systemic than individual measures.

In 2020, the Committee indicated that Spain should "undertake genuine consultation with the author to examine her needs in terms of suitable alternative housing and, if necessary, provide her with such housing; and … reimburse the author for the legal costs reasonably incurred in the processing of the present communication".[154] As a general measure to ensure non-repetition, the Committee indicated that the state should develop mechanisms to ensure the proportionality of evictions.[155] This indicates the ability of systemic measures to discuss

[152] *I.D.G.* v. *Spain*, Committee on Economic, Social and Cultural Rights, Report on the 54h, 55th and 56th Sess., Supp. 2, UN Doc E/C.12/55/D/2 (2014), Views adopted 13 October 2015 at para 16.

[153] *Djazia* v. *Spain*, Comm. No. 5/2015, Committee on Economic, Social and Cultural Rights, UN Doc E/C.12/61/D/5/2015 (2017), Views adopted 20 June 2017 at paras 19–21.

[154] *Rosario Gómez-Limón Pardo* v. *Spain*, Comm. No. 052/2018, Committee on Economic, Social and Cultural Rights, UN Doc E/C.12/67/D/52/2018, 5 March 2020 at para 13.

[155] Ibid. at para 14.

general remedial principles such as the need for proportionality without attempting to specify the precise measures that the state should adopt. Another approach is to eliminate some state responses as insufficient. For example, the Committee has indicated that the availability of accommodation in shelters was not adequate alternative accommodation when a mother with children was evicted in defiance of an interim remedy. The Committee recommended individual measures to ensure that the petitioner had adequate accommodation, including the option of moving up the waitlist for social housing as well as general measures to prevent the repetition of the violation.[156]

8.6.3.4 Colombia and Healthcare

In 2008, the Colombian Constitutional Court recognized that "for over a decade people have had to resort to the action of *tutela* to resolve disputes" relating to healthcare. It held that these cases revealed "flaws in the regulation of the health system, which in turn is the basis for general orders we adopt to correct such problems".[157] In addition to sixteen different orders that required treatment for twenty-two different individuals, the Court ordered various parts of the state to update the lists of medicines paid for by the state. It also required the government to report back to the Court every six months on the steps taken toward the broad goal of universal healthcare. The Court's approach was consistent with a declaration plus approach because it pronounced the broad goal of universal healthcare and retained jurisdiction but did not issue specific orders that could be enforced through penalties.

The government responded with emergency decrees that restricted the treatment that could be provided. These decrees were the subject of much public protest and many were invalidated by the Court. One decree that was not invalidated allowed the government to implement new taxes to finance healthcare.[158] New laws were enacted in 2011 that provided a process for health experts to update treatments that would be excluded from the public scheme. A 2015 law was also upheld by the

[156] *Maribel Viviana López Albán* v. *Spain*, Comm. No. 37/2018, Committee on Economic, Social and Cultural Rights, UN Doc E/C.12/66/D/37/2018, 29 November 2019.

[157] Colombia Constitutional Court, *Decision T-760 of 2008* at para 9, English summary online (pdf): www.escr-net.org/sites/default/files/English_summary_T-760.pdf

[158] Katharine G. Young and Julieta Lemaitre, "The Comparative Fortunes of the Right to Health: Two Tales of Justiciability in Colombia and South Africa" (2013) 26 *Harv. Hum. Rts. J.* 179, 193.

Constitutional Court as a means to implement, with some delays, the remedial goal of universal healthcare.[159]

The pursuit of a two-track remedial strategy in healthcare can capitalize on the particular strengths of all three branches of government. The granting of individual remedies invokes the traditional and intuitive understanding of courts as places where individuals make claims of rights that if accepted result in individual remedies to rectify documented cases of injustice. At the same time, the executive and the legislature have more expertise and ability to ration scarce resources, make reasonable trade-offs and to employ expertise in decision-making.

Courts may erode their legitimacy if they only focus on systemic issues. The many individual remedies that the Colombian Court has ordered provided it with some support in its struggles with the government.[160] In turn, the legislature and the executive, if left to their own devices, may ignore claims by the affected individual in favour of longer-term systemic reform. Although legitimate concerns have been raised in the Colombian context that individual judicial remedies had regressive effects, the legislature also retains the ability to respond dialogically albeit prospectively. The state should be able to justify reasonable allocations of scarce resources with new evidence and new legislation.

8.6.3.5 Canada and Healthcare

The British Columbia Court of Appeal took a two-track approach when it ordered that four children named as plaintiffs be provided with a specific form of autism treatment. This individual remedy was ordered while the government was given the flexibility to select from a broader range of treatments and to determine the appropriate age cut-off for providing treatment. The Court of Appeal noted that such a systemic remedy was "not of particular help to these four infant petitioners who have succeeded in establishing a breach of their right to equality, but who have all, now, reached school age".[161] The result, which was eventually

[159] Everaldo Lamprea, "Colombia's Right-to-Health Litigation in a Context of Health Care Reform" in Colleen Flood and Aeyal Gross (eds.), *The Right to Health at the Public/Private Divide: A Global Comparative Study* (Cambridge: Cambridge University Press, 2014), pp.148–149; Everaldo Lamprea and Johnathan Garcia, "Closing the Gap between Formal and Material Health Care Coverage in Colombia" (2016) 18(2) *Health Hum. Rts.* 49, 65.

[160] David Landau, "Choosing between Simple and Complex Remedies in Socio-Economic Rights Cases" (2019) 69 Supp. 1 *U.T.L.J.* 105, 119.

[161] *Auton (Guardian ad litem of) v. British Columbia (Attorney General)*, 2002 BCCA 53 at para 91 rev'd on the merits [2004] 3 SCR 657.

overturned by the Supreme Court on the merits, provided both individual remedies that recognized the hardships of the litigation while also giving the government an opportunity to devise a systemic response that might have been less generous than that received by the plaintiffs.

Suspended declarations of invalidity have also been used in a two-track manner that provide remedies to individuals applicants while allowing the legislature to formulate systemic remedies.[162] A two-track approach in *Chaoulli* would have exempted the individual applicants from the suspended declaration of invalidity. This would have allowed the two litigants to seek private health insurance while the government crafted a systemic remedy to provide speedy healthcare.[163]

8.6.3.6 South Africa and Housing

Justice Albie Sachs has defended the Constitutional Court's decision to focus on systemic remedies in *Grootboom* in part because the plaintiffs had already received a remedy that the Court had ratified. He defended the Court's deferential systemic remedy on the sound basis that government and not the Court should decide whether the program would be national, provincial or local; whether it should supply only land or land and houses; and the degree to which the private sector should be involved.[164] In the ensuing years, the Court has moved towards a more formal version of the two-track approach that combines individual remedies with longer-term systemic reforms. As Brian Ray has stated, the courts have refused "to allow an eviction where the state cannot provide alternative accommodation" while using other means including engagement orders to minimize "institutional-competence and separation-of-powers concerns"[165] about systemic remedies. The result is a two-track combination of individual and systemic remedies.[166]

[162] *Carter v. Canada* [2016] 1 SCR 13; *Truchon c. Procureur général du Canada*, 2019 QCCS 3792 at 747.

[163] [2005] 1 SCR 791.

[164] Sachs, "The Judicial Enforcement of Socio-Economic Rights: The Grootboom Case", 595–596.

[165] Ray, *Engaging with Social Rights*, p.217.

[166] Christopher Mbazira in *Litigating Socio-Economic Rights in South Africa: A Choice between Corrective and Distributive Justice* (Pretoria: Pretoria University Law Press, 2009) well describes the traditions of both approaches but ultimately maintained that the distributive and systemic approach was best in the South African context. See also Christopher Mbazira, "Appropriate, Just and Equitable Relief in Socio-Economic Rights Litigation: The Tension between Corrective and Distributive Forms of Justice" (2008) 125(1) *S.A. L. J.* 71.

In *Blue Moonlight*, the Court indicated that occupiers of private land could not be evicted unless the city made adequate alternative accommodation available fourteen days before the eviction. At the same time, the Court issued systemic relief to prevent future violations of the rights in similar circumstances by declaring that a Johannesburg policy that excluded those evicted from private property from temporary accommodation was unconstitutional[167]

In *Port Elizabeth Municipality v. Various Occupiers,*[168] the Court restrained the eviction of almost 100 people including twenty-three children who occupied twenty-nine shacks on privately owned vacant land. The Court recognized that the case involved competing constitutional rights of the landowner to property and the applicants to homes. The Court recognized that the municipality sought the eviction after over 1,000 people had complained about the informal settlement. Nevertheless, it urged the municipality to treat the occupiers with respect and not simply take the side of the landowner. Justice Sachs explained his willingness to grant a remedy against evictions in the following eloquent words:

> The inherited injustices at the macro level will inevitably make it difficult for the courts to ensure immediate present-day equity at the micro level. The judiciary cannot of itself correct all the systemic unfairness to be found in our society. Yet it can at least soften and minimise the degree of injustice and inequity which the eviction of the weaker parties in conditions of inequality of necessity entails.[169]

The Court issued the individual remedy that the occupiers not be evicted, but encouraged mediation and active and respectful participation by the applicants and others as the means to develop a just systemic remedy.

The two-track approach was developed more fully in *Occupiers of 51 Olivia Road v. City of Johannesburg.*[170] The trial judge ordered an individual remedy that restrained an eviction pending the implementation of the sort of program for the homeless that the Constitutional Court had contemplated in *Grootboom.*[171] The Court of Appeal overturned the anti-eviction order, but made eviction dependent upon finding

[167] *City of Johannesburg Metropolitan Municipality* v. *Blue Moonlight Properties 39 (Pty) Ltd & Another,* [2011] ZACC 33 at para 104.

[168] [2004] ZACC 7.

[169] Ibid. at para 38.

[170] [2008] ZACC 1.

[171] *City of Johannesburg* v. *Rand Properties (Pty) Ltd.* 2007 (6) SA 417 at 749 (SCA).

alternative accommodations that would be secure, waterproof and have basic water and sanitation services subject to the Court's retention of jurisdiction.[172] The applicants appealed to the Constitutional Court, but two days before the case was to be heard, the Court issued an interim remedy that the parties engage with each other. It extended the deadline for reporting back on the result of the engagement twice. This recognizes that respectful and meaningful engagement will take time. However, it was time well spent because a settlement was eventually reached. It included repair of the buildings and alternative accommodations in the inner city.[173] The settlement was subsequently endorsed by the Court. As Professor Liebenberg has commented, the settlement in this case "arguably went further than an order which even the sympathetic court would have granted".[174] It accommodated the applicant's desire for alternative accommodations that were in the inner city and close to their jobs. The Court also crafted its own systemic remedy by reading into legislation that eviction orders should not be affirmed without meaningful engagement.

In *Schubart Park*, the Court found that an offer devised by the city to find alternative accommodation for residents displaced by a fire was not an adequate form of engagement because it proceeded from "a 'top-down' premise, namely that the City will determine when, for how long and ultimately whether at all, the applicants may return to Schubart Park". Instead, what was required was "meaningful engagement with the applicants at every stage of the re-occupation process".[175] The Court set deadlines for the city to propose a plan for alternative accommodation and for the applicants to respond. It also added that because it was "uncertain how long that process will be", a trial judge should supervise this process.[176] This avoided the rushed dispute resolution form of engagement that Liebenberg has criticized and that is unlikely to result in agreement.

172 Ibid. at *Order* para 2.1.

173 Liebenberg, *Socio-economic Rights*, p.296.

174 Ibid., p.420. For arguments that the engagement remedy can advance participatory democracy but a recognition that engagement should take place after and not before the court has defined the relevant legal entitlement, see Lilian Chenwi, "A New Approach to Remedies in Socio-economic Rights Adjudication: Occupiers of 51 Olivia Road and Others v. City of Johannesburg and Others" (2009) 2 *Constitutional Crt. Rev.* 371.

175 *Schubart Park Residents' Association and Others* v. *City of Tshwane Metropolitan Municipality and Another*, [2012] ZACC 26 at para 51.

176 Ibid. at paras 49–53.

As discussed in Section 8.4 of this chapter, engagement plays two different roles. It can be a means of justifying limits on SEC rights. At its worst, it is a procedural formality dominated by the state that is required before eviction. At its best, it is a source for creative and consensual remedies. The latter result is more likely if courts ensure the integrity of the engagement process and provide interim and individual remedies that address the inequality of bargaining power between those claiming SEC rights and the rights of governments and/or property owners. They can address this inequality by using the declaration plus to declare in general terms a fair process that should be followed and what sort of outcomes are required or precluded by their interpretation of the underlying rights. They can also ensure that those who are being asked to engage with the government are not evicted or suffer irreparable harm during the engagement process. It is perhaps not a coincidence that creative and consensual remedies in a number of South African housing cases have allowed applicants to remain in their homes and neighbourhoods while services and facilities were improved.

8.6.4 Two-Track Remedies and the Minimum Core?

The two-track approach has some similarities with international law approaches to enforcing SEC rights that stress entitlement to a minimum core of rights.[177] The individual remedy might be seen as analogous to the minimum core that can be enforced through adjudication, while the systemic remedy allows the executive and the legislature to pursue the progressive realization of the right. The Colombian Constitutional Court that orders many individual remedies has referred to an "essential nucleus"[178] of rights that must always be respected. It has also upheld a 2015 law on the basis that it implements a minimum core of healthcare rights.[179]

[177] For a defence of such an approach and a critique of South African courts for not enforcing a minimum core, see Bilchitz, *Poverty and Fundamental Rights*.

[178] Colombia Constitutional Court, *Decision T-025 of 2004* in Manuel José Cepeda Espinosa and David Landau, *Colombian Constitutional Law* (New York: Oxford University Press 2017), p.185.

[179] Decision C-313/14, which cites Office of the High Commissioner for Human Rights, *General Comment No. 14: The Right to the Highest Attainable Standard of Health (Art. 12),* Committee on Economic, Social and Cultural Rights, UN Doc E/C.12/2000/4, 22nd Sess. (11 August 2000) with approval.

There are, however, some important differences between individual remedies and the minimum core. The individual remedy is determined on the facts of the case. It is not designed to apply across the board. It places a focus on the specific suffering of specific litigants. It can make the dysfunction of existing policies real. Moreover, it provides courts with a unique and distinct role to participate in societal debates that involve both rights and policies. Many commentators who simply advocate "weak" or "dialogic" remedies may underestimate how the "micro justice" of the individual remedies affirms the court's legitimacy and can make a tangible contribution to larger debates about achieving "macro justice".[180]

Systemic remedies under the two-track approach should not be seen as the simple surrender of the task of progressive realization to the legislature and the executive. To be sure, courts should invite these institutions to devise systemic remedies, but they should also leave open the possibility of further judicial intervention should the state's systemic response not be reasonable. Delay may be accepted in implementing systemic remedies, but it should generally not be open-ended delay. Retention of jurisdiction provides governments with the ability to justify additional delay but also allows the courts to intensify relief should the state prove either incapable or unwilling to devise a systemic solution. The ability of the court to order individual remedies and to point out the repetitive nature of the violation also places pressure on the state should its systemic response fail to prevent similar violations of SEC rights in the future.

8.6.5 The Two-Track Approach and Remedial Failure

As suggested throughout the book, one of the strengths of the two-track approach is that it is responsive to remedial failure. The *Joe Slovo* case discussed above demonstrates how even losses in courts in terms of judicial approval of an eviction order can subsequently be turned into victories – in this case, by renewed and successful efforts at settlement. Lack of success and compliance with systemic remedies also provide the basis for additional legal and political actions.

Two-track approaches respond to the inevitability of remedial failure. Courts may be too deferential to governments in crafting systemic

[180] *Port Elizabeth Municipality* v. *Various Occupiers*, [2004] ZACC 7.

remedies. Fortunately, the availability of individual remedies provides a judicial safety net when someone fall through the cracks of even judicially approved systemic remedies.

Individual remedies can have regressive and even potentially destabilizing effects. Nevertheless, governments can, when necessary, respond to counter these effects by enacting new laws and justifying the reasonableness of their allocation of scarce resources. Legislative activism should, as in Colombia, be the appropriate response to concerns that the courts have engaged in excessive judicial activism in enforcing SEC rights. Governments will always get second chances. Those denied basic SEC rights may not if they do not receive effective individual remedies.

In recent work addressing my two-track approach, David Landau has argued that different political and social contexts can justify exclusive use of individual or systemic remedies. He points to *Grootboom* and the Indian right to food litigation as examples where purely structural approaches were effective.[181] There is also a danger that individual remedies, especially of the magnitude provided in Colombia healthcare cases, will take away resources that could be better used for systemic remedies.[182] As suggested above, however, both *Grootboom* and even the right to food litigation did have some less visible elements that focused on individuals and their claim to remedies. Professor Landau may, however, be correct that there are some contexts where litigants will for good strategic reasons make decisions to ask for exclusively individual or systemic remedies.[183] Such choices by litigants will and should be respected by the courts. Professor Landau's criticisms serve as a useful reminder that the two-track approach is primarily a way of conceptualizing remedies rather than a rigid requirement to be applied in every case and regardless of context.

[181] Landau, "Choosing between Simple and Complex Remedies", 112–113.

[182] Note, however, that some of the individual remedies may not have been justified given that insurance companies helped litigants in order to increase their own profits and the government may not have had a full opportunity to demonstrate that the claim was extravagant.

[183] Litigators that focus only on systemic remedies, however, should take care that they are not placing their institutional interests over the interests of those whose rights have been violated. Derick A. Bell Jr., "Serving Two Masters: Integration Ideals and Client Interests in School Desegregation Litigation" (1976) 85 *Yale L. J.* 470.

8.7 Conclusion

The challenges of devising effective remedies for SEC rights are considerable. Those who ask for remedies that courts may find unmanageable, illegitimate, jumping the queue or too expensive, risk having courts reject the merits of their claim. Narrowly focused litigation that asks for individual remedies for "micro injustices" while taking a more deferential stance on systemic remedies to address "macro injustice" may be a way to affirm the justiciability of SEC rights. The best example of the two-track approach are the South African cases that combine remedies against eviction or alternative accommodation with longer-term strategies including engagement to develop better housing policies.

The experience in Colombia suggests governments can respond to regressive individual remedies by updating and justifying their allocations of scarce resources. If governments cannot justify the choices they have made, courts should order individual remedies if they are to treat SEC rights as justiciable rights. Individual litigants may not be the most deserving, but that is not the appropriate test for a court. Individuals who have established an unjustified rights violation have a legitimate expectation of receiving a remedy. At the same time, the court should more tentatively and modestly pursue systemic remedies through the use of dialogic remedies such as the declaration plus, the delayed declaration of invalidity and engagement orders.

Courts should capitalize on their institutional advantage by doing justice to those litigants who appear before them. There is much intuitive appeal and cathartic drama in the traditional notion of where there is a right, there is a remedy. Given the costs of litigation, there is an element of queue jumping and uneven distributive justice in almost all litigation. A two-track remedial strategy accepts the traditional role of courts in providing individual remedies while recognizing some of their limits in dealing with polycentric problems. The executive and the legislature have more expertise and ability to make justified choices in the rationing of scarce resources. Courts may erode their legitimacy and strain their competence if they only focus on systemic issues. In turn, the legislature and the executive, if left to their own devices, may ignore claims by the affected individual in a way that will produce complacency about the need for systemic reforms to honour SEC rights.

The two tracks can productively interact. The micro-justice provided by an individual remedy restraining evictions or ordering healthcare can address power imbalances when individual and groups work with the state to develop a systemic response. It can increase the chance that engagement will produce creative and consensual remedies as opposed to a justification for limiting SEC rights. The individual remedy also underlines the severe effects of some governmental policies on individuals. It can trigger necessary cycles of individual and systemic remedies that may often be necessary to achieve greater socio-economic justice in the face of the economic, public health and environmental crises that we face.

9

Remedies for Violations of Indigenous Rights

9.1 Introduction

The challenges of devising effective and just remedies for long-standing violations of Indigenous rights are considerable. They include the problem of remedial deterrence discussed in Chapter 8, Section 8.1, in relation to social, economic and cultural (SEC) rights. Such problems are greater in the Indigenous rights context because the harms of colonial dispossession of Indigenous people are so massive.

Even if there is a willingness to recognize harms, there is the added danger that supra-national and national adjudicators may, even with the best of intentions, replicate colonial methods and impose what they perceive to be the best for Indigenous peoples.[1] James Anaya has warned that: "remedies to redress historical violations of self-determination do not necessarily entail a reversion to the status quo ante, but rather are to be developed in accordance with the present-day aspirations of the aggrieved groups, whose character may be substantially altered with the passage of time".[2] Remedies for violations of Indigenous rights should make room for Indigenous self-determination while also recognizing judicial responsibility for effective and meaningful remedies.

Following the two-track approach, courts should take the lead with first-track remedies designed to prevent irreparable harm and provide restitution and reparation for past harms. At the same time, they should be even more deferential than usual with respect to systemic remedies that will help shape the future. Systemic remedies should be based on prior and informed Indigenous consent and the exercise of Indigenous self-determination. The two tracks are, however, linked. First-track reparations and interim remedies are often necessary to create the conditions for free and informed Indigenous consent and systemic remedies that will prevent the re-occurrence of violations. Unfortunately, domestic courts have frequently denied requests for interim injunctions to protect Indigenous rights from irreparable harm sometimes on the basis of majoritarian understandings of the balance of convenience. To make matters worse, they have used interim remedies to prevent Indigenous protest and self-help.

[1] In some early cases, the IACtHR imposed trust fund requirements on the use of the damages, something that has been aptly criticized by a leading commentator as "paternalism": Thomas M. Antkowiak, "A Dark Side of Virtue: The Inter-American Court and Reparations for Indigenous Peoples" (2014) 25 *Duke J. Comp. Int'l. L.* 1, 22.

[2] S. James Anaya, *Indigenous Peoples in International Law*, 2nd ed. (Oxford: Oxford University Press, 2004), p.107. Dean Anaya situates self-determination as the foundational principle. He adds "[n]egotiation makes possible nuanced solutions to potentially complex issues of redistribution of power and resources in diverse circumstances." Ibid., p.187

The enforcement of rights relating to Indigenous languages, medicine, and culture involve many of the dilemmas examined in Chapter 8 in relation to SEC rights. In addition, these remedies need to be developed in a manner that recognizes the right of Indigenous people "to be actively involved in developing and determining health, housing and other economic and social programmes affecting them and, as far as possible, to administer such programmes through their own institutions".[3]

Article 40 of the UN Declaration on the Rights of Indigenous Peoples (UNDRIP) provides a right "to effective remedies". It states that remedial decisions "shall give due consideration to the customs, traditions, rules and legal systems of the Indigenous people concerned and international human rights".[4] UNDRIP thus contemplates a bi-jural approach to remedies that combines Indigenous laws and human rights.

Remedies may have a better chance of embracing bi-juralism than rights. Remedies involve a search for practical and creative solutions compared to rights, where the focus has often been on competing rights.[5] At the same time, Article 40 received little discussion in the travaux preparatoires of UNDRIP perhaps because its reference to remedies was thought to refer more to procedure and access to justice than reparations. Remedies were not neglected in other parts of UNDRIP. Article 28 of UNDRIP contemplates the priority of restitution over compensation and Article 11(2) provides for redress, which may include restitution, with respect to the taking of cultural, intellectual, religious and spiritual property.[6]

UNDRIP[7] makes frequent reference to fair, equitable and just compensation including restitution. Section 9.2 of this chapter will document a regrettable tendency both in supra-national and national courts to

[3] United Nations Declaration on the Rights of Indigenous Peoples, GA Res. 61/295 UNGAOR, 61st Sess., UN Doc A/Res/71/295 (2007), Art. 23 (henceforth UNDRIP). The precise legal status of UNDRIP raises questions beyond the scope of this book. Even non-binding "soft" international law may provide guidance for remedial principles and practice.

[4] Ibid., Art. 40.

[5] There is a danger of a zero-sum approach to conflicts between human rights and Indigenous law. For example in a 1993 case, the Inter-American Court of Human Rights held that the human rights standards of gender equality should prevail over the matrilineal customs of an Indigenous community: *Aloeboetoe* v. *Suriname* (1993), (2015) 37 *Loy. L.A. Int'l. & Comp. L. Rev.* 1591.

[6] Willem van Genugten and Federico Lenzerini "Legal Implementation and International Co-operation and Assistance" in Jessie Hohmann and Marc Weiler (eds.), *The United Nations Declaration on the Rights of Indigenous Peoples* (Oxford: Oxford University Press, 2018) at p.558; Federico Lenzerini "Reparations, Restitution and Redress" in ibid.

[7] UNDRIP Arts. 10 and 28.

under-estimate the pecuniary harms caused by violations of Indigenous rights. The fact that courts also tend to off-set this with a generous approach to assessing non-pecuniary harms relating to cultural loss does not excuse such under-compensation.

Consistent with general international law principles of state responsibility, restitution should be the primary remedy with compensation only being used when restitution is impossible or disproportionate. Return of Indigenous land and resources may require courts to retain jurisdiction. This will be a delicate task because judges who retain jurisdiction need to avoid neo-colonial judicial rule but also ensure that governments comply with what may be costly and unpopular remedies. The declaration plus introduced in Chapter 7, Section 7.4, is an appealing remedy in this context. It avoids detailed judicial management while ensuring that the judiciary can be called upon by the parties to assist in resolving disputes about the meaning and consequences of declarations of Indigenous rights.

The duty of governments to consult Indigenous people is increasingly recognized in domestic and international law. But the duty to consult is an elusive legal concept. The duty to consult, like the South African engagement duty discussed in Chapter 8, Section 8.5, is best used when it results in creative and consensual agreements that themselves provide effective remedies. At a minimum, Indigenous people should be provided interim relief that protects them from suffering irreparable harm while the parties are engaged in a consultation process that should also respect Indigenous law. Unfortunately, it will be suggested that the duty to consult, like the engagement duty, is often used more as a means to authorize resource extraction sometimes with accommodations of Indigenous interests. When the duty to consult is breached, courts often simply give governments a “do over”. This fails to remedy the harms that inadequate and sometimes disrespectful consultation causes to Indigenous people.

The two-track approach can assist in balancing the need for Indigenous rights to have effective judicial remedies with the need for courts to more modestly respect Indigenous self-determination going forward. The two-track approach suggests that courts should be more active with respect to interim remedies designed to prevent irreparable harm. They should maintain the integrity of both consultation and adjudication with interim remedies to prevent irreparable harm to Indigenous rights. They should also recognize the preferred position of restitution as a remedy. If restitution of Indigenous land is impossible or disproportionate, courts should fairly calculate damages. They should not give way to temptations to limit pecuniary damages for often unarticulated reasons related to competing social interests. They should also not attempt to off-set this process with a romanticized but in the end colonial willingness to give generous awards for non-pecuniary cultural harms. With respect to second-track systemic remedies, courts should use declarations and the declaration plus in an attempt to make room for consensual agreements.

Given the durability and harms of colonialism, courts should be especially attentive to the reality of remedial failure. Fortunately, an iterative remedial process may accord with multi-generational worldviews of many Indigenous peoples. The grant of new interim remedies, meaningful remedies for the failure to consult and restitution and reparation for past violations may be a necessary response to the failure of systemic remedies and the stubborn and multi-generational nature of colonial harms. The task of devising effective remedies for long-standing violations of Indigenous rights is, however, urgent. Effective remedies and respect for Indigenous laws may also help mitigate the environmental crises that affect us all.

9.1.1 Outline of This Chapter

Section 9.2 will examine the broad range of remedies that are available for violations of Indigenous rights before supra-national and national courts. The Inter-American Court of Human Rights (IACtHR) has been a leader in trying to return land to Indigenous peoples. Alas courts have not always calculated either the balance of convenience or pecuniary damages for the harms caused to Indigenous rights fairly and transparently.

Section 9.3 will examine the duty to consult in both supra-national and national law. It can act as a means to limit Indigenous claims of rights without Indigenous consent or it can be a source of consensual agreement. In addition, if governments fail to conduct the required consultations, this action itself may be a basis for judicial remedies. The extensive Canadian experience with the duty to consult, however, suggests that these remedies are often weak. They generally only give the government a second chance to perform adequate consultation without compensation for the harms that inadequate consultation causes to Indigenous people. The Canadian approach has been focused on securing regulatory approval of resource extraction, as opposed to producing new Treaties based on Indigenous consent.

Section 9.4 will discuss the application of proportionality principles to remedial decision-making. Special care must be taken to avoid allowing majoritarian and economic interests to dominate balancing of competing interests and rights. The application of proportionality principles should also aspire to be bi-jural. Indigenous laws that regulate harvesting and the use of the environment may provide effective alternative remedies that secure valid and important conservation objectives. The overall balance stage should include Indigenous perspectives, including multi-generational ones and those that honour animals and the environment.

Section 9.5 will apply the two-track approach. Domestic and supra-national courts should focus on providing first-track remedies to prevent irreparable harm to Indigenous rights and provide restitution and reparation for the many past violations of Indigenous rights. Courts should use a lighter touch with respect to systemic remedies in order to encourage modern Treaties and better relations in the future.[8] The relation between first- and second-track remedies is critical. The absence of robust first-track remedies to prevent irreparable harm and provide restitution and reparation will replicate colonial imbalances of power. This is unlikely to result in the genuine consent of Indigenous people who have already survived the harms of colonialism and are determined to exist and thrive as Indigenous people in the future.

9.2 Practice

This section will examine a range of remedies, many of which have been examined in prior chapters, but with an emphasis on their role in enforcing Indigenous rights. In recognition of state threats to those who exercise their Indigenous rights, there will also be a brief discussion of the use of injunctions against Indigenous people. Discussion of the duty to consult, including remedies that may be ancillary to the duty and remedies for the failure to respect it, will be discussed in Section 9.3.

9.2.1 Interim Remedies

Interim remedies can play a critical role in enforcing Indigenous rights in relation to land and resources that are particularly susceptible to

[8] Mark D. Walters, "Rights and Remedies within Common Law and Indigenous Legal Traditions: Can the Covenant Chain Be Judicially Enforced Today?" in John Borrows and Michael Coyle (eds.), *The Right Relationship: Reimagining the Implementation of Historical Treaties* (Toronto: University of Toronto Press, 2017).

irreparable harm. They can provide time either for full litigation of whether a proposed action violates Indigenous rights or for negotiations towards settlements based on Indigenous consent. The grant of interim remedies can address imbalances of power between Indigenous people on the one hand and government and resource extraction corporations on the other.[9] As suggested in Chapter 3, Section 3.5, interim remedies are perhaps the most important judicial remedy and they have not received the scholarly attention they deserve.

Supra-national adjudicators have become much more active in ordering interim remedies. They have recognized that interim remedies can be justified as a means to ensure that the parties do not act in a manner that aggravates a dispute or makes its resolution impossible. This focus on the relations between the parties is particularly important in the context of Indigenous rights given the importance of maintaining good relations. Supra-national courts focus on irreparable harm and not more problematic and potentially majoritarian concepts such as the balance of convenience.

Domestic courts have frequently been reluctant to grant interim relief to enforce Indigenous rights because of concerns about the balance of convenience. In a landmark decision introducing the duty to consult as an alternative to "all or nothing" decisions to grant interim remedies, the Supreme Court of Canada observed (but hopefully did not approve)[10] that "the balance of convenience test tips the scales in favour of protecting jobs and government revenues, with the result that Aboriginal interests tend to "lose" outright pending a final determination of the issue, instead of being balanced appropriately against conflicting concerns".[11] Such a majoritarian and monetized reading of the balance of convenience is hostile to Indigenous rights. It should be repudiated.

[9] Kent Roach, "Remedies for Violation of Aboriginal Rights" (1992) 21 *Man. L. J.* 498; Kent Roach, *Constitutional Remedies in Canada,* 2nd ed. (Toronto: Thomson Reuters, 2013), pp.15.10–15.750.

[10] It will be suggested in Section 9.4 of this chapter that important social interests and competing rights should be considered, but subject to structured proportionality analysis. This analysis should give full weight to the danger of irreparable harm to Indigenous rights and recognize that interim remedies are only temporary and can be adjusted in light of changing circumstances including harms to social interests. Robust interim remedies can address colonial power imbalances and provide a foundation for meaningful settlements based on full and informed Indigenous consent.

[11] *Haida Nation* v. *British Columbia (Minister of Forests),* [2004] 3 SCR 511 at para 14.

9.2.1.1 United Nations Bodies

The Human Rights Committee issued provisional measures against Canada in 1990 in a complaint by the Lubicon Lake Band. The Band had requested but failed to obtain an interim injunction from Canadian courts to enjoin mining in 8,500 square miles of Lubicon traditional lands in Northern Alberta. The Canadian courts ruled that the Band had not established irreparable harm that would prevent hunting and trapping, even while recognizing that explosions and drilling by the mining companies could reduce the wildlife.[12] The Canadian courts also stressed that the mining companies would suffer "a loss of competitive positions"[13] should the injunction be issued. They noted that the Indigenous applicants were unable to undertake to pay any damages suffered by the mining company. Finally, they suggested that the government and the mining companies as agents of the government were immune from injunctive relief.

The Human Rights Committee devoted most of its 1990 communication to refuting claims that the applicants had not exhausted domestic remedies given the ongoing litigation. Its approach to irreparable harm was more generous than the Canadian courts. The Committee accepted that there was a risk of irreparable harm that threatened "the way of life and culture of the Lubicon Lake Band".[14] At the same time, the Committee did not elaborate on the appropriate remedy. As Dean Anaya has suggested: "by not providing guidance on the remedy issue, the Committee left it subject to continuing controversy within Canada's internal processes in which Canada has the upper hand".[15] This confirms the importance but frequent neglect of remedies.

Negotiations between Canada and the Lubicon Lake Band broke down in 2003 and mining continued.[16] In 2006, the Human Rights Committee called on the state to resume negotiations and consult with the Band

[12] *Ominayak* v. *Norcen Energy Resources Ltd.*, 1983 CanLII 1120 (AB QB) at para 17 aff'd 1985 ABCA 12 at para 35.

[13] Ibid. at para 21.

[14] *Lubicon Lake Band v. Canada* (1990), Report of the UNHRC, Comm. No. 167/1984, UN Doc A/45/40, Supp. No. 40, 26 March 1990 at para 30.

[15] Anaya, *Indigenous Peoples in International Law*, p.257.

[16] Amnesty International, *20 Years' Denial of Recommendations Made by the UN Human Rights Committee and the Continuing Impact on the Lubicon Cree* (London: Amnesty International Publications, 2010), online (pdf): www.amnesty.org/download/Documents/36000/amr200032010en.pdf

before granting more mining licences.[17] In 2018, an agreement involving Can$113 million in compensation and recognition of 246 square kilometres of Indigenous land was finally reached between the Lubicon Lake Band and Canadian governments.[18]

In subsequent cases, the Committee took a more cautious approach to interim remedies. It originally requested that Finland "refrain from adopting measures which would cause irreparable harm to the environment which the authors claim is vital to their culture and livelihood".[19] This demonstrates an awareness of the connection between the environment and Indigenous rights. The Committee subsequently withdrew interim measures when the state established that the logging was confined to a relatively small area of 500 hectares. Although the logging would cause some harm, it would not threaten the survival of the reindeer that the Sami relied upon. In a demonstration of the flexibility of interim relief, the Committee suggested that it would reconsider should evidence emerge that the effects of the logging was more serious than was foreseen.[20] This decision also reveals that more narrowly focused interim relief will generally be easier to obtain.

9.2.1.2 Inter-American Court of Human Rights

Article 63(2) of the American Convention on Human Rights contemplates that the IACtHR will order provisional measures in cases of "extreme gravity and urgency, and when necessary to avoid irreparable damage to persons". Consistent with emerging international practice, the IACtHR has characterized interim relief as mandatory, though it has not awarded damages as a remedy for breaches of provisional measures. A unique feature of the Inter-American jurisprudence is that the Court has also been willing to grant provisional measures, even after a final

[17] UN Human Rights Committee, Concluding Observations of the Human Rights Committee: Canada, UN Doc CCPR/C/CAN/CO/5, 20 April 2006.

[18] The Canadian Press, "Alberta Band Settles Long-Standing Land Claim for $113M and Swath of Land", *CBC News* (24 October 2018), online: www.cbc.ca/news/canada/edmonton/lubicon-settle-land-claim-alberta-1.4876940

[19] *J. Lansman* v. *Finland* (1996), Views of the UNHRC, Comm. 671/1995, UN Doc CCPR/C/58/D/671/1995, 58th Sess., 30 October 1996 at para 4.1.

[20] Ibid.; *I. Lansman* v. *Finland* (1994), Report of the UNHRC, Comm. No. 511/1992, UN Doc CCPR/C/52/D/511/1992, 52nd Sess., 26 October 2014; see also Eva Rieter, *Preventing Irreparable Harm Provisional Measures in International Human Rights Adjudication* (Antwerp: Intersentia, 2010), p.456.

judgement designed to protect the applicants from irreparable harm.[21] This could be particularly useful in the Indigenous rights context as a discrete supplement to longer term systemic relief or as part of the consultation process.

In one case from Colombia, the IACtHR ordered provisional measures designed to protect the physical safety of an Indigenous community. It maintained the measures in place from 2004 to 2011.[22] In 2004, the Court ordered protection by interim measures of the lands of an Indigenous community in Ecuador from harms caused by petroleum production.[23] After conducting its first on-site visit, the IACtHR found on the merits for the community. It ordered US$1.4 million in damages and rehabilitation efforts. In 2016, the Court found substantial compliance with its judgement.[24]

The IACtHR has also ordered interim remedies after a final judgement that ordered Nicaragua to demarcate and title their land. The case involved the land rights of the Awas Tingni community of about 600 Mayagna Indigenous people. They successfully litigated in the IACtHR after failing to obtain effective remedies to stop logging in the domestic courts. A year after final judgement, the IACtHR found a situation of "extreme gravity and urgency regarding the property of the Mayagna Community, including the resources therein, which are the basis for their subsistence, culture, and traditions". It ordered the necessary measures to stop such "immediate and irreparable" harms. The applicants should be able "to participate in planning and implementation of those measures and, in general, to keep them informed of progress regarding measures" ordered by the Inter-American Court of Human Rights.[25] This order was less precise than domestic courts would order because of their concerns about enforcement. At the same time, it recognized the importance of Indigenous participation. It also appears

[21] Clara Burbano Herrera, *Provisional Measures in the Case Law of the Inter-American Court of Human Rights* (Antwerp: Intersentia, 2010) p.171

[22] *Kankuamo Indigenous People* (Colombia) (2004), Provisional Measures, Inter-Am. Ct. H.R. (Ser. E.), (5 July 2004) at para. 2.

[23] *Kichwa Indigenous People of Sarayaku* v. *Ecuador* (2004), Provisional Measures, Inter-Am. Ct. H.R. (Ser. C), (6 July 2004).

[24] *Kichwa Indigenous People of Sarayaku* v. *Ecuador* (2014), (2017) 41 *Loy. L.A. Int'l. & Comp. L. Rev.* 1469.

[25] *Mayagna (Sumo) Awas Tingni Community (Nicaragua)* (2002), Provisional Measures, Order of the Court, Inter-Am.Ct. H.R (Ser. C), (September 6, 2002) at *Considering*, para 6.

to have been effective. The state formed a committee with representatives of the community to monitor compliance and enacted laws to allow the property to be titled. The interim measures were lifted five years later because their effect was subsumed in the Court's monitoring of the final judgement.[26]

9.2.1.3 The African Court of Human and Peoples' Rights

The African Court of Human and Peoples' Rights has issued provisional measures to restrain the eviction of 15,000 Ogiek people from their traditional lands.[27] The Court explained that "there is a situation of extreme gravity and urgency, as well as a risk of irreparable harm to the Ogiek of the Mau Forest and also prejudice to the substantive matter before the Court".[28] It unanimously issued a provisional order that "[t]he Respondent immediately reinstates the restrictions it had imposed on land transactions in the Mau Forest Complex and refrains from any act or thing that would or might irreparably prejudice the main application before the Court, until the final determination of the said application".[29] It also ordered the state to report to the Court on the measures taken to implement this Order.

Supra-national courts are generally more prepared than domestic courts to order that the government report back to them about the measures taken to comply with interim measures. They do not assume that compliance is automatic. The reporting requirement provides an opportunity to adjust interim relief if necessary and allows for participation by the parties. This is yet another example where domestic courts could learn from the remedial practice of international courts.

9.2.1.4 Canada

One of Canada's largest and more successful land claims agreements can be related to a decision by a trial judge to restrain massive flooding of Cree land to facilitate hydroelectric development. After a year-long hearing that heard extensive evidence from Cree trappers and forty other experts, Justice Malouf issued an interlocutory injunction against the

[26] *Mayagna (Sumo) Awas Tingni Community* v. *Nicaragua* (2002), at (2014) 36 *Loy. L.A. Int'l & Comp L. Rev.* 1113, 1138. See Eva Rieter, *Preventing Irreparable Harm* (Antwerp: Intersentia, 2010), pp.459–461.

[27] *African Commission on Human and Peoples' Rights* v. *Kenya* (2013), No. 006/2012, Provisional Measures, African Court on Human and Peoples' Rights, 1 AfCLR 193.

[28] Ibid. at para 22.

[29] Ibid. at para 25.

continued construction of four major dams on James Bay. He concluded that the flooding of the land that the Cree and Inuit used to hunt, trap and fish would cause irreparable harm to wildlife and the physical environment. Consistent with the international jurisprudence, he found that the claimed rights and irreparable harm alone justified granting the injunction.[30] He heard evidence estimating damages in halting the dams to be as much as Can$60 million. Nevertheless, he decided that if the case must be decided on the basis of the balance of convenience that the rights of the Indigenous applicants to their way of life on their land should prevail.[31]

The injunction was suspended pending appeal and subsequently overturned. The Quebec Court of Appeal concluded that "the public and general interests of the people of Quebec" should prevail over those "of some two thousand of its inhabitants",[32] namely the Cree and Inuit of James Bay. This decision demonstrates some of the dangers of the balance of convenience concept. The idea that vaguely defined "public interests" of the majority should trump those of Indigenous people is majoritarian, colonial and racist. It ignores that the interests of the "people of Quebec" are economic interests while the interests of the Cree and the Inuit are their rights to be peoples.

The Quebec Court of Appeal re-evaluated the extensive evidence heard by Justice Malouf about the harm to wildlife that would be caused by extensive flooding and that it could be compensated by damages. Justice Turgeon expressed a colonial hope that "*les autochones ont evolue rapidement vers un mode de vie qui est celui des tous les Quebecois*".[33] The Court of Appeal also held that the Cree and the Inuit had not established a likelihood of success on the merits. The Court of Appeal stressed that the development had been authorized by legislation that should be presumed to be constitutional.[34] Today, Canadian courts would err if they required such a high likelihood of success on the merits or presumed that the authorizing legislation was constitutional. Unfortunately, the Quebec Court of Appeal's decision cannot be dismissed as a historic

[30] *Gros-Louis c. Société dé développment de la Baie James*, (1973) 8 CNLR 188 (Que. S.C.) at 355.
[31] Ibid. at 370.
[32] *Gros-Louis c. Société dé développment de la Baie James*, (1973) 8 CNLR 414 (Que. C.A.) at 414.
[33] *Gros-Louis c. Société dé développment de la Baie James*, (1973) 8 CNLR 373 (Que. C.A.) at 399.
[34] Ibid. at 399–400.

footnote. In 1987, the Supreme Court of Canada referred to its decision with approval and stated that the trial judge's grant of the injunction was "a striking illustration of interlocutory relief which could have compromised the common good of the public as a whole".[35]

Despite the Court of Appeal's rulings, the Quebec and federal government continued to negotiate with the Cree and the Inuit. The judgement granting the interim injunction played an important role in educating the public about the irreparable harm that could be caused if the development continued to go ahead. The parties reached a land claims agreement in 1975 that applied to over 6,000 Cree people and over 2,000 Inuit people who approved of the agreement. It included Can$225 million to be paid over ten years in part from hydroelectric royalties. It also included varying levels of Indigenous control over the land, including complete control over forestry rights and exclusive hunting, trapping and fishing rights. The agreement also included the right to education in the Cree and Inuktitut languages, social and health services administered by Cree and Inuit institutions and investment in Indigenous businesses.[36] Some may question whether this modern-day Treaty should be seen as a remedy. In my view, it should. Consistent with the two-track approach, it provided compensation for harm and a systemic framework for future relations.

In subsequent cases, Canadian courts recognized that "a temporary restraining order does not signal victory or defeat to either side" or necessarily represent the remedy that the court would order after a full trial on the merits. After granting an injunction against logging, the British Columbia Court of Appeal added that "the public anticipates that the claims will be resolved by negotiation and settlement".[37] The British Columbia Court of Appeal has upheld an interim injunction against mining. It stressed that mining would cause irreparable harm compared to a temporary delay for the mining company.[38] When granting another interlocutory injunction, another Canadian judge simply stated: "the

35 *Manitoba (A.G)* v. *Metropolitan Stores*, [1987] 1 SCR 110 at para 59.

36 John Ciaccia, *James Bay and Northern Quebec Agreement* (Montreal: Quebec National Library, 1976). For background, see Hans Carlson, "A Watershed of Words: Litigating and Negotiating Nature in Eastern James Bay, 1971–75" (2004) 85(1) *Can. Historical Rev.* 63.

37 *MacMillan Bloedel* v. *Mullin*, [1985] 3 WWR 577 at 607 (BC CA).

38 *Taseko Mines Ltd.* v. *Tsilhqot'in National Government*, 2019 BCCA 479.

minerals, if there, will remain; the caribou, presently there, may not".[39] This confirms what was discussed in Chapter 3, Section 3.1, about the asymmetrical nature of interim relief. In many cases, a denial of an interim remedy will end a dispute and allow state action to proceed despite claims that it may cause irreparable harm to rights. Conversely, a decision to grant interim relief will not necessarily end the dispute. It will allow defendants to argue at trial that they are not violating rights. It will ensure that there can be meaningful and effective remedies should a violation of Indigenous rights be established.

Despite this, applications for interim relief are also frequently denied in Canadian Indigenous rights cases. As mentioned above, the Supreme Court of Canada acknowledged in its leading case on the duty to consult that "the balance of convenience tips the scales in favour of protecting jobs and government revenues"[40] without clearly approving or disapproving of such a majoritarian approach that is hostile to Indigenous rights. It will be suggested in Section 9.4 that courts should use proportionality reasoning so as to avoid the type of reasoning used by the Quebec Court of Appeal in the *James Bay* case.

Canadian courts will generally apply the lenient preliminary test of whether the claim is frivolous or vexatious given the fact specific nature of claims of Indigenous rights. Courts will also generally find that Indigenous people are at a risk of suffering irreparable harm from the state action they challenge.[41] Thus, in many cases both irreparable harm and a serious question to be tried will be present. This means that

[39] *The Hamlet at Baker Lake* v. *The Minister of Indian Affairs and Northern Development* (1978), 87 DLR (3d) 342 at 348 (FCTD). More recently, another judge similarly noted: "[t]he geology will always be there. The ore bed is not going anywhere. The same cannot be said of the habitat that is presently left to the petitioners. Once disturbed, it is lost. Once lost, the exercise of Aboriginal rights is further diminished": *Xeni Gwet'in First Nation* v. *British Columbia*, 2019 BCSC 1271 at paras 64–65. In that case, the judge also did not order the plaintiffs to undertake to pay the damages caused by interim relief should they be unsuccessful on the merits. The Supreme Court of Canada has stated in the human rights context that "the fact that one party may be impecunious does not automatically determine the application in favour of the other party who will not ultimately be able to collect damages, although it may be a relevant consideration". *R. J. R. Macdonald Inc.* v. *Canada (Attorney General),* [1994] 1 SCR 311 at 341.

[40] *Haida Nation* v. *British Columbia (Minister of Forests)*, [2004] 3 SCR 511 at para 14.

[41] *Musqueam Indian Band* v. *Canada*, 2008 FCA 214 (sale of two office buildings in downtown Vancouver will not cause irreparable harm). But see *Musqueam Indian Band* v. *Canada*, 2004 FC 579 (restraining sale of other land). One judge has acknowledged arguments that "it is critical to consider the nature of the potential loss from an Aboriginal perspective ... Aboriginal identity, spirituality, laws, traditions, culture and

whether an interim remedy is granted will depend on the judge's determination of where the balance of convenience and the public interest lies.[42] More narrowly tailored injunctions are more likely to be granted.[43] Courts remain concerned about adverse economic impacts of granting interim relief even at the interim stage.[44] At the same time, the government does not have a monopoly on the public interest and courts have also recognized that granting interim relief can advance the honour of the Crown.[45]

9.2.1.5 Australia

To obtain an interlocutory injunction, an Aboriginal applicant will have to establish a "sufficiently arguable case". Those opposing an injunction may prevail if they "demonstrate that the action brought by the claimant is doomed to fail and to contend that no arguable case for the existence of native title is or can be made out".[46] The Australian High Court applied this merits-based approach to deny an injunction on the basis that native title had been extinguished by a grant of fee simple. Justice Kirby in his concurrence acknowledged that while courts often "take into account the ultimate prospects of success", the grant of fee simple was a special form of "knock out" of the Indigenous claim.[47]

As discussed in Chapter 3, Section 3.3, there are dangers if courts accept weak rights claims as constituting irreparable harm and then balance such claims against the balance of convenience.[48] In such a battle, Indigenous applicants may frequently lose especially if they are unable to undertake to

rights are connected to and arise from this relationship land". Given this, "no amount of money can compensate for its loss". *Platinex Inc.* v. *Kitchenuhmaykoosib Inninuwug First Nation*, 2006 CanLII 26171 (ON SC) at paras 79–80. Note that the same judge after hearing new evidence about the limited effects of limited exploratory drilling subsequently concluded in the same dispute: "[t]he fear of cultural, environmental, and spiritual harm ... cannot reliably be linked to Platinex's proposed development". *Platinex* v. *Kitchenuhmaykoosib Inninuwug First Nation and A.G Ontario*, 2007 CanLII 16637 at para 158 (ON SC).

42 For additional discussion of the Canadian jurisprudence, see Roach, *Constitutional Remedies in Canada*, 15.240–15.750.

43 *Westar Timber Ltd* v. *Gitksan Wet'suwet'en Tribal Council*, (1989) CanLII 2764 (BC CA); *Blueberry River First Nation* v. *Canada*, 2017 BCSC 899.

44 *Canada Forest Products* v. *Sam*, 2013 BCCA 38; *Kruger Inc. c. Première nation des Bestiamites*, 2006 QCCA 569.

45 *Williams* v. *British Columbia*, 2019 BCCA 112 at para 50.

46 *Fejo* v. *Northern Territory*, [1998] HCA 58 at para 41.

47 Ibid. at para 83.

48 Robert J. Sharpe, "Interim Remedies and Constitutional Rights" (2019) 69 Supp. 1 *U.T.L.J.* 9, 24–25.

pay the hefty damages that interim relief may cause to resource companies should the applicants eventually lose on the merits. Thus, it is important for requests for interim relief to be accompanied with the best evidence possible about the strength of the claim and the irreparable harm it will cause to the plaintiff. This will be difficult to do given the fact specific and historical nature of most Indigenous rights. The fact that corporate defendants will generally only suffer monetary harm should also be relevant, as well as the fact that by granting licenses to such corporate defendants, the state may be liable to compensate the corporation for harms caused by interim remedies.

9.2.1.6 New Zealand

In New Zealand, most requests for interim injunctions are decided by specialized Māori courts and tribunals. This could be an important safeguard against applying common law approaches that are more geared to disputes between competing corporations or between corporations and governments.

The Māori Land Court granted an interim injunction on the common law basis of a serious issue to be tried, irreparable harm not compensable by damages and the balance of convenience. At the same time, the Court allowed the respondents bound by the injunction to return to the Court to "seek approval from the Court for payment of any urgent accounts that would otherwise be prevented by the injunction".[49] The Māori Appellate Court has denied interim relief in cases where it held that damages would be an adequate remedy and where those seeking the injunction do not come with "clean hands".[50] Courts that order interim relief should take more responsibility for ensuring that there are productive settlement discussions or that the case is making progress towards a full trial. Because of their centralized nature, supra-national courts may be better at this than domestic courts.

9.2.2 Demarcation and Restitution of Land

9.2.2.1 Inter-American Court of Human Rights

The IACtHR has been perhaps the most ambitious court in ordering various forms of equitable relief for violations of Indigenous rights. As

[49] *Sherard* v. *Povey and Ors – Otakanin Māori Reservation (Haranui Marae)* (2016), 140 Taitokerau MB 60 at para 84.

[50] *Mihaka* v. *Wihapi – Paengaroa North B No. 10A Block* [1992], 8 Waiariki Appellate MB 137, [1992] NZMAC 7.

Thomas Antkowiak has recognized, the Court has ordered "cessation of ongoing violations, land restitution, medical and psychological care, apologies, memorials, cultural initiatives, legislative reform, training programs for state officials, and community development schemes".[51]

In a number of cases, the IACtHR has ordered states to recognize Indigenous land rights. It has generally asked states in consultation with the affected Indigenous group to demarcate land rights and grant title. It has also ordered, as an ancillary remedy, that no additional grants of third party rights over the land be made while the land is returned.[52] As Brenda Gunn has argued, such forms of land restitution are "key for the satisfaction or realization of... the right of Indigenous peoples to use, own, occupy and control their traditional lands".[53]

One instructive order made in the 2007 case of *Saramaka People* v. *Suriname* was:

> The state shall delimit, demarcate and grant collective title over the territory of the members of the Saramaka people, in accordance with their customary laws, and through previous, effective and fully informed consultations, without prejudice to other tribal and indigenous community.[54]

As Professor Gunn notes, an important component of this order is respect for Indigenous law. This remedy is consistent with the aspiration of Article 40 of UNDRIP to have bi-jural remedies that respect both

[51] Antkowiak, "A Dark Side of Virtue", 51.

[52] *Moiwana Community* v. *Suriname* (2005), Preliminary Objections, Merits, Reparations and Costs, Judgment, Inter-Am. Ct. H.R. (Ser. C), (15 June 2005); *Case of the Yakye Axa Indigenous Community* v. *Paraguay* (2005), Merits, Reparations and Costs, Judgment, Inter-Am. Ct. H.R. (Ser. C), (17 June 2005); *Case of the Sawhoyamaxa Indigenous Community* v. *Paraguay* (2006), Merits, Reparations and Costs, Judgment, Inter-Am. Ct. H.R. (Ser. C), (29 March 2006); *Case of the Saramaka People* v. *Suriname* (2007), Preliminary Objections, Merits, Reparations and Costs, Inter-Am Ct. H.R (Ser. C), (28 November 2007); *Garífuna Triunfo de la Cruz Community and Its Members* v. *Honduras* (2012), Report on Merits, Inter-Am. Ct. H.R. (Ser. C), (7 November 2012); *Xákmok Kásek Indigenous Community* v. *Paraguay* (2010), Merits, Reparations and Costs, Judgment, Inter-Am. Ct. H.R. (Ser. C), (24 August 2010); *Yakye Axa Indigenous Community* v. *Paraguay* (2008), Monitoring Compliance with Judgment, Order of the Court, Inter-Am. Ct. H.R. (Ser. E), (8 February 2008) at *Declares* para 1.

[53] Brenda Gunn, "Remedies for Violations of Indigenous Peoples' Human Rights" (2019) 69 Supp. 1 *U.T.L.J.* 150, 163.

[54] Preliminary Objections, Merits, Reparations and Costs, Inter-Am Ct. H.R. (Ser. C), (28 November 2007) at para 214.5. Other remedies included US$75,000 in pecuniary damages for logging and US$600,000 in non-pecuniary damages in the form of a community development fund.

Indigenous law and human rights. Another important feature was that the state and its agents were asked to not adversely affect Indigenous land pending the grant of collective title and that it revisit any grant of third parties rights. Unfortunately, Suriname, a small country and former Dutch colony, has not complied with this and other remedies even though Indigenous people have lived there since 3000 BC.[55]

In *Kalina and Lokono Peoples* v. *Suriname*,[56] the Court gave the state three years to demarcate and grant title to Indigenous land. This allowed time for negotiations with third parties that may have acquired the land or, if necessary, negotiations about the grant of equivalent land. The state was also required to immediately stop granting the Indigenous land to third parties. The Court also complemented this order with a US$1 million community development fund that provided for environmentally damaged land to be rehabilitated as well as the sharing of the benefits of resource development with Indigenous people. Unfortunately, Suriname has again not complied. The UN Committee on the Elimination of Racial Discrimination found that it disregarded the judgement and the rights of Indigenous people who constitute about 4 per cent of the country's population.[57] There have also been suggestions that the Organization of American States, the World Bank and international civil society might help counter Suriname's continued resistance to Indigenous rights.[58] Enforcement actions, though rare in international law, can play an important dialogic role in extreme cases where states defy court orders[59]

[55] (2014) 36 *Loy. L.A. Int'l & Comp. L. Rev.* 2305, 2321–2324. Despite finding non-compliance, the Court has not referred the case to the Organization of American States for enforcement. The Court has also refused to issue new interim measures as requested in an attempt to stop new concessions to gold mining companies: *Saramaka People* v. *Suriname* (2013), Monitoring Compliance with Judgment, Order of the Court, Inter-Am Ct. H.R. (Ser. C), (4 September 2013).

[56] (2017) 40 *Loy. L.A. Int'l. & Comp. L. Rev.* 1213.

[57] The Association of Indigenous Village Leaders in Suriname, The Association of Saramaka Authorities and The Forest Peoples Programme, Report on the Situation of Indigenous and Tribal People in Suriname and Comments on Suriname's 13th–15th Periodic Reports, CERD, 87th Sess., 14 July 2015, online (pdf): https://iachr.lls.edu/sites/default/files/iachr/Court_and_Commission_Documents/2016-2017/kalina_012_committee_on_the_elimination_of_racial_discrimination_july_2015.pdf

[58] Jeanice Koorndjik, "Judgments of the Inter-American Court of Human Rights Concerning Indigenous and Tribal Rights in Suriname" (2019) 23(10) *Int'l. J. Hum. Rts.* 1615.

[59] Jutta Brunée and Stephen Toope, *Legitimacy and Legality in International Law: An Interactional Account* (Cambridge: Cambridge University Press, 2010), pp.109–114,

In a 2015 case, the Court ordered that ownership of Indigenous land be confirmed and that Honduras make no grants of this land to third parties. Unfortunately, the Court did not address whether this had been done in its first follow-up judgement on compliance. It did, however, order Honduras to add US$15 to a US$1.5 million community development fund that had been deducted from the state's transfer of money because of banking charges.[60] Enforcement actions should be reasonable and proportionate to the lack of compliance. This one seems quite trivial. The much more important issue is the return of Indigenous land.

In another case, the Court ordered that Honduras restore ancestral lands, including paying damages to and re-locating others who had settled on the land. It indicated that if this was not possible, the state should give the Indigenous community alternative land.[61] This remedy appropriately recognized the priority of restitution under the international law of state responsibility. In another case, the Court ordered the return of 10,700 hectares of ancestral land within a year. It held that the state could ask for another year's extension but if granted, must pay the community US$10,000 a month during the extension.[62] This provided incentives for the state to comply.

In the *Mayagna (Sumo) Awas Tingni Community* Case,[63] the Court found that Nicaragua had failed to protect Indigenous property rights. The Court again recognized the primacy of restitution. It ordered the state to adopt legislative and administrative measures to protect the land, but to do so in a manner consistent with Indigenous law.[64] This is another example of a bi-jural systemic remedy that would have involved

recognizing that enforcement can be important and respond to a "lack of 'congruence' between existing norms and international practice".

60 *Garífuna Punta Piedra Community and Its Members* v. *Honduras* (2015), (2018) 41 *Loy. L.A. Int'l. & Comp. L. Rev.* 1263, 1283.

61 *Garífuna Triunfo de la Cruz Community and Its Members* v. *Honduras* (2012), Report on Merits, Inter-Am. Ct. H.R. (Ser. C), (7 November 2012).

62 *Xákmok Kásek Indigenous Community* v. *Paraguay* (2010), Merits, Reparations and Costs, Judgment, Inter-Am. Ct. H.R. (Ser. C), (24 August 2010).

63 *Mayagna (Sumo) Awas Tingni Community (Nicaragua)* (2002), Monitoring Compliance with Judgment, Inter-Am. Ct. H.R. (Ser. C), (3 April 2009) at *Considering* para 11. See generally S James Anaya and Claudio Grossman, "The Case of Awas Tingni v. Nicaragua: A Step in the International Law of Indigenous Peoples" (2002) 19 *Ariz. J. Int'l. Comp. L.* 1.

64 *Mayagna (Sumo) Awas Tingni Community (Nicaragua)* (2002), Monitoring Compliance with Judgment, Inter-Am.Ct. H.R (Ser. C), (3 April 2009) at para 164.

the Indigenous community as the keeper of their laws. In 2008, the Court held that the state had made progress, but still not completed the demarcation of Indigenous land seven years after the original judgement. In April 2009, however, the Court found that Nicaragua had fully complied and transferred ownership of over 73,000 hectares of land and that this had been recognized in a ceremony. The Court praised Nicaragua for its actions.[65] Rewards, even informal and symbolic ones, can play a role in enforcing international law.

Unfortunately, this case from Nicaragua is an exception. Most of the IACtHR's follow-up judgements have found a lack of compliance or insufficient information to determine if there has been compliance with land demarcation and restitution. In three cases involving Paraguay, ranch owners were unwilling to sell their land after judgements in favour of Indigenous land rights. In two of those cases, after long delays Indigenous people re-occupied their traditional lands on their own accord. In the third case, alternative land was purchased by the state, but it was not suitable.[66] Lack of state compliance with land return occurs even while registering compliance with other parts of a judgement providing for damages, publication of the judgement and state acknowledgement of wrongdoing. These results suggest state resistance to recognition of land rights and a strategic willingness to cherry pick among multiple remedies and comply with those that are less costly from the perspective of the state and third parties.

9.2.2.2 South Africa

The South African Constitutional Court issued a general declaration that nine Indigenous applicants were entitled to land that they occupied.[67] Unfortunately, there were subsequent problems in implementing the judgement. The land had been consolidated in a large commercial farm owned by a company that had blocked access to traditional graves. The applicants were not included in negotiations with the company. The government also failed to consult with the community. The

65 *Mayagna (Sumo) Awas Tingni Community* v. *Nicaragua* (2002), at (2014) 36 *Loy. L.A. Int'l & Comp L. Rev.* 1113, 1134–1138.

66 Joel E. Correia, "Adjudication and Its After Effects in Three Inter-American Court Cases Brought against Paraguay: Indigenous Land Rights" (2018) (111) *Erasmus L. Rev.* 43, 53–56.

67 *Department of Land Affairs & Others* v. *Goedgelegen Tropical Fruits (Pty) Ltd*, [2007] ZACC 12 at paras 84–85.

applicants expressed disillusionment in a ten-year delay in the return of their land.[68]

The South African Constitutional Court has recognized the need for restitution of traditional lands in a case where the government evicted Indigenous peoples to make way for a diamond mine.[69] The Court indicated that in determining such questions, it would apply Indigenous law so long as it was consistent with the Constitution and constitutionally valid legislation.[70] In this case, Indigenous law required that the land and mineral rights be held communally.[71] The Court affirmed that the Indigenous community was entitled to "restitution of the right to ownership of the subject land (including its minerals and precious stones) and to the exclusive beneficial use and occupation thereof".[72] Demarcation and return of land requires bi-jural remedies that incorporate Indigenous law in the recognition and regulation of land returned to Indigenous people.

9.2.3 *Damages*

Consistent with general international law principles, damages should only be ordered if restitution is impossible or disproportionate.[73] Unfortunately, both supra-national and national courts have not always observed this priority. They have also often under-valued pecuniary losses from violations of Indigenous rights. This failure has only been partially made up by an increasing tendency to award more generous damages for non-pecuniary damage to culture.

9.2.3.1 Inter-American Court of Human Rights

9.2.3.1.1 Community Development Funds and Neo-Colonialism In a 2005 case, the Court ordered a US$1.2 million community development fund for the Indigenous community. The spending of this money was, however, subject to control by a three-person committee, only one of

[68] Bernadette Atuahene and Sanele Sibanda, "From Reparations to Dignity Restoration: The Story of the Popela Community" (2018) 18 *African Hum. Rts. L. J.* 654.

[69] *Alexkor Ltd and Another* v. *Richtersveld Community and Others*, [2003] ZACC 18.

[70] Ibid. at para 51.

[71] Ibid. at paras 62–64.

[72] Ibid. at para 103.

[73] International Law Commission, *Principles of State Responsibility*, of the Commission's fifty-third and fifty-fifth sessions, 23 April–1 June and 2 July–10 August 2001, GA Supplement No. 10, A/56/10, Art. 35.

whom would represent the community. This approach has rightly been criticized as neo-colonial in its desire to "assist" the Indigenous community.[74] In a follow-up judgement two years later, the Court found that while the state had paid individual damages, the collective development funds had not been spent by the committee.[75] A top-down colonial approach to remedies is not only wrong in principle in denying the foundational principle of Indigenous self-determination, but also more likely to be ineffective because of its failure to employ Indigenous law and governance.

By 2012, the Court had abandoned its use of three-person committees to control the use of community development funds. It ordered that another US$1.2 million community development fund be distributed "in accordance with [the petitioner community's] own decision-making mechanisms and institutions".[76] The Court in 2016 found that there was compliance with this part of the judgement.[77] Direct community control is likely more efficient and effective than having the court or government attempt to regulate how funds are spent. It is certainly less colonial.

Similar trends away from neo-colonialism are seen in the remedies that the IACtHR frequently has to order for massacres of Indigenous people. In 2004, the Court ordered, a "specialized program of psychological and psychiatric treatment" be provided free of charge to surviving victims.[78] In a 2012 case, however, the Court seemed more aware of Mayan culture when it quoted with approval an expert witness who testified that "the Mayan peoples never go to psychologists, instead [their] psychology is cared for with the sacred fire [and] with medicinal plants". The Court stated that "based on the representatives request, this medical and psychological care may be provided by healers of the Maya Achi community, in keeping with their own health practices and using traditional medicines".[79] There is a need for courts to respect Indigenous

[74] *Moiwana Community* v. *Suriname* (2005), Preliminary Objections, Merits, Reparations and Costs, Judgment, Inter-Am. Ct. H.R. (Ser. C), (15 June 2005) at para 79.

[75] *Moiwana Community* v. *Suriname*, (2014) 36 *Loy. L.A. Int'l. & Comp. L. Rev.* 2513, 2546.

[76] *Kichwa Indigenous People of Sarayaku* v. *Ecuador* (2012), Merits and Reparations, Judgment, Inter-Am. Ct. H.R. (Ser. C), (27 June 2012) at para 323.

[77] *Kichwa Indigenous People of Sarayaku* v. *Ecuador*, (2017) 40 *Loy. L.A. Int'l. & Comp. L. Rev.* 1469, 1489.

[78] *Case of the Plan de Sanchez Massacre* v. *Guatemala* (2004), Reparations, Judgment, Inter-Am. Ct. H.R. (Ser. C), (19 November 2004) at para 81, 102–110.

[79] *Case of Río Negro Massacres* v. *Guatemala* (2012), Preliminary Objection, Merits, Reparations and Costs, Judgment, Inter-Am. Ct. H.R. (Ser. C), (12 September 2017) at para 289. The Court also called for a program "for the rescue, promotion, dissemination and conservation of... ancestral customs and practices, based on the values, principles

self-determination even when ordering first-track remedies such as damages that are well within the court's traditional competence.

9.2.3.1.2 Under-Valuation of Pecuniary Harms The IACtHR's award of non-pecuniary damages through the vehicle of community development funds is generous. Alas, there is a danger that they are de facto being used as an alternative to full damages for pecuniary losses. One oft-criticized case involved the award of US$75,000 for lost timber in the face of expert evidence from a former World Bank Chief Environmental Advisor that a conservative value of the timber taken from Indigenous lands was US$10 million. This was much greater than even the US$600,000 community development fund awarded in the case.[80]

The trend in undervaluing pecuniary harms has continued. The Court in 2015 found that an Indigenous community whose ancestral lands were the subject of grants to third parties had not presented enough evidence to establish pecuniary damages. The Court did, however, order that the land be returned and a US$1.5 million community development fund be provided.[81] The Court has accepted that in expropriation situations, fair market value is not necessarily payable. It has indicated that all that is required is a "fair balance" between the claimant's interests and "the general interest".[82] As will be explored in Section 9.4 of this chapter, however, courts rarely apply full proportionality reasoning to such a balancing process.

9.2.3.2 United States

In 1954, the United States Supreme Court held that extinguishment of native title was not compensable under the Fifth Amendment because such title was "not a property right".[83] It was only a "right of occupancy"

and philosophies of the Maya Achi people" including a museum. What is not known is whether this order, undoubtedly well-intentioned, accorded with the community's priorities.

80 Antikowiak, "A Dark Side of Virtue", 67–68 in reference to *Case of the Saramaka People* v. *Suriname* (2007), Preliminary Objections, Merits, Reparations and Costs, Inter-Am Ct. H.R (Ser. C), (28 November 2007).

81 *Garífuna Triunfo de la Cruz Community and Its Members* v. *Honduras* (2012), Report on Merits, Inter-Am. Ct. H.R. (Ser. C), (7 November 2012).

82 *Case of Salvador Chiriboga* v. *Ecuador*, Report on Reparations and Costs, Judgment, Inter-Am. Ct. H.R. (Ser. C), (3 March 2011).

83 *Tee Hit Ton Indians* v. *United States*, 348 US 272 (1954).

that states could end without compensation. The Court's decision reflected concerns about the social costs of providing compensation as revealed by a footnote that indicated that damages for violation of native title had been estimated at US$9 billion.[84]

Before the 1954 decision, the Court decided that Congress could legislate in violation of Treaties.[85] It subsequently held that compensation should be paid for the taking of land granted by Treaty. Justice Cardozo reasoned that anything but "just compensation" would be "an act of confiscation".[86] The Court has also awarded damages for breach of fiduciary duty in mismanaging Indian land[87] but only where statutes granted the government extensive powers over the Indigenous interests.[88] In principle, it is difficult to understand why damages can be paid for breach of Treaties and fiduciary duty but not for breach of Indigenous title. One factor may be that the costs of remedies related to extinguishment of title are likely to be larger than the costs of remedies linked to Treaty and fiduciary duty violations.

9.2.3.3 Canada

In 1973, the Supreme Court of Canada divided 3–3 on whether extinguishment of Aboriginal title would result in damages. Justice Hall would have subjected extinguishment to the same presumption of compensation as other "private rights".[89] Given the lack of constitutional protection of any rights at the time, there could be expropriation without compensation but only if authorized by clear legislation. In contrast, Justice Judson would have followed the American approach and not have awarded compensation because of the distinct nature of native title.

The choice between these two alternatives of compensation and no compensation may be too extreme. Full monetary compensation may be too weak with respect to land that is very important to Indigenous people, but also too generous with respect to land that is subject to infrequent Indigenous use. The Supreme Court has subsequently

[84] Ibid. at fn 17.

[85] *Lone Wolf* v. *Hitchcock*, 187 US 553 (1903).

[86] *Shoshone Tribe of Indians of the Wind River Reservation in Wyoming* v. *United States*, 299 US 476 (1937) at 497.

[87] *United States* v. *Mitchell*, 463 US 206 (1983); *United States* v. *White Mountain Apache Tribe*, 537 US 465 (2003).

[88] *United States* v. *Navajo Nation*, 129 S.Ct. 1547 (2009); *United States* v. *Jicarilla Apache Nation*, 131 S.Ct. 2313 (2011) at 2332.

[89] *Calder* v. *British Columbia (Attorney General)*, [1973] SCR 313 at para 96.

expressed some preference for a more flexible approach to remedies that avoids the extremes of compensation and non-compensation. This approach would provide a variety of remedies that depend on the precise nature of the interest. The remedies could include restitution of land, damages, assignment of priority user rights and the use of declarations.[90] In a leading case, the Supreme Court has stated: "ultimately, it is through negotiated settlements, with good faith and give and take on all sides, reinforced by the judgments of this Court, that we will achieve... reconciliation. Let us face it, we are all here to stay".[91]

The Canadian courts have also awarded remedies to Indigenous groups for breach of fiduciary duty by the government, something also recently done by the New Zealand Supreme Court.[92] This approach has the advantage of treating Aboriginal rights as a complex range of rights that include elements of property rights and rights of participation and sharing of resources. The courts have stressed that they have flexible equitable powers to remedy breach of fiduciary duty. These powers could include constructive trusts that could result in restitution of land and the assignment of priority and alternative user rights. Some commentators have argued that the fiduciary duty approach can provide meaningful remedies.[93] At the same time, courts often favour damages as a remedy for breach of fiduciary duty. In the leading case, the Court awarded Can$10 million in damages on an "equitable basis" for breach of fiduciary duty when the government did not consult with the Indigenous community with respect to a lease to a golf course on land that the Indigenous community had surrendered to the Crown.[94]

9.2.3.4 Australia

In its landmark *Mabo*[95] case recognizing native title, the Australian High Court decided 4–3 not to apply the presumption of compensation for

90 *Tsilhqot'in Nation* v. *British Columbia*, 2014 SCC 44 at paras 90–91.
91 *Delgamuukw* v. *British Columbia*, [1997] 3 SCR 1010 at para 186.
92 *Proprietors of Wakatū* v. *Attorney-General*, [2017] NZSC 17.
93 Robert Mainville, *An Overview of Aboriginal and Treaty Rights and Compensation for Their Breach* (Saskatoon: Purich, 2001), pp.87, 94.
94 *Guerin* v. *The Queen*, [1984] 2 SCR 335 at 339.
95 *Mabo* v. *Queensland* (1992), 66 ALJR 408 at 410 per Mason CJ and McHugh J; ibid. at 430 per Brennan J; ibid. at 462 per Dawson J.; Justices Deane and Gaudron dissented: ibid. at 443–445, 452–453 as did Justice Toohey: ibid. at 489–490. As Peter Russell noted, it was "disturbing" that the majority did not apply constitutional protections to Aboriginal title even if they suggested that some takings may infringe ordinary statutes prohibiting racial discrimination: Peter H. Russell, *Recognizing Aboriginal Title* (Toronto:

extinguished title. Dissenting judges would have classified native title as a property interest that would require compensation under section 51 (xxxi) of the Australian Constitution. Legislation was, however, subsequently enacted providing for compensation for extinguishment of native title.[96] Like the overturned James Bay interim injunction, this demonstrates how some legal defeats can result in some political victories.

In a 2019 case, the Australian High Court awarded over AUS$1.3 in damages for extinguishment of native title. It reduced the damage awarded by the trial judge from 80 per cent of the market value of non-Indigenous title to 50 per cent. It reasoned that "native title rights and interests were essentially usufructuary, ceremonial and non-exclusive, without power to prevent other persons entering or using the land. . . and without right to exploit the land for commercial purposes".[97] The economic loss award was AUS$320,250 with an additional AUS$910,100 in interest. The Court rejected the idea that this was discriminatory and that the requirements for compensation of the taking of non-Indigenous land was determinative. It asserted that it was simply valuing the extinguished Aboriginal title on the basis of its actual nature and value. The Court concluded that "[t]here is nothing discriminatory about treating non-exclusive native title as a lesser interest in land than a full exclusive native title or, for that reason, as having a lesser economic value than a freehold estate. To the contrary, it is to treat like as like".[98]

Reflecting a trend also seen in the international jurisprudence, the Court was more generous in awarding AUS$1.3 million in non-pecuniary damages for cultural loss. The Court defined the task of assessing cultural loss as determining "the essentially spiritual relationship which the Ngaliwurru and Nungali Peoples had with their country and to translate the spiritual hurt caused by the compensable acts into compensation".[99] It also noted the damage caused "under their laws and customs when country is harmed",[100] as well as spiritual losses

University of Toronto Press, 2005), p.260. As Russell recounts, the mining industry wanted the act against racial discrimination not to apply. This did not occur, but the Native Title Act validates actions up to its enactment while including an AUS$1.5 billion for compensation and the right to both consultation and compensation for subsequent extinguishment of Native title: ibid., pp.306–310.

[96] Native Title Act, 1993 (Cth).

[97] *Northern Territory* v. *Griffiths and Jones*, [2019] HCA 7 at para 106.

[98] Ibid. at para 74.

[99] Ibid. at para 216.

[100] Ibid. at para 167.

connected to development on the land.[101] This attempts to integrate Indigenous law into remedial decision-making, but the devaluing of the pecuniary value of Indigenous title remains troubling, albeit still more generous than the American approach.

9.2.4 *Injunctive Relief*

9.2.4.1 India

A three-judge panel of the Indian Supreme Court has nullified mining leases granted on traditional tribal lands. It stressed that Indigenous rights are designed not only to prohibit alienation to others "but also to ensure that the tribals remain in possession and enjoyment of the lands in Scheduled areas for their economic empowerment, social status and dignity of their person".[102] The 1997 decision was also forward looking in stating that in cases where Indigenous people could lease land for development, 20 per cent of profits should be reserved for ecology such as re-forestation and supply of water, education, hospitals, houses and sanitation for the Indigenous people.[103] No reference was, however, made to the need to consult Indigenous people about how these profits should be calculated and used. At the same time, this judgement led to demands that the constitutional protection for Indigenous people be repealed. Indigenous people are estimated to be about 8.6 per cent (over 104 million people) of India's population. Their rights, however, are imperilled by forced evictions and proposed resource extraction.[104]

9.2.4.2 United States

Cases involving Treaty rights of Indigenous tribes in the state of Washington have gone to the United States Supreme Court multiple times. In the first case, the Court held that the states could only regulate the fishery for conservation reasons and could not discriminate against the tribes.[105] In a second decision, it held that state regulation of the fishery violated Treaty rights.[106]

[101] Ibid. at para 180.

[102] *Samatha* v. *State of Andhra Pradesh and Ors.* (1997) 8 SCC 191 at para 111.

[103] Ibid. at paras 113–114.

[104] Phutoli Shikhu Chingmak, "International Law and Reparations for Indigenous People in Asia" in Federico Lenzerini (ed.), *Reparations for Indigenous Peoples* (Oxford: Oxford University Press, 2008), p.434.

[105] *Puyallup Tribe* v. *Department of Game of Washington et al.*, 391 US 392 (1968).

[106] *Department of Game of Washington* v. *Puyallup Tribe et al.*, 414 US 44 (1973).

A year after that decision, a lower court held that two out of fourteen tribes were able to regulate their own fishery. The trial judge also ruled that the Tribes were entitled to up to 50 per cent of the fish that could be caught consistent with conservation.[107] Following the model of 1970s American public law litigation discussed in Chapter 7, Section 7.2.1, the trial judge retained jurisdiction over the case and appointed a master and advisory committee to assist in devising decrees.[108] He retained jurisdiction into 1985.[109] His decision was upheld on appeal including in the United States Supreme Court. An appeal court noted that "except for some desegregation cases, the district court has faced the most concerted official and private efforts to frustrate a decree of a federal court witnessed in this century".[110] The trial judge's orders were so numerous that they are contained in two separate volumes of the law reports.[111] The litigation also expanded to another phase concerned with fish raised in hatcheries.[112]

In 2007, there was new litigation as a trial judge issued a declaration that culverts harmed salmon spawning. By 2013, the judge converted the declaration into an injunction. He reasoned that the injunction was consistent with the public interest because all would benefit from addressing declining salmon stocks.[113] This decision demonstrates how declarations in the United States can be modified and become

107 *United States of America, Quinault Tribe of Indians, Queets Band of Indians et al.* v. *State of Washington*, 384 F Supp 312 (1974) aff'd 443 US 658 (1979).

108 Ibid. at 419.

109 Fay Cohen, *Treaties on Trial* (Seattle: University of Washington Press, 1986); Phil Lancaster, *The Structural Injunction as a Remedy for Violations of Aboriginal Constitutional Rights* (Ottawa: Canada Bar Association, 1991); Charles Wilkinson, *Messages from Frank's Landing: A Story of Salmon, Treaties, and the Indian Way* (Seattle: University of Washington Press, 2000).

110 *Puget Sound Gillnetters Association* v. *U.S. Dist. Court*, 573 F.2d 1123 (9th Cir., 1977) at 1126 aff'd *Washington* v. *Commercial Fishing Vessel Association*, 443 US 658 (1979) at 696–97.

111 *United States* v. *State of Washington*, U.S. Dist. Court, Western Dist. of Washington, 1974–1985 (Vol. I) and 1985–2013 (Vol. 2), (Thomson Reuters 2015).

112 *United States* v. *State of Washington (Phase II)*, 506 F. Supp. 187 (W.D. Wash., 1980) aff'd in part 759 F.2d 1353, 1356–1360 (9th Cir. 1982) (en banc); *United States* v. *State of Washington*, 853 F 3d 946 (9th Cir., 2017). This decision was upheld but only because the Supreme Court decision was rendered without an opinion but with a 4–4 tie, caused by Justice Kennedy's recusal because of his previous involvement in the case: *Washington* v. *United States*, 138 S.Ct. 1832 (2018).

113 The Court's injunction gave the state until October 2016 to correct specified culverts, seventeen years to correct other priority culverts and the remainder at the end of the natural life of the culvert or in connection with independent projects. See: *United States*

injunctions, something that is consistent with the declaration plus discussed in Chapter 7, Section 7.4. This decision was also upheld on appeal with the court holding that the state's estimate of US$100 million a year to comply with the injunction was overstated. The Ninth Circuit also put the costs into a larger budgetary perspective by noting that the state's annual transportation budget was US$9.9 billion.[114] It also affirmed that the trial judge could amend the structural injunction in response to new evidence.[115] More litigation, including whether the injunction applies to culverts installed by municipalities, is predicted.[116]

These cases are noteworthy in applying the intensive American model of public law litigation to Indigenous rights. This may be justified in cases of extreme resistance to Indigenous rights and remedies. Nevertheless, it is not ideal, especially if it results in delay in protecting fish and marginalizes Indigenous participation. Such litigation also produced extensive backlash to Indigenous rights. Judges may in extreme cases have to use structural injunctions to enforce Indigenous rights, but consensual agreements are much preferable on all sides.

9.2.5 *Declaratory Relief*

9.2.5.1 Canada

The Canadian courts have traditionally relied upon declarations as opposed to injunctions in part because they leave more space for subsequent negotiations in Indigenous rights cases[117] as well as more space for the government to select the precise means to respond.[118] The state's immunity from injunctions would no longer apply where constitutional rights are infringed.[119] Nevertheless, Canadian courts have remained

v. *Washington*, 827 F.3d 836 (9th Cir., 2016) at 848 (discussing the trial court's injunction).

114 Ibid. at 863–864.

115 Ibid. at 865.

116 Michael Blumm, "Indian Treaty Fishing Rights and the Environment: Affirming the Right to Habitat Protection and Restoration" (2016) 92 *Wash. L. Rev.* 1.

117 *Dumont* v. *Canada (Attorney General)*, [1990] 1 SCR 279; *Manitoba Métis Federation Inc.* v. *Canada (Attorney General)*, [2013] 1 SCR 623; *West Moberly First Nations* v. *British Columbia*, 2020 BCCA 138 at paras 354–356; *Newfoundland and Labrador (Attorney General)* v. *Uashaunnuat (Innu of Uashat and of Mani-Utenam)*, 2020 SCC 4 at para 40.

118 *Daniels* v. *Canada*, [2016] 1 SCR 99 at para 11.

119 *Doucet-Boudreau* v. *Nova Scotia*, 2003 SCC 62 at para 51. This ruling applies to the remedial provisions of s.24(1) of the Charter, which does not include Indigenous rights

cautious about using injunctions to enforce Indigenous rights.[120] In a recent case, the Supreme Court allowed the Innu's claims of Indigenous title spanning areas of both Quebec and the neighbouring provinces of Newfoundland and Labrador to proceed in Quebec courts by stressing that declaratory relief could have extra-territorial effects.[121] Yet at the same time, the majority of the Court was largely silent about the Innu's additional claims for a permanent injunction restraining a mega development, as well as for $900 million in damages and accounting and trusts. It not clear that Quebec courts by themselves could issue injunctions that would be enforceable beyond their borders. To be sure, there is a need for effective remedies to recognize Indigenous title based on prior occupancy that existed before the creation of either province.[122] Nevertheless, it is not clear that the Supreme Court's reliance on declarations will always ensure the most effective remedy especially in cases where governments may have economic and political incentives to resist or minimize a declaration in favour of Indigenous rights.

In a landmark case, the Supreme Court of Canada has stated that remedies for Aboriginal title could include "injunctive relief, damages or an order that consultation or accommodation be carried out".[123] It elaborated that "the usual remedies that lie for breach of interests in land" should be available. These remedies should be "adapted as may be necessary to reflect the special nature of Aboriginal title and the fiduciary obligation owed by the Crown to the holders of Aboriginal title".[124] A finding of Aboriginal title means that the First Nation has "the right to determine, subject to the inherent limits of group title held for future generations, the uses to which the land is put and to enjoy its economic

under s.35. At the same time, the same principles of the supremacy of remedies ordered by the courts to enforce constitutional rights should apply to remedies for violations of Indigenous rights.

120 The British Columbia Court of Appeal has affirmed a permanent injunction against a marina development that would have interfered with a treaty right to fish: *Saanichton Marina Ltd.* v. *Claxton* (1989), 57 DLR (4th) 161.

121 *Newfoundland and Labrador (Attorney General)* v. *Uashaunnuat (Innu of Uashat and of Mani-Utenam)*, 2020 SCC 4.

122 Ibid. at para 40–42. Four judges in dissent would have denied the jurisdiction of the Quebec courts to award any remedy with extra-territorial effects. They characterized the declaration as a slightly stronger remedy than the majority stating that governments should "comply with both the letter and the spirit of the declaration". Ibid. at para 248.

123 *Tsilhqot'in Nation* v. *British Columbia*, 2014 SCC 44 at para 89.

124 Ibid. at para 90.

fruits… it is the right to proactively use and manage the land".[125] This recognizes powers of self-government over the land if Aboriginal title is established. It also creates a space for Indigenous law to govern how the land is used.

In the *Delgamuukw* land claim litigation in British Columbia, plaintiffs representing the Gitksan and Wet'suwet'en First Nation asked for declarations of Aboriginal title. They also asked that the court retain jurisdiction to, if necessary, resolve disputes between the parties about the implementation of the declaration. This was essentially a request for a "declaration plus" as discussed in Chapter 7, Section 7.4. In two different decisions, the British Columbia Court of Appeal rejected the declaration plus approach. In 1986, it stated that it had no jurisdiction to direct the government to negotiate.[126] In 1993, it rejected requests by both the Indigenous applicant and a newly elected government to retain jurisdiction and give the parties two years to negotiate the remaining issue.[127] Two judges dissented. They would have decided "issues properly suitable for legal decisions" while leaving other issues "to be settled by negotiation and by political accommodation". Moreover, the court would retain "the power to deal with the unresolved issues, if necessary, or to work out more detailed orders on the issues that had been resolved".[128] Their approach made space for consensual resolution that could produce creative remedies while at the same time not renouncing judicial responsibility for enforcing Indigenous rights.

The declaration plus allows the court to define the right and expected outcomes in more general terms than would be appropriate in an injunction which can be enforced through contempt. At the same time, a judge familiar with the case remains available to resolve disputes that may arise. A number of trial judges have retained jurisdiction in duty to consult cases, but the Federal Court of Appeal has overturned one such

[125] Ibid. at paras 94, 153.

[126] *Delgamuukw* v. *British Columbia*, [1986] BCJ No. 1413 (December 5, 1986) at para 18 stating: "I can find no jurisdiction in law and, in my view, the Supreme Court has no jurisdiction to declare that the defendants are obligated to negotiate. No one doubts, however, that must of necessity be done. Still less has the Supreme Court the power to direct the defendants to meet with the plaintiffs and negotiate in good faith as sought in paragraph 15 of the prayer for relief".

[127] *Delgamuukw* v. *British Columbia*, (1993) 104 DLR (4th) 470 at 542–543, 601–602 rev'd not on this ground [1997] 3 SCR 1010. I was a legal consultant to the late Joe Arvay OC, QC, who was one of British Columbia's lawyers in this appeal.

[128] Ibid. at 764.

case on the basis that there was no bad governmental conduct that could justify the retention of jurisdiction.[129] As discussed in Chapter 7, Section 7.4, the idea that judicial retention of jurisdiction is a penalty for governments is misguided. It fails to recognize the inevitability of disputes about general declarations. General declarations create space for Indigenous self-determination. There is, however, a special danger that conflicts may arise because of the often very different world views, bargaining power and experiences of the parties in Indigenous rights cases. Courts that retain jurisdiction can help resolve such disputes both through their substantive rulings and their concern about procedural fairness.

9.2.6 *Remedies Involving Legislation*

Different courts have different powers with respect to laws that violate rights. It will be interesting to see if the New Zealand Supreme Court's recent recognition of its ability to make non-binding declarations of incompatibility will be extended to Indigenous rights under the Treaty of Waitangi.[130] Even though non-binding domestically, such declarations could play a role in political responses and supra-national adjudication.

The United States courts favour fact specific and as applied declarations of invalidity or constitutional exemptions from otherwise valid laws for those exercising rights. This approach has been used in the Indigenous rights context.[131] The Court has used a broader approach in its landmark decision holding that no states could regulate gaming on Indigenous reserves.[132] Too fact specific an exemption may require additional litigation by Indigenous people who are charged with violating a law. Too limited or vague an exemption may also increase policing and prosecutorial discretion and chill the exercise of Indigenous rights.

In a landmark Aboriginal title case, the Supreme Court of Canada stated that "if legislation was validly enacted before title was established, such legislation may be rendered inapplicable going forward to the extent that it unjustifiably infringes Aboriginal title".[133] This contemplates that the natural remedy may be an exemption from regulatory statutes of those exercising an Indigenous right even though the Canadian court has

129 *Canada* v. *Long Plain First Nation*, 2015 FCA 177 at paras 150, 152.
130 *Attorney General* v. *Taylor*, [2018] NZSC 104.
131 *Herrera* v. *Wyoming*, 587 US (2019).
132 *California* v. *Cabazon Band of Indians*, 480 US 202 (1987).
133 *Tsilhqot'in Nation* v. *British Columbia*, 2014 SCC 44 at para 92.

been resistant to the use of exemptions in other contexts.[134] As discussed in Chapter 4, Section 4.2.2, Canadian courts have circumvented restrictions on constitutional exemptions by using interpretative remedies.[135] Courts should be as precise and transparent as possible. They need to provide remedies for litigants, but also clearly indicate to the executive and rights holders about what the law requires in the future. This is consistent with the two-track aspiration both to provide litigants with effective remedies but to prevent similar violations in the future.

Another issue is whether suspended declarations of invalidity or prospective rulings can be justified in cases involving Indigenous rights. Such remedies may provide time to negotiate co-management agreements between governments and Indigenous governments. It might also address concerns that judges may have that conflict may result from immediately recognizing Indigenous rights.[136] In one case dealing with a prosecution of a person exercising an Indigenous right to hunt, the Supreme Court of Canada warned that suspended declarations "should continue to be used only in exceptional circumstances in which a court of general jurisdiction deems that giving an immediate effect to an order will undermine the very purpose of that order or otherwise threaten the rule of law".[137] The Court refused to extend a one-year suspension entered by a lower court because it had expired and "chaos does not appear to have ensued".[138] It also indicated that the lower court had rightly exempted the accused Indigenous person from the suspension so that he was not convicted under a law that violated Indigenous rights. In essence a two-track approach had been applied that produced an exemption for the litigant and a finite delay in implementing a systemic remedy to benefit all Métis.

In another case involving a systemic challenge to restrictions on voting in Band elections, the Court has used one of its longest suspensions of eighteen months. It did not exempt the successful Indigenous applicant from the delay even when the applicant requested a rehearing on that basis and the Court had indicated in the case that successful applicants should generally be exempted from suspended declarations of

[134] *R.* v. *Ferguson*, [2008] 1 SCR 96.

[135] *Yahey* v. *British Columbia*, 2020 BCSC 278 at para 75.

[136] This raises all the issues of remedial delay and possible remedial deterrence discussed in Chapter 7, Section 7.2.1, in relation to *Brown* v. *Board of Education II*, 349 US 294 (1955).

[137] *R.* v. *Powley*, [2003] 2 SCR 207 at para 51.

[138] Ibid. at para 52.

invalidity.[139] This demonstrates the lack of consistency in the Canadian jurisprudence on suspended declarations of invalidity discussed in Chapter 4, Section 4.2.5. The two cases can perhaps be reconciled by the reluctance of courts to use suspended declarations in cases that will result in people being convicted under laws that violate rights. Unfortunately, the eighteen-month suspension in the voting rights case did not (despite its intention) facilitate consultation and creative remedies and the government eventually simply extended full voting rights to Band members living off the Band's reserve.[140]

9.2.7 *Injunctions Used against Indigenous Protests*

It is a sign of the precarious nature of Indigenous rights that the subject of the use of injunctions against those who take direct action to defend Indigenous rights must be discussed. A helpful analogy can be drawn with controversies over the labour injunction that led to legislation limiting the ability of courts to issue injunctions against picketing, often replacing them with more expert and conciliatory processes.[141] Felix Frankfurter and Nathan Greene in *The Labor Injunction*[142] demonstrated that the origins of labour injunctions were in hostility to unions[143] and that employers often found allies in the American Federal courts.[144] They also stressed the asymmetrical effects of the grant of interim injunctions against picketing. Such remedies "affects only the strikers; the employer resumes his efforts to defeat the strike, and resumes them free from interdicted interference".[145]

139 *Corbiere* v. *Canada (Minister of Indian and Northern Affairs)*, [1999] 2 SCR 203 rehearing application refused: 2000 CarswellNat 2393 (SCC).

140 Kent Roach, "Remedial Consensus and Dialogue under the Charter" (2002) 35(2) *U.B.C. L. Rev.* 219.

141 I am grateful to John Borrows for pointing out this analogy when reading an earlier draft of this chapter. On Indigenous self-action in Canada, see John Borrows, *Freedom and Indigenous Constitutionalism* (Toronto: University of Toronto, 2016), pp.50–103.

142 (New York: MacMillan, 1930). Their book inspired the 1932 federal legislation depriving Federal Courts of the power to issue such injunctions. The law that remains in force was upheld in a case involving a boycott to persuade a store to hire Black people: *New Negro Alliance* v. *Sanitary Grocery Co*, 303 US 552 (1938). See also *Lauf* v. *E. G. Shinner and Co.*, 303 US 323 (1938) at 330 again affirming the ability of Congress to place limits on remedies that Federal Court could order.

143 Frankfurter and Greene, *The Labor Injunction*, pp.2ff.

144 *In re Debs*, 158 US 564 (1895) (upholding six months in prison for labour leader).

145 Frankfurter and Greene, *The Labor Injunction*, p.201.

Much the same can be said about injunctions issued against Indigenous and other protests against development. They are based on implicit assumptions that the extractive industries that typically obtain such injunctions have an unencumbered right to the land and development in question. There is a more or less straight line from such assumptions to racist and repudiated ideas of terra nullius that deny the existence of Indigenous people as people when Europeans came to their lands. Corporations and the police similarly often find willing allies in courts of ordinary jurisdiction that may not have expertise with Indigenous rights or consider the full background of the dispute. The grant of such injunctions, especially in cases where courts have also refused to grant interim remedies to protect Indigenous rights from irreparable harm, allow state-sponsored resource extraction to proceed without interference.

9.2.7.1 Canada

A 2019 study found over a hundred instances of injunctions being used against Indigenous people in Canada. Most of these injunctions were granted to protect resource companies from economic harm.[146] In 1996 the Supreme Court of Canada affirmed that forestry companies could obtain broad interim injunctions against illegal protests or blockades to stop logging on land claimed by Indigenous people. The injunction did not even need to be directed at specific people but could be directed at Jane and John Doe.[147] As John Borrows has written, the injunction "protected corporate interests rather than Aboriginal rights, though the court's reference to a 'wilful and flagrant defiance of the law' could have easily been applied to those who failed to respect Nuu-chah-nulth legal traditions".[148]

In one case from northern Ontario, a trial judge started out by restraining mining to prevent irreparable harm to Indigenous people. The injunction was, however, limited to five months.[149] The judge refused to order funding for the Indigenous community as it consulted

[146] Yellowhead Institute *Land Back: A Yellowhead Red Paper* (Toronto: Yellowhead Institute, 2019) at 30.

[147] *MacMillan Bloedel Ltd.* v. *Simpson*, [1996] 2 SCR 1048. See also *MacMillan Bloedel Ltd.* v. *Simpson*, 1992 CanLII 1593 (BC SC). But for concerns about overbroad injunctions that could apply to journalists, see *Re Brake; Anderson* v. *Nalcor Energy*, 2019 NLCA 17.

[148] Borrows, *Freedom and Indigenous Constitutionalism*, p.72.

[149] *Platinex Inc.* v. *Kitchenuhmaykoosib Inninuwug First Nation*, 2006 CanLII 26171 at para 138.

with governments and a mining company. After that time, the trial judge concluded that it was now the mining company and not the Indigenous community that risked irreparable harm. In part, this was because the mining company had invested all of its resources in the project. The judge authorized exploratory drilling, but retained jurisdiction over the case and scheduled mediation meetings with the affected parties. At the same time, he endorsed much of the mining company's plan. As Rachel Ariss has argued, this meant that "consultation... took place outside the courtroom in a social context of inequality of resources and expertise". This approach delegitimized the Indigenous community's own plans for land use.[150]

The Indigenous community eventually resorted to self-help. The judge then issued an injunction against the protest and six First Nations leaders were sentenced to six months imprisonment for contempt of court.[151] The Ontario Court of Appeal warned that before granting such injunctions, courts should consider whether the duty to consult has been discharged and that "every effort has been exhausted to obtain a negotiated or legislated solution to the dispute before it".[152] At the same time, the First Nations resistance eventually led to the abandonment of the mining project.[153] This confirms Professor Borrows' conclusions that self-help has often worked for Indigenous people when Canadian law has failed. At the same time, he also warns that civil disobedience is a double-edged sword that can be used against Indigenous people.[154]

Canadian courts remain reluctant to consider violations of Indigenous rights or the duty to consult when enforcing injunctions against protests which are still frequently granted.[155] Canadian courts often assume that any economic harm to extractive industries will cause irreparable

[150] Rachel Ariss, *Keeping the Land* (Halifax: Fernwood Publishing, 2012), p.108.

[151] *Platinex Inc.* v. *Kitchenuhmaykoosib Inninuwug First Nation*, [2008] ONCA 534. Courts cannot in advance declare that those who breach the injunction are guilty of contempt. *Henco Industries Limited* v. *Haudenosaunee Six Nations Confederacy Council*, 2006 CanLII 41649. The Supreme Court has held that Indigenous protesters cannot raise breach of Treaty rights or the duty to consult as a defence to protest and self-help remedies: *Behn* v. *Moulton Construction*, [2013] 2 SCR 227.

[152] *Frontenac Ventures Corp.* v. *Ardoch Algonquin First Nation*, [2008] 3 CNLR 119 at para 48. See also David Milward, "Restless Spirit in the Land: Finding a Place in Canadian Law for Aboriginal Disobedience" (2009) 15 *Int'l. J. Minority Group Rts.* 1.

[153] Ariss, *Keeping the Land*, p.150.

[154] Borrows, *Freedom and Indigenous Constitutionalism*, pp.50–103.

[155] See, for example, *Nalcor Energy* v. *NunatuKavut Community Council Inc.*, 2014 NLCA 46; *Behn* v. *Moulton Construction*, [2013] 2 SCR 227.

harm.[156] This assumption should be re-examined in light of the importance of Indigenous rights and the broader context of the dispute where the state may have improperly granted resource extraction permits to the corporation.[157] Again, the frequent grant of injunctions against Indigenous self-help suggests that the balance of convenience has been defined in a manner that gives greater weight to majoritarian, corporate and economic interests than Indigenous rights.

9.2.7.2 Inter-American Court of Human Rights

Indigenous people too often risk jail for exercising their rights. The IACtHR has ordered expungement of criminal records and compensation for Indigenous people who were wrongly convicted under anti-terrorism laws. The Court has sometimes added systemic remedies to such individual and compensatory remedies. They include training state officials with respect to Indigenous rights and criminal investigations of state officials.[158] The Inter-American response is important because many domestic courts are less sensitive to the history of state law being used to dispossess and repress Indigenous people.[159]

9.3 Duty to Consult: Consensual Remedies or Authorized Development?

Both supra-national and national courts are increasingly imposing a duty on states to consult Indigenous peoples before taking steps that affect their rights. When consultation results in Indigenous consent, it can produce consensual agreements that should avoid the need for judicial remedies. Such agreements should be classified as remedies. They provide a practical way to deal with an apprehended violation of Indigenous

[156] Rick Williams et al., "The New Normal? Natural Resource Development, Civil Disobedience and Injunctive Relief" (2017) 55 *Alta. L. Rev.* 285, 298–302.

[157] There are some examples, however, of judges refusing to order interim injunctions against Indigenous protests while at the same time issuing injunctions requested by Indigenous applicants to restrain resource extraction: *Taseko Mines Ltd.* v. *Phillips*, 2011 BCSC 1675 at paras 59–60; *Taseko Mines Limited* v. *Tsilhqot'in National Government*, 2019 BCSC 1507; *William* v. *Taseko Mines Limited*, 2019 BCCA 479.

[158] *Norín Catrimán et al. (Leaders, Members and Activist of the Mapuche Indigenous People)* v. *Chile*, (2016) 39 *Loy. L.A. Int'l. & Comp. L. Rev.* 1204. The Court ordered criminal convictions to be annulled, rehabilitative treatment provided to the Indigenous protesters who were mistreated, as well as pecuniary and non-pecuniary compensation.

[159] Zia Akhtar, "Mapuche Land Claims: Environmental Protest, Legal Discrimination and Customary Rights" (2013) 20 *Int'l. J. Minority Group Rts.* 551.

rights and are a functional substitute for judicial remedies. They respond to harms and also attempt to govern the future. The agreements can also be bi or even tri-jural and reflect international, domestic and Indigenous law.

The more difficult cases are the frequent ones where consultation does not produce agreements between the state and Indigenous representatives. At this point, consultation can be used by the courts as a way to limit Indigenous rights and claims and approve state-authorized activities such as resource extraction perhaps with some proportionate accommodation of Indigenous rights. As will be seen, this is a particular danger in Canada where courts have increasingly taken a thin approach to consultation that focuses on approving planned projects. This is analogous to what Sandra Liebenberg has criticized as a "dispute resolution" paradigm[160] to the South African engagement remedy, discussed in Chapter 8, Section 8.5.

Canadian courts now allow consultation to be conducted through a variety of administrative, regulatory and environmental approval processes.[161] This means that it is not necessary for Canadian governments to engage respectfully on a state-to-state basis with Indigenous peoples and their governments even though in Canada and in Colombia the duty to consult is an obligation of the state that cannot be delegated to resource extraction companies.[162] Administrative approval processes in Canada also do not have the power to decide on the validity of Aboriginal claims and this means that the consultation process will often occur on the basis of judgments about the reasonableness of executive and not judicial determination of the strength of the Indigenous claims.[163]

The Canadian courts have repeatedly warned that Indigenous people do not have a "veto" over development projects as part of the duty to consult. In addition, they have decided that the consultation process is not meant to deal with past grievances or even provide Indigenous

[160] Sandra Liebenberg, "Participatory Approaches to Socio-economic Litigation" (2012) 32 *Nordic J. Hum. Rts.* 312.

[161] *Chippewas of the Thames First Nation* v. *Enbridge Pipelines Inc.*, 2017 SCC 41, [2017] 1 SCR 1099 holding that the National Energy Board when approving pipelines can discharge the duty to consult for the government.

[162] *Decision SU-039 of* 1997 in Manuel José Cepeda Espinosa and David Landau, *Colombian Constitutional Law* (New York: Oxford University Press, 2017) at 259; *Haida Nation* v. *British Columbia (Minister of Forests)*, [2004] 3 SCR 511.

[163] *Ktunaxa Nation* v. *British Columbia(Forests, Lands and Natural Resource Operations)*, [2017] 2 SCR 386 [84–85]

people with declarations about Indigenous rights that may increase their bargaining power when they deal with states, resource companies and regulatory approval processes.[164] This is disappointing, but perhaps not surprising. The Canadian duty to consult was developed before UNDRIP and never linked to the need for Indigenous consent. Rather, it emerged from a dispute resolution perspective that was concerned that reliance on interim injunctions was too much of a "zero sum" approach.[165]

9.3.1 *Indigenous Consent or "Veto"?*

A critical issue in defining whether the duty to consult will result in consensual agreements or serve as a means to limit Indigenous rights and claims is the degree to which it is tied to Indigenous consent. Writing in 2014, Dwight Newman concluded: "[t]here has not developed an international practice of states having to obtain free, prior and informed consents for all activities affecting Indigenous peoples" that have been the subject of the duty to consult.[166] He cited in support a 2009 report by special rapporteur on the rights of Indigenous people James Anaya. Professor Anaya concluded that Indigenous consent is not required in every case of consultation. At the same time, he warned that framing the question as a binary and simple one of an Indigenous "veto" does not honour the need for consultations to aim towards agreement in every case.[167] The Colombia Constitutional Court has similarly stressed that the veto debate is not helpful for a consultation process that it imagined as "a space for discourse between equals"[168]. In a 2013 report, Anaya concluded that Indigenous consent is the general rule. Lack of Indigenous consent could only be justified on the basis that the rights were subject to necessary and proportionate limitation as contemplated

[164] *Rio Tinto Alcan* v. *Carrier Sekani Tribal Council*, [2010] 2 SCR 650 at paras 45, 50; *Chippewas of the Thames First Nation* v. *Enbridge Pipelines Inc.* at para 41.

[165] *Haida Nation* v. *British Columbia (Minister of Forests)*, [2004] 3 SCR 511; *Ktunaxa Nation v. British Columbia(Forests, Lands and Natural Resource Operations)*, [2017] 2 SCR 386 [114].

[166] Dwight Newman, *Revisiting the Duty to Consult Aboriginal Peoples* (Saskatoon: Purich Publishing, 2014), pp.163–164.

[167] Anaya concluded that focusing on a veto "is not in line with the spirit or character of the principles of consultation and consent as they have developed in international human rights law and have been incorporated into the Declaration". *Annual Report of the United Nations Special Rapporteur on the Rights and Fundamental Freedoms of Indigenous People*, UN Doc A/HRC/12/34 (15 July 2009) at para 48.

[168] Decision T-129 of 2011 in *Colombian Constitutional Law* at 269.

in Article 46(2) of UNDRIP.[169] His approach recognizes that consultation should generally result in consensual agreements, but can also serve as a means to limit Indigenous rights including obtaining accommodations for such rights.

Thomas Antkowiak has criticized the IACtHR's consultation jurisprudence for not consistently recognizing the Indigenous right to consent. He argues that the burdens that consultation places on governments are "a small price to pay for a literal gold mine".[170] In *Kichwa Peoples of Sarayaku* v. *Ecuador*,[171] the Court stressed that the state should consult with the Indigenous people before granting third parties rights that could harm Indigenous rights, but did not stress the need for consent as it had in a landmark 2007 decision.[172] The free and informed consent standard has not been rigorously enforced. Courts have often failed to provide a full justification for not requiring Indigenous consent. In any event, the consultation process should be governed in order to maximize the opportunity for gaining consent.

9.3.2 Substantive, Treaty and Consent Seeking Consultation

James Ananya and Sergio Puig have argued that a substantive approach to the duty to consult can lead "to 'free, prior and informed consent' on terms that are protective of the rights implicated".[173] A substantive approach would also require careful attention to the difficult question

[169] *Annual Report of the United Nations Special Rapporteur on the Rights and Fundamental Freedoms of Indigenous People*, UN Doc A/HRC/24/41 (1 July 2013) at para 32.

[170] Thomas M. Antkowiak, "Rights, Resources, and Rhetoric: Indigenous Peoples and the Inter-American Court" (2013) 35 *U. Pa. J. Int'l. L.* 113, 171. See also Lucas Lixinski, "Case of the Kalina and Lokono Peoples v. Suriname" (2017) 111(1) *Am. J. Int'l. L.* 147.

[171] Merits and Reparations, Judgment, Inter-Am. Ct. H.R. (Ser. C), (June 27, 2012).

[172] *Case of the Saramaka People* v. *Suriname* (2007), Preliminary Objections, Merits, Reparations and Costs, Inter-Am Ct. H.R. (Ser. C) No. 172, (28 November 2007) at para 134; see Antkowiak, "Dark Side of Virtue", 54–55. In that case, however, the court qualified its reference to consent in a request for re-interpretation by indicating that consent was only required when the survival of the Indigenous people were threatened. *Case of the Saramaka People* v. *Suriname* (2007), (2014) 36 *Loy. L.A. Int'l. & Comp. L. Rev.* 2305 at 2320 in relation to Judgment on Interpretation of Judgment Inter-Am Ct. H.R. (Ser. C) No. 185.

It also subsequently refused to grant a provisional measure to prevent mining even though the systemic remedy of demarcation of the land had not been completed. Ibid. 2324 in relation to Judgment on Compliance (September 4. 2013).

[173] S. James Anaya and Sergio Puig, "Mitigating State Sovereignty: The Duty to Consult with Indigenous Peoples" (2017) 67 *U.T.L.J.* 435, 446.

of what is the appropriate body of Indigenous people that should be consulted.[174] Jody Wilson-Raybould has written about how Indigenous governance reform is required to make the right to consult meaningful. She also warns that obtaining the agreement of some Indigenous people may not necessarily be the agreement of all and of the limits of a checklist approach to the duty.[175]

Consultation should respect Indigenous law if it is to be respectful. Karen Drake has argued that short timelines may themselves violate the laws of some Indigenous communities by not allowing adequate time for Indigenous governance to play out.[176] The Supreme Court has paid rhetorical homage to a more respectful approach by referring to the consultation process as one of modern treaty making.[177] Unfortunately, the Court has not backed this rhetoric up with an approach to the duty to consult that respects government-to-government relations. It also seems to have considered the duty to consult as a duty that will often be discharged in a shorter time frame than would be required to take an Indigenous rights claims to trial, perhaps after the grant of an interim injunction. This all points in the direction of the Canadian duty to consult being focused more on efficient dispute resolution than a genuine search for Indigenous consent.

9.3.3 Procedural and Regulatory Approval Seeking Consultation

In contrast to a substantive and consent-seeking process of consultation, Anaya and Puig describe minimalist and instrumental approaches that obscure "concern for any substantive rights that may be implicated".[178]

174 John Borrows, "Wise Practices in Indigenous Economic Development and Environmental Protection" in John Borrows et al. (eds.), *Wise Practices: Exploring Indigenous Economic Justice and Self-Determination* (Toronto: University of Toronto, forthcoming).

175 Jody Wilson Raybould, *From Where I Stand: Rebuilding Indigenous Nations for a Stronger Canada* (Vancouver: Purich Books, 2019), pp.154ff.

176 Karen Drake, "The Trials and Tribulations of Ontario's Mining Act: The Duty to Consult and Anishinaabek Law" (2015) 11(2) *J.S.D.L.P.* 183. For a recent example of approval of a three-month adjournment by a regulatory board to allow consultation, see *Nova Scotia (Attorney General)* v. *Nova Scotia (Utility and Review Board)*, 2019 NSCA 66.

177 *Beckman* v. *Little Salmon*, [2010] 3 SCR 310 at paras 143–144, 67.

178 Anaya and Puig, "Mitigating State Sovereignty". On the dangers that an exclusive focus on consultation in relation to unproven claims could diminish the strength of remedies for stronger claims including the role of damages and injunctions, see Roach, *Constitutional Remedies in Canada*, pp.15.820–15.980.

Such an approach can limit the participation of Indigenous groups "to either accepting the project wholesale or rejecting it".[179] The Canadian version of the duty to consult has consistently stated that it "does not give Aboriginal groups a veto over what can be done with land pending final proof of the claim".[180] It has also restricted the duty to consult by holding that it is not generally the Court's place to consider past grievances[181] or to obtain declarations about the existence of Indigenous rights.[182] The reluctance to make such rulings can exacerbate inequalities of bargaining power and a lack of attention to the underlying Indigenous right.

Citing the Supreme Court of Canada's landmark decision in *Haida Nation* in support, Dwight Newman writes that "the duty to consult doctrine – as compared to an approach founded on interlocutory injunctions during litigation or negotiation – fosters appropriate incentives for negotiation and is thus preferable on the grounds of what will promote the best negotiation processes".[183] This is essentially a dispute resolution understanding of the duty to consult that avoids the extremes of either blocking development through an interim injunction or allowing it. Professor Newman has warned that "Aboriginal communities need to recognize that the courts' decision to adopt the duty to consult rather than a system of injunctions means that governments still have the power to make many decisions"[184]

Several Canadian scholars have taken a less optimistic view of the duty to consult than Professor Newman. Shin Imai has written that "[t]he problem with the *consult* standard is that the community feels powerless, because they *are* powerless. It is difficult for people to trust a process of discussion when they know no matter what happens, the final decision is

[179] Anaya and Puig, "Mitigating State Sovereignty", 452. See also Stephen Young, "The Deification of Process in the Duty to Consult" (2019) 52 *U.B.C. L. Rev.* 1065; Richard Stacey, "Honour in Sovereignty: Can Crown Consultation with Indigenous People Erase Canada's Sovereignty Deficit?" (2018) 68 *U.T.L.J.* 405, 437.

[180] *Haida Nation* v. *British Columbia*, [2004] 3 SCR 511 at para 48.

[181] *Chippewas of the Thames First Nation* v. *Enbridge Pipelines Inc.*, [2017] 1 SCR 1099 at para 41 (the duty to consult is not triggered by historical impacts. It is not the vehicle to address historical grievances). See generally Robert Hamilton and Joshua Nichols, "The Tin Ear of the Court" (2019) 56(3) *Alta. L. Rev.* 729.

[182] *Ktunaxa First Nation* v. *British Columbia (Forest, Lands and Natural Resources Operations)*, [2017] 1 SCR 386 at paras 83–84.

[183] Newman, *Revisiting the Duty to Consult Aboriginal Peoples*, p.29.

[184] Dwight Newman *The Rule and Role of Law: Duty to Consult, Aboriginal Communities and the Canadian Natural Resource Sector* (Ottawa: MacDonald Laurier Institute, 2014), p.20

not in their hands". He adds: "it is through recognition of the necessity of *consent* that the Indigenous community will have power that can be a balance to the superior economic power of the mining company and the superior power of government".[185] Sarah Morales has written that the Canadian duty to consult has frequently failed because of "the power imbalance inherent within this framework and the failure of these consultative processes to adequately consider and rely upon Indigenous legal traditions".[186] One way to address power imbalances in the consultation processes is for courts to ensure that the proposed project does not go ahead to cause irreparable harm to Indigenous rights during the consultation process. As will be seen, courts do not always even take this minimal step.

9.3.3.1 New Zealand

In a 1989 case dealing with the grant of mining licences, the New Zealand Court of Appeal affirmed not only a duty to consult the Māori, but that "the Crown should take no further action... in selling, disposing or otherwise alienating the said lands until such time as the Crown has established a scheme of protection in respect of the rights of the plaintiffs".[187] The duty to consult can be accompanied by what are, in effect, interim remedies that restrain encroachment on Indigenous rights pending the completion of consultation.

9.3.3.2 Colombia

The Colombian Constitutional Court has been divided on the appropriateness of interim relief pending consultation. In a 5–4 1997 decision, it granted a tutela prohibiting oil exploration on U'wa land and ordered that consultation take place within thirty days. Four judges dissented and concluded that the summary tutela was not appropriate.[188] In 2003, the Court affirmed that judges could enforce the duty to consult through the tutela and contemplated a three-month period to complete consultation. Nevertheless, the Court refused to halt aerial spraying in the meantime to

[185] Shin Imai, "Consult, Consent and Veto: International Norms and Canadian Vetos" in Borrows and Coyle (eds.)., *The Right Relationship*, pp.385–386 (emphasis in original).

[186] Sarah Morales, "Braiding the Incommensurables" in John Borrows et al. (eds.), *Braiding Legal Orders: Implementing the United Nations Declaration on the Rights of Indigenous Peoples* (Waterloo: Centre for International Governance, 2019), p.69.

[187] *Tainui Māori Trust* v. *Attorney General*, [1989] 2 NZLR 513 at 527 (C.A.). See also *New Zealand Māori Council* v. *Attorney General*, [1989] 2 NZLR 142.

[188] Decision SU-039 of 1997 in *Colombian Constitutional Law* at 259.

eradicate coca plants. Three judges dissented. They warned that there was a danger that the chemical used for the spraying could affect "several generations of living beings (men, animal, plants etc.)" and the damage will be irreversible".[189] The first decision is preferable in producing a consultation process that will be informed by Indigenous rights and address the inevitably greater powers that governments will have in their dealings with Indigenous people.

9.3.3.3 Canada

In its 2004 *Haida Nation* case recognizing the duty to consult, the Supreme Court of Canada presented the duty to consult as an alternative to "the all-or-nothing solution" of interim injunctions. At the same time, it somewhat paradoxically indicated that "[t]o unilaterally exploit a claimed resource during the process of proving and resolving the Aboriginal claim to that resource, may be to deprive the Aboriginal claimants of some or all of the benefit of the resource. That is not honourable".[190] Other parts of the judgement seem to qualify the requirement "of taking steps to avoid irreparable harm" to cases "where a strong *prima facie* case exists for the claim, and the consequences of the government's proposed decision may adversely affect it in a significant way…".[191] This would seem to impose a higher standard of proving the merits than typically required to obtain an interim injunction. Any delay

[189] Decision SU-383 of 2003 per Justice Araujo in dissent in *Colombian Constitutional Law* at 264. Recent empirical research suggests that tutelas are granted in about 75 per cent of cases and that they have halted infrastructure projects in Colombia in twenty-three cases and resource extraction in seventeen cases. Juan Herrera "Judicial Dialogue and Transformative Constitutionalism: The Case of Indigenous Peoples and Afro-Descendants" (2019) 43 *Revista Derecho del Estado* 191 at 207–208. For an analysis of the Colombian jurisprudence on the duty to consent see Jose Parra, "The Role of Domestic Courts in International Human Rights Law: The Constitutional Court of Columbia and Free, Prior and Informed Consent" (2016) 23(3) *Intl. J. Minority Group Rights* 355.

[190] *Haida Nation* v. *British Columbia*, [2004] 3 SCR 511 at para 27. Chief Justice McLachlin added that waiting for a full trial "risks unfortunate consequences. When the distant goal of proof is finally reached, the Aboriginal peoples may find their land and resources changed and denuded. This is not reconciliation. Nor is it honourable". Ibid at 33. For suggestions that the general rule should be no Crown action threatening Indigenous interests until the consultation is completed, see Sonia Lawrence and Patrick Macklem "From Consultation to Reconciliation: Aboriginal Rights and the Crown's Duty to Consult" (2000) 79 *Can Bar Rev.* 252 at 275–276.

[191] Ibid. at para 47.

to proposed projects during the duty to consult might be less than the time to have a full Indigenous claim go to trial.

Some Canadian courts have granted temporary injunctions to restrain development during the consultation process.[192] In one case, the British Columbia Court of Appeal indicated that the Crown could not sell contested land for two years so as to allow consultation to take place and that courts should retain jurisdiction.[193] At the same time, the Federal Court of Appeal has reversed an order restraining the government from selling lands until there was adequate consultation. It suggested that the trial judge erred in retaining jurisdiction in a declaration plus manner to resolve disputes about the law that frequently arises in the consultation process.[194]

In 2014, the Supreme Court suggested that courts can "preserve the Aboriginal interest pending final resolution of the claim" but only in cases "where a claim is particularly strong – for example, shortly before a court declaration of title".[195] This statement seems to backtrack from the its *Haida Nation* statement that it would not be honourable for the state unilaterally to exploit a resource while consultation or even proof of the claim was ongoing. The vast majority of consultation cases will not occur in a situation where a court is soon prepared to declare the existence of title. This adds to concerns that Canada has taken a procedural and regulatory approving approach to consultation. The focus on the strength of the claim also suggests a possible higher standard than with respect to interim injunctions. Even if there is something equivalent to an interim remedy, it will only last until the consultation process is completed, as opposed to when a full trial on the merits is complete.

9.3.4 Remedial Consequences of Breach of the Duty to Consult: More than a Re-Do?

The Supreme Court of Canada has stressed a spectrum approach to the duty to consult and matched this with an equally flexible approach to remedies. The remedies for breach of the duty range "from injunctive

[192] *Wahgoshig First Nation* v. *Ontario*, 2011 ONSC 7708 appeal dismissed as moot: 2013 ONSC 632 (Div. Ct.).

[193] *Musqueam Indian Band* v. *British Columbia* (Minister of Sustainable Resource Management), 2005 BCCA 128 at para 101.

[194] *Canada (Attorney General)* v. *Long Plain First Nation*, 2015 FCA 177 at para 148ff.

[195] *Tsilhqot'in Nation* v. *British Columbia*, 2014 SCC 44 at para 91.

relief against the threatening activity altogether, to damages, to an order to carry out the consultation prior to proceeding further with the proposed government conduct".[196] The Court's most frequent remedy for breach of the duty to consult has been the quashing of decisions of governments and regulatory boards that allow development to proceed as a remedy for the lack of consultation.[197] In essence, this is a "re-do"[198] remedy.

Re-do remedies have generally not been accompanied by damages or injunctions against proposed resource extraction that may cause irreparable harm. This means that not only does the duty to consult not result in modern Treaties, but it may impose uncompensated harms on Indigenous people. It may also require them to engage in consultation while pipelines are being built, mining is starting and trees are being cut. The duty to consult may require Indigenous communities to devote their own limited resources and time to consultation including developing procedures for whom should represent the community. As one judge has recognized, an Indigenous community may be "disinclined to spend its 'community resources' to review someone else's project. This is a reasonable position".[199]

A limited quashing or re-do remedy simply gives the government a second chance. It imposes more uncompensated burdens on Indigenous people. It should be accompanied by compensatory damages. It should also be accompanied with judicial declarations that could encourage any new consultation to respect Indigenous protocols and laws.[200]

9.3.5 *Summary*

Despite its potential to produce consensual bi-jural agreements based on prior and informed Indigenous consent, there is a real danger that the

[196] *Rio Tinto Alcan* v. *Carrier Sekani Tribal Council*, [2010] 2 SCR 650 at para 37.

[197] *Mikisew Cree First Nation* v. *Canada*, [2005] 3 SCR 388; *Clyde River* v. *Petroleum Geo-Service*, 2017 SCC 40; *First Nation of Nacho Nyak Dun* v. *Yukon*, [2017] 2 SCR 576.

[198] *Tsleil-Waututh Nation* v. *Canada* (Attorney General), 2018 FCA 153 at 771. The government then successfully redid the consultation gaining approval of a pipeline: *Coldwater First Nation* v. *Canada* (Attorney General), 2020 FCA 34 leave to appeal denied 2020 CanLII 43130 (SCC).

[199] *Saugeen First Nation* v. *Ontario*, 2017 ONSC 3456 at para 158.

[200] As Ryan Beaton has pointed out in comments on an earlier draft, a number of Canadian Indigenous communities have their own consultation protocols that could be used as a basis for better consultation.

duty to consult will be used as a procedural means to obtain regulatory approvals of resource extraction and justify limits on Indigenous rights and claims. The duty to consult can play a role in revealing ways to accommodate Indigenous interests that may be relevant to deciding whether limits placed on Indigenous rights are justified and proportionate.

9.4 Proportionality and Accommodation

Courts have struggled to avoid colonial dominance especially when assessing whether the balance of convenience favours interim relief to protect Indigenous rights over land from irreparable harm. Given this, there are reasons to be sceptical of judicial balancing of interests even when informed by proportionality principles. As suggested in the last section, Indigenous consent is always preferable.

Attention to proportionality principles requires disciplined and transparent justification of any limits on remedies, as well as rights. One of the purposes of the duty to consult is to find ways in which social objectives can be reconciled with Indigenous rights through various forms of accommodation. The Colombian Courts have stressed that even if there is no agreement after the duty to consult has been conducted that the survival of Indigenous people must be guaranteed and that unreasonable and disproportionate state actions that infringe their rights should not be allowed.[201] The Canadian courts have also emphasized that proportionality principles should inform both the government's duty to consult and any limit place on Indigenous rights.[202]

201 The Constitutional Court indicated that some actions would require Indigenous consent "not by the now obsolete discussion on existence or not of a right to a veto, but because it is openly unreasonable and disproportionate". *Decision C-389 of 2016* as quoted in Juan Herrera "Judicial Dialogue and Transformative Constitutionalism: The Case of Indigenous Peoples and Afro-Descendants" (2019) 43 *Revista Derecho del Estado* 191 at 212–213.

202 Chief Justice McLachlin has explained: "the Crown's fiduciary duty infuses an obligation of proportionality into the justification process. Implicit in the Crown's fiduciary duty to the Aboriginal group is the requirement that the incursion is necessary to achieve the government's goal (rational connection); that the government go no further than necessary to achieve it (minimal impairment); and that the benefits that may be expected to flow from that goal are not outweighed by adverse effects on the Aboriginal interest (proportionality of impact). The requirement of proportionality is inherent in the *Delgamuukw* process of reconciliation and was echoed in *Haida*'s insistence that the Crown's duty to consult and accommodate at the claims stage "is proportionate to a preliminary assessment of the strength of the case supporting the existence of the right

It is necessary in a book about remedies to engage with these issues because of the danger of remedial deterrence where judges refuse to recognize rights because of the fear of remedial consequences. Much like in Chapter 8, Section 8.1, the alternative to the use of proportionality to limit remedies may not be a "right maximizing"[203] approach to remedies. Rather, it may be no recognition of either rights or the provision of remedies that are inadequate to compensate for past violations or prevent future violations. This is not a good thing, but part of the tragic reality of remedies.

9.4.1 *Objectives*

Given the state's superior resources and its duty to be honourable in dealings with Indigenous peoples, it should bear the burden of justification of demonstrating why remedies requested by Indigenous peoples should not be granted or delayed. Article 46(2) of UNDRIP contemplates a strict standard that limits on Indigenous rights "shall be non-discriminatory and strictly necessary" and limited to respecting other rights or "the just and most compelling requirements of a democratic society".[204]

Legitimate objectives to limit remedies should not include objections to the right or attempts to re-litigate a failed attempt to justify general limits on a right. Courts should also be cautious about accepting abstract, inflated or symbolic statements of social interests as a legitimate objective. For example, there may be a tendency to refer to the social interests in "general economic development" or "the building of infrastructure"[205] as a competing objective.[206] Such formulations overstate social interests. Courts should be as specific as possible in describing the objective that the state claims justifies a limit on remedies. In a report as UN special rapporteur on Indigenous rights, James Anaya has suggested that "mere commercial interests" should not be considered a "valid public purpose" for limiting Indigenous rights.[207] Alas and as discussed in Section 9.2,

or title, and to the seriousness of the potentially adverse effect upon the right or title claimed'". *Tsilhqot'in Nation* v. *British Columbia*, 2014 SCC 44 at para 87.

203 Paul Gewirtz, "Remedies and Resistance" (1983) 92 *Yale L. J.* 4.

204 UNDRIP Art. 46(2).

205 *Delgamuukw* v. *British Columbia*, [1997] 3 SCR 1010 at para 165; *R* v. *Gladstone*, [1996] 2 SCR 723; *R* v. *Sparrow*, [1990] 1 SCR 1075.

206 Ibid.

207 *Annual Report of the United Nations Special Rapporteur on the Rights and Fundamental Freedoms of Indigenous People*, UN Doc A/HRC/24/41, (1 July 2013) at paras 32, 35.

these interests have at times prevailed especially when courts have given resource companies injunctions to restrain Indigenous self-help remedies.

9.4.2 *Other Parts of the Proportionality Test*

Another check on over-inflated state objectives is the need for a rational connection between the competing objective and the proposed limit. For example, there will generally not be a rational connection between not ordering that resource extraction be stopped at a particular site and the state's whole economy. The government should precisely detail the harms that will emerge from the grant of remedies such as injunctions and damages.

Many states now have a duty to consult Indigenous people before undertaking actions that may infringe Indigenous rights. One of the purposes of the duty to consult is to ensure that states consider impacts on Indigenous communities that they might otherwise not appreciate. A failure by states to engage in meaningful consultation will often mean that it is premature for the court to conclude that limits on Indigenous rights or remedies have been justified.

The critical step in most proportionality analysis is whether there is a better way to reconcile rights (or remedies) with the competing social interests. Here, courts should pay attention to the scope of the remedy. Less drastic and sweeping remedies will cause less harms to social interests than more sweeping remedies. At the same time, the state has a duty to accommodate Indigenous rights.

Article 40 of UNDRIP suggests that courts should consider whether Indigenous laws, governance and regulations can effectively implement legitimate state objectives such as the need for conservation and effective management of resources. Indigenous laws vary from community to community, but many recognize the importance of conservation for future generations.[208] Some Indigenous communities in Canada have prepared elaborate articulations of how their own Indigenous laws would guide their self-regulation of resources.[209] These should be considered as

[208] John Borrows, *Law's Indigenous Ethics* (Toronto: University of Toronto Press, 2019), pp.125–126.

[209] See, for example, Heiltsuk Tribal Council, *To Look at Our Traditional Laws* (2016), online (pdf): www.heiltsuknation.ca/wp-content/uploads/2018/10/Heiltsuk_Adjudication_Report.pdf; Deshkan Ziibiing and Chippewas of the Thames First

an alternative way to implement valid concerns that governments may have.

The final stage of proportionality is a comparison of the overall balance. This requires judges to compare the effects on Indigenous people of limiting a remedy or ordering no remedy against the effects on the competing social interests. The courts have in some interim injunction cases appropriately stressed that allowing resource extraction may cause irreparable harm whereas a delay in development may simply result in financial loss. The overall balance should also be applied in a way that is sensitive to Indigenous perspectives including relations to the land, water, animals and future generations.

9.5 Towards a Two-Track Approach

Can the two-track approach be adapted to the distinctive context of Indigenous rights? Gordon Christie has stressed the importance of Indigenous self-determination with respect to remedies when he writes: "[t]he Crown cannot simply act to repair fractures or bring people together. That is essentially the business of Indigenous peoples". At the same time, he recognizes that "in many cases... Indigenous communities cannot make significant headway without the cessation of destructive activities by the Crown".[210]

Professor Christie's insights can be applied to the two-track approach. They suggest that courts should focus on the first-track in providing compensation for the harms of violations of Indigenous rights and in preventing ongoing or imminent violations that will cause irreparable harm. At the same time, courts should use a lighter touch in the second systemic track in order to maximize Indigenous participation and self-determination.

Remedial approaches that focus on only one track to the exclusion of the other will be inadequate. Moreover, the two tracks are related and reinforce each other. Compensation for past harms and cessation of ongoing violations may be necessary for sustainable and effective remedies to govern the future. In the Indigenous rights context, there is a

Nation, *Wiindmaagewin Consultation Protocol* (26 November 2016), online (pdf): www.cottfn.com/wp-content/uploads/2016/02/Wiindmaagewin-CONSULTATION-PROTOCOL-Final-Nov-2016-2.pdf

210 Gordon Christie, "Indigenous Legal Orders, Canadian Law and UNDRIP" in Borrows et al. (eds.), *Braiding Legal Orders*, pp.51–52.

serious danger that judicial failures to order effective first-track remedies will mean that systemic second-track remedies will only replicate colonial imbalances of power. In other words, the absence of effective first-track remedies will make it difficult for Indigenous people to give consent that will result in modern Treaties that are our best hope for sustainable systemic remedies.

9.5.1 *Indigenous Self-determination and Negotiated Remedies*

Writing in the context of the rights of Indigenous Hawaiians, James Anaya has stated that the ultimate remedy should be: "[n]egotiation or other procedures responsive to Native Hawaiian demands".[211] Anaya recognizes that self-determination will require negotiations between Indigenous peoples and governments with the aim of achieving consensual remedies or new Treaties. Such negotiations and settlements may also require work by Indigenous people to ensure democratic and legitimate forms of self-governance that have often been lost because of colonialism. This process may involve Indigenous people reclaiming and developing their Indigenous laws.

9.5.2 *Bi-Jural Remedies*

Mark Walters has suggested that remedies should be viewed "as a cross-cultural legal question".[212] He recounts the negotiations of the 1764 Niagara Treaty where the Europeans demanded remedies for a past "rebellion" but the Indigenous people were focused on "re-establishing, in a forward-looking manner, a relationship of trust and care".[213] In some ways, this reflects the traditional European emphasis on remedies for past wrongs and the Indigenous focus on relationships. Dean Walters is right to be drawn to remedies in discussing the potential for cross cultural understandings. Remedies are more flexible than rights. At the same time, he recognizes that western judges brought up with European "right to a remedy" traditions may be reluctant to recognize remedies that are dependent on Indigenous participation and self-determination.

211 S. James Anaya, "The Native Hawaiian People and International Human Rights Law: Towards a Remedy for Past and Continuing Wrongs" (1994) 28 *Geo. L. Rev.* 309, 362.
212 Walters, "Rights and Remedies within Common Law and Indigenous Legal Traditions" in Borrows and Coyle, *The Right Relationship*, p.190.
213 Ibid., p.197.

Like both Christie and Anaya, Walters concludes that a cross-cultural approach "cannot be restored through a simple judicial order".[214] There is much wisdom in their consensus on this subject. Adjudicators should be respectful of the resilience and wisdom of Indigenous peoples and their laws. There is a need for judicial humility. As Professor Christie notes, much of the remedial process should be "the business of Indigenous people". At the same time, however, there is a fine line between needed judicial humility and judicial abdication. Remedies for past violations and stopping ongoing violations should, when Indigenous people ask for them, be the business of the courts.

Article 40 of UNDRIP supports an emphasis on cross-cultural and bijural remedies by calling for effective remedies that "shall give due consideration to the customs, traditions, rules and legal systems of the indigenous peoples concerned and international human rights".[215] Article 40 is deliberately agnostic about the particular process used to develop such remedies. Ryan Beaton has argued that Article 27 of UNDRIP encourages the creation by governments and Indigenous people of tribunals to adjudicate "the rights of Indigenous peoples pertaining to their land, territories and resources" in a manner that gives "due recognition to indigenous peoples' laws, traditions, customs and land tenure systems".[216] He contemplates that such a tribunal would have a role to play in deciding whether limits on Indigenous rights are justified and that such determinations should be made before any encroachment on Indigenous rights.[217]

9.5.3 *Treaty of Waitangi Tribunal*

The Treaty of Waitangi Tribunal generally makes non-binding recommendations. It can make binding recommendations relating to Crown land, but even those recommendations allow the parties to negotiate a

[214] Ibid., p.199.
[215] UNDRIP Art. 40.
[216] Ryan Beaton, "Articles 27 and 46(2): UNDRIP Signposts Pointing towards the Justified Infringement Section 35 Morass" in Centre for International Governance Innovation and Wiyasiwewin Mikiwahp Native Law Centre, *UNDRIP Implementation: More Reflections on the Braiding of International, Domestic and Indigenous Laws* (Saskatchewan: Center for International Governance Innovation, 2018), pp.111–120, online (pdf): www.cigionline.org/sites/default/files/documents/UNDRIP%202018%20lowres.pdf
[217] Ibid.

different solution within ninety days.[218] The Tribunal frequently encourages negotiation over the remedy while retaining jurisdiction to have a hearing if negotiations break down.[219] The Tribunal sometimes makes tentative remedial suggestions or canvasses a variety of possible remedies. This suggests that attention to Indigenous self-determination and law may require flexible remedies and judicial humility.

A recent case indicates some tensions between the emphasis on the right to a remedy in the first-track and the Tribunal's approach. In a case dealing with multiple claims by Māori to Crown land, the Tribunal refused to make binding recommendations because of concerns that an individual remedy would not be fair to other Māori. The Tribunal concluded that it would be impossible for it to divide the disputed land fairly among the Māori. This may have represented attention to legal pluralism and a preference for a negotiated settlement among the different groups. On judicial review, however, the courts found the Tribunal's approach to be unlawful.[220] This demonstrates some continued tension between state courts that have stressed efficient dispute resolution and the Tribunal that has placed more of an emphasis on consensual resolution – especially in cases involving intra-Māori disputes.

At the same time, the Tribunal does provide remedies, including interim remedies. It has determined that the Crown has an obligation to "restore to Māori ownership where practicable, where past wrongful dispossessions are established and not to alienate lands so as to prejudice Māori claims to them".[221] It has indicated that there is "a right to a remedy and corresponding obligation on the Crown to negotiate redress for the wrongful loss of a legal right".[222] Specialized tribunals with Indigenous participation are one way to encourage a bi-jural approach

[218] Treaty of Waitangi Act, 1975 No. 114, s.8B(4)(a) and s.8HC(4)(a) (in respect of claims made relating to Crown forest land).

[219] John Dawson, "The Remedies Report" in Janine Hayward and Nicola R. Wheel (eds.), *The Waitangi Tribunal: Te Roopu Whakamana i te Titri o Waitangi* (Wellington: Williams, 2004), p.128. Settlements after their reports typically include property and cash, agreements about Indigenous participation in decision-making about land and cultural redress including changing names to reflect Indigenous origins. Andrew Erueti, "Reparations for Indigenous People" in Corrine Lennox and Damien Short (eds.), *Routledge Handbook of Indigenous Peoples' Rights* (Abington: Routledge, 2016), p.106.

[220] *Haronga* v. *Waitangi Tribunal*, [2016] NZCA 626.

[221] Waitangi Tribunal Report, *Interim Report on Sylvia Park and Auckland Crown Asset Disposal* (1993), (Wai 276, 72 and 121) in MSR Palmer, *The Treaty of Waitangi in New Zealand's Law and Constitution* (Wellington, Victoria University Press, 2008), p.119.

[222] Waitangi Tribunal Report, *The Ngai Tahu Report* (1991), (Wai 27) at 4.6.17 in Palmer, *The Treaty of Waitangi*, p.120.

to remedies, but there is a need to understand that the very concept of remedy may sometime differ in western and Indigenous understandings.

9.5.4 *First-Track Remedies Are Necessary but Not Sufficient*

Interim remedies pending either fulfilment of duties of consultation or trials on the merits are critical. They create needed space and security to allow for potentially just settlements. Courts can apply proportionality reasoning to determine if such relief will cause disproportionate harm to legitimate social interests. They can alter such interim injunctions if circumstances change.

Restitution and, if that is impossible or disproportionate, damages can also be an appropriate first-track remedy that recognizes past acts of injustice. As outlined in Section 9.2.3 of this chapter, there are many examples of supra-national and national courts not awarding full pecuniary damages for lost Indigenous land or resources while sometimes being more generous in awarding non-pecuniary damages in relation to loss of culture. Courts should ensure that their approach to damages is non-discriminatory and does not romanticize the Indigenous experience as simply one that focuses on culture. In this respect, the Australian High Court asked itself the right question when it assessed whether its decision to award 50 per cent of market value for Indigenous land was discriminatory.[223] Not all may agree with the High Court's conclusion that it was not discriminatory.

When awarding compensation as a first-track remedy, courts should require a causal connection between the violation of Indigenous rights and the damages provided. When awarding forward-looking remedies such as community development funds, causation requirements are less important. As in other contexts, first-track remedies alone will not be sufficient. They will leave Indigenous rights vulnerable to violations in the future. Reliance on them will also require constant litigation over matters such as the duty to consult and requests for interim remedies. This may strain the limited resources of Indigenous communities and create uncertainty and harms to better relations.

9.5.5 *The Dangers of an Exclusively Systemic Approach*

As in other areas, first-track remedies play an important role in maximizing the opportunity for successful systemic remedies. Without first-

[223] *Northern Territory* v. *Griffiths and Jones*, [2019] HCA 7.

track remedies, systemic remedies including settlements are likely to reflect colonial imbalances of power. They may also focus on the future without attempting to make amends for an unjust past.

Systemic remedies that are pursued by the courts also risk neo-colonialism. A few American courts have used extensive public law litigation with respect to fishing rights in Washington but conflict and litigation has continued. Most supra-national and national courts have had the humility to recognize that sustainable systemic remedies will require negotiated agreements or negotiation about the means to implement remedies such as restitution and demarcation of land.

9.5.6 Examples of Two-Track Approaches

Consistent with a pattern seen throughout the book, supra-national adjudicators are more comfortable with the two-track approach than domestic courts. The UN Committee on the Elimination of Racial Discrimination recognized that the Western Shoshone peoples' land claims required a long-term systemic remedy to be negotiated between the Indigenous Nation and the United States. At the same, however, the Committee also contemplated a variety of interim remedies including orders against implementing plans to privatize ancestral lands.[224] Some interim relief was subsequently ordered by American domestic courts with respect to concerns about irreparable environmental damage.[225] Indigenous claims demonstrate how two-track relief can be sought under both domestic and international human rights law.

Another example of the two-track approach is when the IACtHR ordered as a systemic and bi-jural remedy that Nicaragua "carry out the delimitation, demarcation and titling of the corresponding lands of the Mayagna (Sumo) Awas Tingni Community" in a manner that respected the Indigenous community's laws. At the same time, the Court also ordered first-track remedies in the form of interim orders that the state would not adversely affect the land and not allow third parties to do so while the longer-term land demarcation remedy was

[224] United Nations Committee on the Elimination of all forms of Racial Discrimination, Decision 1(68) (United States of America), UN ESCOR, CERD, 68th Sess., UN DOC CERD/C/USA/Dec/1 (11 April 2006).

[225] *South Fork Band Council of the Western Shoneshone Nation* v. *United States* 588 F.3d. 718 (9th Cir, 2009).

pursued.[226] After seven different compliance hearings,[227] the Court concluded in 2009 that there had been full compliance with both parts of the remedy.

Domestic courts pursuing a two-track approach must aspire to give meaningful and non-discriminatory remedies to compensate for past violations and stop continuing violations while leaving space for Indigenous self-determination to guide systemic remedies to govern the future. In a landmark recognizing the importance of the spirit of the Treaty of Waitangi, the New Zealand Court of Appeal under the leadership of Lord Cooke did just that. It combined judicial remedies that prevented the government from alienating disputed resources while also ordering the government within twenty-one days to provide a plan to ensure that the transfer of Crown lands to state owned enterprises would not prejudice Māori claims. The Māori National Council (the applicants in the case) were then to be given twenty-one days to comment, with the Court ultimately retaining jurisdiction to determine whether the plan should be approved. President Cooke made clear that the Treaty of Waitangi would prevail, but also that both sides are partners who, under the Treaty, should "act towards each other reasonably and with the utmost good faith".[228] The Court of Appeal approved the settlement reached in this case, congratulating the parties on their agreement which was consistent with the spirit of the Treaty. This case combined judicial remedies against irreparable harm with judicial encouragement of settlements that can constitute bi-jural, consensual and sustainable second-track systemic remedies.[229] Lord Cooke's approach in this and other similar cases was informed by his appreciation that "[p]referably –

226 On the trend away from such paternalistic restraints, see *infra* Section 9.2.

227 On the difficulties of implementation, see Leonardo J. Alvardo, "Prospects and Challenges in the Implementation of Indigenous Peoples' Human Rights in International Law: Lessons from the Case of Awas Tingni v. Nicaragua" (2007) 24(3) *Ariz. J. Int'l. Comp. L.* 609.

228 *New Zealand Maori Council* v. *Attorney-General*, [1987] 1 NZLR 641 at 667. See also *New Zealand Maori Council* v. *Attorney General*, [2013] NZSC 6 recognizing the importance of the 1987 case but also distinguishing it on the basis that the Crown could if it retained 51% ownership still provide remedies for any Treaty breaches.

229 New Zealand has also moved to a more bi-jural approach in two pieces of legislation that protect areas of special significance by giving the land in question its own legal status and by appointing guardians for the land, see Te Urewera Act, 2014 No. 51 and Te Awa Tupua Act, 2017, No. 7. See generally Catherine J. Iorns Magallanes, "Improving the Global Environmental Rule of Law by Upholding Indigenous Rights: Examples from Aotearoa New Zealand" (2018) 7 *Global J. Comp. L.* 61.

and I am confident that the Waitangi Tribunal would agree with this – the Treaty partners should work out their own agreement. The principles of the Treaty require that they make a genuine effort to do so". He contemplated that "judicial resolution should be very much a last resort".[230]

Unfortunately, it is more difficult to find Canadian examples of a two-track approach that combines first- and second-track remedies even though Canada's Royal Commission on Aboriginal Peoples recommended in 1996 that "courts should design their remedies to facilitate negotiations between First Nations, governments and other affected interests".[231] In one case, a Canadian court took a declaration plus approach by ordering that the government eliminate discrimination in services in consultation with the Indigenous applicant. It characterized the relief as innovative. Rothstein JA noted that the trial judge's order "is not a mandamus in a traditional sense – no public officer is ordered to carry out a legal duty. Rather, it is more akin to a declaration of unconstitutionality coupled with an order directing the government to remedy the infringement of… rights".[232] The Court's retention of jurisdiction provided an opportunity for the parties to return to the court if necessary.

In other cases, Canadian courts have been more reluctant to use innovative remedies that "would require the ongoing involvement and supervision of the court".[233] They have also been reluctant to combine their emphasis on the duty to consult with interim remedies that prevent incursions on Indigenous rights during consultation. Canadian courts

[230] *Tainui Maori Trust Board* v. *Attorney-General*, [1989] 2 NZLR 513 at 529.

[231] Government of Canada, *Report of the Royal Commission on Aboriginal Peoples* (Ottawa: Supply and Services, 1996), p.564; see also Shin Imai, "Sound Science, Careful Policy Analysis, and Ongoing Relationships: Integrating Litigation and Negotiation in Aboriginal Lands and Resources Disputes" (2003) 41(4) *Osgoode Hall L. J.* 587. For a recognition that the decisions courts make (or do not make) about rights will affect the negotiation process, see Dwight G Newman, "Negotiated Rights Enforcement" (2006) 69 *Sask. L. Rev.* 119.

[232] *Ardoch Algonquin First Nation* v. *Canada (Attorney General)*, 2003 FCA 473 at para 42. This remedy does not fully comply with the declaration plus model because the trial judge did not retain jurisdiction: *Ardoch Algonquin First Nation* v. *Canada (Attorney General)*, 2002 FCT 1058; [2003] 2 FC 350.

[233] *Chippewas of Sarnia Band* v. *Canada*, 2000 CanLII 16991 (ON CA) at para 282, leave to appeal refused; *Delgamuukw* v. *British Columbia*, [1986] 2 ACWS (3d) 262 (BC CA); *Delgamuukw* v. *British Columbia*, [1993], 41 ACWS 93d) 234 (BC CA); *R* v. *Perry* (1997), 148 DLR(4th) 96, leave to appeal denied: [1997] 3 SCR xii; Roach, Constitutional Remedies in Canada, at 15.1370–15.1470.

have allowed requests for declarations about past violations made "in aid of extra-judicial claims"[234] but only on the basis that the applicants were not seeking compensatory remedies. This is a systemic approach that skips first-track remedies that by providing compensation for past harms and preventing on-going irreparable harm help counter inequality of bargaining power during the consultation process and make consensual agreements more likely. At the same time, this may be one of those cases where the litigants made a choice to seek only second-track systemic remedies. As discussed in Chapter 2, Section 2.4.4, such choices should generally be respected by courts.

9.5.7 Remedial Failure, Colonialism and Remedial Cycles

Many are reluctant to discuss the reality of remedial failure. Federico Lenzerini has recognized this "dark side" of remedies. He writes about "the scarce effectiveness of the protection of human rights in the real world, on account of the enormous figure of breaches of fundamental rights committed every day… As many Europeans know, with their longer history, no country escapes its past, to begin anew, morally fresh".[235] David Williams has suggested that the United States has been unable to fully recognize harms to Indigenous people because of an "impulse to moral perfectionism".[236] Examining remedies as opposed to rights forces one to confront failure and even tragedy.

One of the virtues of the two-track approach is that it can respond to remedial failure. A key to this response in the Indigenous rights context will be the willingness of courts to employ first-track remedies starting with interim remedies when previous systemic remedies have failed to prevent subsequent violations of Indigenous rights. If domestic courts are not responsive to rights claims or fail to order effective remedies, people in many democracies are able to appeal to a variety of supra-national adjudicators, including some regional human rights courts and some UN bodies. The important remedial work of the IACtHR has not resulted in

[234] *Dumont* v. *Canada (Attorney General)*, [1990] 1 SCR 279; *Manitoba Métis Federation* v. *Canada*, 2013 SCC 14.

[235] Federico Lenzerini, "Reparations for Indigenous Peoples in International and Comparative Law: An Introduction" in Lenzerini (ed)., *Reparations for Indigenous Peoples*, p.7.

[236] David Williams, "In Praise of Guilt: How the Yearning for Moral Purity Blocks Reparations to Native Americans" in Lenzerini (ed)., *Reparations for Indigenous Peoples*, pp.248–249.

full compliance by states, but it demonstrates how courts can continue monitoring compliance and, if necessary, make findings that states have not fully complied often with the more ambitious parts of court judgements that implicate their economic interests. It will require staying power and hard work[237] to re-enforce social commitments to Indigenous rights and remedies, but hopefully there will be broader social support if only because of coming environmental crises. A final case study involves an example of such a remedial cycle.

In 2003, the New Zealand Court of Appeal reversed a prior precedent that held that Crown sovereignty had extinguished Māori rights and that the Crown owned the seabed and foreshore.[238] The decision generated a populist legislative backlash that resulted in the Foreshore and Seabed Act, 2004. This law purported to extinguish any Māori rights to the seabed.[239] Like so many Indigenous peoples, the Māori did not give up. They continued to fight the legislation in both domestic and international forums. Domestically, the Treaty of Waitangi Tribunal ruled that the legislation was discriminatory and that it provided for expropriation without compensation. In an example of a bi-jural approach, the Tribunal concluded that the law violated both the rule of law honoured by European settlers and Indigenous law governing relations to the land and water. The Tribunal outlined possible approaches to remedies that might be applied by the High Court and the Maori Land court.[240] The multiple remedial options provided by the Tribunal demonstrated the power of proportionality analysis to outline a number of remedial options. Alas, none were taken up.

The Māori next switched to a supra-national forum. The Committee on the Elimination of Racial Discrimination expressed concerns about the majoritarian "political atmosphere" and speed in which the 2004 law was enacted.[241] It concluded that the law contained "discriminatory aspects against the Māori, in particular, in its extinguishment of the

237 Brunée and Toope, *Legality and Legitimacy in International Law*.

238 *Ngati Apa* v. *Attorney-General*, [2003] NZCA 117.

239 There was concern that the Māori would prohibit common use of beaches even though the Māori said they had no intention of doing so: Richard P. Boast, "Foreshore and Seabed, Again" (2011) 9 *N.Z. J. Pub. Int'l. L.* 271, 273.

240 Waitangi Tribunal Report, *Report on the Crown's Foreshore and Seabed Policy* (2004), (Wai 1071), online (pdf): https://forms.justice.govt.nz/search/Documents/WT/wt_DOC_68000605/Foreshore.pdf

241 United Nations Committee on the Elimination of all forms of Racial Discrimination, Decision 1(66) (New Zealand), UN DOC CERD/C/66/NZL/Dec.1 (2004) at para 3.

possibility of establishing Māori customary title over the foreshore and seabed and its failure to provide a guaranteed right of redress, notwithstanding the State party's obligations under articles 5 and 6 of the Convention" on the Elimination of All Forms of Racial Discrimination.[242] Consistent with the iterative remedial approach often taken by supra-national institutions, the Committee asked New Zealand to report back on steps it had taken to provide remedies.[243] James Anaya, then the UN special rapporteur on Indigenous rights, also called for the repeal of the legislation.[244]

The 2004 act was eventually repealed by new legislation in 2011. The preamble to the new law acknowledged the criticism that the prior act had received including from international bodies. It recognized inherent Māori rights and translated them into new forms of legal interests that are "inalienable, enduring, and able to be exercised so as to sustain all the people of New Zealand and the coastal marine environment for future generations".[245] The eventual outcome suggests that sustained opposition to discriminatory legislation can be effective even in the Indigenous rights context, at least when Indigenous people are a significant (15 per cent of New Zealand's population) minority and the Māori party holds the balance of power. The UN special rapporteur has praised the abolition of the 2004 law, but raised some concerns about the 2011 legislation.[246] This only affirms the iterative nature of a remedial process that involves both domestic and international law.

9.6 Conclusion

Devising remedies for violations of Indigenous rights is perhaps the most challenging of all the topics examined in this book. It is thus fitting that this chapter on remedies for violations of Indigenous rights is the last substantive chapter in this book.

[242] Ibid. at para 6.

[243] Ibid. at paras 8–9.

[244] United Nations Commission on Human Rights, Economic and Social Council, *Report of the Special Rapporteur on the Situation of Human Rights and Fundamental Freedoms of Indigenous People*, UN Doc E/CN.4/2006/78/Add.3 (13 March 2006), p.15; see also S. James Anaya, "Report of the Special Rapporteur on the Rights of Indigenous Peoples in the Situation of Maori People in New Zealand" (2015) 32 *Ariz. J. Int'l. Comp. L.* 1.

[245] Marine and Coastal Area (Takutai Moana) Act 2011, No. 3.

[246] Anaya, "Report of the Special Rapporteur on the Rights of Indigenous Peoples in the Situation of Maori People in New Zealand", pp.18–25.

Article 40 of UNDRIP speaks to the need for effective remedies, but also the need to take a bi-jural approach to remedies that is attentive to both relevant Indigenous law and human rights law. The two-track approach can be adapted so that courts provide first track remedies to protect Indigenous right from irreparable harm. They can also provide restitution and when that is not possible or disproportionate, full reparation for past harms. The IACtHR's jurisprudence demonstrates that restitution of land should be accomplished in a bi-jural way that involves both state and Indigenous law. At the same time with respect to second-track systemic remedies, courts should make room for Indigenous self-determination and free and informed prior consent. Even judges with the best of intentions should be careful to avoid the dangers of imposing neo-colonial solutions on Indigenous peoples.

Defensive remedies may be necessary for Indigenous people who undertake self-help or resistance to state actions. Courts should not hesitate to craft exemptions from otherwise valid laws for those exercising Indigenous rights. Courts should also pay attention to Indigenous claims and the state's duty to consult with Indigenous people when asked to grant injunctions against Indigenous protests in the defence of Indigenous lands and natural resources.

As in the last chapter dealing with SEC rights, the danger of remedial deterrence looms large in the area of Indigenous rights. It may explain why Canadian courts have retreated from ordering interim relief to halt developments that may cause irreparable harm to Indigenous rights and why the subsequent Canadian jurisprudence on the government's duty to consult stresses that Indigenous people do not have a veto over proposed developments. There is a danger that the duty to consult will degenerate into a procedural checklist that is more about gaining approval for resource extraction than creating modern Treaties. The duty to consult should be exercised in a manner that maximizes the possibility of consent and does not simply rely on the simplistic and self-defeating slogan of "no veto". It should aspire to produce consent and not focus on mandatory duties and checklists. Interim remedies should protect Indigenous people from irreparable harm as they consult. If the duty to consult is breached, there should be effective remedies including compensation and directions to ensure more respectful consultation in the future. Giving the state a second chance or a "re-do" is not sufficient.

Proportionality reasoning is preferable to vague reference to the equities of the case or the need for balancing when ordering remedies. Courts should not accept vague and inflated state objectives such as "economic development". Courts should also attempt to integrate Indigenous perspectives, including multi-generational and environmental thinking, into their assessment of the overall balance struck when selecting between the remedies requested by Indigenous people and lesser or no remedies requested by the state.

With respect to future oriented systemic remedies, domestic and supra-national courts should have the humility to recognize that Indigenous communities are in the best position to determine their own future. When devising remedies for laws and state activities that violate Indigenous rights, domestic and supra-national courts should also recognize that Indigenous people have their own legal systems that can play an important role in regulating how Indigenous people exercise their land, harvesting, social, economic and cultural rights. More than in other contexts examined in this book, courts need to defer to the superior ability of other actors to devise systemic remedies. To be sure, courts should not hesitate to impose first-track remedies to prevent and repair violations of Indigenous rights. But they should also recognize the importance of consensual remedies to create a better future for us all.

10

Conclusion

10.1 Introduction

In this concluding chapter, I highlight four points about the methodology used in this book and five substantive points about remedies for violations of human rights.

10.2 Methodological Contributions

10.2.1 Remedies as Under-Studied

Judges continue to make remedial decisions with brief and sometimes no reasoning. Scores of texts on domestic and supra-national human rights law continue to lack chapters on remedies. With some exceptions, human rights are studied as a matter of either theory or doctrine, both disembodied from practical enforcement. This can make human rights seem other-worldly. Lack of effective remedies also contributes to cynicism about human rights.

One reason why remedies for human rights remain under-studied is that they cross the boundaries of procedural and substantive law. They implicate civil, administrative, criminal law and Indigenous law. Another reason is that remedies often involve the executive and the legislature as well as courts. This requires attention not only to the work of the courts but also the executive and the legislature.[1]

In the supra-national field, remedies are less neglected. Supra-national courts have to justify their existence in a way that domestic courts do not. Hence, there is much work on whether governments comply with their remedies,[2] something that seems to be complacently assumed domestically. The challenges faced by the large caseload of the European Court of Human Rights (ECtHR) has placed the remedial work of that court in dealing with repetitive violations into the spotlight. Similarly, the innovative remedies ordered by the Inter-American Court of Human Rights (IACtHR) have drawn much attention,[3] as have interim remedies ordered by the International Court of Justice (ICJ) and other supra-national courts.[4] International lawyers generally accept that remedies are an iterative[5] and interactionalist[6] process and one that often fails.

[1] Important work has also been done on the new remedies of suspended declarations of invalidity and declarations of incompatibility. Robert Leckey, *Common Law Bill of Rights* (Cambridge: University of Cambridge Press, 2015); Aruna Sathanapally, *Beyond Disagreement: Open Justice in Human Rights Adjudication* (Oxford: Oxford University Press, 2012).

[2] Yuval Shany, *Assessing the Effectiveness of International Courts* (Oxford: Oxford University Press, 2014); Courtney Hillebrecht, *Domestic Politics and International Human Rights Tribunals: The Problem of Compliance* (Cambridge: Cambridge University Press, 2014).

[3] Jo Pasqualucci, *The Practice and Procedure of the Inter-American Court of Human Rights*, 2nd ed. (New York: Cambridge University Press, 2013).

[4] Eva Rieter, *Preventing Irreparable Harm Provisional Measures in International Human Rights Adjudication* (Antwerp: Intersentia, 2010).

[5] Abram Chayes and Antonia Handler Chayes, *The New Sovereignty: Compliance with International Regulatory Agreements* (Cambridge: Harvard University Press, 1996).

[6] Jutta Brunée and Stephen Toope, *Legality and Legitimacy in International Law: An Interactional Account* (Cambridge: Cambridge University Press, 2010); Clara Sandoval, Philip Leach and Rachel Murray, "Monitoring, Cajoling and Promoting Dialogue: What Role for Supranational Human Rights Bodies in the Implementation of Individual Decisions" (2020) 12 *Journal of Human Rights Practice* 71.

10.2.2 *Domestic and Supra-national Remedies Combined*

As discussed in Chapter 1, Section 1.4, this book follows in the footsteps of a few scholars such as Edwin Borchard and Abram Chayes who have studied domestic and supra-national human rights together. They were open to the perhaps counter-intuitive idea that domestic law could learn from supra-national law when it comes to remedies.

Borchard's work brought declarations as a preventive remedy from international to domestic law. He also challenged the common law orthodoxy still accepted in the United States that the state could not be held directly responsible for damages. Chayes recognized that complex relief in American law was an iterative and negotiated process, something that he also found to be the case in international law.

Domestic courts can still learn much from international law. International courts have increasingly used interim relief to prevent irreparable harm to rights. They have required states to report at the interim stage and even ordered provisional measures after final judgements. International law principles stress restitution and creative forms of reparation not limited to damages. International criminal courts use a broader range of alternative remedies than domestic criminal courts. They also formulate remedies for crime victims. The experience of international courts is relevant as courts move away from command and control strategies with respect to complex relief.[7]

Domestic and supra-national remedies should also be studied together because they frequently interact. Domestic remedies must generally be exhausted before seeking supra-national remedies. It is not possible to understand declarations of incompatibility under section 4 of the UK's Human Rights Act, 1998, without understanding the possibility of subsequent review by the ECtHR. This understanding also helps distinguish the United Kingdom's use of declarations of incompatibility from similar remedies used in Australia and New Zealand.

10.2.3 *Remedies as an Important Window on Comparative Law*

This book confirms Robert Leckey's insight that the study of remedies can reveal much about comparative law.[8] For example, it suggests that

[7] William Simon and Charles Sabel, "Destabilization Rights: How Public Law Litigation Succeeds" (2004) 117 *Harv. L. Rev.* 1016.

[8] Leckey, Common Law Bills of Rights; Robert Leckey "Remedial Practice beyond Constitutional Text" (2016) 64 *Am. J. Comp. L.* 1.

Mark Tushnet's dichotomy of strong and weak form judicial review can obscure more than it reveals.[9] For example, the UK courts have been driven to strong interpretative remedies so as to avoid the use of non-binding declarations of incompatibility. Moreover, the American courts often use narrow as applied declarations of invalidity and they accept legislative restrictions on damages and injunctions. The American experience is largely a story of courts restricting and not granting remedies.[10] Most remedial innovations come from the global South, often in the context of social, economic and cultural (SEC) rights.[11]

The theme of American remedial exceptionalism runs throughout the book. It starts with the decision in *Marbury* v. *Madison*[12] not to award a remedy while paying rhetorical homage to right to a remedy reasoning. The sovereign immunity of the state (except municipalities) that Edwin Borchard criticized almost a hundred years ago remains in place. The remaining promise of constitutional torts against state officials has died with increasingly robust qualified immunities. Legislative reform in the wake of the police killing of George Floyd holds out the only hope of reform.[13] The result is a legalistic form of impunity for human rights violations abuses that I have criticized elsewhere as American "extra-legalism".[14]

There has been much litigation but frequent delay and failure in desegregating American public schools and prisons. The exclusionary rule and the *Bivens* constitutional tort remedy might be abolished by the Supreme Court in the near future. In any event, both remedies provide illusory restraints on the American police. The victory of extending habeas corpus to military detention at Guantanamo Bay has been eroded by lower courts. The Supreme Court's recent 5–4 decision to uphold Trump's "Muslim ban" is an ominous sign,[15] but it does underline the

9 Mark Tushnet, *Weak Courts Strong Rights* (Princeton: Princeton University Press, 2004).

10 James Pfander, *Constitutional Torts and the War against Terror* (Oxford: Oxford University Press, 2017).

11 Brian Ray, *Engaging with Social Rights* (Cambridge: University of Cambridge Press, 2016).

12 5 US 137 (1803).

13 George Floyd Justice in Policing Act, 2020 (H.R. 7120) s.102 (passed by House of Representatives, 25 June 2020).

14 Kent Roach, *The 9/11 Effect: Comparative Counter-Terrorism* (Cambridge: Cambridge University Press, 2011), pp.161–238.

15 *Trump* v. *Hawaii,* 138 S.Ct. 2392 (2018).

importance of interim remedies and the Court's willingness to take a merits-based approach to them.

Perhaps reflecting greater trust in government, Canadian courts use general declarations much more than specific injunctions that can be enforced with contempt. They are hesitantly reaching towards the intermediate remedy of the "declaration plus" that allows courts to retain jurisdiction to resolve disputes about the declaration.[16] Canadian prison cases have like those in Europe resulted in legislative reform encouraged by suspended declarations of invalidity and some recent class action damage awards.[17] The suspended declaration of invalidity looks to legislatures but has come with the price of not always producing individual remedies. Nevertheless, recent assisted dying cases have combined remands to the legislatures for systemic remedies with the ability of courts to fashion individual remedies through exemptions from overly restrictive laws.[18] The duty to consult with Indigenous people is much litigated. Unfortunately, it is more often used as a means to obtain regulatory approvals than as an instrument to formulate modern Treaties in a respectful government-to-government manner and based on Indigenous consent.

The South African courts demonstrate less trust in government than the Canadian courts. For example, they use interim remedies to instruct the executive on how to administer laws when they suspend declarations of invalidity. In the same-sex marriage case, they made it clear that the legalization of same-sex marriage was required. In recent years, they have started to use more prescriptive structural injunctions and even the contempt power. Second generation housing cases are promising in

[16] *Reference Re Manitoba Language Rights*, [1985] 1 SCR 721; supplemental reasons [1985] 2 SCR 347; [1990] 3 SCR 1417; [1992] 1 SCR 212; *Doucet-Boudreau* v. *Nova Scotia*, 2003 SCC 62. See *infra* Chapter 7, Section 7.4.5.

[17] *British Columbia Civil Liberties Association* v. *Canada (Attorney General)*, 2019 BCCA 228 (declarations and suspended declarations of invalidity); *Canadian Civil Liberties Association* v. *Canada*, 2019 ONCA 243 (declaration of a fifteen-day limit on solitary confinement); *Brazeau* v. *Canada* 2020 ONCA 184 (Can$20 million class action award in relation to harms caused by solitary confinement). The reform legislation is found in S.C. 2019 c.27, but it may well be challenged by requests for both individual and systemic remedies. This illustrates the importance of remedial cycles discussed *infra* Chapter 10, Section 10.3.5.

[18] *Carter* v. *Canada*, [2016] 1 SCR 13; *Truchon* v. *Canada* 2020 QCSC 2019 *Truchon v. Quebec* 2020 QCSC 4388 (extending suspended declarations of invalidity but also allowing exemptions and other individual remedies); *Ontario v. G* 2020 SCC 38 (combining suspension and immediate remedy in a two-track manner).

combining anti-eviction remedies with engagement orders. At the same time, there are concerns that courts do not say enough about rights to inform the results of engagement. The engagement remedy, like the duty to consult Indigenous people, can be a two-faced remedy. It can result in creative and consensual agreements, but it can also be used to justify limits on rights and authorize evictions.

The Australian High Court has resisted the innovations of declarations of incompatibility and prospective rulings as unwarranted departures from the traditional judicial role in providing individual remedies. Australia also remains committed to a dualism that sharply distinguishes between international and domestic law.[19] In contrast to Australia, New Zealand has been a source of remedial innovation despite the absence of a remedies provision in its statutory Bill of Rights. It has pioneered the use of damages[20] and recently accepted the declaration of incompatibility.[21] Until 2002, it employed a prima facie rule of exclusion of evidence. The New Zealand courts have also recognized the utility of proportionality principles in remedial decision-making. The work of the Treaty of Waitangi Tribunal creates a potential for a bi-jural approach to remedies for violations of Indigenous rights.

The UK courts have been more willing than Australian and New Zealand courts to use robust interpretative remedies to make laws consistent with rights. This may reflect right to a remedy traditions of the common law,[22] but also concerns about compliance with the European Convention on Human Rights that are also seen in Parliament's generally favourable response to declarations of incompatibility. At the same time, the UK courts have followed specific instructions in the Human Rights Act, 1998 to follow the ECtHR's anaemic jurisprudence on damages. This has led to strong arguments that a return to the common law would be best.[23] Remedies may change in a post-Brexit Britain under a proposed British Bill of Rights and especially if the country was to continue its move towards less integration by renouncing the jurisdiction of the ECtHR.

19 Hilary Charlesworth et al., *No Country Is an Island: Australia and International Law* (Sydney: University of New South Wales Press, 2006). But for a different perspective outside of the human rights context, see James Crawford and Rose Cameron, "International Law in Australia Revisited" (2019) 40(1) *Adel. L. Rev.* 199.

20 *Simpson* v. *Attorney-General* (*Baigent's Case*), [1994] 3 NZLR 667.

21 *Attorney-General* v. *Taylor*, [2018] NZSC 104.

22 Kent Roach, "Dialogic Remedies" (2019) 17 *I. Con.* 760.

23 Jason Varuhas, *Damages and Human Rights* (Oxford: Hart Publishing, 2016).

This book also confirms some insights about countries in the global South being more inclined to engage in remedial activism and experimentation than courts in more established and prosperous democracies.[24] India's right to food litigation demonstrates the power of interim measures, use of existing laws and programs and careful monitoring. At the same time, some of India's public law litigation seems to be dominated by courts and the amicus they have appointed. This has failed to produce effective remedies and has even produced remedies with counterproductive effects.

The Colombian Constitutional Court has been criticized for using individual healthcare remedies with regressive effects. Nevertheless, the Court has, in consolidated cases about healthcare and the rights of displaced persons, acted in a dialogic manner to prompt legislative and executive reforms.[25] Like supra-national courts, the Colombian Court has been aware of the threats that repetitive violations present both to rights but also to the Court itself.[26] It has also rejected the unhelpful question of a veto in enforcing the duty to consult with Indigenous people and in some but not all cases enjoined state activity pending the results of a consultation process.[27] The Colombian experience also demonstrates how individual remedies can produce some limited remedial success and support for the Court.

The regional human rights courts also reveal some interesting comparative insights. The ECtHR still relies on damages with more complex remedies being subject to the not always transparent supervision and diplomacy in the Committee of Ministers. The IACtHR's use of apologies, commemoration and community development funds has been more creative than the ECtHR. The San Jose court's follow-ups to its judgements, however, reveal significant lack of compliance with its more ambitious remedies. Both courts make use of vague concepts of equity to balance conflicting interests when awarding remedies. The African Court of Human and Peoples' Rights has not yet placed its own stamp on remedies. Unfortunately, there is no regional human rights court for

[24] Daniel Bonilla Maldonado (ed.), *Constitutionalism of the Global South: The Activist Tribunals of India, South Africa and Colombia* (Cambridge: Cambridge University Press, 2013).

[25] Decision T-205 of 2004 (individual and systemic remedies for displaced persons); Decision T-760 of 2008 (individual and systemic remedies for healthcare).

[26] Gerald L. Neuman, "Bi-level Remedies for Human Rights Violations" (2014) 55 *Harv. J. Int'l. L.* 2.

[27] Decision T-129 of 2011, Colombia Constitutional Court.

Asia. Hopefully, in the next decade the global South will play a greater role in supra-national remedies. To borrow from Upenda Baxi: remedies, perhaps more than rights, can be responsive to "the voices of suffering" and the "lived and embodied experience" of "violated peoples".[28]

As Mark Tushnet notes, comparative law is not only concerned with the expressive differences between the laws of different countries, but also their functional similarities.[29] Most courts are reluctant to issue remedies before a full trial and to retain jurisdiction over a case. The American courts are a good exception here in their willingness to take a more merits-based approach to interim relief and to retain jurisdiction. All of the courts examined in this book tend to value human rights quite cheaply in their assessment of damages. There are also common trends to balancing competing interests before staying proceedings or excluding evidence even while somewhat inconsistently retaining individualistic standing and causation requirements. Although the Canadian and New Zealand courts have made reference to proportionality concepts and many courts discuss alternative remedies, there has not been a full application of proportionality principles when balancing the competing interests when formulating remedies. Courts seem to have an interest in emphasizing their remedial discretion while not always providing full justifications for how it is used. There is also a common movement towards the duty to consult Indigenous peoples but a reluctance to require Indigenous consent.

10.2.4 Theory and Context

Remedial decision-making is inherently contextual. For this reason, this book has devoted separate chapters to institutional cases, socio-economic and cultural rights and Indigenous rights. Each remedy tells its own story and sometimes it is a long story.

Context cannot, however, be everything. The idea that judges must have unfettered remedial discretion to deal with context can undermine the very idea of rights itself.[30] It can produce pathologies where courts focus on only individual or systemic remedies when both are needed.

[28] Upendra Baxi, *The Future of Human Rights* (Oxford: Oxford University Press, 2008), pp.7–8.

[29] Tushnet, *Weak Courts, Strong Rights*, pp.3–4.

[30] Peter Birks, "Three Kinds of Objections to Discretionary Remedialism" (2000) 29 *W. Aust. L. Rev.* 1.

The two-track approach to remedies which lies at the heart of this book is an attempt to inject some theory, or at least some conceptual thinking, into remedies. It is not a recipe for what remedies should be ordered or which will be effective. That does depend on context.

The two-track concept can be applied across a range of remedies. It suggests that individual remedies that respond to past violations and attempt to repair the harms they caused are important and at the core of the judicial role. At the same time, such individual remedies by themselves will generally fail to prevent similar violations in the future. Even if, as David Landau has argued,[31] my two-track approach is not possible or advisable in every context, it provides a reminder of important remedial work that still has to be accomplished. It can help litigants and judges to think about what is missing in their remedial approaches.

The two-track approach also engages indirectly with the extensive work done on interactionalist or dialogic approaches to enforcing human rights. Following from legal process foundations, it suggests that courts have a special role in providing effective remedies for litigants who have established rights violations. At the same time, it accepts that courts will generally need assistance from the executive, the legislature and society itself to formulate more complex systemic remedies to minimize future violations.

10.3 Substantive Contributions

10.3.1 Only Transparent and Proportional Limits on Remedies

As discussed in Chapter 1, Section 1.8, general principles such as respect for subsidiarity and the separation of powers[32] should guide remedial decision-making. They avoid the extremes of strong and unjustified exercise of discretion or the constraints of rigid rules that will not be responsive to particular remedial contexts.[33] Another principle that should guide remedial decision-making is proportionality.

[31] David Landau, "Choosing between Simple and Complex Remedies in Socio-Economic Cases" (2019) 69 Supp. 1 *U.T.L.J.* 105.

[32] See *infra* Chapter 1, Section 1.8, for a discussion of how supra-national adjudicators and domestic courts should always consider subsidiarity and the separation of powers even though the precise weight and constraints of these general principles will depend on the particular context.

[33] *Ontario (Attorney General) v. G* 2020 SCC 38 at para 89-93 quoting Kent Roach, "Principled Remedial Discretion under the Charter" (2004) 25 *S.C.L.R.*(2d) 101. See *infra* Chapter 1, Section 1.7, for additional discussion.

Although there are plenty of criticisms of proportionality principles in human rights law,[34] they are an apt tool for remedial decision-making. Remedies require a form of practical reasoning that optimizes respect for rights and the provision of effective remedies. There are few examples in remedial decision-making of an absolutist approach that focuses only on rights.[35]

Making judges more conscious of the need to discuss and justify how they allow concerns about competing social interests and rights to temper remedies has the potential to make remedial-decision making more disciplined and transparent. It can result in a better jurisprudence of remedies that may help in giving remedies the attention they deserve.

The state should have the onus of justifying limits on the remedies applicants propose. In Canada's leading damages case, the Court clearly held that once the applicant established a violation and a need for a remedy to compensate, vindicate or deter a rights violation, the state should have an opportunity to justify either a less drastic alternative to damages such as a declaration or limits on the damage award or even no damage award at all.[36] Placing the burden on the state will require the government to support their arguments with evidence about the negative consequences of proposed remedies and to propose alternative remedies. It allows applicants for remedies to challenge these arguments and propose different remedies. The whole process can help counter the tendency of remedies being a brief afterthought in much human rights litigation.

The objectives that can justify limits on remedies are open-ended but must be legitimate and not constitute objections to the very idea of rights or remedies. They also should not constitute attempts by the state to re-argue that rights were not violated or that general limits on rights had been justified. The familiar steps of proportionality analysis can be applied at the remedy stage. There should be a rational connection between the competing objective and the state's proposed limit on the remedy. Alternative remedies that can better reconcile the need for a remedy with competing interests should be considered. This is already an established part of remedial practice. Whether an interim remedy will be

[34] Gregoire Webber, *The Negotiable Constitution* (New York: Cambridge University Press, 2009).

[35] Paul Gewirtz, "Remedies and Resistance" (1983) 92 *Yale L. J.* 4.

[36] *Ward* v. *Vancouver (City)*, 2010 SCC 27. For a recent re-affirmation of this approach after some earlier decisions that imposed qualified immunities, see *Conseil scolaire francophone de la Colombie-Britannique* v. *British Columbia*, 2020 SCC 13.

ordered often depends on the adequacy or inadequacy of damages after a full trial. Courts consider the adequacy of less drastic alternatives to stays of proceedings or whether a declaration will be sufficient even though an applicant has requested an injunction. There should not be a mechanical preference for the least drastic remedy if it does not achieve the applicant's interest in receiving an effective and full remedy.

Finally, close attention should be paid to the overall balance struck by comparing how the state and the applicant are affected by any proposed remedy.[37] This should force the judge to consider the consequences and harms of giving the applicant a requested remedy, a less drastic remedy or no remedy at all. If all of these steps are followed, it may often be difficult to justify providing an aggrieved individual with no remedy. At the same time, it may be easier to justify limits and delays on broader systemic remedies.

Proportionality reasoning is superior to either rules that are inevitably over- or under-inclusive or strong forms of remedial discretion that do not require justification. In the damage context, qualified immunities that require the applicant to establish not only a rights violation but some set level of fault are examples of rules that attempt to vindicate legitimate state interests in a manner that may not be necessary in all cases. Conversely, the idea that the determination of the quantum of damages is simply a matter of equity means that judges exercise a strong discretion over how much damages are examined without careful attention to the effects of damage awards on both applicants and states.

Finally, the use of familiar proportionality principles can make remedial decision-making more transparent. It can contribute to informed debate. It recognizes that those who have had their rights violated require a good justification if they receive no remedy or a different remedy than they requested. Proportionality principles are a form of evidence-based practical reasoning. They can allow courts to change their remedial decisions in response to new evidence. They are a much needed improvement to remedial decision-making.

10.3.2 The Need for the Declaration Plus

Domestic judges often face an impossible choice between issuing declarations that are intended to be general statements about what rights and remedies require or making specific injunctions that provide fair notice in the case that punishment is required if the court order is violated.

[37] *Hislop* v. *Canada*, 2007 SCC 10.

Courts have opted for the former course sometimes with tragic results that have resulted in continued rights violations.[38] The use of declarations means that domestic courts, unlike supra-national courts, rarely retain jurisdiction over a case that allows them to respond to continued disputes about what rights require.

The declaration plus can combine the best of declarations and injunctions while avoiding many of their limits. It can fill a remedial gap between the two remedies. As courts have recognized, declarations respect subsidiarity and the separation of powers. At the same time, they can prolong disputes if there are disagreements about the adequacy of the state's response. Injunctions allow the court to retain jurisdiction but can require specificity that may impinge on the separation of powers. Fortunately, there is a trend in public law litigation away from command and control strategies to more declaration-like strategies that allow the government to select the precise means to achieve desired outcomes.[39] This more flexible approach can also facilitate consultation and engagement with those who are supposed to benefit from the remedy.[40] The declaration plus[41] where courts make general declarations but retain jurisdiction may be an appropriate and needed remedy especially in the early stages of cases involving institutions, SEC rights and Indigenous rights.

10.3.3 Engagement and the Duty to Consult: Creative and Consensual Remedies and/or Authorizing Limits on Rights

There are some important similarities between the South African Constitutional Court's novel use of engagement as a systemic remedy and the government's duty to consult Indigenous people. Both strive to achieve consensual and creative agreements that will involve free and informed consent by the rights-holders. In the Indigenous rights context, they can produce bi-jural agreements or modern Treaties that honour the aspiration of Article 40 of the United Nations Declaration on the Rights

[38] *Minister of Health* v. *Treatment Action Campaign (No. 2)*, [2002] ZACC 16 at para 129. See *infra* Chapter 8, Section 8.2.4, for additional discussion.

[39] *Eldridge* v. *British Columbia* [1997] 2 SCR 13; *Rail Commuters Action Group* v. *Transnet Ltd t/a Metrorail*, (2005) (2) SA 359 (CC) at para 108.

[40] Simon and Sabel, "Destabilization Rights: How Public Law Litigation Succeeds".

[41] See *infra* Chapter 7, Section 7.4, for discussion of a few cases, most notably *Doucet-Boudreau* v. *Nova Scotia* [2003] 3 SCR 3, where Canadian courts have made declarations that were not specific enough to be enforced by contempt but also retained jurisdiction.

of Indigenous People of producing remedies that respect both Indigenous and human rights law.

But what if there is no agreement? Engagement and consultation then can be used as a means to justify de facto limits on housing rights by authorizing evictions[42] or resource extraction in the face of claims of Indigenous rights.[43] To be sure, consultation can produce some accommodation of the interests of rights holders, but at the end of the day, the state's project, whether it be evictions or resource extraction, proceeds.

Engagement/consultation holds the most promise when it results in consensual agreements. Courts can maximize the chance for such agreements by addressing inevitable power imbalances in the consultation process. There should be interim remedies to protect those consulted from being evicted or having their lands subject to irreparable harm during the consultation process. Courts should also avoid the simplistic "no veto" slogan and design and if necessary supervise a process that maximizes the chances of agreement. Consultation should not be conducted in a hurried or top down manner. It should be done in a manner that recognizes the dignity, grievances and customs and laws of those who are being consulted. If the consultation is inadequate, there should be real remedies. The state should not simply get a "do-over" that will place more burdens on those who rights are or may be violated by state action. There should be compensation, judicial assistance in designing a more respectful process and judicial declarations about the rights in play. In this (and other) contexts, the declaration plus may be an apt remedy.

10.3.4 A Two-Track Approach That Seeks both Individual and Systemic Remedies

The heart of this book is its advocacy of a two-track approach to remedies. The two-track idea finds inspiration in the distinction that supra-national adjudicators make between individual and general measures. The former are provided to redress the harms suffered by litigants.

[42] *Residents of Joe Slovo Community, Western Cape* v. *Thubelisha Homes and Others*, [2009] ZACC 16.

[43] *Beckman* v. *Little Salmon/Carmacks First Nation*, 2010 SCC 53, [2010] 3 SCR103; *Chippewas of the Thames First Nation* v. *Enbridge Pipelines Inc.*, 2017 SCC 41, [2017] 1 SCR 1099.

The latter are designed to prevent similar violations in the future. The two-track approach allows courts to aim low and achieve relatively easy success in terms of crafting remedies for individual violations while also aiming higher in terms of systemic reforms to reduce violations in the future.[44] It recognizes that more ambitious systemic remedies "require high levels of institutional co-ordination, technical knowledge, financial resources, and significant time for completion".[45]

The two-track model is also inspired by Chayes' traditional and public law models of adjudication.[46] Both Chayes and Owen Fiss suggested that the traditional model would fade away. Writing in 1979, Fiss wrote that the "judgment – of a right without a remedy – hardly seemed plausible when the remedy imagined was of modest proportions – a damage judgment, or a preventive judgment aimed at some discrete act . . . But not so once the perspective broadens".[47] Chayes and Fiss did an enormous service in outlining the new public law model. In their pioneering excitement, however, they neglected the importance of the traditional model both to the meaning of rights and the legitimacy of courts.

The two-track approach demands that courts be attentive to what Justice Albie Sachs has called both "micro" and "macro" injustices.[48] It recognizes that courts traditionally exist to provide a remedy to successful litigants. Individual remedies for SEC rights have been criticized as illegitimate queue jumping, but this criticism ultimately seems designed to undermine the justiciability of those rights. The fact that courts cannot do justice to everyone who has suffered a similar violation has never taken away from their obligation to provide remedies for those who have gone to court and established that their rights have been violated. Perfect justice should not be the enemy of individual justice. In addition, governments can generally respond when individual remedies have regressive effects.

At the same time, the two-track approach also counsels against judicial hubris by suggesting that judges should approach the difficult task of

44 Shany, *Assessing the Effectiveness of International Courts*, pp.126, 128.

45 Thomas Antkowiak and Alejandra Gonza, *The American Convention on Human Rights* (New York: Oxford University Press, 2017), p.313.

46 Abram Chayes, "The Role of the Judge in Public Law Litigation" (1976) 89 *Harv. L. Rev.* 7.

47 Owen Fiss, *The Civil Rights Injunction* (Bloomington: Indiana University Press, 1979), p.91.

48 *Port Elizabeth Municipality* v. *Various Occupiers*, [2004] ZACC 7 at para 38. See *infra* Chapter 8, Section 8.3, for additional discussion.

systemic reform with deference towards the knowledge and expertise possessed by both the state and the parties. Both supra-national and national courts must engage with governments and society to produce effective systemic remedies that will minimize rights violations in the future. In healthy states, this should not require judges to run prisons or the police but to monitor reform processes that will draw on the ability of the state to train and discipline the executive.

The two-track approach warns about dysfunctions when remedies are only pursued on one track. Purely individual remedies will fail to stop repetitive violations. The most obvious pathology is that governments can simply pay the occasional price of the modest amounts of damages that are awarded by domestic and supra-national courts for the violation of rights. Less obvious are the thousands of remedies that domestic courts award in the criminal process without paying attention to their systemic causes of rights violations in criminal justice institutions – most notably, the police.[49]

The tragedy of purely individual remedies is that they could easily be converted into a two-track approach simply by making domestic courts more aware of the repetitive nature of many human rights violations. Supra-national courts such as the ECtHR are aware of this in large part because of their own institutional interests in not being flooded with repetitive petitions.[50] Domestic courts should follow their lead. They should be more willing to ask the state what, if anything, it is doing to prevent similar violations. They then should factor in the state's answer to their selection of both individual and systemic remedies.

An exclusive focus on systemic remedies is not the answer. Courts that have taken this route both in the United States and India have forgotten about the individuals who continue to have their rights violated. The tragedy of purely systemic remedies is that individuals whose rights are violated and who deserve some individual remedy get lost in an often futile quest by the court to achieve systemic reform. Although many have applauded the United States Supreme Court's narrow affirmation of an injunction ordering California to only operate their prisons at 137.5 per cent capacity,[51] this ignores the prisoners who have received inadequate health treatment

[49] Craig Bradley, *The Failure of the Criminal Procedure Revolution* (Philadelphia: University of Pennsylvania Press, 1993); William Stuntz *The Collapse of American Criminal Justice* (Cambridge: Harvard University Press, 2011).

[50] Neuman, "Bi-Level Remedies".

[51] *Brown* v. *Plata*, 563 US 493 (2011). See, for example, Jonathan Simon, *Mass Incarceration on Trial: A Remarkable Court Decision and the Future of American Prisons* (New York: New Press, 2014).

and deserve some compensation for their suffering. Individual remedies for prisoners who need medical treatment can achieve some remedial success and make real the individual consequences of systemic violations.

There are plenty of examples that suggest that the choice between individual and systemic remedies or between strong and weak remedies is often an unnecessary and false choice.[52] The ECtHR is able to award some individual measures even in cases where it uses the Committee of Ministers to persuade states to engage in legislative and executive reforms to prevent similar violations. As discussed in Chapter 7, Section 7.2.2, its approach to prison cases uses all of the tools of the legal process compared to the American approach which has relied on costly and controversial structural injunctions that have often neglected the very individual violations that courts have traditionally focused on and brought to public attention. The IACtHR also uses a two-track approach that employs a broader and more creative range of individual remedies than modest damage awards while also monitoring whether the state has adopted executive and legislative reforms to prevent future violations.

Some domestic courts have also used a two-track approach. For example, South African courts are combining individual remedies that prevent evictions or provide temporary accommodation with other more gradual and participatory remedies to improve housing. Colombian courts started with many individual healthcare remedies but in part because of their interest in not being flooded with claims have pursued a more dialogic and systemic approach that has resulted in legislative reform. Canadian courts are dealing with the difficult but pressing issues of medical assistance in dying through individual remedies so as to prevent unnecessary suffering while also allowing the legislature time to devise, and if necessary revise, a regulatory structure. The commitment to both individual and systemic remedies provides for cycles of reform and learning when systemic remedies inevitably fail to prevent all future violations.

10.3.5 Remedial Failures and Cycles

Thinking about remedies requires engagement with the reality of our collective failure to respect rights. It can provide an antidote to the perfectionism of rights and the increasing sense by many that rights are

[52] See generally Roach, "Dialogic Remedies".

simply pretty rhetoric and that states violate the rights of unpopular and sometimes demonized minorities with impunity.

The two-track approach has been designed to be attentive and responsive to the pervasive reality of remedial failure. When systemic reforms fail to prevent similar violations in the future, those whose rights are violated should have an incentive to seek both individual remedies and stronger systemic remedies. Courts should be attentive to the reasons that explain a repetitive violation. Whether those reasons be rooted in governmental intransigence or incompetence,[53] courts may have to order more robust individual and systemic remedies. If states are not able to prevent violations, judges will still have to do something. This is consistent with both subsidiarity and the separation of powers which defer to states but allow judicial intervention when the state and its executive fails to respect rights. At the same time, however, the state may be able to demonstrate that the violation was a one-off or that more systemic remedies are not required because the state has taken reasonable measures to prevent the repetition of the violation.

The two-track approach provides a guide to weather the harsh reality of remedial failure and the need for iterative cycles of remedies. Courts should resist the temptation to ignore the individual violations that prompt their reconsideration of the adequacy of systemic remedies. The facts of the individual violation matter. Even if individual remedies like damages do not fully undo the harm, they should still be ordered both to honour the integrity of adjudication[54] and to publicize and humanize the consequences of the violation.[55] Sometimes, inadequate remedies are better than no remedies at all. The fact that the remedy is inadequate should provoke debate and inspire us to do better.

Recognition of the reality of remedial failure and the lack of full compliance bring domestic and supra-national human rights law closer together. It promotes a recognition that effective remedies often require an ongoing and perhaps never-ending iterative process. This process will involve courts being in continued dialogue with governments and society. Courts can make distinct and necessary contributions to this dialogue through their focus on discrete events and their commitment to provide effective remedies. An effective remedy should respond to litigants who have established

[53] Kent Roach and Geoff Budlender, "Mandatory Relief and Supervisory Jurisdiction: When Is It Appropriate, Just and Equitable" (2005) 122 *S.A. L.J.* 325.

[54] Lon Fuller, "The Forms and Limits of Adjudication" (1978) 92 *Harv. L. Rev.* 353.

[55] Charles Epp, *Making Rights Real: Activists, Bureaucrats and the Creation of the Legalistic State* (Chicago: University of Chicago Press, 2009).

that their rights have been violated and attempt to prevent similar violations in the future. Courts may have to repeat this process many times, perhaps forever, to honour our frequently broken promises of human rights.

10.4 Conclusion

Focusing on remedies as opposed to rights confronts a world of repetitive violations and grave harms that unfortunately often can never be undone. This does not mean that this is a book only about failure, though it has been about that. Understanding remedies as a jurisprudence of persuasion that is attentive to the input of all parties and a range of domestic and supra-national institutions can also make remedies a site for transformation. Many rights exist only on paper. Better remedies have the potential to make rights more meaningful. But remedies are complex. They require attention to both the past and the future. They also require courts to work with other institutions of governance, the claimants and society itself.

Examining domestic and international law expands the remedial imagination and reveals many common issues. Both the domestic concept of respecting the separation of powers and the supra-national concept of respecting subsidiarity should be interpreted in a flexible and dialogic manner. They both suggest that courts should exercise one of their core functions by providing effective remedies for individual litigants. At the same time, courts should be concerned about preventing similar violations in the future. They should initially be deferential to governments, but should play a greater role if governments fail to provide effective individual and systemic remedies. A continued commitment to the two-track approach can produce successive cycles of remedies.

Remedies – what former Canadian Supreme Court Chief Justice McLachlin calls "the law stripped of pretensions"[56] – have been neglected for too long. They should not be dismissed as an afterthought or a site for the exercise of remedial discretion. We live in a world where rights seem like empty promises for too many. If we do not pay more attention to the intractable problems presented by remedies, there is a danger that disillusioned and angry publics will renounce rights, first at the supra-national level and later at the national level.

[56] Beverley McLachlin, "Rights and Remedies – Remarks" in Robert J. Sharpe and Kent Roach (eds.), *Taking Remedies Seriously* (Ottawa: Canadian Institute for the Administration of Justice, 2010), pp.22–23, 30.

SELECT BIBLIOGRAPHY

General

Barak, Aharon, *Proportionality: Constitutional Rights and Their Limitations* (Cambridge: Cambridge University Press, 2012).

Bates, Ed, *The Evolution of the European Convention on Human Rights* (Oxford: Oxford University Press, 2010).

Beatty, David, *The Ultimate Rule of Law* (Oxford: Oxford University Press, 2004).

Bickel, Alexander, *The Morality of Consent* (New Haven: Yale University Press, 1975).

The Supreme Court and the Idea of Progress (New Haven: Yale University Press, 1978).

The Least Dangerous Branch: The Supreme Court at the Bar of Politics (New Haven: Yale University Press, 1986).

Bilchitz, David and Landau, David (eds.), *The Evolution of the Separation of Powers* (Northampton: Edward Elgar, 2018).

Birks, Peter, "Three Kinds of Objections to Discretionary Remedialism" (2000) 29 *W. Aust. L. Rev.* 1.

Borchard, Edwin, *The Diplomatic Protection of Citizens Abroad* (New York: Banks Law Publishing, 1916).

"Government Responsibility in Tort VI" (1926) 36 *Yale L. J.* 8.

"Tort Liability of the State" (1930) 12 *J. Comparative Int'l. L.* 1.

"Judicial Relief for Peril or Insecurity" (1931) 45 *Harv. L. Rev.* 791.

"Declaratory Judgments in International Relations" (1935) 98 *World Affairs* 3.

Declaratory Judgments, 2nd ed. (Cleveland: Banks: Baldwin, 1941).

Brunée, Jutta and Toope, Stephen, *Legality and Legitimacy in International Law: An Interactional Account* (Cambridge: Cambridge University Press, 2010).

Calabresi, Guido, *The Common Law in the Age of Statutes* (Cambridge: Harvard University Press, 1982).

Calabresi, Guido and Bobbitt, Philip, *Tragic Choices: The Conflicts Society Confronts in the Allocation of Tragically Scarce Resources* (New York: W. W. Norton & Company, 1978).

Calabresi, Guido and Melamed, Douglas, "Property Rules and Liability Rules: One View of the Cathedral" (1972) 85 *Harv. L. Rev.* 1089.

Carozza, Paolo G., "Subsidiarity as a Structural Principle of International Human Rights Law" (2003) 97(1) *Am. J. Intn'l. L.* 38.

Chayes, Abram, "The Role of the Judge in Public Law Litigation" (1976) 89 *Harv. L. Rev.* 7.

Chayes, Abram and Chayes Handler, Antonia, "On Compliance" in Lisa L. Martin and Beth A. Simmons (eds.), *International Institutions: An International Organization Reader* (Cambridge and London: The MIT Press, 1993).

The New Sovereignty: Compliance with International Regulatory Agreements (Cambridge: Harvard University Press, 1996).

Chayes, Abram, Ehrlich, Thomas and Lowenfeld, Andreas, *International Legal Process* (Boston: Little Brown, 1968).

Donald, Alice, Long, Debra and Speck, Anna-Katrin, "Identifying and Assessing the Implementation of Human Rights Decisions" (2020) 12 *Journal of Human Rights Practice* 125.

Eisenberg, Theodore and Yeazell, Stephen C., "The Ordinary and Extraordinary in Litigation" (1980) 93 *Harv. L. Rev.* 465.

Fiss, Owen, "Forward: The Forms of Justice" (1979) 93 *Harv. L. Rev.* 1.

"Against Settlement" (1984) 93 *Yale L. J.* 1073.

Fuller, Lon. "Some Reflections on Legal and Economic Freedoms: A Review of Robert Hale's Freedom through Law" (1954) 54 *Colum L. Rev.* 70.

The Morality of Law (New Haven: Yale University Press, 1969).

"The Forms and Limits of Adjudication" (1978) 92 *Harv. L. Rev.* 353.

Fuller L. L. and Purdue, William R., "The Reliance Interest in Contracts" (1936) 46 *Yale. L. J.* 1.

Gewirtz, Paul, "Remedies and Resistance" (1983) 92 *Yale L. J.* 4.

Gilden, Gary, "Damages Caused by Violations of the Charter: The Relevance of American Constitutional Remedies Jurisprudence" (2009) 24 *Nat'l. J. Const. L.* 121.

Goldsmith, Jack and Posner, Eric, *The Limits of International Law* (Oxford: Oxford University Press, 2005).

Hart, Henry and Sacks, Albert, *The Legal Process: Basic Problems in the Making and Application of the Law* (Westbury: The Foundation Press, 1994).

Hickman, Tom, "Bill of Rights Reform and the Case for Going beyond the Declaration of Incompatibility Model" (2015) 2015 *N.Z. L. Rev.* 35.

Hoole, Grant, "Proportionality as a Remedial Principle: A Framework for Suspended Declarations of Invalidity in Canadian Constitutional Law" (2011) 49 *Alta. L. Rev.* 107.

Huneeus, Alexandra, "Courts Resisting Courts: Lessons from the Inter-American Court's Struggle to Enforce Human Rights" (2011) 44 *Cornell Int'l. L. J.* 3.

Koh Hongju, Harold, "Why Do Nations Obey International Law?" (1997) 106 *Yale L. J.* 2599.

Landau, David, "Choosing between Simple and Complex Remedies in Socio-Economic Rights Cases" (2019) 69 Supp. 1 *U.T.L.J.* 120.

Levinson, Daryl J., "Rights Essentialism and Remedial Equilibration" (1999) 99 *Colum. L. Rev.* 4.

Leckey, Robert, "The Harms of Remedial Discretion" (2016) 14 *I. Con.* 3.

"Remedial Practice beyond Constitutional Text" (2016) 64 *Am. J. Comp. L.* 1.

Maladonado, Daniel, *Constitutionalism of the Global South* (Cambridge: Cambridge University Press, 2013).

McLachlin, Beverley, "Rights and Remedies – Remarks" in Robert J. Sharpe and Kent Roach (eds.), *Taking Remedies Seriously* (Ottawa: Canadian Institute for the Administration of Justice, 2010).

Roach, Kent, "Constitutionalizing Disrepute" (1986) 44 *U. Toronto Fac. L. Rev.* 209.

"What Is New and Old about the Legal Process" (1997) 47 *U.T.L.J.* 363.

"Principled Remedial Discretion under the Charter" (2004) 25 *S.C.L.R.(2d)* 101.

Constitutional Remedies in Canada, 2nd ed. (Aurora: Thomson Reuters, 2013).

"The Judicial, Legislative and Executive Role in Enforcing the Constitution: Three Manitoba Stories" in Richard Albert and David Cameron (eds.), *Canada in the World* (Cambridge: Cambridge University Press, 2018).

"Dialogue in Canada and the Dangers of Simplified Comparative Law and Populism" in Geofferey Sigalet, Gregoire Webber and Rosalind Dixon (eds.), *Constitutional Dialogue Rights and Institutions* (New York: Cambridge University Press, 2019).

Rosenberg, Gerald N., *The Hollow Hope: Can Courts Bring about Social Change?*, 2nd ed. (Chicago: University of Chicago Press, 1991).

Rudovsky, David, "Running in Place: The Paradox of Expanding Rights and Restricted Remedies" (2005) 2005 *U. Ill. L. Rev.* 5.

Sandoval, Clara, Leach, Philip and Murray, Rachel, "Monitoring, Cajoling and Promoting Dialogue: What Role for Supra-national Bodies in the Implementation of Individual Decisions?" (2020) 12 *Journal of Human Rights Practice* 71.

Shany, Yuval, *Assessing the Effectiveness of International Courts* (Oxford: Oxford University Press, 2014).

Sharpe, Robert J., *Good Judgment: Making Judicial Decisions* (Toronto: University of Toronto Press, 2018).

Sharpe, Robert J. and Roach, Kent, *The Canadian Charter of Rights and Freedoms*, 6th ed. (Toronto: Irwin Law, 2017).

Shelton, Dinah, *Remedies in International Human Rights Law*, 3rd ed. (New York: Oxford University Press, 2015).

Simpson, A. W. Brian, *Human Rights and the End of Empire* (Oxford: Oxford University Press, 2001).

Smith, Stephen A., "Rights and Remedies: A Complex Relationship" in Robert Sharpe and Kent Roach (eds.), *Taking Remedies Seriously* (Ottawa: Canadian Institute for the Administration of Justice, 2010).

Starr, Sonja B., "Rethinking 'Effective Remedies' and Remedial Deterrence in International Courts" (2008) 83 *N.Y.U. L. Rev.* 693.

Thomas, Tracy A., "Proportionality and the Supreme Court's Jurisprudence of Remedies" (2007) 59(1) *Hastings L. J.* 73.

Trindade, Antônio Augusto Cançado, *Access to International Justice* (Oxford: Oxford University Press, 2011).

Tushnet, Mark and Jackson, Vicki (eds.), *Proportionality: New Frontiers New Challenges* (Cambridge: Cambridge University Press, 2017).

Waddams, Stephen, *Principle and Policy in Contract Law* (New York: Cambridge University Press, 2011).

Webber, Gregoire, *The Negotiable Constitution* (Cambridge: Cambridge University Press, 2009).

Wojtyczek, Krzysztof, "Judicial and Non-Judicial Elements in the Enforcement Mechanism of the European Convention on Human Rights" in Paula Pinto de Albuquerque and Krzysztof Wojtyczek (eds.), *Judicial Power in a Globalized World* (Berlin: Springer, 2019).

Yap, Po Jen (ed.), *Constitutional Remedies in Asia*, 1st ed. (London: Routledge, 2019).

Chapter 2 Two-Track Approach

Antkowiak, Thomas M., "An Emerging Mandate for International Courts: Victim-Centered Remedies and Restorative Justice" (2011) 47(2) *Stanford J. Int'l. L.* 279.

Aristotle, *The Nicomachean Ethics*, D. Ross (trans.), J. L. Ackrill and J. O. Urmson (rev. eds.), (Oxford: Oxford University Press, 1980).

Blackstone, William, *Commentaries on the Laws of England* (Oxford: Clarendon Press, 1765).

Buyse, Antoine, "The Pilot Judgment Procedure at the European Court of Human Rights: Possibilities and Challenges" (2009) *Greek L. J.* 1.

Chayes, Abram, "How Does the Constitution Establish Justice?" (1988) 101 *Harv. L. Rev.* 1026.

Contesse, Jorge, "Settling Human Rights Violations" (2019) 60 *Harv. Int'l. L. J.* 317.

Dicey, A. V., *Introduction to the Study of the Law of the Constitution*, 10th ed. (London: MacMillan, 1959).

Epp, Charles R., "Implementing the Rights Revolution: Repeat Players and the Interpreting of Diffuse Legal Messages" (2008) 71 *L. Contemp. Problems* 2.

Espinosa, Manuel José Cepeda and Landau, David, *Colombian Constitutional Law* (New York: Oxford University Press, 2017).

Fallon, Richard H. and Meltzer, Daniel J., "New Law, Non-retroactivity and Constitutional Remedies" (1991) 194 *Harv. L. Rev.* 8.

Friedland, M. L., "Prospective and Retrospective Judicial Lawmaking" (1974) 24 *U.T.L.J.* 170.

Fuller, Lon L. and Winston, Kenneth I., "The Forms and Limits of Adjudication" (1978) 92 *Harv. L. Rev.* 2.

Glas, Lize, "The European Court of Human Rights Supervising the Execution of Its Judgments" (2019) 37(3) *Netherlands Q. Hum. Rts.* 228.

Greer, Stephen, *The European Convention on Human Rights: Achievements, Problems and Prospects* (Cambridge: Cambridge University Press, 2006).

"What's Wrong with the European Convention on Human Rights" (2008) 30 *Hum. Rts. Q.* 680.

Hawkins, Darrin and Jacoby, Wade, "Partial Compliance: A Comparison of the European and Inter-American American Courts for Human Rights" (2010) 6 *J. Int'l. L. Int'l. Rltns.* 35.

Hillebrecht, Courtney, *Domestic Politics and International Tribunals: The Problem of Compliance* (New York: Cambridge University Press, 2014).

Hodgson, Jacqueline and Roach, Kent, "Disenfranchisement as Punishment: European Court of Human Rights, UK and Canadian Responses to Prisoner Voting" (2017) *Public Law* 450.

Horwitz, Donald, *The Courts and Social Policy* (Washington: Brookings Institute, 1977).

Keller, Hellen and Marti, Cedric, "Reconceptualizing Implementing: The Judicialization of the Execution of European Court of Human Rights Judgements" (2016) 26(4) *E. J. L.* 829.

Kurban, Dilek, "Forsaking Individual Justice: The Implications of the European Court of Human Rights Pilot Judgment Procedure for Victims of Gross and Systemic Violations" (2016) 16 *Hum. Rts. L. Rev.* 731.

Leckey, Robert, "Enforcing Laws That Infringe Rights" (2016) *Public Law* 206.

Liebenberg, Sandra, "Participatory Justice in Social Rights Adjudication" (2018) 18 *Hum. Rts L. Rev.* 623.

Neuman, Gerald L., "Bi-level Remedies for Human Rights Violations" (2014) 55 *Harv. J. Int'l. L.*

Pfander, James, "Dicey's Nightmare: An Essay on the Rule of Law" (2019) 107 *Calif. L. Rev.* 737.

Ray, Brian, *Engaging with Social Rights: Procedure, Participation and Democracy in South Africa's Second Wave* (Cambridge: Cambridge University Press, 2016).

Roach, Kent, "Polycentricity and Queue Jumping in Public Law Remedies" (2016) 66 *U.T.L.J.* 3.

"Remedies for Laws That Violate Human Rights" in John Bell et al. (eds.) *Public Law Adjudication in Common Law Systems* (Oxford: Hart Publishing, 2016).

"Dialogic Remedies" (2019) 17 *I. Con.* 860.

Rodriguez-Garavito, Cesar and Rodriguez-Franco, Diana, *Radical Deprivation on Trial: The Impact of Judicial Activism on Socio-economic Rights* (Cambridge University Press, 2015).

Ryder, Bruce, "Suspending the Charter" (2003) 21 *S.C.L.R.* (2d) 267.
Sachs, Albie, "The Judicial Enforcement of Socio-economic Rights: The Grootboom Case" (2003) 56(1) *Current Legal Problems* 579.
Sainati, Tatiana, "Human Rights Class Actions: Rethinking the Pilot-Judgment Procedure at the European Court of Human Rights" (2015) 56(1) *Harv. Int'l. L. J.* 147.
Schlanger, Margo, "Civil Rights Injunctions Over Time: A Case Study of Jail and Prison Court Orders" (2006) 81 *N.Y.U L. Rev.* 2.
Schoenbroad, David S., and Sandler, Ross, *Democracy by Decree* (New Haven: Yale University Press, 2003).
Sicilianos, Linos-Alexander, "The Involvement of the European Court of Human Rights in the Implementation of Its Judgments" (2014) 32 *Netherlands Q. Hum. Rts.* 235.
Steiner, Henry, "Individual Claims in a World with Massive Rights Violations: What Role for the Human Rights Committee?" in Phillip Alston and James Crawford (eds.), *The Future of UN Human Rights Treaty Monitoring* (New York: Cambridge University Press, 2000).
Tushnet, Mark, "Public Law Litigation and the Ambiguities of Brown" (1992) 61 *Fordham L. Rev.* 23.
Tushnet, Mark, *Weak Courts, Strong Rights: Judicial Review and Social Welfare Rights in Comparative Constitutional Law* (Princeton: Princeton University Press, 2004).
Vladek, Stephen, "The New National Security Canon" (2012) 61 *Amer. Univ. L. Rev.* 1295.
Wadham J., and Said, T., "What Price the Right of Individual Petition: Report of the Evaluation Group to the Committee of Ministers on the European Court of Human Rights" (2002) 2 *Eur. Hum. Rts. L. Rev.* 169.
Weinrib, Ernest, *Corrective Justice* (Oxford: Oxford University Press, 2012).
Wildhaber, Luzius, "Pilot Judgments in Cases of Structural or Systemic Problems on the National Level" in Rudiger Wolfrum and Ulkrike Deutsch (eds.), *The European Court of Human Rights Overwhelmed by Applications: Problems and Possible Solutions* (Berlin: Springer, 2009).
Young, Katharine G., "Rights and Queues: On Distributive Contests in the Modern State" (2016) 55 *Colum. J. Transnt'l. L.* 65.

Chapter 3 Interim Relief

Bates, Bethany M., "Reconciliation after Winter: The Standard for Preliminary Injunctions in Federal Courts" (2011) 111 *Colum. L. Rev.* 1522.
Bray, Samuel, "Multiple Chancellors: Reforming the National Injunction" (2017) 131 *Harv. L. Rev.* 418.
Brewer-Carias, Allan R., *Constitutional Protection of Human Rights in Latin America* (Cambridge: Cambridge University Press, 2009).

Brown, Chester, *A Common Law of International Adjudication* (New York City: Oxford University Press, 2007).

Burbano-Herrera, Clara, *Provisional Measures in the Case Law of the Inter-American Court of Human Rights* (Antwerp: Intersentia, 2010).

"The Inter-American Court of Human Rights and Its Role in Preventing Violations of Human Rights through Provisional Measures" in Yves Haeck, Oswaldo Ruiz-Chiriboga and Clara Burbano-Herrera (eds.), *The Inter-American Court of Human Rights: Theory and Practice, Present and Future* (Antwerp: Intersentia, 2015).

Burbano-Herrera, Clara and Haeck, Yves, "Letting States off the Hook? The Paradox of the Legal Consequences Following State Non-Compliance with Provisional Measures in the Inter-American and European Human Rights Systems" (2017) 28 *Netherlands Q. Hum. Rts.* 3.

Burgenthal, Thomas, "Interim Measures in the Inter-American Court of Human Rights" in Rudolf Bernhardt (ed.), *Interim Measures Indicated by International* Courts (Berlin: Springer, 1994).

Cassels, Jamie, "An Inconvenient Balance: The Injunction as a Charter Remedy" in Jeffrey Berryman (ed.), *Remedies, Issues and Perspectives* (Thomas Professional Publishing, 1991).

Chayes, Abram and Chayes Handler, Antonia, "Compliance without Enforcement: State Behaviour under Regulatory Treaties" (1991) 7 *Negotiation Journal* 311.

Fitzmaurice, Sir Gerald, *The Law and Procedure of the International Court of Justice*, Vols. I–II (Cambridge: Grotius Publications Limited, 1986).

Franklin, Beatrice, "Irreparability, I Presume? On Assuming Irreparable Harm for Constitutional Violations in Preliminary Injunctions" (2014) 45 *Colum. Hum. Rts. Rev.* 362.

Ghandi, Sandy, "The Human Rights Committee and Interim Measures of Relief" (2007) 12 *Canterbury L. Rev.* 203.

Gray, Christine, *Judicial Remedies in International Law* (Oxford: Clarendon Press, 1990).

Haeck, Yves, Burbano-Herrera, Clara and Zwaak, Leo, "Non-Compliance with a Provisional Measure Automatically Leads to a Violation of the Right of Individual Application... or Doesn't It: Strasbourg Court Takes Away Any Remaining Doubts and Broadens Its Pan-American Protection" (2008) 4 *Eur. Const. L. Rev.* 41.

Haeck, Yves, Ruiz-Chiriboga, Oswaldo and Burbano-Herrera, Clara (eds.), *The Inter-American Court of Human Rights: Theory and Practice, Present and Future* (Antwerp: Intersentia, 2015).

Harrington, Joanna, "Punting Terrorists, Assassins and Other Undesirables: Canada, the Human Rights Committee and Requests for Interim Measures of Protection" (2003) 48 *McGill L. J.* 55.

Jorem, Henrik, "Protecting Human Rights in Cases of Urgency: Interim Measures and the Right of Individual Application under Article 34 ECHR" (2012) 30 *Nordic J. Hum. Rts.* 404.

Laycock, Douglas, *The Death of the Irreparable Injury Rule* (Oxford: Oxford University Press, 1991).

Lee-Iwamoto, Yoshiyuki, "The Repercussions of the LaGrand Judgment: Recent ICJ Jurisprudence on Provisional Measures" (2012) 55 *Japanese Y.B. Int'l. L.* 237.

Leubsdorf, John, "The Standard for Preliminary Injunctions" (1978) 91 *Harv. L. Rev.* 525.

McCormick, Pamela, "Risk of Irreparable Damage: Interim Measures in Proceedings before the European Court of Human Rights" (2010) 12 *Cambridge Y.B. Eur. Leg. Stud.* 313.

Miles, Cameron, *Provisional Measures before International Courts and Tribunals* (Cambridge University Press, 2017).

"Provisional Measures and the 'New' Plausibility in the Jurisprudence of the International Court of Justice" (2018) *Br. Y.B. Intn'l L.*

Naldi, Gino, "Interim Measures in the UN Human Rights Committee" (2004) 53 *Int'l. Comp. L. Q.* 445.

Okpaluba, Chuks and Mhango, Mtendeweka, "Between Separation of Powers and Justiciability: Rationalising the Constitutional Court's Judgement in the Gauteng E-Tolling Litigation in South Africa" (2017) 21 *L. Democ. Dvpmn't.* 1.

Pasqualucci, Jo M., "Interim Measures in International Human Rights: Evolution and Harmonization" (2005) 38 *Vanderbilt J. Transnt'l. L.* 1.

Pasqualucci, Jo *The Practice and Procedure of the Inter-American Court of Human Rights*, 2nd ed. (New York: Cambridge University Press, 2013)

Raboshakga, Ngwako, "The Separation of Powers in Interim Interdict Applications" (2014) 5 *Constitutional Ct. Rev.* 366.

Rieter, Eva, *Preventing Irreparable Harm Provisional Measures in International Human Rights Adjudication* (Antwerp: Intersentia, 2010).

"Provisional Measures: Binding and Persuasive?" (2012) 16 *Netherlands Intn'l. L. Rev.* 165.

Sharpe, Robert J., "Interim Remedies and Constitutional Rights" (2019) 69 Supp. 1 *U.T.L.J.* 9.

Swart, Mia and Coggin, Thomas, "The Road Not Taken: Separation of Powers: Interim Interdicts, Rationality Review and E-Tolling in National Treasury v. Opposition to Urban Tolling" (2014) 5 *Constitutional Ct. Rev.* 346.

Trindade, Cançado A.A., "The Evolution of Provisional Measures of Protection under the Case-law of the Inter-American Court of Human Rights (1987–2002)" (2003) 24 *Hum. Rts. J.* 162.

Trindade, Cançado, *International Law for Humankind*, 2nd ed. (Leiden: Martinus Nijhoff Publishers, 2013).

Chapter 4 Remedies for Laws That Violate Human Rights

Berger, Benjamin, "A More Lasting Comfort? The Politics of Minimum Sentences, the Rule of Law and *R* v. *Ferguson*" (2009) 47 *The Supreme Court Law Review: Osgoode Annual Constitutional Cases Conference* 1.

Calabresi, Guido, "Foreword: Antidiscrimination and Constitutional Accountability (What the Bork-Brennan Debate Ignores)" (1991) 105 *Harv. L. Rev.* 80.

Carolan, Eoin, "A 'Dialogue-oriented Departure' in Constitutional Remedies? The Implications of NHV v. Minister for Justice for Inter-Branch Roles and Relationships" (2017) 40 *Dublin U. L.J.(N.S.)*. 191.

Chandrachud, Chintan, *Balanced Constitutionalism Courts and Legislatures in India and the United Kingdom* (Oxford: Oxford University Press, 2017).

Choudhry, Sujit and Roach, Kent, "Putting the Past behind Us? Prospective Judicial and Legislative Constitutional Remedies" (2003) 21 *S.C.L.R. (2d)* 205.

Crawford, Christopher, "Dialogue and Declarations of Incompatibility under Section 4 of the Human Rights Act 1998" (2013) 25 *Denning L. J.* 43.

Davis, Fergal and Mead, David, "Declarations of Incompatibility, Dialogue and the Criminal Law" (2014) 43 *Common L. World Rev.* 62.

De Londras, Fiona, "Declarations of Incompatibility under the ECHR 2003 Act: A Workable Transplant?" (2014) 35 *Statute L. Rev.* 50.

Dixon, Rosalind, "A Minimalist Charter of Rights for Australia?" (2009) 37 *Fed. L. Rev.* 335.

Donald, Alice and Leach, Philip, *Parliaments and the European Court of Human Rights* (Oxford: Oxford University Press, 2016).

Duclos, Nitya and Roach, Kent, "Constitutional Remedies as "Constitutional Hints": A Comment on R v. Schachter" (1991) 36 *McGill L. J.* 1.

Fallon, Richard H. Jr., "Fact and Fiction about Facial Challenges" (2011) 99 *Calif. L. Rev.* 915.

Fish, Eric, "Severability as Conditionality" (2015) 64 *Emory L. J.* 1293.

Fish, Eric S., "Choosing Constitutional Remedies" (2016) 63 *U.C.L.A L. Rev.* 2.

"Judicial Amendment of Statutes" (2016) 84 *Geo. Wash. L. Rev.* 3.

Kameny, Fred, "Are Inseverability Clauses Constitutional?" (2005) 68 *Alta. L. Rev.* 997.

Kavanagh, Aileen, *Constitutional Review under the UK Human Rights Act* (Cambridge University Press, 2009).

Kenny, David, "Remedial Innovation, Constitutional Culture, and the Supreme Court at a Crossroads" (2017) 40 *Dublin U. L. J.(N.S.)* 85.

Kommers, Donald and Miller, Russell, *The Constitutional Jurisprudence of the Federal Republic of Germany*, 3rd ed. (Durham: Duke University Press, 2012).

Geiringer, Claudia, "The Constitutional Role of the Courts under the NZ Bill of Rights: Three Narratives from Attorney-General v. Taylor" (2017) 48 *V.U.W. L. Rev.* 4.

Ginsburg, Ruth Bader, "Some Thoughts on Judicial Authority to Repair Unconstitutional Legislation" (1979) 28 *Clev. St. L. Rev.* 301.

Hickman, Tom, *Public Law after the Human Rights Act* (Oxford: Hart Publishing, 2010).

Jacobi, Tonja, "Sharing the Love: The Political Power of Remedial Delay in Same-Sex Marriage" (2006) 15 *L. Sexuality* 11.

King, Jeff, "Parliament's Role Following Declarations of Incompatibility" in Murray Hunt, Hayley Hooper and Paul Yowell (eds.), *Parliament and Human Rights* (Oxford: Hart Publishing, 2015).

Kronman, Anthony T., "Alexander Bickel's Philosophy of Prudence" (1985) 94 *Yale L. J.* 7.

Lau, Holning, "Comparative Perspectives on Strategic Remedial Delays" (2016) 91 *Tul. L. Rev.* 259.

Lauterpacht, Hersh, *The International Bill of Rights* (Oxford: Oxford University Press, 2014).

Leckey, Robert, *Bills of Rights in the Common Law* (Cambridge: Cambridge University Press, 2015).

"Assisted Dying, Suspended Declarations and Dialogue's Time" (2019) 69 Supp. 1 *U.T.L.J.* 64.

Leigh, Ian and Lustgarten, Laurence, "Making Rights Real: The Courts, Remedies, and the Human Rights Act" (1999) 58 *Cambridge L. J.* 3.

Mason, Anthony, "Human Rights: Interpretation, Declarations of Inconsistency and the Limits of Judicial Power" (2011) 9 *N.Z. J. Pub. Int'l L.* 1.

Peltomaa, Arthur, *Understanding Unconstitutionality* (Toronto: Teja Press, 2018).

Petrie, Nicholas, "Indications of Inconsistency" (2019) 78 *Cambridge L. J.* 3.

Philipson, Gavin, "Deference, Discretion and Democracy in the Human Rights Era" (2007) 60 *Current Legal Problems* 40.

Roach, Kent, "The Dangers of a Charter-Proof and Crime-Based Response to Terrorism" in Ronald Daniels et al. (eds.), *The Freedom of Security: Essays on Canada's Anti-Terrorism Bill* (Toronto: University of Toronto Press, 2001).

"Remedial Consensus and Challenge: General Declarations and Delayed Declarations of Invalidity" (2002) 35 *U.B.C. Law Rev.* 211.

"Dialogic Judicial Review and Its Critics" (2004) 23 *S.C.L.R.* (2d) 49.

"New and Problematic Restrictions on Constitutional Remedies" (2004) 49 *C.L.Q.* 253.

"Constitutionalized Interpretation, Reading Down/In and the Wisdom of Schachter" (2016) 36 *N.J.C.L.* 2.

The Supreme Court on Trial: Judicial Activism or Democratic Dialogue, 2nd ed. (Toronto: Irwin Law, 2016).

Rupp-von Brunneck, Wiltraut, "Germany: The Federal Constitutional Court" (1972) 20 *Am. J. Comp. L.* 3.

Rogerson, Carol, "The Judicial Search for Appropriate Remedies under the Charter: The Examples of Overbreadth and Vagueness" in Robert J. Sharpe (ed.), *Charter Litigation* (Toronto: Butterworths, 1987).

Sathanapally, Aruna, *Beyond Disagreement: Open Remedies in Human Rights Adjudication* (Oxford: Oxford University Press, 2012).

Stewart, Hamish, "A Defence of Constitutionalized Interpretation" (2016) 36 *N.J.C.L.* 2.

Stiansen, Oyvind, "Delayed but Not Derailed: Legislative Compliance with European Court of Human Rights Judgments" (2019) 23 *Int'l. J. Hum. Rts.* 8.

Sunstein, William N., "If People Would Be Outraged by Their Rulings, Should Judges Care?" (2007) 60 *Stan. L. Rev.* 155.

Yap, Po Jen, "New Democracies and Novel Remedies" (2017) 2017 *Public Law* 30.

Constitutional Remedies in Asia (London: Routledge, 2019).

"Remedial Discretion and Dilemmas in Asia" (2019) 69 Supp. 1 *U.T.L.J.* 84.

Zeidler, Wolfgang, "Federal Constitutional Court of the Federal Republic of Germany: Decisions on the Constitutionality of Legal Norms" (1986) 62 *Notre Dame L. Rev.* 4.

Chapter 5 Damages

Aronson, Mark, "Some Australian Reflections on Roncarelli v. Duplessis" (2010) 55 *McGill L. J.* 615.

Antkowiak, James and Gonza, Alejandra, *The American Convention on Human Rights* (Oxford: Oxford University Press, 2017).

Berryman, Jeff and Carroll, Robyn, "Cy-Près as a Class Action Remedy" in Kit Barker and Darryn Jenson (eds.), *Private Law: Key Encounters with Public Law* (Cambridge: Cambridge University Press, 2013).

Carroll, Robyn, "You Can't Order Sorriness, so Is There Any Value in an Ordered Apology – An Analysis of Ordered Apologies in Anti-Discrimination Cases" (2010) 33 *U.N.S.W. L.J.* 2.

"Apologies as a Legal Remedy" (2013) 35(2) *Sydney L. Rev.* 317.

Chan, Johannes, "Vindicatory Damages for Violations of Constitutional Rights: A Comparative Approach" in Mark Elliott, Jason Varuhas and Shona Stark (eds.), *The Unity of Public Law?* (Oxford: Hart Publishing, 2018).

Charles, W. H., *Understanding Charter Damages* (Toronto: Irwin Law, 2016).

Cichero, Agnostina and Green-Martinez, Sebastian, "Punitive Damages and the Principle of Full Reparation in the Case Law of the Inter-American Court of

Human Rights" in Yves Haeck et al. (eds.), *The Inter-American Court of Human Rights: Theory and Practice, Present and Future* (Cambridge: Intersentia, 2015).

Citroni, Gabriella, "Measures of Reparation for Victims of Gross Human Rights Violations: Developments and Challenges in the Jurisprudence of Two Regional Human Rights Courts" (2012) 5 *Inter-Am. Eur. Hum. Rts. J.*

Cooper-Stephenson, Kenneth, *Charter Damage Claims* (Toronto: Carswell, 1990).

Cooper-Stephson, Kenneth *Constitutional Damages Worldwide* (Toronto: Thomson Reuters, 2013).

Crawford, James, *The International Law Commission's Articles on State Responsibility* (Cambridge: Cambridge University Press, 2002).

de Albuquerque, Pinto and Van Aaken, Anne, "Punitive Damages in Strasbourg" in Anne van Aaken and Julia Motoc (eds.), *The European Convention on Human Rights and General International Law* (Oxford: Oxford University Press, 2017).

Epp, Charles, *Making Rights Real: Activists, Bureaucrats and the Creation of the Legalistic State* (Chicago: University of Chicago Press, 2009).

Fallon, Richard, "Bidding Farewell to Constitutional Torts" (2019) 107 *Calif. L. Rev.* 933.

Fikfak, Veronika, "Changing State Behaviour: Damages before the European Court of Human Rights" (2019) 29(4) *E. J. I. L.* 1091.

Flaherty, Michele, "Trends in Human Rights Damages" (2017) 20 *Can. Lab. Emp. L. J.* 355.

Harlow, Carol, "Damages and Human Rights" (2004) *N.Z. L. Rev.* 429.

State Liability: Tort Liability and Beyond (Oxford: Oxford University Press, 2004).

Ichim, Octavian, *Just Satisfaction under the European Convention on Human Rights* (Cambridge: Cambridge University Press, 2015).

Jeffries Jr., John, "Reversing the Order of Battle in Constitutional Torts" (2009) *Sup. Ct. L. Rev.* 115.

"The Liability Rule for Constitutional Torts" (2013) 99 *Virg. L. Rev.* 207.

Laplante, Lisa, "Bringing Effective Remedies Home: The Inter-American Human Rights System, Reparations and the Duty of Prevention" (2004) 22 *Netherlands Q. Hum. Rts.* 347.

Laurin, Jennifer, "Trawling for Herring: Lessons in Doctrinal Borrowing" (2011) 111 *Colum. L. Rev.* 670.

Levinson, Daryl J., "Making Government Pay: Markets Politics and the Allocation of Constitutional Costs" (2000) 67 *U. Chi. L. Rev.* 2.

Linden, Allen, "Charter Damage Claims: New Dawn or Mirage?" (2012) 39 *Adv. Q.* 426.

Lord Scott of Foscote, Holland, Justice Randy, and Varner, Chilton, "The Role of Extra-compensatory Damages for Violations of Fundamental Human Rights in the United Kingdom and the United States" (2006) 46 *Va. J. Intnl. L.* 475.

Love, J. C., "Damages: A Remedy for the Violation of Constitutional Rights" (1979) 67 *Calif. L. Rev.* 1242.

McLay, Geoff, "Damages for Breach of the New Zealand Bill of Rights: Why Aren't They Sufficient Remedy" (2008) 2008 *N.Z. L. Rev.* 333.

Mullan, David, "Roncarelli v. Duplessis and Damages for Abuse of Power: For What Does It Stand in 1959 and for What Does It Stand in 2009?" (2010) 55 *McGill L. J.* 587.

Pfander, James, *Constitutional Torts and the War on Terror* (New York: Oxford University Press, 2017).

Pfander, James, Reinert, Alexander and Schwartz, Joanna, "The Myth of Personal Liability" (2020) 72 *Stan. L. Rev.* 561.

Psutska, Michelle and Sheehy, Elizabeth, "Strip Searching of Women in Canada: Wrongs and Rights" (2016) 94 *Can. Bar Rev.* 241.

Roach, Kent, "A Promising Late Spring for Charter Damages: *Ward* v. *British Colombia*" (2011) 29 *N.J.C.L.* 135.

"Substitute Justice? Indirect Challenges to American Counter-Terrorism Activities in non-American Courts" (2012) 82 *Miss. L. J.* 4.

"Blaming the Victim: Canadian Law, Causation and Residential Schools" (2014) 64 *U.T.L.J.* 566.

"The Disappointing Remedy? Damages as a Remedy for Violations of Human Rights" (2019) 69 Supp. 1 *U.T.L.J.* 33.

Rubio-Marin, Ruth (ed.), *The Gender of Reparations: Unsettling Sexual Hierarchies While Redressing Human Rights Violations* (Cambridge: Cambridge University Press, 2009).

Rubio-Marin, Ruth, Sandoval, Clara and Diaz, Catalina, "Repairing Family Members: Gross Human Rights Violations and Communities of Harm" in Ruth Rubio-Marin (ed.), *The Gender of Reparations: Unsettling Sexual Hierarchies While Redressing Human Rights Violations* (Cambridge: Cambridge University Press, 2009).

Sampson-Jones, Ted, "The Myth of Ashby v. Wright" (2010) 8 *St Thomas L. Rev.* 40.

Schmeiser, Douglas, *Civil Liberties in Canada* (Oxford: Oxford University Press, 1964).

Schuck, Peter, *Suing Government* (New Haven: Yale University Press, 1983).

Schwartz, Joanna C., "How Qualified Immunity Fails" (2017) 127 *Yale L. J.* 2.

"The Case against Qualified Immunity" (2018) 93 *Notre Dame L. Rev.* 5.

Steele, Jenny, "Damages and Tort under the Human Rights Act" (2008) 67 *C. L. J.* 606.

Trengove, Win, "Judicial Remedies for Violations of Socio-economic Rights" (1999) 1 *E.S.R. Rev.* 8.

Trindade, Antonio Augusto Cançado, "The Human Person and International Justice" (2008) 47 *Colum. J. Transn'l. L.* 16.

van Dijk, Gijs, "The Ordered Apology" (2017) 37 *Oxford J. Leg. Studies* 562.
Varuhas, Jason, *Damages and Human Rights* (Oxford: Hart Publishing, 2016).
"The Development of the Damage Remedy under the New Zealand Bill of Rights: From Torts to Administrative Law" (2016) *N.Z. L. Rev.* 213.
Wagatsuma, Hiroshi and Rosett, Arthur, "The Implications of Apology: Law and Culture in Japan and the United States" (1986) 20 *L. Soc'y. Rev.* 461.
White, Brent T., "Say You're Sorry: Court-ordered Apologies as a Civil Rights Remedy" (2006) 91 *Cornell L. Rev.* 6.

Chapter 6 Remedies in the Criminal Process

Amsterdam, Anthony, "Speedy Criminal Trial: Rights and Remedies" (1975) 27 *Stan. L. Rev.* 3.
Bettinger-Lopez, Caroline, "The Challenge of Domestic Implementation of International Human Rights Law in the Cotton Field Case" (2012) 15(2) *N.Y. City L. Rev.* 315, 329.
Bloom, Robert and Delaney, Erin, "When Rights Become Empty Promises: Promoting an Exclusionary Rule That Vindicates Personal Rights" (2012) 46 *Irish Jurist (N.S.)* 38.
Bradley, Craig, *The Failure of the Criminal Procedure Revolution* (Pennsylvania: University of Pennsylvania Press, 1993).
Criminal Procedure: A Worldwide Study, 2nd ed. (Durham: Carolina Academic Press, 2007).
Bradley, Craig M., "Is the Exclusionary Remedy Dead?" (2012) 102 *J. Crim. L. Criminology* 1.
Calabresi, Guido, "The Exclusionary Rule" (2003) 26 *Harv. J. L. and Pub. Pol'y.* 112.
Chappell, Louise, "The Gender Injustice Cascade" (2017) 21(9) *Int'l J. Hum. Rts.* 1223.
Choo, Andrew, *Abuse of Process and Judicial Stays of Proceedings*, 2nd ed. (Oxford: Oxford University Press, 2008).
Code, Michael, *Trial within a Reasonable Time* (Toronto: Carswell, 1992).
Cover, Robert M. and Aleinikoff, T. Alexander, "Dialectical Federalism: Habeas Corpus and the Court" (1977) 86 *Yale L. J.* 1035.
Doernberg, Donald L., "'The Right of the People': Reconciling Collective and Individual Interests under the Fourth Amendment" (1983) 58 *N.Y.U. L. Rev.* 240.
Dutton, Anne and Ni Aolain, Fionnuala, "Between Reparations and Repair: Assessing the Work of the ICC Trust Fund for Victims" (2019) 19 *Chi. J. Int'l. L.* 490.
Engle, Karen, "Anti-impunity and the Turn to Criminal Law in Human Rights" (2015) 100 *Cornell L. Rev.* 1069.
Farbey, Judith, Sharpe, Robert J. and Atrill, Simon, *The Law of Habeas Corpus*, 3rd ed. (Oxford University Press, 2011).

Farrell, Brian, *Habeas Corpus in International Law* (Cambridge: Cambridge University Press, 2017).

Garrett, Brandon, *Convicting the Innocent* (Cambridge: Harvard University, 2011).

Garrett, Brandon L., "Aggregation in Criminal Law" (2007) 95 *Cal. L. Rev.* 383.

"Aggregation and Constitutional Rights" (2012) 88 *Notre Dame L. Rev.* 2.

Giannoulopoulos, Dimitrios, *Improperly Obtained Evidence in Anglo-American and Continental Law* (Oxford: Hart Publishing, 2019).

Hodgson, Jacqueline, *The Metamorphosis of Criminal Justice* (Oxford: Oxford University Press, 2020).

Huneeus, Alexandra, "International Criminal Law by Other Means" (2013) 107 *Am. J. Int'l. L.* 1.

Jackson, John D. and Summers, Sarah, *The Internationalisation of Criminal Evidence* (Cambridge: Cambridge University Press, 2012).

Jeffries Jr., John C., "The Right-remedy Gap in Constitutional Law" (1999) 109 *Yale L. J.* 87.

Kamisar, Yale, "Does (Did) (Should) the Exclusionary Rule Rest on a 'Principled Basis' Rather than an 'Empirical Proposition'" (1983) 16 *Creighton L. Rev.* 565.

"In Defence of the Exclusionary Rule" (2003) 26 *Harv. J. L. Pub. Pol'y.* 119.

King, Nancy and Hoffman, Joseph, *Habeas for the Twenty-First Century: Uses, Abuses, and the Future of the Great Writ* (Chicago: University of Chicago Press, 2011).

Kuijer, Martin, "The Right to a Fair Trial and the Council of Europe's Efforts" (2013) 13 *Hum. Rts. L. Rev.* 4.

Lamer, Rt. Hon Antonio, "Protecting the Administration of Justice from Disrepute" (1998) 42 *St Louis U. L. J.* 345.

Levine, Kay, Turner, Jenia and Wright, Ronald, "Evidence Laundering in a Post-Herring World" (2016) 106 *J. Crim. L. Criminology* 627.

Mahoney, Richard, "Exclusion of Evidence" in Paul Rishworth et. al (eds.), *The New Zealand Bill of Rights* (Oxford: Oxford University Press, 2003).

Mandel, Michael, *How America Gets Away with Murder* (London: Pluto Press, 2004).

Marshall, Peter, "Sentence Reductions as a BORA Remedy" (2012) 2012 *N.Z. L. J.* 24.

McFadden, Patrick M., "Provincialism in United States Courts" (1995–1996) 81 *Cornell L. Rev.* 4.

McGrath, Declan, "The Exclusionary Rule in respect of Unconstitutionally Obtained Evidence" (2004) 26 *Dublin Univ. L. J.* 108.

Mégret, Frédéric, "Justifying Compensation by the International Criminal Court's Victims Trust Fund: Lessons from Domestic Compensation Schemes" (2010) 36 *Brook. J. Int'l. L.* 123.

Mégret, Frédéric and Calderon, Jean-Paul, "The Move towards a Victim-Centred Concept of Criminal Law and the 'Criminalization' of Inter-American

Human Rights Law: A Case of Human Rights Law Devouring Itself?" in Yves Haeck, Oswaldo Ruiz-Chiriboga, Clara Burbano-Herrera (eds.), *The Inter-American Court of Human Rights: Theory and Practice, Present and Future* (Cambridge: Intersentia, 2015).

Michell, Paul, "English-Speaking Justice: Evolving Responses to Transnational Forcible Abduction after Alvarez-Machain" (1996) 29 *Cornell Int'l. U.* 2.

Moffatt, Luke, "Reparative Complemtarity" (2013) 17(3) *Int'l. J. Hum. Rts.* 368.

Naymark, Daniel, "Violations of Rights of the Accused at International Criminal Tribunals: The Problem of Remedy" (2008) 4 *J. Int'l. L. Int'l. Rltns.* 2.

Optican, Scott L. and Sankoff, Peter J., "The New Exclusionary Rule: A Preliminary Assessment of R. v. Shaheed" (2003) 2003 *N.Z. L. Rev.* 1.

Paciocco, David, "Section 24(2): Lottery or Law – The Appreciable Limits of Purposive Reasoning" (2011) 58 *C.L.Q.* 15.

Primus, Eve Brensike, "A Structural Vision of Habeas Corpus" (2010) 98 *Cal. L. Rev.* 1.

Rappaport, John, "How Private Insurers Regulate Public Police" (2017) 130 *Harv. L. Rev.* 6.

Roach, Kent, "Constitutionalizing Disrepute: Exclusion of Evidence after Therens" (1986) 44 *U. Toronto Fac. L. Rev.* 209.

"The Evolving Fair Trial Test" (1996) 1 *Can. Crim. L. Rev.* 69.

Due Process and Victims' Rights: The New Law and Politics of Criminal Justice (Toronto: University of Toronto Press, 1999).

The 9/11 Effect: Comparative Counter-Terrorism (Cambridge: Cambridge University Press, 2011).

"Reclaiming Prima Facie Exclusionary Rules in Canada, Ireland, New Zealand and the United States: The Importance of Compensation, Proportionality and Non-Repetition" (2020) 43 *Manitoba Law Journal* 1.

Rubio-Marín, Ruth and Sandoval, Clara, "Engendering the Reparations Jurisprudence of the Inter-American Court of Human Rights: The Promise of the "Cotton Field" Judgment" (2011) 33 *Hum. Rts. Q.* 1062.

Sandoval, Clara and Duttwiler, Michael. "Redressing Non-Pecuniary Damages of Torture Survivors: The Practice of the Inter-American Court of Human Rights" in Geoff Gilbert et. al. (eds.), *The Delivery of Human Rights* (London: Routledge, 2010).

Seibert-Fohr, Anja, *Prosecuting Serious Human Rights Violations* (Oxford: Oxford University Press, 2009).

Shereshevsky, Yahli, "Monetary Compensation as a Remedy for Fair Trial Violations under International Criminal Law" (2015) 18 *New Crim. L. Rev.* 71.

Sikkink, Kathryn, *The Justice Cascade: How Human Rights Prosecutions Are Changing World Politics* (New York: W.W. Norton and Company, 2011).

Starr, Sonja B., "Sentence Reduction as a Remedy for Prosecutorial Misconduct" (2009) 97 *Geo. L. J.* 6.

Stuntz, William, *The Collapse of American Criminal Justice* (Cambridge; Harvard University Press, 2011).

Tomkovicz, James J., *Constitutional Exclusion: The Rules, Rights, and Remedies That Strike the Balance between Freedom and Order* (New York: Oxford University Press, 2011).

Turner, Jenia Iontcheva, "Policing International Prosecutors" (2012) 45 *N.Y.U. J. Int'l. L. Pol'y*. 1.

"The Accountability of International Prosecutors" in Stahn, Carsten (ed.), *The Law and Practice of the International Criminal Court* (Oxford: Oxford University Press, 2015), Chapter 17.

Viebig, Petra, *Illicitly Obtained Evidence in the International Criminal Court* (Berlin: Springer, 2016).

Chapter 7 Declarations, Injunctions and the Declaration Plus

Attaran, Amir and Khan, Jon, "Solving the 'Khadr' Problem: Retention of Jurisdiction- A Comparative Analysis" (2015) 34 *N.J.C.L.* 145.

Baxi, Upendra, "Law, Politics and Constitutional Hegemony" in Sujit Choudhry, Madhav Khosla and Pratap Bhanu Mehta (eds.), *The Oxford Handbook of the Indian Constitution* (Oxford University Press, 2016)

Bell, Derrick, *Silent Covenants: Brown v. Board of Education and the Unfulfilled Hopes for Racial Reform* (New York: Oxford University Press, 2005).

Bell, Derick A. Jr., "Serving Two Masters: Integration Ideals and Client Interests in School Desegregation Litigation" (1976) 85 *Yale L. J.* 470.

Bhagwati, P. N., "Judicial Activism and Public Interest Litigation" (1985) 23 *Colum. J. Transntn'l. L.* 561.

Bhwanania, Anuj, *Courting the People Public Interest Litigation in Post-Emergency India* (Cambridge: Cambridge University Press, 2017).

Bray, Samuel, "The Myth of the Mild Declaratory Judgment" (2014) 63 *Duke L.J.* 1091.

Budlender, Steven, Marcus, Gilbert and Ferreira, Nick, *Public Interest Litigation and Social Change in South Africa: Strategies, Tactics and Lessons* (The Atlantic Philanthropies, 2014).

Buyse, Antoine, "The Pilot Judgment Procedure at the European Court of Human Rights: Possibilities and Challenges" (2009) 57 *Nomiko Vima* 1890.

Carter, Robert L., "The Warren Court and Desegregation" (1968) 67(2) *Mich. L. Rev.* 236.

Chandrachud, Chintan, "Structural Injunctions and Public Interest Litigation in India" in Po Jen Yap (ed.), *Constitutional Remedies in Asia*, 1st ed. (London: Routledge, 2019).

Chayes, Abram, "Public Law Litigation and the Burger Court" (1982) 96 *Harv. L. Rev.* 4.

Chen, Jim, "With All Deliberate Speed: Brown II and Desegregation's Children" (2006) 24 *L. Ineq.* 1.

Chiang, Emily, "Reviving the Declaratory Judgment: A New Path to Structural Reform" (2015) 63(3) *Buff. L. Rev.* 549.

Choudhry, Sujit, Khosla, Madhav and Bhanu Mehta, Pratap, "Locating Indian Constitutionalism" in Sujit Choudhry, Madhav Khosla and Pratap Bhanu Mehta (eds.), *The Oxford Handbook of the Indian Constitution* (Oxford University Press, 2016).

Conklin, William and Morrison, Jodi, "Public Law Issues in a Private Law World: The Appointment of a Receiver as a Case Study" (1986) 26 *Osgoode Hall L. J.* 45.

Donald, Alice and Speck, Anne-Katrin, "The European Court of Human Rights' Remedial Practice and Its Impact on the Execution of Judgments" (2019) 19(1) *Hum. Rts. L. Rev.* 83.

Dunn, Joshua, *Complex Justice: The Story of Missouri v. Jenkins* (Chapel Hill: University of North Carolina Press, 2008).

Eisenberg, Theodore and Yeazell, Stephen, "The Ordinary and Extraordinary in Institutional Litigation" (1980) 93 *Harv. L. Rev.* 465.

Feeley, Malcolm and Rubin, Edward, *Judicial Policy-Making and the Modern State* (Cambridge: Cambridge University Press, 1998).

Fiss, Owen, "Dombrowski" (1977) 86 *Yale L. J.* 1103.

The Civil Rights Injunction (Bloomington: Indiana University Press, 1979).

Fuller, Lon, "Mediation – Its Forms and Functions" (1971) 44 *S. Cal. L. Rev.* 305.

Gerards, Janneke H. and Glas, Lize R., "Access to Justice in the European Convention on Human Rights System" (2017) 35 *Netherlands Q. Hum. Rts.* 11.

Gilles, Myriam, "Reinventing Structural Reform: Deputizing Private Citizens in the Enforcement of Civil Rights" (2000) 100 *Colum. L. Rev.* 1384.

Guetzkow, Joshua and Schoon, Eric, "If You Build It, They Will Fill It: The Consequences of Prison Overcrowding Litigation" (2015) 49(2) *L. Soc'y. Rev.* 401.

Hirschhorn, James M., "Where the Money Is: Remedies to Finance Compliance with Structural Injunctions" (1984) 82(8) *Mich. L. Rev.* 1815.

Hoffer, Peter, *The Law's Conscience Equitable Constitutionalism in America* (Chapel Hill: University of North Carolina Press, 1999).

Horowitz, Donald, *The Courts and Social Policy* (Washington: Brookings, 1977).

Huneeus, Alexandra, "Reforming the State from Afar: Structural Reform Litigation at the Human Rights Courts" (2015) 40 *Yale L. J.* 1.

Jackson, Michael, *Prisoners of Isolation* (Toronto: University of Toronto Press, 1980).

Jansen, Rudolph and Tendayi Achiume, Emily, "Prison Conditions in South Africa and the Role of Public Interest Litigation since 1994" (2011) 27(1) *S.A. J. Hum. Rts.* 183.

Kindt, Eline, "Giving up on Individual Justice?" (2018) 36 *Netherlands Q. Hum. Rts.* 173.

Klarman, Michael, *From Jim Crow to Civil Rights* (New York: Oxford University Press, 2004).

Brown v. Board of Education and the Civil Rights Movement (New York: Oxford University Press, 2007).

Kluger, Richard, *Simple Justice: The History of Brown v. Board of Education and Black America's Struggle for Equality* (New York: Knopf, 1975).

Mackintosh, Gordon, "Heading Off Bilodeau: Attempting Constitutional Amendment" (1986) 15 *Man. L. J.* 271.

Maldonado, Daniel Bonilla (ed.), *Constitutionalism of the Global South: The Activist Tribunals of India, South Africa and Colombia* (Cambridge: Cambridge University Press, 2013).

McLachlin, Beverley, "The Charter: A New Role for the Judiciary" (1991) 29 *Atla. L. Rev.* 540.

Minor, Janet and Wilson, James, "Reflections of a Supervisory Order Sceptic" in Robert J. Sharpe and Kent Roach, *Taking Remedies Seriously* (Ottawa: Canadian Institute for the Administration of Justice, 2010).

Mowbry, Alistair, "An Examination of the European Court of Human Rights Indication of General Measures" (2017) 17 *Hum. Rts. L. Rev.* 451.

Noonan, Kathleen, Lipson, Jonathan and Simon, William, "Reforming Institutions: The Judicial Function in Bankruptcy and Public Law Litigation" (2019) 94 *Indiana L. J.* 491.

Ogletree, Charles J. Jr. and Eaton, Susan, "From Little Rock to Seattle and Louisville: Is All Deliberate Speed Stuck in Reverse" (2008) 30(2) *U. Ark. Little Rock L. Rev.* 279.

Parker, Wendy, "The Supreme Court and Public Law Remedies: A Tale of Two Kansas Cities" (1999) 50 *Hastings L. J.* 475.

Parkin, Jason, "Aging Injunctions and the Legacy of Institutional Reform Litigation" (2017) 70 *Vanderbilt L. Rev.* 167.

Parrillo, Nicholas, "The Endgame of Administrative Law: Governmental Disobedience and the Judicial Contempt Power" (2018) 131 *Harv. L. Rev.* 685.

Pillay, Anashri, "Process and Substance in Economic and Social Rights Adjudication" in Mark Elliott, Jason Varuhas and Shona Wilson Stark (eds.), *The Unity of Public Law* (Oxford: Hart Publishing, 2018).

Roach, Kent, "The Limits of Corrective Justice and the Potential of Equity in Constititional Remedies" (1991) 33 *Ariz. L. Rev.* 859.

"The Supreme Court at the Bar of Politics: The Afghan Detainee and Omar Khadr Cases" (2010) 28 *N.J.C.L.* 115.

"Charter Remedies" in Peter Oliver, Patrick Macklem and Nathalie Des Rosiers (eds.), *The Oxford Handbook of the Canadian Constitution* (New York: Oxford University Press, 2017).

Roach, Kent and Budlender, Geoff, "Mandatory Relief and Supervisory Jurisdiction: When Is It Appropriate, Just and Equitable" (2005) 122 *S.A. L. J.* 325.

Rouleau, Paul and Sherman, Linsey, "Doucet-Boudreau, Dialogue and Judicial Activism" (2010) 41(2) *Ottawa L. Rev.* 171.

Rushin, Stephen, "Structural Reform Litigation in American Police Departments" (2015) 99 *Minn. L. Rev.* 1343.

Sabel, Charles F. and Simon, William H., "Destabilization Rights: How Public Law Litigation Succeeds" (2004) 117 *Harv. L. Rev.* 1016.

Schlanger, Margo, "Beyond the Hero Judge: Institutional Reform Litigation as Litigation" (1999) 97 *Mich. L. Rev.* 6.

"*Plata* v. *Brown* and Realignment: Jails, Prisons, Courts and Politics" (2013) 48 *Harv. C.R.-C.L. L. Rev.* 145.

"Trends in Prison Litigation, as the PLRA Enters Adulthood" (2015) 5 *U.C. Irvine L. Rev.* 153.

Simon, Jonathan, *Mass Incarceration on Trial: A Remarkable Court Decision and the Future of American Prisons* (New York: New Press, 2014).

Taylor, Helen, "Forcing the Court's Remedial Hand: Non-Compliance as a Catalyst for Remedial Innovation" (2019) 9 *Constitutional Ct. Rev.* 247.

Tushnet, Mark, "Public Law Litigation and the Ambiguities of Brown" (1992) 61 *Fordham L. Rev.* 23.

Viljoen, Sue-Mari and Makama, Saul Porsche, "Structural Relief – A Context-Sensitive Approach" (2018) 34 *S.A J. Hum. Rts.* 209.

Yackle, Larry, *Reform and Regret: The Story of Federal Involvement in the Alabama Prison System* (New York: Oxford University Press, 1989).

Yoo, John, "Who Measures the Chancellor's Foot: The Inherent Remedial Authority of the Federal Courts" (1996) 84 *Calif. L. Rev.* 1121.

Chapter 8 Remedies for Social, Economic and Cultural Rights

Bilchitz, David, *Poverty and Fundamental Rights* (Oxford: Oxford University Press, 2008).

Brown, George D., "Binding Advisory Opinions: A Federal Court's Perspective on State Court School Finance Decisions" (1994) 35(3) *B.C. L. Rev.* 543.

Budlender, Geoff, "The Right to Alternative Accommodations in Forced Evictions" in John Squires et al. (eds.), *The Road to a Remedy: Current Issues in the Litigation of Economic, Social and Cultural Rights* (Sydney: University of New South Wales Press, 2005).

Calabresi, Guido and Bobbit, Philip, *Tragic Choices: The Conflicts Society Confronts in the Allocation of Tragically Scarce Resources* (New York: Norton, 1978).

Cassels, Jamie, "Judicial Activism and Public Interest Litigation in India: Attempting the Impossible?" (1989) 37(3) *Am. J. Comp. L.* 495.

Černič, Jernej Letnar, "The European Court of Human Rights, Rule of Law and Socio-Economic Rights in Times of Crises" (2016) 8 *Hague J. Rule Law* 227.

Chenwi, Lilian, "A New Approach to Remedies in Socio-economic Rights Adjudication: Occupiers of 51 Olivia Road and Others v. City of Johannesburg and Others" (2009) 2 *Constitutional Crt. Rev.* 371.

Chitalkar, Poorvi and Gauri, Varun, "India: Compliance with Orders on the Right to Food" in Mal Langford, Cesar Rodriguez-Garavito and Julieta Rossi, *Social Rights Judgments and the Politics of Compliance: Making It Stick* (Cambridge: Cambridge University Press, 2017).

Cullet, Philippe, "The Right to Water in Rural India" in Malcom Langford *The Human Right to Water: Theory, Practice and Prospects* (Cambridge University Press, 2017).

Dixon, Rosalind, "Creating Dialogue about Socio-Economic Rights" (2007) 5 *I. Con.* 391.

Ferraz, Octavio, "Brazil: Are Collective Suits Harder to Enforce?" in Mal Langford, Cesar Rodriguez-Garavito and Julieta Rossi, *Social Rights Judgments and the Politics of Compliance: Making It Stick* (Cambridge: Cambridge University Press, 2017).

Ferraz, Octavio Luiz Motta, "Social Rights, Judicial Remedies and the Poor" (2019) 18(3) *Wash. U. Global Studies L. Rev.* 569.

Flood, Colleen, "Chaoulli's Legacy for the Future of Canadian Health Care Policy" (2006) 44 *Osgoode Hall L. J.* 273.

Flood, Colleen M., Kent Roach and Lorne Sossin (eds.), *Access to Care, Access to Justice: The Legal Debate Over Private Health Insurance in Canada* (Toronto: University of Toronto Press, 2005).

Gomez-Ceballos, Diego and Craverier, Isabel, "Judicialization of the Right to Health" (2019) 34 *Int'l. J. Health Plan. Mgmt.* 1277.

Hunter, Molly, "All Eyes Forward: Public Engagement and Educational Reform in Kentucky" (1999) 28 *J. L. Edu.* 485.

Jackson, Vicki C. and Tushnet, Mark (eds.), *Proportionality: New Frontiers, New Challenges* (Cambridge: Cambridge University Press, 2019).

Kapczynski, Amy and Berger, Jonathan M., "Story of the TAC Case: The Potential and Limits of Socio-Economic Rights Litigation in South Africa" in Deena Hurwitz and Margaret Slaitterwaite, *Human Rights Advocacy Stories* (New York: Foundation Press, 2009).

King, Jeff, *Judging Social Rights* (Cambridge: Cambridge University Press, 2012).

Lamprea, Everaldo, "Colombia's Right-to-Health Litigation in a Context of Health Care Reform" in Colleen Flood and Aeyal Gross (eds.), *The Right to Health at the Public/Private Divide: A Global Comparative Study* (Cambridge: Cambridge University Press, 2014).

Lamprea, Everaldo and Garcia, Johnathan, "Closing the Gap between Formal and Material Health Care Coverage in Colombia" (2016) 18(2) *Health Hum. Rts.* 49.

Landau, David, "The Reality of Social Rights Enforcement" (2012) 53 *Harv. J. Int'l. L.* 189.

Landau, David and Dixon, Rosalind, "Constitutional Non-Transformation?" in Katharine Young (ed.), *The Future of Economic and Social Rights* (Cambridge: Cambridge University Press, 2019).

Langford, Mal, Rodriguez-Garavito, Cesar and Rossi, Julieta, *Social Rights Judgments and the Politics of Compliance: Making It Stick* (Cambridge: Cambridge University Press, 2017).

Liebenberg, Sandra, *Socio-Economic Rights: Adjudication under a Transformative Constitution* (Claremont, South Africa: Juta, 2010).

"Participatory Approaches to Socio-Economic Rights: Tentative Lessons from South Africa's Evictions Law" (2014) 32(4) *Nordic J. Hum. Rts.* 312.

Mbazira, Christopher, "Appropriate, Just and Equitable Relief in Socio-Economic Rights Litigation: The Tension between Corrective and Distributive Forms of Justice" (2008) 125(1) *S.A. L. J.* 71.

"Non-Implementation of Court Orders in Socio-Economic Rights Litigation in South Africa: Is the Cancer Here to Stay?" (2008) 9(4) *ESR Rev.: Econ. Soc. Rts. S.A.* 2.

Litigating Socio-Economic Rights in South Africa: A Choice between Corrective and Distributive Justice (Pretoria: Pretoria University Law Press, 2009).

McLean, Kirsty, "Meaningful Engagement: One Step Forward or Two Back: Some Thoughts on Joe Slovo" (2010) 3 *Con. Ct. Rev.* 223.

Melish, Tara, "Rethinking the 'Less as More' Thesis: Supranational Litigation of Economic, Social and Cultural Rights in the Americas" (2006) 39 *N.Y.U. J. Int'l. L. Pol'y.* 171.

Naznin, Atia and Alam, Shawkat, "Judicial Remedies for Forced Slum Evictions in Bangladesh" (2019) 6(1) *Asian J. L. Soc'y* 99.

Pieterse, Marius, "Coming to Terms with Judicial Enforcement of Socio-economic Rights" (2004) 20 *S.A. J. Hum. Rts.* 383.

Pillay, Anashri, "Towards Effective Social Economic Rights Adjudication: The Role of Meaningful Engagement" (2012) 10(3) *I. Con.* 732.

"Revisiting the Indian Experience of Economic and Social Rights Adjudication: The Need for a Principled Approach to Judicial Activism and Restraint" (2014) *I.C.L.Q.* 385.

Roach, Kent, "Constitutional, Remedial and International Dialogues about Rights: The Canadian Experience" (2005) 40 *Texas Int'l. L. J.* 537.

"The Courts and Medicare: Too Much or Too Little Judicial Activism?" in Colleen M. Flood, Kent Roach and Lorne Sossin (eds.), *Access to Care, Access to Justice: The Legal Debate Over Private Health Insurance in Canada* (Toronto: University of Toronto Press, 2005).

"The Challenge of Crafting Remedies for Violations of Socio-Economic Rights" in Mal Langford (ed.), *Social Rights Jurisprudence* (Cambridge: Cambridge University Press, 2008).

Rodriguez-Garavito, Cesar, "Beyond Enforcement: Assessing and Enhancing Judicial Impact" in Mal Langford, Cesar Rodriguez-Garavito and Julieta Rossi, *Social Rights Judgments and the Politics of Compliance: Making It Stick* (Cambridge: Cambridge University Press, 2017).

Rebell, Michael, *Courts and Kids: Pursuing Educational Equity through the State Courts* (Chicago: University of Chicago Press, 2009).

Rebell, Michael A. and Hughes, Robert, "Schools, Communities, and the Courts: A Dialogical Approach to Educational Reform" (1996) 14 *Yale L. Pol'y. Rev.* 99.

"Efficacy and Engagement: The Remedies Problem Posed by Sheff v. O'Neill and a Proposed Solution" (1997) 29 *Conn. L. Rev.* 1115.

Rooney, James, "Class Actions and Public Interest Standing in South Africa: Practical and Participatory Perspectives" (2017) 33(3) *S.A. J. Hum. Rts.* 406.

Sachs, Albie, "The Judicial Enforcement of Socio-economic Rights: The Grootboom Case" (2003) 56 *Current Leg. Prob.* 579.

"Enforcement of Social and Economic Rights" (2006) 22 *Am. U. Int'l. L. Rev.* 673.

Schuck, Peter H., "Public Law Litigation and Social Reform" (1993) 102 *Yale L. J.* 1763.

Sengupta, Arghya et al., "Legislating Human Rights" in Katharine Young (ed.), *The Future of Economic and Social Rights* (Cambridge: Cambridge University Press, 2019).

Sharpe, Robert J., "Injunctions and the Charter" (1984) 22(3) *Osgoode Hall L. J.* 474.

Sturm, Susan, "A Normative Theory of Public Law Remedies" (1991) 79 *Geo. L. J.* 1355.

Sunstein, Cass, "Social and Economic Rights? Lessons from South Africa" (2001) 11(4) *Constitutional Forum* 123.

Young, Katharine, *Constituting Economic and Social Rights* (Oxford: Oxford University Press, 2012).

"Proportionality, Reasonableness and Economic and Social Rights" in Vicki C. Jackson and Mark Tushnet (eds.) *Proportionality: New Frontiers, New Challenges* (Cambridge: Cambridge University Press, 2019).

Young, Katharine (ed.), *The Future of Economic and Social Rights* (Cambridge: Cambridge University Press, 2019).

Young, Katherine G., "Holism and Separatism in Economic and Social Rights Adjudication" (2019) 69 Supp. 1 *U.T.L.J.* 124.

Young, Katharine G. and Lemaitre, Julieta, "The Comparative Fortunes of the Right to Health: Two Tales of Justiciability in Colombia and South Africa" (2013) 26 *Harv. Hum. Rts. J.* 179, 193.

Chapter 9 Remedies for Violations of Indigenous Rights

Akhtar, Zia, "Mapuche Land Claims: Environmental Protest, Legal Discrimination and Customary Rights" (2013) 20(4) *Int'l. J. Minority Group Rts.* 551.

Alvardo, Leonardo J., "Prospects and Challenges in the Implementation of Indigenous Peoples' Human Rights in International Law: Lessons from the Case of Awas Tingni v. Nicaragua" (2007) 24(3) *Ariz. J. Int'l. Comp. L.* 609.

Anaya, S. James, "The Native Hawaiian People and International Human Rights Law: Towards a Remedy for Past and Continuing Wrongs" (1994) 28 *Geo. L. Rev.* 309.

Indigenous Peoples in International Law, 2nd ed. (Oxford: Oxford University Press, 2004).

"Report of the Special Rapporteur on the Rights of Indigenous Peoples in the Situation of Maori People in New Zealand" (2015) 32 *Ariz. J. Int'l. Comp. L.* 1.

Anaya, S. James and Grossman, Claudio, "The Case of Awas Tingni v. Nicaragua: A Step in the International Law of Indigenous Peoples" (2002) 19 *Ariz. J. Int'l. Comp. L.* 1.

Anaya, S. James and Puig, Sergio, "Mitigating State Sovereignty: The Duty to Consult with Indigenous Peoples" (2017) 67 *U.T.L.J.* 435.

Antkowiak, Thomas M., "Rights, Resources, and Rhetoric: Indigenous Peoples and the Inter-American Court" (2013) 35 *U. Pa. J. Int'l. L.* 113.

"A Dark Side of Virtue: The Inter-American Court and Reparations for Indigenous Peoples" (2014) 25 *Duke J. Comp. Int'l. L.* 1.

Ariss, Rachel, and Cutfeet, John, *Keeping the Land: Kitchenuhmaykoosib Inninuwug, Reconciliation and Canadian Law* (Halifax: Fernwood Publishing, 2012).

Atuahene, Bernadette and Sibanda, Sanele, "From Reparations to Dignity Restoration: The Story of the Popela Community" (2018) 18 *African Hum. Rts. L. J.* 654.

Barelli, Mauro, "Free, Prior and Informed Consent in the Aftermath of the UN Declaration on the Rights of Indigenous Peoples: Developments and Challenges Ahead" (2012) 16 *Int'l. J. Hum. Rts.* 10.

Beaton, Ryan, "Articles 27 and 46(2): UNDRIP Signposts Pointing towards the Justified Infringement Section 35 Morass" in Centre for International Governance Innovation and Wiyasiwewin Mikiwahp Native Law Centre, *UNDRIP Implementation: More Reflections on the Braiding of International, Domestic and Indigenous Laws* (Saskatchewan: Center for International Governance Innovation, 2018).

Blumm, Michael, "Indian Treaty Fishing Rights and the Environment: Affirming the Right to Habitat Protection and Restoration" (2016) 92 *Wash. L. Rev.* 1.

Boast, Richard P., "Foreshore and Seabed, Again" (2011) 9 *N.Z. J. Pub. Int'l. L.* 271.

Borrows, John, *Freedom and Indigenous Constitutionalism* (Toronto: University of Toronto, 2016).

Law's Indigenous Ethics (Toronto: University of Toronto Press, 2019).

Wise Practices: Exploring Indigenous Economic Justice and Self-Determination (Toronto: University of Toronto, forthcoming).

Borrows, John and Coyle, Michael (eds.), *The Right Relationship: Reimagining the Implementation of Historical Treaties* (Toronto: University of Toronto Press, 2017).

et al. (eds.), *Braiding Legal Orders: Implementing the United Nations Declaration on the Rights of Indigenous Peoples* (Waterloo: Centre for International Governance, 2019).

Carlson, Hans, "A Watershed of Words: Litigating and Negotiating Nature in Eastern James Bay, 1971–75" (2004) 85(1) *Can. Historical Rev.* 63.

Chingmak, Phutoli Shikhu, "International Law and Reparations for Indigenous People in Asia" in Federico Lenzerini (ed.), *Reparations for Indigenous Peoples* (Oxford University Press, 2008).

Ciaccia, John, *James Bay and Northern Quebec Agreement* (Montreal: Quebec National Library, 1976).

Cohen, Fay, *Treaties on Trial* (Seattle: University of Washington Press, 1986).

Correia, Joel E., "Adjudication and Its After Effects in Three Inter-American Court Cases Brought against Paraguay: Indigenous Land Rights" (2018) 11(1) *Erasmus L. Rev.* 43.

Dawson, John, "The Remedies Report" in Janine Hayward and Nicola R. Wheel (eds.), *The Waitangi Tribunal: Te Roopu Whakamana i te Titri o Waitangi* (Wellington: Williams, 2004).

Drake, Karen, "The Trials and Tribulations of Ontario's Mining Act: The Duty to Consult and Anishinaabek Law" (2015) 11(2) *J.S.D.L.P.* 183.

Frankfurter, Felix and Greene, Nathan, *The Labor Injunction* (New York: MacMillan, 1930).

Gunn, Brenda, "Remedies for Violations of Indigenous Peoples' Human Rights" (2019) 69 Supp. 1 *U.T.L.J.* 150.

Hamilton, Robert and Nichols, Joshua, "The Tin Ear of the Court" (2019) 56(3) *Alta. L. Rev.* 729.

Herrera, Juan, "Judicial Dialogue and Transformative Constitutionalism: The Case of Indigenous Peoples and Afro-Descendants" (2019) 43 *Revista Derecho del Estado* 191, 212–213.

Imai, Shin, "Sound Science, Careful Policy Analysis, and Ongoing Relationships: Integrating Litigation and Negotiation in Aboriginal Lands and Resources Disputes" (2003) 41(4) *Osgoode Hall L. J.* 587.

Koorndjik, Jeanice, "Judgments of the Inter-American Court of Human Rights Concerning Indigenous and Tribal Rights in Suriname" (2019) 23(10) *Int'l. J. Hum. Rts.* 1615.

Lancaster Phil, The Structural Injunction as a Remedy for Violations of Aboriginal Constitutional Rights (Ottawa: Canada Bar Association, 1991).

Lawrence, Sonia and Macklem, Patrick, "From Consultation to Reconciliation: Aboriginal Rights and the Crown's Duty to Consult" (2000) 79 *Can. Bar Rev.* 252.

Lenzerini, Federico (ed.), *Reparations for Indigenous Peoples* (Oxford University Press, 2008).

Lenzerini, Frederico, "Reparations, Restitution and Redress" in Jessie Hohmann and Marc Weiler (eds.), *The United Nations Declaration on the Rights of Indigenous Peoples* (Oxford: Oxford University Press, 2018).

Magallanes Iorns, Catherine J., "Improving the Global Environmental Rule of Law by Upholding Indigenous Rights: Examples from Aotearoa New Zealand" (2018) 7 *Global J. Comp. L.* 61.

Mainville, Robert, *An Overview of Aboriginal and Treaty Rights and Compensation for their Breach* (Saskatoon: Purich, 2001).

Milward, David, "Restless Spirit in the Land: Finding a Place in Canadian Law for Aboriginal Disobedience" (2009) 15 *Int'l. J. Minority Group Rts.* 1.

Morales, Sarah, "Braiding the Incommensurables" in John Borrows et al. (eds.), *Braiding Legal Orders: Implementing the United Nations Declaration on the Rights of Indigenous Peoples* (Waterloo: Centre for International Governance, 2019).

Newman, Dwight, "Negotiated Rights Enforcement" (2006) 69 *Sask. L. Rev.* 119.

Revisiting the Duty to Consult Aboriginal Peoples (Saskatoon: Purich Publishing, 2014).

The Rule and Role of Law: Duty to Consult, Aboriginal Communities and the Canadian Natural Resource Sector (Ottawa: MacDonald Laurier Institute, 2014).

Palmer, MSR, *The Treaty of Waitangi in New Zealand's Law and Constitution* (Wellington, Victoria University Press, 2008).

Patzer, Jeremy, "Indigenous Rights and the Legal Politics of Canadian Coloniality: What Is Happening to Free and Informed Consent in Canada?" (2019) *Int'l. J. Hum. Rts.* 214.

Roach, Kent, "Remedies for Violation of Aboriginal Rights" (1992) 21 *Man. L. J.* 498.

Russell, Peter H., *Recognizing Aboriginal Title* (Toronto: University of Toronto Press, 2005).

Stacey, Richard, "Honour in Sovereignty: Can Crown Consultation with Indigenous People Erase Canada's Sovereignty Deficit?" (2018) 68 *U.T.L.J.* 405.

van Genugten, Willem and Frederico Lenzerini, "Legal Implementation and International Co-operation and Assistance" in Jessie Hohmann and Marc Weiler (eds.), *The United Nations Declaration on the Rights of Indigenous Peoples* (Oxford: Oxford University Press, 2018).

Ventura Robles, Manuel, "Impact of the Reparations Ordered by the Inter-American Court of Human Rights" in Yves Haeck, Oswaldo Ruiz-Chiriboga, and Clara Burbano-Herrera (eds.) *The Inter-American Court of Human Rights: Theory and Practice, Present and Future* (Antwerp: Intersentia, 2015).

Walters, Mark D., "Rights and Remedies within Common Law and Indigenous Legal Traditions: Can the Covenant Chain Be Judicially Enforced Today?" in John Borrows and Michael Coyle (eds.), *The Right Relationship: Reimagining the Implementation of Historical Treaties* (Toronto: University of Toronto Press, 2017).

Wilkinson, Charles, *Messages From Frank's Landing: A Story of Salmon, Treaties, and the Indian Way* (Seattle: University of Washington Press, 2000).

Williams, Rick et al., "The New Normal? Natural Resource Development, Civil Disobedience and Injunctive Relief" (2017) 55 *Alta. L. Rev.* 285.

Wilson Raybould, Jody, *From Where I Stand: Rebuilding Indigenous Nations for a Stronger Canada* (Vancouver: Purich Books, 2019).

Young, Stephen, "The Deification of Process in the Duty to Consult" (2019) 52 *U.B.C. L. Rev.* 1065.

INDEX

Introductory Note

References such as "178–179" indicate (not necessarily continuous) discussion of a topic across a range of pages. Wherever possible in the case of topics with many references, these have either been divided into sub-topics or only the most significant discussions of the topic are listed. Because the entire work is about "human rights", the use of this term (and certain others that occur constantly throughout the book) as an entry point has been minimized. Information will be found under the corresponding detailed topics.

CPSIA information can be obtained
at www.ICGtesting.com
Printed in the USA
LVHW011101120922
728117LV00001B/215